MICROSOFT

PowerPoint 2000

Comprehensive Concepts and Techniques

Gary B. Shelly
Thomas J. Cashman
Susan L. Sebok

COURSE TECHNOLOGY
ONE MAIN STREET
CAMBRIDGE MA 02142

Thomson Learning™

SHELLY
CASHMAN
SERIES®

Australia • Canada • Denmark • Japan • Mexico • New Zealand • Philippines
Puerto Rico • Singapore • South Africa • Spain • United Kingdom • United States

PHOTO CREDITS: Microsoft PowerPoint 2000 *Project 1, pages PP 1.4-5* COMDEX/Canada, COMDEX/Las Vegas, conference presentation, Courtesy of 2D Events; IBM computer, Courtesy of International Business Machines; First Apple computer, Courtesy of Apple Computer, Inc.; portable computer, Courtesy of Compaq Computer Corporation; *Project 2, pages PP 2.2-3* Business meeting, man and woman working on laptop computer, woman next to desk, Courtesy of PhotoDisc, Inc.; *Project 3, pages PP 3.2-3* Businessman, woman at computer, teacher and students, Courtesy of PhotoDisc, Inc.; *page PP 3.5* Couple kayaking, Courtesy of PhotoDisc, Inc.; *Project 4, pages PP 4.2-3* Hawaiian vacation brochure, fish, Courtesy of MetaTools, BMW, Courtesy of BMW North America, Inc.; *page PP 4.5* Palm trees, Courtesy of MetaTools; Couple on the beach, Courtesy of Corel Corporation; *Project 5, pages PP 5.2-3* Workers, eye, Courtesy of PhotoDisc, Inc.; globes, Courtesy of Map Art by Cartesia Software; *Project 6, pages PP 6.2-3* Help Wanted sign, classified advertisements, hand on keyboard, two workers, Courtesy of PhotoDisc, Inc.

ISBN 0-7895-5611-1

1 2 3 4 5 6 7 8 9 10   BC   04 03 02 01 00

MICROSOFT

PowerPoint 2000

Comprehensive Concepts and Techniques

CONTENTS

Microsoft PowerPoint 2000

● PROJECT 1

USING A DESIGN TEMPLATE AND AUTOLAYOUTS TO CREATE A PRESENTATION

Preface

The Shelly Cashman Series® offers the finest textbooks in computer education. We are proud of the fact that our *Microsoft PowerPoint 4*, *Microsoft PowerPoint 7*, and *Microsoft PowerPoint 97* textbooks have been the most widely used presentation books in education. Each edition of our PowerPoint textbooks has included innovations, many based on comments made by the instructors and students who use our books. The *Microsoft PowerPoint 2000* books continue with the innovation, quality, and reliability that you have come to expect from the Shelly Cashman Series.

In our *Microsoft PowerPoint 2000* books, you will find an educationally sound and easy-to-follow pedagogy that combines a step-by-step approach with corresponding screens. All projects and exercises in this book are designed to take full advantage of the PowerPoint 2000 enhancements. The popular Other Ways and More About features offer in-depth knowledge of PowerPoint 2000. The project openers provide a fascinating perspective of the subject covered in the project. The project material is developed carefully to ensure that students will see the importance of learning PowerPoint 2000 for future course work.

Objectives of This Textbook

Microsoft PowerPoint 2000: Comprehensive Concepts and Techniques is intended for a two- to three-unit course that presents Microsoft PowerPoint 2000. No experience with a computer is assumed, and no mathematics beyond the high school freshman level is required. The objectives of this book are:

- To teach the fundamentals of Microsoft PowerPoint 2000
- To expose students to practical examples of the computer as a useful tool
- To acquaint students with the proper procedures to create presentations suitable for course work, professional purposes, and personal use
- To develop an exercise-oriented approach that allows learning by example
- To encourage independent study, and help those who are working alone
- To demonstrate the proposed Expert level skill set for the Microsoft Office User Specialist Exam

Approved by Microsoft as Courseware for the Microsoft Office User Specialist Program – Proposed Expert Level

This book has been approved by Microsoft as courseware for the Microsoft Office User Specialist (MOUS) program. After completing the projects and exercises in this book, students will be prepared to take the proposed Expert level examination for the Microsoft Office User Specialist Exam for Microsoft PowerPoint 2000. By passing the certification exam for a Microsoft software application, students demonstrate their proficiency in that application to employers. This exam is offered at participating centers, participating corporations, and participating employment agencies. See Appendix D for additional information on the MOUS program and for a table that includes the Microsoft PowerPoint 2000 MOUS skill sets for both Core level and the proposed Expert level and corresponding page numbers where a skill is discussed in the book, or visit the Web site at www.mous.net.

The Shelly Cashman Series Microsoft Office User Specialist Center Web page (Figure 1) has more than fifteen Web pages you can visit to obtain additional information on the MOUS Certification program. The Web page (www.scsite.com/off2000/cert.htm) includes links to general information on certification, choosing an application for certification, preparing for the certification exam, and taking and passing the proposed certification exam.

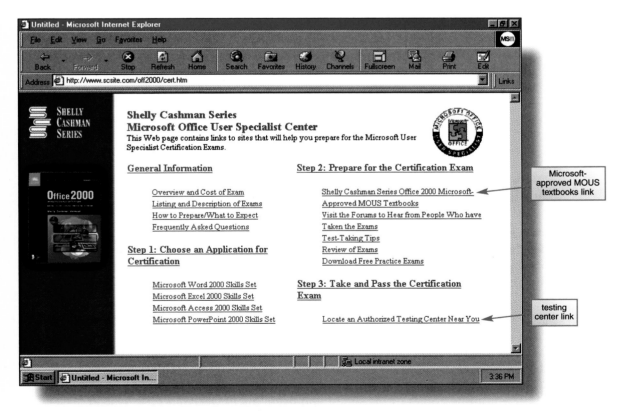

FIGURE 1

The Shelly Cashman Approach

Features of the Shelly Cashman Series PowerPoint books include:

- **Project Orientation:** Each project in the book presents a practical problem and complete solution in an easy-to-understand approach.

- **Step-by-Step, Screen-by-Screen Instructions:** Each of the tasks required to complete a project is shown using a step-by-step, screen-by-screen approach. The screens are shown in full color.

- **Thoroughly Tested Projects:** Every screen in the book is correct because it is produced by the author only after performing a step, resulting in unprecedented quality.

- **Other Ways Boxes and Quick Reference Summary:** PowerPoint 2000 provides a variety of ways to carry out a given task. The Other Ways boxes displayed at the end of most of the step-by-step sequences specify the other ways to do the task completed in the steps. Thus, the steps and the Other Ways box make a comprehensive reference unit. A Quick Reference Summary, available in the back of this book and on the Web, summarizes the way specific tasks can be completed.

- **More About Feature:** These marginal annotations provide background information that complements the topics covered, adding depth and perspective.

- **Integration of the World Wide Web:** The World Wide Web is integrated into the PowerPoint 2000 learning experience by (1) More Abouts that send students to Web sites for up-to-date information and alternative approaches to tasks; (2) a MOUS information Web page and a MOUS map Web page so students can better prepare for the Microsoft Office Use Specialist (MOUS) Certification examinations; (3) a PowerPoint 2000 Quick Reference Summary Web page that summarizes the ways to complete tasks (mouse, menu, shortcut menu, and keyboard); and (4) project reinforcement Web pages in the form of true/false, multiple choice, and short answer questions, and other types of student activities.

Other Ways

1. Click Run Macro button on Visual Basic toolbar
2. On Tools menu point to Macro, click Macros on Macro submenu, double-click macro name
3. Press ALT+F8, double-click macro name

More About 2000

Chart Types

PowerPoint has a variety of 2-D, bubble, and 3-D chart types. For 2-D charts, you can change the chart type of either a group of data or the entire chart. For bubble charts, you can change only the type of the entire chart. For 3-D bar and column charts, you can change the data series to the cone, cylinder, or pyramid chart types. For most other 3-D charts, you change the entire chart when you change the chart type.

Organization of This Textbook

Microsoft PowerPoint 2000: Comprehensive Concepts and Techniques provides detailed instruction on how to use PowerPoint 2000. The material is divided into six projects, two Web Features, an Integration Feature, four appendices, and a Quick Reference Summary.

Project 1 – Using a Design Template and AutoLayouts to Create a Presentation In Project 1, students are introduced to PowerPoint terminology, the PowerPoint window, and the basics of creating a multi-level bulleted list presentation. Topics include selecting a design template; increasing font size; changing font style; ending a slide show with a black slide; saving a presentation; viewing the slides in a presentation; checking a presentation for spelling and style errors; changing line spacing on the Slide Master; printing copies of the slides; and using the PowerPoint Help system.

Project 2 – Using Outline View and Clip Art to Create a Slide Show In Project 2, students create a presentation in outline view, insert clip art, and add animation effects. Topics include creating a slide presentation by promoting and demoting text in outline view; changing slide layouts; inserting clip art; changing clip art size; adding slide transition effects; adding text animation effects; animating clip art; running an animated slide show; printing audience handouts from an outline; and e-mailing a slide show from within PowerPoint.

Web Feature – Creating a Presentation on the Web Using PowerPoint In the Web Feature, students are introduced to saving a presentation as a Web page. Topics include saving an existing PowerPoint presentation as an HTML file; viewing the presentation as a Web page; editing a Web page through a browser; and viewing the editing change.

Project 3 – Using Embedded Visuals to Enhance a Slide Show In Project 3, students create a presentation from a Microsoft Word outline and then enhance it with embedded visuals. Topics include creating a slide background using a picture; customizing graphical bullets; creating and embedding an organization chart; creating and formatting a PowerPoint table; scaling objects; ungrouping and modifying clip art; and applying slide transition and text preset animation effects.

Project 4 – Creating a Presentation Containing Interactive OLE Documents In Project 4, students customize the presentation created in Project 3 by updating the information on the slides and using object linking and embedding to create a slide containing action buttons and hyperlinks. Topics include creating a WordArt object; adding special text effects; modifying organization chart content and formatting; modifying a PowerPoint table; hiding a slide; using guides to position and size objects; adding a summary slide automatically; and running a slide show to display a hidden slide in an active interactive document.

Integration Feature – Importing Clips from the Microsoft Clip Gallery Live Web Site In the Integration Feature, students are introduced to downloading clips from a source on the Internet and adding them to a presentation. Topics include connecting to the Clip Gallery Live Web site; searching for and downloading motion and sound clips to Microsoft Clip Gallery 5.0; importing clips into a presentation; and positioning the clips on a slide.

Project 5 – Creating a Self-Running Presentation Using Animation Effects In Project 5, students create a self-running presentation to view at a kiosk. Topics include inserting an animated slide from another presentation; embedding animated clip art, an Excel chart, a PowerPoint chart, and a Word table; inserting and formatting an AutoShape; removing background objects from a slide; using custom animation effects; and setting automatic slide timings.

Project 6 – Using Visual Basic for Applications (VBA) with PowerPoint In Project 6, students use VBA to develop an electronic career portfolio designed for viewing during a job interview. The slides are customized for each interview and include clip art, a photograph, and a video clip. Topics include creating a new toolbar and adding buttons; using the macro recorder to create a macro that prints handouts displaying four slides per page; and assigning the macro to a command on the File menu.

Web Feature – Distributing Presentations to Remote Audiences In this Web Feature, students learn to use the Pack and Go Wizard to condense files and include the PowerPoint Viewer. Topics include downloading a file from a Web server; setting discussion options; and subscribing to a publication.

Appendices

Appendix A presents a detailed step-by-step introduction to the Microsoft PowerPoint Help system. Students learn how to use the Office Assistant and the Contents, Answer Wizard, and Index sheets in the PowerPoint Help window. Appendix B describes how to publish PowerPoint Web pages to a Web server. Appendix C shows students how to reset the menus and toolbars. Appendix D introduces students to the Microsoft Office User Specialist (MOUS) Certification program and includes a MOUS map that lists a page number in the book for each of the MOUS activities for Core level and the proposed Expert level.

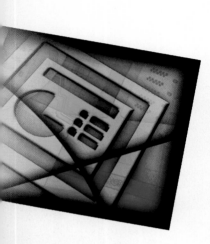

Quick Reference Summary

In PowerPoint, you can accomplish a task in a number of ways, such as using the mouse, menu, shortcut menu, and keyboard. The Quick Reference Summary at the back of this book provides a quick reference to the different ways to complete each task presented in this textbook. The Quick Reference Summary also is available on the Web at www.scsite.com/off2000/qr.htm.

End-of-Project Student Activities

A notable strength of the Shelly Cashman Series PowerPoint 2000 books is the extensive student activities at the end of each project. Well-structured student activities can make the difference between students merely participating in a class and students retaining the information they learn. The activities in the Shelly Cashman Series PowerPoint 2000 books include the following.

- ○ **What You Should Know** A listing of the tasks completed within a project together with the pages where the step-by-step, screen-by-screen explanations appear. This section provides a perfect study review for students.

- ○ **Project Reinforcement on the Web** Every project has a Web page (www.scsite.com/off2000/reinforce.htm). The Web page includes true/false, multiple choice, and short answer questions, and additional project-related reinforcement activities that will help students gain confidence in their PowerPoint 2000 abilities. The Project Reinforcement exercises also are included on the Shelly Cashman Series Teaching Tools CD-ROM.

- ○ **Apply Your Knowledge** This exercise requires students to open and manipulate a file on the Data Disk. To obtain a copy of the Data Disk, follow the instructions on the inside back cover of this book.

- ○ **In the Lab** Three in-depth assignments per project require students to apply the knowledge gained in the project to solve problems on a computer.

- ○ **Cases and Places** Up to seven unique case studies that require students to apply their knowledge to real-world situations.

Shelly Cashman Series Teaching Tools

A comprehensive set of Teaching Tools accompanies this textbook in the form of a CD-ROM. The CD-ROM includes an Instructor's Manual and teaching and testing aids. The CD-ROM (ISBN 0-7895-4636-1) is available through your Course Technology representative or by calling one of the following telephone numbers: Colleges and Universities, 1-800-648-7450; High Schools, 1-800-824-5179; Career Colleges, 1-800-477-3692; Canada, 1-800-268-2222; and Corporations and Government Agencies, 1-800-340-7450.

- Instructor's Manual The Instructor's Manual is made up of Microsoft Word files. The files include lecture notes, solutions to laboratory assignments, and a large test bank. The files allow you to modify the lecture notes or generate quizzes and exams from the test bank using your own word processing software. Where appropriate, solutions to laboratory assignments are embedded as icons in the files. When an icon appears, double-click it and the application will start and the solution will display on the screen. The Instructor's Manual includes the following for each project: project objectives; project overview; detailed lesson plans with page number references; teacher notes and activities; answers to the end-of-project exercises; test bank of 110 questions for every project (25 multiple-choice, 50 true/false, and 35 fill-in-the-blank) with page number references; and transparency references. The transparencies are available through the Figures in the Book. The test bank questions are numbered the same as in Course Test Manager. Thus, you can print a copy of the project test bank and use the printout to select your questions in Course Test Manager.

- Figures in the Book Illustrations for every screen and table in the textbook are available in JPEG format. Use this ancillary to create a slide show from the illustrations for lecture or to print transparencies for use in lecture. You also may create your own PowerPoint presentations and insert these illustrations.

- Course Test Manager Course Test Manager is a powerful testing and assessment package that enables instructors to create and print tests from the large test bank. Instructors with PowerPoint to a networked computer lab (LAN) can administer, grade, and track tests online. Students also can take online practice tests, which generate customized study guides.

- Course Syllabus Any instructor who has been assigned a course at the last minute knows how difficult it is to come up with a course syllabus. For this reason, sample syllabi are included for each of the PowerPoint 2000 products that can be customized easily to a course.

- Lecture Success System Lecture Success System files are for use with the application software, a personal computer, and projection device to explain and illustrate the step-by-step, screen-by-screen development of a project in the textbook without entering large amounts of data.

- Instructor's Lab Solutions Solutions and required files for all the In the Lab assignments at the end of each project are available.

- Lab Tests/Test Outs Tests that parallel the In the Lab assignments are supplied for the purpose of testing students in the laboratory on the material covered in the project or testing students out of the course.

- Project Reinforcement True/false, multiple choice, and short answer questions, and additional project-related reinforcement activities for each project help students gain confidence in their PowerPoint 2000 abilities.

- Student Files All the files that are required by students to complete the Apply Your Knowledge exercises are included.

- Interactive Labs Eighteen hands-on interactive labs that take students from ten to fifteen minutes each to step through help solidify and reinforce mouse and keyboard usage and computer concepts. Student assessment is available.

- WebCT Content This ancillary includes book-related content that can be uploaded to your institution's WebCT site. The content includes a sample syllabus, practice tests, a bank of test questions, a list of book-related links, and lecture notes from the Instructor's Manual.

Acknowledgments

The Shelly Cashman Series would not be the leading computer education series without the contributions of outstanding publishing professionals. First, and foremost, among them is Becky Herrington, director of production and designer. She is the heart and soul of the Shelly Cashman Series, and it is only through her leadership, dedication, and tireless efforts that superior products are made possible. Becky created and produced the award-winning Windows series of books.

Under Becky's direction, the following individuals made significant contributions to these books: Doug Cowley, production manager; Ginny Harvey, series specialist and developmental editor; Ken Russo, senior Web designer; Mike Bodnar, associate production manager; Stephanie Nance, graphic artist and cover designer; Mark Norton, Web designer; Meena Mohtadi, production editor; Marlo Mitchem, Chris Schneider, Hector Arvizu, Kenny Tran, Kathy Mayers, and Dave Bonnewitz, graphic artists; Jeanne Black and Betty Hopkins, Quark experts; Nancy Lamm, Lyn Markowicz, Margaret Gatling, and Laurie Sullivan, copyeditors; Marilyn Martin, Kim Kosmatka, Cherilyn King, Mary Steinman, and Pat Hadden, proofreaders; Cristina Haley, indexer; Sarah Evertson of Image Quest, photo researcher; and Susan Sebok and Ginny Harvey, contributing writers.

Special thanks go to Richard Keaveny, managing editor; Jim Quasney, series consulting editor; Lora Wade, product manager; Erin Bennett, associate product manager; Francis Schurgot, Web product manager; Scott Wiseman, online developer; Rajika Gupta, marketing manager; and Erin Runyon, editorial assistant.

Gary B. Shelly
Thomas J. Cashman
Susan L. Sebok

Shelly Cashman Series – Traditionally Bound Textbooks

For more information, see your Course Technology representative, call 1-800-648-7450, or visit Shelly Cashman Online at **www.scseries.com**

COMPUTERS	
Computers	Discovering Computers 2000: Concepts for a Connected World, Web and CNN Enhanced
	Discovering Computers 2000: Concepts for a Connected World, Web and CNN Enhanced Brief Edition
	Teachers Discovering Computers: A Link to the Future, Web and CNN Enhanced
	Discovering Computers 98: A Link to the Future, World Wide Web Enhanced
	Discovering Computers 98: A Link to the Future, World Wide Web Enhanced Brief Edition
	Exploring Computers: A Record of Discovery 2e with CD-ROM
	Study Guide for Discovering Computers 2000: Concepts for a Connected World
	Essential Introduction to Computers 3e (32-page)
	Discovering Computer Certification: Planning, Prerequisites, Potential
	Discovering Internet Companies: Doing Business in the New Millennium

WINDOWS APPLICATIONS	
Microsoft Office	Microsoft Office 2000: Essential Concepts and Techniques (5 projects)
	Microsoft Office 2000: Brief Concepts and Techniques (9 projects)
	Microsoft Office 2000: Introductory Concepts and Techniques (15 projects)
	Microsoft Office 2000: Advanced Concepts and Techniques (11 projects)
	Microsoft Office 2000: Post Advanced Concepts and Techniques (11 projects)
	Microsoft Office 97: Introductory Concepts and Techniques, Brief Edition (6 projects)
	Microsoft Office 97: Introductory Concepts and Techniques, Essentials Edition (10 projects)
	Microsoft Office 97: Introductory Concepts and Techniques, Enhanced Edition (15 projects)
	Microsoft Office 97: Advanced Concepts and Techniques
Microsoft Works	Microsoft Works 4.5[1]
Windows	Microsoft Windows 98: Essential Concepts and Techniques (2 projects)
	Microsoft Windows 98: Introductory Concepts and Techniques (3 projects)
	Microsoft Windows 98: Introductory Concepts and Techniques Web Style Edition (3 projects)
	Microsoft Windows 98[2]: Complete Concepts and Techniques (6 projects)
	Microsoft Windows 98: Comprehensive Concepts and Techniques (9 projects)
	Introduction to Microsoft Windows NT Workstation 4
	Microsoft Windows 95: Introductory Concepts and Techniques (2 projects)
	Introduction to Microsoft Windows 95 (3 projects)
	Microsoft Windows 95[1]: Complete Concepts and Techniques (6 projects)
Word Processing	Microsoft Word 2000[2] • Microsoft Word 97[1] • Microsoft Word 7[1]
	Corel WordPerfect 8 • Corel WordPerfect 7 • WordPerfect 6.1[1]
Spreadsheets	Microsoft Excel 2000[2] • Microsoft Excel 97[1] • Microsoft Excel 7[1] • Microsoft Excel 5[1] • Lotus 1-2-3 97[1]
Database	Microsoft Access 2000[2] • Microsoft Access 97[1] • Microsoft Access 7[1]
Presentation Graphics	Microsoft PowerPoint 2000[2] • Microsoft PowerPoint 97[1] • Microsoft PowerPoint 7[1]
Desktop Publishing	Microsoft Publisher 2000[1]
Graphic Design	Microsoft PhotoDraw 2000: Essential Concepts and Techniques

PROGRAMMING	
Programming	Microsoft Visual Basic 6: Complete Concepts and Techniques[1]
	Microsoft Visual Basic 5: Complete Concepts and Techniques[1]
	QBasic • QBasic: An Introduction to Programming • Microsoft BASIC
	Structured COBOL Programming, Second Edition

INTERNET	
Browser	Microsoft Internet Explorer 5: An Introduction • Microsoft Internet Explorer 4: An Introduction
	Netscape Navigator 4: An Introduction
Web Page Creation	HTML: Complete Concepts and Techniques[1] • Microsoft FrontPage 2000: Complete Concepts and Techniques[1] • Microsoft FrontPage 98: Complete Concepts and Techniques[1] • Netscape Composer • JavaScript: Complete Concepts and Techniques[1]

SYSTEMS ANALYSIS/DATA COMMUNICATIONS	
Systems Analysis	Systems Analysis and Design, Third Edition
Data Communications	Business Data Communications: Introductory Concepts and Techniques, Second Edition

[1]Also available as an Introductory Edition, which is a shortened version of the complete book
[2]Also available as an Introductory Edition, which is a shortened version of the complete book and also as a Comprehensive Edition, which is an extended version of the complete book

Shelly Cashman Series – **Custom Edition**® Program

If you do not find a Shelly Cashman Series traditionally bound textbook to fit your needs, the Shelly Cashman Series unique **Custom Edition** program allows you to choose from a number of options and create a textbook perfectly suited to your course. Features of the **Custom Edition** program are:

- Textbooks that match the content of your course
- Windows- and DOS-based materials for the latest versions of personal computer applications software
- Shelly Cashman Series quality, with the same full-color materials and Shelly Cashman Series pedagogy found in the traditionally bound books
- Affordable pricing so your students receive the **Custom Edition** at a cost similar to that of traditionally bound books

The table on the right summarizes the available materials.

For more information, see your Course Technology representative or call one of the following telephone numbers: Colleges and Universities, 1-800-648-7450; High Schools, 1-800-824-5179; Career Colleges, 1-800-477-3692; Canada, 1-800-268-2222; and Corporations and Government Agencies, 1-800-340-7450.

For Shelly Cashman Series information, visit Shelly Cashman Online at **www.scseries.com**

COMPUTERS	
Computers	Discovering Computers 2000: Concepts for a Connected World, Web and CNN Enhanced
	Discovering Computers 2000: Concepts for a Connected World, Web and CNN Enhanced Brief Edition
	Discovering Computers 98: A Link to the Future, World Wide Web Enhanced
	Discovering Computers 98: A Link to the Future, World Wide Web Enhanced Brief Edition
	A Record of Discovery for Exploring Computers 2e (available with CD-ROM)
	Study Guide for Discovering Computers 2000: Concepts for a Connected World, Web and CNN Enhanced
	Essential Introduction to Computers 3e (32-page)
OPERATING SYSTEMS	
Windows	Microsoft Windows 98: Essential Concepts and Techniques (2 projects)
	Microsoft Windows 98: Introductory Concepts and Techniques (3 projects)
	Microsoft Windows 98: Introductory Concepts and Techniques Web Style Edition (3-project)
	Microsoft Windows 98: Complete Concepts and Techniques (6 projects)
	Microsoft Windows 98: Comprehensive Concepts and Techniques (9 projects)
	Microsoft Windows 95: Introductory Concepts and Techniques (2 projects)
	Introduction to Microsoft Windows NT Workstation 4
	Introduction to Microsoft Windows 95 (3 projects)
	Microsoft Windows 95: Complete Concepts and Techniques
DOS	Introduction to DOS 6 (using DOS prompt)
WINDOWS APPLICATIONS	
Microsoft Office	Microsoft Office 2000: Brief Concepts and Techniques (5 projects)
	Microsoft Office 97: Introductory Concepts and Techniques, Brief Edition (396-pages)
	Microsoft Office 97: Introductory Concepts and Techniques, Essentials Edition (672-pages)
	Object Linking and Embedding (OLE) (32-page)
	Microsoft Outlook 97 • Microsoft Schedule+ 7
	Using Microsoft Office 97 (16-page)
	Using Microsoft Office 95 (16-page)
	Introduction to Integrating Office 97 Applications (48-page)
	Introduction to Integrating Office 95 Applications (80-page)
Word Processing	Microsoft Word 2000* • Microsoft Word 97* • Microsoft Word 7* Corel WordPerfect 8 • Corel WordPerfect 7 •
Spreadsheets	Microsoft Excel 2000* • Microsoft Excel 97* • Microsoft Excel 7* Lotus 1-2-3 97* • Quattro Pro 6
Database	Microsoft Access 2000* • Microsoft Access 97* • Microsoft Access 7*
Presentation	Microsoft PowerPoint 2000* • Microsoft PowerPoint 97*
Graphics	Microsoft PowerPoint 7*
INTERNET	
Internet	The Internet: Introductory Concepts and Techniques (UNIX)
Browser	Netscape Navigator 4 • Netscape Navigator 3
	Microsoft Internet Explorer 5 • Microsoft Internet Explorer 4
	Microsoft Internet Explorer 3
Web Page Creation	Netscape Composer

*Also available as a mini-module

Microsoft PowerPoint 2000

PROJECT

1

Using a Design Template and AutoLayouts to Create a Presentation

OBJECTIVES

You will have mastered the material in this project when you can:

- Start a presentation as a New Office document
- Describe the PowerPoint window
- Select a design template
- Create a title slide
- Describe and use text attributes such as font size and font style
- Save a presentation
- Add a new slide
- Create a multi-level bulleted list slide
- Move to another slide in normal view
- End a slide show with a black slide
- View a presentation in slide show view
- Quit PowerPoint
- Open a presentation
- Check the spelling and consistency of a presentation
- Edit a presentation
- Change line spacing on the slide master
- Display a presentation in black and white
- Print a presentation in black and white
- Use the PowerPoint Help system

Puttin' on the Glitz

Presentations Help COMDEX Shine

Microsoft's Bill Gates will be there. So will thousands of the world's computer industry executives. And they will be joined by hundreds of thousands of curious technology affectionados seeking the latest trends in hardware, software, and the Internet.

They will be attending COMDEX, North America's largest trade show. COMDEX/Fall is held in Las Vegas each November, and COMDEX/Spring is held in Chicago in April. Both shows feature speeches by industry leaders, tutorials on the latest technologies, and thousands of square feet of exhibits showcasing the latest in computer technology.

Information technology (IT) experts headline COMDEX as the premier IT event in the world. Indeed, more than 10,000 new products are unveiled at the Fall show. Since COMDEX's inception in 1979, some of the more notable product launches have been the IBM PC in 1981, COMPAQ's suitcase-sized portable computer, Microsoft's first version of Windows, Apple's original Macintosh computer, and CD-ROM drives.

Attendance and industry representation have grown steadily. The first show featured 150 exhibitions seen by 4,000 curious visitors. Six years later, more than 1,000 companies displayed their wares for more than 100,000 techies. Recent shows have produced as many as 2,400 booths visited by 250,000-plus attendees.

Computer companies realize their sales forces need to capture their audiences' attention, so they add sensory cues to their exhibits. They treat the trade show visitors to a multimedia blitz of sound, visuals, and action with the help of presentation software such as Microsoft PowerPoint 2000. This program enhances the presenters' speeches by highlighting keywords in the presentation, displaying graphs, pictures, and diagrams, and playing sound and video clips.

In this project, you will learn to use PowerPoint 2000 to create a presentation, which also is called a slide show, concerning effective study skills. You then will run the slide show and print handouts for the audience. In later projects you will add animation, pictures, and sound.

PowerPoint's roots stem from the innovative work performed by a small company called Forethought, Inc. Programmers at this pioneering business coined the phrase, desktop presentation graphics, for formal slide shows and created a complete software package that automated creating slides containing text, charts, and graphics. Microsoft liked the visual appeal of the software and acquired Forethought in 1987. Company executives decided to market the software to Apple Macintosh users because Mac computers were considered clearly superior to IBM-based personal computers for graphics applications.

Microsoft PowerPoint became a favorite among Mac users. Meanwhile, Lotus Freelance Graphics and Software Publishing Harvard Graphics were popular within the PC community. This division ceased, however, when Microsoft released Windows 3.0 in 1990 and subsequently developed a Windows version of PowerPoint to run on PCs.

Since that time, Macintosh and PC users alike have utilized the presentation power of PowerPoint. The package has grown to include animation, audio and video clips, and Internet integration. Certainly the technology gurus at COMDEX have realized PowerPoint's dazzling visual appeal. So will you as you complete the exercises in this textbook.

Microsoft **PowerPoint 2000**

Microsoft PowerPoint 2000

Using a Design Template and AutoLayouts to Create a Presentation

P R O J E C T

1

C A S E   P E R S P E C T I V E

Excellent study habits are the keys to college success. What matters is not how long people study — it is how well they use their time. Students who study well can maximize their hours, have time for other activities, make the highest grades, and have a better chance to get accepted to their desired school. Ultimately, they generally earn higher incomes because their good study habits carry over to the working environment.

Advisers in Seaview College's Counseling Department spend many hours each semester helping students organize their study times, maximize their classroom experiences, and read their textbooks for ultimate comprehension. Dr. Ramon Martinez, the dean of counseling, has asked you to develop a short presentation to run at next semester's Freshmen Orientation sessions. You agree to create the presentation using a computer and PowerPoint software with the theme of effective study habits. In addition, you will print handouts of the presentation for the incoming students and also print a copy of the presentation on transparency film to enable the advisers to project the slides using an overhead projector.

What Is Microsoft PowerPoint 2000?

Microsoft PowerPoint 2000 is a complete presentation graphics program that allows you to produce professional-looking presentations. A PowerPoint **presentation** also is called a **slide show**. PowerPoint gives you the flexibility to make presentations using a projection device attached to a personal computer (Figure 1-1a) and using overhead transparencies (Figure 1-1b). In addition, you can take advantage of the World Wide Web and run virtual presentations on the Internet (Figure 1-1c). PowerPoint also can create paper printouts of the individual slides, outlines, and speaker notes.

PowerPoint contains several features to simplify creating a slide show. For example, you can instruct PowerPoint to create a predesigned presentation, and then you can modify the presentation to fulfill your requirements. You quickly can format a slide show using one of the professionally designed presentation design templates. To make your presentation more impressive, you can add tables, charts, pictures, video, sound, and, animation effects. You also can check the spelling of your slide show as you type or after you have completed designing the presentation. For example, you can instruct PowerPoint to restrict the number of bulleted items on a slide or limit the number of words in each paragraph. Additional PowerPoint features include the following:

- ❯ **Word processing** — create bulleted lists, combine words and images, find and replace text, and use multiple fonts and type sizes.
- ❯ **Outlining** — develop your presentation using an outline format. You also can import outlines from Microsoft Word or other word processing programs.
- ❯ **Charting** — create and insert charts into your presentations. The two chart types are: standard, which includes bar, line, pie, and xy (scatter) charts; and custom, which displays floating bars, colored lines, and three-dimensional cones.

(a) Projection Device Connected to a Personal Computer

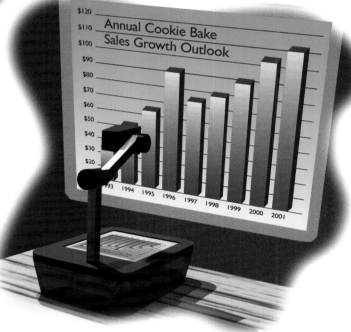

(b) Overhead Transparencies

FIGURE 1-1

(c) PowerPoint Presentation Over the World Wide Web

Projection Devices

Multimedia projectors have become the standard for today's presenters. The newest devices are about the size of a deli sandwich, weigh just five pounds, and fill the room with brilliant, clear images. For more information, visit the PowerPoint 2000 More About Web page (www.scsite.com/pp2000/more.htm) and click Projection.

▶ **Drawing** —form and modify diagrams using shapes such as arcs, arrows, cubes, rectangles, stars, and triangles.

▶ **Inserting multimedia** — insert artwork and multimedia effects into your slide show. Clip Gallery 5.0 contains hundreds of clip art images, pictures, photos, sounds, and video clips. You can search for clips by entering words or phrases that describe the subject you want, by looking for clips with similar artistic styles, colors, or shapes, or by connecting to a special Web site reserved for Clip Gallery users. You also can import art from other applications.

▶ **Web support** — save presentations or parts of a presentation in HTML format so they can be viewed and manipulated using a browser. You can publish your slide show to the Internet or to an intranet. You also can insert action buttons and hyperlinks to create a self-running or interactive Web presentation.

▶ **E-mailing** — send an individual slide as an e-mail message or your entire slide show as an attachment to an e-mail message.

▶ **Using Wizards** — quickly and efficiently create a presentation by answering prompts for specific content criteria. For example, the **AutoContent Wizard** gives prompts for the type of slide show you are planning, such as communicating bad news or motivating a team, and the type of output, such as an on-screen presentation or black and white overheads. If you are planning to run your presentation on another computer, the **Pack and Go Wizard** helps you bundle everything you need, including any objects associated with that presentation. If you cannot confirm that this other computer has PowerPoint installed, you also can include the **PowerPoint Viewer**, a program that allows you to run, but not edit, a PowerPoint slide show.

Project One — Effective Study Skills

This book presents a series of projects using PowerPoint to produce slides similar to those you would develop in an academic or business environment. Project 1 uses PowerPoint to create the presentation shown in Figures 1-2a through 1-2d. The objective is to produce a presentation, called Effective Study Skills, to be displayed using an overhead projector. As an introduction to PowerPoint, this project steps you through the most common type of presentation, which is a bulleted list. A **bulleted list** is a list of paragraphs, each preceded by a bullet. A **bullet** is a symbol such as a heavy dot (•) or other character that precedes text when the text warrants special emphasis.

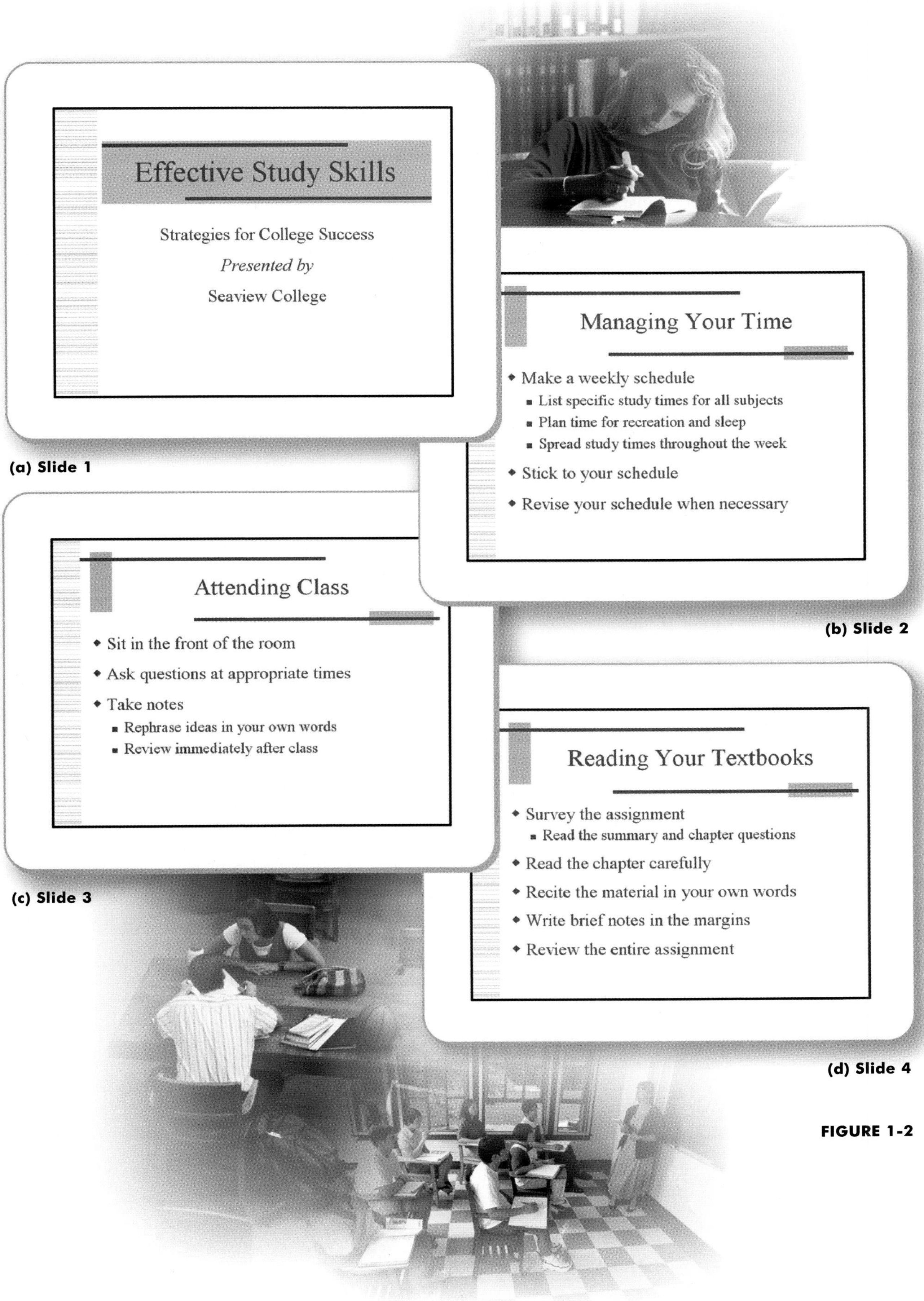

(a) Slide 1

(b) Slide 2

(c) Slide 3

(d) Slide 4

FIGURE 1-2

Starting a Presentation as a New Office Document

The quickest way to begin a new presentation is to use the **Start button** on the **taskbar** at the bottom of your screen. When you click the Start button, the **Start menu** displays several commands for simplifying tasks in Windows. When Microsoft Office 2000 is installed, the Start menu displays the New Office Document and Open Office Document commands. You use the **New Office Document command** to designate the type of Office document you are creating. The Open Office Document command is discussed later in this project. Perform these steps to start a new presentation, or ask your instructor how to start PowerPoint on your system.

To Start a New Presentation

1 **Click the Start button on the taskbar and then point to New Office Document.**

The programs on the Start menu display above the Start button (Figure 1-3). The New Office Document command is highlighted on the Start menu. Your computer system displays the time on the clock in the tray status area on the taskbar.

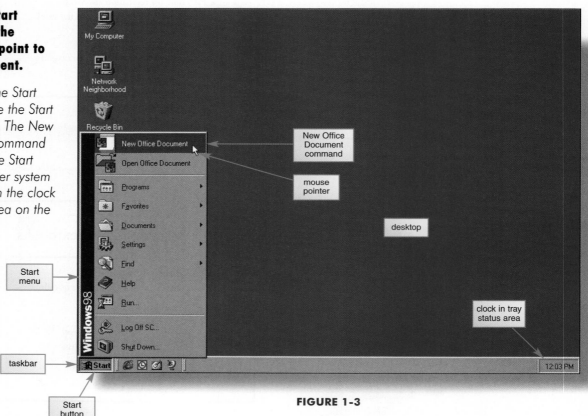

FIGURE 1-3

2 **Click New Office Document. If necessary, click the General tab in the New Office Document dialog box, and then click the Blank Presentation icon.**

Office displays several icons on the General sheet in the New Office Document dialog box (Figure 1-4). Each icon represents a different type of document you can create in Microsoft Office. In this project, you will create a new presentation using Microsoft PowerPoint, starting with a blank presentation.

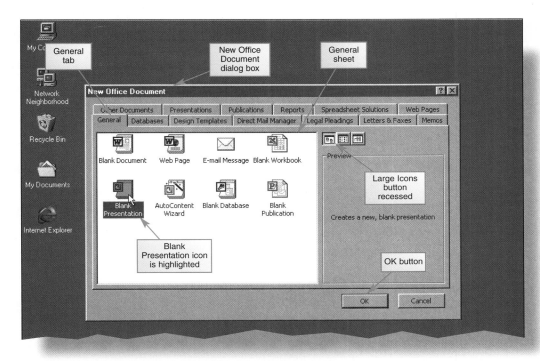

FIGURE 1-4

3 **Click the OK button. If necessary, enlarge the PowerPoint window by double-clicking its title bar. If the Office Assistant displays, right-click the Office Assistant and then click Hide on the shortcut menu. Point to the OK button in the New Slide dialog box.**

The New Slide dialog box displays (Figure 1-5). The Title Slide AutoLayout is selected, and its name displays in the lower-right corner of the New Slide dialog box. The Office Assistant will be discussed later in this project.

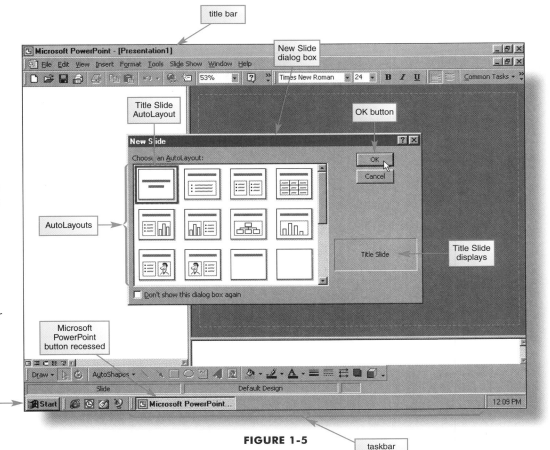

FIGURE 1-5

4 Click the OK button.

PowerPoint displays the Title Slide AutoLayout and the Default Design template on Slide 1 (Figure 1-6). The title bar identifies this window as a Microsoft PowerPoint presentation currently titled [Presentation1]. The status bar displays information about the current slide: the slide number and the name of the current design template.

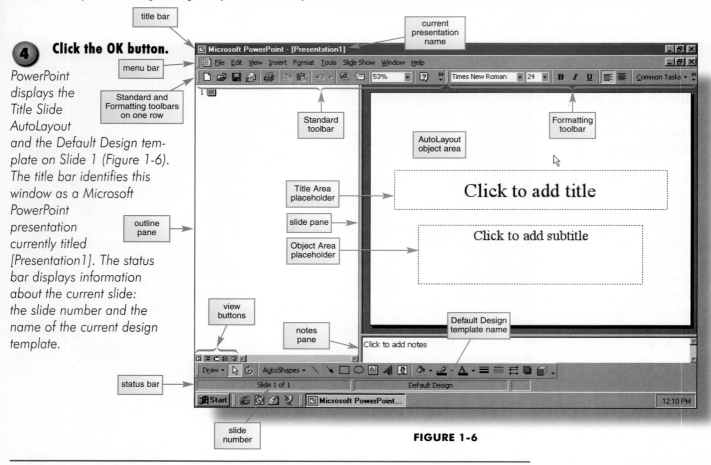

FIGURE 1-6

When an application is open, its name displays on a button in the **taskbar button area**. The **active application** is the one displaying on the foreground of the desktop. That application's corresponding button in the taskbar button area displays recessed.

The basic unit of a PowerPoint presentation is a **slide**. A slide contains one or many **objects**, such as a title, text, graphics, tables, charts, and drawings. An object is the building block for a PowerPoint slide. PowerPoint assumes the first slide in a new presentation is the **title slide**. The title slide's purpose is to introduce the presentation to the audience.

The PowerPoint Window

In PowerPoint, you have the option of using the PowerPoint default settings or establishing your own. A **default setting** is a particular value for a variable that PowerPoint assigns initially. It controls the placement of objects, the color scheme, the transition between slides, and other slide attributes, and it remains in effect unless you cancel or override it. **Attributes** are the properties or characteristics of an object. For example, if you underline the title of a slide, the title is the object, and the underline is the attribute. When you start PowerPoint, the default **slide layout** is **landscape orientation**, where the slide width is greater than its height. In landscape orientation, the slide size is preset to 10 inches wide and 7.5 inches high. The slide layout can be changed to **portrait orientation**, so that the slide height is greater than its width, by clicking Page Setup on the File menu. In portrait orientation, the slide width is 7.5 inches, and the height is 10 inches.

PowerPoint Views

PowerPoint has five views: normal view, outline view, slide view, slide sorter view, and slide show. A **view** is the mode in which the presentation displays on the screen. You may use any or all views when creating your presentation, but you can use only one at a time. Change views by clicking one of the view buttons found in the lower-left of the PowerPoint window above the status bar (Figure 1-6). The PowerPoint window display is dependent on the view. Some views are graphical while others are textual.

You generally will use normal view and slide sorter view when you are creating your presentation. Normal view is composed of three panes, which are the **outline pane**, **slide pane**, and **notes pane**. You can drag the pane borders to adjust the size of the panes. They allow you to work on various aspects of your presentation simultaneously (Figure 1-6). You can type the text of your presentation in the outline pane and easily rearrange bulleted lists, paragraphs, and individual slides. As you type in the outline pane, you can view this text in the slide pane. You also can enter text, graphics, animations, and hyperlinks directly in the slide pane. You can type notes and additional information in the notes pane. This text can consist of notes to yourself or remarks to share with your audience. After you have created at least two slides, **scroll bars**, **scroll arrows**, and **scroll boxes** will display below and to the right of the windows, and you can use them to view different parts of the panes.

Slide sorter view is helpful when you want to see all the slides in your presentation simultaneously. A miniature version of each slide displays, and you can rearrange their order, add transitions and timings to switch from one side to the next in your presentation, add and delete slides, and preview animations.

Table 1-1 identifies the view buttons and provides an explanation of each view.

More About

PowerPoint Views

The three panes in normal, outline, and slide views allow you to work on all aspects of your presentation simultaneously. You can drag the pane borders to make each area larger or smaller.

Table 1-1	View Buttons and Functions	
BUTTON	NAME	FUNCTION
	Normal View	Displays three panes: the outline pane, the slide pane, and the notes pane.
	Outline View	Displays a presentation in an outline format showing slide titles and text. It is best used for organizing and developing the content of your presentation. You can rearrange paragraphs and bullet points in this view.
	Slide View	Displays a single slide as it appears in your presentation. Slide view is used to incorporate text, graphics, video, audio, hyperlinks, and animation and also to create line-by-line progressive disclosure, called build effects. Use slide view to create or edit a presentation.
	Slide Sorter View	Displays miniature versions of all slides in your presentation. You then can copy, cut, paste, or otherwise change slide position to modify your presentation. Slide sorter view also is used to add timings, to select animated transitions, and to preview animations.
	Slide Show View	Displays your slides as an electronic presentation on the full screen of your computer's monitor. Looking much like a slide projector display, you can see the effect of transitions, build effects, slide timings, and animations.

Placeholders, Title Area, Object Area, Mouse Pointer, and Scroll Bars

The PowerPoint window contains elements similar to the document windows in other Microsoft Office 2000 applications. Other features are unique to PowerPoint. The main elements are the Title Area and Object Area placeholders, the mouse pointer, and scroll bars.

PLACEHOLDERS **Placeholders** are boxes that display when you create a new slide. All AutoLayouts except the Blank AutoLayout contain placeholders. Depending on the particular slide layout selected, placeholders display for the slide title, text, charts, tables, organization charts, media clips, and clip art. You type titles, body text, and bulleted lists in **text placeholders**; you place graphic elements in chart placeholders, table placeholders, organizational chart placeholders, and clip art placeholders. A placeholder is considered an **object**, which is a single element of your slide. An empty placeholder is called an **unfilled object**; a placeholder containing text or graphics is called a **filled object**. When a filled object contains text, it is called a **text object**.

TITLE AREA Surrounded by a dotted outline, the **Title Area** is the location of the text placeholder where you will type the main heading of a new slide (Figure 1-6 on page PP 1.12).

OBJECT AREA Surrounded by a dotted outline, the **Object Area** is the empty area that displays below the Title Area on a slide. It can contain various placeholders for displaying subtitle or supporting information such as clip art and charts (Figure 1-6).

MOUSE POINTER The **mouse pointer** can have a different shape depending on the task you are performing in PowerPoint and the pointer's location on the screen. The different shapes are discussed when they display in subsequent projects.

SCROLL BARS When you add a second slide to your presentation, **vertical scroll bars** display on the right side of the outline and slide panes. PowerPoint allows you to use the scroll bars to move forward or backward through your presentation.

The **horizontal scroll bar** also displays when you add a second slide to your presentation. It is located on the bottom of the slide pane and allows you to display a portion of the slide when the entire slide does not fit on the screen.

Menu Bar, Standard Toolbar, Formatting Toolbar, Drawing Toolbar, and Status Bar

The menu bar, Standard toolbar, and Formatting toolbar display at the top of the screen just below the title bar (Figure 1-6). The Standard and Formatting toolbars are by default on one row. The Drawing toolbar and status bar display at the bottom of the screen above the Windows taskbar.

MENU BAR The menu bar displays the PowerPoint menu names (Figure 1-7a). Each menu name represents a menu of commands that you can use to retrieve, store, print, and manipulate objects in your presentation. When you point to a menu name on the menu bar, the area of the menu bar containing the name changes to a button. To display a menu, such as the Insert menu, click the Insert menu name on the menu bar (Figures 1-7b and 1-7c). If you point to a command with an arrow on the right, a submenu displays from which you can choose a command.

When you click a menu name on the menu bar, a **short menu** displays listing the most recently used commands (Figure 1-7b). If you wait a few seconds or click the arrows at the bottom of the short menu (Figure 1-7b), the full menu displays. The **full menu** shows all the commands associated with a menu (Figure 1-7c). As you use PowerPoint, it automatically personalizes the menus for you based on how often you use commands. In this book, when you display a menu, wait a few seconds or click the arrows at the bottom of the menu so the long menu displays. The **hidden commands** that display on the full menu are recessed. **Dimmed commands** (gray background) indicate they are not available for the current selection.

The menu bar can change to include other menu names depending on the type of work you are doing. For example, if you are adding a chart to a slide, Data and Chart menu names are added to the menu bar with commands that reflect charting options.

More About

The Mouse Pointer

The Microsoft IntelliMouse® pointing device can help you build presentations efficiently. For example, you can roll the wheel forward or backward instead of clicking a scroll bar. You also can have your document scroll automatically. For more information, visit the PowerPoint 2000 More About Web page (www.scsite.com/pp2000/more.htm) and click IntelliMouse.

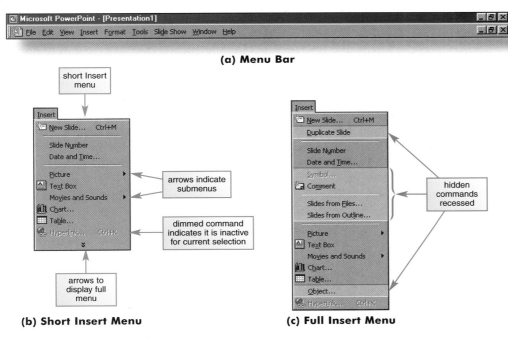

(a) Menu Bar

(b) Short Insert Menu

(c) Full Insert Menu

FIGURE 1-7

STANDARD, FORMATTING, AND DRAWING TOOLBARS The Standard toolbar (Figure 1-8a), Formatting toolbar (Figure 1-8b), and Drawing toolbar (Figure 1-8c) contain buttons and list boxes that allow you to perform frequent tasks more quickly than when using the menu bar. For example, to print a slide show, you click the Print button on the Standard toolbar. Each button has an image on the button that helps you remember the button's function. When you move the mouse pointer over a button or box, the name of the button or box also displays below it. This name is called a **ScreenTip**.

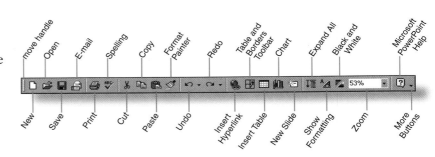

(a) Standard Toolbar

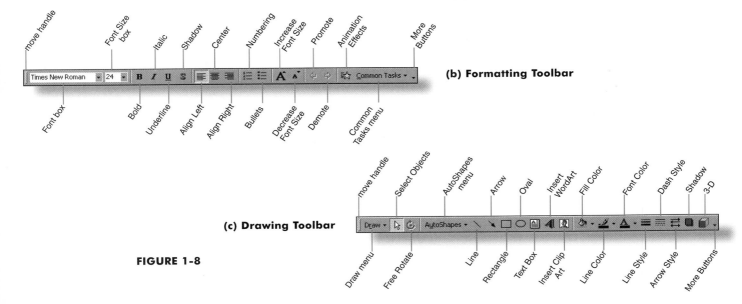

(b) Formatting Toolbar

(c) Drawing Toolbar

FIGURE 1-8

Toolbars

To display more of the PowerPoint window, you can hide a toolbar you no longer need. To hide a toolbar, right-click any toolbar and then click the check mark next to the toolbar you want to hide.

Figures 1-8a, 1-8b, and 1-8c on the previous page illustrate the Standard, Formatting, and Drawing toolbars and describe the functions of the buttons. Each of the buttons and list boxes will be explained in detail when they are used in the projects.

Remember, both the Standard and Formatting toolbars are by default on the same row immediately below the menu bar. Usually, the Standard toolbar displays on the left of the row and the Formatting toolbar displays on the right (Figure 1-9a).

To view the entire Formatting toolbar, double-click the move handle on its left edge or drag the move handle to the left. When you show the complete Formatting toolbar, a portion of the Standard toolbar is hidden (Figure 1-9b). To display the entire Standard toolbar, double-click its move handle. PowerPoint slides the Formatting toolbar to the right so the toolbars return to the way they look in Figure 1-9a.

An alternative to sliding one toolbar over another is to use the More Buttons button on a toolbar to display the buttons that are hidden (Figure 1-9c).

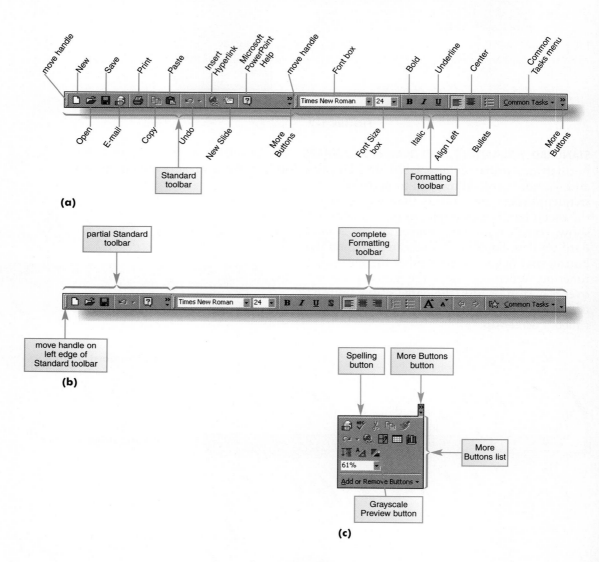

FIGURE 1-9

As with the menus, PowerPoint will personalize the toolbars. That is, if you use a hidden button on a partially displayed toolbar, PowerPoint will remove the button from the More Buttons list (Figure 1-9c) and place it on the toolbar. For example, if you click the Spelling button and then the Grayscale Preview button on the Standard toolbar (Figure 1-9c), PowerPoint will display these buttons on the Standard toolbar and remove buttons from the Standard or Formatting toolbars to make room on the row.

STATUS BAR Immediately above the Windows taskbar at the bottom of the screen is the status bar. The **status bar** consists of a message area and a presentation design template identifier (Figure 1-11 on page PP 1.18). Generally the message area displays the current slide number and the total number of slides in the slide show. For example, in Figure 1-11 the message area displays Slide 1 of 1. Slide 1 is the current slide, and of 1 indicates the slide show contains only 1 slide. The template identifier displays Default Design, which is the template PowerPoint uses initially.

PowerPoint has several additional toolbars you can display by pointing to Toolbars on the View menu and then clicking the respective name on the Toolbars submenu. You also can display a toolbar by pointing to a toolbar and right-clicking to display a shortcut menu, which lists the available toolbars. A **shortcut menu** contains a list of commands or items that relate to the item to which you are pointing when you right-click.

Resetting Menus and Toolbars

Each project in this book begins with the menu bars and toolbars appearing as they did at initial installation of the software. To reset your toolbars and menus so they appear exactly as shown in this book, follow the steps outlined in Appendix C.

Displaying the Formatting Toolbar in Its Entirety

Perform the following steps to display the entire Formatting toolbar.

More About

Personalizing

Have some fun building your presentation by adding sound cues. You can download files from the Microsoft Web site that play sounds when you scroll, open dialog boxes, and zoom in or out. For more information, visit the PowerPoint 2000 More About Web page (www.scsite.com/pp2000/more.htm) and click Personalizing.

 To Display the Formatting Toolbar in Its Entirety

1 Point to the move handle on the Formatting toolbar (Figure 1-10).

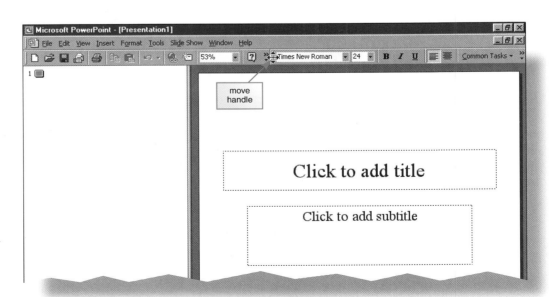

FIGURE 1-10

Microsoft **PowerPoint** 2000

2 Double-click the move handle on the Formatting toolbar.

The entire Formatting toolbar displays (Figure 1-11).

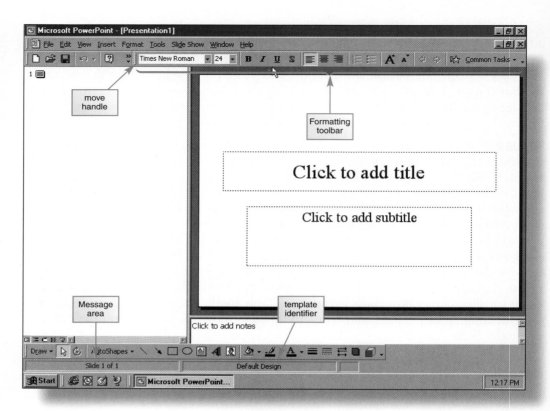

FIGURE 1-11

Choosing a Design Template

A **design template** provides consistency in design and color throughout the entire presentation. It determines the color scheme, font and font size, and layout of your presentation. Perform the following steps to choose a design template.

Steps **To Choose a Design Template**

1 Click the Common Tasks menu button on the Formatting toolbar and then point to Apply Design Template (Figure 1-12).

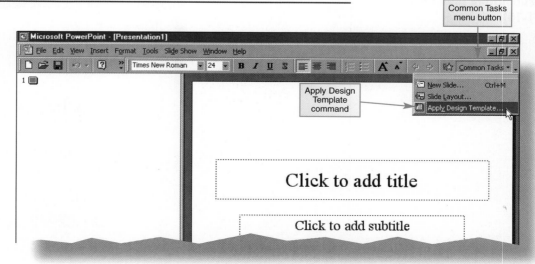

FIGURE 1-12

2 **Click Apply Design Template.**

The Apply Design Template dialog box displays (Figure 1-13). Numerous design template names display in the list box. Artsy is highlighted in the list, and a thumbnail view of the Artsy design template displays in the preview area. If the preview area does not display, click the Views button arrow and then click Preview. The Cancel button or the Close button can be used to close the Apply Design Template dialog box if you do not want to apply a new template.

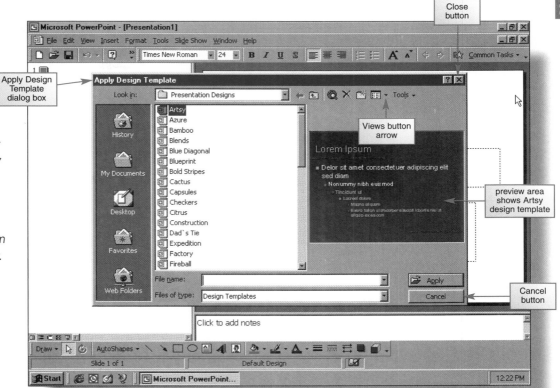

FIGURE 1-13

3 **Click the down scroll arrow to scroll down the list of design templates until Straight Edge appears. Click Straight Edge. Point to the Apply button.**

A preview of the Straight Edge design template displays in the preview area (Figure 1-14).

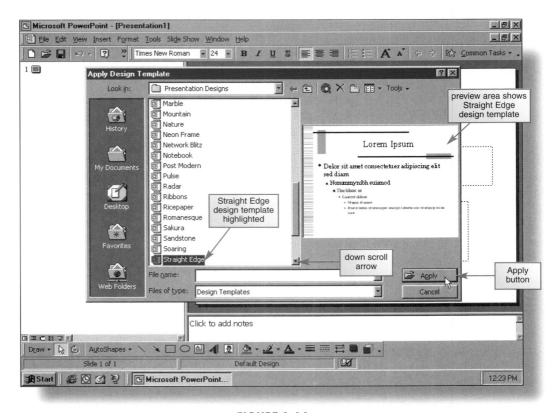

FIGURE 1-14

4 **Click the Apply button.**

Slide 1 displays with the Straight Edge design template (Figure 1-15).

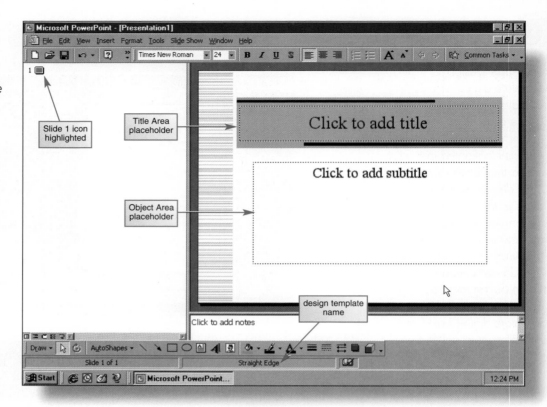

FIGURE 1-15

Other Ways

1. Double-click Straight Edge in list
2. On Format menu click Apply Design Template, scroll down to select Straight Edge, click Apply
3. Double-click Default Design on status bar, scroll down to select Straight Edge, click Apply

Creating a Title Slide

With the exception of a blank slide, PowerPoint also assumes every new slide has a title. To make creating your presentation easier, any text you type after a new slide displays becomes the title object. The AutoLayout for the title slide has a Title Area placeholder near the middle of the window and an Object Area placeholder directly below the Title Area placeholder (Figure 1-15).

Entering the Presentation Title

The presentation title for Project 1 is Effective Study Skills. As you begin typing in the Title Area placeholder, the title text displays immediately after the Slide 1 icon in the outline pane. Perform the following steps to create the title slide for this project.

Steps To Enter the Presentation Title

1 **Click the label, Click to add title, located inside the Title Area placeholder.**

The insertion point is in the Title Area placeholder (Figure 1-16). The *insertion point* is a blinking vertical line (|), which indicates where the next character will display. The mouse pointer changes to an I-beam. A *selection rectangle* displays around the Title Area placeholder. The placeholder is selected as indicated by the border and sizing handles displaying on the edges.

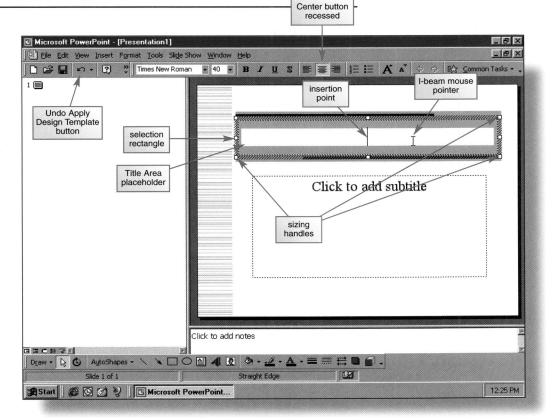

FIGURE 1-16

2 **Type** Effective Study Skills **in the Title Area placeholder. Do not press the ENTER key.**

The title text, Effective Study Skills, displays in the Title Area placeholder and in the outline pane (Figure 1-17). The current title text displays with the default font (Times New Roman) and default font size (40).

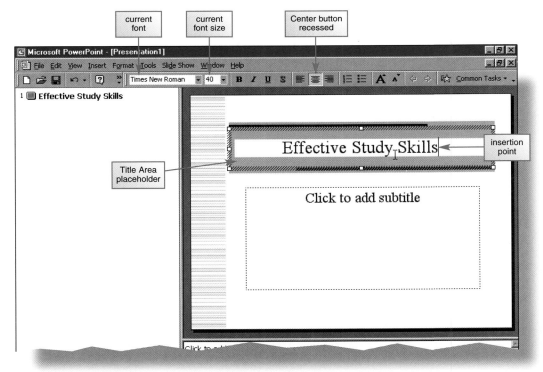

FIGURE 1-17

Enhancements

Microsoft touts the AutoFit text feature as an important PowerPoint 2000 upgrade. Other ease-of-use enhancements are the tri-pane view, the ability to create tables easily, and the self-paced introduction, which gives a useful overview of PowerPoint's key features. For more information, visit the PowerPoint 2000 More About Web page (www.scsite.com/pp2000/more.htm) and click Enhancements.

Notice that you do not press the ENTER key after the word Skills. If you press the ENTER key after typing the title, PowerPoint creates a new line, which would be a new second paragraph in the Title Area. You want only one paragraph in this text placeholder. A **paragraph** is a segment of text with the same format that begins when you press the ENTER key and ends when you press the ENTER key again. Therefore, do not press the ENTER key unless you want to create a two-paragraph title. Additionally, PowerPoint **line wraps** text that exceeds the width of the placeholder. For example, if the slide title was Effective College Study Skills, it would exceed the width of the Title Area placeholder and display on two lines.

One of PowerPoint's new features is **AutoFit text**. If you are creating your slide and need to squeeze an extra line in the text placeholder, PowerPoint will resize the existing text in the placeholder so that this extra line will fit on the screen.

Correcting a Mistake When Typing

If you type the wrong letter and notice the error before pressing the ENTER key, press the BACKSPACE key to erase all the characters back to and including the one that is incorrect. If you mistakenly press the ENTER key after entering the title and the insertion point is on the new line, simply press the BACKSPACE key to return the insertion point to the right of the letter s in the word Skills.

When you install PowerPoint, the default setting allows you to reverse up to the last 20 changes by clicking the **Undo button** on the Standard toolbar. The ScreenTip that displays when you point to the Undo button changes to indicate the type of change just made. For example, if you type text in the Title Area placeholder and then point to the Undo button, the ScreenTip that displays is Undo Typing. For clarity, when referencing the Undo button in this project, the name displaying in the ScreenTip is referenced. Another way to reverse changes is to click the Undo command on the Edit menu. Like the Undo button, the Undo command reflects the last type of change made to the presentation.

You can reapply a change that you reversed with the Undo button by clicking the Redo button on the Standard toolbar. Clicking the **Redo button** reverses the last undo action. The ScreenTip name reflects the type of reversal last performed.

Entering the Presentation Subtitle

The next step in creating the title slide is to enter the subtitle text into the Object Area placeholder. Perform the following steps to enter the presentation subtitle.

To Enter the Presentation Subtitle

1 **Click the label, Click to add subtitle, located inside the Object Area placeholder.**

The insertion point is in the Object Area placeholder (Figure 1-18). The mouse pointer changes to an I-beam indicating the mouse is in a text placeholder. The selection rectangle indicates the placeholder is selected. The default Object Area text font size is 32.

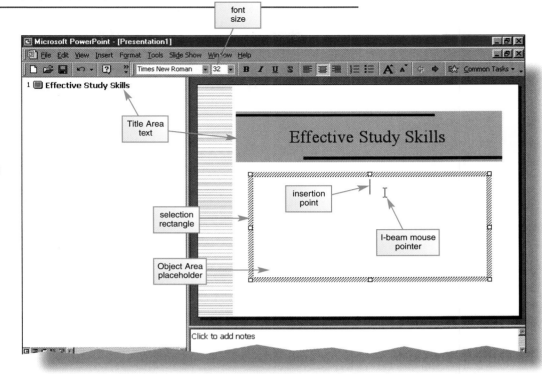

FIGURE 1-18

2 **Type** Strategies for College Success **and then press the ENTER key. Type** Presented by **and then press the ENTER key. Type** Seaview College **but do not press the ENTER key.**

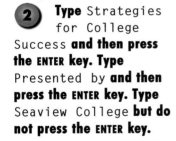

The text displays in the Object Area placeholder and the outline pane (Figure 1-19). The insertion point displays after the letter e in College. A red wavy line displays under the word, Seaview, to indicate a possible spelling error. A light bulb may display in the top-left corner of the text placeholder, depending on your computer's settings. The Office Assistant generates this light bulb to give you design tips.

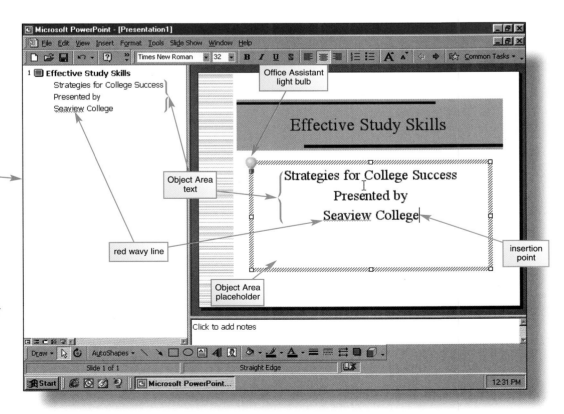

FIGURE 1-19

The previous section created a title slide using an AutoLayout for the title slide. PowerPoint displayed the title slide layout because you created a new presentation. You clicked the Title Area placeholder to select it and then typed your title. In general, to type text in any text placeholder, click the text placeholder and begin typing. You could, however, enter text in the Title Area placeholder without selecting this placeholder because PowerPoint assumes every slide has a title. You also added subtitle text in the Object Area placeholder. While this information identifying the presenter is not required, it often is useful for the audience.

More About

Text Attributes

An extensive glossary of typography terms is available at the Microsoft Web site. The information includes a diagram illustrating the text attributes. For more information, visit the PowerPoint 2000 More About Web page (www.scsite.com/pp2000/more.htm) and click Attributes.

Text Attributes

This presentation is using the Straight Edge design template. Each design template has its own text attributes. A **text attribute** is a characteristic of the text, such as font, font size, font style, or text color. You can adjust text attributes any time before, during, or after you type the text. Recall that a design template determines the color scheme, font and font size, and layout of your presentation. Most of the time, you use the design template's text attributes and color scheme. Occasionally you may want to change the way your presentation looks, however, and still keep a particular design template. PowerPoint gives you that flexibility. You can use the design template and change the text's color, font size, font, and font style. Table 1-2 explains the different text attributes available in PowerPoint.

Table 1-2 Design Template Text Attributes	
ATTRIBUTE	**DESCRIPTION**
Color	Defines the color of text. Displaying text in color requires a color monitor. Printing text in color requires a color printer or plotter.
Font	Defines the appearance and shape of letters, numbers, and special characters.
Font size	Specifies the size of characters on the screen. Character size is gauged by a measurement system called points. A single point is about 1/72 of an inch in height. Thus, a character with a point size of eighteen is about 18/72 (or 1/4) of an inch in height.
Font style	Defines text characteristics. Font styles include plain, italic, bold, shadowed, and underlined. Text may have one or more font styles at a time.
Subscript	Defines the placement of a character in relationship to another. A subscript character displays or prints slightly below and immediately to one side of another character.
Superscript	Defines the placement of a character in relationship to another. A superscript character displays or prints above and immediately to one side of another character.

The next two sections explain how to change the font size and font style attributes.

Changing the Font Size

The Straight Edge design template default font size is 40 points for title text and 32 points for body text. A point is 1/72 of an inch in height. Thus, a character with a point size of 40 is about 40/72 (or 5/9) of an inch in height. Slide 1 requires you to increase the font size for the paragraph, Effective Study Skills. Perform the following steps to increase the font size.

To Increase Font Size

1 **Position the mouse pointer in the Title Area placeholder and then triple-click.**

PowerPoint selects the entire line (Figure 1-20). You select an entire line quickly by triple-clicking any area within the Title Area placeholder.

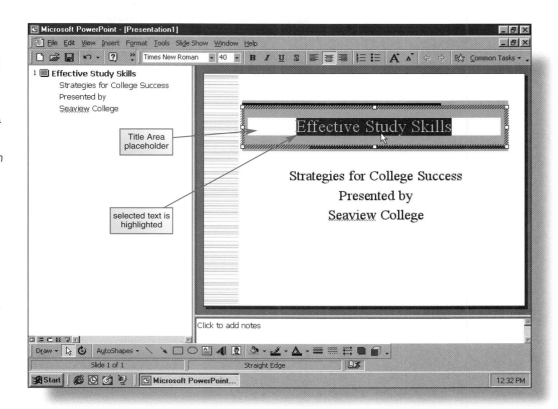

FIGURE 1-20

3 **With Effective Study Skills highlighted, point to the Font Size box arrow in the Font Size box on the Formatting toolbar.**

When you point to a button or other areas on a toolbar, PowerPoint displays a Screen-Tip. A ScreenTip contains the name of the tool to which you are pointing. When pointing to the Font Size box or the Font Size box arrow, the ScreenTip displays the words, Font Size (Figure 1-21). The Font Size box indicates that the title text is 40 points.

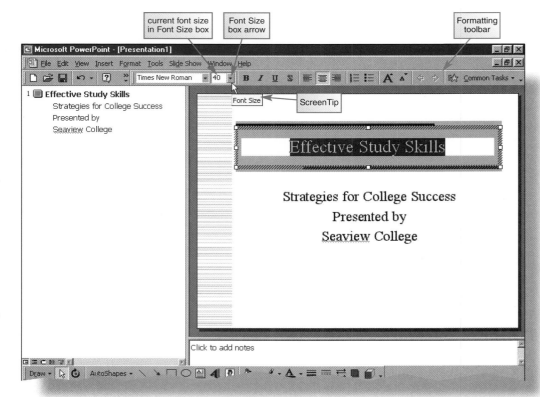

FIGURE 1-21

4 **Click the Font Size box arrow, click the down scroll arrow on the Font Size scroll bar until 54 appears, and then point to 54.**

*When you click the **Font Size box arrow**, a list of available font sizes displays in the Font Size list box. The font sizes displayed depend on the current font, which is Times New Roman. Font size 54 is highlighted (Figure 1-22).*

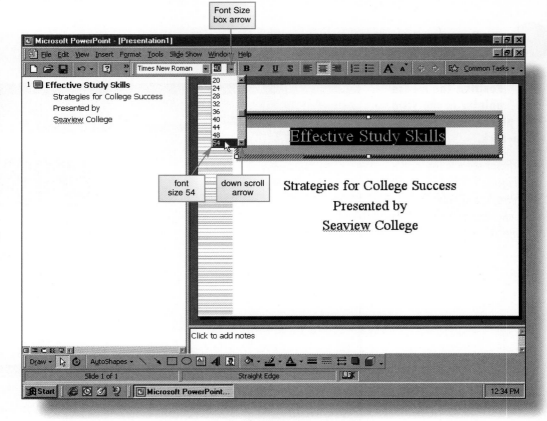

FIGURE 1-22

5 **Click 54.**

The title text, Effective Study Skills, increases in font size to 54 points (Figure 1-23). The Font Size box on the Formatting toolbar displays 54, indicating the selected text has a font size of 54.

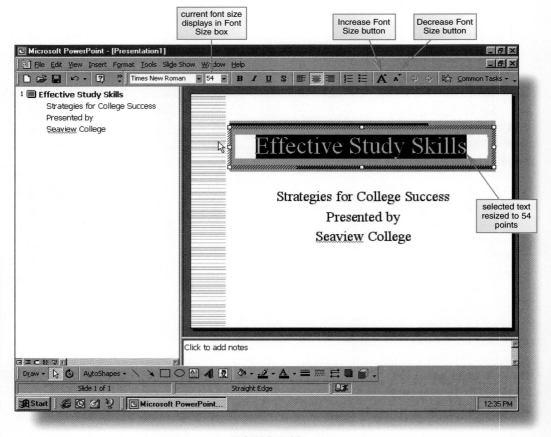

FIGURE 1-23

Other Ways

1. Right-click selected text, click Font on shortcut menu, type new font size in Size box

2. Click Increase Font Size button on Formatting toolbar

3. Click Font Size box on Formatting toolbar, type font size between 1 and 4000

4. On Format menu click Font, click new font size in Size box, or type font size between 1 and 4000

You also can use the **Increase Font Size button** on the Formatting toolbar to increase the font size. Each time you click the button, the font size becomes larger in preset increments. If you need to decrease the font size, click the Font Size box arrow and select a size smaller than 40. Another method is to click the **Decrease Font Size button** on the Formatting toolbar. The font size will become smaller in preset increments each time you click the button.

Changing the Style of Text to Italic

Text font styles include plain, italic, bold, shadowed, and underlined. PowerPoint allows you to use one or more text font styles in your presentation. Perform the following steps to add emphasis to the title slide by changing plain text to italic text.

 To Change the Text Font Style to Italic

1 **Triple-click the paragraph, Presented by, in the Object Area text placeholder, and then point to the Italic button on the Formatting toolbar.**

The paragraph, Presented by, is highlighted (Figure 1-24). The Italic button is three-dimensional.

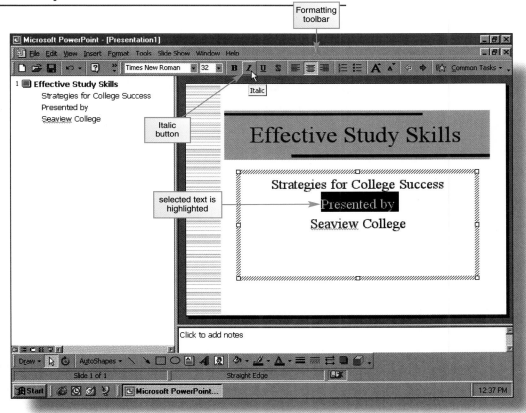

FIGURE 1-24

2 Click the Italic button.

The text is italicized in both the slide and outline panes, and the Italic button is recessed on the Formatting toolbar (Figure 1-25).

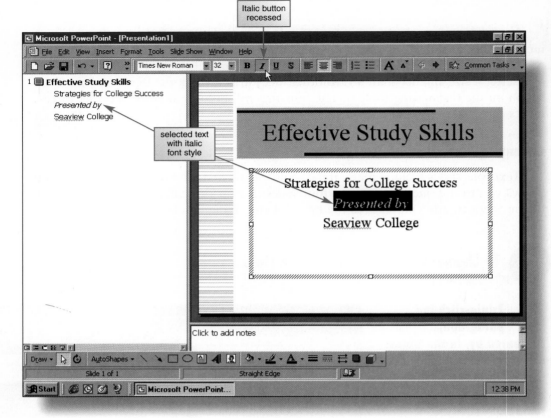

FIGURE 1-25

To remove italics from text, select the italicized text and then click the Italic button. As a result, the Italic button is not recessed, and the text does not have the italic font style.

Saving the Presentation on a Floppy Disk

While you are building your presentation, the computer stores it in main memory. It is important to save your presentation frequently because the presentation will be lost if the computer is turned off or you lose electrical power. Another reason to save your work is that if you run out of lab time before completing your project, you may finish the project later without starting over. You must, therefore, save any presentation you will use later. Before you continue with Project 1, save the work completed thus far. Perform the following steps to save a presentation on a floppy disk using the Save button on the Standard toolbar.

Steps To Save a Presentation on a Floppy Disk

1 Insert a formatted floppy disk in drive A and then click the Save button on the Standard toolbar.

The Save As dialog box displays (Figure 1-26). The default folder, My Documents, displays in the Save in box. Effective Study Skills displays highlighted in the File name box because PowerPoint uses the words in the Title Area placeholder as the default file name. Presentation displays in the Save as type box. Clicking the Cancel button closes the Save As dialog box.

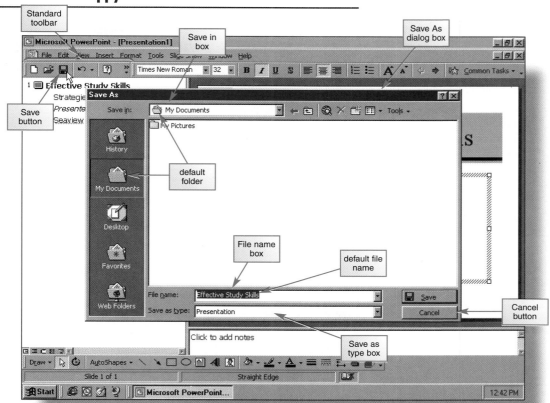

FIGURE 1-26

2 Type Studying in the File name box. Do not press the ENTER key after typing the file name.

The name, Studying, displays in the File name box (Figure 1-27).

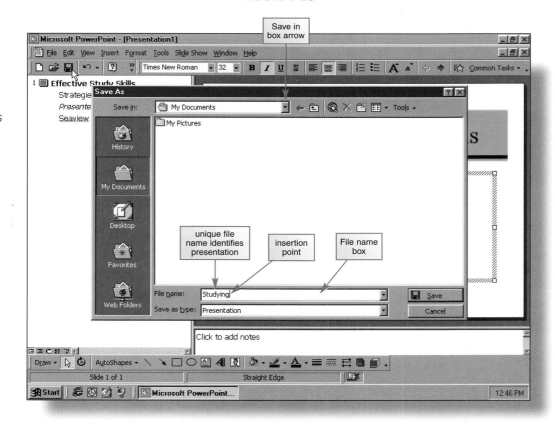

FIGURE 1-27

3 Click the Save in box arrow. Point to 3½ Floppy (A:) in the Save in list.

The Save in list displays a list of locations to which you can save your presentation (Figure 1-28). Your list may look different depending on the configuration of your system. 3½ Floppy (A:) is highlighted.

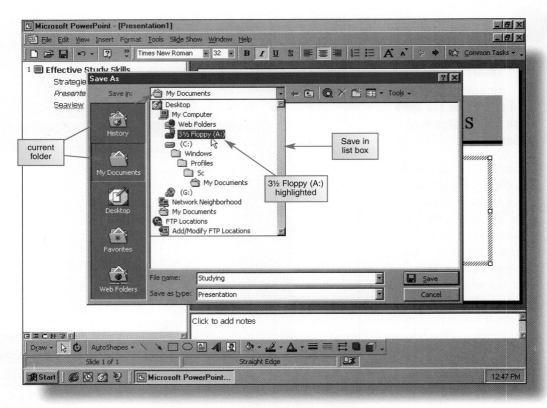

FIGURE 1-28

4 Click 3½ Floppy (A:) and then point to the Save button.

Drive A becomes the destination location for the presentation (Figure 1-29).

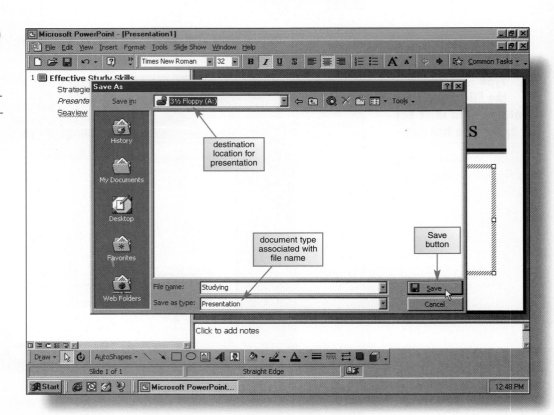

FIGURE 1-29

5 **Click the Save button.**

PowerPoint saves the presentation to your floppy disk in drive A. The title bar displays the file name, Studying, used to save the presentation (Figure 1-30).

file name displays on title bar

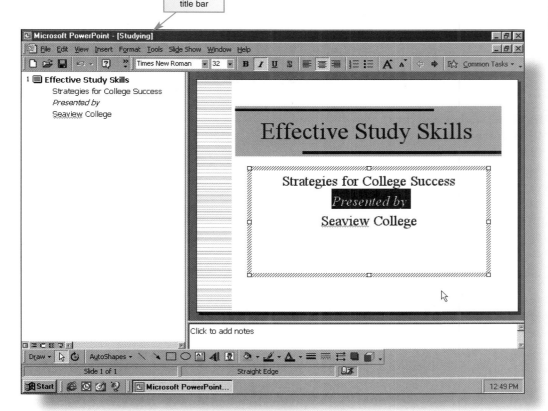

FIGURE 1-30

Other Ways

1. On File menu click Save As
2. Press CTRL+S or press SHIFT+F12

PowerPoint automatically appends the extension .ppt to the file name, Studying. The **.ppt** extension stands for **P**ower**P**oin**t**. Although the slide show, Studying, is saved on a floppy disk, it also remains in main memory and displays on the screen.

It is a good practice to save periodically while you are working on a project. By doing so, you protect yourself from losing all the work you have done since the last time you saved.

Adding a New Slide to a Presentation

The title slide for your presentation is created. The next step is to add the first bulleted list slide immediately after the current slide in Project 1. Usually when you create your presentation, you add slides with text, graphics, or charts. When you add a new slide, PowerPoint displays a dialog box for you to choose one of the 24 different AutoLayouts. These AutoLayouts have placeholders for various objects. Some placeholders allow you to double-click the placeholder and then access other PowerPoint objects. More information about using AutoLayout placeholders to add graphics follows in subsequent projects. Perform the steps on the next page to add a new slide using the Bulleted List AutoLayout.

Steps To Add a New Slide Using the Bulleted List AutoLayout

1 Double-click the move handle on the Standard toolbar and then point to the New Slide button (Figure 1-31).

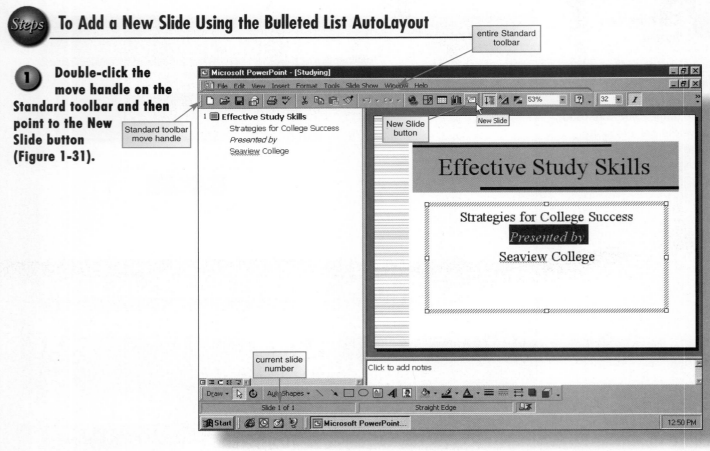

FIGURE 1-31

2 Click the New Slide button. When the New Slide dialog box displays, point to the OK button.

The New Slide dialog box displays (Figure 1-32). The Bulleted List AutoLayout is selected, and the AutoLayout title, Bulleted List, displays at the bottom-right corner of the New Slide dialog box.

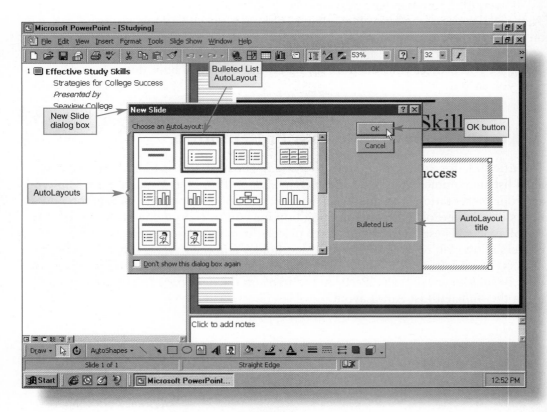

FIGURE 1-32

③ Click the OK button.

Slide 2 displays keeping the attributes of the Straight Edge design template using the Bulleted List AutoLayout (Figure 1-33). Slide 2 of 2 displays on the status bar. The vertical scroll bar displays in the slide pane. The bullet appears as a diamond.

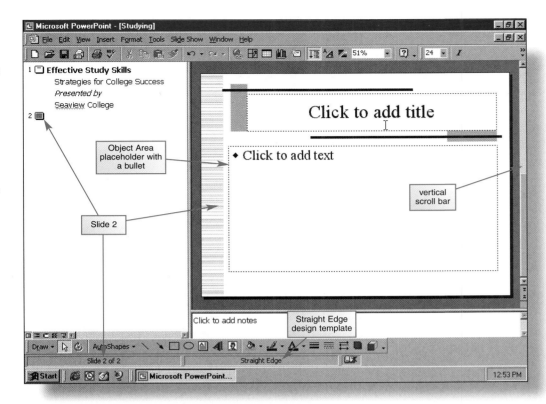

FIGURE 1-33

Because the Bulleted List AutoLayout was selected, PowerPoint displays Slide 2 with a Title Area placeholder and an Object Area placeholder with a bullet. You can change the layout for a slide at any time during the creation of your presentation by clicking the Common Tasks menu button on the Formatting toolbar and then clicking the Slide Layout button. You then can double-click the AutoLayout of your choice.

Other **Ways**

1. Click Common Tasks menu button on Formatting toolbar, click New Slide
2. On Insert menu click New Slide
3. Press CTRL+M

Creating a Bulleted List Slide

The bulleted list slides in Figure 1-2 on page PP 1.9 contain more than one level of bulleted text. A slide with more than one level of bulleted text is called a **multi-level bulleted list slide**. A **level** is a position within a structure, such as an outline, that indicates a magnitude of importance. PowerPoint allows for five paragraph levels. Each paragraph level has an associated bullet. The bullet font is dependent on the design template. Figure 1-34 on the next page identifies the five paragraph levels and the bullet fonts for the Straight Edge design template. Beginning with the Second level, each paragraph indents to the right of the preceding level.

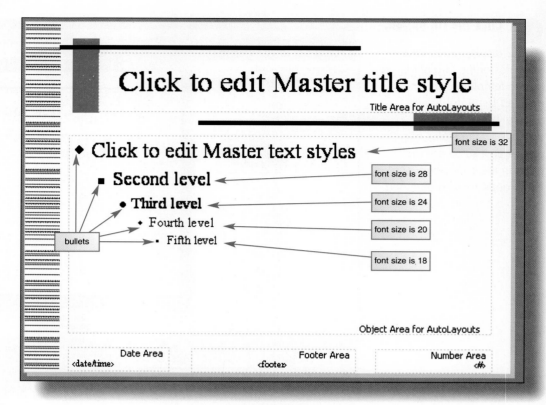

FIGURE 1-34

An indented paragraph is **demoted,** or pushed down to a lower level. For example, if you demote a First level paragraph, it becomes a Second level paragraph. This lower-level paragraph is a subset of the higher-level paragraph. It usually contains information that supports the topic in the paragraph immediately above it. You demote a paragraph by clicking the **Demote button** on the Formatting toolbar.

When you want to raise a paragraph from a lower level to a higher level, you **promote** the paragraph by clicking the **Promote button** on the Formatting toolbar.

Creating a multi-level bulleted list slide requires several steps. Initially, you enter a slide title in the Title Area placeholder. Next, you select the Object Area text placeholder. Then you type the text for the multi-level bulleted list, demoting and promoting paragraphs as needed. The next several sections explain how to add a multi-level bulleted list slide.

Entering a Slide Title

PowerPoint assumes every new slide has a title. The title for Slide 2 is Managing Your Time. Perform the following step to enter this title.

More *About*

Slide Masters

Each design template has a corresponding slide master designed by Microsoft graphic artists. The text attributes and color schemes are developed to coordinate with each other and to evoke audience reactions, such as excitement or relaxation.

To Enter a Slide Title

1 **If necessary, click the Title Area placeholder and then type** Managing your Time **as the title. Do not press the ENTER key.**

The title, Managing Your Time, displays in the Title Area placeholder and in the outline pane (Figure 1-35). The insertion point displays after the e in Time.

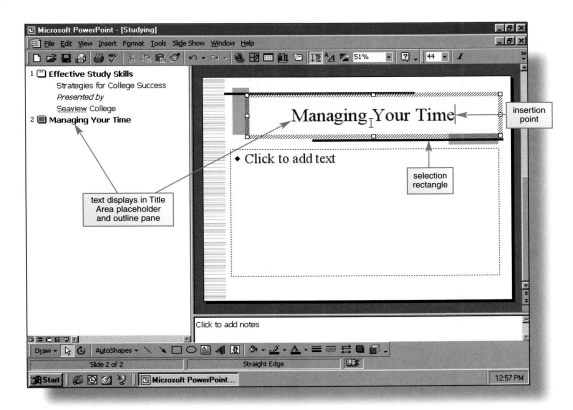

FIGURE 1-35

Selecting an Object Area Placeholder

Before you can type text in the Object Area placeholder, you first must select it. Perform the step on the next page to select the Object Area placeholder on Slide 2.

To Select an Object Area Placeholder

1 **Click the bulleted paragraph labeled, Click to add text.**

The insertion point displays immediately after the bullet on Slide 2 (Figure 1-36). The mouse pointer may change shape if you move it away from the bullet.

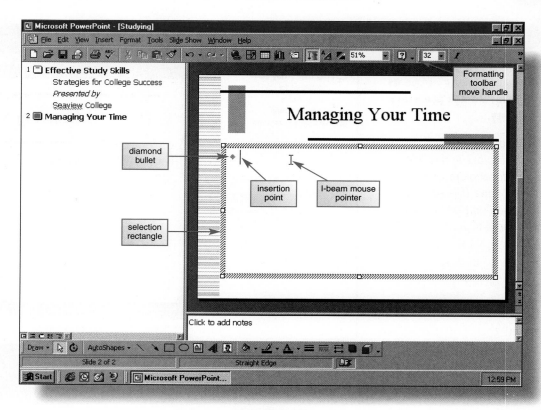

FIGURE 1-36

1. Press CTRL+ENTER

Typing a Multi-level Bulleted List

Recall that a bulleted list is a list of paragraphs, each of which is preceded by a bullet. Also recall that a paragraph is a segment of text ended by pressing the ENTER key. The next step is to type the multi-level bulleted list, which consists of the six entries (Figure 1-2 on page PP 1.9). Perform the following steps to type a multi-level bulleted list.

Steps To Type a Multi-level Bulleted List

1 **Double-click the move handle on the Formatting toolbar. Type** Make a weekly schedule **and then press the ENTER key.**

The paragraph, Make a weekly schedule, displays (Figure 1-37). The font size is 32. The insertion point displays after the second bullet. When you press the ENTER key, PowerPoint ends one paragraph and begins a new paragraph. Because you are using the Bulleted List Auto-Layout, PowerPoint places a diamond bullet in front of the new paragraph.

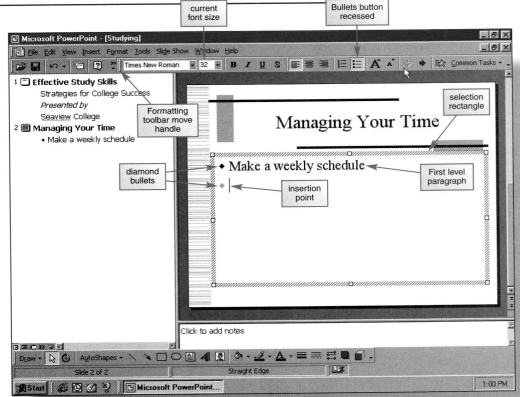

FIGURE 1-37

2 **Point to the Demote button (Figure 1-38).**

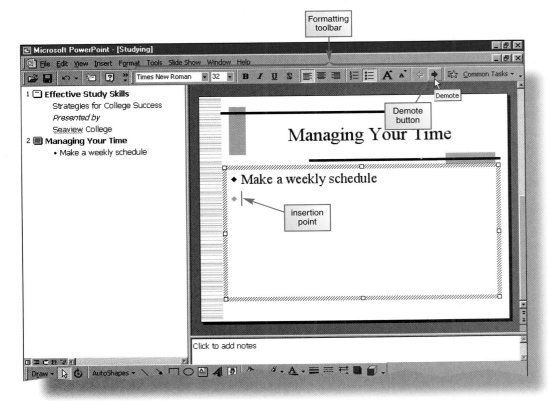

FIGURE 1-38

3 **Click the Demote button.**

The second paragraph indents under the first and becomes a Second level paragraph (Figure 1-39). Notice the bullet in front of the second paragraph changes from a diamond to a box, and the font size for the demoted paragraph now is 28. The insertion point displays after the box.

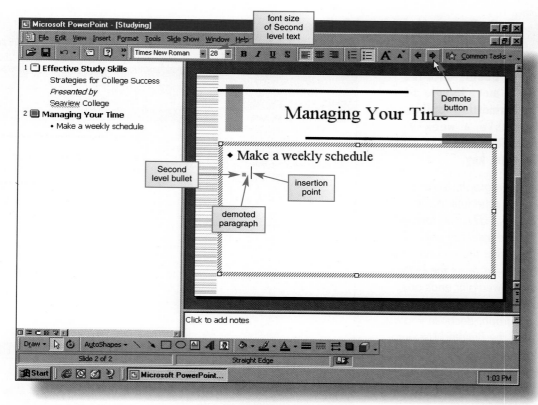

FIGURE 1-39

4 **Type** List specific study times for all subjects **and then press the ENTER key. Type** Plan time for recreation and sleep **and then press the ENTER key. Type** Spread study times throughout the week **and then press the ENTER key. Point to the Promote button.**

Three new Second level paragraphs display with boxes in both the slide and outline panes (Figure 1-40). When you press the ENTER key, PowerPoint adds a new paragraph at the same level as the previous paragraph.

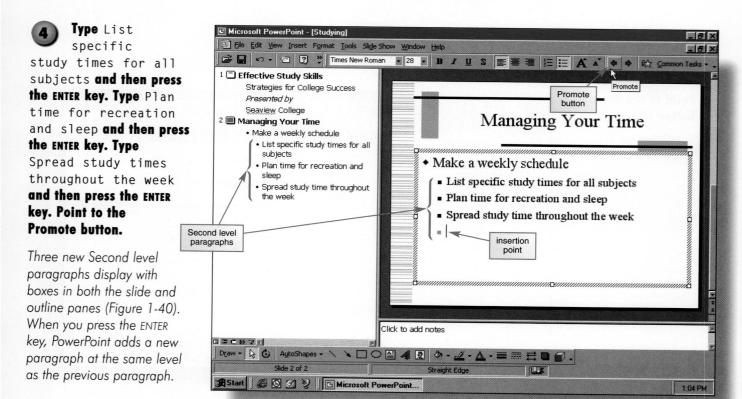

FIGURE 1-40

5 **Click the Promote button.**

The Second level paragraph becomes a First level paragraph (Figure 1-41). The bullet in front of the new paragraph changes from a box to a diamond, and the font size for the promoted paragraph is 32. The insertion point displays after the diamond bullet.

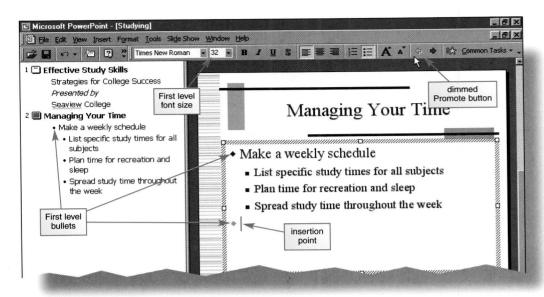

FIGURE 1-41

Perform the following steps to complete the text for Slide 2.

TO TYPE THE REMAINING TEXT FOR SLIDE 2

1 Type Stick to your schedule and then press the ENTER key.

2 Type Revise your schedule when necessary but do not press the ENTER key.

The insertion point displays after the y in necessary (Figure 1-42).

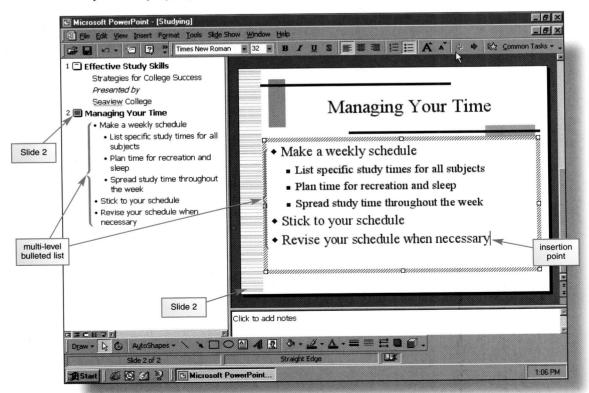

FIGURE 1-42

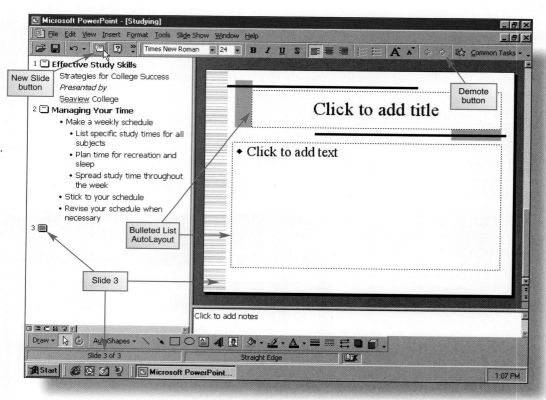
Notice that you did not press the ENTER key after typing the last bullet line in Step 2. If you press the ENTER key, a new bullet displays after the last entry on this slide. To remove an extra bullet, press the BACKSPACE key.

Adding New Slides with the Same AutoLayout

When you add a new slide to a presentation and want to keep the same AutoLayout used on the previous slide, PowerPoint gives you a shortcut. Instead of clicking the New Slide button and clicking an AutoLayout in the New Slide dialog box, you can press and hold down the SHIFT key and then click the New Slide button. Perform the following step to add a new slide (Slide 3) and keep the Bulleted List AutoLayout used on the previous slide.

 To Add a New Slide with the Same AutoLayout

1 **Press and hold down the SHIFT key, click the New Slide button on the Standard toolbar, and then release the SHIFT key.**

Slide 3 displays the Bulleted List AutoLayout (Figure 1-43). Slide 3 of 3 displays on the status bar.

FIGURE 1-43

Slide 3 is added to the presentation. Perform the following steps to add text to Slide 3 and to create a multi-level bulleted list.

TO COMPLETE SLIDE 3

 Type Attending Class in the Title Area placeholder.

 Press CTRL+ENTER to move the insertion point to the Object Area placeholder.

3 Type Sit in the front of the room and then press the ENTER key.

4 Type Ask questions at appropriate times and then press the ENTER key.

5 Type Take notes and then press the ENTER key.

6 Click the Demote button.

7 Type Rephrase ideas in your own words and then press the ENTER key.

8 Type Review immediately after class but do not press the ENTER key.

Slide 3 displays as shown in Figure 1-44. The Office Assistant light bulb may display to offer design help. If so, you may click the light bulb next to the Office Assistant to see a tip. For additional help on using the Office Assistant, refer to Appendix A.

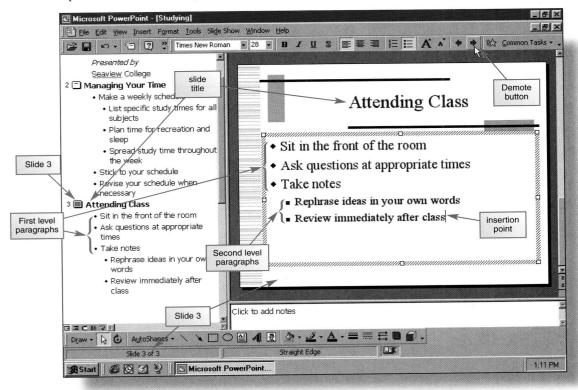

FIGURE 1-44

Slide 4, also a multi-level bulleted list, is the last slide in this presentation. Perform the following steps to create Slide 4.

TO CREATE SLIDE 4

1 Press and hold down the SHIFT key, click the New Slide button on the Standard toolbar, and then release the SHIFT key.

2 Type Reading Your Textbooks in the Title Area placeholder.

3 Press CTRL+ENTER to move the insertion point to the Object Area placeholder.

4 Type Survey the assignment and then press the ENTER key.

5 Click the Demote button. Type Read the summary and chapter questions and then press the ENTER key.

6 Click the Promote button. Type Read the chapter carefully and then press the ENTER key.

7 Type Recite the material in your own words and then press the ENTER key.

8 Type Write brief notes in the margins and then press the ENTER key.

9 Type Review the entire assignment but do not press the ENTER key.

The Title Area and Object Area text objects display in the slide and outline panes (Figure 1-45). The Office Assistant light bulb may display to offer design help.

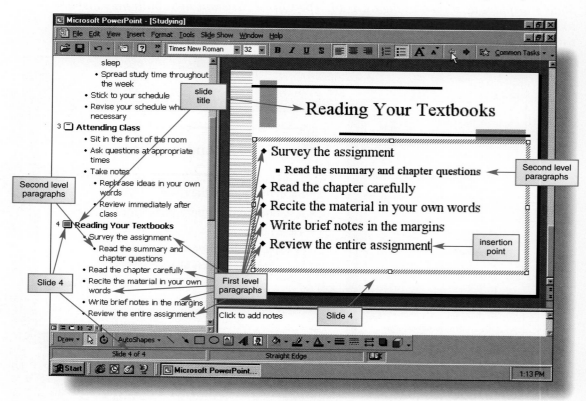

FIGURE 1-45

All slides for the Studying presentation are created. This presentation consists of a title slide and three multi-level bulleted list slides.

Ending a Slide Show with a Black Slide

After the last slide in the slide show displays, the default PowerPoint setting is to end your presentation with a black slide. This black slide displays only when the slide show is running and concludes your slide show gracefully so your audience never sees the PowerPoint window. A black slide ends all slide shows until the option setting is deactivated. Perform the following steps to verify the End with black slide option is activated.

 **To End a Slide Show with a Black Slide**

1 Click Tools on the menu bar and then point to Options (Figure 1-46).

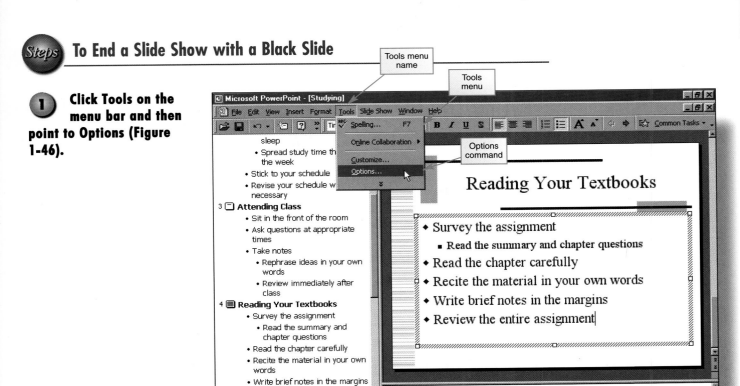

FIGURE 1-46

2 Click Options. If necessary, click the View tab when the Options dialog box opens. Verify a check mark displays in the End with black slide check box. If a check mark does not display, click the End with black slide check box.

The Options dialog box displays (Figure 1-47). The View sheet contains settings for the overall PowerPoint display and for a particular slide show.

3 Click the OK button.

The End with black slide option is activated.

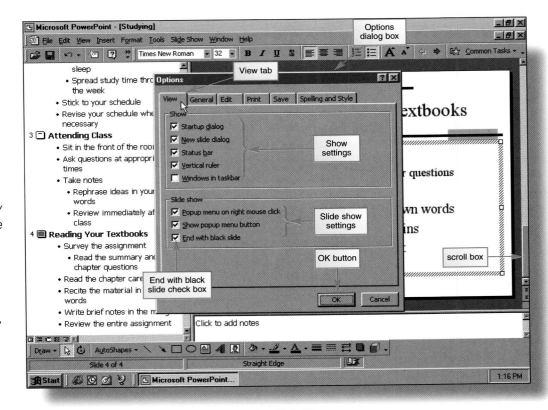

FIGURE 1-47

Now that all aspects of the presentation are complete, you need to save the additions and changes you have made to your Studying presentation.

Saving a Presentation with the Same File Name

Saving frequently cannot be overemphasized. When you first saved the presentation, you clicked the Save button on the Standard toolbar and the Save dialog box displayed. When you want to save the changes made to the presentation after your last save, you again click the Save button. This time, however, the Save dialog box does not display because PowerPoint updates the document called Studying.ppt on your floppy disk. Perform the following steps to save the presentation again.

TO SAVE A PRESENTATION WITH THE SAME FILE NAME

(1) Be sure your floppy disk is in drive A.

(2) Click the Save button on the Standard toolbar.

PowerPoint overwrites the old Studying.ppt document on the floppy disk in drive A with the revised presentation document. Slide 4 displays in the PowerPoint window.

Moving to Another Slide in Normal View

When creating or editing a presentation in normal view, you often want to display a slide other than the current one. You can move to another slide using several methods. In the outline pane, you can point to any of the text in a particular slide to display that slide in the slide pane, or you can drag the scroll box on the vertical scroll bar up or down to move through the text in your presentation. In the slide pane, you can click the **Previous Slide** or **Next Slide** buttons on the vertical scroll bar. Clicking the Next Slide button advances to the next slide in the presentation. Clicking the Previous Slide button backs up to the slide preceding the current slide. You also can drag the scroll box on the vertical scroll bar. When you drag the scroll box, the **slide indicator** displays the number and the title of the slide you are about to display. Releasing the mouse button displays the slide.

A slide's **Zoom setting** affects the portion of the slide displaying in the slide pane. PowerPoint defaults to a setting of approximately 50% so the entire slide displays. This percentage depends on the size and type of your monitor. If you want to display a small portion of the current slide, you would zoom in by clicking the Zoom box arrow and then clicking the desired magnification. You can display the entire slide in the slide pane by clicking Fit in the Zoom list. The Zoom setting affects the action of the vertical and horizontal scroll bars. If Zoom is set so that the entire slide is not visible in the slide pane, clicking the up scroll arrow on the vertical scroll bar displays the next portion of your slide, not the previous slide.

Using the Scroll Box on the Slide Pane to Move to Another Slide

Before continuing with Project 1, you want to display the title slide. Perform the following steps to move from Slide 4 to the Slide 1 using the scroll box on the slide pane vertical scroll bar.

More *About*

Zoom

You can increase your Zoom setting to as large as 400% when you want to see details on small objects. Likewise, you can decrease your Zoom setting to as small as 10%.

To Use the Scroll Box on the Slide Pane to Move to Another Slide

1 **Position the mouse pointer on the scroll box. Press and hold down the left mouse button.**

Slide: 4 of 4 Reading Your Textbooks displays in the slide indicator (Figure 1-48). The Slide 4 icon is shaded in the outline pane.

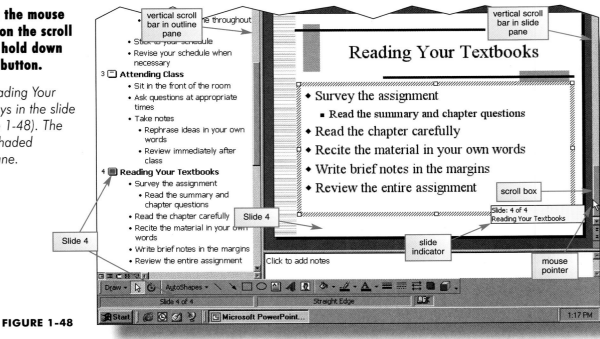

FIGURE 1-48

2 **Drag the scroll box up the vertical scroll bar until Slide: 1 of 4 Effective Study Skills displays in the slide indicator.**

Slide: 1 of 4 Effective Study Skills displays in the slide indicator (Figure 1-49). Slide 4 still displays in the PowerPoint window, and the Slide 4 icon is shaded in the outline pane.

3 **Release the left mouse button.**

Slide 1, titled Effective Study Skills, displays in the PowerPoint window. The Slide 1 icon is shaded in the outline pane.

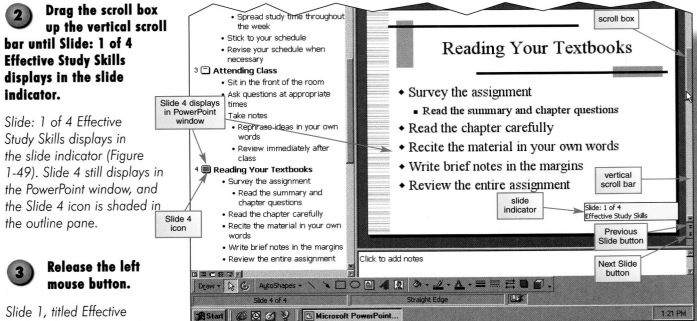

FIGURE 1-49

Other **Ways**

1. Click Next Slide button or Previous Slide button to move forward or back one slide

2. Press PAGE DOWN or PAGE UP to move forward or back one slide

Viewing the Presentation Using Slide Show

The **Slide Show button**, located at the lower-left of the PowerPoint window above the status bar, allows you to display your presentation electronically using a computer. The computer acts like a slide projector, displaying each slide on a full screen. The full screen slide hides the toolbars, menus, and other PowerPoint window elements. Slide show view is used when making a presentation. You can start slide show view from any view: normal view, outline view, slide view, or slide sorter view.

Starting Slide Show View

Slide show view begins when you click the Slide Show button in the lower-left of the PowerPoint window above the status bar. PowerPoint then displays the current slide on the full screen without any of the PowerPoint window objects, such as the menu bar or toolbars. Perform the following steps to start slide show view.

 To Start Slide Show View

1 **Point to the Slide Show button in the lower-left of the PowerPoint window above the status bar.**

The Normal View button is recessed because you still are in normal view (Figure 1-50).

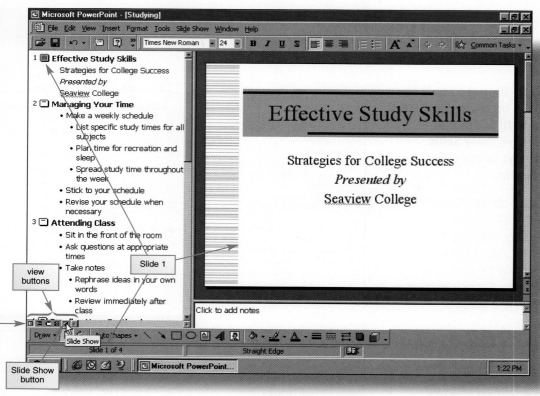

FIGURE 1-50

2 **Click the Slide Show button.**

The title slide fills the screen (Figure 1-51). The PowerPoint window is hidden.

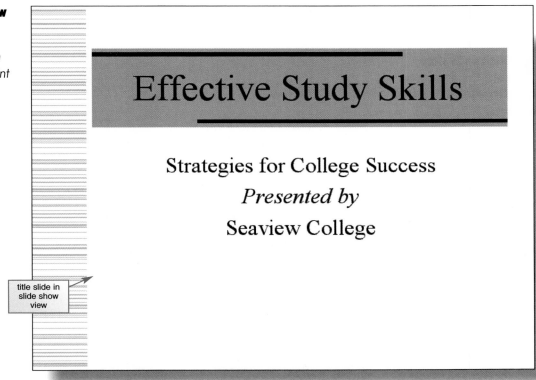

Effective Study Skills

Strategies for College Success
Presented by
Seaview College

title slide in slide show view

FIGURE 1-51

Advancing Through a Slide Show Manually

After you begin slide show view, you can move forward or backward through your slides. PowerPoint allows you to advance through your slides manually or automatically. Automatic advancing is discussed in a later project. Perform the steps on the next page to move manually through your slides.

Other **Ways**

1. On View menu click Slide Show
2. Press F5

To Move Manually Through Slides in a Slide Show

1 **Click each slide until the Reading Your Textbooks slide (Slide 4) displays.**

Each slide in your presentation displays on the screen, one slide at a time. Each time you click the mouse button, the next slide displays.

2 **Click Slide 4.**

The black slide displays (Figure 1-52). The message at the top of the slide announces the end of the slide show. To return to normal view, click the black slide.

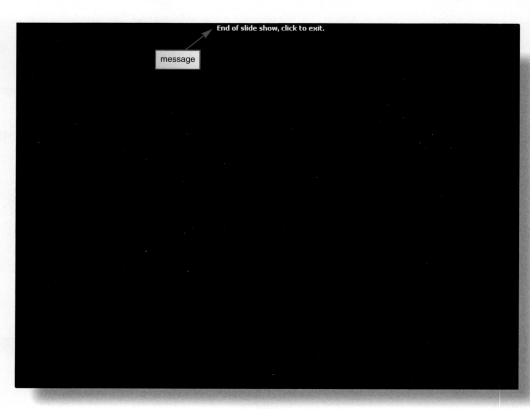

End of slide show, click to exit.

message

FIGURE 1-52

 Other Ways

1. Press PAGE DOWN to advance one slide at a time, or press PAGE UP to go backward one slide at a time

2. Press RIGHT ARROW key to advance one slide at a time, or press LEFT ARROW key to go backward one slide at a time

Using the Popup Menu to Go to a Specific Slide

Slide show view has a shortcut menu, called **Popup menu**, that displays when you right-click a slide in slide show view. This menu contains commands to assist you during a slide show. For example, clicking the **Next command** moves you to the next slide. Clicking the **Previous command** moves you to the previous slide. You can go to any slide in your presentation by pointing to the **Go command** and then clicking Slide Navigator. The **Slide Navigator dialog box** contains a list of the slides in your presentation. Go to the requested slide by double-clicking the name of that slide.

Perform the following steps to go to the title slide (Slide 1) in your presentation.

To Display the Popup Menu and Go to a Specific Slide

1 **With the black slide displaying in slide show view, right-click the slide. Point to Go on the Popup menu, and then point to Slide Navigator on the Go submenu.**

The Popup menu displays on the black slide, and the Go submenu displays (Figure 1-53). Your screen may look different because the Popup menu displays near the location of the mouse pointer at the time you right-click.

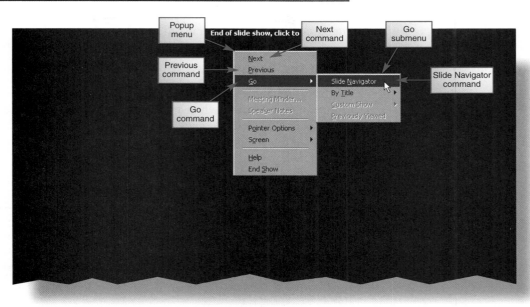

FIGURE 1-53

2 **Click Slide Navigator. When the Slide Navigator dialog box displays, point to 1. Effective Study Skills in the Slide titles list.**

The Slide titles list contains the title text of the slides in your presentation (Figure 1-54). You want to go to Slide 1 in your presentation. Slide 4 is the last slide viewed during your slide show.

3 **Double-click 1. Effective Study Skills.**

The title slide, Effective Study Skills, displays.

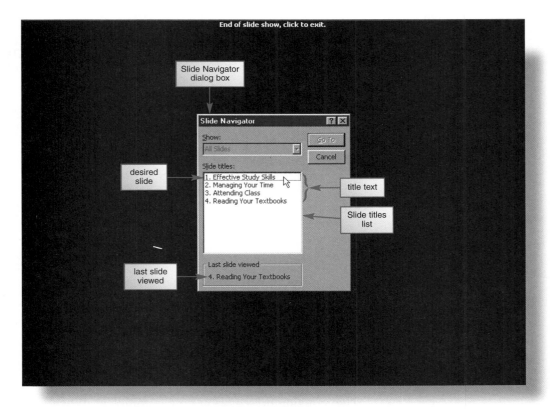

FIGURE 1-54

Additional Popup menu commands allow you to write meeting minutes or to create a list of action items during a slide show, change the mouse pointer to a pen that draws in various colors, blacken the screen, and end the slide show. Popup menu commands are discussed in subsequent projects.

Using the Popup Menu to End a Slide Show

The **End Show command** on the Popup menu exits slide show view and returns to the view you were in when you clicked the Slide Show button. Perform the following steps to end slide show view and return to normal view.

To Use the Popup Menu to End a Slide Show

1 **Right-click the title slide.**

The Popup menu displays on Slide 1.

2 **Point to End Show on the Popup menu.**

Your Popup menu may display in a different location (Figure 1-55).

3 **Click End Show.**

PowerPoint exits slide show view and returns to normal view. Slide 1 displays because it is the last slide displayed in slide show view.

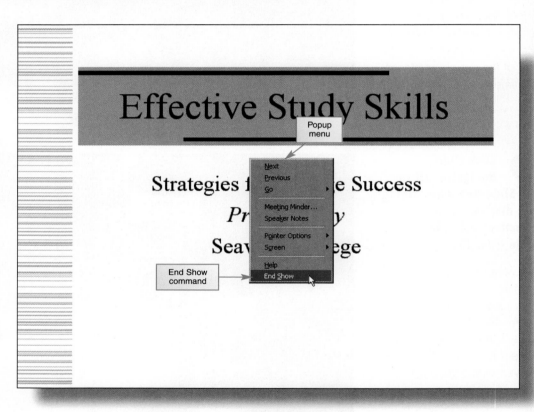

FIGURE 1-55

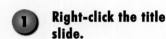

1. Click last slide in presentation to return to slide at which you began slide show view
2. Press ESC to display slide last viewed in slide show view

Quitting PowerPoint

The Studying presentation now is complete. When you quit PowerPoint, PowerPoint prompts you to save any changes made to the presentation since the last save, closes all PowerPoint windows, and then quits PowerPoint. Closing PowerPoint returns control to the desktop. Perform the following steps to quit PowerPoint.

Steps **To Quit PowerPoint**

1 **Point to the Close button on the title bar (Figure 1-56).**

2 **Click the Close button.**

PowerPoint closes and the Windows desktop displays. If you made changes to the presentation since your last save, a Microsoft PowerPoint dialog box displays the question, Do you wish to save the changes you made to Studying?. Click the Yes button to save the changes to the presentation before closing PowerPoint. Click the No button to quit PowerPoint without saving the changes. Click the Cancel button to return to the presentation.

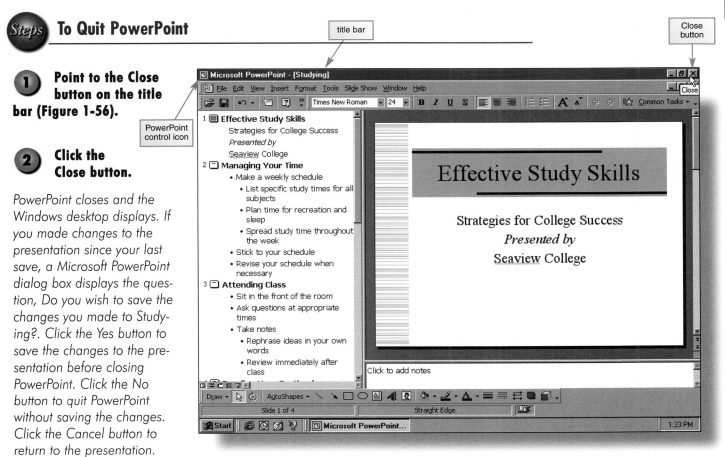

FIGURE 1-56

Other Ways

1. On title bar double-click PowerPoint control icon; or on title bar click PowerPoint control icon, click Close
2. On File menu click Exit
3. Press CTRL+Q or press ALT+F4

Opening a Presentation

Earlier, you saved the presentation on a floppy disk using the file name, Studying.ppt. Once you create and save a presentation, you may need to retrieve it from the floppy disk to make changes. For example, you may want to replace the design template or modify some text. Recall that a presentation is a PowerPoint document. Use the **Open Office Document command** to open an existing presentation.

Opening an Existing Presentation

Ensure that the floppy disk used to save Studying.ppt is in drive A. Then perform the steps on the next page to open the Studying presentation using the Open Office Document command on the Start menu.

Steps **To Open an Existing Presentation**

1 **Click the Start button on the taskbar and then point to Open Office Document.**

The Windows Start menu displays (Figure 1-57). Open Office Document is highlighted.

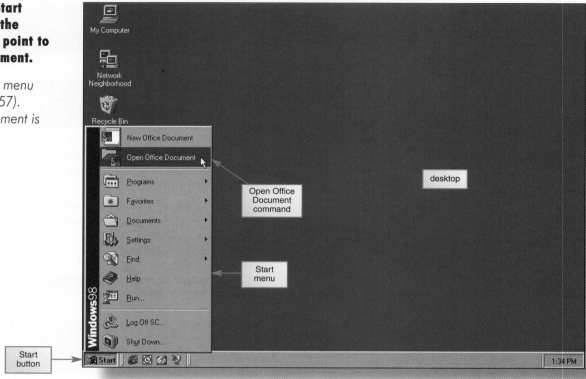

FIGURE 1-57

2 Click Open Office Document. When the Open Office Document dialog box displays, if necessary, click the Look in box arrow and then click 3½ Floppy (A:) (see Figures 1-28 and 1-29 on page 1.30 to review this process).

The Open Office Document dialog box displays (Figure 1-58). A list of existing files on drive A displays because your floppy disk is in drive A. Notice that Office Files displays in the Files of type box. The file, Studying, is highlighted. Your list of existing files may be different depending on the files saved on your floppy disk.

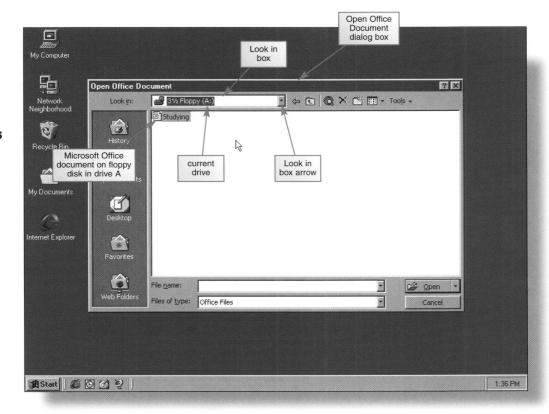

FIGURE 1-58

3 Double-click Studying.

PowerPoint starts, opens Studying.ppt from drive A into main memory, and displays the first slide on the screen. The presentation displays in normal view because PowerPoint opens a presentation in the same view in which it was saved.

Other Ways

1. Click Open Office Document button on Microsoft Office Shortcut Bar, click folder or drive name in Look in list, double-click document name
2. On Start menu click Documents, click document name

When you start PowerPoint and open Studying.ppt, this application and the file name display on a recessed button in the taskbar button area. When more than one application is open, you can switch between applications by clicking the button labeled with the name of the application to which you want to switch.

Checking a Presentation for Spelling and Consistency

After you create a presentation, you should check it visually for spelling errors and style consistency. In addition, you can use PowerPoint's Spelling and Style tools to identify possible misspellings and inconsistencies.

Checking a Presentation for Spelling Errors

PowerPoint checks your entire presentation for spelling mistakes using a standard dictionary contained in the Microsoft Office group. This dictionary is shared with the other Microsoft Office applications such as Word and Excel. A **custom dictionary** is available if you want to add special words such as proper names, cities, and acronyms. When checking a presentation for spelling errors, PowerPoint opens the standard dictionary and the custom dictionary file, if one exists. When a word displays in the Spelling dialog box, you perform one of the actions listed in Table 1-3.

More *About*

Dictionaries

Microsoft has partnered with publishing companies to produce the world's first global dictionary. More than 250 people worked to compile the three million English words contained in this work. The terms are used worldwide, for more than 80 percent of the world's computer-based communication uses the English language.

Table 1-3 Summary of Spelling Checker Actions	
FEATURE	*DESCRIPTION*
Ignore the word	Click Ignore when the word is spelled correctly but not found in the dictionaries. PowerPoint continues checking the rest of the presentation.
Ignore all occurrences of the word	Click Ignore All when the word is spelled correctly but not found in the dictionaries. PowerPoint ignores all occurrences of the word and continues checking the rest of the presentation.
Select a different spelling	Click the proper spelling of the word from the list in the Suggestions box. Click Change. PowerPoint corrects the word and continues checking the rest of the presentation.
Change all occurrences of the misspelling to a different spelling	Click the proper spelling of the word from the list in the Suggestions box. Click Change All. PowerPoint changes all occurrences of the misspelled word and continues checking the rest of the presentation.
Add a word to the custom dictionary	Click Add. PowerPoint opens the custom dictionary, adds the word, and continues checking the rest of the presentation.
View alternative spellings	Click Suggest. PowerPoint lists suggested spellings. Click the correct word from the Suggestions box or type the proper spelling. Then click Change. PowerPoint continues checking the rest of the presentation.
Add spelling error to AutoCorrect list	Click AutoCorrect. PowerPoint adds the spelling error and its correction to the AutoCorrect list. Any future misspelling of the word is corrected automatically as you type.
Close	Click Close to exit from the spelling checker and to return to the PowerPoint window.

The standard dictionary contains commonly used English words. It does not, however, contain proper names, abbreviations, technical terms, poetic contractions, or antiquated terms. PowerPoint treats words not found in the dictionaries as misspellings.

Starting the Spelling Checker

Start the Spelling checker by clicking the Spelling command on the Tools menu. Perform the following steps to start the Spelling checker and check your entire presentation.

To Start the Spelling Checker

1 **Double-click the move handle on the Standard toolbar. Point to the Spelling button on the Standard toolbar (Figure 1-59).**

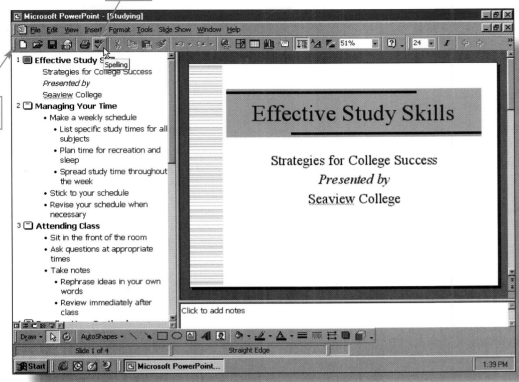

FIGURE 1-59

2 **Click the Spelling button. When the Spelling dialog box displays, point to the Ignore button.**

PowerPoint launches the Spelling checker and displays the Spelling dialog box (Figure 1-60). The word, Seaview, displays in the Not in Dictionary box. Depending on your custom dictionary, Seaview may not be recognized as a misspelled word.

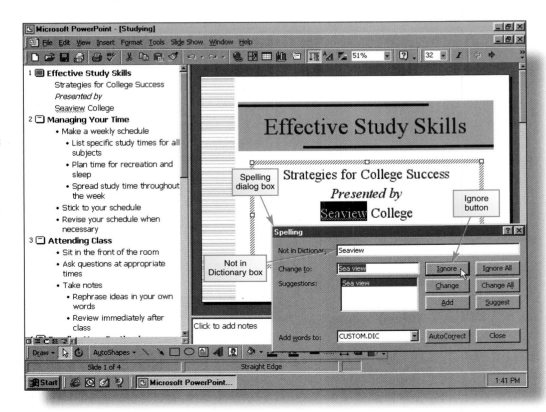

FIGURE 1-60

Click the Ignore button.

PowerPoint ignores the word, *Seaview,* and continues searching for additional misspelled words. PowerPoint may stop on additional words depending on your typing accuracy. When PowerPoint has checked all slides for misspellings, it displays the Microsoft PowerPoint dialog box informing you that the spelling check is complete (Figure 1-61).

 Click the OK button.

PowerPoint closes the Spelling checker and returns to the current slide, Slide 1, or to the slide where a possible misspelled word appeared.

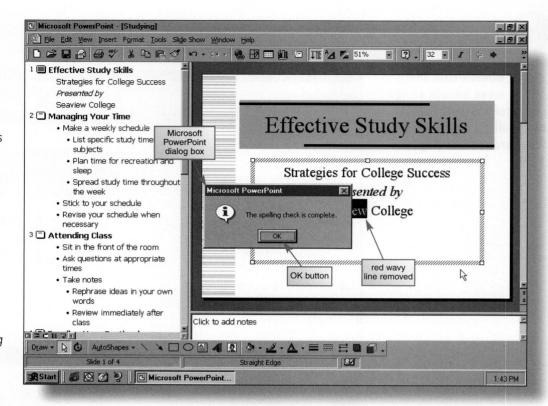

FIGURE 1-61

1. Press ALT+T, press S; when finished, press ENTER

The red wavy line under the word, Seaview, is gone because you instructed PowerPoint to ignore that word, which does not appear in the standard dictionary. You also could have added that word to the dictionary so it would not be flagged as a possible misspelled word in subsequent presentations you create using that word.

Checking a Presentation for Style Consistency

Recall that the Office Assistant may have generated a light bulb in the text placeholder when you were typing your title slide (see Figure 1-19 on page PP 1.23). The Office Assistant recognized you were starting to prepare a slide show and offered design tips. These tips can range from suggesting clip art to ensuring your presentation meets predefined criteria for style consistency. For example, in this Studying presentation the first word in each line of text begins with a capital letter, and each line does not end with a period. The Office Assistant automatically checks for case and end punctuation consistency and for visual clarity. It identifies problems on a screen by displaying a light bulb. You then can choose to correct or to ignore the elements PowerPoint flags. You can change the options to suit your design specifications. Table 1-4 identifies each option available in the Style checker and each default setting.

Table 1-4	Style Checker Options and Default Settings
OPTION	SETTING
CASE	
Slide title style	Title Case
Body text style	Sentence case
END PUNCTUATION	
Slide title punctuation	Paragraphs have punctuation
Body punctuation	Paragraphs have consistent punctuation
VISUAL CLARITY	
Number of fonts should not exceed	3
Title text size should be at least	36
Body text size should be at least	20
Number of bullets should not exceed	6
Number of lines per title should not exceed	2
Number of lines per bullet should not exceed	2

Correcting Errors

After creating a presentation and running the Spelling checker, you may find that you must make changes. Changes may be required because a slide contains an error, the scope of the presentation shifts, or the style is inconsistent. This section explains the types of errors that commonly occur when creating a presentation.

Types of Corrections Made to Presentations

You generally make three types of corrections to text in a presentation: additions, deletions, and replacements.

▶ **Additions** — are necessary when you omit text from a slide and need to add it later. You may need to insert text in the form of a sentence, word, or single character. For example, you may want to add the rest of the presenter's first name on your title slide.

▶ **Deletions** — are required when text on a slide is incorrect or is no longer relevant to the presentation. For example, one of your slides may look cluttered. Therefore, you may want to remove one of the bulleted paragraphs to add more space.

▶ **Replacements** — are needed when you want to revise the text in your presentation. For example, you may want to substitute the word, their, for the word, there.

Editing text in PowerPoint is basically the same as editing text in a word processing package. The following sections illustrate the most common changes made to text in a presentation.

Deleting Text

You can delete text using one of three methods. One is to use the BACKSPACE key to remove text just typed. The second is to position the insertion point to the left of the text you wish to delete and then press the DELETE key. The third method is to drag through the text you wish to delete and then press the DELETE key. (Use the third method when deleting large sections of text.)

Replacing Text in an Existing Slide

When you need to correct a word or phrase, you can replace the text by selecting the text to be replaced and then typing the new text. As soon as you press any key on the keyboard, the highlighted text is deleted and the new text displays.

PowerPoint inserts text to the left of the insertion point. The text to the right of the insertion point moves to the right (and shifts downward if necessary) to accommodate the added text.

Changing Line Spacing

The bulleted lists on Slides 2, 3, and 4 look crowded; yet, there is ample blank space that could be used to separate the paragraphs. You can adjust the spacing on each slide, but when several slides need to be changed, you should change the slide master. Each PowerPoint component (slides, title slides, audience handouts, and speaker's notes) has a **master**, which controls its appearance. Slides have two masters, title master and slide master. The **title master** controls the appearance of the title slide. The **slide master** controls the appearance of the other slides in your presentation.

Table 1-5	Summary of Slide Master Components
ELEMENT	*DESCRIPTION*
Background items	Any object other than the title object or text object. Typical items include borders and graphics such as a company logo, page number, date, and time.
Color scheme	A coordinated set of eight colors designed to complement each other. Color schemes consist of background color, line and text color, shadow color, title text color, object fill color, and three different accent colors.
Date	Inserts the special symbol used to print the date the presentation was printed.
Font	Defines the appearance and shape of letters, numbers, and special characters.
Font size	Specifies the size of the characters on the screen. Character size is gauged by a measurement system called points. A single point is about 1/72 of an inch in height. Thus, a character with a point size of eighteen is about 18/72 of an inch in height.
Font style	Font styles include plain, italic, bold, shadowed, and underlined. Text may have more than one font style at a time.
Slide number	Inserts the special symbol used to print the slide number.
Text alignment	Position of text in a paragraph is left-aligned, right-aligned, centered, or justified. Justified text is proportionally spaced across the object.
Time	Inserts the special symbol used to print the time the presentation was printed.

Each design template has a specially designed slide master. If you select a design template but want to change one of its components, you can override that component by changing the slide master. Any change to the slide master results in changing every slide in the presentation, except the title slide. For example, if you change the line spacing to .5 inches before each paragraph on the slide master, each slide (except the title slide) changes line spacing after each paragraph to .5 inches. The slide master components more frequently changed are listed in Table 1-5.

Additionally, each view has its own master. You can access the master by holding down the SHIFT key while clicking the appropriate view button. For example, holding down the SHIFT key and clicking the Slide View button displays the slide master. To exit a master, click the view button to which you wish to return. To return to slide view, for example, click the Slide View button.

Displaying the Slide Master

Before you can change line spacing on the slide master, you first must display it. Perform the following steps to display the slide master.

Steps **To Display the Slide Master**

1 **Click the Next Slide button on the slide pane to display Slide 2. Press and hold down the SHIFT key and then point to the Slide View button.**

When you hold down the SHIFT key, the ScreenTip displays Slide Master View (Figure 1-62).

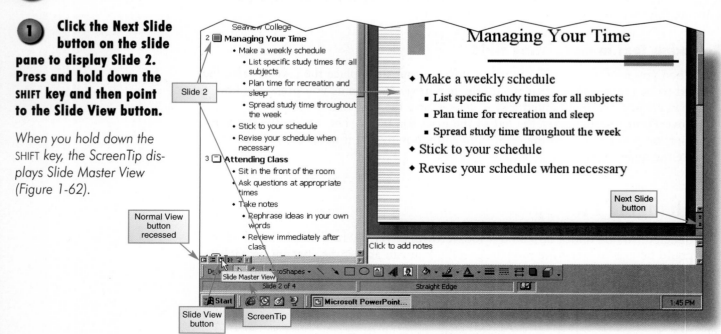

FIGURE 1-62

2 While holding down the SHIFT key, click the Slide Master View button. Then release the SHIFT key.

The slide master and Master toolbar display (Figure 1-63).

FIGURE 1-63

Changing Line Spacing on the Slide Master

Change line spacing by clicking the Line Spacing command on the Format menu. When you click the **Line Spacing command**, the Line Spacing dialog box displays. The Line Spacing dialog box contains three boxes, Line spacing, Before paragraph, and After paragraph, which allow you to adjust line spacing within a paragraph, before a paragraph, and after a paragraph, respectively.

Before paragraph line spacing is controlled by establishing the number of units before a paragraph. Units are either lines or points; lines are the default unit. Points may be selected by clicking the down arrow next to the Before paragraph box (see Figure 1-66 on page PP 1.61). Recall from page PP 1.24 that a single point is about 1/72 of an inch in height.

The Line spacing, Before paragraph, and After paragraph boxes each contain an amount of space box and a unit of measure box. To change the amount of space displaying between paragraphs, click the amount of space box up arrow or down arrow in the Line spacing box. To change the amount of space displaying before a paragraph, as you did in this project, click the amount of space box up arrow or down arrow in the Before paragraph box. To change the amount of space displaying after a paragraph, click the amount of space box up arrow or down arrow in the After paragraph box. To change the unit of measure from Lines to Points in the Line Spacing dialog box, click the arrow next to the appropriate unit of measure box and then click Points in the list.

In this project, you change the number in the amount of space box to increase the amount of space that displays before every paragraph, except the first paragraph, on every slide. For example, increasing the amount of space box to 0.5 lines increases the amount of space that displays before each paragraph.

Other **Ways**

1. On View menu point to Master, click Slide Master

More **About**

Line Spacing

Blank space on a slide can be advantageous. The absence of text, called white space, helps the viewer focus attention on the presenter. Do not be afraid to increase line spacing to give your text some breathing room.

The first paragraph on every slide, however, does not change because of its position in the Object Area placeholder. Perform the following steps to change the line spacing.

 To Change Line Spacing on the Slide Master

1 **Click the bulleted paragraph in the Object Area placeholder labeled, Click to edit Master text styles.**

The insertion point displays at the point you clicked (Figure 1-64). The Object Area placeholder is selected.

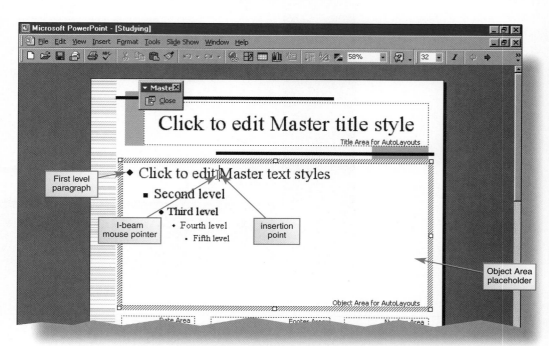

FIGURE 1-64

2 **Click Format on the menu bar and then point to Line Spacing. (Remember that you might have to wait a few seconds for the entire menu to display.)**

The Format menu displays (Figure 1-65).

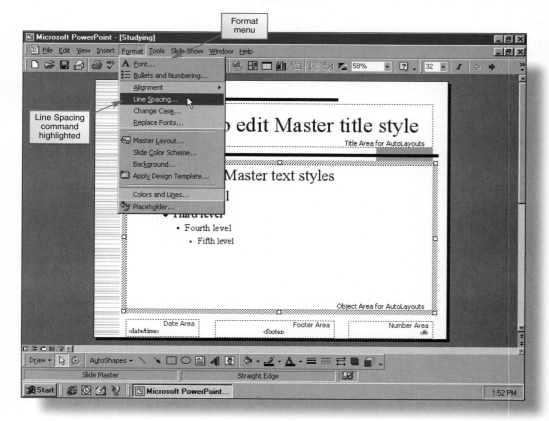

FIGURE 1-65

**③ Click Line Spacing.
Point to the Before
Paragraph amount of space
box up arrow.**

*PowerPoint displays the Line
Spacing dialog box (Figure
1-66). The default Before
paragraph line spacing is set
at 0.2 Lines.*

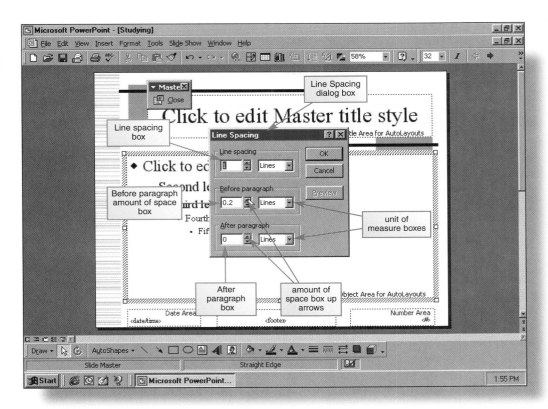

FIGURE 1-66

**④ Click the Before
paragraph amount
of space box up arrow six
times.**

*The Before paragraph
amount of space box displays
0.5 (Figure 1-67). The Preview button is available after
this change is made in the
Line Spacing dialog box. If
you click the Preview button,
PowerPoint temporarily
updates your presentation
with the new amount of
space setting. This new setting is not actually applied
until you click the OK button.*

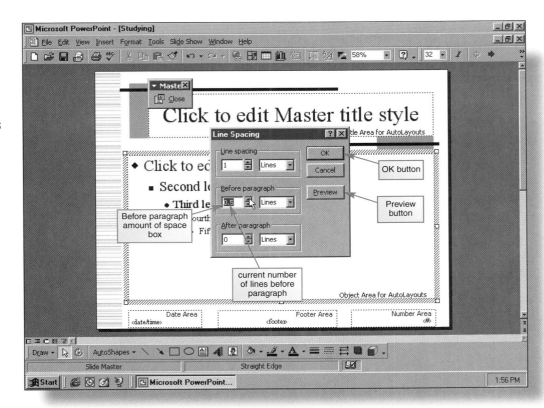

FIGURE 1-67

5 **Click the OK button.**

The slide master Object Area placeholder displays the new line spacing (Figure 1-68). Depending on the video drivers installed, the spacing on your screen may appear slightly different than this figure.

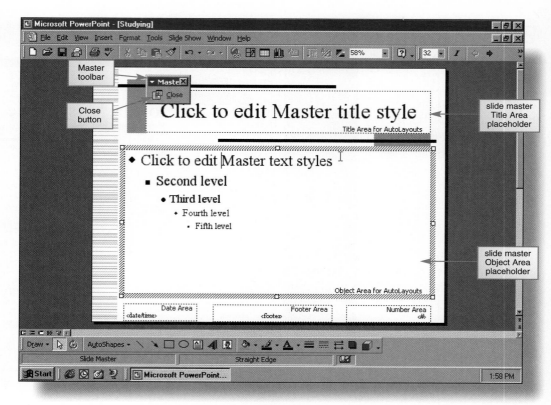

FIGURE 1-68

6 **Click the Close button on the Master toolbar to return to normal view.**

Slide 2 displays with the Before paragraph line spacing set to 0.5 Lines (Figure 1-69).

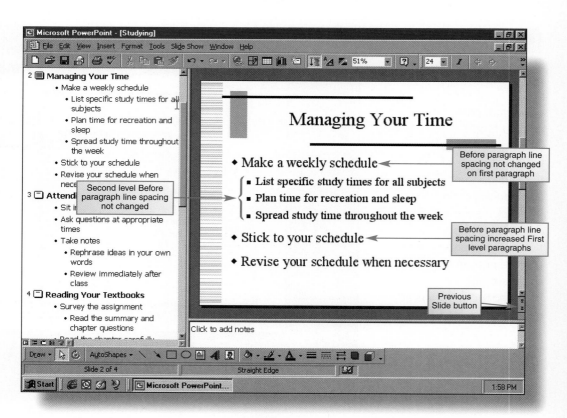

FIGURE 1-69

To display line spacing changes without making them permanent, click the Preview button in the Line Spacing dialog box. If you want to close the Line Spacing dialog box without applying the changes, click the Cancel button.

The placeholder at the top of the slide master (Figure 1-68) is used to edit the Master title style. The Object Area placeholder under the Master Title Area placeholder is used to edit the Master text styles. Here you make changes to the various bullet levels. Changes can be made to line spacing, bullet font, text and line color, alignment, and text shadow.

Displaying a Presentation in Black and White

You want to print handouts of your presentation and create overhead transparencies. The **Grayscale Preview button** allows you to display the presentation in black and white before you print. Table 1-6 identifies how PowerPoint objects display in black and white.

Perform the following steps to display the presentation in black and white.

Table 1-6 Appearance in Black and White View	
OBJECT	DISPLAY
Text	Black
Text shadows	Hidden
Embossing	Hidden
Fills	Grayscale
Frame	Black
Pattern fills	Grayscale
Lines	Black
Object shadows	Grayscale
Bitmaps	Grayscale
Slide backgrounds	White

Steps To Display a Presentation in Black and White

1 **Click the Previous Slide button to display Slide 1. Point to the Grayscale Preview button on the Standard toolbar.**

Slide 1 displays. The Grayscale Preview ScreenTip displays (Figure 1-70).

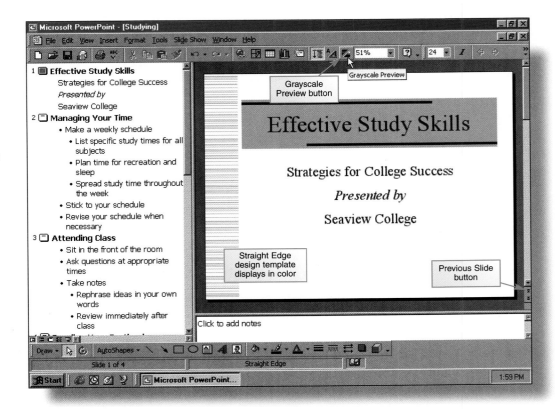

FIGURE 1-70

Click the Grayscale Preview button.

Slide 1 displays in black and white (Figure 1-71). The Grayscale Preview button is recessed on the Standard toolbar.

Click the Next Slide button three times to view all slides in the presentation in black and white.

Click the Grayscale Preview button.

Slide 4 displays with the default Straight Edge color scheme.

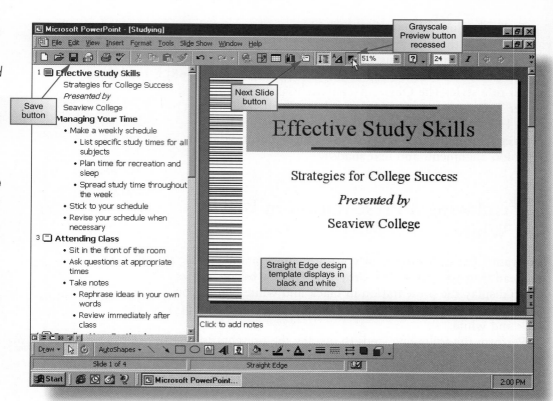

FIGURE 1-71

Other Ways

1. On View menu click Black and White

After you view the text objects in your presentation in black and white, you can make any changes that will enhance printouts produced from a black and white printer or photocopier.

Printing a Presentation

After you create a presentation, you often want to print it. A printed version of the presentation is called a **hard copy**, or **printout**. The first printing of the presentation is called a **rough draft**. The rough draft allows you to proofread the presentation to check for errors and readability. After correcting errors, you print the final copy of your presentation.

Saving a Presentation Before Printing

Prior to printing your presentation, you should save your work in the event you experience difficulties with the printer. You occasionally may encounter system problems that can be resolved only by restarting the computer. In such an instance, you will need to reopen your presentation. As a precaution, always save your presentation before you print. Perform the following steps to save the presentation before printing.

TO SAVE A PRESENTATION BEFORE PRINTING

1 Verify that your floppy disk is in drive A.

2 Click the Save button on the Standard toolbar.

All changes made after your last save now are saved on a floppy disk.

Printing the Presentation

After saving the presentation, you are ready to print. Clicking the **Print button** on the Standard toolbar causes PowerPoint to print all slides in the presentation. Perform the following steps to print the presentation slides.

 To Print a Presentation

1 **Ready the printer according to the printer instructions. Then click the Print button on the Standard toolbar.**

The printer icon in the tray status area on the taskbar indicates a print job is processing (Figure 1-72). After several moments, the slide show begins printing on the printer. When the presentation is finished printing, the printer icon in the tray status area on the taskbar no longer displays.

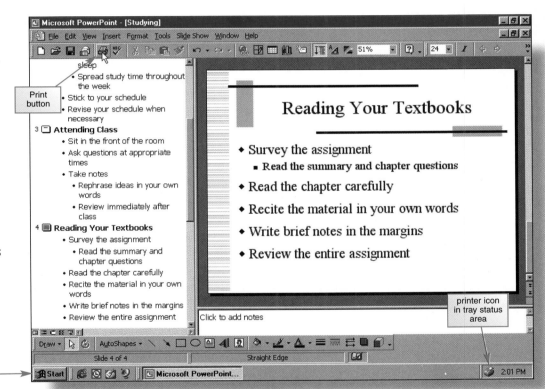

FIGURE 1-72

(2) **When the printer stops, retrieve the printouts of the slides.**

The presentation, Studying, prints on four pages (Figures 1-73a through 1-73d).

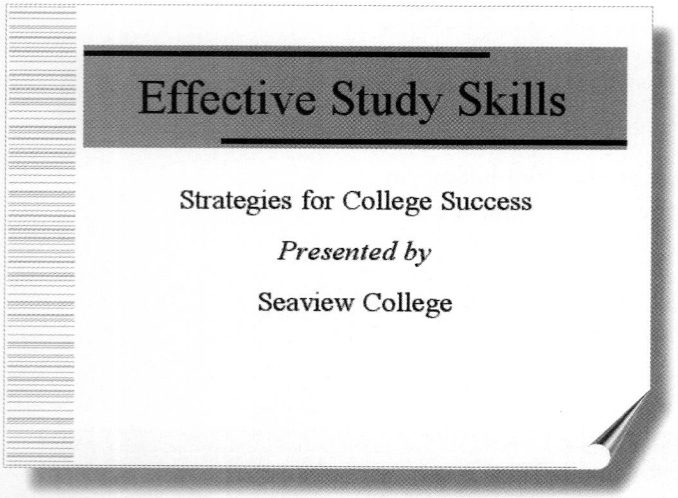

Effective Study Skills

Strategies for College Success

Presented by

Seaview College

(a) Slide 1

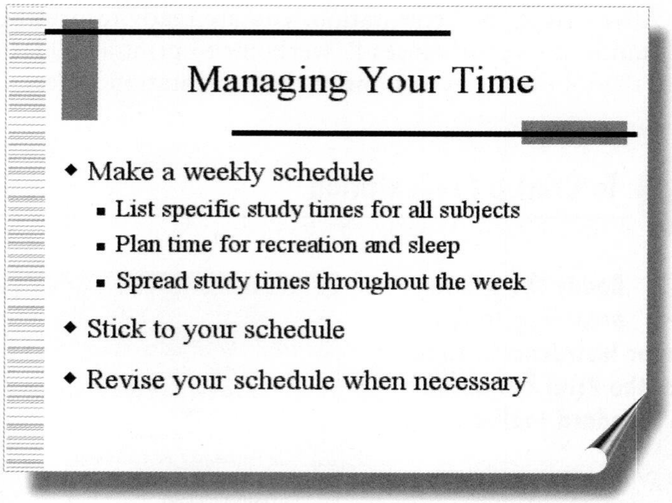

Managing Your Time

- ◆ Make a weekly schedule
  - ▪ List specific study times for all subjects
  - ▪ Plan time for recreation and sleep
  - ▪ Spread study times throughout the week
- ◆ Stick to your schedule
- ◆ Revise your schedule when necessary

(b) Slide 2

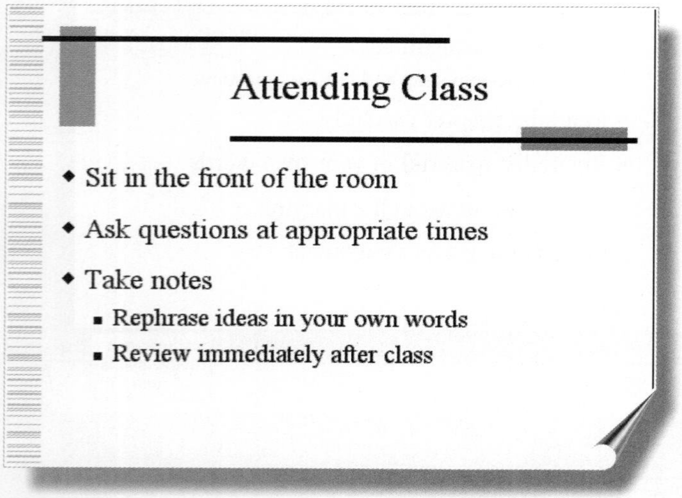

Attending Class

- ◆ Sit in the front of the room
- ◆ Ask questions at appropriate times
- ◆ Take notes
  - ▪ Rephrase ideas in your own words
  - ▪ Review immediately after class

(c) Slide 3

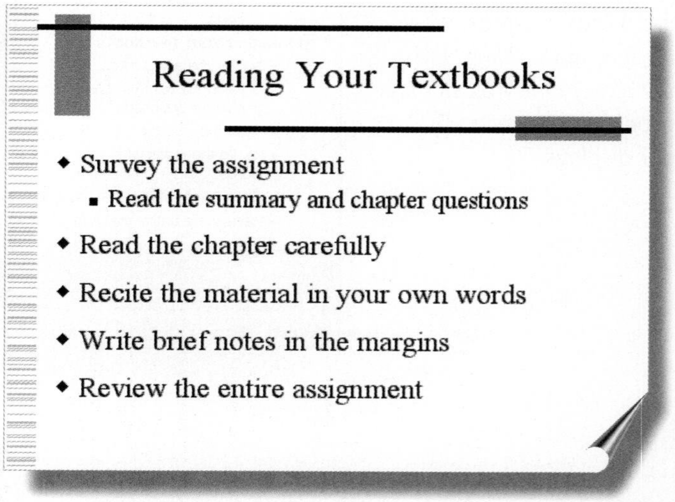

Reading Your Textbooks

- ◆ Survey the assignment
  - ▪ Read the summary and chapter questions
- ◆ Read the chapter carefully
- ◆ Recite the material in your own words
- ◆ Write brief notes in the margins
- ◆ Review the entire assignment

(d) Slide 4

FIGURE 1-73

Other Ways

1. On File menu click Print
2. Press CTRL+P or press CTRL+SHIFT+F12

You can click the printer icon next to the clock in the tray status area on the taskbar to obtain information about the presentations printing on your printer and to delete files in the print queue that are waiting to be printed.

Making a Transparency

Now that you have printed handouts, you want to make overhead transparencies. You can make transparencies using one of several devices. One device is a printer attached to your computer, such as an ink-jet printer or a laser printer. Transparencies produced on a printer may be in black and white or color, depending on the printer. Another device is a photocopier. Because each of these devices requires a special transparency film, check the user's manual for the film requirement of your specific device, or ask your instructor.

PowerPoint Help System

You can get answers to PowerPoint questions at any time by using the **PowerPoint Help system**. Used properly, this form of online assistance can increase your productivity and reduce your frustrations by minimizing the time you spend learning how to use PowerPoint. The following section shows how to get answers to your questions using the Office Assistant.

Using the Office Assistant

The **Office Assistant** answers your questions and suggests more efficient ways to complete a task. With the Office Assistant active, for example, you can type a question, word, or phrase in a text box and the Office Assistant provides immediate help on the subject. Also, as you create a worksheet, the Office Assistant accumulates tips that suggest more efficient ways to do the tasks you completed while building a presentation, such as formatting, printing, and saving. This tip feature is part of the **IntelliSense™ technology** that is built into PowerPoint, which understands what you are trying to do and suggests better ways to do it. When the light bulb displays above the Office Assistant, click it to see a tip.

The following steps show how to use the Office Assistant to obtain information on formatting a presentation.

More About 2000

Help

In previous versions of Microsoft PowerPoint and other software, users had to spend hours pouring through thick reference manuals to find relevant information. This task was particularly difficult for novice computer users. Today, the Office Assistant helps you search for relevant information instantly and easily.

Steps **To Obtain Help Using the Office Assistant**

1 **If the Office Assistant is not on the screen, click Show the Office Assistant on the Help menu. With the Office Assistant on the screen, click it. Type** how do i take meeting minutes **in the What would you like to do? text box in the Office Assistant balloon. Point to the Search button (Figure 1-74).**

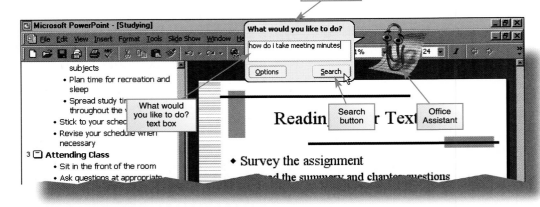

FIGURE 1-74

2 Click the Search button. Point to the topic Take notes or meeting minutes during a slide show in the Office Assistant balloon.

The Office Assistant displays a list of topics relating to the question how do i take meeting minutes (Figure 1-75). The mouse pointer changes to a hand.

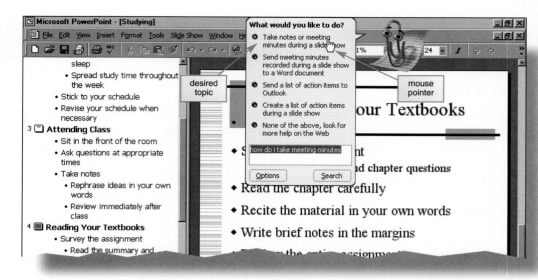

FIGURE 1-75

3 Click Take notes or meeting minutes during a slide show.

The Office Assistant displays a Microsoft PowerPoint Help window that provides Help information on taking notes or meeting minutes during a slide show (Figure 1-76).

4 Click the Close button on the Microsoft PowerPoint Help window title bar.

The Microsoft PowerPoint Help window closes, and the worksheet again is active.

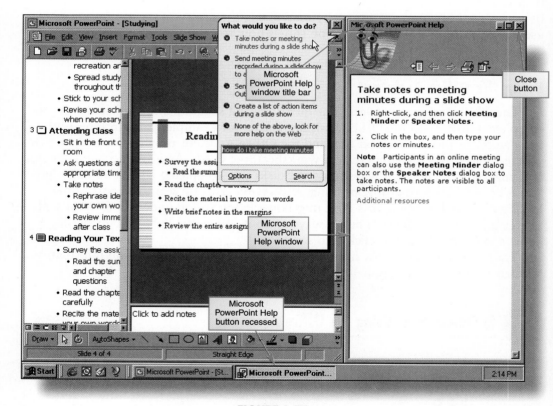

FIGURE 1-76

Table 1-7 summarizes the eight categories of help available to you. Because of the way the PowerPoint Help system works, please review the right-most column of Table 1-7 if you have difficulties activating the desired category of help.

Table 1-7 PowerPoint Help System

TYPE	DESCRIPTION	HOW TO ACTIVATE	TURNING THE OFFICE ASSISTANT ON AND OFF
Answer Wizard	Similar to the Office Assistant in that it answers questions that you type in your own words.	Click the Microsoft PowerPoint Help button on the Standard toolbar. If necessary, maximize the Help window by double-clicking its title bar. Click the Answer Wizard tab.	If the Office Assistant displays, right-click it, click Options, click the Use the Office Assistant check box, and then click the OK button.
Contents sheet	Groups Help topics by general categories. Use when you know only the general category of the topic in question.	Click the Office Assistant button on the Standard toolbar. If necessary, maximize the Help window by double-clicking its title bar. Click the Contents tab.	If the Office Assistant displays, right-click it, click Options, click the Use the Office Assistant check box, and then click the OK button.
Detect and Repair	Automatically finds and fixes errors in the application.	Click Detect and Repair on the Help menu.	
Hardware and Software Information	Shows Product ID and allows access to system information and technical support information.	Click About Microsoft PowerPoint on the Help menu and then click the System Information or Technical Information button.	
Index sheet	Similar to an index in a book; use when you know exactly what you want.	Click the Microsoft PowerPoint Help button on the Standard toolbar. If necessary, maximize the Help window by double-clicking its title bar. Click the Index tab.	If the Office Assistant displays, right-click it, click Options, click Use the Office Assistant check box, and then click the OK button.
Office Assistant	Answers questions that you type in your own words, offers tips, and provides Help for a variety of PowerPoint features.	Click the Microsoft PowerPoint Help button on the Standard toolbar.	If the Office Assistant does not display, close the Microsoft PowerPoint Help window and then click Show the Office Assistant on the Help menu.
Office on the Web	Accesses technical resources and download free product enhancements on the Web.	Click Office on the Web on the Help menu.	
Question Mark button and What's This? command	Identifies unfamiliar items on the screen.	Click the Question Mark button and then click an item in the dialog box. Click What's This? on the Help menu, and then click an item on the screen.	

You can use the Office Assistant to search for Help on any topic concerning PowerPoint. For additional information on using the PowerPoint Help system, see Appendix A.

Quitting PowerPoint

Project 1 is complete. The final task is to close the presentation and quit PowerPoint. Perform the following steps to quit PowerPoint.

TO QUIT POWERPOINT

1 Click the Close button on the title bar.

2 If prompted to save the presentation before quitting PowerPoint, click the Yes button in the Microsoft PowerPoint dialog box.

More About

Quick Reference

For a table that lists how to complete the tasks covered in this book using the mouse, menu, shortcut menu, and keyboard, visit the Shelly Cashman Series Office Web page (www.scsite.com/off2000/qr.htm) and then click Microsoft PowerPoint 2000.

CASE PERSPECTIVE SUMMARY

Your Effective Study Skills PowerPoint slide show should help Dr. Martinez and the counseling staff present essential college survival skills to incoming freshmen attending orientation sessions at your school. The four slides display the key study habits all students need to succeed throughout college. The title slide identifies the topic of the presentation, and the next three slides give key pointers regarding time management, class attendance, and textbook usage. The counselors will use your overhead transparencies to organize their speeches, and the students will keep handouts of your slides for future reference.

Project Summary

Project 1 introduced you to starting PowerPoint and creating a multi-level bulleted list presentation. You learned about PowerPoint design templates, objects, and attributes. This project illustrated how to create an interesting introduction to a presentation by changing the text font style to italic and increasing font size on the title slide. Completing these tasks, you saved your presentation. Then, you created three multi-level bulleted list slides to explain how to study effectively in college. Next, you learned how to view the presentation in slide show view. Then you learned how to quit PowerPoint and how to open an existing presentation. You used the Spelling checker to search for spelling errors and learned how the Office Assistant Style checker identifies inconsistencies in design specifications. Using the slide master, you quickly adjusted the Before paragraph line spacing on every slide to make better use of white space. You learned how to display the presentation in black and white. Then, you learned how to print hard copies of your slides in order to make overhead transparencies. Finally, you learned how to use the PowerPoint Help system.

What You Should Know

Having completed this project, you now should be able to perform the following tasks:

- Add a New Slide Using the Bulleted List AutoLayout *(PP 1.32)*
- Add a New Slide with the Same AutoLayout *(PP 1.40)*
- Change Line Spacing on the Slide Master *(PP 1.60)*
- Change the Text Font Style to Italic *(PP 1.27)*

- Choose a Design Template *(PP 1.18)*
- Complete Slide 3 *(PP 1.40)*
- Create Slide 4 *(PP 1.41)*
- Display a Presentation in Black and White *(PP 1.63)*
- Display the Formatting Toolbar in its Entirety *(PP 1.17)*
- Display the Popup Menu and Go to a Specific Slide *(PP 1.49)*
- Display the Slide Master *(PP 1.58)*
- End a Slide Show with a Black Slide *(PP 1.43)*
- Enter a Slide Title *(PP 1.35)*
- Enter the Presentation Subtitle *(PP 1.23)*
- Enter the Presentation Title *(PP 1.21)*
- Increase Font Size *(PP 1.25)*
- Move Manually Through Slides in a Slide Show *(PP 1.48)*
- Obtain Help Using the Office Assistant *(PP 1.67)*
- Open an Existing Presentation *(PP 1.52)*

- Print a Presentation *(PP 1.65)*
- Quit PowerPoint *(PP 1.51, 1.69)*
- Save a Presentation Before Printing *(PP 1.65)*
- Save a Presentation on a Floppy Disk *(PP 1.29)*
- Save a Presentation with the Same File Name *(PP 1.44)*
- Select an Object Area Placeholder *(PP 1.36)*
- Start a New Presentation *(PP 1.10)*
- Start Slide Show View *(PP 1.46)*
- Start the Spelling Checker *(PP 1.55)*
- Type a Multi-level Bulleted List *(PP 1.37)*
- Type the Remaining Text for Slide 2 *(PP 1.39)*
- Use the Popup Menu to End a Slide Show *(PP 1.50)*
- Use the Scroll Box on the Slide Pane to Move to Another Slide *(PP 1.45)*

Apply Your Knowledge

✚ Project Reinforcement at www.scsite.com/off2000/reinforce.htm

1 Computer Buying Basics

Instructions: Start PowerPoint. Open the presentation Apply-1 from the PowerPoint Data Disk. See the inside back cover for instructions for downloading the PowerPoint Data Disk or see your instructor for information on accessing the files required for this book. This slide lists questions to consider when buying a computer. Perform the following tasks to change the slide so it looks like the one in Figure 1-77.

Buying a Computer?

- Ask these questions:
  - Hardware
    - How fast is the microprocessor?
    - How large is the hard drive?
    - How much RAM is included?
  - Software
    - Will I be using graphics?
    - Will I be computing my finances and taxes?

FIGURE 1-77

1. Click the Common Tasks menu button on the Formatting toolbar, and then click the Apply Design Template command. Choose the Blends design template.
2. Press and hold down the SHIFT key, and then click the Slide Master View button to display the slide master. Click the paragraph, Click to edit Master text styles. Click Format on the menu bar and then click Line Spacing. Increase the Before paragraph line spacing to 1 Lines. Click the OK button. Then click the Close button on the Master toolbar to return to normal view.
3. Select the text in the Title Area placeholder. Click the Bold button on the Formatting toolbar.
4. If necessary, select the text in the Title Area placeholder. Click the Font Size box arrow on the Font Size button on the Formatting toolbar. Click the down scroll arrow and then scroll down and click font size 48.
5. Click the paragraph in the Object Area placeholder, How fast is the microprocessor?. Click the Demote button on the Formatting toolbar.
6. Demote the four other paragraphs that end with a question mark.
7. Click File on the menu bar and then click Save As. Type Buying a Computer in the File name box. If drive A is not already displaying in the Save in box, click the Save in box arrow, and then click 3½ Floppy (A:). Click the Save button.
8. Click the Grayscale Preview button on the Standard toolbar to display the presentation in black and white.
9. Click the Print button on the Standard toolbar.
10. Click the Close button on the menu bar to quit PowerPoint.
11. Write your name on the printout, and hand it in to your instructor.

In the Lab

NOTE: These labs require you to create presentations based on notes. When you design these slide shows, use the 7 x 7 rule, which states that each line should have a maximum of seven words, and each slide should have a maximum of seven lines.

1 Financial Freedom at Community Savings & Loan

Problem: You work at the Community Savings & Loan. The institution's vice president wants you to help her prepare a presentation for an upcoming seminar for the community regarding achieving financial freedom. She hands you the notes in Figure 1-78, and you create the presentation shown in Figures 1-79a through 1-79d.

I) **Money Sense –**
Gaining Financial Freedom
  A) Presented by:
  B) Rich Jackson
  C) Community Savings & Loan
II) **Start Saving Now**
  A) Use the benefits of compounding interest
    1) Search for investments with high returns
    2) Consider stocks and stock mutual funds
  B) Have an emergency money fund
    1) Try to save six months' living expenses
    2) Put in easily liquidated accounts
III) **Spend Within Your Means**
  A) Make a budget and stick to it
  B) Watch for bargains
    1) Shop at pre-season and post-season sales
  C) Buy classic clothes and furnishings
    1) They will not seem dated years later
IV) **Pay Yourself First**
  A) You are your primary financial obligation
    1) Be completely committed to saving regularly
  B) Save 10 percent of your gross income
    1) As your salary grows, increase this amount
  C) Use direct deposit to ensure a transaction

FIGURE 1-78

In the Lab

**Money Sense –
Gaining Financial Freedom**

Presented by:
Rich Jackson
Community Savings & Loan

(a) Slide 1

Start Saving Now

- Use the benefits of compounding interest
  - Search for investments with high returns
  - Consider stocks and stock mutual funds

- Have an emergency money fund
  - Try to save six months' living expenses
  - Put in easily liquidated accounts

(b) Slide 2

Spend Within Your Means

- Make a budget and stick to it

- Watch for bargains
  - Shop at pre-season and post-season sales

- Buy classic clothes and furnishings
  - They will not seem dated years later

(c) Slide 3

Pay Yourself First

- You are your primary financial obligation
  - Be completely committed to saving regularly

- Save 10 percent of your gross income
  - As your salary grows, increase this amount

- Use direct deposit to ensure a transaction

(d) Slide 4

FIGURE 1-79

Instructions: Perform the following tasks.

1. Create a new presentation using the Capsules design template.
2. Using the typed notes illustrated in Figure 1-78, create the title slide shown in Figure 1-79a using your name in place of Rich Jackson. Decrease the font size of the paragraph, Presented by:, to 24. Decrease the font size of the paragraph, Community Savings & Loan, to 20.
3. Using the typed notes in Figure 1-78, create the three bulleted list slides shown in Figures 1-79b through 1-79d. Increase the Before paragraph spacing to .8 Lines.
4. Click the Spelling button on the Standard toolbar. Correct any errors.
5. Save the presentation on a floppy disk using the file name, Money Freedom.
6. Display the presentation in black and white.
7. Print the black and white presentation. Quit PowerPoint.

In the Lab

2 Lake Shore Mall Fashion Show

Problem: You work in a clothing store at Lake Shore Mall, and your manager has asked you to participate in the annual fashion show. You decide to get involved with the segment promoting clothing to wear on job interviews. You determine that a PowerPoint presentation would help the commentator present key points as the models display accompanying clothing. You interview fashion coordinators at various stores in the mall and organize the list in Figure 1-80. Then you select a PowerPoint design template and decide to modify it. *Hint*: Use the PowerPoint Help system to solve this problem.

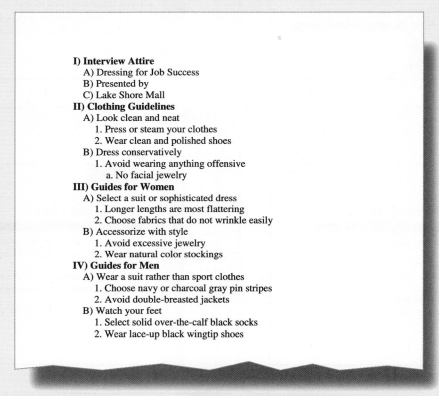

I) **Interview Attire**
    A) Dressing for Job Success
    B) Presented by
    C) Lake Shore Mall
II) **Clothing Guidelines**
    A) Look clean and neat
        1. Press or steam your clothes
        2. Wear clean and polished shoes
    B) Dress conservatively
        1. Avoid wearing anything offensive
          a. No facial jewelry
III) **Guides for Women**
    A) Select a suit or sophisticated dress
        1. Longer lengths are most flattering
        2. Choose fabrics that do not wrinkle easily
    B) Accessorize with style
        1. Avoid excessive jewelry
        2. Wear natural color stockings
IV) **Guides for Men**
    A) Wear a suit rather than sport clothes
        1. Choose navy or charcoal gray pin stripes
        2. Avoid double-breasted jackets
    B) Watch your feet
        1. Select solid over-the-calf black socks
        2. Wear lace-up black wingtip shoes

FIGURE 1-80

Instructions: Perform the following tasks.

1. Create a new presentation using the Post Modern design template.
2. Using the notes in Figure 1-80, create the title slide shown in Figure 1-81a. Increase the font size of the paragraph, Dressing for Job Success, to 36. Decrease the font size of the paragraph, Presented by, to 28.
3. Using the notes in Figure 1-80, create the three multi-level bulleted list slides shown in Figures 1-81b through 1-81d.
4. Display the slide master. Click the paragraph, Click to edit Master title style. Click the Bold button on the Formatting toolbar.
5. Click the paragraph, Click to edit Master text styles. On the Format menu, click Line Spacing, and then increase the Before paragraph line spacing to 0.75 Lines. Click the paragraph, Second level. On the Format menu, click Line Spacing, and then increase the After paragraph spacing to 0.25 Lines.

In the Lab

(a) Slide 1

Interview Attire

Dressing for Job Success

Presented by

Lake Shore Mall

9/12/01   Student Name   1

(b) Slide 2

Clothing Guidelines

- Look clean and neat
  - Press or steam your clothes
  - Wear clean and polished shoes
- Dress conservatively
  - Avoid wearing anything offensive
    - No facial jewelry

9/12/01   Student Name   2

(c) Slide 3

Guides for Women

- Select a suit or sophisticated dress
  - Longer lengths are most flattering
  - Choose fabrics that do not wrinkle easily
- Accessorize with style
  - Avoid excessive jewelry
  - Wear natural color stockings

9/12/01   Student Name   3

(d) Slide 4

Guides for Men

- Wear a suit rather than sport clothes
  - Choose navy or charcoal gray pin stripes
  - Avoid double-breasted jackets
- Watch your feet
  - Select solid over-the-calf black socks
  - Wear lace-up black wingtip shoes

9/12/01   Student Name   4

FIGURE 1-81

6. Drag the scroll box in the slide pane down to display the title master. Click the paragraph, Click to edit Master title style. Click the Bold button on the Formatting toolbar.

7. Return to normal view. On the View menu, click Header and Footer. If necessary, click the Slide tab. Add the date (so it updates automatically), a slide number, and your name to the footer. Display the footer on all slides.

8. Drag the scroll box to display Slide 1. Click the Slide Show button to start slide show view. Then click to display each slide.

9. Save the presentation on a floppy disk using the file name, Interview Attire. Display and print the presentation in black and white. Quit PowerPoint.

In the Lab

3 Cholesterol Basics at the Community Wellness Center

Problem: At your visit to the South Suburban Community Wellness Center last week, staff nurse Debbie Ortiz explained the fundamentals of cholesterol to you and several other patients. You decide she can use a presentation and handouts to better educate clinic visitors. *Hint*: Use the PowerPoint Help system to solve this problem.

Instructions: Using the list in Figure 1-82, design and create a presentation. The presentation must include a title slide and three bulleted list slides. Perform the following tasks.

1. Create a new presentation using the Dad's Tie design template.

2. Create a title slide titled, Cholesterol Highs and Lows. Include a subtitle, using your name in place of Debbie Ortiz. Decrease the font size for paragraphs Presented by: and South Suburban Wellness Center to 32. Italicize your name.

3. Using Figure 1-82, create three multi-level bulleted list slides. On Slide 2, use check marks instead of square bullets for the three main Cholesterol Basics paragraphs.

4. Adjust Before paragraph and After paragraph line spacing to utilize the available white space.

5. Insert a footer on every slide except the title slide that includes the current date, your name, and the slide number.

6. View the presentation in slide show view to look for errors. Correct any errors.

7. Check the presentation for spelling errors.

8. Save the presentation to a floppy disk with the file name, Cholesterol Basics. Print the presentation slides in black and white. Quit PowerPoint.

I) **Cholesterol Highs and Lows**
  A) Presented by:
  B) Debbie Ortiz
  C) South Suburban Wellness Center
II) **Cholesterol Basics**
  A) Needed by:
    1) Every cell in your body
  B) Builds:
    1) Brain and nerve tissues; bile
  C) Manufactured by:
    1) Liver and small intestine
III) **HDL (high density lipids)**
  A) H stands for "Healthy"
  B) Good for your heart
    1) Delivers cholesterol deposits in body to liver
      a) Liver disposes or recycles these deposits
IV) **LDL (low density lipoproteins)**
  A) L stands for "Lethal"
  B) Enemy of the heart
    1) Transports needed cholesterol to cells
    2) Dumps excess on arterial walls and tissues

FIGURE 1-82

Cases and Places

The difficulty of these case studies varies:
▶ are the least difficult; ▶▶ are more difficult; and ▶▶▶ are the most difficult.

1 ▶ Dr. Doug Gordon, chief ophthalmologist at the North Shore Eye Clinic, knows that many people take their eyesight for granted. They visit an eye doctor only when they are having difficulties, such as eye pain or extreme redness. He urges everyone, from newborns to senior citizens, to preserve their eyesight by scheduling regular eye exams. The times for these checkups varies by age. Dr. Gordon has contacted you to help him prepare a presentation that will be delivered at community fairs and at the local shopping mall. He has prepared the notes in Figure 1-83 and has asked you to use them to develop a title slide and additional slides that can be used on an overhead projector. Use the concepts and techniques introduced in this project to create the presentation.

The Eyes Have It
When Is Checkup Time?
Dr. Doug Gordon
North Shore Eye Clinic

Children
Newborns
    When: In nursery
    Potential problems: infections, abnormalities
Infants (to 6 months)
    When: once
    Potential problems: eye misalignment
Youngsters (ages 1 to 6)
    When: every 1 to 3 years
    Potential problems: nearsightedness, farsightedness, astigmatism, lazy eye
School-age children (ages 7 to 17)
    When: every 1 to 2 years
    Potential problems: nearsightedness, farsightedness, astigmatism
Adults
Ages 18 to 40
    When: every 1 to 2 years
    Potential problems: needing reading glasses, early stages of glaucoma
Ages 41 – 64
    When: every 1 to 2 years
    Potential problems: glaucoma, cataracts, macular degeneration
Seniors (ages 65+)
When: annually
Potential problems: glaucoma, cataracts, macular degeneration

FIGURE 1-83

Cases and Places

2 ▶▶ This past holiday season, the Highland Shores police and fire departments experienced an unusually high number of calls for assistance. Many of these problems were the result of mishaps that easily could have been prevented. Police Chief Victor Halen and Fire Chief Norton Smits want to inform community residents at local block parties next summer about how they can follow a few safety precautions to reduce their chances of injuries. The chiefs want you to help them prepare a slide show and handouts for the community. They have typed safety tips for you (Figure 1-84), and they have asked you to prepare five slides that can be used on an overhead projector and as handouts. They want the title slide to introduce them and their topic. Use the concepts and techniques introduced in this project to create the presentation.

Seasonal Safety

Using Candles
Never burn unattended or in drafts
Burn on a heat-resistant surface
Trim wick to ¼ inch before lighting
   Do not drop wick trimming into candle
Burn for 2 – 3 hours at a time
   Allow to cool before relighting
Decorating
Be mindful of children
   Hang ornaments, tinsel on high branches
   Keep dangerous plants out of reach
      Mistletoe, poinsettia, and holly contain toxic substances
Lighting
Use the right lights
   Choose lights with the UL label
   Check for defects
      Cracked sockets, frayed wires, loose connections
   Turn off lights before leaving house
Cooking
Reduce the risk of bacterial growth
   Keep food on table two hours maximum
      Egg dishes should be refrigerated hourly
      Rotate foods occasionally
Do not leave food unattended on stovetops

FIGURE 1-84

Cases and Places

3 ▶▶ CPU-4-U is a computer repair store near campus that specializes in repairing computer systems and building custom computers. The co-owners, Warren Shilling and Mary Burg, want to attract new customers, and they have asked you to help them design a PowerPoint advertising campaign. Having graduated from your college, they are familiar with the hardware and software students need for their classes. Computer users can make appointments to bring their computers to the shop or to arrange for on-site service 24 hours a day. CPU-4-U also carries a complete line of supplies, including toner cartridges, paper, and labels. Many students consult with the technicians to plan for future computer purchases and to arrange financing for their new systems. The store is located in Tinley Mall, 6302 South State Street, Ypsilanti, Michigan. For more information call 555-2297. Using the techniques presented in this project, prepare a title slide and three bulleted list slides to be used for their presentation and for handouts.

4 ▶▶ The Poochy Humane Society in your town wants to increase community awareness of its services and facilities. The society's director, Jennifer Durkin, has decided that one way she can promote the shelter is by informing community residents on how they should react when a loose dog approaches them. She decides to address residents who regularly participate in activities at the local park district and who are walking, jogging, and biking in the community park. She wants to inform them that they can react in one of three ways when a stray dog approaches. They can be friendly by talking softly and by extending one of their hands palm down. Another behavior is to assert dominance. Using this approach, they should look at the dog sternly and yell, "Go away!" A third reaction is to act submissively by relaxing their muscles and glancing to the side. This technique is especially useful for an encounter with a big dog that thinks it is in control. The Poochy Humane Society is located at 10836 Windy Terrace; the telephone number is 555-DOGS. Using the concepts and techniques presented in this project, prepare a title slide and three bulleted list slides to be used on an overhead projector and as handouts for community residents.

5 ▶▶ Fat is one of the three essential components your body needs. The other two are protein and carbohydrates. Unfortunately, many people throughout the world consume too much fat in their diets. Although fat intake needs vary based on age and weight, following a low-fat diet can reduce the risk of heart disease. Some fats are healthy and actually help give energy, prevent blood clotting, and reduce cholesterol and triglyceride levels. These fats, commonly called essential fatty acids (EFAs) or Vitamin F, are found in cold-water fish and cold-temperature plant oils, such as flax seed and black currant. Monounsaturated fats also are healthy for the body. They are found in olive, almond, and canola oils, they all are liquid at room temperature, and they generally come from plant seeds. Although polyunsaturated fats can decrease cholesterol levels, they also can decrease the percentage of healthy HDL cholesterol (see In the Lab Project 3). Like monounsaturated fats, they come from plant seeds and are liquid at room temperature. They are found in safflower oil and corn oil. Saturated fats and hydrogenated fats are unhealthy because they can clog arteries and elevate cholesterol levels. They are found in animal foods, such as butter, margarine, and meat. Using the concepts and techniques presented in this project, prepare a presentation describing the various type of fats in our foods and their benefits or dangers to our health. Create a title slide and at least three additional slides that can be used with an overhead projector and as handouts.

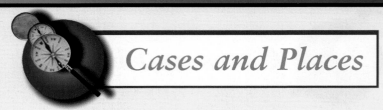

Cases and Places

6 ▶▶ Every day, two Americans are killed in collisions between trains and cars or between trains and pedestrians. Many more people suffer serious injuries from these accidents. Lighting is not a significant factor, for more than 50 percent of these accidents occur at crossings marked with gates and flashing lights, and more than 70 percent occur during the day. People involved in train accidents have one or more of these three personality traits: impatient, and not wanting to wait for a train; inattentive, and daydreaming or listening to loud music; or ignorant, and not aware of the impending danger. Drivers and pedestrians can reduce the risk of train accidents by looking both ways before crossing the tracks, never walking down a track, and assuming that a train can come at any time in either direction on any track. If your car stalls on a railroad track when a train is approaching, get out immediately and run away from the track in the same direction from which the train is coming. (If you run in the same direction the train is traveling, the train will hit your car, which can potentially hit you.) Using the concepts and techniques presented in this project, prepare a presentation to warn drivers and pedestrians of the dangers involved in crossing railroad tracks. Create a title slide and at least three additional slides that can be used with an overhead projector and as handouts.

7 ▶▶▶ In the Lab Project 1 discusses the need for developing techniques to achieve financial freedom. One of the suggestions is to invest in stocks or in stock mutual funds. These mutual funds pool shareholders' money and invest in a diversified portfolio of funds. Interview a financial planner or research the Internet for information on the various types of mutual funds and how they are managed. Determine the fees and expenses involved in this type of investment. Then, using the concepts and techniques presented in this project, prepare a presentation to report your findings. Create a title slide and at least three additional slides that can be used with an overhead projector and as handouts.

Microsoft PowerPoint 2000

PROJECT 2

Using Outline View and Clip Art to Create a Slide Show

You will have mastered the material in this project when you can:

- Create a presentation from an outline
- Start a presentation as a new PowerPoint document
- Use outline view
- Create a presentation in outline view
- Add a slide in outline view
- Create multi-level bulleted list slides in outline view
- Create a closing slide in outline view
- Save and review a presentation
- Change the slide layout
- Insert clip art from Microsoft Clip Gallery 5.0
- Move clip art
- Change clip art size
- Add a header and footer to outline pages
- Add animation and slide transition effects
- Apply animation effects to bulleted slides
- Animate clip art objects
- Format and animate a title slide
- Run an animated slide show
- Print a presentation outline
- E-mail a slide show from within PowerPoint

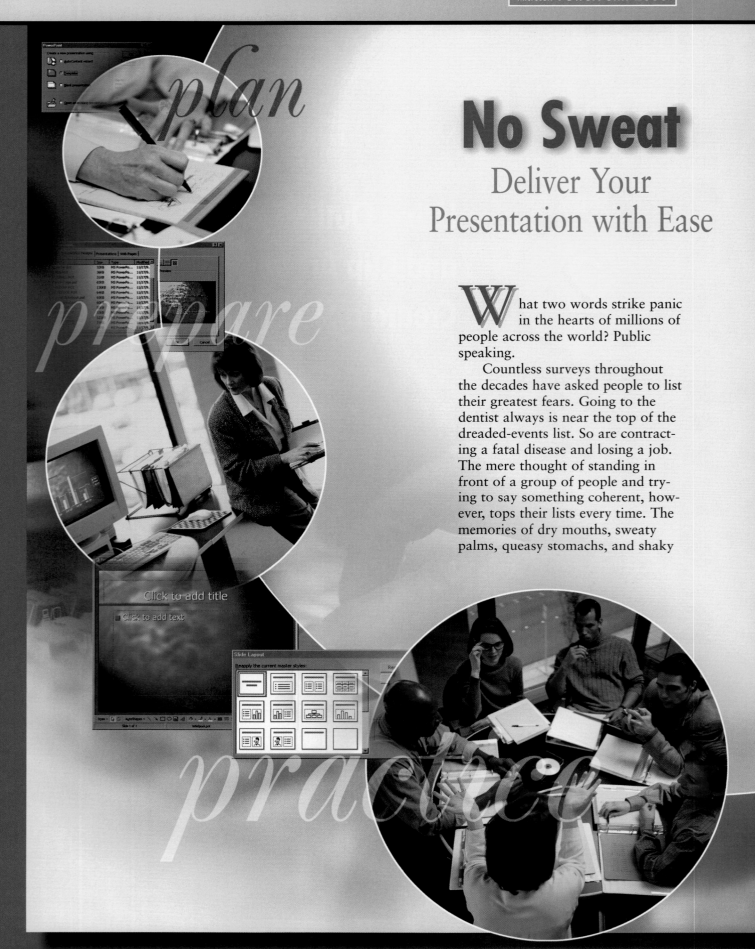

plan

prepare

practice

Click to add title

Click to add text

No Sweat

Deliver Your Presentation with Ease

What two words strike panic in the hearts of millions of people across the world? Public speaking.

Countless surveys throughout the decades have asked people to list their greatest fears. Going to the dentist always is near the top of the dreaded-events list. So are contracting a fatal disease and losing a job. The mere thought of standing in front of a group of people and trying to say something coherent, however, tops their lists every time. The memories of dry mouths, sweaty palms, queasy stomachs, and shaky

knees are enough to guarantee a lifetime of nightmares.

Fortunately, PowerPoint has eased the pain of speechmaking somewhat. As you learned in Project 1, this software helps you organize your thoughts and present your information in an orderly, attractive manner. In Project 2, you will add to your knowledge base by learning to change layouts and then insert drawings and photos in your slides. Ultimately, your slide shows will have visual appeal and ample content.

While the PowerPoint slide shows help you plan your speeches, they also help your audience absorb your message. People learn most effectively when their five senses are involved. Researchers have determined that individuals remember 10 percent of what they read, 20 percent of what they hear, 30 percent of what they see, and an amazing 70 percent when they both see and hear. That is why it is important to attend class instead of copying your classmate's notes. When you see and hear your instructor deliver a lecture and write your own notes, you are apt to interpret the concepts correctly and recall this information at the ever-important final exam.

The synergy of the speech-graphics combo is recognized in a variety of venues. For example, some college administrators and instructors are requiring students to register for their communications and PowerPoint classes concurrently. Bill Clinton's maps and Ross Perot's charts are staples in their speech repertoires.

The theories of structuring effective communication presentations are deep rooted. Dale Carnegie wrote *How to Win Friends and Influence People* in 1936, and the millions of people who have read that book have learned practical advice on achieving success through communication. He formed the Dale Carnegie Institute, which has taught 4.5 million graduates worldwide the techniques of sharing ideas effectively and persuading others. Microsoft has included Carnegie's four-step process — plan, prepare, practice, and present — in the PowerPoint Help system.

In the days prior to PowerPoint, slides and overhead transparencies were the domain of artists in a corporation's graphic communications department. With the influx of Microsoft Office on desktops throughout a company, however, employees from all departments now develop the slide shows. According to Microsoft, the average PowerPoint user now creates nine presentations each month, which is double the number produced in 1995.

With all these presentations, that means a lot of sweaty palms and shaky knees. But with planning and practice — and powerful PowerPoint presentations — these speakers can deliver their messages confidently and successfully.

Microsoft PowerPoint 2000

Microsoft PowerPoint 2000

Using Outline View and Clip Art to Create a Slide Show

P R O J E C T

2

CASE PERSPECTIVE

A college education no longer is considered an extravagance; instead, it is essential for landing and advancing in many jobs. The college experience has a price, however. Students often find their budgets maximized and their bank accounts drained. Financial aid in the form of scholarships, loans, and grants can help ease this burden. Each year millions of dollars of scholarship money go unclaimed because students do not know where or how to find these funds. Fortunately, a little effort can uncover an assortment of scholarship sources.

Many financially strapped students at your college visit the Office of Financial Aid in hopes of finding some relief. Dr. Mary Halen, the director of financial aid, has asked you to help prepare a student lecture on the topic of searching for scholarships. You suggest developing a short PowerPoint presentation to accompany her talk. The slide show will give an overview of researching scholarship sources, applying for the funds, considering merit scholarships and private sources, and surfing the Internet for additional information. You decide to add clip art and animation to increase visual interest. Then you e-mail the completed presentation to her.

Creating a Presentation from an Outline

At some time during either your academic or business life, you probably will make a presentation. The presentation may be informative by providing detailed information about a specific topic. Other presentations may be persuasive by selling a proposal or a product to a client, convincing management to approve a new project, or persuading the board of directors to accept the new fiscal budget. As an alternative to creating your presentation in the slide pane in normal view, as you did in Project 1, PowerPoint provides an outlining feature to help you organize your thoughts. When the outline is complete, it becomes the foundation for your presentation.

You can create your presentation outline using outline view. When you create an outline, you type all the text at one time, as if you were typing an outline on a sheet of paper. This technique differs from creating a presentation in the slide pane in normal view, where you type text as you create each individual slide and the text displays in both the slide and outline panes. PowerPoint creates the presentation as you type the outline by evaluating the outline structure and displaying a miniature view of the slide. Regardless of the view in which you build a presentation, PowerPoint automatically creates the five views discussed in Project 1: normal, outline, slide, slide sorter, and slide show.

The first step in creating a presentation in outline view is to type a title for the outline. The **outline title** is the subject of the presentation and later becomes the presentation title slide. Then you type the remainder of the outline, indenting appropriately to establish a structure or hierarchy. Once the outline is complete, you make your presentation more persuasive by adding graphics. This project uses outlining to create the presentation and clip art graphics to support the text visually.

Project Two — Searching for Scholarships

Project 2 uses PowerPoint to create the six-slide Searching for Scholarships presentation shown in Figures 2-1a through 2-1f. You create the presentation from the outline in Figure 2-2 on the next page.

(a) Slide 1

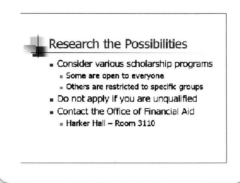

(b) Slide 2

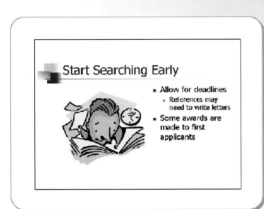

(c) Slide 3

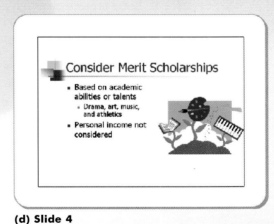

(d) Slide 4

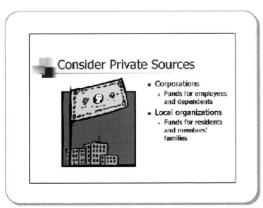

(e) Slide 5

(f) Slide 6

FIGURE 2-1

I. Searching for Scholarships
  A. Finding Cash for College
  B. Presented by
  C. The Office of Financial Aid
II. Research the Possibilities
  A. Consider various scholarship programs
    1. Some are open to everyone
    2. Others are restricted to specific groups
  B. Do not apply if you are unqualified
  C. Contact the Office of Financial Aid
    1. Harker Hall – Room 3110
III. Start Searching Early
  A. Allow for deadlines
    1. References may need to write letters
  B. Some awards are made to first applicants
IV. Consider Merit Scholarships
  A. Based on academic abilities or talents
    1.Drama, art, music, and athletics
  B. Personal income not considered
V. Consider Private Sources
  A. Corporations
    1. Funds for employees and dependents
  B. Local organizations
    1. Funds for residents and members' families
VI. Additional Information
  A. College Board Online
    1. www.collegeboard.org
  B. U.S. Department of Education
    1. www.ed.gov
  C. Financial Aid Information Page
    1. www.finaid.org

FIGURE 2-2

Starting a New Presentation

Project 1 introduced you to starting a presentation document, choosing an AutoLayout, and applying a design template. The following steps summarize how to start a new presentation, choose an AutoLayout, apply a design template, and display the entire Formatting toolbar. For a more detailed explanation, see pages PP 1.10 through PP 1.20 in Project 1. To reset your toolbars and menus so they display exactly as shown in this book, follow the steps outlined in Appendix B. Perform the following steps to start a new presentation.

More About 2000

Using PowerPoint

The word "PowerPoint" traditionally is used as a noun to refer to the software you are using in these projects to create presentations. With our ever-changing language, however, the word has evolved into a synonym for the term presentation. You now can ask your instructor, Did you grade my PowerPoint?

TO START A NEW PRESENTATION

1 Click the Start button on the taskbar.

2 Click New Office Document. If necessary, click the General tab in the New Office Document dialog box.

3 Double-click the Blank Presentation icon.

4 Click the OK button when the New Slide dialog box displays to select the Title Slide AutoLayout.

5 Double-click Default Design on the status bar. Double-click the Blends design template in the Presentation Designs list in the Apply Design template dialog box.

6 If the Office Assistant displays, right-click the Office Assistant and then click Hide on the shortcut menu.

7 Double-click the move handle on the Formatting toolbar in the Microsoft PowerPoint window to display it in its entirety.

PowerPoint displays the Title Slide AutoLayout and the Blends design template on Slide 1 in normal view (Figure 2-3).

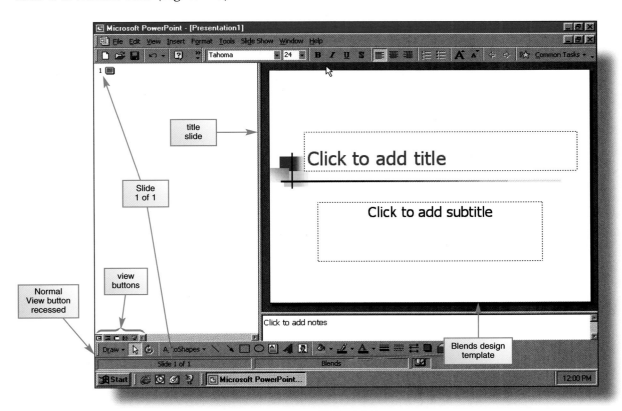

FIGURE 2-3

Using Outline View

Outline view provides a quick, easy way to create a presentation. Outlining allows you to organize your thoughts in a structured format. An outline uses indentation to establish a hierarchy, which denotes levels of importance to the main topic. An **outline** is a summary of thoughts, presented as headings and subheadings, often used as a preliminary draft when you create a presentation.

Heading Levels

While PowerPoint gives you six heading levels to use on each slide, graphic designers suggest you limit your slides to three levels. The details on all six levels may overwhelm audiences. If you find yourself needing more than three levels, consider combining content in one level or using two different slides.

The three panes — outline, slide, and notes — shown in normal view also display in outline view. In outline view, however, the outline pane occupies the largest area on the left side of the window, and the slide pane shrinks to the upper-right corner to display how the current slide will look in normal view, slide view, slide sorter view, and slide show view. The notes pane displays under the slide pane. In the outline pane, the slide text displays along with a slide number and a slide icon. Body text is indented under the title text. Graphic objects, such as pictures, graphs, or tables, do not display in outline view. The slide icon is blank when a slide does not contain graphics. The attributes for text in outline view are the same as in normal view except for color and paragraph style.

PowerPoint limits the number of heading levels to six. The first heading level is the slide title and is not indented. The remaining five heading levels are the same as the five indent levels in slide view. Recall from Project 1 that PowerPoint allows for five indent levels and that each indent level has an associated bullet.

The outline begins with a title on **heading level 1**. The title is the main topic of the slide. Text supporting the main topic begins on **heading level 2** and indents under heading level 1. **Heading level 3** indents under heading level 2 and contains text to support heading level 2. **Heading level 4, heading level 5**, and **heading level 6** indent under heading level 3, heading level 4, and heading level 5, respectively. Use heading levels 4, 5, and 6 as required. They generally are used for very detailed scientific and engineering presentations. Business and sales presentations usually focus on summary information and use heading level 1, heading level 2, and heading level 3.

PowerPoint initially displays in normal view when you start a new presentation. Change from normal view to outline view by clicking the Outline View button at the lower left of the PowerPoint window. Perform the following steps to change the view from normal view to outline view.

Steps To Change the View to Outline View and Display the Outline Toolbar

1 Point to the Outline View button located at the lower left of the PowerPoint window (Figure 2-4).

Click to add title

Click to add subtitle

view buttons

Click to add notes

Outline View button

Outline View

Slide 1 of 1   Blends

Start   Microsoft PowerPoint...   12:01 PM

ScreenTip

FIGURE 2-4

2 Click the Outline View button.

3 Click View on the menu bar and then point to Toolbars. Point to Outlining on the Toolbars submenu.

PowerPoint displays in outline view and the Toolbars submenu displays (Figure 2-5).

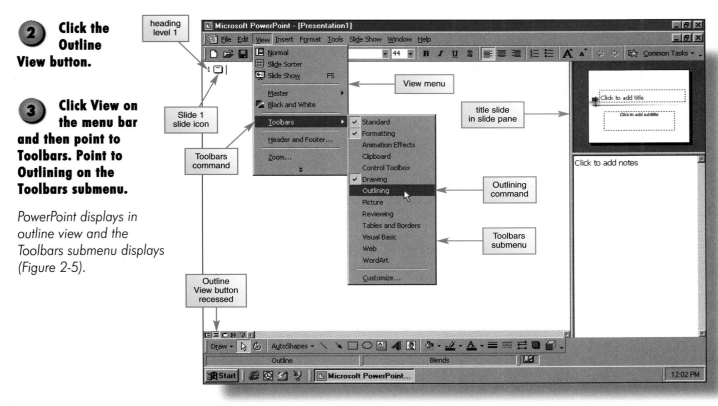

FIGURE 2-5

4 Click Outlining.

PowerPoint displays in outline view with the Outlining toolbar (Figure 2-6). PowerPoint displays the color view of Slide 1 in the slide pane.

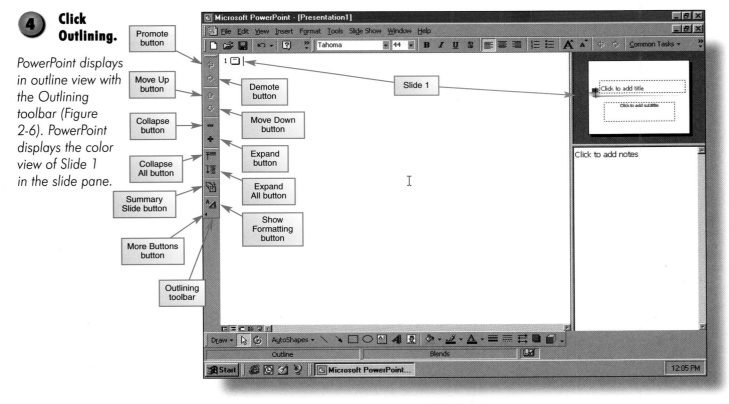

FIGURE 2-6

You can create and edit your presentation in outline view. Outline view also makes it easy to sequence slides and to relocate title text and body text from one slide to another. In addition to typing text to create a new presentation in outline view, PowerPoint can produce slides from an outline created in Microsoft Word or another word processor, if you save the outline as an RTF file or as a plain text file. The file extension **RTF** stands for **R**ich **T**ext **F**ormat.

The PowerPoint Window in Outline View

The PowerPoint window in outline view differs from the window in normal view because the Outlining toolbar displays, the outline pane occupies the majority of the window, and the slide pane displays a miniature version of the current slide. Table 2-1 describes the buttons on the Outlining toolbar.

Table 2-1	Buttons on the Outlining Toolbar	
BUTTON	BUTTON NAME	DESCRIPTION
	Promote	Moves the selected paragraph to the next-higher heading level (up one level, to the left).
	Demote	Moves the selected paragraph to the next-lower heading level (down one level, to the right).
	Move Up	Moves a selected paragraph and its collapsed (temporarily hidden) subordinate text above the preceding displayed paragraph.
	Move Down	Moves a selected paragraph and its collapsed (temporarily hidden) subordinate text down, below the following displayed paragraph.
	Collapse	Hides all but the title of selected slides. Collapsed text is represented by a gray line.
	Expand	Displays the titles and all collapsed text of selected slides.
	Collapse All	Displays only the title of each slide. Text other than the title is represented by a gray line below the title.
	Expand All	Displays the titles and all the body text for each slide.
	Summary Slide	Creates a new slide from the titles of the slides you select in slide sorter or normal view. The summary slide creates a bulleted list from the titles of the selected slides. PowerPoint inserts the summary slide in front of the first selected slide.
	Show Formatting	Shows or hides character formatting (such as bold and italic) in normal view. In slide sorter view, switches between showing all text and graphics on each slide and displaying titles only.
	More Buttons	Allows you to select the particular buttons you want to display on the toolbar.

Creating a Presentation in Outline View

Outline view enables you to view title and body text, add and delete slides, drag and drop slide text, drag and drop individual slides, promote and demote text, save a presentation, print an outline, print slides, copy and paste slides or text to and from other presentations, apply a design template, and import an outline. When you **drag and drop** slide text or individual slides, you change the order of the text or the slides by selecting the text or slide you want to move or copy and then dragging the text or slide to its new location.

Developing a presentation in outline view is quick because you type the text for all slides on one screen. Once you type the outline, the presentation fundamentally is complete. If you choose, you then can go to normal view or slide view to enhance your presentation with graphics.

Creating a Title Slide in Outline View

Recall from Project 1 that the title slide introduces the presentation to the audience. In addition to introducing the presentation, Project 2 uses the title slide to capture the attention of the students in your audience by using a design template with colorful graphics. Perform the following steps to create a title slide in outline view.

Design Templates

You can change design templates easily, even when you have completed creating each slide in your presentation. Each design template changes the color scheme, font attributes, and graphic objects throughout the entire file. For more information, visit the PowerPoint 2000 More About Web page (www.scsite.com/pp2000/more.htm) and click Design Templates.

Steps **To Create a Title Slide in Outline View**

1 **Type** Searching for Scholarships **and then press the ENTER key.**

Searching for Scholarships is the title for Slide 1 and is called heading level 1. A slide icon displays to the left of each slide title. The font for heading level 1 is Tahoma and the font size is 44 points. Pressing the ENTER key moves the insertion point to the next line and maintains the same heading level. The insertion point is in position for typing the title for Slide 2 (Figure 2-7).

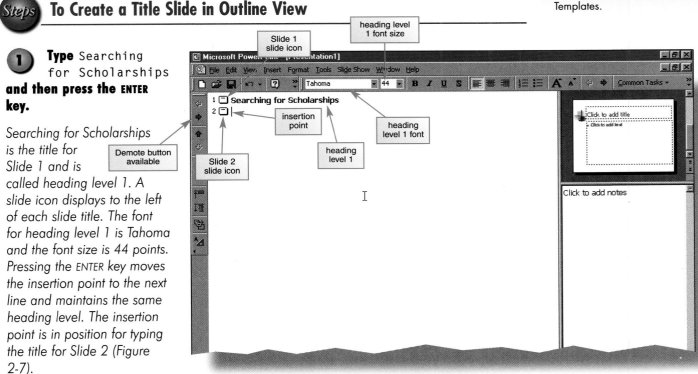

FIGURE 2-7

2 **Point to the Demote button.**

The Demote ScreenTip displays (Figure 2-8).

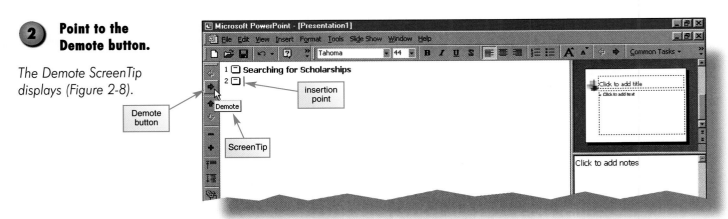

FIGURE 2-8

3 **Click the Demote button on the Outlining toolbar. Type** Finding Cash for College **and then press the ENTER key. Type** Presented by **and then press the ENTER key. Type** The Office of Financial Aid **and then press the ENTER key.**

The paragraphs, Finding Cash for College, Presented by, and The Office of Financial Aid, are subtitles on the title slide (Slide 1) and demote to heading level 2 (Figure 2-9). Heading level 2 is indented to the right under heading level 1. The heading level 2 font is Tahoma and the heading level 2 font size is 32 points. The Slide 2 slide icon does not display.

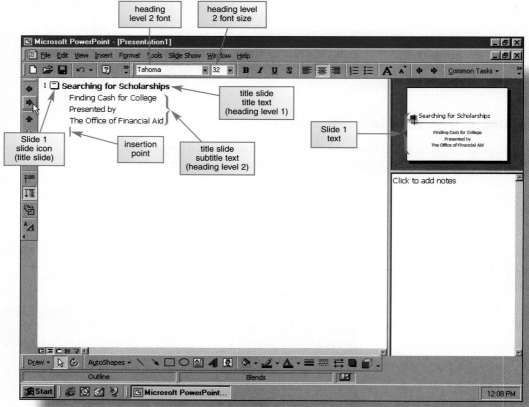

FIGURE 2-9

Auto-Fit Text

PowerPoint will reduce the point size of text automatically when you reach the bottom of the Object Area placeholder and need to squeeze an additional line on the slide. If you do not want to use this Auto-Fit feature, you can deactivate it by clicking Tools on the menu bar, clicking Options, clicking the Edit tab, clicking the Auto-fit text to text placeholder check box, and clicking OK.

The title slide text for the Searching for Scholarships presentation is complete. The next section explains how to add a slide in outline view.

Adding a Slide in Outline View

Recall from Project 1 that when you add a new slide in normal view, PowerPoint defaults to the Bulleted List AutoLayout. This action occurs in outline view as well. One way to add a new slide in outline view is to promote a paragraph to heading level 1 by clicking the Promote button on the outlining toolbar until the insertion point or the paragraph displays at heading level 1. A slide icon displays when the insertion point or paragraph reaches heading level 1. Perform the following steps to add a slide in outline view.

To Add a Slide in Outline View

1 **Point to the Promote button on the Outlining toolbar.**

The insertion point still is positioned at heading level 2 (Figure 2-10).

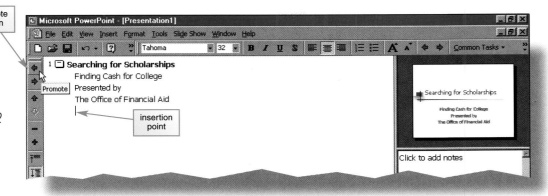

FIGURE 2-10

2 **Click the Promote button.**

The Slide 2 slide icon displays indicating a new slide is added to the presentation (Figure 2-11). The insertion point is in position to type the title for Slide 2 at heading level 1.

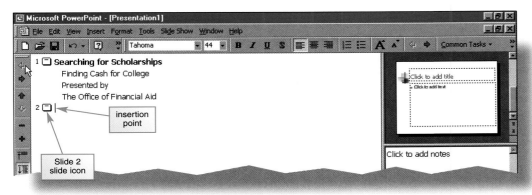

FIGURE 2-11

After you add a slide, you are ready to type the slide text. The next section explains how to create a multi-level bulleted list slide in outline view.

Creating Multi-level Bulleted List Slides in Outline View

To create a multi-level bulleted list slide, you demote or promote the insertion point to the appropriate heading level and then type the paragraph text. Recall from Project 1 that when you demote a paragraph, PowerPoint adds a bullet to the left of each heading level. Depending on the design template, each heading level has a different bullet font. Also recall that the design template determines font attributes, including the bullet font.

Slide 2 is the first **informational slide** for Project 2. Slide 2 introduces the main topic: students can conduct searches to find many scholarships available to them. Each of the three major points regarding finding scholarship information displays as heading level 2, and the first and third points have two supporting paragraphs, which display as heading level 3. The steps on the next page explain how to create a multi-level bulleted list slide in outline view.

Other Ways

1. Click New Slide button on Standard toolbar, click OK button

2. On Insert menu click New Slide, click OK button

3. Press ALT+I, press N, press ENTER

4. Press CTRL+M, press ENTER

5. Press and hold SHIFT, press TAB until paragraph or insertion point displays at heading level 1, release TAB

Steps ## To Create a Multi-level Bulleted List Slide in Outline View

1 **Type** Research the Possibilities **and then press the ENTER key. Click the Demote button on the Outlining toolbar to demote to heading level 2.**

The title for Slide 2, Research the Possibilities, displays and the insertion point is in position to type the first bulleted paragraph (Figure 2-12). A bullet displays to the left of the insertion point.

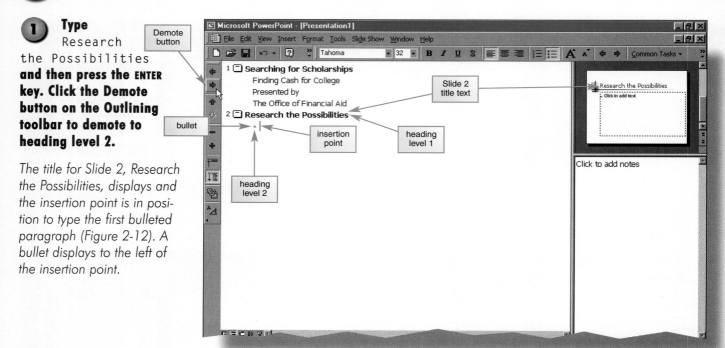

FIGURE 2-12

2 **Type** Consider various scholarship programs **and then press the ENTER key. Click the Demote button on the Outlining toolbar to demote to heading level 3. Type** Some are open to everyone **and then press the ENTER key.**

Slide 2 displays three heading levels: the title, Research the Possibilities, on heading level 1, the first bulleted paragraph on heading level 2, and the third bulleted paragraph and insertion point on heading level 3 (Figure 2-13). The heading level 3 font is Tahoma and the font size is 28 points.

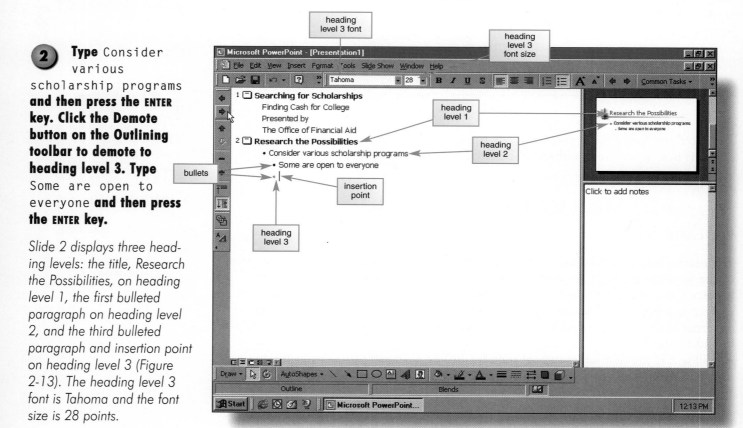

FIGURE 2-13

3 **Type** Others are restricted to specific groups **and then press the ENTER key. Click the Promote button on the Outlining toolbar to promote to heading level 2. Type** Do not apply if you are unqualified **and then press the ENTER key. Type** Contact the Office of Financial Aid **and then press the ENTER key. Click the Demote button on the Outlining toolbar to demote to heading level 3. Type** Harker Hall — Room 3110 **and then press the ENTER key.**

The text for Slide 2 is complete (Figure 2-14). Pressing the ENTER key begins a new paragraph at the same heading level as the previous paragraph. A red wavy line displays under the word Harker to indicate that particular word is not found in the Microsoft main dictionary or open custom dictionaries.

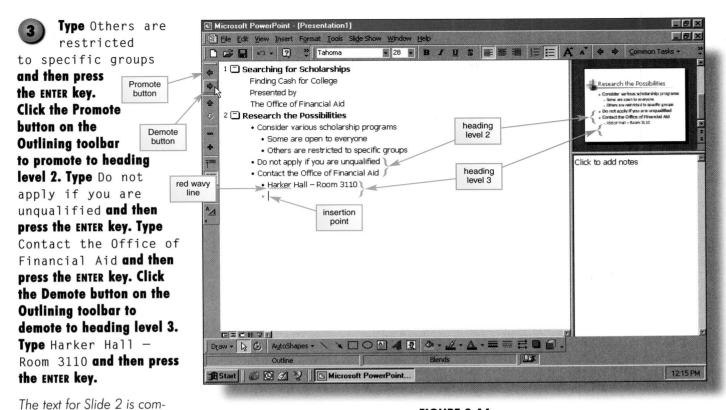

FIGURE 2-14

Creating Subordinate Slides

When developing your presentation, begin with a main topic and follow with **subordinate slides**, which are slides to support the main topic. Placing all your information on one slide may overwhelm your audience. In Project 1 you learned about the 7 x 7 rule, which recommends that each line should have a maximum of seven words, and each slide should have a maximum of seven lines. The steps on the next page use this 7 x 7 rule and explain how to create subordinate slides giving techniques for finding scholarships. The information on the next slide, Slide 3, provides information explaining the importance of looking for scholarships in a timely manner. Slides 4 and 5 list information on merit and private scholarships.

TO CREATE A SUBORDINATE SLIDE

1 Click the Promote button on the Outlining toolbar two times so that Slide 3 is added after Slide 2.

2 Type Start Searching Early and then press the ENTER key.

3 Click the Demote button on the Outlining toolbar to demote to heading level 2.

4 Type Allow for deadlines and then press the ENTER key.

5 Click the Demote button to demote to heading level 3.

6 Type References may need to write letters and then press the ENTER key.

7 Click the Promote button to promote to heading level 2.

8 Type Some awards are made to first applicants and then press the ENTER key.

The completed Slide 3 displays (Figure 2-15).

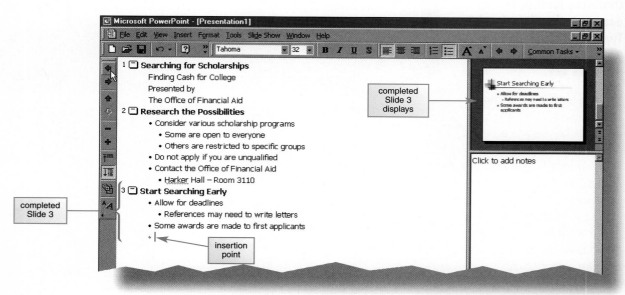

FIGURE 2-15

Creating a Second Subordinate Slide

The next step is to create Slide 4, which discusses merit scholarships. Perform the following steps to create this subordinate slide.

TO CREATE A SECOND SUBORDINATE SLIDE

1 Click the Promote button on the Outlining toolbar to add Slide 4 after Slide 3. Type Consider Merit Scholarships and then press the ENTER key.

2 Click the Demote button on the Outlining toolbar to demote to heading level 2. Type Based on academic abilities or talents and then press the ENTER key.

3 Click the Demote button to demote to heading level 3. Type Drama, art, music, and athletics and then press the ENTER key.

4 Click the Promote button to promote to heading level 2. Type Personal income not considered and then press the ENTER key.

The completed Slide 4 displays (Figure 2-16).

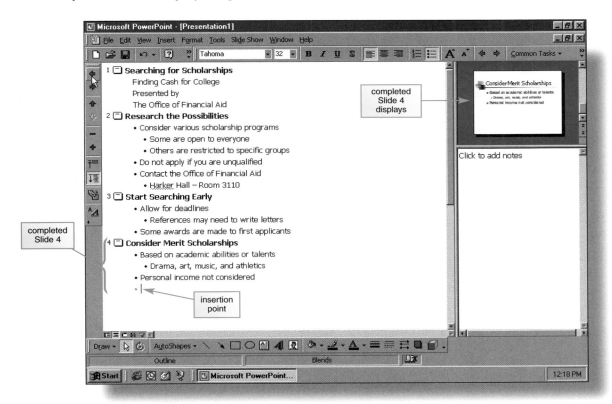

FIGURE 2-16

Creating a Third Subordinate Slide

The next step is to create Slide 5, which gives details on private sources of scholarship funds. Perform the following steps to create this subordinate slide.

TO CREATE A THIRD SUBORDINATE SLIDE

1 Click the Promote button on the Outlining toolbar to add Slide 5 after Slide 4. Type Consider Private Sources and then press the ENTER key.

2 Click the Demote button on the Outlining toolbar to demote to heading level 2. Type Corporations and then press the ENTER key.

3 Click the Demote button to demote to heading level 3. Type Funds for employees and dependents and then press the ENTER key.

4 Click the Promote button to promote to heading level 2. Type Local organizations and then press the ENTER key.

5 Click the Demote button to demote to heading level 3. Type Funds for residents and members' families and then press the ENTER key.

The completed Slide 5 displays (Figure 2-17 on the next page).

More About 2000

Smart Quotes

When you type an apostrophe and quotation marks, PowerPoint automatically converts these symbols to smart quotes, which also are called curly quotes. These symbols are in the shape of a dot and curved line (' " ") instead of a straight line (' "). If you want to use straight quotes instead, click Options on the Tools menu, click the Edit tab, and the click the Replace straight quotes with smart quotes check box.

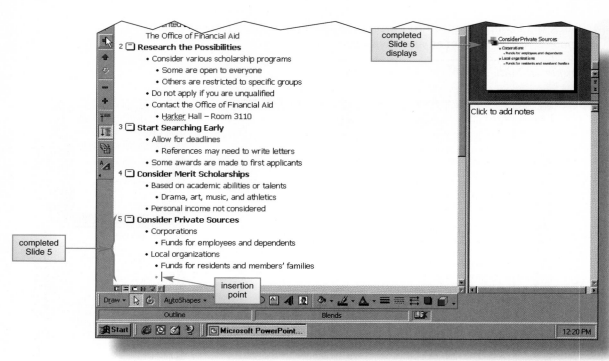

FIGURE 2-17

Creating a Closing Slide in Outline View

The last slide in your presentation is the closing slide. A **closing slide** gracefully ends a presentation. Often used during a question and answer session, the closing slide usually remains on the screen to reinforce the message delivered during the presentation. Professional speakers design the closing slide with one or more of these methods.

1. List important information. Tell the audience what to do next.
2. Provide a memorable illustration or example to make a point.
3. Appeal to emotions. Remind the audience to take action or accept responsibility.
4. Summarize the main points of the presentation.
5. Cite a quotation that directly relates to the main points of the presentation. This technique is most effective if the presentation started with a quotation.

The closing slide in this project lists three links to sites on the World Wide Web that have additional information on scholarships. Perform the following steps to create this closing slide.

TO CREATE A CLOSING SLIDE IN OUTLINE VIEW

1 Click the Promote button on the Outlining toolbar two times so that Slide 6 is added to the end of the presentation. Type `Additional Information` as the slide title and then press the ENTER key.

2 Click the Demote button on the Outlining toolbar to demote to heading level 2. Type `College Board Online` and then press the ENTER key.

3 Click the Demote button to demote to heading level 3. Type `www.collegeboard.org` and then press the ENTER key.

4 Click the Promote button to promote to heading level 2. Type `U.S. Department of Education` and then press the ENTER key.

5 Click the Demote button to demote to heading level 3. Type `www.ed.gov` and then press the ENTER key.

6 Click the Promote button to promote to heading level 2. Type `Financial Aid Information Page` and then press the ENTER key.

7 Click the Demote button to demote to heading level 3. Type `www.finaid.org` but do not press the ENTER key.

The completed Slide 6 displays (Figure 2-18). PowerPoint automatically displays the first two Internet addresses underlined and with a font color of red.

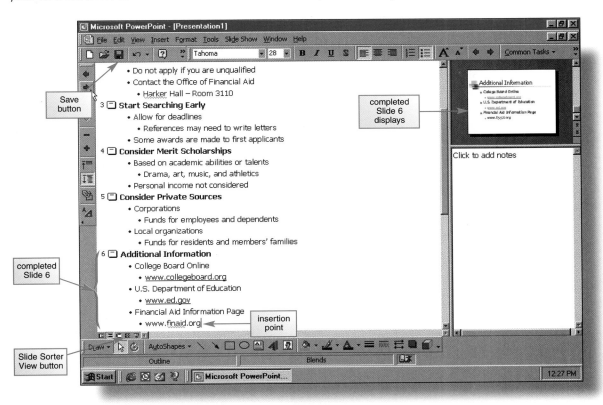

FIGURE 2-18

The outline now is complete and the presentation should be saved. The next section explains how to save the presentation.

Saving a Presentation

Recall from Project 1 that it is wise to save your presentation frequently. Now that you have created all the text for your presentation, you should save your presentation. For a detailed explanation of the following summarized steps, refer to pages PP 1.28 through PP 1.31 in Project 1.

TO SAVE A PRESENTATION

1 Insert a formatted floppy disk in drive A and then click the Save button on the Standard toolbar.

2 Click the Save in box arrow. Click 3½ Floppy (A:) in the Save in list.

Quick Reference

For a table that lists how to complete the tasks covered in this book using the mouse, menu, shortcut menu, and keyboard, visit the Office 2000 Web page (www.scsite.com/off2000/qr.htm) and then click Microsoft PowerPoint.

3 Click the Save button in the Save As dialog box.

The presentation is saved on the floppy disk in drive A under the file name Searching for Scholarships. PowerPoint uses the first text line in your presentation as the default file name. The file name displays on the title bar.

Reviewing a Presentation in Slide Sorter View

In Project 1, you displayed slides in slide show view to evaluate the presentation. Slide show view, however, restricts your evaluation to one slide at a time. Outline view is best for quickly reviewing all the text for a presentation. The slide sorter view allows you to look at several slides at one time, which is why it is the best view to use to evaluate a presentation for content, organization, and overall appearance. Perform the following step to change from outline view to slide sorter view.

 To Change the View to Slide Sorter View

1 **Click the Slide Sorter View button at the lower left of the PowerPoint window.**

PowerPoint displays the presentation in slide sorter view (Figure 2-19). Slide 6 is selected because it was the current slide in outline view.

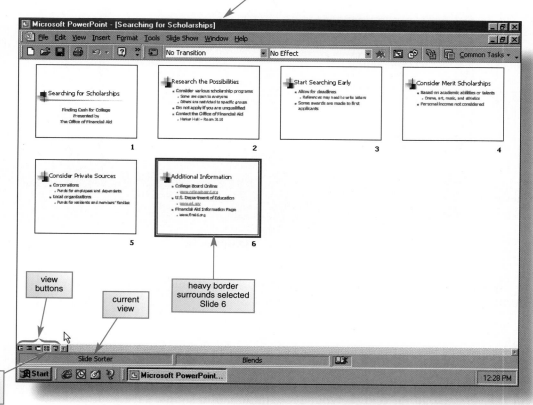

FIGURE 2-19

Other Ways

1. On View menu click Slide Sorter
2. Press ALT+V, press D

You can review the six slides in this presentation all in one window. Notice the slides have a significant amount of white space and look drab. These observations indicate a need to add visual interest to the slides by using graphics, such as clip art. The next several sections explain how to improve the presentation by changing slide layouts and adding clip art.

You can make changes to text in normal view, outline view, and slide view. It is best, however, to change the view to slide view when altering the slide layouts so you can see the result of your changes. Perform the following steps to change the view from slide sorter view to slide view.

 To Change the View to Slide View

1 Point to the Slide 3 slide miniature (Figure 2-20).

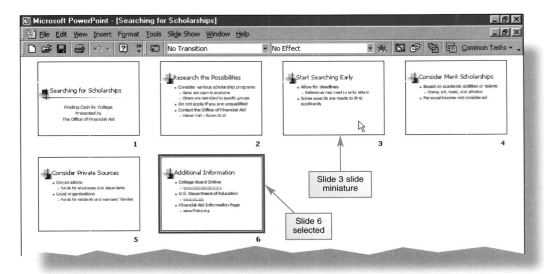

FIGURE 2-20

2 Click the Slide 3 slide miniature. Click the Slide View button at the lower left of the PowerPoint window.

Slide 3 displays in slide view (Figure 2-21). The Slide View button is recessed at the lower left of the PowerPoint window. The Slide 3 icon is highlighted in the outline pane.

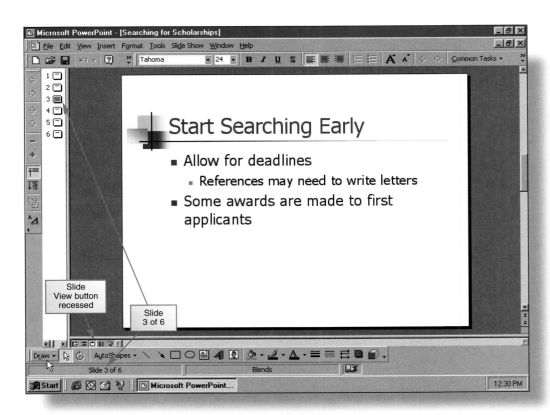

FIGURE 2-21

Changing Slide Layout

More About

Toolbar Buttons

You can customize your toolbars by using buttons that are larger than the ones normally displayed. To enlarge the buttons, click Customize on the Tools menu, click the Options tab, and then select the Large icons check box. This setting will affect all of your Microsoft Office programs.

When you began developing this presentation, PowerPoint displayed the New Slide dialog box with the default Title Slide AutoLayout selected. When you added the five new slides to your presentation, PowerPoint used the default Bulleted List Auto-Layout. After creating a slide, you can change its layout by clicking the **Common Tasks button** on the Formatting toolbar and then clicking the Slide Layout command on the Common Tasks button menu. The Slide Layout dialog box then displays.

Like the AutoLayout dialog box, the **Slide Layout dialog box** allows you to choose one of the 24 different AutoLayouts that has placeholders arranged in various configurations for the title, text, clip art, graphs, tables, and media clips. The placement of the text, in relationship to nontext objects, depends on the slide layout. The nontext Object Area placeholder may be to the right or left of the text, above the text, or below the text. Additionally, some slide layouts are constructed with two nontext object placeholders.

When you change the layout of a slide, PowerPoint retains the text and graphics and repositions them into the appropriate placeholders. Using slide layouts eliminates the need to resize objects and the font size because PowerPoint automatically sizes the objects and text to fit the placeholders. If the objects are in landscape orientation, PowerPoint sizes them to the width of the placeholders. If the objects are in portrait orientation, PowerPoint sizes them to the height of the placeholder.

Before you insert clip art into an AutoLayout placeholder, you first must select one of the slide layouts that includes an Object Area placeholder with a clip art region. This Object Area placeholder contains instructions to open Microsoft Clip Gallery 5.0. Double-clicking the clip art region in the Object Area placeholder activates the instructions. The Object Area placeholders on Slides 3, 4, and 5 will hold clip art. Adding clip art to these slides requires two steps. First, change the slide layout to Clip Art & Text or Text & Clip Art. Then insert clip art into the Object Area placeholder. Perform the following steps to change the slide layout on Slide 3 from a bulleted list to Clip Art & Text.

 To Change Slide Layout to Clip Art & Text

1 Click the Common Tasks button on the Formatting toolbar and then point to Slide Layout (Figure 2-22).

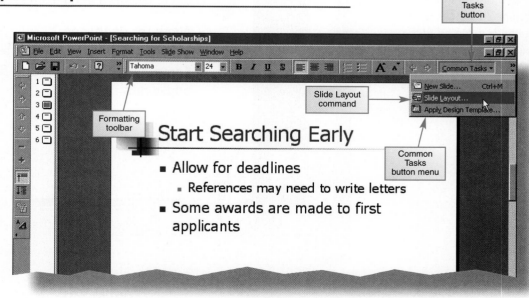

FIGURE 2-22

2 Click Slide Layout on the Common Tasks button menu. Click the Clip Art & Text slide layout located in row three, column two when the Slide Layout dialog box displays. Point to the Apply button.

The Slide Layout dialog box displays (Figure 2-23). The Clip Art & Text slide layout is selected. When you click a slide layout, its name displays in the box at the lower-right corner of the Slide Layout dialog box.

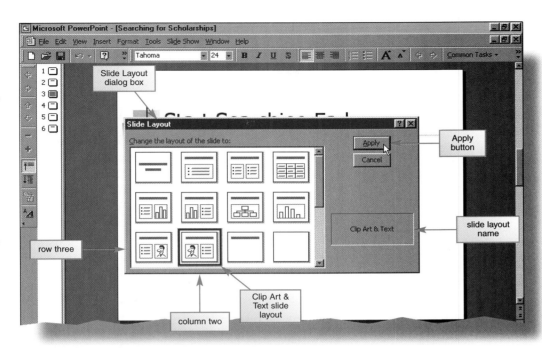

FIGURE 2-23

3 Click the Apply button.

Slide 3 displays the Clip Art & Text AutoLayout (Figure 2-24). PowerPoint moves the text object containing the bulleted list to the right side of the slide and automatically resizes the text to fit the object. The left side of the Object Area placeholder displays the message, Double click to add clip art.

Other Ways

1. Right-click slide anywhere except Title Area or Object Area placeholders, click Slide Layout, double-click desired slide layout
2. Click Common Tasks menu button, click Slide Layout, double-click desired slide layout
3. On Format menu click Slide Layout, double-click desired slide layout
4. Press ALT+O, press L, press arrow keys to select desired slide layout, press ENTER

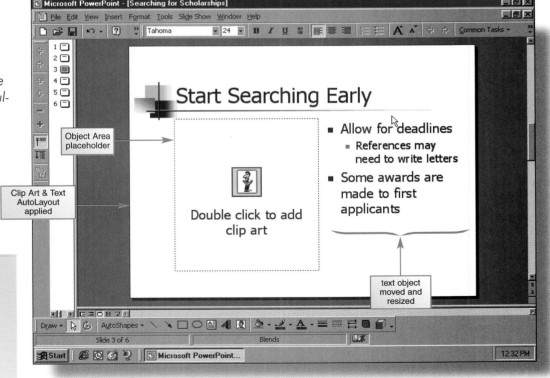

FIGURE 2-24

PowerPoint reduced the heading level 2 text in the Slide 3 placeholder from a font size of 32 points to 28 points and the heading level 3 text from 28 points to 24 points so all the words would fit into the text object.

Adding Clip Art to a Slide

More *About*

Legal Use of Clip Art

Be certain you have the legal right to use clip art, photographs, sounds, and movies in your slide show. Read the copyright notices that accompany clip art software and are posted on Web sites. The owners of these images and files often ask you to give them credit for using their work, which may be accomplished by stating where you obtained the images.

Clip art offers a quick way to add professional-looking graphic images to your presentation without creating the images yourself. One clip art source is the Microsoft Clip Gallery 5.0. **Microsoft Clip Gallery 5.0** is a tool that accompanies Microsoft Office 2000 and allows you to insert pictures, photographs, audio clips, and video clips to a presentation. It contains a wide variety of clip art images and is shared with other Microsoft Office applications. Microsoft Clip Gallery 5.0 combines topic-related clip art images into categories, such as Academic, Business, Entertainment, and Healthcare & Medicine.

Table 2-2 shows four of the 51 categories from Microsoft Clip Gallery 5.0 and keywords of various clip art files in those categories. Clip art images have one or more keywords associated with various entities, activities, labels, and emotions. In most instances, the keywords give the name of the physical object and related categories. For example, an image of a horse in the Animals category has the keywords, animals, nature, creatures, mammals, domestic animals, and horses. You can enter these keywords in the Search for clips text box to find clip art when you know one of the words associated with the clip art image. Otherwise, you may find it necessary to scroll through several categories to find an appropriate picture.

Table 2-2 Microsoft Clip Gallery 5.0 Category and Keyword Examples	
CATEGORY	**CLIP ART KEYWORDS**
Academic	Books; activities; graduations; schools; academic, music, school bells; academic, books, education; academic, office, office
Business	Risks; decisions; light bulbs; goals; motivation; challenges; workers; teamwork; activities
Entertainment	Musicians; musical notes; magic; dance; motion pictures; juggling priorities
Healthcare & Medicine	Research; vaccinations; equipment; medical; surgery; nursing; chiropractors; veterinary medicine; dentistry

Depending on the installation of Microsoft Clip Gallery 5.0 on your computer, you may not have the clip art pictures used in this project. Contact your instructor if you are missing clip art when you perform the following steps.

Inserting Clip Art into an Object Area Placeholder

Now that the Clip Art & Text layout is applied to Slide 3, you insert clip art into the Object Area placeholder. Perform the following steps to insert clip art to the Object Area placeholder on Slide 3.

To Insert Clip Art into an Object Area Placeholder

1 **Position the mouse pointer anywhere within the clip art region of the Object Area placeholder.**

The mouse pointer is positioned inside the clip art region of the Object Area placeholder (Figure 2-25). The mouse pointer becomes a four-headed arrow. It is not necessary to point to the picture inside the placeholder.

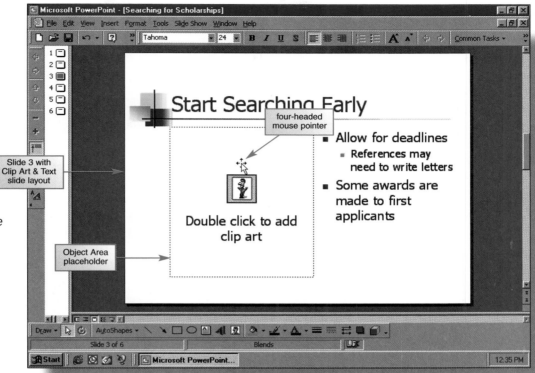

FIGURE 2-25

2 **Double-click the left side of the Object Area placeholder on Slide 3.**

PowerPoint displays the Microsoft Clip Gallery dialog box (Figure 2-26). The Pictures sheet displays clip art images by category, and New Category is the selected category. The Search for clips text box displays, Type one or more words. . . , as the entry.

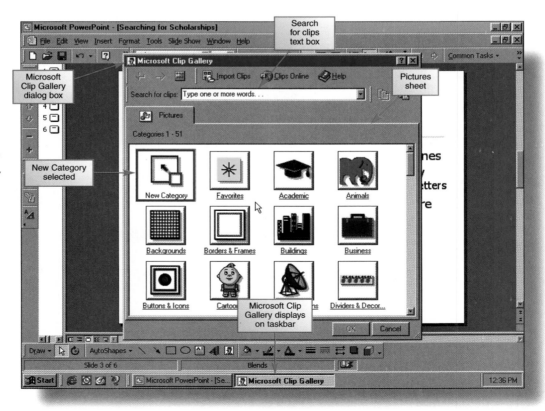

FIGURE 2-26

3 **Click the Search for clips text box. Type** books papers **and then press the ENTER key.**

The Microsoft Clip Gallery searches for and displays all pictures having the keywords, books and papers (Figure 2-27). The desired clip art image of a man looking in a book displays. Your images may be different depending on the clip art installed on your computer.

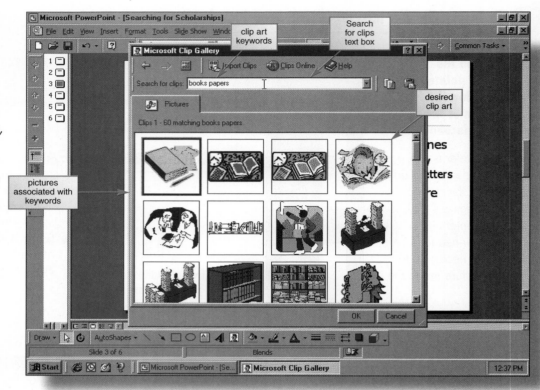

FIGURE 2-27

4 **Click the desired picture and then point to the Insert clip button.**

When you click the desired picture, a Pop-up menu displays (Figure 2-28). If you want to see a larger image of the selected image, you would click Preview clip on the Pop-up menu.

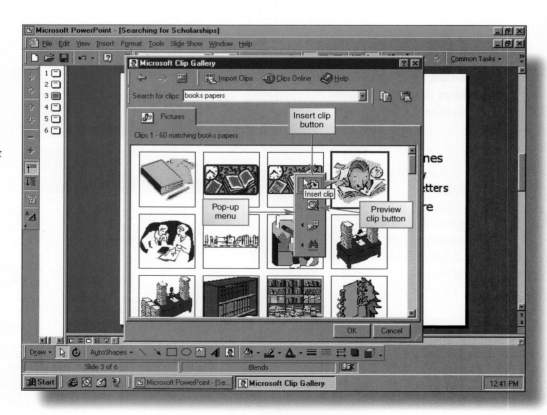

FIGURE 2-28

⑤ Click the Insert clip button on the Pop-up menu.

The selected picture is inserted into the Object Area placeholder on Slide 3 (Figure 2-29). PowerPoint automatically sizes the picture to fit the placeholder.

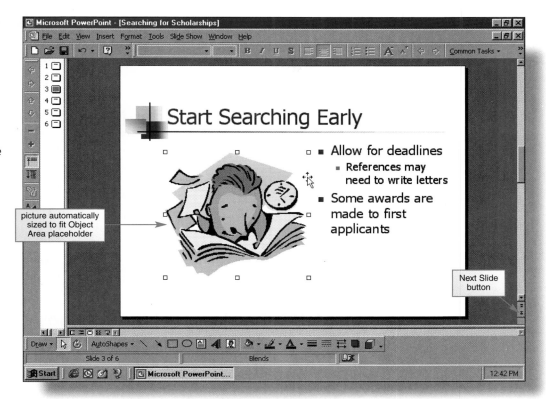

picture automatically sized to fit Object Area placeholder

Next Slide button

FIGURE 2-29

Inserting Clip Art on Other Slides

Slide 3 is complete, and you now want to add other clip art to Slides 4 and 5. Slide 5 also uses the Clip Art & Text slide layout, but Slide 4 uses the Text & Clip Art slide layout so the text displays on the left side of the slide and the clip art displays on the right side. Perform the following steps to change the slide layouts and then add clip art to Slide 4.

TO CHANGE THE SLIDE LAYOUT TO TEXT & CLIP ART AND INSERT CLIP ART

① Click the Next Slide button on the vertical scroll bar to display Slide 4.

② Click the Common Tasks menu button on the Formatting toolbar and then click Slide Layout.

③ Double-click the Text & Clip Art slide layout located in row three, column one.

④ Double-click the clip art region of the Object Area placeholder on the right side of Slide 4.

⑤ Type art music in the Search for clips text box and then press the ENTER key.

⑥ If necessary, scroll to display the desired clip art displaying a book, an artist's palette, and a keyboard. Click the desired clip art and then click Insert clip on the Pop-up menu.

The selected picture is inserted into the Object Area placeholder on Slide 4 (Figure 2-30 on the next page). PowerPoint automatically sizes the picture to fit the placeholder.

Microsoft **PowerPoint 2000**

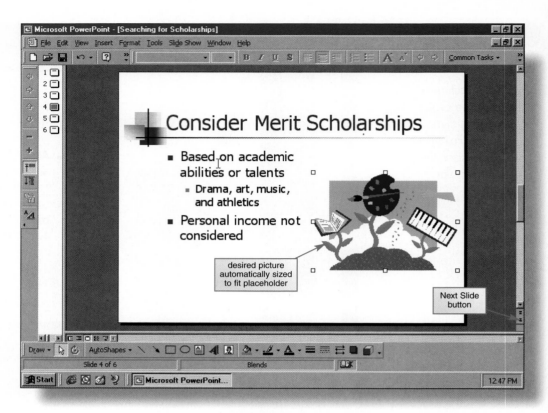

FIGURE 2-30

Slide 4 is complete. Your next step is to add other clip art to Slide 5, which also uses the Clip Art & Text slide layout you used in Slide 3. Perform the following steps to change the slide layouts and then add clip art to Slide 5.

TO CHANGE THE SLIDE LAYOUT TO CLIP ART & TEXT AND INSERT CLIP ART

1 Click the Next Slide button on the vertical scroll bar to display Slide 5.

2 Click the Common Tasks menu button on the Formatting toolbar and then click Slide Layout.

3 Double-click the Clip Art & Text slide layout located in row three, column two.

4 Double-click the clip art region of the Object Area placeholder on the left side of Slide 5.

5 Type buildings money in the Search for clips text box and then press the ENTER key.

6 If necessary, scroll to display the desired clip art displaying buildings with money on a flagpole. Click the desired clip art and then click Insert clip on the Pop-up menu.

The selected picture is inserted into the Object Area placeholder on Slide 5 (Figure 2-31). PowerPoint automatically sizes the picture to fit the placeholder.

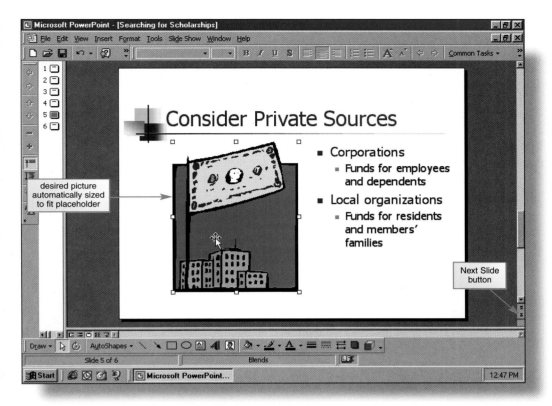

FIGURE 2-31

In addition to the clip art images in Microsoft Clip Gallery 5.0, other sources for clip art include retailers specializing in computer software, the Internet, bulletin board systems, and online information systems. Some popular online information systems are The Microsoft Network, America Online, CompuServe, and Prodigy. A **bulletin board system** is a computer system that allows users to communicate with each other and share files. Microsoft has created Clip Gallery Live, a special page on its World Wide Web site with new clips you can review and add to your Clip Gallery.

Besides clip art, you can insert pictures into your presentation. These may include scanned photographs, line art, and artwork from compact discs. To insert a picture into a presentation, the picture must be saved in a format that PowerPoint can recognize. Table 2-3 identifies some of the formats PowerPoint recognizes.

You can import files saved with the .emf, .gif, .jpg, .png, .bmp, .rle, .dib, and .wmf formats directly into your presentations. All other file formats require separate filters that are shipped with the PowerPoint installation software and must be installed. You can download additional graphics filters from the Microsoft Office Update Web site.

Table 2-3 Primary File Formats Recognized by PowerPoint	
FORMAT	*FILE EXTENSION*
Computer Graphics Metafile	*.cgm
CorelDRAW	*.cdr, .cdt, .cmx, and .pat
Encapsulated PostScript	*.eps
Enhanced Metafile	*.emf
FlashPix	*.fpx
Graphics Interchange Format	*.gif
Hanako	*.jsh, .jah, and .jbh
Joint Photographic Experts Group (JPEG)	*.jpg
Kodak Photo CD	*.pcd
Macintosh PICT	*.pct
PC Paintbrush	*.pcx
Portable Network Graphics	*.png
Tagged Image File Format	*.tif
Windows Bitmap	*.bmp, .rle, .dib
Microsoft Windows Metafile	*.wmf
WordPerfect Graphics	*.wpg

Design

Graphic artists suggest designing a presentation in black and white and then adding color to emphasize particular areas on the slide. By starting with black letters on a white background, basic design principles, such as balance, contrast, rhythm, and harmony, are evident.

Inserting Clip Art on a Slide without a Clip Art Region

PowerPoint does not require you to use an AutoLayout containing a clip art region in the Object Area placeholder to add clip art to a slide. You can insert clip art on any slide regardless of its slide layout. On Slides 3, 4, and 5, you added clip art images that enhanced the message in the text. Recall that the slide layout on Slide 6 is the Bulleted List AutoLayout. Because this AutoLayout does not contain a clip art region, you click the Insert Clip Art button on the Drawing toolbar to start Microsoft Clip Gallery 5.0. The picture for which you are searching has money coming out of a computer monitor. Its keywords are computer and dollars. Perform the following steps to insert the picture of this monitor on a slide that does not have a clip art region.

 To Insert Clip Art on a Slide without a Clip Art Region

1 **Click the Next Slide button on the vertical scroll bar to display Slide 6.**

2 **Point to the Insert Clip Art button on the Drawing toolbar.**

Clicking the Insert Clip Art button on the Drawing toolbar performs the same action as double-clicking an Object Area placeholder (Figure 2-32).

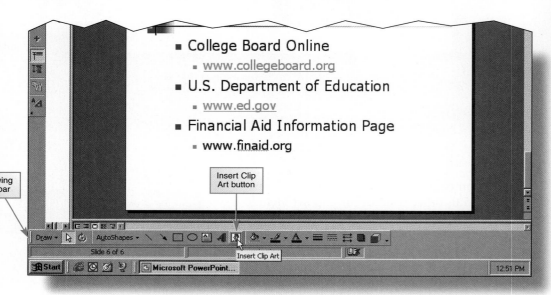

FIGURE 2-32

3 **Click the Insert Clip Art button.**

4 **Type** computer dollars **in the Search for clips text box and then press the ENTER key. If necessary, scroll to display the desired clip art displaying a computer monitor with money.**

The clip art image of money floating out of a computer monitor displays (Figure 2-33).

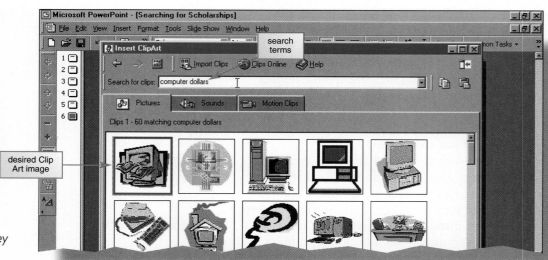

FIGURE 2-33

5 **Click the desired clip art and then click Insert clip on the shortcut menu. Point to the Close button on the Insert Clip Art title bar.**

PowerPoint inserts the desired clip art on Slide 6. Slide 6, however, is not visible until you close the Insert ClipArt dialog box (Figure 2-34).

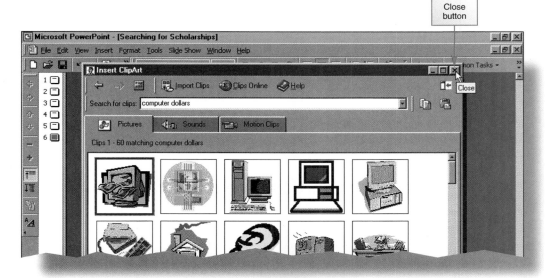

FIGURE 2-34

6 **Click the Close button on the Insert ClipArt title bar.**

The selected picture is inserted on Slide 6 (Figure 2-35). Sizing handles indicate the clip art is selected.

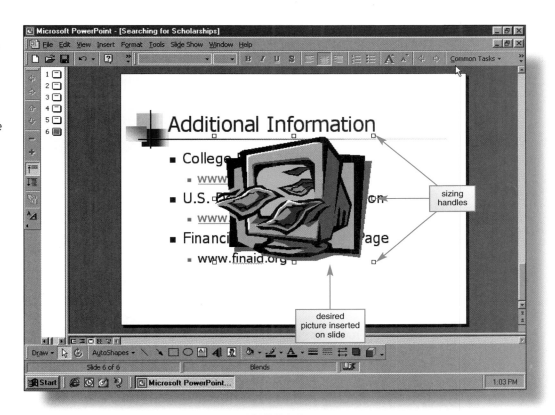

FIGURE 2-35

Moving Clip Art

After you insert clip art on a slide, you may want to reposition it. The picture of the monitor on Slide 6 overlays the bulleted list. You want to move the picture away from the text to the bottom-right corner of the slide. First move the picture and then change its size. Perform the steps on the next page to move the monitor to the bottom-right side of the slide.

To Move Clip Art

1 If the picture of the monitor is not already selected, use the mouse pointer to point to the monitor and then click.

2 Press and hold down the left mouse button. Drag the picture of the monitor to the bottom-right corner of the slide. Release the left mouse button.

When you drag an object, a dotted box displays. The dotted box indicates the new position of the object. When you release the left mouse button, the picture of the monitor displays in the new location (Figure 2-36). Sizing handles display at the corners and along the edges of the monitor.

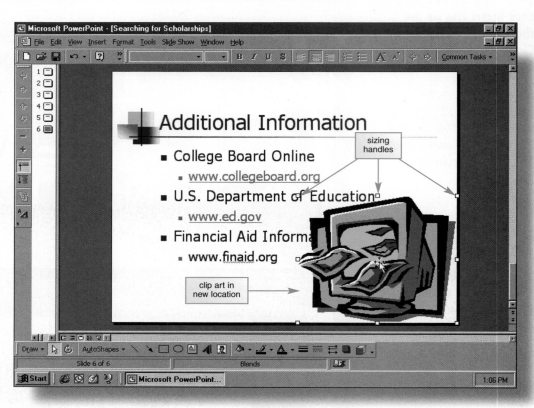

FIGURE 2-36

 Other Ways

1. Select clip art, press arrow keys to move to new position

 **More About**

Changing Clip Art

If you alter a clip art image, be certain you have the legal right to make these modifications. For example, corporate logos are designed using specific colors and shapes and often cannot be changed. Photographs and illustrations cannot damage a person's reputation by casting them in a "false light," such as inserting a photograph of your teacher on the FBI's Top Ten Most Wanted list.

Changing the Size of Clip Art

Sometimes it is necessary to change the size of clip art. For example, on Slide 6, the monitor covers some of the bulleted text. To make the picture fit onto the slide, you reduce its size. To change the size of a clip art picture by an exact percentage, use the **Format Picture command**. The Format Picture dialog box contains six tabbed sheets with several options for formatting a picture. The **Size sheet** contains options for changing the size of a picture. You either enter the exact height and width in the Size and rotate area, or enter the height and width as a percentage of the original picture in the Scale area. When the **Lock aspect ratio check box** displays a check mark, the height and width settings change to maintain the aspect ratio of the original picture. **Aspect ratio** is the relationship between the height and width of an object. For example, a 3-by-5-inch picture scaled to 50 percent would become a 1½-by-2½-inch picture. Perform the following steps to reduce the size of the monitor.

Steps **To Change the Size of Clip Art**

1 **Right-click the monitor picture. Point to Format Picture (Figure 2-37).**

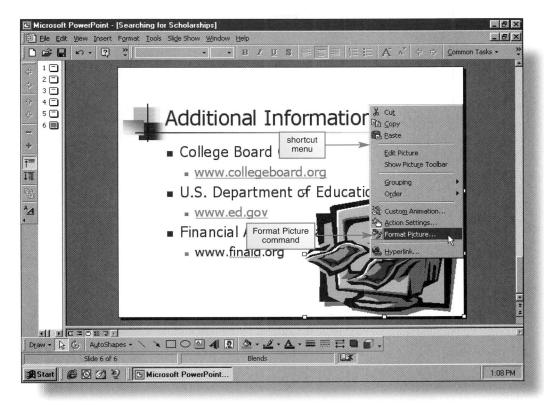

FIGURE 2-37

2 **Click Format Picture on the shortcut menu. Click the Size tab when the Format Picture dialog box displays.**

The Size sheet in the Format Picture dialog box displays (Figure 2-38). The Height and Width text boxes in the Scale area display the current percentage of the monitor picture, 100. Check marks display in the Lock aspect ratio and Relative to original picture size check boxes.

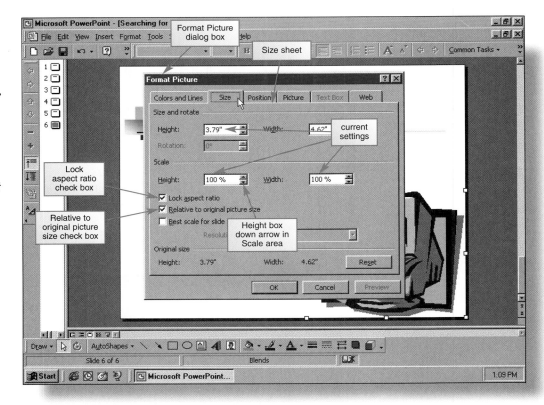

FIGURE 2-38

3 **Click the Height box down arrow in the Scale area until 65% displays and then point to the OK button.**

Both the Height and Width text boxes in the Scale area display 65% (Figure 2-39). PowerPoint automatically changes the Height and Width text boxes in the Size and rotate area to reflect changes made in the Scale area.

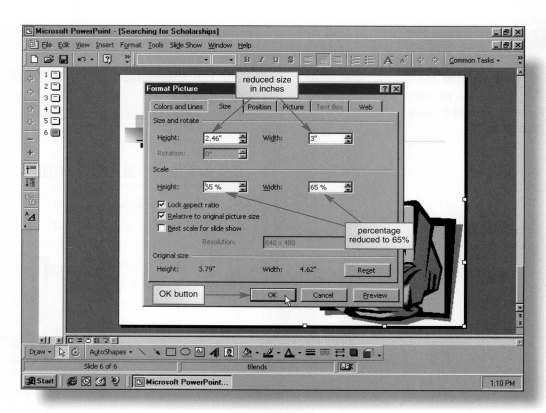

FIGURE 2-39

4 **Click the OK button. Drag the picture of the monitor to the bottom-right corner of the slide.**

PowerPoint closes the Format Picture dialog box and displays the reduced monitor picture in the desired location (Figure 2-40).

Other Ways

1. Click clip art object, on Format menu click Picture, click Size tab, click Height box up or down arrow in Scale area, click OK

2. Press ALT+O, press I, press CTRL+TAB three times to select Size tab, press TAB to select Height text box in Scale area, press up or down arrow keys to increase or decrease size, press ENTER

3. Click clip art object, drag a sizing handle until object is desired shape and size

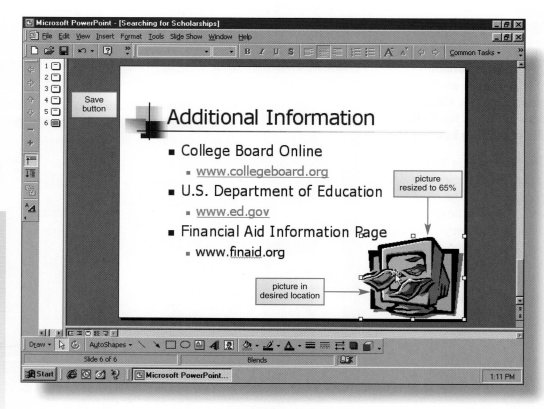

FIGURE 2-40

Creating a Hyperlink

The Internet address in the last bulleted item on Slide 6 does not appear underlined and with a font color of red. When you were creating that slide, you typed the first two Web page addresses for the College Board Online and the U.S. Department of Education and then pressed the ENTER key after each address. When you performed this action, PowerPoint enabled the **AutoFormat as you type** option and changed the addresses' appearances to display as **hyperlinks**. A hyperlink is a shortcut that allows a user to jump from the presentation to another destination, such as a Web page on the Internet or another document on your computer. You did not press the ENTER key after you typed the address for the Financial Aid Information Web site, so the text did not change appearance and become a hyperlink. You can check to see if the AutoFormat as you type option is enabled by clicking Tools on the menu bar, clicking Options, and then verifying the AutoFormat as you type check box is selected.

To change the last bulleted line to a hyperlink, perform the following steps.

TO CREATE A HYPERLINK

1. Click the end of the last bulleted line, www.finaid.org.

2. Press the ENTER key.

3. Press the BACKSPACE key twice.

The last Internet address displays underlined and with a font color of red.

Saving the Presentation Again

To preserve the work completed, perform the following step to save the presentation again.

TO SAVE A PRESENTATION

1. Click the Save button on the Standard toolbar.

The changes made to the presentation after the previous save are saved on a floppy disk.

A default setting in PowerPoint allows for fast saves, which save only the changes made since the last time you saved. If you want to full save a copy of the complete presentation, click Tools on the menu bar, click Options on the Tools menu, and then click the Save tab. Remove the check mark in the Allow fast saves check box by clicking the check box and then click the OK button.

Adding a Header and Footer to Outline Pages

A printout of the presentation outline often is used as an audience handout. Distributing a copy of the outline provides the audience with paper on which to write notes or comments. Another benefit of distributing a copy of the outline is to help the audience see the text on the slides when lighting is poor or the room is too large. To help identify the source of the printed outline, add a descriptive header and footer. A **header** displays at the top of the sheet of paper or slide, and a **footer** displays at the bottom. Both contain specific information, such as the presenter's name or the company's telephone number. In addition, the current date and time and the slide or page number can display beside the header or footer information.

More About

Footers

If you are going to turn your PowerPoint slides into overhead transparencies, consider using page numbers and the presentation name in the footer. This information will help keep the transparencies organized.

Using the Notes and Handouts Sheet to Add Headers and Footers

You add headers and footers to outline pages by clicking the Notes and Handouts sheet in the Header and Footer dialog box and entering the information you wish to print. Perform the following steps to add the current date, header information, the page number, and footer information to the printed outline.

Steps **To Use the Notes and Handouts Sheet to Add Headers and Footers**

1 **Click View on the menu bar and then point to Header and Footer (Figure 2-41).**

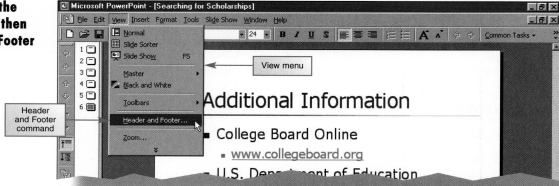

FIGURE 2-41

2 **Click Header and Footer on the View menu. Click the Notes and Handouts tab when the Header and Footer dialog box displays.**

The Notes and Handouts sheet in the Header and Footer dialog box displays (Figure 2-42). Check marks display in the Date and time, Header, Page number, and Footer check boxes. The Fixed option button is selected.

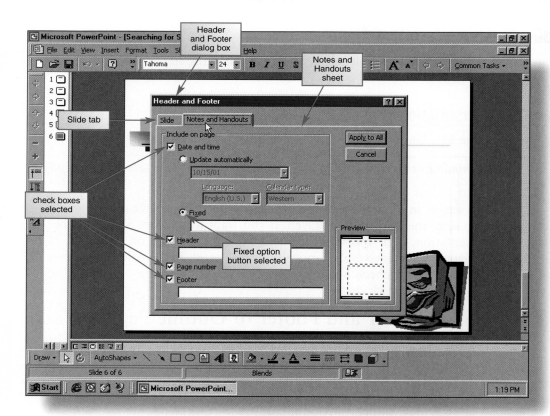

FIGURE 2-42

3 **Click the Update automatically option button and then click the Header text box. Type** Searching for Scholarships **in the Header text box. Click the Footer text box. Type** Office of Financial Aid **in the Footer text box and then point to the Apply to All button (Figure 2-43).**

4 **Click the Apply to All button.**

PowerPoint applies the header and footer text to the outline, closes the Header and Footer dialog box, and displays Slide 6. You cannot see header and footer text until you print the outline (see Figure 2-67 on page PP 2.53).

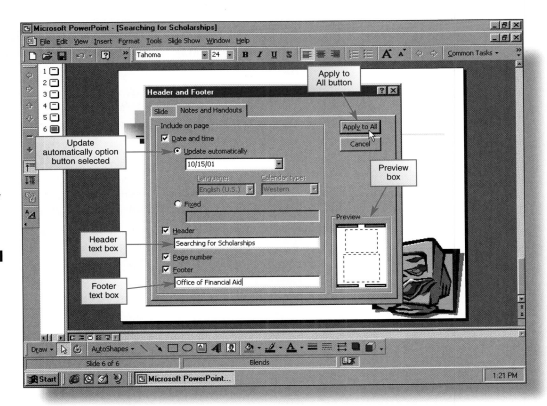

FIGURE 2-43

Adding Animation Effects

PowerPoint provides many animation effects to make your slide show presentation look professional. In this project you use slide transition and custom animation. A **slide transition** is a special effect used to progress from one slide to the next in a slide show. **Custom animation effects** define animation types and speeds and sound effects on a slide. The following pages discuss each of these animation effects in detail.

Slide Sorter Toolbar

PowerPoint provides you with multiple methods for accomplishing most tasks. Generally, the fastest method is to right-click to display a shortcut menu. Another frequently used method is to click a toolbar button. For example, you can apply slide transition effects by clicking the Slide Transition Effects list box on the Slide Sorter toolbar.

The Slide Sorter toolbar displays only when you are in slide sorter view. It displays to the right of the Standard toolbar, in place of the Formatting toolbar. The Slide Sorter toolbar contains tools to help you quickly add animation effects to your slide show. Table 2-4 on the next page explains the function of the buttons and boxes on the Slide Sorter toolbar.

Table 2-4 Buttons and Boxes on the Slide Sorter Toolbar

BUTTON/BOX	BUTTON/BOX NAME	FUNCTION
	Slide Transition	Adds or changes the special effect that introduces a slide during a slide show. For example, you can play a sound when the slide displays, or you can make the slide fade from black.
Split Vertical Out	Slide Transition Effects	Adds or changes the special effect that introduces a slide during a slide show. For example, you can play a sound when the slide displays, or you can make the slide fade from black.
Zoom In From Screen Center	Animation Effects	Adds or changes animation effects on the current slide. Animation effects include sounds, text and object movements, and movies that occur during a slide show.
	Animation Preview	Runs all the animation effects for the current slide in a slide-miniature window so you can see how the animation will work during the slide show.
	Hide Slide	Hides the selected slide. If you are in slide view, hides the current slide so that it is not displayed automatically during an electronic slide show.
	Rehearse Timings	Runs your slide show in rehearsal mode, in which you can set or change the timing of your electronic slide show.
	Summary Slide	Creates a new slide from the titles of the slides you select in slide sorter view or normal view. The summary slide creates a bulleted list from the titles of the selected slides. PowerPoint inserts the summary slide in front of the first selected slide.
	Speaker Notes	Displays the speaker notes for the current slide. You can include speaker notes on your printed handouts, or you can print them to remember key points during a presentation.
Common Tasks ▾	Common Tasks	Contains the three more frequently used commands: New Slide, Slide Layout, and Apply Design Template.
	More Buttons	Allows you to select the particular buttons you want to display on the toolbar.

Adding Slide Transitions to a Slide Show

Slide Transitions

Graphic designers suggest using a maximum of two different slide transition effects in one presentation. Any more than two can cause audience members to fixate on the visual effects and not on the slide content or the speaker.

PowerPoint allows you to control the way you advance from one slide to another by adding slide transitions to a slide show. PowerPoint has 42 different slide transitions, and you can vary the speed of each in your presentation. The name of the slide transition characterizes the visual effect that displays. For example, the slide transition effect, Split Vertical Out, displays the next slide by covering the previous slide with two vertical boxes moving from the center of the screen until the two boxes reach the left and right edges of the screen. The effect is similar to opening draw drapes over a window.

PowerPoint requires you to select at least one slide before applying slide transition effects. In this presentation, you apply slide transition effects to all slides except the title slide. Because Slide 6 already is selected, you must select Slides 2, 3, 4, and 5. The technique used to select more than one slide is the SHIFT+click technique. To perform the SHIFT+click technique in slide sorter view, press and hold down the SHIFT key as you click the starting and ending range of desired slides. After you click the slides to which you want to add animation effects, release the SHIFT key.

In the Searching for Scholarships presentation, you wish to display the Wipe Down slide transition effect between slides. That is, all slides begin stacked on top of one another, like a deck of cards. As you click the mouse to view the next slide, the new slide enters the screen by starting at the top of the slide and gliding down to the bottom of the slide. This effect resembles pulling down a window shade. Perform the following steps to apply the Wipe Down slide transition effect to the Searching for Scholarships presentation.

Steps ## To Add Slide Transitions to a Slide Show

1 **Click the Slide Sorter View button at the lower left of the PowerPoint window.**

PowerPoint displays the presentation in slide sorter view (Figure 2-44). Slide 6 is selected. Slide 6 currently does not have a slide transition effect, as noted in the Slide Transition Effects box on the Slide Sorter toolbar.

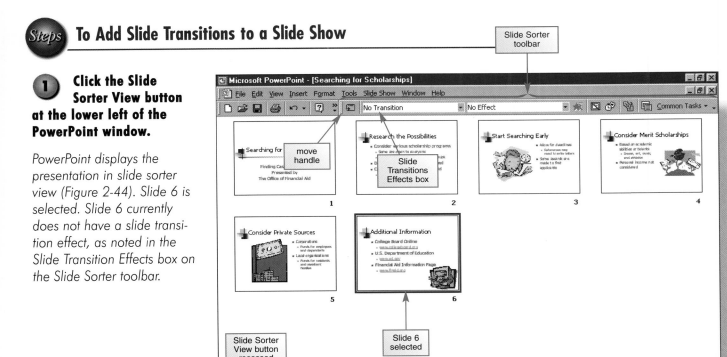

FIGURE 2-44

2 **Press and hold down the SHIFT key and then click Slide 2. Release the SHIFT key.**

Slides 2 through 6 are selected, as indicated by the heavy border around each slide (Figure 2-45).

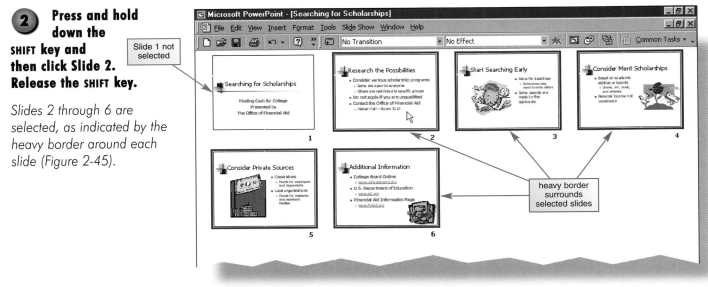

FIGURE 2-45

3 Point to Slide 2 and right-click. Point to Slide Transition (Figure 2-46).

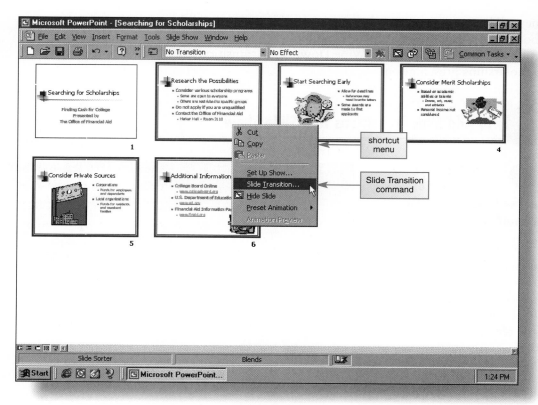

FIGURE 2-46

4 Click Slide Transition on the shortcut menu. Click the Effect box arrow when the Slide Transition dialog box displays. Scroll down to display the Wipe Down effect in the Effect list, and then point to Wipe Down.

The Slide Transition dialog box displays (Figure 2-47). The Effect list displays available slide transition effects.

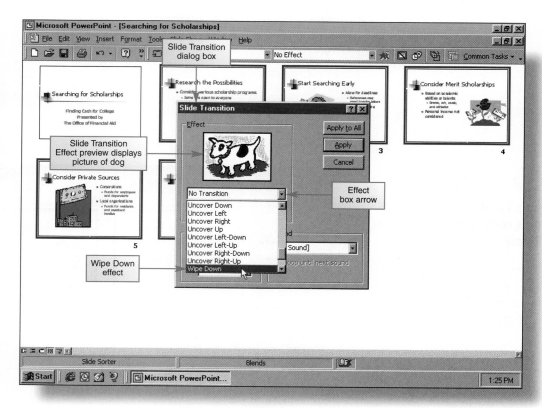

FIGURE 2-47

5 **Click Wipe Down in the list. Point to the Apply button.**

The Slide Transition Effect preview demonstrates the Wipe Down effect (Figure 2-48). To see the demonstration again, click the picture in the Slide Transition Effect preview.

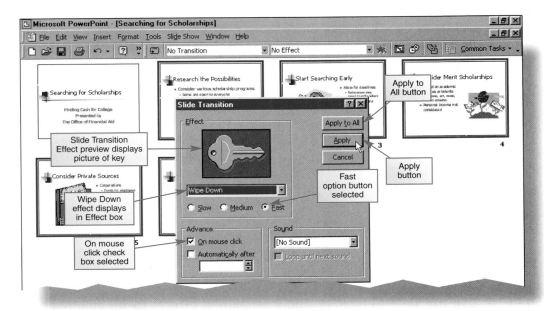

FIGURE 2-48

6 **Click the Apply button.**

PowerPoint displays the presentation in slide sorter view (Figure 2-49). A slide transition icon displays under each selected slide, which indicates that a slide transition effect has been added to those slides. The current slide transition effect, Wipe Down, displays in the Slide Transition Effects box.

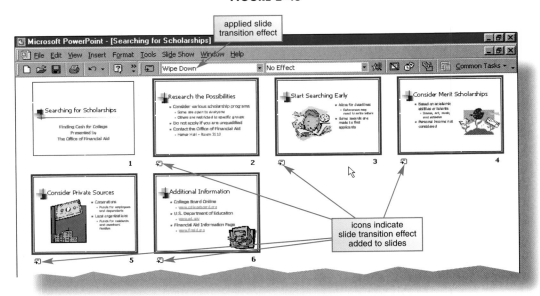

FIGURE 2-49

To adjust the speed at which the special effect runs during the slide show, click Slow, Medium, or Fast in the Effect area in the Slide Transition dialog box. When you click a particular speed option, PowerPoint runs that effect in the sample picture.

To apply slide transition effects to every slide in the presentation, right-click a slide, click Slide Transition on the shortcut menu, choose the desired slide transition effect, and then click the Apply to All button.

To remove slide transition effects when displaying the presentation in slide sorter view, select the slides to which slide transition effects are applied, click the Slide Transition Effects box arrow, and select No Transition.

The Wipe Down slide transition effect has been applied to the presentation. The next step in creating this slide show is to add animation effects to individual slides.

Other Ways

1. Select slide, right-click selected slide, click Slide Transition, click Effect box arrow, select desired effect, click Apply button

2. Select slide, on Slide Show menu click Slide Transition, click Effect box arrow, select desired effect, click Apply button

More)About

Clip Gallery Live

Microsoft's Clip Gallery Live is an outstanding place to locate additional clip art. This Web site also contains movie clips, pictures, and sounds. To connect to the Clip Gallery Live site, click the Insert Clip Art button on the Drawing toolbar and then click the Clips Online button. Another method of connecting to this area is to visit the PowerPoint 2000 More About Web page (www.scsite.com/pp2000/more.htm) and click Clip Gallery Live.

Applying Animation Effects to Bulleted Slides

Animation effects can be applied to text as well as to objects, such as clip art. When you apply animation effects to bulleted text, you progressively disclose each bulleted paragraph. As a result, you build the slide paragraph by paragraph during the running of a slide show to control the flow of information. PowerPoint has a wide variety of custom animation effects and the capability to dim the paragraphs already displaying on the slide when the new paragraph is displayed.

The next step is to apply the Zoom In From Screen Center animation effect to Slides 2, 3, 4, 5, and 6 in the Searching for Scholarships presentation. All slides, except the title slide, will have the Zoom In From Screen Center animation effect. Recall from Project 1 that when you need to make a change that affects all slides, make the change to the slide master. Perform the following steps to apply animation effects to the bulleted paragraphs in this presentation.

 To Use the Slide Master to Apply Animation Effects to All Bulleted Slides

---

1 Press and hold down the SHIFT key and then click the Slide Master View button at the lower left of the PowerPoint window.

The slide master displays (Figure 2-50).

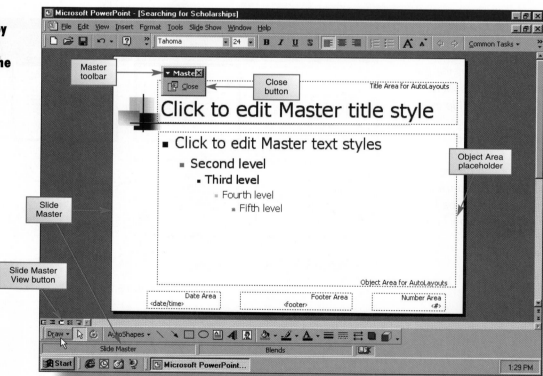

FIGURE 2-50

2 Right-click the Object Area placeholder in the slide master. Point to Custom Animation (Figure 2-51).

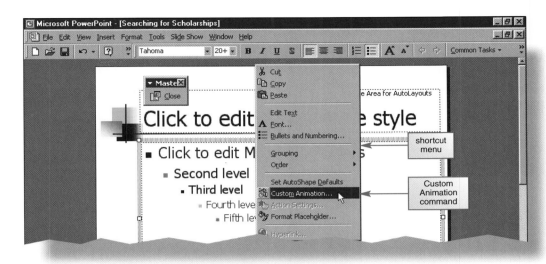

FIGURE 2-51

3 Click Custom Animation on the shortcut menu. If necessary, click the Effects tab when the Custom Animation dialog box displays.

The Custom Animation dialog box displays (Figure 2-52).

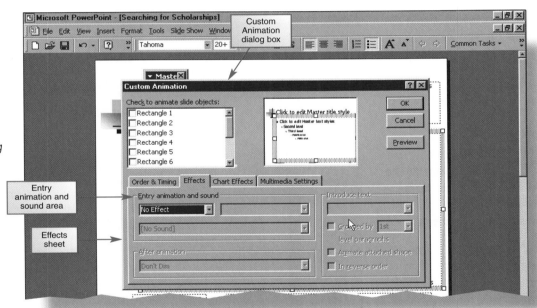

FIGURE 2-52

4 Click the left Entry animation and sound box arrow. Scroll down the list until Zoom displays and then point to Zoom (Figure 2-53).

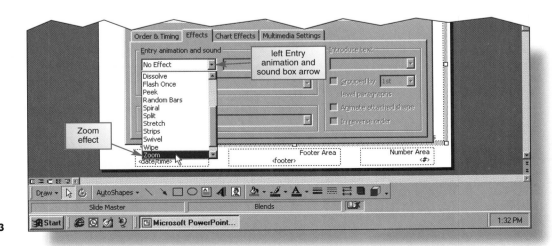

FIGURE 2-53

5 Click Zoom in the list. Click the right Entry animation and sound box arrow and then point to In From Screen Center (Figure 2-54).

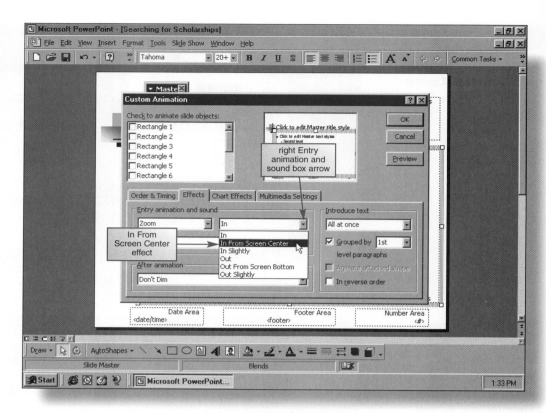

FIGURE 2-54

6 Click In From Screen Center in the list and then point to the Grouped by level paragraphs box arrow.

The Entry animation and sound boxes display Zoom and In From Screen Center, respectively (Figure 2-55). A check mark displays in the Grouped by level paragraphs box, and 1st level paragraphs is the default setting.

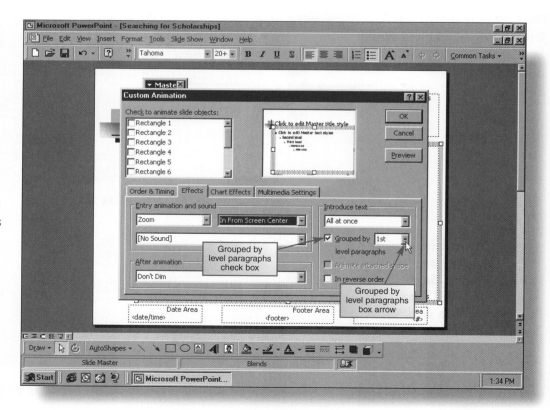

FIGURE 2-55

7 **Click the Grouped by level paragraphs box arrow and then point to 3rd.**

3rd is highlighted in the Grouped by level paragraphs list (Figure 2-56).

8 **Click 3rd in the list and then click the OK button.**

PowerPoint applies the animation effects to the slide master, closes the Custom Animation dialog box, and then displays the slide master.

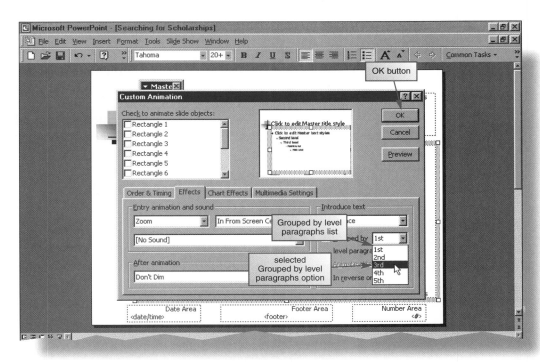

FIGURE 2-56

9 **Click the Close button on the Master toolbar.**

PowerPoint closes the slide master and returns to slide sorter view (Figure 2-57). The icons next to the slide transition effect icons indicate animation effects have been added to the slides.

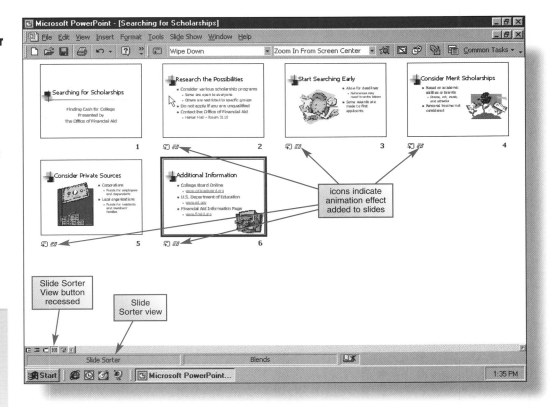

FIGURE 2-57

Other Ways

1. On View menu point to Master, click Slide Master, right-click Object Area placeholder, on Slide Show menu click Custom Animation, click Effects tab, click Entry animation and sound box arrow, click desired animation effect, click Grouped by level paragraphs box arrow, click appropriate paragraph level, click OK

The Zoom In From Screen Center animation effect displays for each bulleted paragraph on paragraph level 1, 2, or 3 on Slides 2 through 6 when the slide show is running.

To remove animation effects from the slide master, press and hold down the SHIFT key, click the Slide Master View button, release the SHIFT key, right-click the slide master, click Custom Animation, click the left Entry animation and sound box arrow, click No effect in the Entry animation and sound list, click the OK button, and then click the Close button on the Master toolbar.

Animating Clip Art Objects

To add visual interest to your presentation, you want the monitor clip art on Slide 6 to rise from the bottom of the screen. Animating a clip art object takes several steps. First, display the slide containing the clip art (Slide 6) in slide view. Then select the clip art object and display the Custom Animation dialog box. Next, select the animation effect. Finally, apply the animation effect as described in the following sections.

Displaying a Slide in Slide View

PowerPoint requires you to display a slide in slide view before adding animation effects to clip art. Before continuing with the animation of the monitor on Slide 6, display the slide in slide view as described in the following step.

TO DISPLAY A SLIDE IN SLIDE VIEW

 Double-click Slide 6.

Slide 6 displays in slide view.

With Slide 6 displaying in slide view, you are ready to animate the monitor clip art as explained in the next section.

Animating Clip Art

PowerPoint allows you to animate clip art along with animating text. Because Slide 6 lists three sources on the Internet for current scholarship information, you want to emphasize these sites by having the monitor clip art pass from the left side of the screen to the right. One way of animating clip art is to select options in the Custom Animation dialog box, similarly to what you did to animate text. A quicker way is to choose an animation option from the Preset Animation list. Perform the following steps to add the Flying animation effect to the monitor on Slide 6.

Steps **To Animate Clip Art**

1 **Click the monitor clip art object. Click Slide Show on the menu bar, point to Preset Animation, and then point to Flying.**

Animation options display in the Preset Animation sub-menu (Figure 2-58). The monitor clip art is selected.

2 **Click Flying on the Preset Animation submenu.**

PowerPoint applies the Flying animation effect to the clip art. You will see this effect when you run your slide show.

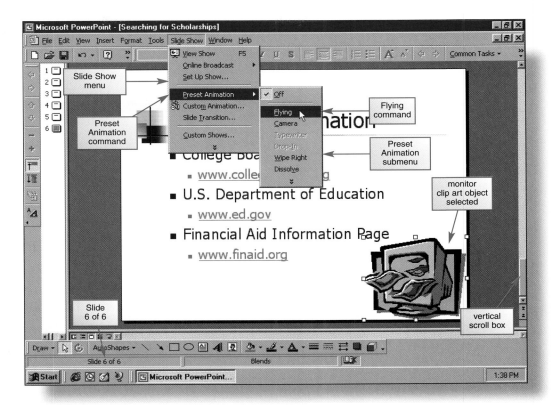

FIGURE 2-58

When you run the slide show, the names of each of the three Internet sites will display, and then the monitor clip art will begin moving from the left side of the slide and stop at the position where you inserted it onto Slide 6.

Formatting and Animating a Title Slide

The title slide of every presentation should seize the attention of the audience. In order to excite the audience with the Searching for Scholarships presentation, you want to intensify the subtitle object on the title slide. First, you italicize the words Presented by, and then you increase the size of the words, Finding Cash for College. Finally, you add animation effects to the subtitle.

The first step is to display Slide 1 and then format the title slide subtitle. Perform the following steps to format the subtitle object on Slide 1.

TO CHANGE TEXT FONT STYLE TO ITALIC AND INCREASE FONT SIZE

1 Drag the vertical scroll box to display Slide 1.

2 Triple-click the paragraph, Finding Cash for College.

3 Click the Font Size box arrow on the Formatting toolbar and then select the font size 40 in the list.

Other **Ways**

1. Click clip art, on Slide Show menu click Custom Anima-tion, click Effects tab, click Entry animation and sound box arrows, click desired animation effects, click OK

2. Press TAB until clip art is selected, press ALT+D, press M, press DOWN ARROW key until desired animation effect selected, press ENTER

Triple-click the paragraph, Presented by, and then click the Italic button on the Formatting toolbar.

The formatted subtitle on Slide 1 displays (Figure 2-59). The paragraph, Finding Cash For College, displays in font size 40, and the words, Presented by, display the italic font style.

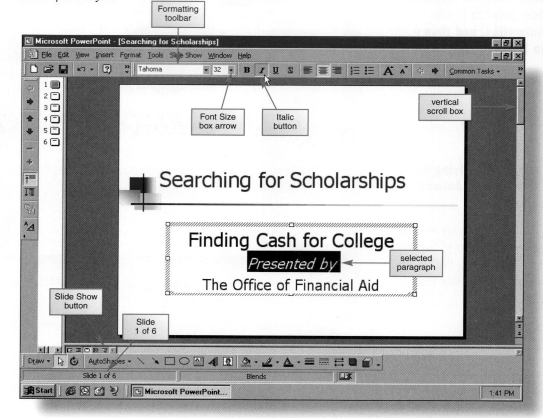

FIGURE 2-59

The next step is to apply the Dissolve animation effect to the subtitle text. Perform the following steps to animate the paragraphs in the subtitle object on Slide 1.

TO ANIMATE TEXT

1 Right-click the Object Area placeholder and then click Custom Animation on the shortcut menu.

2 If necessary, click the Effects tab in the Custom Animation dialog box.

3 Click the left Entry animation and sound box arrow.

4 Scroll down the list until Dissolve displays and then click Dissolve in the list.

5 Click the OK button.

The Object Area object, Text 2, is selected in the preview box and in the Check to animate slide objects box. Dissolve displays in the Entry animation and sound box. By default, the subtitle text is grouped by first level paragraphs. PowerPoint applies the animation effect, closes the Custom Animation dialog box, and then displays Slide 1.

Animation effects are complete for this presentation. You now are ready to review the presentation in slide show view.

Saving the Presentation Again

The presentation is complete. Perform the following step to save the finished presentation on a floppy disk before running the slide show.

TO SAVE A PRESENTATION ON A FLOPPY DISK

 Click the Save button on the Standard toolbar.

PowerPoint saves the presentation on your floppy disk by saving the changes made to the presentation since the last save.

Running an Animated Slide Show

Project 1 introduced you to using slide show view to look at your presentation one slide at a time. This project introduces you to running a slide show with slide transition effects and text and object animation effects. When you run a slide show with slide transition effects, PowerPoint displays the slide transition effect when you click the mouse button to advance to the next slide. When a slide has text animation effects, each paragraph level displays as determined by the animation settings. Animated clip art objects display the selected animation effect in the sequence established in the Custom Animation dialog box. Perform the following steps to run the animated Searching for Scholarships slide show.

More About

Giving a Slide Show

PowerPoint's Projector Wizard automatically sets the optimum screen resolution for your monitor or projector when you are running your presentation in a large room. To start the Project Wizard, click Set Up Show on the Slide Show menu, click the Projector Wizard button, and follow the instructions. If you are using two monitors, you can display your slide show on one monitor and view your notes, outline, and slides on the second monitor.

 To Run an Animated Slide Show

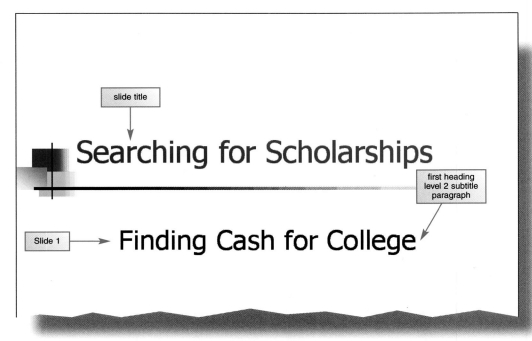

1 **With Slide 1 displaying, click the Slide Show button at the lower left of the PowerPoint window. When Slide 1 displays in slide show view, click the slide anywhere.**

PowerPoint first displays the title slide title object, Searching for Scholarships (Figure 2-60). When you click the slide, the first heading level 2 subtitle paragraph, Finding Cash for College, displays using the Dissolve animation effect.

FIGURE 2-60

Click the slide again.

PowerPoint displays the second heading level 2 subtitle paragraph, Presented by, using the Dissolve animation effect (Figure 2-61). If the Popup Menu buttons display when you move the mouse pointer, do not click them.

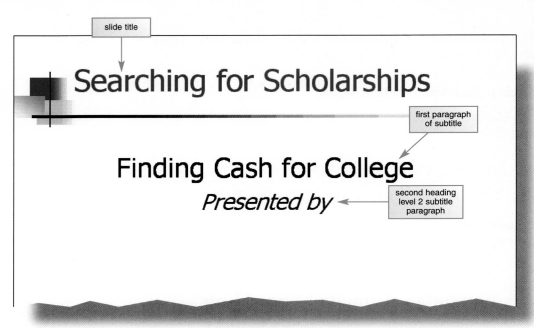

FIGURE 2-61

 Click the slide again.

PowerPoint displays the third heading level 2 subtitle paragraph, The Office of Financial Aid, beneath the second heading level 2 subtitle paragraph. PowerPoint again uses the Dissolve animation effect (Figure 2-62).

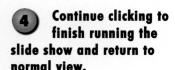 **Continue clicking to finish running the slide show and return to normal view.**

Each time a new slide displays, PowerPoint first displays the Wipe Down slide transition effect and then displays only the slide title. Then, PowerPoint builds each slide based on the animation settings. When you click the slide after the last paragraph displays on the last slide of the presentation, PowerPoint displays a blank slide. When you click again, PowerPoint exits slide show view and returns to normal view.

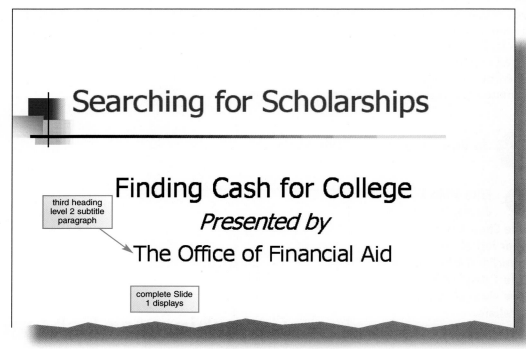

FIGURE 2-62

Other **Ways**

1. On Slide Show menu click View Show, click slide until slide show ends
2. Press ALT+D, press V, press ENTER until slide show ends

Now that the presentation is complete and you have tested the animation effects, the last step is to print the presentation outline and slides.

Printing in Outline View

When you click the Print button on the Standard toolbar, PowerPoint prints a hard copy of the presentation component last selected in the Print what box in the Print dialog box. To be certain to print the component you want, such as the presentation outline, use the Print command on the File menu. When the Print dialog box displays, you can select the appropriate presentation component in the Print what box. The next two sections explain how to use the Print command on the File menu to print the presentation outline and the presentation slides.

Printing an Outline

During the development of a lengthy presentation, it often is easier to review your outline in print rather than on the screen. Printing your outline also is useful for audience handouts or when your supervisor or instructor wants to review your subject matter before you develop your presentation fully.

Recall that the Print dialog box displays print options. When you wish to print your outline, select Outline View in the Print what list located in the Print dialog box. The outline, however, prints as last viewed in outline view. This means that you must select the Zoom setting to display the outline text as you wish it to print. If you are uncertain of the Zoom setting, you should return to outline view and review it prior to printing. Perform the following steps to print an outline from slide view.

More About

Outlines

You can send your PowerPoint outline to Microsoft Word and then create handouts and other documents using that text. To perform this action, click the Grayscale Preview button on the Standard toolbar, click File on the menu bar, point to Send To, click Microsoft Word, and then select the desired page layout.

Steps — To Print an Outline

1 **Ready the printer according to the printer manufacturer's instructions. Click File on the menu bar and then point to Print.**

The File menu displays (Figure 2-63). The **Collapse All button** *on the Outlining toolbar is recessed, so the entire outline will not print. If you want to print all the lines of text on the slides, you would click the* **Expand All button.**

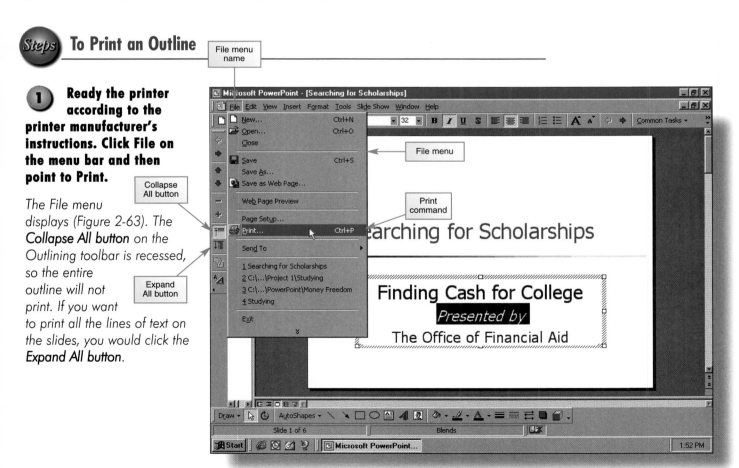

FIGURE 2-63

Microsoft **PowerPoint 2000**

2 **Click Print on the File menu.**

The Print dialog box displays (Figure 2-64).

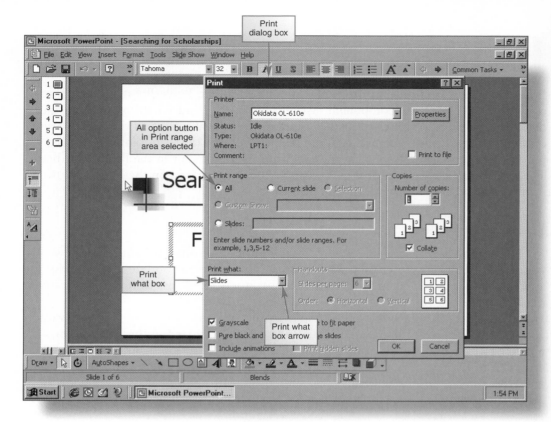

FIGURE 2-64

3 **Click the Print what box arrow and then point to Outline View.**

Outline View displays highlighted in the Print what list (Figure 2-65).

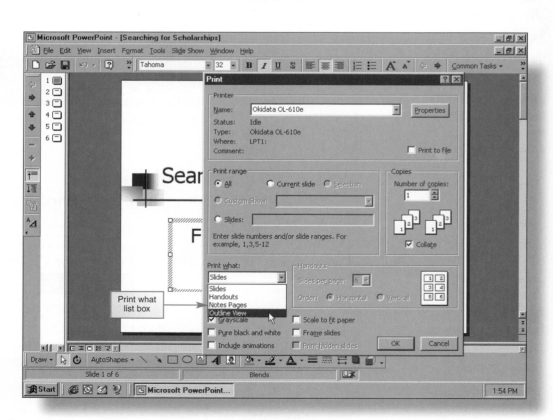

FIGURE 2-65

4 Click Outline View in the list and then point to the OK button (Figure 2-66).

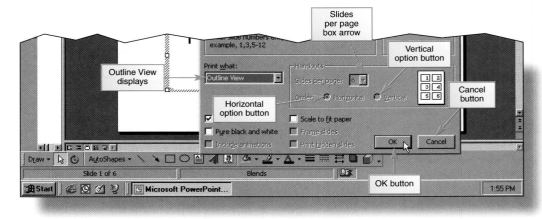

FIGURE 2-66

5 Click the OK button.

The outline prints. Clicking the Cancel button, cancels the printing request.

6 When the printer stops, retrieve the printout of the outline (Figure 2-67).

The six PowerPoint slides display in outline form. The words, Searching for Scholarships, and the current date display in the header, and the words, Office of Financial Aid, and the page number display in the footer.

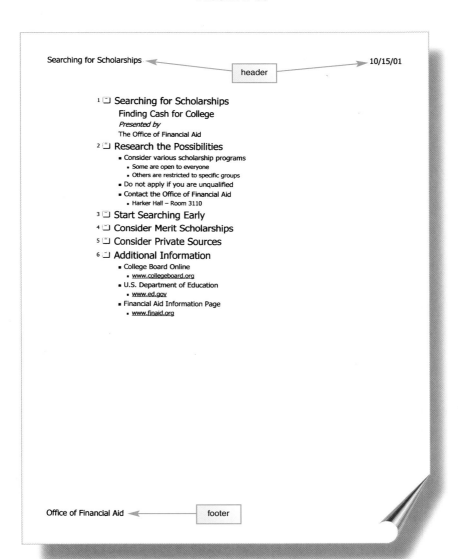

FIGURE 2-67

You may select the Print command from the File menu while in any view except slide show view.

Other Ways

1. Press ALT+F, press P, press TAB, press W, press down arrow until Outline View selected, press ENTER, press ENTER

Printing

If your printer seems to print slowly, Microsoft suggests clearing at least two megabytes of space on your hard drive and also closing any unnecessary programs that are running simultaneously.

The Print what list in the Print dialog box contains options for printing handouts, and the Handouts area allows you to specify whether you want two, three, four, six, or nine slide images to display on each page. Printing handouts is useful for reviewing a presentation because you can analyze several slides displaying simultaneously on one page. Additionally, many businesses distribute handouts of the slide show before a presentation so the attendees can refer to a copy. To print handouts, click Handouts in the Print what box, click the Slides per page box arrow in the Handouts area, and then click 2, 3, 4, 6, or 9. You can change the order in which the Searching for Scholarships slides display on a page by clicking the Horizontal option button in the Order area, which displays Slides 1 and 2, 3 and 4, and 5 and 6 adjacent to each other, or the Vertical option button in the Order area, which displays Slides 1 and 4, 2 and 5, and 3 and 6 adjacent to each other.

Printing Presentation Slides

After correcting errors, you will want to print a final copy of your presentation. If you made any changes to your presentation since your last save, be certain to save your presentation before you print.

Perform the following steps to print the presentation.

TO PRINT PRESENTATION SLIDES

1. Ready the printer according to the printer manufacturer's instructions.

2. Click File on the menu bar and then click Print on the File menu.

3. When the Print dialog box displays, click the Print what box arrow.

4. Click Slides in the list.

5. Click the OK button. When the printer stops, retrieve the slide printouts.

The printouts should resemble the slides shown in Figures 2-68a through 2-68f.

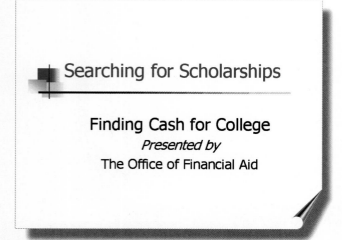

(a) Slide 1

(b) Slide 2

FIGURE 2-68

(c) Slide 3

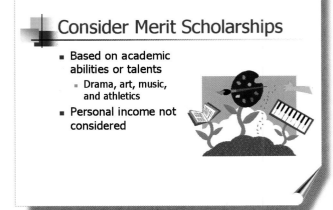

(d) Slide 4

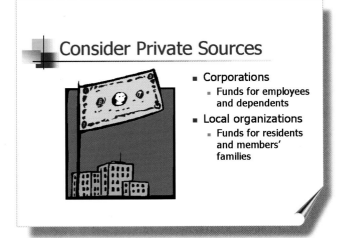

(e) Slide 5

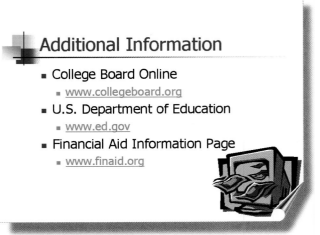

(f) Slide 6

FIGURE 2-68 (continued)

E-mailing a Slide Show from within PowerPoint

Billions of e-mail messages are sent throughout the world each year. Computer users use this popular service on the Internet to send and receive plain text e-mail or to send and receive rich e-mail content that includes graphics, links to other Web pages, and file attachments. These attachments can include Office files, such as Word documents or PowerPoint slide shows. Using Office 2000, you can e-mail the presentation directly from within PowerPoint. In previous versions of Microsoft Office, to send a presentation you would have had to save it, close the file, launch your e-mail program, and then attach the presentation to the e-mail before sending it.

For these steps to work properly, users need an e-mail address and a 32-bit e-mail program compatible with a Messaging Application Programming Interface, such as Outlook, Outlook Express, or Microsoft Exchange Client. Free e-mail accounts are available at www.hotmail.com. The steps on the next page show how to e-mail the slide show from within PowerPoint to Dr. Mary Halen. Assume her e-mail address is mary_halen@hotmail.com. If you do not have an E-mail button on the Standard toolbar, then this activity is not available to you.

E-mail

UCLA Professor Leonard Kleinrock sent the first e-mail message in 1969 to a colleague at Stanford University. Today, Americans send more than 2.2 billion e-mail messages daily, as compared to fewer than 300 million pieces of first-class mail.

Steps **To E-mail a Slide Show from within PowerPoint**

1 **Double-click the move handle on the Standard toolbar and then click the E-mail button on the Standard toolbar. If necessary, click the Send the entire presentation as an attachment option button or click the same message displayed by the Office Assistant. Point to the OK button.**

The E-mail dialog box displays (Figure 2-69).

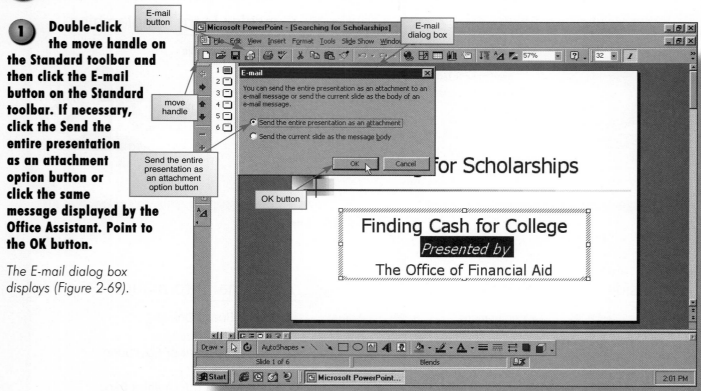

FIGURE 2-69

2 **Click the OK button. When the New Message window displays, type** mary_halen@ hotmail.com **in the To box. Type** Scholarships presentation **in the Subject box. Click the Message box.**

PowerPoint displays the E-mail area, which includes the title bar, menu bar, Standard Buttons toolbar, the To, Cc, Subject, and Attach boxes, and the Formatting Bar toolbar (Figure 2-70). The insertion point is in the Message box so you can type a message to Dr. Mary Halen.

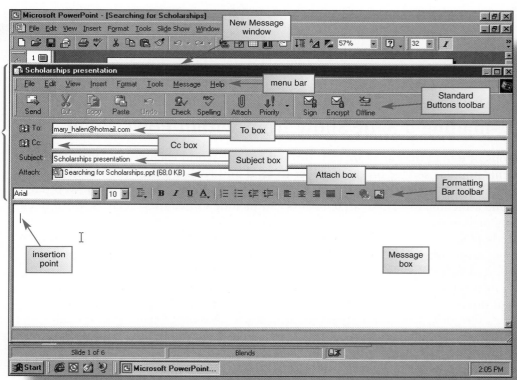

FIGURE 2-70

3 **Type** Attached is the PowerPoint presentation you can use to accompany your lecture on scholarships. **in the Message box. Point to the Send button.**

This message helps Dr. Halen understand the purpose of your e-mail when she opens her mail (Figure 2-71).

4 **Click the Send button on the Standard Buttons toolbar.**

The e-mail with the attached presentation is sent to mary_halen@hotmail.com.

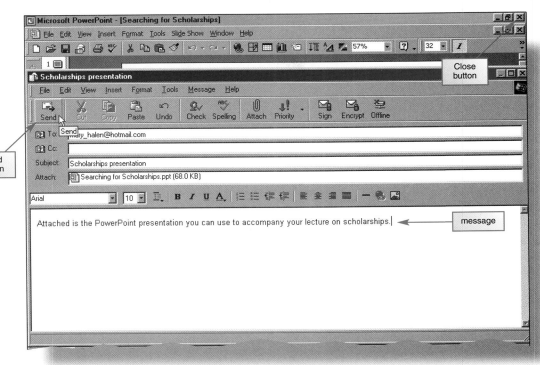

FIGURE 2-71

Because the slide show was sent as an attachment, Dr. Halen can save the attachment and then open the presentation in PowerPoint. The alternative in the E-mail dialog box in Figure 2-69 on page PP 2.56 is to send a copy of the current slide as the e-mail message. In this case, Mary would be able to see the slide in her e-mail, but she would not be able to open it in PowerPoint.

You can choose many more options when you send e-mail from within PowerPoint. For example, the Apply Stationery command on the Format menu in the Outlook Express window adds graphics to your message, such as colorful candles for a birthday message or chicken soup for a get well note. In addition, the Encrypt message on the Standard Buttons toolbar allows you to send secure messages that only your intended recipient can read.

Saving and Quitting PowerPoint

If you made any changes to your presentation since your last save, you should save it again before quitting PowerPoint. For more details on quitting PowerPoint, refer to pages PP 1.50 through PP 1.51 in Project 1. Perform the following steps to save changes to the presentation and quit PowerPoint.

TO SAVE CHANGES AND QUIT POWERPOINT

1 Click the Close button on the Microsoft PowerPoint window title bar.

2 If prompted, click the Yes button.

PowerPoint saves any changes made to the presentation since the last save and then quits PowerPoint.

More *About*

Microsoft Certification

The Microsoft Office User Specialist (MOUS) Certification program allows you to prove your knowledge of essential PowerPoint 2000 skills. For more information, see Appendix D or visit the Shelly Cashman Series MOUS Web page at www.scsite.com/off2000/cert.htm.

CASE PERSPECTIVE SUMMARY

The Searching for Scholarships slide show should help some students at your school find sources of financial aid. These classmates viewing your presentation in the Office of Financial Aid will realize that many sources of scholarships are overlooked. When Dr. Halen runs your slide show, she will describe and expand upon the available scholarships you list in your slides. The audience members should have a better understanding of potential sources of scholarship money by knowing possible aid sources, the benefits of searching early, the difference between merit and private scholarships, and places to look on the Internet for more details.

Project Summary

Project 2 introduced you to outline view, clip art, and animation effects. You created a slide presentation in outline view where you entered all the text in the form of an outline. You arranged the text using the Promote and Demote buttons. Once your outline was complete, you changed slide layouts and added clip art to the Object Area placeholders. After adding clip art to another slide without a clip art region in the Object Area placeholder, you moved and sized the picture. You added slide transition effects and text animation effects. Then you applied animation effects to clip art. You learned how to run an animated slide show demonstrating slide transition and animation effects. Finally, you printed the presentation outline and slides using the Print command on the File menu and e-mailed the presentation.

What You Should Know

Having completed this project, you now should be able to perform the following tasks:

▶ Add a Slide in Outline View *(PP 2.13)*
▶ Add Slide Transitions to a Slide Show *(PP 2.39)*
▶ Animate Clip Art *(PP 2.47)*
▶ Animate Text *(PP 2.48)*
▶ Change the Size of Clip Art *(PP 2.33)*
▶ Change Slide Layout to Clip Art & Text *(PP 2.22)*
▶ Change the Slide Layout to Clip Art & Text and Insert Clip Art *(PP 2.28)*
▶ Change the Slide Layout to Text & Clip Art and Insert Clip Art *(PP 2.27)*
▶ Change the View to Outline View and Display the Outline Toolbar *(PP 2.8)*
▶ Change the View to Slide Sorter View *(PP 2.20)*
▶ Change the View to Slide View *(PP 2.21)*
▶ Change Text Font Style to Italic and Increase Font Size *(PP 2.47)*
▶ Create a Closing Slide in Outline View *(PP 2.18)*
▶ Create a Hyperlink *(PP 2.35)*
▶ Create a Multi-level Bulleted List Slide in Outline View *(PP 2.14)*
▶ Create a Second Subordinate Slide *(PP 2.16)*
▶ Create a Third Subordinate Slide *(PP 2.17)*

▶ Create a Subordinate Slide *(PP 2.16)*
▶ Create a Title Slide in Outline View *(PP 2.11)*
▶ Display a Slide in Slide View *(PP 2.46)*
▶ E-mail a Slide Show from within PowerPoint *(PP 2.56)*
▶ Insert Clip Art into an Object Area Placeholder *(PP 2.25)*
▶ Insert Clip Art on a Slide without a Clip Art Region *(PP 2.30)*
▶ Move Clip Art *(PP 2.32)*
▶ Print an Outline *(PP 2.51)*
▶ Print Presentation Slides *(PP 2.54)*
▶ Run an Animated Slide Show *(PP 2.49)*
▶ Save a Presentation *(PP 2.19, 2.35)*
▶ Save a Presentation on a Floppy Disk *(PP 2.49)*
▶ Save Changes and Quit PowerPoint *(PP 2.57)*
▶ Start a New Presentation *(PP 2.7)*
▶ Use the Notes and Handouts Sheet to Add Headers and Footers *(PP 2.36)*
▶ Use the Slide Master to Apply Animation Effects to All Bulleted Slides *(PP 2.42)*

Apply Your Knowledge

⊕ Project Reinforcement at www.scsite.com/off2000/reinforce.htm

1 Intensifying a Presentation by Applying a Design Template, Changing Slide Layout, Inserting Clip Art, and Applying Animation Effects

Instructions: Start PowerPoint. Open the presentation Antique from the Data Disk. See the inside back cover of this book for instructions for downloading the Data Disk or see your instructor for information on accessing the files required in this book. Perform the following tasks to change the presentation to look like Figures 2-72a through 2-72e.

1. Apply the Dad's Tie design template. Add the current date, slide number, and your name to the notes and handouts footer.

2. On Slide 1, italicize the paragraph, Midwest College Art Department, and then decrease the font size to 28 points. Insert the gramophone clip art image shown in Figure 2-72a. Scale the clip art to 90% using the Format Picture command on the shortcut menu. Drag the gramophone clip art image to align the upper-left corner of the dotted box below the letter w in the word Show, as shown in Figure 2-72a. Apply the Spiral custom animation effect to the clip art.

(a) Slide 1

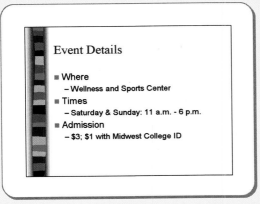

(b) Slide 2

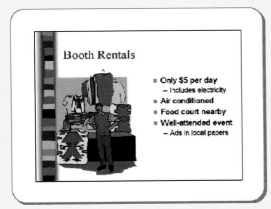

(c) Slide 3

(d) Slide 4

(e) Slide 5

FIGURE 2-72

(continued)

Apply Your Knowledge

Project Reinforcement at www.scsite.com/off2000/reinforce.htm

Intensifying a Presentation by Applying a Design Template, Changing Slide Layout, Inserting Clip Art, and Applying Animation Effect *(continued)*

3. Go to Slide 3. Change the slide layout to Clip Art & Text. Insert the vendor clip art image shown in Figure 2-72c. Change the size of the vendor clip art image to 275%. Move the vendor clip art image so the left edge of the selection rectangle aligns with the blue strip running down the slide.

4. Go to Slide 4. Change the slide layout to 2 Column Text. Select the bottom three categories (Furniture, Jewelry, Arts & Crafts), press and hold down the left mouse button, and drag the text to the right placeholder.

5. Go to Slide 5. Change the slide layout to Text & Clip Art. Insert the treasure chest clip art image shown in Figure 2-72e. Change the size of the treasure chest to 100%.

6. Add the Uncover Right slide transition effect to all slides except the title slide.

7. Save the presentation on a floppy disk using the file name, Antique Show.

8. Print the presentation in black and white. Print the presentation outline. Quit PowerPoint.

In the Lab

1 Adding Clip Art and Animation Effects to a Presentation Created in Outline View

Problem: Every fall and winter you experience the "winter blues." You feel depressed and lethargic, and you notice your friends are feeling the same symptoms. In the spring and summer months, however, these symptoms fade away. In your Health 101 class, you learn that these "winter blues" feelings are attributed to Seasonal Affective Disorder, commonly called SAD. They result from fewer hours of daylight, cold temperatures, and inclement weather. One of the assignments in this class is a research paper and accompanying five-minute presentation. You decide to conduct additional research on SAD and create the outline shown in Figure 2-73 to prepare your presentation. You use the outline to create the slide show shown in Figures 2-74a through 2-74d.

Instructions: Perform the following tasks.

1. Create a new presentation using the Sandstone design template.

2. Using the outline shown in Figure 2-73, create the title slide shown in Figure 2-74a.

I. Seasonal Affective Disorder
  A. Jacob Heilman
  B. Health 101
II. Symptoms of SAD
  A. Frequent depression
  B. Increasing appetite
    1. Craving carbohydrates
  C. Oversleeping
  D. Being irritable
III. Causes of SAD
  A. Increased melatonin
    1. A natural tranquilizer
    2. Secreted in greater amounts in darkness
  B. Internal clock desynchronized
IV. Relief for SAD
  A. Use light therapy
    1. Use bright lights in the morning
    2. Take a walk outside
  B. Avoid overeating
  C. Think spring!

FIGURE 2-73

In the Lab

Use your name instead of the name Jacob Heilman. Decrease the font size of the class name to 28 points. Insert the clip art that has the keywords, emotions, hearts, sadness, broken. Center the clip art under the class name.

3. Using the outline in Figure 2-73, create the three bulleted list slides shown in Figures 2-74b through 2-74d.

4. Change the slide layout on Slide 2 to Text & Clip Art. Using the Object Area placeholder, insert the clip art shown in Figure 2-74b that has the keywords, sorrow, grief, sadness, tears. Scale the clip art to 200%.

5. Change the slide layout on Slide 3 to Clip Art & Text. Using the Object Area placeholder, insert the clip art shown in Figure 2-74c that has the keywords, medicine, body parts, healthcare.

6. On Slide 4, change the slide layout to Text & Clip Art. Insert the clip art shown in Figure 2-74d that has the keywords, emotions, nature, seasons. Animate the sun clip art using the Spiral custom animation effect.

7. Add the slide number and your name to the slide footer. Display the footer on all slides except the title slide. Add your name to the outline header and your school's name to the outline footer.

8. Apply the Fade Through Black slide transition effect to Slides 2, 3, and 4.

9. Save the presentation on a floppy disk using the file name, SAD.

10. Print the presentation outline. Print the presentation. Quit PowerPoint.

(a) Slide 1

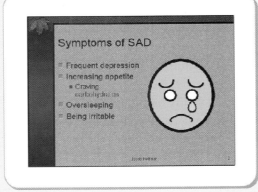

(b) Slide 2

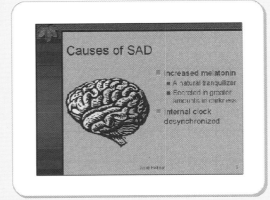

(c) Slide 3

(d) Slide 4

FIGURE 2-74

In the Lab

2 Animating a Slide Show

Problem: The park district in your community wants to develop a PowerPoint presentation that encourages residents to consider Nordic skiing at South Shore Park for fun and recreation. You have been active in many park district activities, so the marketing director asks you for assistance. She approves the outline you developed in Figure 2-75. When you practice your presentation, you decide to add animation effects to the slide show. The completed slide show is shown in Figures 2-76a through 2-76d. *Hint*: Use Help to solve this problem.

Instructions: Perform the following tasks.

1. Create a new presentation using the Nature design template and the outline shown in Figure 2-75.
2. On the title slide, increase the font size of Fun and Fitness to 36 points. Decrease the font size of the word, at, to 28 points. Using Figure 2-76a as a reference, insert the clip art that has the keywords, people, person, sports. Scale the clip art to 95% and drag it to the upper-right corner of the slide.
3. On Slide 2, change the slide layout to 2 Column Text. Drag the text into the right column placeholder so your slide looks like Slide 2 in Figure 2-76b.
4. On Slide 3, change the slide layout to Text & Clip Art. Insert the clip art shown in Figure 2-76c that has the keywords, animals, cartoons, nature, birds. Scale the clip art to 115%.
5. On Slide 4, change the slide layout to Clip Art & Text. Insert the clip art shown in Figure 2-76d that has the keywords, household, hats, clothes. Scale the clip art to 200%.
6. Add the current date, slide number, and your name to the slide footer. Display the footer on all slides except the title slide. Include the current date and your name on the outline header. Include South Shore Park and the page number on the outline footer.

> I. Nordic Skiing
>   A. Fun and Fitness
>   B. at
>   C. South Shore Park
> II. Have Fun
>   A. Enjoy touring with friends and family
>   B. Join enthusiasts in a race, or slip into solitude
>   C. Snow conditions require quality gear
>   1. No wax skis are convenient
>   2. Waxable skis perform best
> III. Get Fit
>   A. Use a variety of styles
>   1. Slow and easy
>   2. Fast and hard
>   B. Take lessons
>   1. Qualified instructors have certification
> IV. Dress Right
>   A. Skiing builds heat and requires light clothing
>   B. Dress in layers
>   C. Always wear a hat
>   1. 50% of heat may be lost through the head

FIGURE 2-75

7. Apply the Box Out slide transition effect to Slide 2 through 4. Apply the Peek From Top custom animation effect to the subtitle text on Slides 1 through 4. On Slide 1, introduce text grouped by 3rd level paragraphs.
8. Animate the clip art on Slide 1 using the Fly From Right custom animation effect so it displays immediately after the slide title when you run the slide show. Animate clip art on Slide 3 using the Fly From Top custom animation effect.
9. Save the presentation on a floppy disk using the file name, Nordic Skiing.
10. Print the presentation outline. Print the presentation slides. Print a handout with all four slides arranged vertically on one page. Quit PowerPoint.

(a) Slide 1

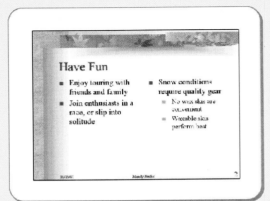

(b) Slide 2

(c) Slide 3

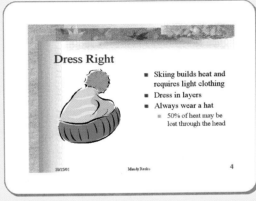

(d) Slide 4

FIGURE 2-76

3 Creating a Presentation in Outline View, Inserting Clip Art, and Applying Slide Transition and Animation Effects

Problem: Bernice Simpson, the director of student life at your school, has asked you to help her prepare a lecture for students on the topic of stress management. You suggest developing a short PowerPoint presentation to accompany her talk. The slide show will describe how stress develops, how it affects studying and sleeping patterns, and what techniques can combat stress. It will conclude with describing how combating stress will improve the students' overall health and outlook toward life. You create the presentation using the outline shown in Figure 2-77 on the next page. You then refine the presentation using clip art, slide transitions, and animation effects to create the slide show shown in Figures 2-78a through 2-78f on page PP 2.65. *Hint*: Use Help to solve this problem.

Instructions: Perform the following tasks.

1. Create a new presentation using the Notebook design template and the outline in Figure 2-77.
2. On the title slide, animate the three subtitles with the Dissolve custom animation effect.

(continued)

In the Lab

Creating a Presentation in Outline View, Inserting Clip Art, and Applying Slide Transition and Animation Effects *(continued)*

3. Use Figure 2-78c as a reference. Change the slide layout on Slide 3 to Clip Art & Text. Then insert clip art that has the keywords, office, people, people at work.

4. Change the slide layout on Slide 4 (Figure 2-78d) to Text & Clip Art. Insert clip art that has the keywords household, people, signs, symbols.

5. On Slide 5 (Figure 2-78e), change the slide layout to Clip Art & Text. Insert the clip art that has the keyword, graduations.

6. On Slide 6 (Figure 2-78f), change the slide layout to Text & Clip Art. Insert the clip art that has the keywords, academic, people, schools. Scale the clip art to 100%.

7. Add the current date, your name,

and slide number to the slide footer. Display the footer on all slides. Display your name and the current date on the outline header, and display the page number and the name of your school on the outline footer.

8. Apply the Wipe Down slide transition effect to Slides 2 through 6. Change the animation order so the clip art displays before the bulleted text. Apply the Split Horizontal In custom animation effect to all heading level 2 and 3 paragraphs on Slides 2 through 6. Apply the Fly From Right custom animation effect to the clip art on Slide 6.

9. Save the presentation on a floppy disk using the file name, Dealing With Stress.

10. Run the slide show.

11. Print the presentation outline. Print the presentation slides. Print a handout with all six slides arranged horizontally on one page. E-mail the presentation to Bernice using the address Bernice_Simpson@hotmail.com. Quit PowerPoint.

I. Dealing with Stress
    A. Managing Stress in Your Life
    B. Presented by
    C. The Office of Student Life
II. What Causes Stress
    A. You react physically and emotionally
    B. Positive stress helps you think and perform
    C. Negative stress makes you tense and frustrated – and will not go away
        1. 50% of you suffer negative stress regularly
        2. Symptoms include headaches, indigestion
III. How Can I Study Better?
    A. Keep good posture
    B. Take deep breaths
    C. Hide the clock
    D. Make a schedule
        1. Schedule time for homework and fun
IV. How Can I Sleep Better?
    A. Do not exercise at night
        1. Try morning workouts
    B. Avoid caffeine, alcohol, fried foods
    C. Turn off the phone
V. What Else Can I Do?
    A. Laugh and be flexible
    B. Imagine pleasant thoughts
        1. Graduating with honors
        2. Being with friends
VI. What Are the Benefits?
    A. You can improve immediately
    B. Changes will affect you forever
    C. You will be healthier and energized

FIGURE 2-77

In the Lab

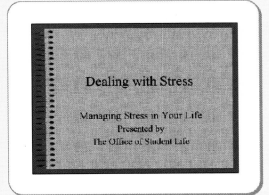

(a) Slide 1

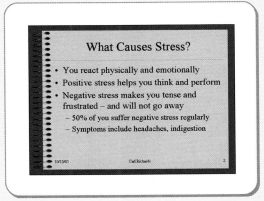

(b) Slide 2

(c) Slide 3

(d) Slide 4

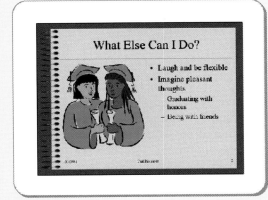

(e) Slide 5

(f) Slide 6

FIGURE 2-78

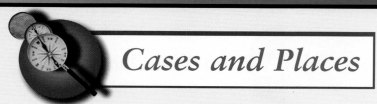

Cases and Places

The difficulty of these case studies varies: ▶ is the least difficult; ▶▶ is more difficult.

1 ▶ The dispatcher at the Brook Highlands Police Station is noticing an increase in the number of calls made to the emergency 911 telephone number. These calls, unfortunately, are not always emergencies. Community residents have been calling the number to obtain information on everything from the times of movies at the local theatre to the names of the local city trustees. Police Chief Wilbur Thiel wants to inform homeowners of the importance of using the 911 service cor-rectly. He created the following outline (Figure 2-79) and asks you to help him prepare an accompanying PowerPoint pre-sentation to show at the local mall and food stores. Using the concepts and techniques intro-duced in this project, together with Chief Thiel's outline, develop slides for a slide show. Include clip art and animation effects to add interest. Print the outline and slides as a one-page handout so they can be distrib-uted to residents at the conclusion of the presentation.

I. 911   A Call for Help
A. Presented by
B. Chief Wilbur Thiel
C. Brook Highlands Police Department
II. What It Is For
A. When you need an emergency response
 1. Fire
 2. Police
 3. Emergency Medical Personnel
B. When disaster occurs
 1. Tornadoes, earthquakes, floods
III. How To Help
A. Do not call for general information
 1. Consult local telephone directories
B. If you call by mistake
 1. Tell the dispatcher you have misdialed
C. Wait if you hear a recording
IV. Other Information
A. Tell the telephone company if you change your name or address
 1. This info displays on the dispatcher's screen
 2. The dispatcher relies on this information
B. Be certain your house number can be seen from the street

FIGURE 2-79

2 ▶▶ About 25 percent of the population suffers from the flu each year from October through May. Flu-related symptoms generally last for two weeks and include sudden headaches, chills, dry coughs, high fevers, and body aches. Serious complications are common, and an estimated 20,000 Americans die each year from the disease. Annual flu shots can help prevent the illness, and they are recommended for high-risk individuals such as the elderly and healthcare workers. Some drugs will help shorten the duration of the illness and decrease its severity if given within 48 hours after symptoms appear. General health tips include eating a balanced diet, getting enough rest, staying home when ill, exercising fre-quently, and washing hands frequently with warm, soapy water. Your campus' health services depart-ment wants to develop a presentation for students informing them about the flu and giving advice to stay healthy. Using the techniques introduced in the project, create a presentation about the flu. Include appropriate clip art and animation effects.

Microsoft **PowerPoint 2000**

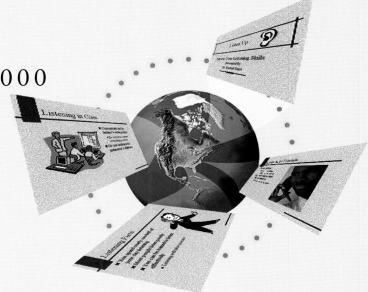

Microsoft PowerPoint 2000

Creating a Presentation on the Web Using PowerPoint

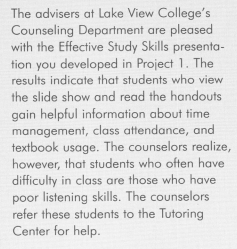

CASE PERSPECTIVE

The advisers at Lake View College's Counseling Department are pleased with the Effective Study Skills presentation you developed in Project 1. The results indicate that students who view the slide show and read the handouts gain helpful information about time management, class attendance, and textbook usage. The counselors realize, however, that students who often have difficulty in class are those who have poor listening skills. The counselors refer these students to the Tutoring Center for help.

Now the Tutoring Center wants you to develop a similar presentation describing how students can improve their listening skills. Dr. Rachel Sims, the Tutoring Center director, knows that students can improve their listening capability by practicing some techniques. Dr. Sims decides the most effective way to disseminate this information is to have you prepare a PowerPoint slide show highlighting these skills and then make the presentation available on the World Wide Web to all students. The slide show, called Listen Up, will contain this information along with clip art and animation effects for visual interest. Dr. Sims then wants you to publish the presentation on the World Wide Web.

Introduction

The graphic design power of PowerPoint allows you to create vibrant presentations that convey information in a clear, interesting manner. Some of these presentations are created for small, specific audiences, such as a subcommittee planning a department golf outing. In this case, the presentation may be shown in an office conference room. On the other hand, other presentations are designed for large, general audiences, such as workers at a corporation's various offices across the country learning about a new computer system being installed. These employees can view the presentation on their company's **intranet**, which is an internal network that uses Internet technologies. On a grand scale, you can inform the entire world about the contents of your presentation by posting your slide show to the World Wide Web. To publish to the World Wide Web, you need an **FTP (File Transfer Protocol)** program to copy your presentation and related files to an **Internet service provider (ISP)** computer.

PowerPoint allows you to create Web pages in three ways. First, you can start a new presentation, as you did in Projects 1 and 2 when you produced the Effective Study Skills and Searching for Scholarships presentations. PowerPoint provides a Web Presentation template in the **AutoContent Wizard** option when you start PowerPoint. The wizard provides design and content ideas to help you develop an effective slide show for an intranet or for the Internet by opening a sample presentation that you can alter by adding your own text and graphics.

Second, by using the **Save as Web Page** command, you can convert an existing presentation to a format compatible with popular Web browsers, such as Microsoft Internet Explorer. This command allows you to create a Web page from a single slide or from a multiple-slide presentation. This Web feature illustrates opening the Listen Up presentation on the Data Disk and then saving the presentation as a Web page. PowerPoint will start your default browser and open your HTML file so you can view the presentation (Figures 1a through 1e). Finally, you will edit the presentation, save it again, and view it in your default browser.

FIGURE 1

Third, in PowerPoint you can preview your presentation as a Web page. This action opens your presentation in your default Web browser without saving HTML files. You could use this feature to review and modify your work in progress until you develop a satisfactory presentation.

Because you are converting the Listen Up presentation on the Data Disk to a Web page, the first step in this project is to open the Listen Up file. Then you will save the file as a Web page and view the presentation in your default browser. For instructional purposes in this Web feature, you create and save your Web page on a floppy disk. At times, this saving process may be slow, so you must be patient.

Saving a PowerPoint Presentation as a Web Page

Once a PowerPoint slide show is complete, you want to save it as a Web page so you can publish and then view it in a Web browser. PowerPoint allows you to **publish** the presentation by saving the pages to a Web folder or to an FTP location. The procedures for publishing Web pages to the World Wide Web in Microsoft Office are discussed in Appendix B. When you publish your presentation to the Web, it is available for other computer users to view on the Internet or through other means.

You can save and then view the presentation in two ways. First, you can save the entire presentation as a Web page, quit PowerPoint, open your browser, and open the Web page in your browser. Second, in this Web feature you will combine these steps by saving the presentation to drive A and then viewing the presentation. In this case, PowerPoint automatically will start the browser and display your presentation. Perform the steps on the next page to save and publish the Listen Up presentation as a Web page.

More About 2000

The World Wide Web

More than three-fourths of college graduates use the World Wide Web for their job hunting efforts. They search for specific information on their careers, and then they turn to corporate Web sites for information on job vacancies and the annual report. They also e-mail their resumes to potential employers and post their resumes on online job services. For more information, visit the PowerPoint 2000 More About Web page (www.scsite.com/pp2000/more.htm) and click Jobs.

To Save a PowerPoint Presentation as a Web Page

1 **Start PowerPoint and then open the Listen Up file on the Data Disk. Reset your toolbars as described in Appendix C. Click the notes pane and then type** We receive most of our information by listening to others, yet few people have had listening training. **Click File on the menu bar and then point to Save as Web Page.**

PowerPoint opens and displays the presentation in normal view (Figure 2). The notes pane lets you type speaker notes to remind you of information you want to share with your audience. The File menu displays.

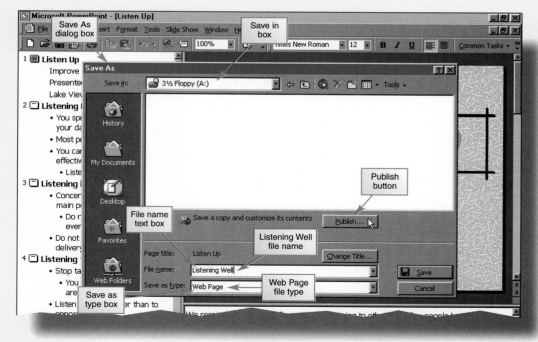

FIGURE 2

2 **Click Save as Web Page. When the Save As dialog box displays, type** Listening Well **in the File name text box.**

PowerPoint displays the Save As dialog box (Figure 3). Web Page displays in the Save as type box.

FIGURE 3

3 Click the Publish button. If the Office Assistant displays, click No, don't provide help now. When the Publish as Web Page dialog box displays, triple-click the Publish a copy as File name text box and then type A:\Listening Well in the text box. Be certain the Open published Web page in browser check box is selected. Point to the Publish button.

The Publish as Web Page dialog box displays (Figure 4). PowerPoint defaults to publishing the complete presentation, although you can choose to publish one or a range of slides. The Open published Web page in browser check box is selected, which means the Listening Well presentation will open in your default browser when you click the Publish button.

4 Click the Publish button.

PowerPoint saves the presentation as Listening Well.htm on your Data Disk in drive A. After a few seconds, PowerPoint opens your default Web browser in a separate window (Figure 5).

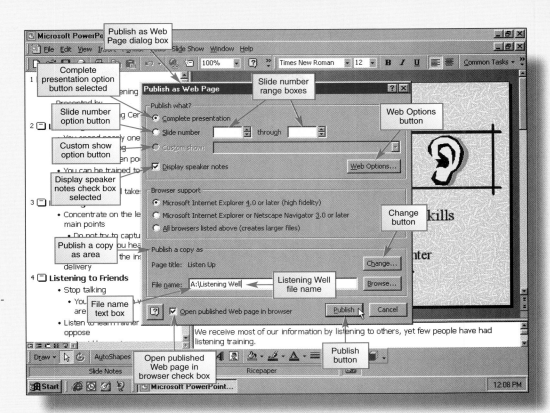

FIGURE 4

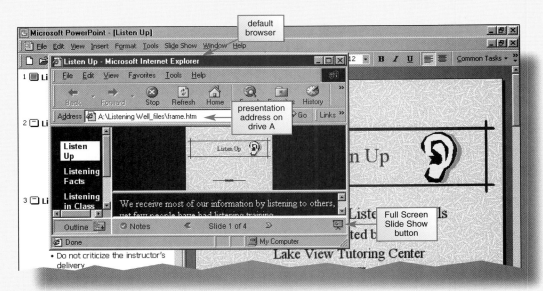

FIGURE 5

Other Ways

1. Press ALT+F, press G, type new file name, press SHIFT+TAB two times, press P, change file name in Publish copy as box, press ENTER

Publishing provides customizing options that are not available when you merely save the entire publication and then start your browser. The Publish as Web Page dialog box provides several options to customize your Web page. For example, you can change the page title that displays in the browser's title bar and history list. People visiting your Web site can store a link to your Web page, which will display in their favorites list. To change the page title, you click the Change button in the Publish a copy as area (see Figure 4 on the previous page) and then type a new title.

The Publish what? area of the Publish as Web Page dialog box allows you to publish parts of your presentation. PowerPoint defaults to publishing the complete presentation, but you can select specific slides by clicking the Slide number option button and then entering the range of desired slide numbers. In addition, you can publish a custom show you have created previously. A **custom show** is a subset of your presentation that contains slides tailored for a specific audience. For example, you may want to show Slides 1, 2, and 4 to one group and Slides 1, 3, and 4 to another group.

You can choose to publish only the publication slides, and not the accompanying speaker notes. By default, the **Display speaker notes check box** is selected in the Publish what? area. You typed speaker notes for Slide 1 of this presentation, so they will display in the browser window. If you do not want to make your notes available to users, click the Display speaker notes check box to remove the check mark.

The Web Options button in the Publish what? area allows you to select options to determine how your presentation will look when viewed in a Web browser. You can choose options such as allowing slide animation to show, selecting the screen size, and having the notes and outline panes display when viewing the presentation in a Web browser.

Now that you have opened the Listen Up file and saved the presentation as a Web page, you want to view the slide show using your default browser.

Viewing a Presentation as a Web Page

PowerPoint makes it easy to create a presentation and then view how it will display on an intranet or the World Wide Web. By viewing your slide show, you can decide which features look good and which need modification. The left side of the window contains the outline pane showing a table of contents consisting of each slide's title text. You can click the **Expand/Collapse Outline button** below the outline pane to view the complete slide text. The right side displays the complete slide in the slide pane. The speaker notes display in the notes pane under the slide pane. Perform the following steps to view your Listening Well presentation as a Web page.

More About

Speaker Notes

When you prepare speaker notes for your presentation, remember that audiences want to hear you explain the concepts on the slides. Each slide should list the key points, and your notes should guide you with the supplemental information you will deliver. Your listeners can retain a maximum of six major points you make, so these facts and your explanation should comprise the majority of your presentation. For more information, visit the PowerPoint 2000 More About Web page (www.scsite.com/pp2000/more.htm) and click Speaker Notes.

More About

Viewing Presentations

The PowerPoint Viewer allows users to see your Web presentation without installing PowerPoint. This application is handy when you are going to deliver your slide show at a remote site on a computer other than your own. Microsoft distributes this software free of charge. For more information, visit the PowerPoint 2000 More About Web page (www.scsite.com/pp2000/more.htm) and click Viewer.

Steps ## To View a Presentation as a Web Page

1 If necessary, double-click the Microsoft Internet Explorer title bar to maximize the browser window. Point to the Full Screen Slide Show button.

The title text and ear clip art of the first slide of the Listening Well presentation display in the slide pane in the browser window (Figure 6). The outline pane contains the table of contents, which consists of the title text of each slide. The notes pane displays the speaker notes.

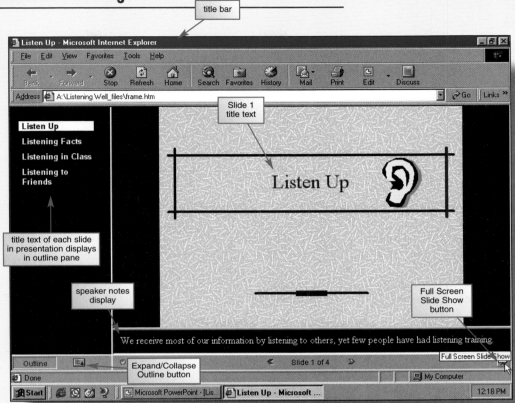

FIGURE 6

2 **Click the Full Screen Slide Show button.**

Slide 1 fills the entire screen (Figure 7). The Slide 1 title text and ear clip art display.

3 **Click to display the first line of the Object Area placeholder text.**

The first line of the Slide 1 Object Area placeholder text displays.

4 **Continue clicking each slide in the presentation. When the black slide displays, click it. Point to the Expand/ Collapse Outline button below the outline pane.**

Each of the four slides in the Listening Well presentation displays. The message on the black slide, End of slide show, click to exit., indicates the conclusion of the slide show.

5 **Click the Expand/ Collapse Outline button.**

The text of each slide displays in the outline pane (Figure 8). Lines display to the left and under the text of the current slide in this pane. To display only the title of each slide, you would click the Expand/ Collapse Outline button again.

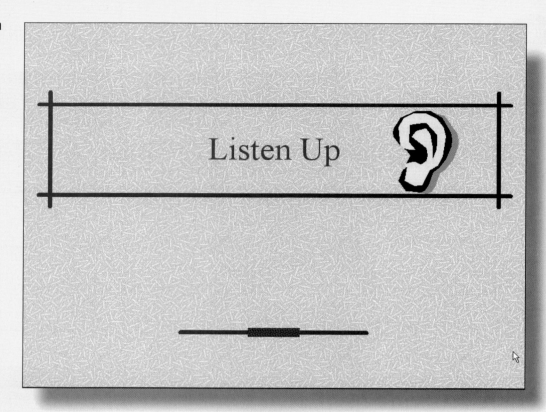

FIGURE 7

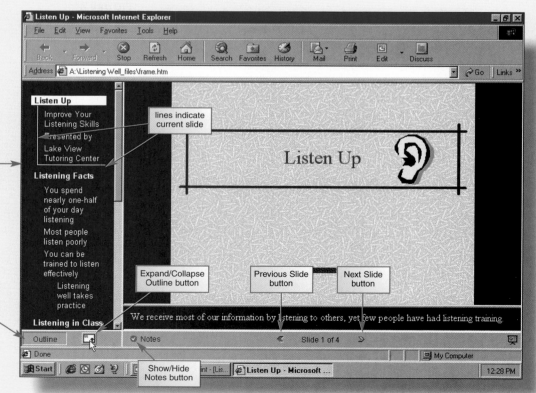

FIGURE 8

You can alter the browser window by choosing to display or hide the outline and notes panes. To eliminate the outline pane, click the **Show/Hide Outline button** below the outline pane. If you later want to display the outline pane, you would click the Show/Hide Outline button again. Similarly, the **Show/Hide Notes button** below the slide pane allows you to display or conceal the speaker notes on a particular slide.

To advance through the Web pages, click the **Next Slide button** below the slide pane. Likewise, to display a slide appearing earlier in the slide show, click the **Previous Slide button**.

Editing a Web Page through a Browser

Dr. Rachel Sims, the Tutoring Center director, informs you that she wants her name to display on the title slide so that students can contact her for further information. She suggests you change the last line of the Slide 1, Lake View Tutoring Center, to her name. Perform the following steps to modify Slide 1.

More About

Persuading Audiences

As you choose to show or hide your outline and notes, consider the needs of your audience. Some researchers believe listeners are more attentive on Sundays, Mondays, and Tuesdays because they are more relaxed than at the middle and end of a week. Thus, you may need to provide more information via the outline and notes when your audience is less focused.

 To Edit a Web Page through a Browser

1 **Point to the Edit button** on the **Standard Buttons toolbar.**

Slide 1 displays in the browser (Figure 9). The ScreenTip, Edit with Microsoft PowerPoint for Windows, indicates you can modify the presentation using PowerPoint directly from the browser window. Your computer may indicate other editing options, such as using Windows Notepad.

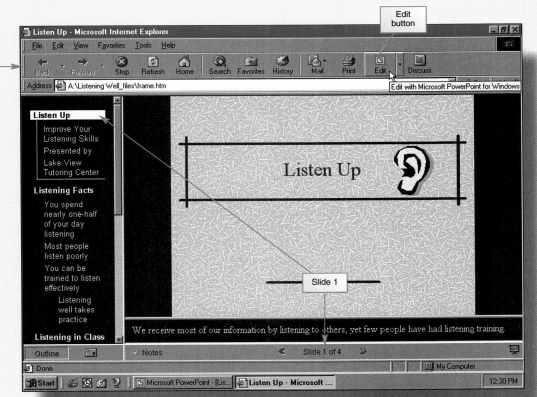

FIGURE 9

2 **Click the Edit button. Triple-click the last second level line, Lake View Tutoring Center.**

When you click the Edit button, PowerPoint returns control to the PowerPoint window, as indicated by the title bar and the recessed Microsoft PowerPoint – [Listening Well] button (Figure 10). A selection rectangle displays around the Object Area placeholder text. The last line is highlighted.

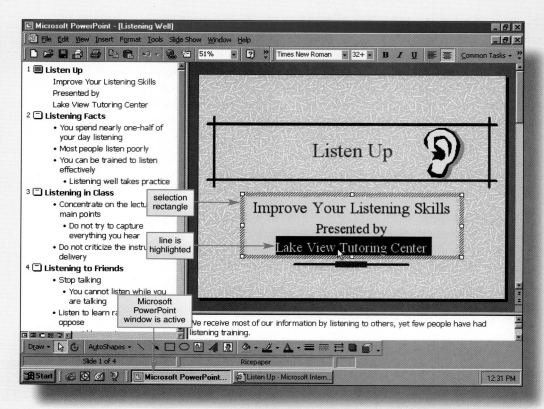

FIGURE 10

3 **Type** Dr. Rachel Sims **and then point to the Save button on the Standard toolbar.**

The last line is modified (Figure 11).

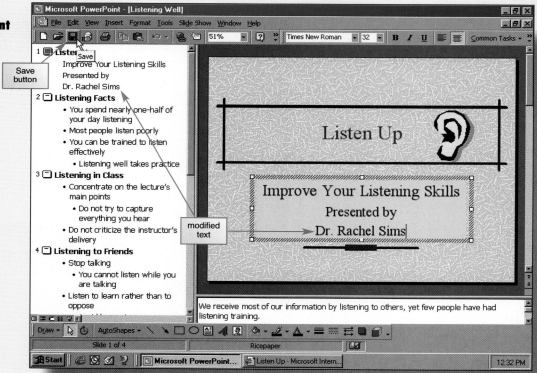

FIGURE 11

4 Click the Save button. Point to the Listen Up – Microsoft Internet Explorer button on the taskbar.

PowerPoint saves the changes to the Listening Well.htm file on the Data Disk. The buttons on the taskbar indicate that both PowerPoint and the browser are open (Figure 12).

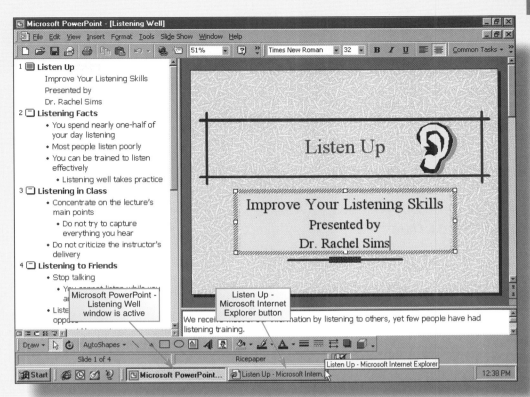

FIGURE 12

5 Click the Listen Up – Microsoft Internet Explorer button and then point to the Refresh button on the Standard Buttons toolbar.

The browser window displays the title text and clip art on Slide 1 (Figure 13). Clicking the Refresh button displays the most current version of the Web page.

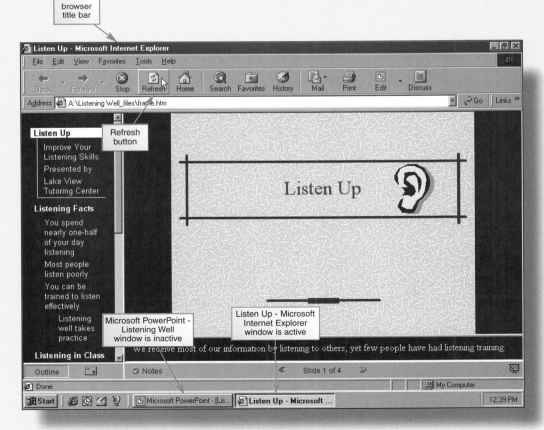

FIGURE 13

 **6** **Click the Refresh button. Click the slide three times to display all the Object Area placeholder text. Point to the Close button on the browser title bar.**

The complete Slide 1 displays (Figure 14). The last line reflects the editing changes.

 **7** **Click the Close button.**

PowerPoint closes the Listening Well Web presentation, and the PowerPoint window redisplays in normal view.

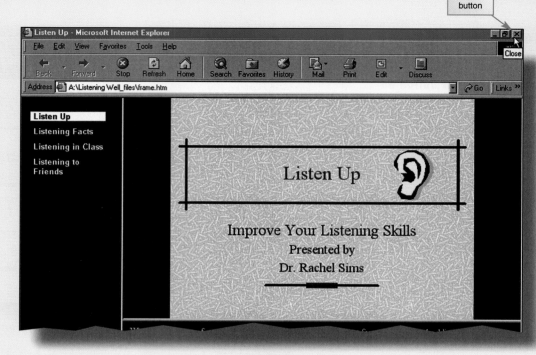

FIGURE 14

The Web page now is complete. The next step is to make your Web presentation available to others on your network, an intranet, or the World Wide Web. Ask your instructor how you can publish your presentation.

CASE PERSPECTIVE SUMMARY

Students attending Dr. Rachel Sims' lecture in the Tutoring Center should learn techniques that will improve their listening skills. Your Listen Up slide show will help to reinforce the key points presented, including facts about listening effectively. The students will be able to apply the theories when they are in class and with their friends. Dr. Sims can publish your presentation to the World Wide Web so that students who cannot attend the lecture also can gain the useful information presented.

Web Feature Summary

This Web feature introduced you to creating a Web page by saving an existing PowerPoint presentation as an HTML file. You then viewed the presentation as a Web page in your default browser. Next, you modified Slide 1. Finally, you reviewed your Slide 1 change using your default browser. Now that your Listen Up presentation is converted to a Web page, you can post the file to an intranet or to the World Wide Web.

What You Should Know

Having completed this Web feature, you now should be able to perform the following tasks:

▶ Edit a Web Page through a Browser *(PPW 1.9)*
▶ Save a PowerPoint Presentation as a Web Page *(PPW 1.4)*

▶ View a Presentation as a Web Page *(PPW 1.7)*

In the Lab

1 Creating a Web Page from the Studying Presentation

Problem: The advisers at Seaview College want to expand the visibility of the Effective Study Skills presentation created for them in Project 1. They believe the World Wide Web would be an excellent vehicle to help students throughout the campus and at other colleges, and they have asked you to help transfer the presentation to the Internet.

Instructions: Start PowerPoint and then perform the following steps with a computer.

1. Open the Studying presentation shown in Figures 1-2a through 1-2d on page PP 1.9 that you created in Project 1. (If you did not complete Project 1, see your instructor for a copy of the presentation.)
2. Use the Save as Web Page command on the File menu to convert and publish the presentation. Save the Web page using the file name, Effective Studying.
3. View the presentation in a browser.
4. Modify Slide 3 by adding a First level line that states, Arrive a few minutes before class starts, as the last line on the screen.
5. View the modified Web page in a browser.
6. Ask your instructor for instructions on how to post your Web page so others may have access to it.

2 Creating a Web Page from the Scholarship Presentation

Problem: The Searching for Scholarships presentation you developed in Project 2 for the Office of Financial Aid is generating much interest. Students are visiting the office, which has moved to Room 4321, and requesting a date to hear the lecture and to see the slide show. Dr. Mary Halen, the Financial Aid director, has asked you to post the presentation to the school's intranet.

Instructions: Start PowerPoint and then perform the following steps with a computer.

1. Open the Searching for Scholarships presentation shown in Figures 2-1a through 2-1f on page PP 2.5 that you created in Project 2. (If you did not complete Project 2, see your instructor for a copy of the presentation.)
2. Use the Save as Web Page command on the File menu to convert and publish the presentation. Save the Web page using the file name, Scholarship Sources.
3. View the presentation in a browser.
4. Modify Slide 2 by changing the room number to 4321.
5. Modify Slide 4 by changing the word, athletics, to the word, writing, in the Second level paragraph.
6. View the modified Web page in a browser.
7. Ask your instructor for instructions on how to post your Web page so others may have access to it.

3 Creating a Personal Presentation

Problem: You have decided to apply for a job at a company several hundred miles from your campus. You are preparing to send your resume and cover letter to the human resources department, and you want to develop a unique way to publicize your computer expertise. You decide to create a personalized PowerPoint presentation emphasizing your academic strengths and extra-curricular activities. You refer to this presentation in your cover letter and inform the company officials that they can view this presentation because you have saved the presentation as a Web page and posted the page to your school's server.

Instructions: Start PowerPoint and then perform the following steps with a computer.

1. Prepare a presentation highlighting your academic strengths. Create a title slide and at least three additional slides. Use appropriate clip art, animation effects, and slide transition effects.
2. Use the Save as Web Page command to convert and publish the presentation. Save the Web page using the file name, Supplemental Information.
3. View the presentation in a browser.
4. Ask your instructor for instructions on how to post your Web page so others may have access to it.

Microsoft **PowerPoint 2000**

Microsoft PowerPoint 2000

PROJECT

3

Using Embedded Visuals to Enhance a Slide Show

You will have mastered the material in this project when you can:

- Create exciting presentations using embedded visuals
- Import an outline created in Microsoft Word
- Create a slide background using a picture
- Customize graphical bullets
- Create and embed an organization chart
- Insert a table into a slide
- Create and format a table
- Create a PowerPoint clip art object
- Scale objects
- Apply slide transition and text preset animation effects
- Print handouts

Preparation, Palpitations, & Exciting Presentations

If the thought of getting up to speak in front of a group of strangers gives you palpitations, you are not unusual or in a class by yourself. On the list of the things that individuals fear most, public speaking leads the list.

Although speakers sometimes are faced with obstacles of their own making, if those moments unnerve you out of all proportion, you may think of taking some assertiveness training, or joining groups such as Toastmasters International or Dale Carnegie. An easier way, however, is to personalize your presentations and create a one-of-a-kind, eye-catching look that turns the focus away from your nervousness.

Accomplished speakers agree that the key to overcoming nervousness and hesitation when giving a public speech is preparation. To help you prepare, you can create your presentation with PowerPoint, as you will do in this project. Using a template, you will learn the techniques to enhance your slide show by adding visuals, slide transitions, and animations.

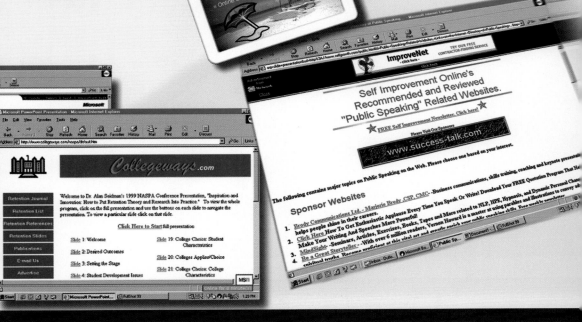

Appropriate visuals help set the tone, which in turn, helps you create a relaxed atmosphere, putting you at ease with your listeners. Then, build your confidence through practice; and you will leave your audience eager for more.

Fortunately, this help is available because leaders in business, government, science, religion, and virtually all vocations agree that the ability to present one's views clearly, while keeping the audience involved, is fundamental to a successful career. Though you probably spend more time in front of the lectern than behind it, your college years are a good time to get a head start on the competition by learning how to develop

power presentations on your PC.

Even with this help, however, it is not enough merely to present dry, static details. A presentation needs zest to grab and hold the attention of today's sophisticated audiences.

Among PowerPoint's many features are the capabilities of adding organizational charts, graphs, and tables in a slide show to give the audience a visual association to help assimilate the speaker's words. Going one step further, a variety of pleasing transitions can be achieved to make one image blend into the next, rather than making abrupt frame changes.

Build effects allow a concept to be presented one point at a time, preventing the visual overload that occurs if all the information is presented at once. In psychology, this is called, chunking, recognizing that the human brain absorbs information more readily in small bites than in one huge mass.

Finally, turning your preparation into a successful presentation, the palpitations subside, and the excitement remains.

Microsoft PowerPoint 2000

Using Embedded Visuals to Enhance a Slide Show

C A S E   P E R S P E C T I V E

The 1960s film classic *Where the Boys Are* affirmed the fact that students just want to get away and have fun during Spring Break in Ft. Lauderdale. Since that time, millions of young people have made their way to sunny destinations for a week of relaxation and fun. Today, students have a multitude of places from which to choose, most notably Daytona Beach and Key West in Florida and South Padre Island in Texas.

The Student Government Association (SGA) at your school wants to sponsor a college-wide trip to the three destinations. The SGA president, Marla Pervan, has asked you to help with the marketing efforts. She knows you have extensive computer experience and wants you to develop a PowerPoint presentation that advertises the three trips and the highlights of each. She has asked you to use an appropriate photograph as a background and clip art for visual appeal. You agree to create the project, which will be published on your college's intranet for the student body to view.

Create Exciting Presentations Using Embedded Visuals

Bulleted lists and simple graphics are the starting point for most presentations, but they can become boring. Advanced PowerPoint users want exciting presentations — something to impress their audiences. With PowerPoint, it is easy to develop impressive presentations by creating a custom background, customizing bullets, embedding organization charts and tables, and creating new graphics.

One problem you may experience when developing a presentation is finding the proper graphic to convey your message. One way to overcome this obstacle is to modify clip art from the Microsoft Clip Gallery. Another solution is to create a table. PowerPoint design templates offer a limited number of slide backgrounds and allow you to create your own background using a picture or clip art.

This project introduces several techniques to make your presentations more exciting.

Project Three — Fun in the Sun Spring Break

Project 3 expands on PowerPoint's basic presentation features by importing existing files and embedding objects. This project creates a presentation that is used to promote the Student Government Associations' Spring Break trips to Daytona Beach, Key West, and South Padre Island (Figures 3-1a through 3-1e). The project begins by building the presentation from an outline created in Microsoft Word and saved as a Rich Text Format (RTF) file. Then, several objects are inserted to customize the presentation. These objects include customized bullets, an organization chart, a table, and clip art.

(e) Slide 5

(d) Slide 4

(c) Slide 3

(b) Slide 2

(a) Slide 1

FIGURE 3-1

Importing Text Created in Another Application

In your classes, you may be asked to make an oral presentation. For example, in your English composition class, your instructor may require you to summarize a research paper you wrote. You can use a PowerPoint presentation to help you construct and deliver your presentation.

PowerPoint can use text created in other programs to create a new slide show. This text may have originated in Microsoft Word or another word processing program, or it may have appeared in a Web page. Microsoft Word files use the **.doc extension** in their file names. Text originating in other word processing programs should be saved in Rich Text Format (.rtf) or plain text format (.txt), and Web page documents should have an HTML extension (.htm).

An outline created in Microsoft Word or another word processing program works well as a shell for a PowerPoint presentation. Instead of typing text in PowerPoint, as you did in Projects 1 and 2, you can import this outline, add visual elements such as clip art, photos, graphical bullets, animation, and slide transitions, and ultimately create an impressive slide show. If you did not create an outline to help you write your word processing document, you can create one by saving your paper with a new file name, removing all text except the topic heading, and then saving the file again.

The advantage of using an outline saved as a Microsoft Word document is that text attributes and outline heading levels are maintained. Documents saved as plain text files can be opened in PowerPoint but do not maintain text attributes and outline heading levels. Consequently, each paragraph becomes a slide title.

To create a presentation using an existing outline, select All Outlines from the Files of type box in the Open dialog box. When you select **All Outlines**, PowerPoint displays a list of outlines. Next, you select the file that contains the outline. PowerPoint then creates a presentation using your outline. Each major heading in your outline becomes a slide title, and subheadings become a bulleted list.

Opening an Outline Created in Another Application

After starting PowerPoint, the first step in this project is to open an outline created in Microsoft Word. PowerPoint can produce slides from an outline created in Microsoft Word or another word processing program if the outline was saved in a format that PowerPoint can recognize. The outline you import in this project was saved as an RTF file (.rtf extension).

Opening an outline into PowerPoint requires two steps. First, you must tell PowerPoint you are opening an existing presentation. Then, to open the outline, you need to select the proper file type from the Files of type box in the Open dialog box. The following steps summarize how to start a new presentation and open an outline created in Microsoft Word. To reset your toolbars and menus so they display exactly as shown in this book, follow the steps outlined in Appendix C. Perform the following steps to start a new presentation and open an outline.

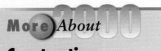

More About

Constructing Presentations

Mark Twain once said, "The difference between the right word and almost the right word is the difference between 'lightning' and 'lightning bug.'" The goal in constructing powerful, PowerPoint presentations is to convey information precisely. Use the thesaurus, readability statistics, and other tools available in a word processing program, such as Microsoft Word, to help develop effective outlines to import into your slide shows.

To Start PowerPoint and Open an Outline

1 **Insert your Data Disk into drive A. Click the Start button on the taskbar. Click New Office Document on the Start menu. If necessary, click the General tab in the New Office Document dialog box.**

2 **Double-click the Blank Presentation icon. Click the Cancel button when the New Slide dialog box displays.**

PowerPoint begins Presentation1 using the Default Design template.

3 **Click File on the menu bar and then point to Open.**

The File menu displays (Figure 3-2). You want to open the outline created in Microsoft Word and saved on your Data Disk.

4 **Click Open. Click the Look in box arrow and then click 3½ Floppy (A:). Click the Files of type box arrow and then scroll down and click All Outlines.**

The Open dialog box displays (Figure 3-3). A list displays the outline files that PowerPoint can open. Your list may be different depending on the software installed on your computer.

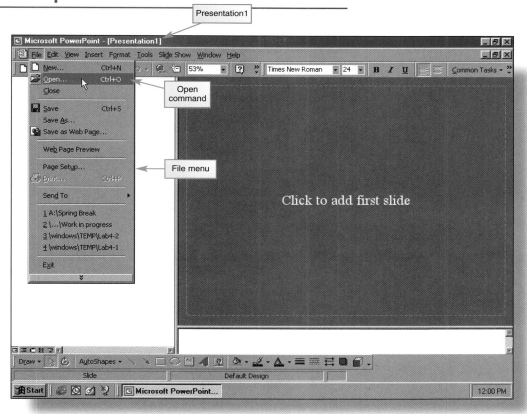

FIGURE 3-2

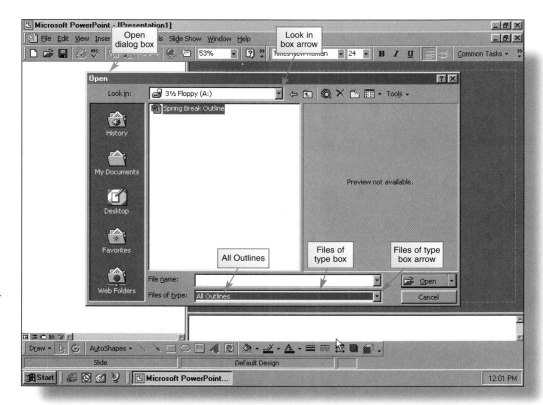

FIGURE 3-3

5 Double-click Spring Break Outline in the list.

PowerPoint opens the Spring Break Outline (Figure 3-4). The outline displays in the outline pane, and Slide 1 displays in the slide pane. Bullets display in the outline text, indicating the slide layout is Bulleted List.

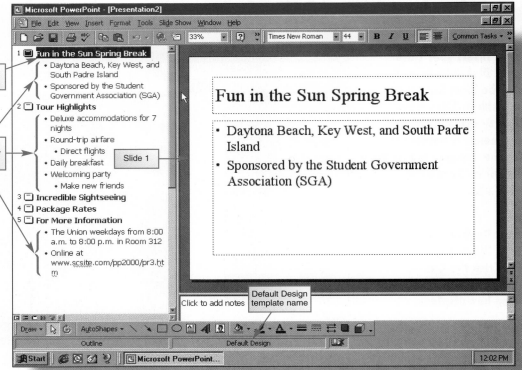

FIGURE 3-4

Copying Slides

Opening a Microsoft Word outline is one way of deriving information for a slide show. Another way is to copy slides from other presentations directly into your new presentation. To do so, display the slide in your presentation that precedes the slide you want to insert, on the Insert menu click Slides from Files, select the presentation containing the slide you want to copy, click Display, select the slide or slides you want to copy to your presentation, and then click Insert. If you want to copy an entire presentation, click Insert All.

When PowerPoint opens a file created in Microsoft Word or a presentation graphics program, such as Harvard Graphics or Lotus Freelance, it picks up the outline structure from the styles used in the file. As a result, heading level one becomes a title, heading level two becomes the first level of text, and so on.

A file saved as a Text Only file in Microsoft Word is saved without formatting. This **plain text file**, which has the **.txt file extension**, does not contain heading styles, so PowerPoint uses the tabs at the beginning of paragraphs to define the outline structure. Imported outlines can contain up to nine outline levels, whereas PowerPoint outlines are limited to six levels (one for titles and five for text). When you import an outline, all text in outline levels six through nine is treated as outline level six.

Changing Presentation Design Templates

Recall that **design templates** format the look of your presentation. You can change the design template any time you want to change the appearance of your presentation, not just when you create a new presentation. The current design template is Default Design. The Whirlpool design template compliments the custom slide background you will create later in this project. Perform this step to change design templates.

TO CHANGE DESIGN TEMPLATES

 Double-click Default Design on the status bar. Scroll down and double-click the Whirlpool design template in the Presentation Designs list in the Apply Design Template dialog box.

PowerPoint applies the Whirlpool design template as indicated by the change to the layout and bullets (Figure 3-5).

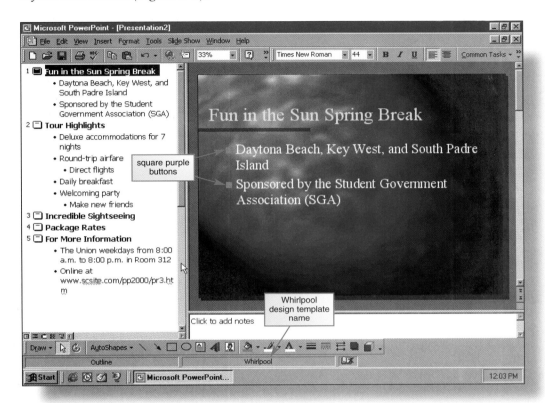

FIGURE 3-5

Recall that slide attributes change when you select a different design template. The Whirlpool design template format determines the slide attributes of the slide master and the title master. For example, when you compare Figure 3-4 with your screen, you see the bullets changed from small black dots to purple squares.

Changing the Font

When you imported the Spring Break Outline file, PowerPoint retained the Times New Roman font used in the Microsoft Word document. You want to change this font to Tahoma, which is the font used in the Whirlpool design template. Perform the steps on the next page to change the font from Times New Roman to Tahoma.

Other Ways

1. Click Common Tasks button on Formatting toolbar, click Apply Design Template, click Whirlpool, click Apply

2. On Format menu click Apply Design Template, scroll down to select Whirlpool, click Apply

To Change the Font

1 **Click Edit on the menu bar and then point to Select All (Figure 3-6).**

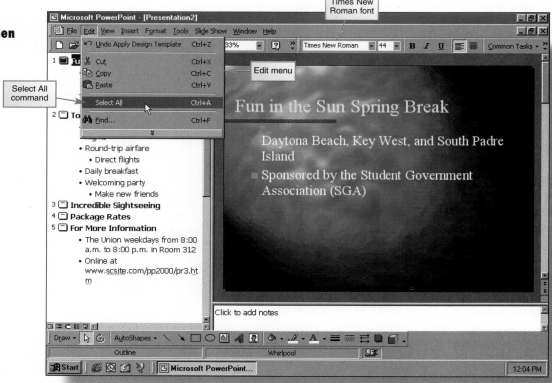

FIGURE 3-6

2 **Click Select All.**

All characters in the outline are selected (Figure 3-7).

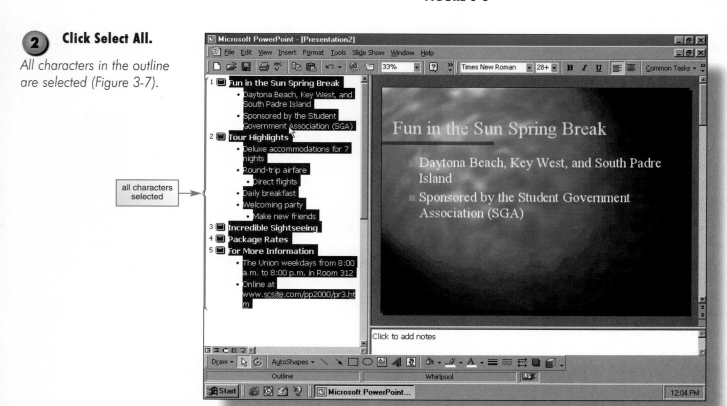

FIGURE 3-7

3 **Click the Font box arrow on the Formatting toolbar, scroll through the list until Tahoma displays, and then point to Tahoma.**

PowerPoint displays a list of available fonts (Figure 3-8). Your list of available fonts may be different depending on the type of printer you are using.

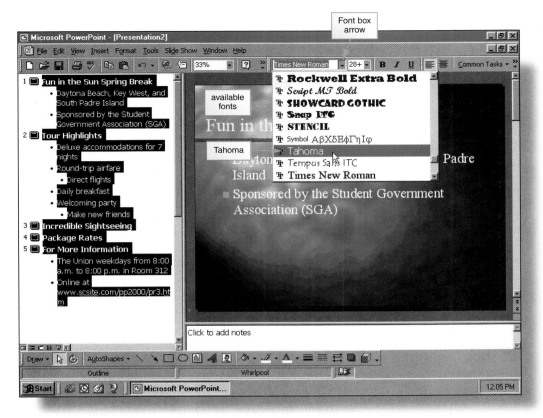

FIGURE 3-8

4 **Click Tahoma.**

Slide 1 displays with the Tahoma font (Figure 3-9).

5 **Click anywhere on Slide 1 except the Title Area or the Object Area placeholders.**

The outline text no longer is selected.

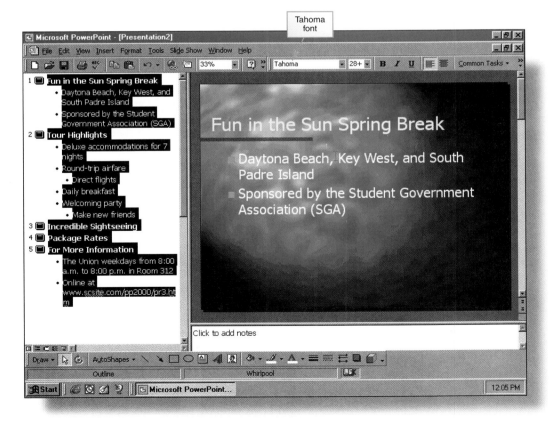

FIGURE 3-9

Saving the Presentation

You now should save your presentation because you created a presentation from an outline file and changed the design template and font. The following steps summarize how to save a presentation.

TO SAVE A PRESENTATION

1 Click the Save button on the Standard toolbar.

2 Type Spring Break in the File name text box.

3 Click the Save in box arrow. Click 3½ Floppy (A:) in the Save in list.

4 Click the Save button in the Save As dialog box.

The presentation is saved on the floppy disk in drive A with the file name Spring Break. This file name displays on the title bar.

Creating a Custom Background

PowerPoint has a variety of design templates in the Presentation Designs folder. Sometimes, however, you may want a background that is not found in one of the design templates, such as the picture of the beach in Figures 3-1a through 3-1e on page PP 3.5. PowerPoint allows you to create that background by inserting a picture. PowerPoint also allows you to customize the background color, shading, pattern, and texture.

You perform two tasks to create the customized background for this presentation. First, you change the slide layout of Slide 1 to the Title Slide AutoLayout. Then, you create the slide background by inserting a picture of a beach.

The next two sections explain how to create a slide background using a picture.

Changing the Slide Layout to Title Slide

When you import an outline to create a presentation, PowerPoint assumes the text is bulleted text. Because Slide 1 is the title slide for this presentation, you want to change the AutoLayout to the Title Slide AutoLayout.

The following steps summarize how to change the layout of Slide 1 to the Title Slide layout.

TO CHANGE THE SLIDE LAYOUT TO TITLE SLIDE

1 Click the Common Tasks button on the Formatting toolbar.

2 Click Slide Layout on the Common Tasks button menu.

3 Double-click Title Slide, the first AutoLayout in the Slide Layout dialog box.

Slide 1 displays with the Title Slide AutoLayout (Figure 3-10).

Backgrounds

Some researchers have determined that audience members prefer viewing photographs instead of line art on a slide, although the line art may be more effective in carrying the desired message. In addition, viewers prefer color graphics as compared to black-and-white objects. The various colors, however, do not affect the amount of information retained. For more information, visit the PowerPoint 2000 Project 3 More About page (www.scsite.com/pp2000/more.htm) and click Backgrounds.

new
presentation title

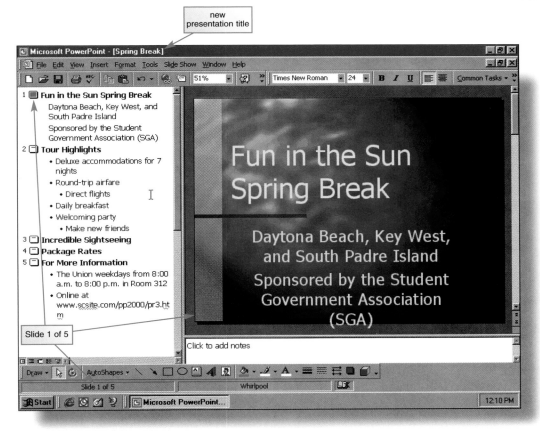

FIGURE 3-10

PowerPoint provides two alternative methods to double-clicking the AutoLayout in Step 3 above. The first alternative is to type the AutoLayout number of one of the 24 AutoLayouts and then press the ENTER key. A layout number corresponds to each AutoLayout, with the four slides in the first row numbered one through four from left to right, the next row of AutoLayouts numbered five through eight, and so on. The second alternative is to type the AutoLayout number and then click the Apply button. PowerPoint interprets the number you type as the corresponding AutoLayout and applies it when you press the ENTER key (alternative one) or click the Apply button (alternative two). For example, the Title Slide AutoLayout is layout number one. When the Slide Layout dialog box displays, you would type the number 1 and then press the ENTER key instead of double-clicking the Title Slide AutoLayout.

Changing the Font Size

When you imported the Spring Break Outline file, PowerPoint placed the first line, Fun in the Sun Spring Break, in the Title Area placeholder and the next two paragraphs in the Object Area placeholder. The text in the Object Area placeholder spills out of the slide, so you want to reduce the font size of the second paragraph, Sponsored by the Student Government Association (SGA).

The steps on the next page summarize how to change the last paragraph on Slide 1 from a font size of 40 to a font size of 24.

More About

AutoLayouts

PowerPoint's AutoLayouts give a balanced, professional look to your presentations. In addition to the AutoLayouts used thus far in this text, additional layouts include areas for media clips, charts, title text, and a maximum of four objects, and one large object. The Blank AutoLayout allows you to add text and graphic elements and place them anywhere on the slide.

TO CHANGE THE FONT SIZE

1 Click to the immediate left of the letter S at the beginning of the second paragraph in the Object Area placeholder, Sponsored by the Student Government Association (SGA). Press the ENTER key to insert a blank line.

2 Triple-click this second paragraph.

3 Click the Font Size box arrow on the Formatting toolbar and then click 24 in the list.

The last paragraph in the Object Area placeholder, Sponsored by the Student Government Association (SGA), moves toward the bottom of the slide and displays in font size 24 (Figure 3-11).

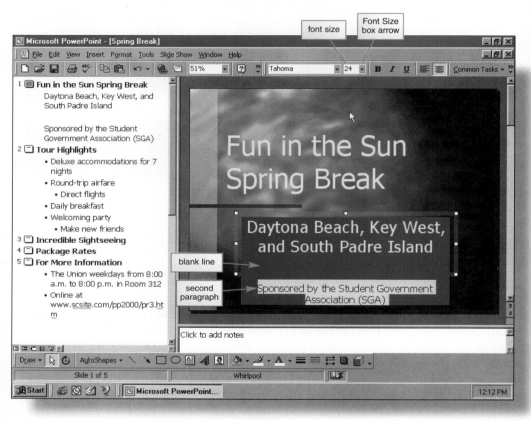

FIGURE 3-11

Customizing Pictures

You can crop pictures added to slides so the focus is on the essential elements of the picture and not the extraneous details. To crop a picture, first select the picture and then click the Crop button on the Picture toolbar. Place the cropping tool over a sizing handle and drag to frame the portion of the picture you want to include on your slide. You also can specify an exact percentage for the object's height and width. If you plan to save your PowerPoint slide show as a Web page, size the picture to a specific dimension less than 50 percent. You later can restore the cropped picture to its original image.

Inserting a Picture to Create a Custom Background

The next step in creating the Spring Break presentation is to insert a picture of a beach to create a custom background. In PowerPoint, a **picture** is any graphic created in another application. Pictures usually are saved in one of two **graphic formats**: bitmap or vector.

This beach picture is a **bitmap graphic**, which is a piece of art that has been stored as a series of small dots, called pixels, that form shapes and lines. A **pixel**, short for **picture element**, is one dot in a grid. A picture that is produced on the computer screen or on paper by a printer is composed of thousands of these dots. Just as a bit is the smallest unit of information a computer can process, a pixel is the smallest element that can display or that print hardware and software can manipulate in creating letters, numbers, or graphics. The beach picture you use in this project has the dimensions of 600 pixels wide and 396 pixels high.

Bitmap graphics are created by digital cameras or in paint programs such as Microsoft Paint. Bitmap graphics also can be produced from **digitizing** art, pictures, or photographs by passing the artwork through a scanner. A **scanner** is a hardware device that converts lines and shading into combinations of the binary digits 0 and 1 by sensing different intensities of light and dark. The scanner shines a beam of light on the picture being scanned. The beam passes back and forth across the picture, sending a digitized signal to the computer's memory. A **digitized signal** is the conversion of input, such as the lines in a drawing, into a series of discrete units represented by the binary digits 0 and 1. **Scanned pictures** are bitmap pictures and have jagged edges. The jagged edges are caused by the individual pixels that create the picture. Bitmap graphics also are known as **raster images**. Pictures in the Microsoft Clip Gallery that have the file extensions of **.jpg** and **.bmp** are examples of bitmap graphic files.

Bitmap files cannot be ungrouped and converted to smaller PowerPoint object groups. They can be manipulated, however, in an imaging program such as Microsoft Photo Editor. This program allows you to rotate or flip the pictures and then insert them in your slides.

The other graphic format in which pictures are stored is vector graphics. A **vector graphic** is a piece of art that has been created by a drawing program such as CorelDRAW or Adobe Illustrator. The clip art pictures used in Project 2 and in this project are vector graphic objects. In contrast to the patterns of individual dots (pixels) that comprise bitmap graphics, vector graphics are created as a collection of lines. Vector graphic files store data either as picture descriptions or as calculations. These files describe a picture mathematically as a set of instructions for creating the objects in the picture. These mathematical descriptions determine the position, length, and direction in which the lines are to be drawn. These calculations allow the drawing program to re-create the picture on the screen as necessary. Because vector graphic objects are described mathematically, they also can be layered, rotated, and magnified with relative ease. Vector graphics also are known as **object-oriented pictures**. Clip art pictures in the Microsoft Clip Gallery that have the file extension of **.wmf** are examples of vector files. Vector files can be ungrouped and manipulated by their component objects. You will ungroup the umbrella clip art used on Slide 5 in this project.

PowerPoint allows you to insert vector files because it uses **graphic filters** to convert the various graphic formats into a format PowerPoint can use. These filters are installed with the initial PowerPoint installation or can be added later by running the Setup program.

The Spring Break presentation will be used to help promote the Student Government Association's trip, so you want to emphasize the beautiful beach scenery. To create the desired effect, you insert a picture of a beach to cover the Whirlpool design template.

Perform the steps on the next page to create a custom background.

More *About*

Digitizing

Digitizing produces some dazzling objects that add interest to presentations. Many artists have traded their paint brushes and easels for the mouse and monitor. To view some of their creations, visit the PowerPoint 2000 Project 3 More About page (www. scsite.com/pp2000/more.htm) and click Digitizing.

Steps To Insert a Picture to Create a Custom Background

1 **Right-click anywhere on Slide 1 except the Title Area or the Object Area placeholders. Click Background on the shortcut menu. When the Background dialog box displays, point to the Background fill box arrow.**

The Background dialog box displays (Figure 3-12).

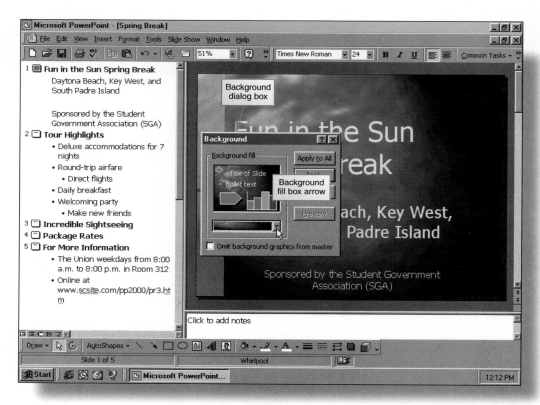

FIGURE 3-12

2 **Click the Background fill box arrow. Point to Fill Effects on the menu.**

The Background fill box menu containing options for filling the slide background displays (Figure 3-13). The current background fill is Automatic, which is the Whirlpool design template default. Fill Effects is highlighted.

FIGURE 3-13

3 Click Fill Effects. If necessary, click the Picture tab, and then click the Select Picture button. Click the Look in box arrow and then click 3½ Floppy (A:). If necessary, click Beach in the list. Point to the Insert button.

The Select Picture dialog box displays (Figure 3-14). The selected file, Beach, displays in the preview box.

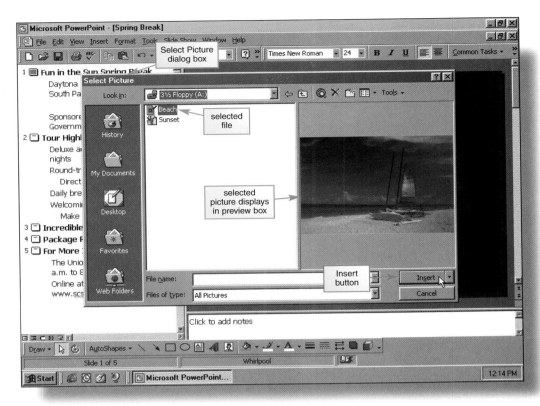

FIGURE 3-14

4 Click the Insert button. When the Fill Effects dialog box displays, click the OK button. When the Background dialog box displays, point to the Apply to All button.

The Background dialog box displays the Beach picture in the Background fill area (Figure 3-15).

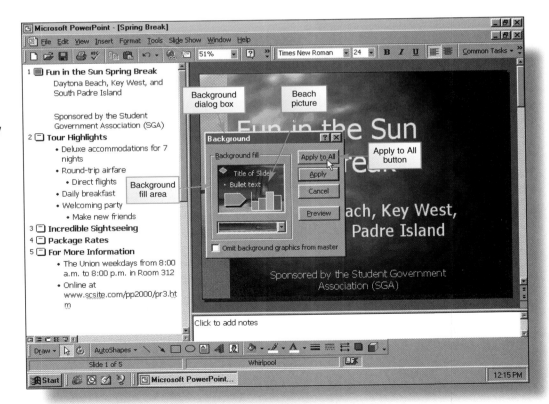

FIGURE 3-15

Click the Apply to All button.

Slide 1 displays the Beach picture as the slide background (Figure 3-16). Although not shown in this figure, the Beach picture is the background for all slides in the presentation. The Whirlpool design template text attributes display on the slide.

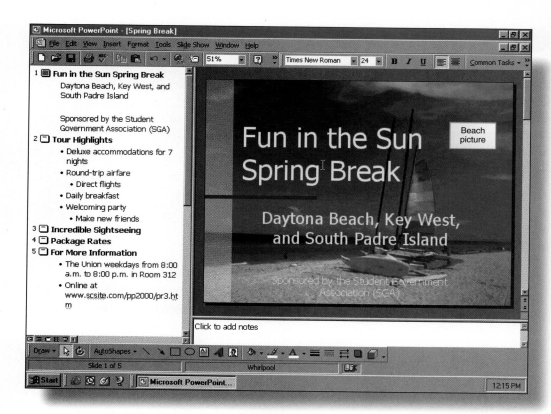

FIGURE 3-16

AutoNumber Bullets

Graphical bullets allow you to customize your presentation. Numbered bullets also give your slides a customized look. PowerPoint's AutoNumber feature adds numbers to the beginning of each slide paragraph. To use this feature, first remove any bullets by pressing the BACKSPACE key. Then type the number 1 or the Roman numeral one and either a period or a closing parenthesis. Type the paragraph text and then press the ENTER key. PowerPoint will add the next consecutive number or Roman numeral. You can modify the slide master to change the default numbering settings.

When you customize the background, the design template text attributes remain the same, but the slide background changes. For example, inserting the Beach picture for the slide background changes the appearance of the slide background but maintains the text attributes of the Whirlpool design template.

Adding Graphical Bullets

PowerPoint allows you to change the appearance of bullets in a slide show. The Bulleted List, Clip Art & Text, and Text & Clip Art AutoLayouts use default bullet characters. You may want to change these characters, however, to add visual interest and variety to your slide show. The graphical character of a beach umbrella fits the theme of your presentation.

The Whirlpool design template uses purple rectangles for the Second level paragraphs and aqua rectangles for the Third level paragraphs. Changing these bullets to graphical characters adds visual interest to your presentation. Creating the graphical bullets requires you to change the default rectangular bullets to the beach umbrella bullets. Perform the following steps to change the bullets from the default rectangles to the graphical umbrellas on Slide 2.

To Add Graphical Bullets

1 **Click the Next Slide button on the vertical scroll bar to display Slide 2.**

Slide 2 displays with the Bulleted List AutoLayout (Figure 3-17).

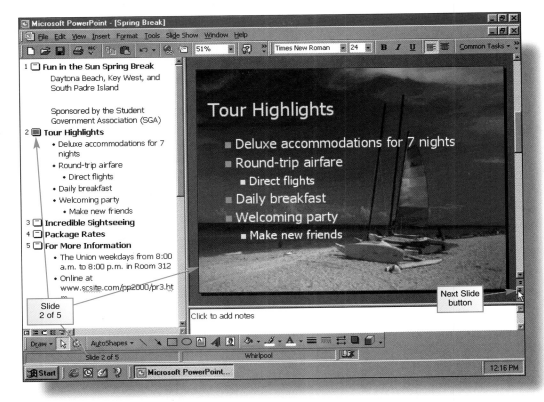

FIGURE 3-17

2 **Click and then drag through all the paragraphs in the Object Area placeholder. Right-click the Object Area placeholder and then point to Bullets and Numbering on the shortcut menu.**

The Object Area placeholder is selected (Figure 3-18). The six paragraphs in the Object Area placeholder are selected.

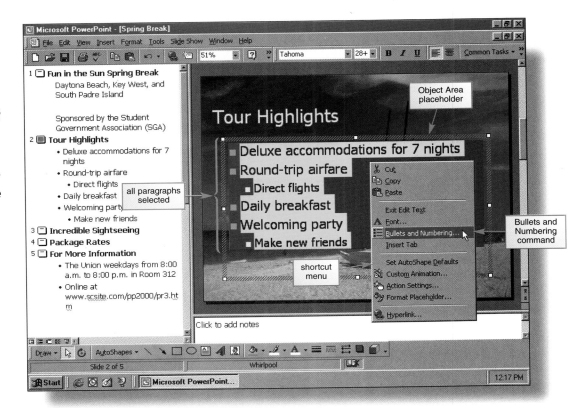

FIGURE 3-18

③ Click Bullets and Numbering. When the Bullets and Numbering dialog box displays, point to the Character button.

The Bullets and Numbering dialog box displays (Figure 3-19).

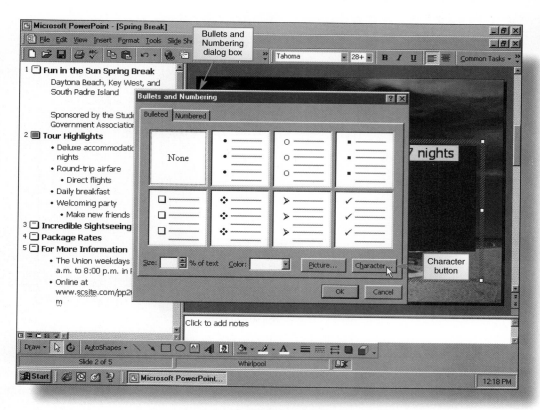

FIGURE 3-19

④ Click the Character button. When the Bullet dialog box displays, click the Bullets from box arrow. Point to Vacation MT.

PowerPoint displays a list of available character fonts (Figure 3-20). The character fonts list may differ depending on your system. The default rectangular purple and aqua bullets on Slide 2 are part of the Wingdings character fonts.

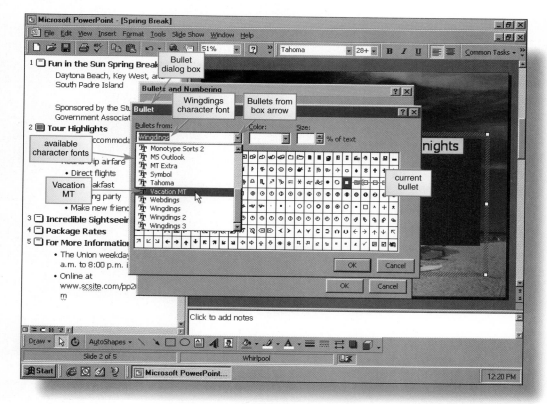

FIGURE 3-20

5 **Click Vacation MT. When the Vacation MT character fonts display in the Bullet dialog box, click the beach umbrella bullet (row 2, column 6). Point to the OK button.**

The desired beach umbrella bullet enlarges to reveal its shape (Figure 3-21). The Vacation MT bullets are graphical images of activities and symbols related to leisure-time activities.

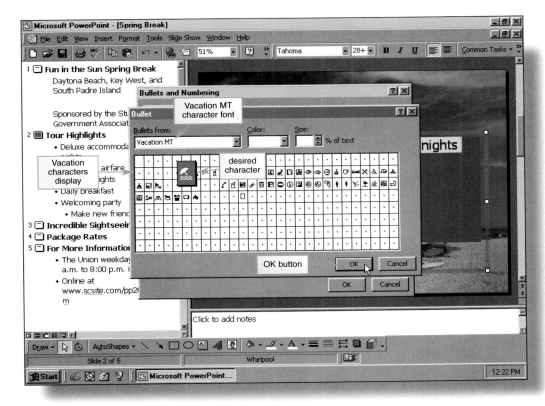

FIGURE 3-21

6 **Click the OK button.**

The beach umbrella bullets replace the default rectangular bullets (Figure 3-22). The First level paragraphs have a purple bullet that is 80 percent of the text size, and the Second level paragraphs have an aqua bullet that is 70 percent of the text size.

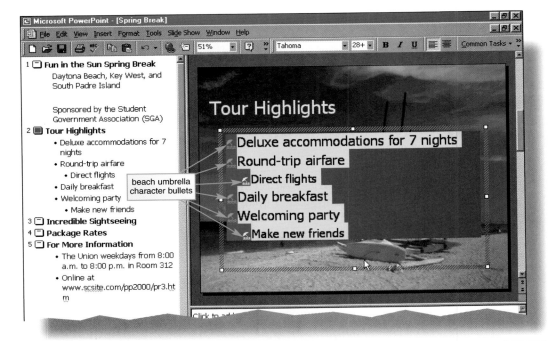

FIGURE 3-22

Other Ways

1. Highlight text, on Format menu click Bullets and Numbering, select character font, click Character, click desired character, click OK button

PowerPoint displays the new character bullets in front of each paragraph on Slide 2. This slide now is complete. The next section describes how to embed an organization chart in a slide.

Creating and Embedding an Organization Chart

Slide 3 contains a chart that elaborates on the sightseeing activities for each of the Spring Break locations, as shown in Figure 3-23. This type of chart is called an **organization chart**, which is a hierarchical collection of elements depicting various functions or responsibilities that contribute to an organization or to a collective function. Typically, you would use an organization chart to show the structure of people or departments within an organization, hence the name, organization chart.

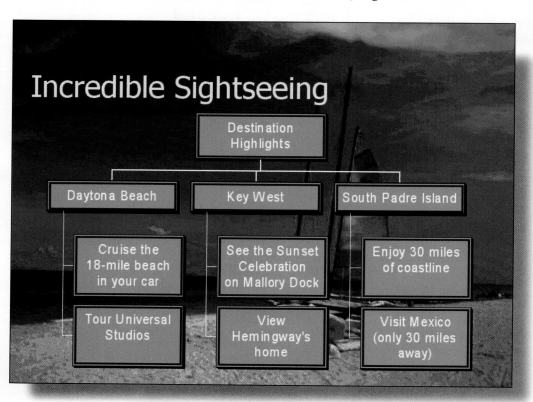

FIGURE 3-23

Organization charts are used in a variety of ways to depict relationships. For example, a company uses an organization chart to describe the relationships between the company's departments. In the information sciences, often organization charts show the decomposition of a process or program. When used in this manner, the chart is called a **hierarchy chart**.

PowerPoint contains a supplementary application called **Microsoft Organization Chart 2.0** that allows you to create an organization chart. When you open Microsoft Organization Chart, its menus, buttons, and tools are available to you directly in the PowerPoint window. Microsoft Organization Chart is an object linking and embedding (OLE) application. The organization chart you create for Slide 3 (Figure 3-23) is an embedded object because it is created in an application other than PowerPoint.

Creating an organization chart requires several steps. First, you display the slide that will contain the organization chart and change the AutoLayout to the Organization Chart AutoLayout. Then, you open the Microsoft Organization Chart application. Finally, you enter and format the contents of the boxes in the organization chart window.

Perform the following steps to create the organization chart for this project.

Changing Slide Layouts

Before you open Microsoft Organization Chart, you need to perform the following steps to display Slide 3 and change the AutoLayout to the Organization Chart AutoLayout.

TO DISPLAY THE NEXT SLIDE AND CHANGE THE SLIDE LAYOUT

1 Click the Next Slide button on the vertical scroll bar to display Slide 3.

2 Click Slide Layout on the Common Tasks button menu.

3 When the Slide Layout dialog box displays, type the number 7 to select the Organization Chart AutoLayout from the 24 available AutoLayouts. Then, click the Apply button.

Slide 3 displays the placeholder for the organization chart and the slide title (Figure 3-24).

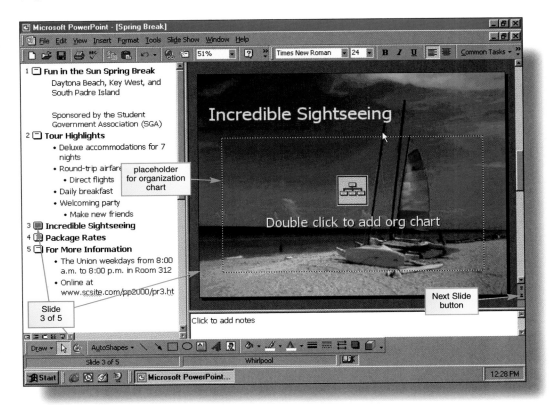

FIGURE 3-24

Slide 3 now displays the placeholder for the organization chart. The next section explains how to open the Microsoft Organization Chart application.

Opening the Microsoft Organization Chart Application

To create the organization chart on Slide 3, you first must open the organization chart application, Microsoft Organization Chart 2.0, which is included within PowerPoint. Recall that when this supplementary application is active, the menus, buttons, and tools in the organization chart application are made available in the

Other Ways

1. Press PAGE DOWN, on Format menu click Slide Layout, double-click Organization Chart AutoLayout

PowerPoint window. Once active, Microsoft Organization Chart displays a sample four-box organization chart in a work area in the middle of the PowerPoint window, as explained in the following step. Perform the following step to open Microsoft Organization Chart.

Steps **To Open Microsoft Organization Chart**

1 **Double-click the placeholder for the organization chart in the middle of Slide 3.**

Microsoft Organization Chart displays the Microsoft Organization Chart - [Object in Spring Break] window in a work area in the PowerPoint window (Figure 3-25). Notice the sample organization chart is composed of four boxes connected by lines. When Microsoft Organization Chart is active, the first line of the top box automatically is selected. Depending on the version of Microsoft Organization Chart installed on your computer, the display on the screen may vary slightly.

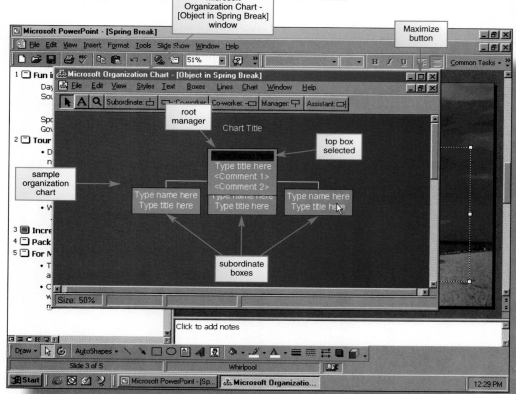

FIGURE 3-25

Microsoft Organization Chart displays a sample organization chart to help you create your chart. The sample is composed of one **manager box**, located at the top of the chart, and three **subordinate boxes**. A manager box has one or more subordinates. The topmost manager is called the **root manager**. A subordinate box is located at a lower level than its manager. A subordinate box has only one manager. When a lower-level subordinate box is added to a higher-level subordinate box, the higher-level subordinate box becomes the manager of the lower-level subordinate box.

In this presentation, each of the three Spring Break trips has two suggested sightseeing activities. As a result, your organization chart will consist of three boxes on level two immediately below the root manager and two boxes immediately under each subordinate manager. These organization chart layouts for each trip are identical, so you create the structure for the Daytona Beach trip, copy it, and make editing changes for the Key West and South Padre Island trips.

Maximizing the Microsoft Organization Chart Window

When Microsoft Organization Chart is active, the Microsoft Organization Chart window is not maximized. Maximizing the Microsoft Organization Chart window makes it easier to create your organization chart because it displays a larger area in which to view the chart. Perform this step to maximize the Microsoft Organization Chart window.

TO MAXIMIZE THE MICROSOFT ORGANIZATION CHART WINDOW

 Click the Maximize button in the upper-right corner of the Microsoft Organization Chart window.

The Microsoft Organization Chart window fills the desktop. Clicking the Restore button returns the Microsoft Organization Chart window to its original size.

Creating the Title for the Root Manager Box

In this presentation, the organization chart is used to describe the various sightseeing activities. The topmost box, the root manager, identifies the purpose of this organization chart: Incredible Sightseeing. Recall that when Microsoft Organization Chart becomes active, the first line in the root manager box is selected. The following step explains how to create the title for the root manager box.

Steps To Create the Title for the Root Manager Box

 Type Destination **in the root manager box on level one and then press the ENTER key. Type** Highlights **on the second line.**

Destination Highlights displays in the root manager box (Figure 3-26). Comment 1 and Comment 2 prompts display in brackets under the root manager box title.

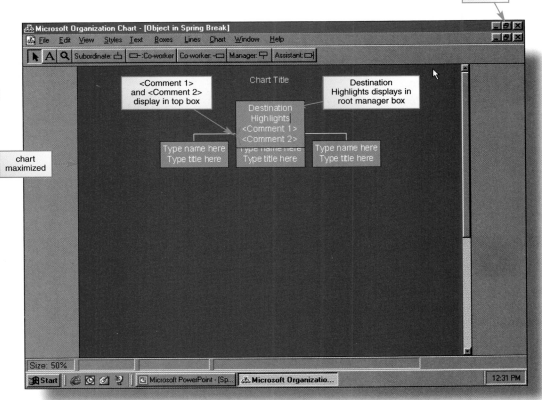

FIGURE 3-26

Titling the Subordinate Boxes

The process of adding a title to a subordinate box is the same as adding the title to the root manager box except that first you must select the subordinate box. The following steps explain how to title subordinate boxes.

 To Title the Subordinate Boxes

1 **Click the left subordinate box.** **Type** Daytona Beach **and then press the ENTER key. Press the DELETE key.**

Daytona Beach displays as the title for the left subordinate box (Figure 3-27). You pressed the DELETE key because only one line of text is needed.

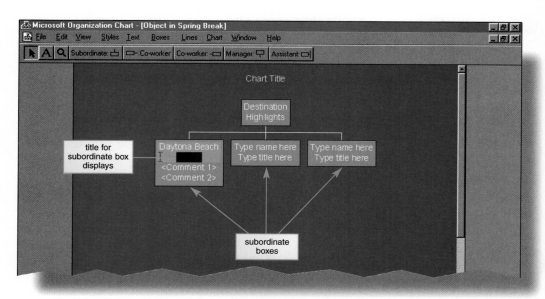

FIGURE 3-27

2 **Click the middle subordinate box.** **Type** Key West **and then press the ENTER key. Press the DELETE key.**

Key West displays as the title for the middle subordinate box.

3 **Click the right subordinate box.** **Type** South Padre Island **and then press the ENTER key. Press the DELETE key.**

South Padre Island displays as the title for the right subordinate box (Figure 3-28).

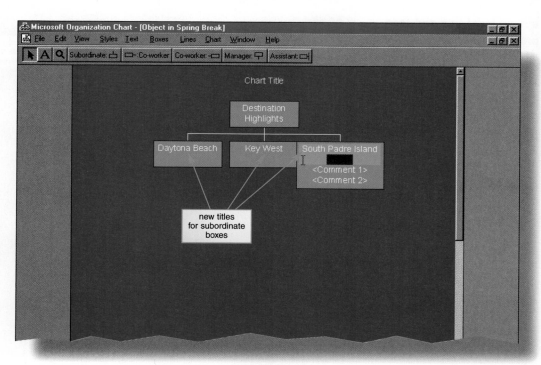

FIGURE 3-28

Adding Subordinate Boxes

Microsoft Organization Chart has five **types of boxes** you can add to a chart. Each box type has a corresponding **box tool** on the Microsoft Organization Chart window **icon bar**. Because each Spring Break trip offers several sightseeing activities, you need to add two subordinate boxes to each of the Spring Break trips.

To add a single subordinate box, click the **Subordinate box tool** and then click the box on the organization chart to which the subordinate reports. When you want to add several subordinate boxes, you can click the Subordinate box tool once for each box you want to add to the organization chart. For example, if you want to add two subordinate boxes, click the Subordinate box tool two times. If the Subordinate box tool is recessed and you decide to not add subordinate boxes, you can deselect the Subordinate box tool by clicking the **Select box tool** on the Microsoft Organization Chart window icon bar or by pressing the ESC key.

The following steps explain how to use the Subordinate box tool to add two subordinate boxes to the Daytona Beach box.

 To Add Multiple Subordinate Boxes

1 **Click the Subordinate box tool on the Microsoft Organization Chart window icon bar two times. Point to the Daytona Beach box.**

The Subordinate box tool is recessed (Figure 3-29). The status bar displays the number of subordinate boxes Microsoft Organization Chart is creating, which is two. The mouse pointer changes shape to a subordinate box.

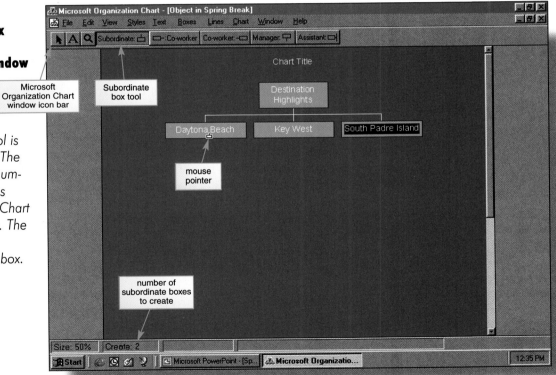

FIGURE 3-29

2 **Click the Daytona Beach box.**

Two subordinate boxes display below the Daytona Beach box (Figure 3-30). The new subordinate boxes display one level lower than the box to which they are attached. Daytona Beach now is the manager to the new subordinate boxes. The left subordinate box on level three is selected.

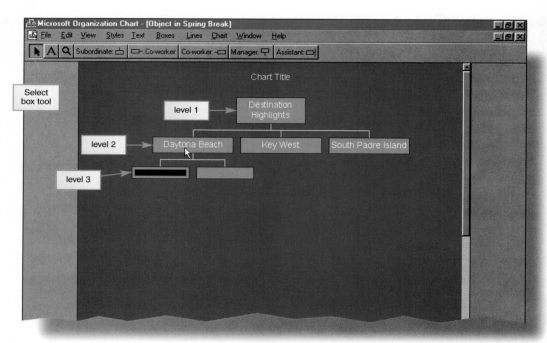

FIGURE 3-30

The basic structure of the left side of the organization chart is complete. The next step is to add titles to the boxes in the chart.

Adding Names to the Subordinate Boxes

To complete the organization chart, you must add names to all subordinate boxes to the Daytona Beach box. After adding the subordinate boxes, the Select box tool is recessed, meaning it is active. When this tool is active, the mouse pointer displays as a left-pointing block arrow. Because the subordinate boxes in this project have names but do not have titles, the Title, Comment 1, and Comment 2 prompts display in brackets under the box name when the box is selected. The brackets indicate the label is optional, and it displays only when replaced by text. The following steps summarize adding a title to each level 3 subordinate box.

TO ADD NAMES TO SUBORDINATE BOXES

1 If necessary, click the left subordinate box on level 3. Type `Cruise the` in the subordinate box and then press the ENTER key. Type `18-mile beach` and then press the ENTER key. Type `in your car` in the subordinate box.

2 Click the right subordinate box on level 3. Type `Tour Universal` in the subordinate box and then press the ENTER key. Type `Studios` and then press the ENTER key.

Both level 3 subordinate boxes under the Daytona Beach box display sightseeing activities (Figure 3-31).

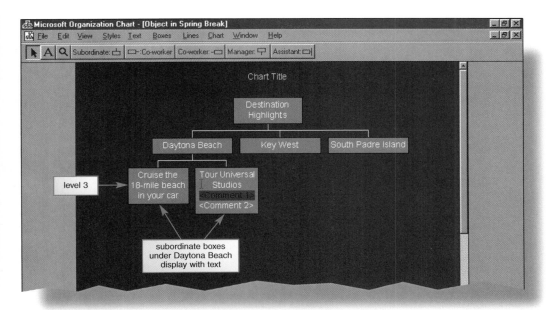

FIGURE 3-31

Changing Organization Chart Styles

Now that the boxes for the Daytona Beach branch are labeled, you want to change the way the organization chart looks. With the addition of each new box, the chart expanded horizontally. Before you add the Key West and South Padre Island activities, you will change the style of selected boxes from horizontal to vertical.

 To Change the Organization Chart Style

1 **Click anywhere outside the organization chart boxes. Press and hold the SHIFT key. Click the two lowest-level boxes: Cruise the 18-mile beach in your car and Tour Universal Studios. Release the SHIFT key.**

The two lowest-level boxes are selected (Figure 3-32).

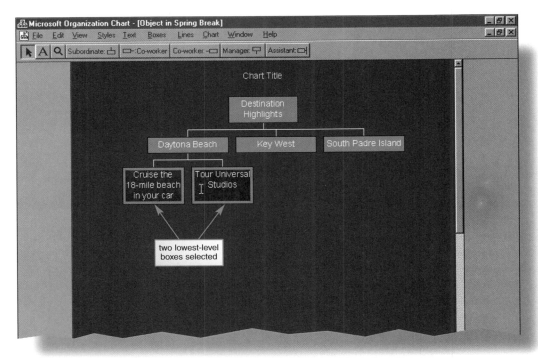

FIGURE 3-32

2 **Click Styles on the menu bar and then point to the vertical styles menu icon (row 1, column 2) in the top set of Groups styles.**

The default group style is selected, which is indicated by the recessed icon (Figure 3-33). The vertical styles menu icon is highlighted.

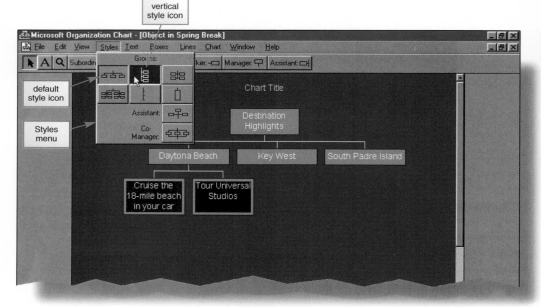

FIGURE 3-33

3 **Click the vertical style icon.**

The organization chart displays the two sightseeing activities vertically under the Daytona Beach box (Figure 3-34).

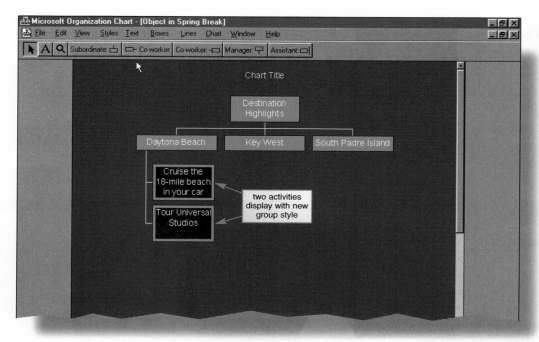

FIGURE 3-34

The **Styles menu** icons allow you to change the arrangement of boxes in your chart. The top set of styles changes the arrangement of boxes in a group. The middle style creates assistant boxes. The bottom style is used to show co-managers. If you select an incorrect style or want to return to the previous style, click the Undo Chart Style command on the Edit menu or press CTRL+Z.

Now that the Daytona Beach activities are complete, you need to compile the Key West and South Padre Island sightseeing lists.

Copying a Branch of an Organization Chart

Instead of creating the Key West and South Padre Island activities by adding and labeling boxes, you copy Daytona Beach's list and add it under the other two Spring Break destinations. When you work with a whole section of an organization chart, it is referred to as working with a **branch**, or an appendage, of the chart. The following steps explain how to copy a branch of the chart.

To Copy a Branch of an Organization Chart

1 **If not already selected, press and hold the SHIFT key, click the two level 3 boxes, Cruise the 18-mile beach in your car and Tour Universal Studios, and then release the SHIFT key. Right-click one of the selected boxes and then point to Copy on the shortcut menu.**

The shortcut menu displays (Figure 3-35).

2 **Click Copy.**

Microsoft Organization Chart copies the Daytona Beach activities branch of the organization chart to the Clipboard. Recall that the Clipboard is a temporary storage area.

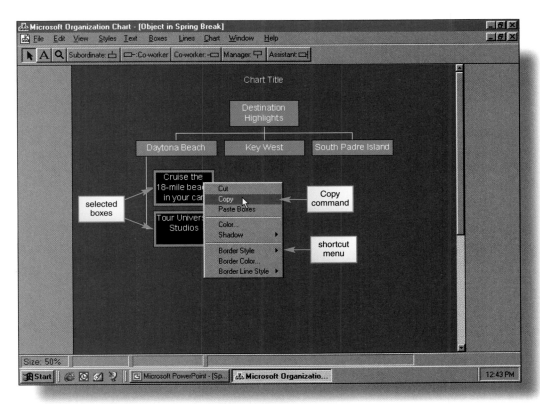

FIGURE 3-35

The next section explains how to paste the Daytona Beach activities branch of the organization chart to two other locations on the chart.

Pasting a Branch of an Organization Chart

Now that a copy of the Daytona Beach branch of the organization chart is on the Clipboard, the steps on the next page are to paste it from the Clipboard to the Key West and South Padre Island areas.

To Paste a Branch of an Organization Chart

 Right-click the middle root manager box, Key West. Then point to Paste Boxes on the shortcut menu.

The shortcut menu displays (Figure 3-36). The Key West box is selected.

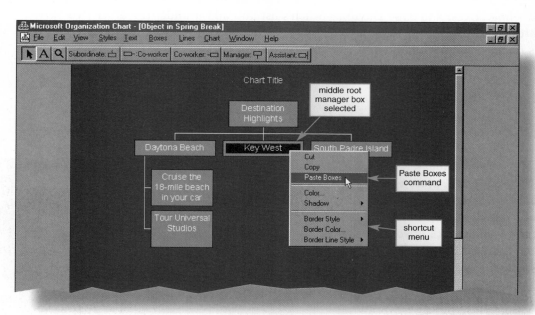

FIGURE 3-36

2 Click Paste Boxes.

The organization chart displays the two sightseeing activities under the Key West box.

3 Right-click the right root manager box, South Padre Island. Click Paste Boxes on the shortcut menu.

The organization chart displays the two sightseeing activities under the South Padre Island box (Figure 3-37).

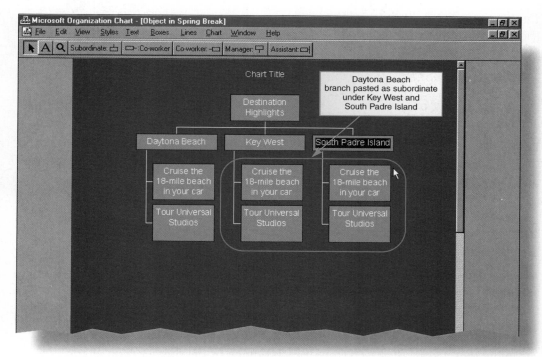

FIGURE 3-37

Editing an Organization Chart

After you have copied and pasted a branch of the organization chart, you need to **edit** the two sightseeing activities for the Key West and South Padre Island trips. Editing a box requires you first to select the box and then make your edits.

Steps **To Edit Text in an Organization Chart**

1 **Click the Cruise the 18-mile beach in your car box under the Key West branch of the organization chart. Type** See the Sunset **in the subordinate box and then press the ENTER key. Type** Celebration **and then press the ENTER key. Type** on Mallory Dock **and then point to the Tour Universal Studios box under the Key West branch of the organization chart.**

The three lines of text replace the original wording (Figure 3-38).

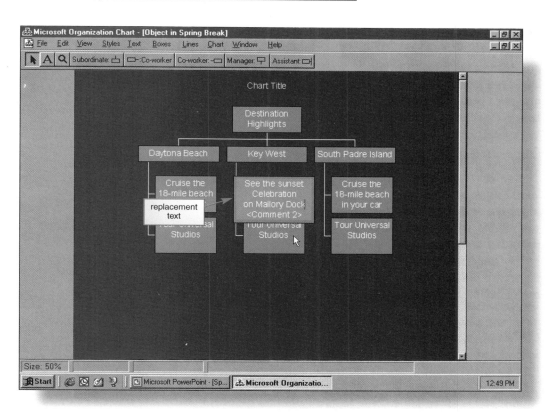

FIGURE 3-38

2 **Click the Tour Universal Studios box under the Key West branch. Type** View **in the subordinate box and then press the ENTER key. Type** Hemingway s **and then press the ENTER key. Type** home **and then point to the Cruise the 18-mile beach in your car box under the South Padre Island branch.**

The editing changes for the Key West branch are complete (Figure 3-39).

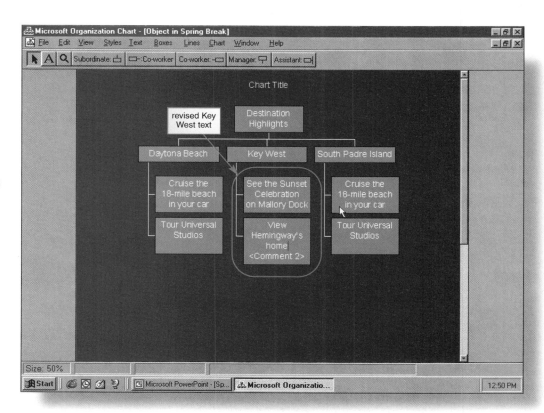

FIGURE 3-39

3 Click the Cruise the 18-mile beach in your car box under the South Padre Island branch. **Type** Enjoy 30 miles **and then press the** ENTER **key. Type** of coastline **and then press the** ENTER **key. Press the** DELETE **key.**

4 Click the bottom-right box, type Visit Mexico **and then press the** ENTER **key. Type** (only 30 miles **and then press the** ENTER **key. Type** away) **and then click anywhere outside the organization chart boxes.**

All editing changes for the Destination Highlights organization chart are complete (Figure 3-40).

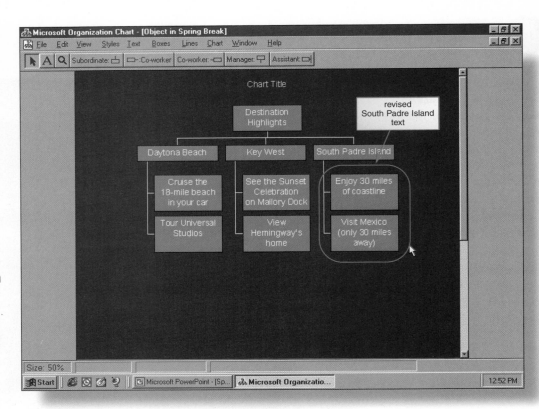

FIGURE 3-40

The Clipboard

When you copy text or an object, it is stored on the Office Clipboard. You then can paste this item repeatedly in your presentation or in other Microsoft Office programs. The Clipboard allows you to copy up to 12 items and then paste any number of these items on your slides or in another Office application. The first 50 characters of text or "Picture *n*" or "Item *x*" displays when you rest your mouse on the item button on the Clipboard. If the Clipboard toolbar does not display, click Copy on the Edit menu. To paste multiple items stored on the Clipboard simultaneously, click the area where you want these items to display and then click Paste all on the Clipboard toolbar.

All the necessary text now appears on the organization chart. The next section explains how to format an organization chart.

Formatting an Organization Chart

Microsoft Organization Chart allows you to format a box simply by selecting it. To make your organization chart look like the chart shown in Figure 3-23 on page PP 3.22, you add shadow effects and a border to every box. The following sections explain how to select all the boxes in the chart and change the shadow and border box attributes.

To Select All Boxes in an Organization Chart

① **Click Edit on the menu bar, point to Select, and then point to All (Figure 3-41).**

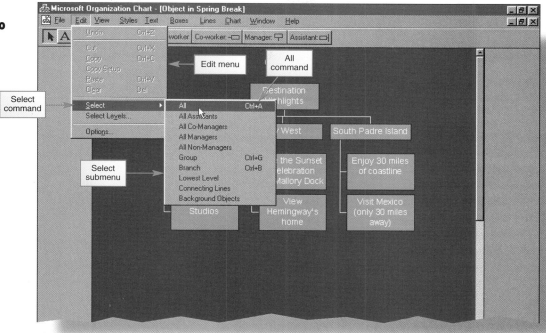

FIGURE 3-41

② **Click All on the Select submenu.**

Microsoft Organization Chart selects all the boxes in the chart (Figure 3-42).

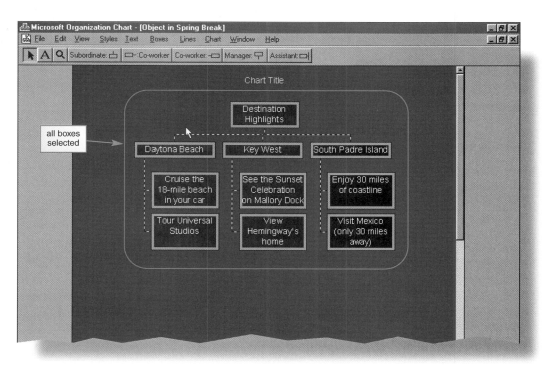

FIGURE 3-42

Other Ways

1. Press CTRL+A

Adding Shadow Effects to Boxes in an Organization Chart

Now that all the boxes are selected, you add shadow effects. Microsoft Organization Chart has eight shadow effects from which to choose. One style is None, which has no shadow. Perform the following steps to add shadow effects to all the boxes in an organization chart.

To Add Shadow Effects to Boxes in an Organization Chart

1 **With all the boxes in the organization chart selected, right-click one of the selected boxes. Point to Shadow on the shortcut menu and then point to the shadow style in row 3, column 2 on the Shadow submenu.**

Microsoft Organization Chart displays the Shadow submenu (Figure 3-43). The default shadow style for Microsoft Organization Chart is None. The desired shadow style is selected.

2 **Click the shadow style on the Shadow submenu.**

Microsoft Organization Chart adds the shadow effect to all boxes in the organization chart.

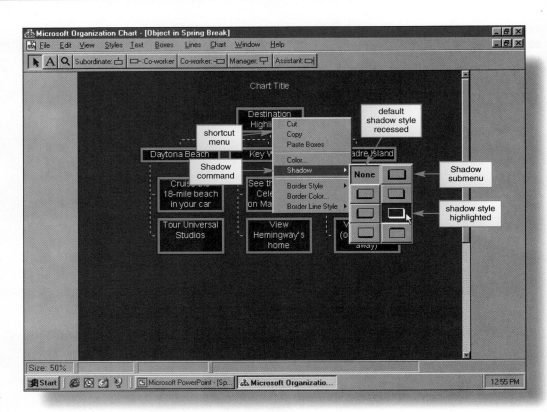

FIGURE 3-43

Changing Border Styles in an Organization Chart

To enhance the boxes in the organization chart, you want to change the border style. Microsoft Organization Chart has 12 border styles from which to choose. One style is None, which has no border. The default border style is a thin line. Perform the following steps to change border styles.

Steps To Change the Border Style

1 **With all the boxes in the organization chart selected, right-click one of the selected boxes. Point to Border Style on the shortcut menu and then point to the border style option in row 4, column 1 on the Border Style submenu.**

Microsoft Organization Chart displays the Border Style submenu (Figure 3-44). The default border style for Microsoft Organization Chart is recessed in row 2, column 1. The desired border style is selected.

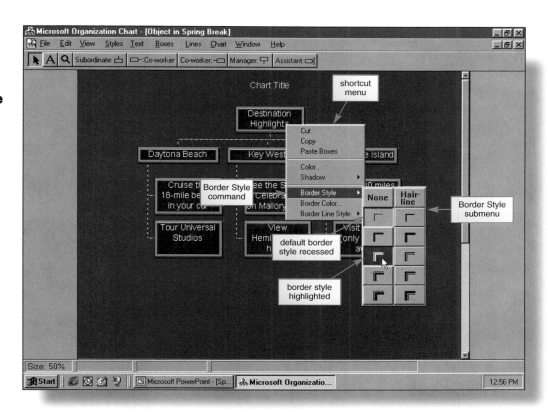

FIGURE 3-44

2 **Click the highlighted border style on the Border Style submenu.**

Microsoft Organization Chart applies the new border style to all boxes in the organization chart (Figure 3-45).

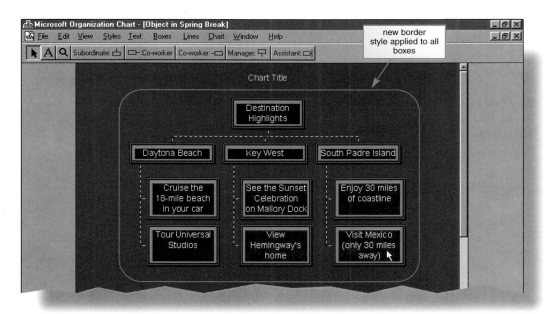

FIGURE 3-45

The organization chart now is complete. The step on the next page is to return to the PowerPoint window.

Quitting Microsoft Organization Chart and Returning to the PowerPoint Window

After you create and format an organization chart, you quit Microsoft Organization Chart and return to the PowerPoint window. The following steps explain how to return to the PowerPoint window.

 To Quit Microsoft Organization Chart and Return to the PowerPoint Window

1 **Click the Close button on the Microsoft Organization Chart - [Object in Spring Break] title bar. When the Microsoft Organization Chart dialog box displays, point to the Yes button.**

The Microsoft Organization Chart dialog box warns you that the organization chart object has changed and asks you if you want to update the object in the PowerPoint presentation, Spring Break, before proceeding (Figure 3-46).

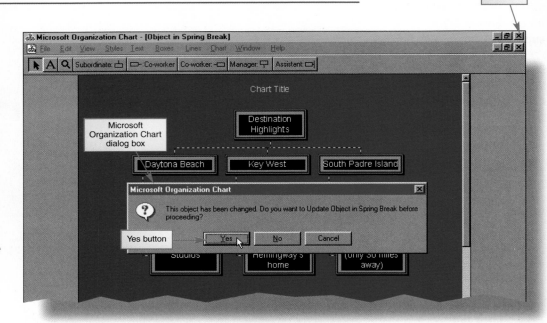

FIGURE 3-46

2 **Click the Yes button.**

Microsoft Organization Chart updates the organization chart object and closes, and then PowerPoint displays the organization chart on Slide 3 (Figure 3-47).

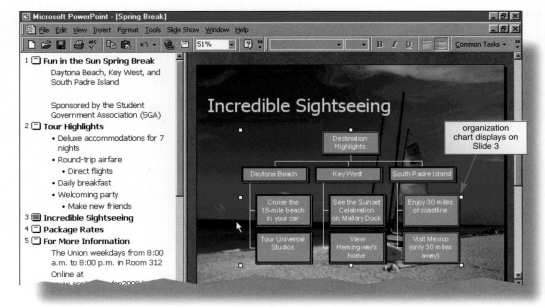

FIGURE 3-47

Scaling an Organization Chart Object

The organization chart on Slide 3 is sized to fit the placeholder for the organization chart, so it needs to be enlarged. The **Scale command** allows you to enlarge or reduce an object by precise amounts while retaining the object's original proportions.

Perform the following steps to scale an organization chart object.

TO SCALE AN ORGANIZATION CHART OBJECT

1 Right-click the selected organization chart object and then click Format Object on the shortcut menu.

2 Click the Size tab. Click the Height box up arrow in the Scale area until 120% displays.

3 Click the OK button.

The organization chart is scaled to 120 percent of its original size (Figure 3-48).

> **Other Ways**
>
> 1. On Format menu click Object, click Size tab, type 120 in Scale Height text box, click OK button

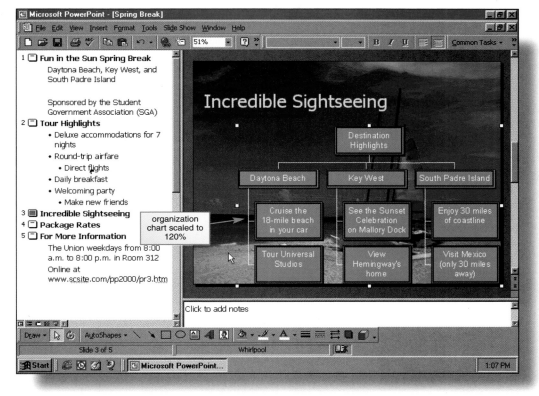

FIGURE 3-48

Moving the Organization Chart

Now that the organization chart is scaled to a readable size, you need to move it onto the slide. To move the organization chart, perform the following step.

TO MOVE THE ORGANIZATION CHART

1 Drag the organization chart onto the middle of the blank area of Slide 3.

The organization chart displays in the center of the slide (Figure 3-49 on the next page).

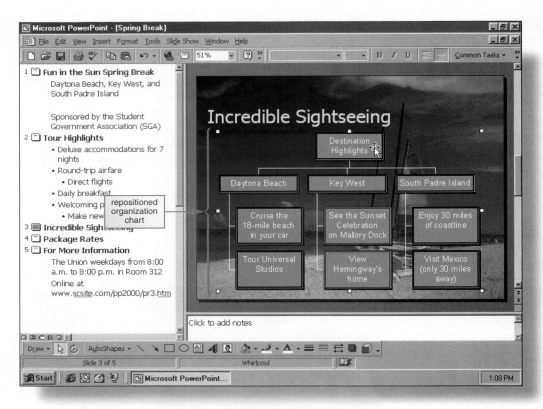

FIGURE 3-49

Slide 3 now is complete. The next section introduces you to inserting a table into a slide.

Inserting a Table into a Slide

Slide 4 is included in this presentation to inform students of the costs of each vacation package. You list each destination and the total package cost. To make this information visually appealing, you arrange the figures in a table. Then you format the table by formatting the column heading font, adding a border, and making the background dark purple.

Inserting a Table into a Slide

The first step is to display the next slide and select the Object Area placeholder.

TO DISPLAY THE NEXT SLIDE AND CHANGE THE SLIDE LAYOUT

1 Click the Next Slide button on the vertical scroll bar to display Slide 4.

2 Click the Common Tasks button on the Formatting toolbar and then click Slide Layout.

3 Double-click the Table slide layout located in row 1, column 4.

Slide 4 displays the Package Rates title and the placeholder for the table with a small table and the words, Double click to add table (Figure 3-50).

Plagiarizing Text

When you gather information for your table or for other aspects of your presentation, be certain to acknowledge the source of this information on the slide or verbally when you give your presentation. The plagiarism rules that you use when writing research papers also apply to your slide shows. Give credit where credit is due. For more information about acknowledging sources, visit the PowerPoint 2000 Project 3 More About page (www.scsite.com/pp2000/more.htm) and click Plagiarism.

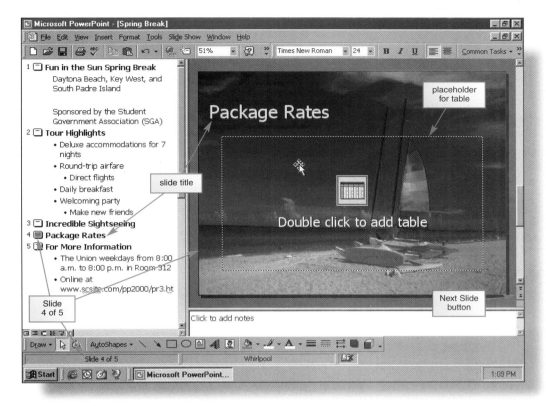

FIGURE 3-50

Now that the AutoLayout is changed to Table and the placeholder for the table is selected, you can insert a table with two columns and four rows. Perform these steps to create the Package Rates table.

 To Create a Table

1 **Double-click anywhere in the placeholder for the table. Point to the Number of rows box up arrow in the Insert Table dialog box.**

The Insert Table dialog box displays. The default settings are two columns and two rows (Figure 3-51).

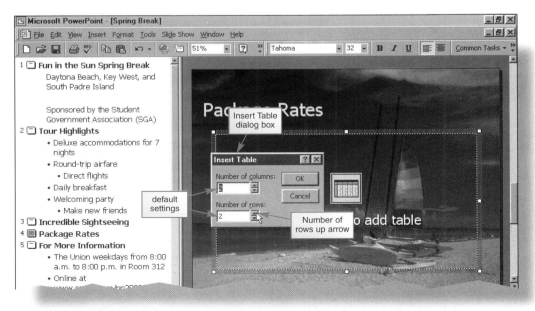

FIGURE 3-51

2 **Click the Number of rows up box arrow twice and then point to the OK button.**

The Number of rows box displays 4 (Figure 3-52).

FIGURE 3-52

3 **Click the OK button.**

PowerPoint displays a table with two columns and four rows (Figure 3-53). The mouse pointer changes to a pencil. The insertion point is in the upper-left cell, which is selected. The Tables and Borders toolbar displays.

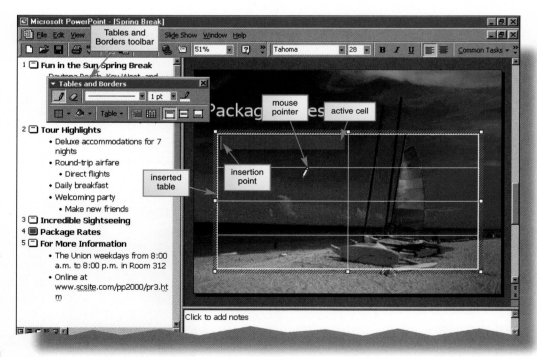

FIGURE 3-53

Other Ways

1. Click Insert Table button on Standard toolbar, drag to select desired number of rows and columns, enter text
2. On Insert menu click Table, type desired number of rows and columns, click OK button

The Tables and Borders toolbar displays when you insert a table. This toolbar contains buttons and menus that allow you to perform frequent table drawing and formatting functions more quickly than when using the menu bar. Figure 3-54 shows the name of each button on the Tables and Borders toolbar.

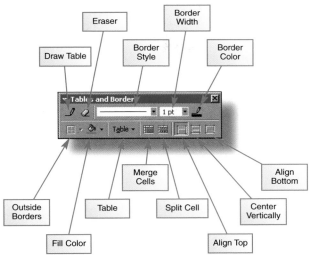

FIGURE 3-54

Entering Data in a Table

The table on Slide 4 has two columns: one for the Spring Break destinations, and one for the package prices. A heading will identify each column. The destinations and prices are summarized in Table 3-1.

Perform the following steps to enter data in the table.

Table 3-1 Destinations and Prices	
DESTINATION	TOTAL COST
Daytona Beach	$529
Key West	$669
South Padre Island	$549

 To Enter Data in a Table

---

1 **Type** Destination **and then press the RIGHT ARROW key.**

The first column title, Destination, displays in the top-left cell and the top-right cell is the active cell (Figure 3-55). You also can press the TAB key to advance to the next cell.

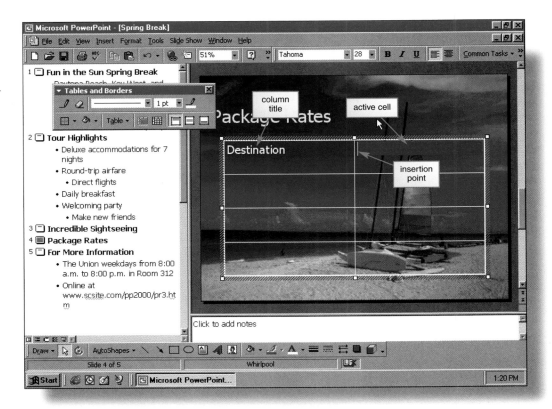

FIGURE 3-55

2 **Repeat Step 1 for the remaining column title and for the other table cells by using Table 3-1 as a guide. Enter** Total Cost **in row 1, column 2,** Daytona Beach **in row 2, column 1,** $529 **in row 2, column 2,** Key West **in row 3, column 1,** $669 **in row 3, column 2,** South Padre Island **in row 4, column 1, and** $549 **in row 4, column 2.**

The three Spring Break destinations and package rates display (Figure 3-56). All entries are left-aligned and display in 28-point Tahoma font.

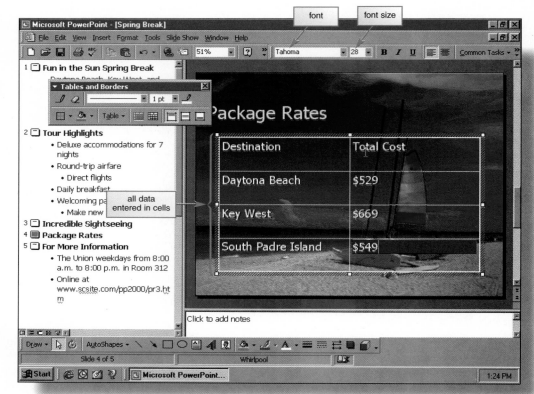

FIGURE 3-56

The next step is to format the table. You **format** the table to emphasize certain entries and to make it easier to read and understand. In this project, you will change the column heading alignment and font style and size, add borders, change the border line color, and make the background dark purple. The process required to format the table is explained in the remainder of this section. Although the format procedures will be carried out in a particular manner, you should be aware that you can make these format changes in any order.

Formatting a Table Cell

You format an entry in a cell to emphasize it or to make it stand out from the rest of the table. Perform the following steps to bold and center the column headings and then increase the font size.

To Format a Table Cell

1 **Click the top-left cell, Destination. Press and hold the SHIFT key and then click the top-right cell, Total Cost. Release the SHIFT key. Click the Font Size box arrow on the Formatting toolbar. Scroll down and then point to 36.**

The two column headings, Destination and Total Cost, are selected and the Font Size list displays (Figure 3-57).

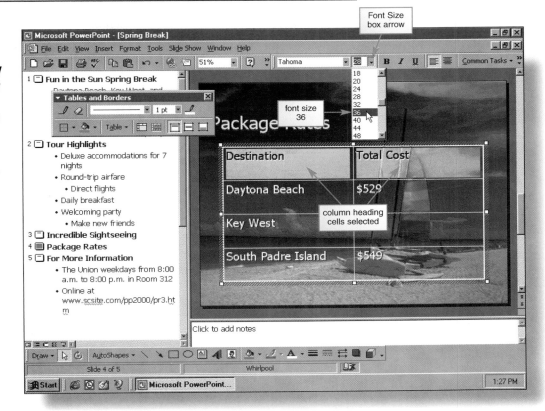

FIGURE 3-57

2 **Click 36. Point to the Bold button on the Formatting toolbar.**

The text in the heading cells displays in 36-point Tahoma font (Figure 3-58).

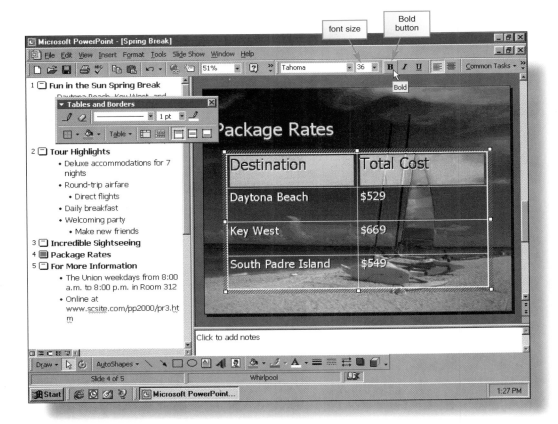

FIGURE 3-58

Click the Bold button and then point to the Center button on the Formatting toolbar.

The text displays in bold and is left-aligned in the cells (Figure 3-59).

 Click the Center button.

The text is centered in the cells.

FIGURE 3-59

You can change the font type, size, or style at any time while the table is selected. Some PowerPoint users prefer to change font and cell alignments before they enter any data. Others change the font and alignment while they are building their table or after they have entered all the data.

Formatting a Table

The next step is to format the table by adding borders and a background color. A **border** is the visible line around the edge of an object. The border draws attention to the object by defining its edges. A border has line style and line color attributes. The **line style** determines the line thickness and line appearance of the border. For example, you could choose a thick, solid line for your border. **Line color** determines the color of the line that forms the border. Your table on Slide 4 will have a dashed purple border with a width of three points.

To draw the attention of the audience to the table, add color to the lines of the border. Recall that the design template establishes the attributes of the title master and the slide master. When you click the Border Color button or the Fill Color button arrow on the Tables and Borders or Drawing toolbar, a list displays line color options. A portion of the list includes the eight colors used to create the design template. One of the colors is identified as the line color, and another is identified as the fill color. Both colors are listed as the Automatic option in the color list.

Perform the following steps to format the table on Slide 4 by adding borders, changing the border style, width, and color, and adding a background color.

Line Styles

A border's line style and color affect the attention a viewer gives to a picture or to an object. A thick border draws more attention than a thin border, and warm colors, such as red and yellow, draw more attention than cool colors, such as green or violet.

Steps To Format a Table

1 Click the Table button on the Tables and Borders toolbar and then point to Select Table.

The formatting changes will be made to the entire table, so you need to select all the cells and borders (Figure 3-60).

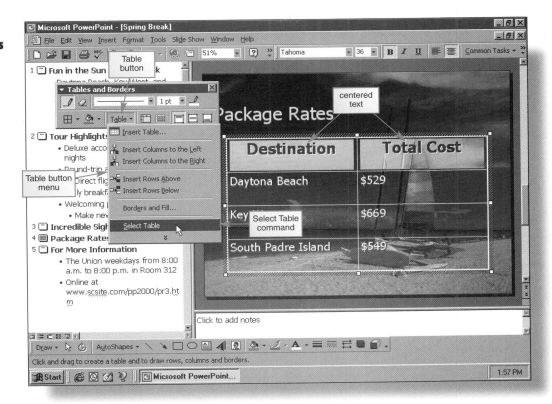

FIGURE 3-60

2 Click Select Table. Click the Border Style box arrow on the Tables and Borders toolbar and then point to the fifth border style in the list as shown in Figure 3-61.

PowerPoint provides 10 border styles or a No Border option.

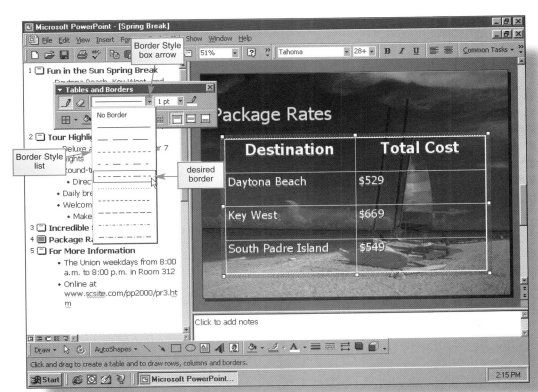

FIGURE 3-61

3 Click the fifth border style. Click the Border Width box arrow on the Tables and Borders toolbar and then point to 3 pt.

The desired border is three-points wide (Figure 3-62). PowerPoint provides nine possible widths in the border list.

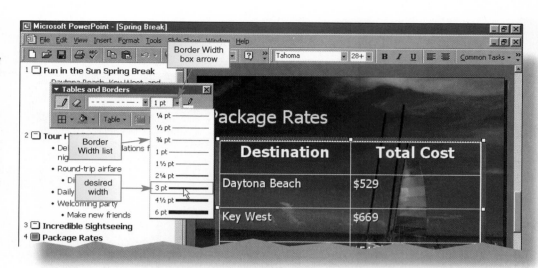

FIGURE 3-62

4 Click 3 pt. Click the Border Color button on the Tables and Borders toolbar and then point to the color purple (color five in the row).

The color purple is the default border color in the Whirlpool design template color scheme (Figure 3-63). The default line color is white.

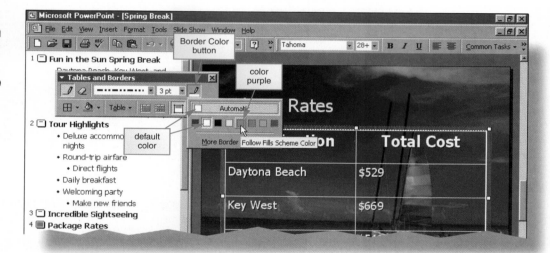

FIGURE 3-63

5 Click the color purple. Click the Outside Borders button arrow on the Tables and Borders toolbar. Point to the All Borders style in row 1, column 2.

You can choose 12 possible border styles (Figure 3-64). The Outside Borders style is the default border style.

FIGURE 3-64

6 Click the All Borders style. Click the Fill Color button arrow on the Tables and Borders toolbar. Point to the color dark blue (color one in the row).

The new purple border style is applied to the table. The default fill color is purple, the same color as the new border (Figure 3-65).

FIGURE 3-65

7 Click the color dark blue. Click the Close button on the Tables and Borders toolbar title bar.

The table background is dark blue (Figure 3-66). The Tables and Borders toolbar is not used in the remainder of this project.

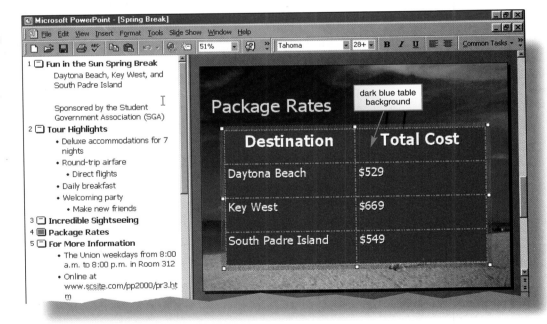

FIGURE 3-66

Slide 4 now is complete. The next section describes how to ungroup clip art and insert pieces of it in your closing slide in the on-screen slide show.

Other Ways

1. On Format menu click Table, click Borders tab, select style, color, and width preferences, click diagram or use buttons to apply borders, click Fill tab, click Fill color arrow, select background color, click OK button

Creating a PowerPoint Clip Art Object

A **clip art picture** is composed of many objects grouped together to form one object. PowerPoint allows you to alter the clip art picture by disassembling it into the objects. **Disassembling** a clip art picture, also called **ungrouping**, separates one object into multiple objects. Once ungrouped, you can manipulate the individual objects as needed to form a new object. When you ungroup a clip art picture in PowerPoint, it becomes a **PowerPoint object** and loses its link to the Microsoft Clip Gallery. Therefore, you cannot double-click the new picture to open the Microsoft Clip Gallery.

Slide 5 contains a modified version of a beach umbrella picture from the Microsoft Clip Gallery. You may want to modify a clip art picture for various reasons. Many times you cannot find a clip art picture that precisely illustrates your topic. For example, you want a picture of a man and woman shaking hands, but the only available clip art picture has two men and a woman shaking hands.

Occasionally you may want to remove or change a portion of a clip art picture or you may want to combine two or more clip art pictures. For example, you can use one clip art picture for the background and another picture as the foreground. Still other times, you may want to combine a clip art picture with another type of object. The types of objects you can combine with a clip art picture depend on the software installed on your computer. The Object type box in the Insert Object dialog box identifies the types of objects you can combine with a clip art picture. In this presentation, the beach umbrella clip art picture contains a beach ball that you do not want to display on your slide, so you will ungroup the clip art picture and remove the ball.

Modifying the clip art picture on Slide 5 requires several steps. First, you display Slide 5 and increase the width of the Object Area placeholder. Then, you insert the beach umbrella clip art picture into the slide. In the next step you scale the clip art picture to increase its size. Finally, you ungroup the clip art picture and delete unwanted pieces. The steps on the following pages explain in detail how to insert, scale, and ungroup a clip art picture.

Increasing the Object Area Placeholder Width

For aesthetic reasons, the second bulleted paragraph on Slide 5, Online at www.scsite.com/pp2000/pr3.htm, should display on one line. To change the width of the Object Area placeholder, perform the following steps.

To Increase the Object Area Placeholder Width

1 **Click the Next Slide button on the vertical scroll bar to display Slide 5. Click a bulleted paragraph to display the Object Area placeholder and then point to the right-center sizing handle on the right side of the object.**

*The selection rectangle indicates the placeholder is selected (Figure 3-67). Recall that a **selection rectangle** is the box framed by the sizing handles when an image is selected. The mouse pointer displays as a two-headed arrow.*

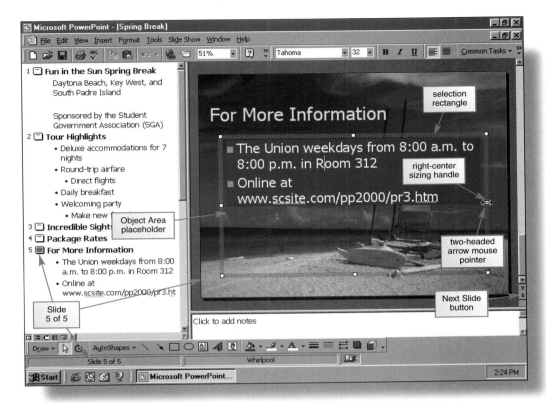

FIGURE 3-67

2 **Drag the sizing handle to the black border along the right edge of the slide.**

The second bulleted paragraph displays on one line (Figure 3-68).

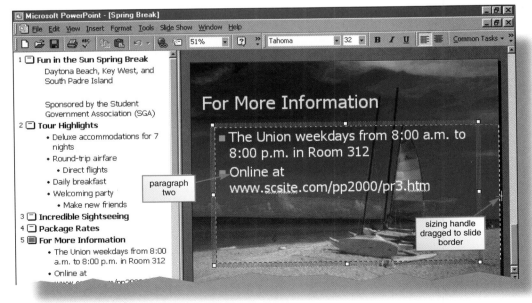

FIGURE 3-68

The area below the bulleted paragraphs is increased to allow more room for the beach umbrella clip art picture. You now can locate and insert the desired picture.

Inserting a Clip Art Picture

The first step in modifying a clip art picture is to insert the picture on a slide. You insert the beach umbrella clip art picture from the Microsoft Clip Gallery. In later steps, you modify the clip art picture.

The following steps explain how to insert the beach umbrella clip art picture on Slide 5 of this presentation.

TO INSERT A CLIP ART PICTURE

(1) Click the Insert Clip Art button on the Drawing toolbar.

(2) When the Insert ClipArt window displays, type beach umbrella in the Search for clips text box and then press the ENTER key.

(3) Click the beach umbrella clip art picture shown in Figure 3-69 and then click the Insert clip button on the shortcut menu.

(4) Click the Close button on the Insert ClipArt window title bar.

Slide 5 displays the beach umbrella clip art picture (Figure 3-69). The Picture toolbar displays.

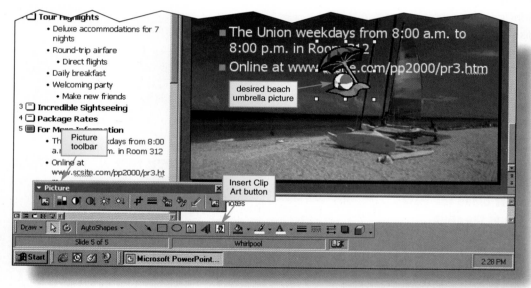

FIGURE 3-69

FIGURE 3-70

The **Picture toolbar** displays when you insert the clip art picture. This toolbar contains buttons and menus that allow you to perform frequent picture formatting functions more quickly than when using the menu bar. Figure 3-70 shows the name of each button on the Picture toolbar.

Scaling and Moving Clip Art

Now that the beach umbrella clip art picture is inserted on Slide 5, you must increase its size by **scaling**. Perform the following steps to scale and move the clip art picture.

TO SCALE AND MOVE A CLIP ART PICTURE

1 If necessary, select the beach umbrella clip art picture and then click the Format Picture button on the Picture toolbar.

2 Click the Size tab in the Format Picture dialog box.

3 Click the Height box up arrow in the Scale area until 185% displays.

4 Click the OK button.

5 Drag the beach umbrella clip art picture to the bottom of the slide near the left corner so the upper-left sizing handle is directly below the bullet for the second paragraph in the Object Area placeholder.

The beach umbrella clip art picture is scaled to 185 percent of its original size and is moved to a desirable location (Figure 3-71).

FIGURE 3-71

Ungrouping a Clip Art Picture

The next step is to ungroup the beach umbrella clip art picture on Slide 5. When you **ungroup** a clip art picture, PowerPoint breaks it into its component objects. A clip art picture may be composed of a few individual objects or several complex groups of objects. These groups can be ungrouped repeatedly until they decompose into individual objects.

Perform the steps on the next page to ungroup a clip art picture.

Steps **To Ungroup a Clip Art Picture**

① **With the beach umbrella clip art picture selected, right-click the clip art. Point to Grouping on the shortcut menu, and then point to Ungroup on the Grouping submenu (Figure 3-72).**

FIGURE 3-72

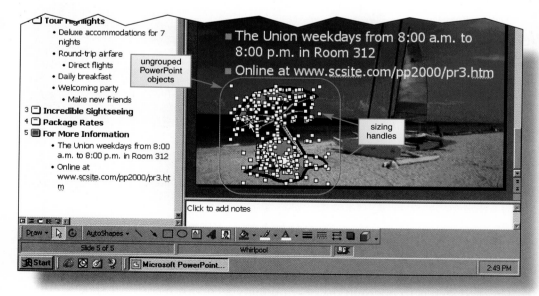

② **Click Ungroup. Click the Yes button in the Microsoft PowerPoint dialog box.**

The clip art picture now displays as many PowerPoint objects and sizing handles display around the ungrouped objects (Figure 3-73). The message in the Microsoft PowerPoint dialog box explains that this clip art picture is an imported picture. Converting it to a Microsoft Office drawing permanently discards any embedded data or linking information it contains.

FIGURE 3-73

 Other **Ways**

1. On Draw menu click Ungroup

Because a clip art picture is a collection of complex groups of objects, you may need to ungroup a complex object into less complex objects before being able to modify a specific object. When you ungroup a clip art picture and click the Yes button in the Microsoft PowerPoint dialog box (Step 2 above), PowerPoint converts the clip art picture to a PowerPoint object. The Picture toolbar no longer displays. Recall that a PowerPoint object is an object *not* associated with a supplementary application. As a result, you lose the capability to double-click the clip art picture to open the Microsoft Clip Gallery.

To replace a PowerPoint object with a clip art picture, click the Insert Clip Art button on the Drawing toolbar or click Insert on the menu bar. Click Object and then click Microsoft Clip Gallery. If for some reason you decide not to ungroup the clip art picture, click the No button in the Microsoft PowerPoint dialog box. Clicking the No button terminates the Ungroup command, and the clip art picture displays on the slide as a clip art picture.

Recall that a clip art picture is an object imported from the Microsoft Clip Gallery. Disassembling imported, embedded, or linked objects eliminates the embedding data or linking information the object contains that ties it back to its original source. Use caution when objects are not completely regrouped. Dragging or scaling affects only the selected object, not the entire collection of objects. To **regroup** the individual objects, select all the objects, click the Draw button on the Drawing toolbar, and then click Group.

Deselecting Clip Art Objects

All of the ungrouped objects in Figure 3-73 are selected. Before you can manipulate an individual object, you must **deselect** all selected objects to remove the selection rectangles, and then you must select the object you want to manipulate. For example, in this slide you will remove the beach ball under the umbrella. The following step explains how to deselect objects.

TO DESELECT A CLIP ART OBJECT

 Click outside the clip art object area.

Slide 5 displays without selection rectangles around the objects.

The beach umbrella clip art picture now is ungrouped into many objects. The next section explains how to delete the unwanted beach ball.

Deleting a PowerPoint Object

Now that the beach umbrella picture is ungrouped, you can delete the beach ball object. Perform the steps on the next page to delete the beach ball object.

More About

Printing Speaker Notes

As you add visual elements to your presentations, think about how you are going to discuss these objects in an oral presentation. When you get an idea, type it in the notes pane. Then you can print these speaker notes in a variety of formats. For example, you can add headers and footers that contain page numbers and the current date and time. You specify this information in the speaker notes master, which prints the slide in the upper half of the sheet and your notes in the notes body area in the lower half.

To Delete a PowerPoint Object

1 **Click near the shoreline on the right side of the umbrella pole as shown in Figure 3-74 and then drag diagonally through the beach ball to the lower-left corner of the brown beach blanket.**

A dotted line square displays around the beach ball as you drag. If you inadvertently select a different area, click the shoreline and retry.

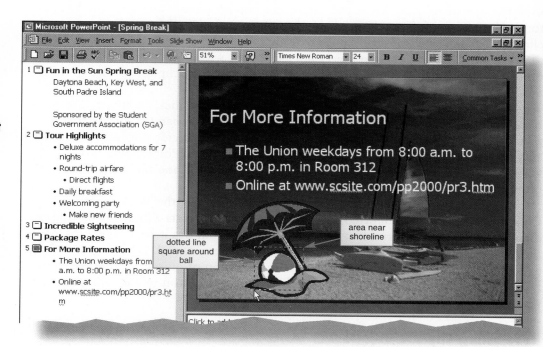

FIGURE 3-74

2 **Release the mouse button. Press the DELETE key.**

The beach ball object is deleted (Figure 3-75). If pieces of the beach ball remain, select each piece and then press the DELETE key.

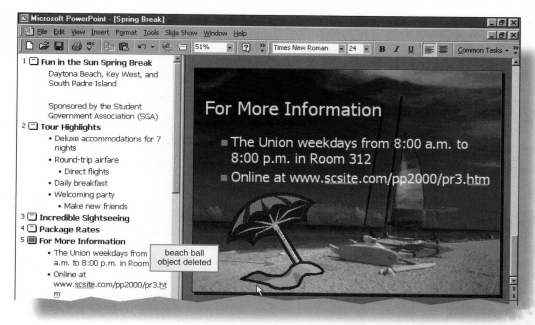

FIGURE 3-75

1. On Edit menu click Clear

Grouping PowerPoint Objects

All of the ungrouped objects in the beach umbrella picture must be regrouped so they are not accidentally moved or manipulated. Perform the following steps to regroup these objects.

Steps **To Group PowerPoint Objects**

1 **Click directly below the bullet for the second paragraph in the Object Area placeholder and then drag diagonally to the bottom-right corner of the beach umbrella picture.**

A dotted line rectangle displays around the beach umbrella picture as you drag (Figure 3-76). You want to group the objects within this area.

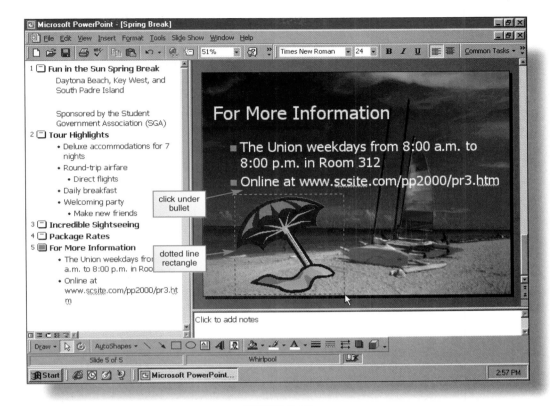

FIGURE 3-76

2 **Release the mouse button. Click the Draw button on the Drawing toolbar and then point to Group.**

Sizing handles display on all the selected components of the beach umbrella picture. You may have to wait a few seconds for the full Draw menu to display (Figure 3-77).

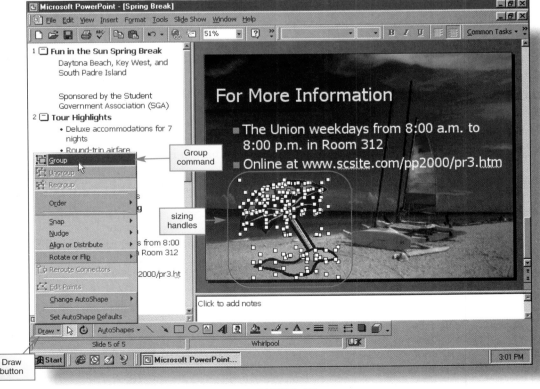

FIGURE 3-77

Click Group on the Draw menu.

The eight sizing handles displaying around the entire beach umbrella picture indicate the object is grouped (Figure 3-78).

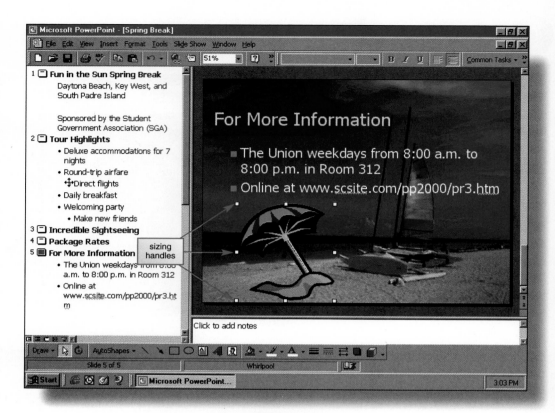

FIGURE 3-78

All the components of the beach umbrella picture now are grouped into one object. Slide 5 now is complete. The next section shows you how to add effects for switching from one slide to the next when you give your presentation.

Adding Slide Transition and Text Preset Animation Effects

The final step in preparing the Spring Break presentation is to add slide transition and text preset animation effects. Perform the following steps to add the slide transition and text preset animation effects.

TO ADD SLIDE TRANSITION AND TEXT PRESET ANIMATION EFFECTS

1. Click the Slide Sorter View button in the lower-left of the PowerPoint window.

2. Press and hold down the SHIFT key and then click Slide 2. Release the SHIFT key.

3. Click the Slide Transition Effects box arrow. Scroll down and then click Strips Right-Down.

4. Click the Preset Animation box arrow. Scroll down and then click Zoom In From Screen Center.

The presentation displays in Slide Sorter View (Figure 3-79). Slide transition effects and preset animation effects are applied to Slides 2, 3, 4, and 5.

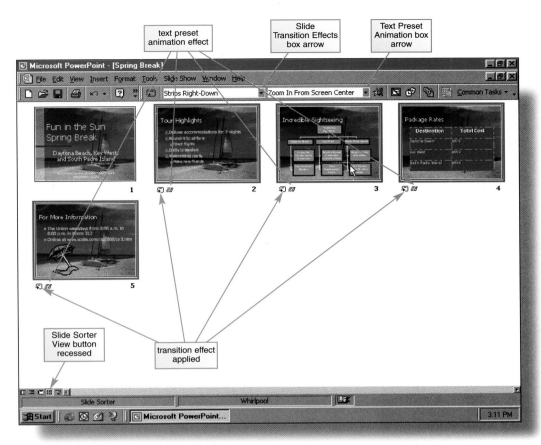

FIGURE 3-79

Printing Slides as Handouts

Perform the following steps to print the presentation slides as handouts, six slides per page.

TO PRINT SLIDES AS HANDOUTS

(1) Ready the printer according to the printer manufacturer's instructions.

(2) Click File on the menu bar and then click Print on the File menu.

(3) Click the Print what box arrow and then click Handouts in the list.

(4) Click Pure black and white and then click the OK button.

The handout prints as shown in Figure 3-80 on the next page. The background beach picture does not print.

Other Ways

1. In Slide View or Slide Sorter View, select slide to add transitions, right-click selected slide, click Slide Transition on shortcut menu, click Effect box arrow, choose desired transition, click Apply button

2. Select slide to add transitions, on Slide Show menu click Slide Transition, click Effect box arrow, choose desired transition, click Apply button

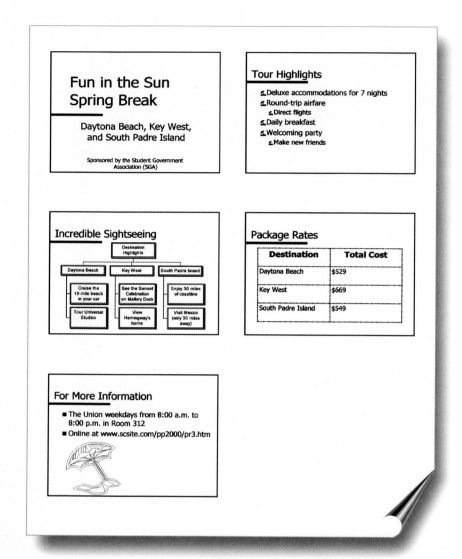

FIGURE 3-80

The Spring Break presentation now is complete. The final step is to make your slide show available to others on an intranet. Ask your instructor how you can publish your presentation.

Project Summary

Project 3 introduced you to several methods of enhancing a presentation with embedded visuals. You began the project by creating the presentation from an outline that was created in Word. Then, you learned how to create a special slide background using a picture. When you created Slide 2, you learned how to insert graphical bullets. Slide 3 introduced you to creating and embedding an organization chart using the supplementary application Microsoft Organization Chart. You then learned how to create and format a table on Slide 4. Next, you learned how to ungroup objects on Slide 5. Finally, you learned how to print your presentation slides as handouts.

What You Should Know

Having completed this project, you now should be able to perform the following tasks:

- Add Graphical Bullets *(PP 3.19)*
- Add Multiple Subordinate Boxes *(PP 3.27)*
- Add Names to Subordinate Boxes *(PP 3.28)*
- Add Shadow Effects to Boxes in an Organization Chart *(PP 3.36)*
- Add Slide Transition and Text Preset Animation Effects *(PP 3.58)*
- Change the Border Style *(PP 3.37)*
- Change Design Templates *(PP 3.9)*
- Change the Font *(PP 3.10)*
- Change the Font Size *(PP 3.14)*
- Change the Organization Chart Style *(PP 3.29)*
- Change the Slide Layout to Title Slide *(PP 3.12)*
- Copy a Branch of an Organization Chart *(PP 3.31)*
- Create a Table *(PP 3.41)*
- Create the Title for the Root Manager Box *(PP 3.25)*
- Delete a PowerPoint Object *(PP 3.56)*
- Deselect a Clip Art Object *(PP 3.55)*
- Display the Next Slide and Change the Slide Layout *(PP 3.23, 3.40)*
- Edit Text in an Organization Chart *(PP 3.33)*
- Enter Data in a Table *(PP 3.43)*
- Format a Table *(PP 3.47)*
- Format a Table Cell *(PP 3.45)*
- Group PowerPoint Objects *(PP 3.57)*
- Increase the Object Area Placeholder Width *(PP 3.51)*
- Insert a Picture to Create a Custom Background *(PP 3.16)*
- Insert a Clip Art Picture *(PP 3.52)*
- Maximize the Microsoft Organization Chart Window *(PP 3.25)*
- Move the Organization Chart *(PP 3.39)*
- Open Microsoft Organization Chart *(PP 3.24)*
- Paste a Branch of an Organization Chart *(PP 3.32)*
- Print Slides as Handouts *(PP 3.59)*
- Quit Microsoft Organization Chart and Return to the PowerPoint Window *(PP 3.38)*
- Save a Presentation *(PP 3.12)*
- Scale an Organization Chart Object *(PP 3.39)*
- Scale and Move a Clip Art Picture *(PP 3.53)*
- Select All Boxes in an Organization Chart *(PP 3.35)*
- Start PowerPoint and Open an Outline *(PP 3.7)*
- Title the Subordinate Boxes *(PP 3.26)*
- Ungroup a Clip Art Picture *(PP 3.54)*

Apply Your Knowledge

⊕ Project Reinforcement at www.scsite.com/off2000/reinforce.htm

1 Creating a Presentation from an Outline, Inserting a Clip Art Picture, Changing Bullets, and Changing the Slide Background

Instructions: Start PowerPoint. Open the outline, Hot Outline, from the Data Disk. See the inside back cover of this book for instructions for downloading the Data Disk or see your instructor for information on accessing the files required in this book. Perform the following tasks.

1. Apply the Blue Diagonal design template.
2. Change the AutoLayout for Slide 1 to Title Slide (Figure 3-81a).
3. Create the custom background shown in Figure 3-81a using the Sunset picture file on the Data Disk.
4. On Slide 2, insert the sleeping clip art picture shown in Figure 3-81b. Scale the height of the clip art picture to 110%.
5. Change the bullets to the sun located in the Almanac MT character fonts.
6. Apply the Blinds Vertical slide transition effect. Then apply the Split Vertical In text preset animation effect.
7. Save the presentation with the file name, Heat.
8. Print the presentation.
9. Quit PowerPoint.

FIGURE 3-81a

Apply Your Knowledge

Project Reinforcement at www.scsite.com/off2000/reinforce.htm

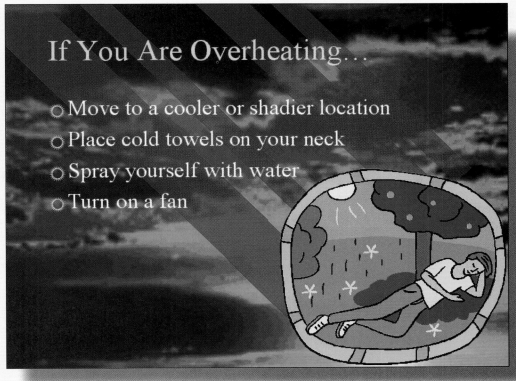

FIGURE 3-81b

In the Lab

1 Creating a Custom Slide

Problem: Communicating effectively among employees is a major problem at your job. Part of the problem stems from reluctance to give and receive instructions. Senior management realizes the problem and wants to schedule a workshop to improve communication skills. Your manager has asked you to prepare a slide show to publicize the goals of the workshop. You want a title slide showing people working together on the job and expressing communication difficulties. You import a picture from the Microsoft Clip Gallery and then modify it to create the slide shown in Figure 3-82 on the next page.

Instructions: Start PowerPoint and perform the following tasks with a computer.

1. Choose the Title Only AutoLayout and then apply the Post Modern design template.
2. Type Communication Skills Workshop for the slide title. Change the font size to 54. Bold this text.

(continued)

In the Lab

Creating a Custom Slide *(continued)*

3. Insert the clip art picture from the Microsoft Clip Gallery with the description, telephones, people. Scale the picture to 300%.

4. Ungroup the picture. Then delete the purple buildings and the blue background. Delete the men's red ties.

5. Insert the clip art picture with the description, communications technology. Scale the picture to 120%.

6. Ungroup this picture and delete the blue background and road so that only the three bubbles with the green question mark, the red exclamation point, and the brown exclamation point and plus sign remain. Group each bubble and move them to the locations shown in Figure 3-82.

FIGURE 3-82

7. Change the fill effect of the slide background stationery by using the Texture sheet in the Fill Effects dialog box.

8. Group all the PowerPoint objects.

9. Save the presentation with the file name, Workshop.

10. Print the slide using the Pure black and white option.

11. Quit PowerPoint.

2 Embedding an Organization Chart and Inserting a Picture

Problem: Community leaders have announced plans to remodel and upgrade the park district's fitness center. The changes include additional aerobics classes, nutritional counseling, and personal training. The marketing director has asked you to help her publicize the facility, and you want to create a slide show to display at the local mall. Part of your presentation will be the slide shown in Figure 3-83a highlighting the upgrades, and another will be the organization chart shown in Figure 3-83b on page PP 3.66 depicting the individuals involved in organizing the class schedule, the nutrition center, and the personal training workouts.

In the Lab

Instructions: Start PowerPoint and perform the following tasks with a computer.

1. Apply the Text & Clip Art AutoLayout and the LaVerne design template.
2. Type Coming Soon in the Title Area placeholder and then press the ENTER key. Type Your New Fitness Center on the second line.
3. Type the bulleted text shown in Figure 3-83a.

FIGURE 3-83a

4. Change the bullets to the heart character that is part of the Monotype Sorts character fonts. Change the heart color to pink.
5. Insert the clip art picture shown in Figure 3-83a with the description, fitness. Add a pink border to the picture using the 4½ pt thin-thick line.
6. Insert a new slide and apply the Organization Chart AutoLayout.
7. Type Meet Your Fitness Center Staff in the Title Area placeholder. Create the organization chart shown in Figure 3-83b on the next page. Type your name in the Director box.
8. Change the box color for the director to lime green (row 2, column 2). Change the box color for the assistant editor to red (row 1, column 9). Change the box color for the three specialty classes staff members to light green (row 1, column 4). Change the box color for the two nutrition services staff members to yellow (row 2, column 1). Do not change the box color for the four personal training staff members.

(continued)

In the Lab

Embedding an Organization Chart and Inserting a Picture *(continued)*

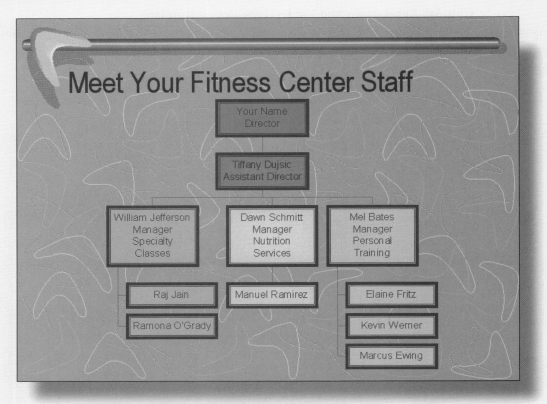

FIGURE 3-83b

9. Add borders to all boxes. Use the border style in the last row, column 2 Border Style submenu. Change the border color for all boxes to royal blue (row 1, column 5).
10. Change the line color to red (row 1, column 9).
11. Quit Microsoft Organization Chart and return to Slide 2. Scale the organization chart to 125%. Then drag the organization chart onto the center of the blank area under the Title Area placeholder.
12. Save the presentation with the file name, Fitness Center.
13. Print handouts (2 slides per page). Quit PowerPoint.

3 Opening an Existing Outline, Adding Graphical Bullets, and Creating a New Clip Art Picture

Problem: Your company softball team is getting organized for the new season, and you have been asked to help with the recruiting efforts. You decide to develop a presentation that includes information about the team. Create the opening slide of the presentation starting with the Softball Outline on your Data Disk. Then add and modify the clip art picture and bullets shown in Figure 3-84.

Instructions: Start PowerPoint and perform the following tasks with a computer.

In the Lab

1. Open the Softball Outline on your Data Disk.
2. Apply the Citrus design template. Change the Auto-Layout to Bulleted List.
3. Select the title text and change the font size to 60.
4. Move the bulleted text to the lower-right corner. Change the bullets to the arrows shown in Figure 3-84 that are part of the Wingdings 3 character fonts. Add a lime green border around the bulleted text using a 1 pt line.

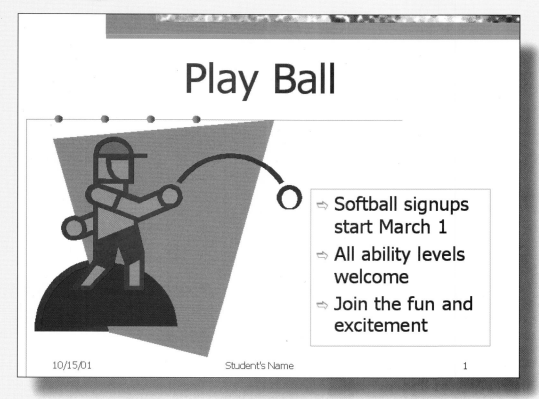

FIGURE 3-84

5. Insert the clip art picture with the description, softball. Enlarge the clip art to 275% and move it to the lower-left corner of the slide.
6. Ungroup the clip art picture. Delete the base. Then, change the color of the shirt to light gray and the shorts to black, which are your team colors. Change the color of the background shape to orange. Enlarge the ball to 120%.
7. Group all the individual objects in the clip art picture into one object.
8. Place the date, your name, and the slide number in the slide footer.
9. Save the presentation with the file name, Play Ball. Print the presentation and then quit PowerPoint.

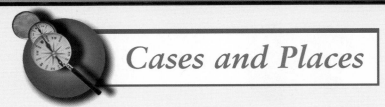

Cases and Places

The difficulty of these case studies varies:
❱ are the least difficult; ❱❱ are more difficult; and ❱❱❱ are the most difficult.

1 ❱ Hiking has become a popular activity for people of all ages. Especially appealing are forest pre-
serves and parks designed for family treks. Families comprise one of the fastest growing hiking groups as
parents introduce their children to the wonders of nature. When parents pack the supplies for the hike,
they should include water, sunscreen with an SPF of 45 or higher, insect repellent, and the children's
favorite wholesome foods, such as fruit and pretzels. They should dress in layers so they can add or peel
off layers as conditions change. Hikers also should wear long pants and a long sleeve shirt to protect
against ticks and cuts. A hat is a must, as it protects eyes against glare and keeps the body warm in winter. Families can have more fun hiking by singing and doing educational activities such as bird watching,
identifying trees and flowers, and looking for animal tracks. It is important to stop frequently and rest.
Prepare a presentation that promotes family hiking by describing how to pack, what to wear, and how
to enjoy the outing. Create a custom background. Include a title slide and a clip art picture.

2 ❱❱ Car theft is on the rise, so your campus police chief wants to give students some simple tips they
can use to protect their cars from thieves. He gives some anti-theft basics, such as installing a good security device and putting stickers on the windows announcing the alarm system. The alarm should sound
when the car is tilted or moved. This system will decrease insurance premiums. Another device is a rein-
forced collar that fits over the steering column casing and has to be removed to start the vehicle. He also
gives some parking tips, such as parking in a well-lit area after dark, turning the wheels sharply to the
right or left so the car is pointed inward when parking against a curb, and having a panic switch on the
remote door opener that triggers the siren and flashes the parking lights to startle potential thieves and
attackers. Another technique is etching the vehicle identification number (VIN) on the parts thieves sell
to body shops. These parts are windows, doors, fenders, bumpers, and fancy wheels. Also, install a toggle switch on the wire running from the ignition to the starter to deter thieves from starting the car. The
switch disables the vehicle's starter circuit. Use the concepts and techniques introduced in this project to
create a presentation. Use a title slide and apply slide transition and text preset animation effects. Create
handouts to distribute to students.

3 ❱❱❱ Producing your campus' student newspaper is an extraordinary task. Reporters, copy editors,
advertising salespeople, and artists must coordinate their activities to generate stories and meet deadlines. Visit the student newspaper office at your school and obtain the names and titles of the editors
and their staffs. Then create a presentation that includes a hierarchy chart explaining this chain of command. Format the hierarchy chart to highlight the newspaper's sections, such as news, features, and
sports. Include a slide showing the staff's accomplishments, such as awards received in competitions or
goals achieved, a short biography of the editor in chief, and appropriate clip art pictures.

P R O J E C T

4

Microsoft PowerPoint 2000

Creating a Presentation Containing Interactive OLE Documents

You will have mastered the material in this project when you can:

O B J E C T I V E S

- Open an existing presentation and save it with a new file name
- Create a WordArt object
- Add a special text effect
- Scale a WordArt object
- Create an interactive document
- Create a slide using action buttons and hyperlinks
- Use guides to position and size an object
- Modify an organization chart
- Edit a PowerPoint table
- Hide a slide
- Change the order of slides
- Automatically add a summary slide
- Run a slide show to display a hidden slide and activate an interactive document

Visual Exhilaration
Brings Audiences Back for More

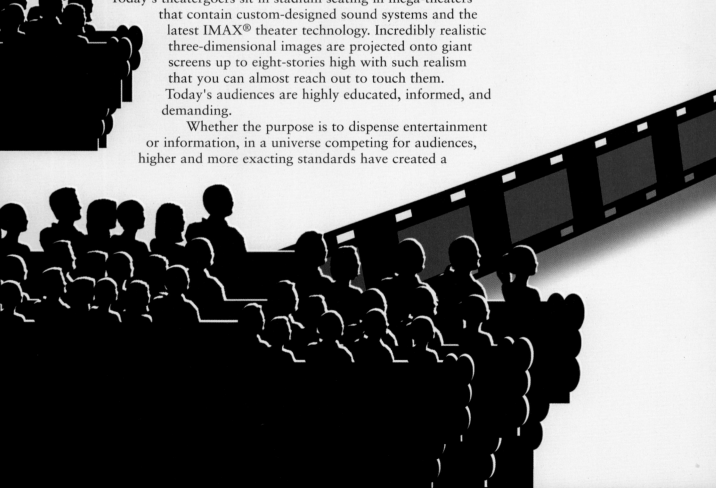

In the fast-paced world of instant communications and live video-conferencing; multimedia and virtual reality; and the dawn of the twenty-first century, people around the world are networked together for the purposes of exchanging information, providing goods, services and entertainment, reporting global news, and searching the vast resources of the Internet.

Baby boomers and the X Generation both have grown up with technological advances beyond the wildest dreams of former generations. Consider moviegoers of 50 and 60 years ago who viewed reel-to-reel films shot on studio lots projected onto the silver screen in movie palaces such as the Mann's Chinese Theater in Hollywood.

Today's theatergoers sit in stadium seating in mega-theaters that contain custom-designed sound systems and the latest IMAX® theater technology. Incredibly realistic three-dimensional images are projected onto giant screens up to eight-stories high with such realism that you can almost reach out to touch them.

Today's audiences are highly educated, informed, and demanding.

Whether the purpose is to dispense entertainment or information, in a universe competing for audiences, higher and more exacting standards have created a

high-tech society that demands excitement and stimulation in everything it sees. Presentations are no exception. In exchange for their time and attention, people expect presentations to be entertaining, as well as informative.

Fortunately for those who face the daunting task of presenting a visually stimulating, rewarding experience to exacting viewers, Microsoft has provided its own answer to theater technology. Far simpler to use than most software in its class, PowerPoint supplies another kind of tool, called Object Linking and Embedding, otherwise known as OLE (pronounced olay). OLE gives users the capability of importing and embedding objects from another source, such as an image on the Web, a Clip Gallery picture, or a scanned-in photo. With the literally thousands of images in commercially available clip art libraries, it is possible to include in a slide any subject whatsoever in the forms of

pictures, sounds, and motion clips with very little effort.

The freedom to create a picture to the author's specifications is a decided plus over other static preparation tools. After embedding a graphics object, the object can be manipulated in several ways: changing its size, extracting part of the image, rearranging the individual components of the image, or adding objects from other sources to the original.

The capability of importing from other applications, such as Excel or Word, adds another powerful tool to the presenter's arsenal. Via this route, interactive documents, graphs, charts, tables, worksheets, and special text effects created with WordArt add to the excitement.

High-tech in the new millennium focuses on the development of advanced information technology such as electronic education and e-commerce. With the excitement derived from a satisfied audience, PowerPoint presentations will be showing well into the new century.

Microsoft PowerPoint 2000

Creating a Presentation Containing Interactive OLE Documents

P R O J E C T

4

C A S E   P E R S P E C T I V E

The PowerPoint presentation for the Fun in the Sun Spring Break trip you created in Project 3 was a great success. Marla Pervan, the Student Government Association (SGA) president, is pleased that your impressive marketing presentation on the three beach destinations gave valuable information and helped recruit students. All three trips were booked solid, and the Student Government Association made a $5,000 profit.

Many students have been discussing cruises as a Spring Break option for next year. Marla thought the initial PowerPoint presentation could be altered to contain marketing information for two cruises. She asked if you would help change the original Spring Break presentation and add information about cruises to the Eastern and Western Caribbean islands. You agree to update the original presentation with the new information. You also create and add a heading using WordArt, replace one slide with another that contains interactive documents, and add the capability of hiding a slide if time limitations occur.

Introduction

Every presentation is created for a specific audience. Occasionally an existing presentation can be modified to fit the needs of a new audience. For example, another audience may have a different knowledge base or have specific interests. Sometimes, when running a slide show, you want to open another application to show more detailed information about a particular topic. For example, when presenting cruise information, you may want to show the cost of the cruise during the slide show without leaving PowerPoint. PowerPoint allows you to do so using interactive documents. An **interactive document** is a file created in another application, such as Microsoft Word, and then opened during the running of a slide show. Other times you may wish to refrain from showing one or more slides because you are short on time or the slides are not applicable to a particular audience.

PowerPoint has the capability of hiding slides. As the presenter, you decide whether to display them. Occasionally, you want to add a more graphical heading to call attention to the slide show topic. Project 4 customizes the Spring Break presentation created in Project 3 (see Figures 3-1a through 3-1e on page PP 3.5) and creates the slide show shown in Figures 4-1a through 4-1h.

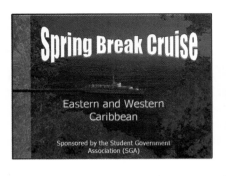

(a) Slide 1

(b) Slide 2

(c) Slide 3

(d) Slide 4

(e) Slide 5

(f) Slide 6

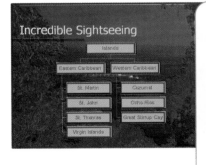

(g) Slide 7

(h) Slide 8

FIGURE 4-1

More About 2000

Presentation Power

An effective PowerPoint presentation helps an audience retain the information a speaker is conveying. Audience members remember 70% of what they see and hear, but only 30% of what they see, 20% of what they hear, and 10% of what they read.

Project Four — Customizing an Existing Presentation

As the first step in customizing the Spring Break presentation created in Project 3, open the Spring Break file. To ensure that the original presentation remains intact, you must save it using a new file name, Spring Break Cruise. Later in this project, you will modify the new presentation's slides by changing the slide background, replacing bulleted text, changing the chart and table, and adding one new slide. The following steps illustrate these procedures.

Opening a Presentation and Saving It with a New File Name

To begin, open the Spring Break presentation saved in Project 3 and save it with the file name, Spring Break Cruise. This procedure should be done immediately to prevent inadvertently saving the presentation with the original file name. Perform the following steps to open an existing presentation and save it with a new file name. If you did not complete Project 3, see your instructor for a copy of the presentation. To reset your toolbars and menus so they display exactly as shown in this book, follow the steps in Appendix C.

TO OPEN A PRESENTATION AND SAVE IT WITH A NEW FILE NAME

1 Insert your Data Disk into drive A. Click the Start button on the taskbar and then click Open Office Document.

2 Click the Look in box arrow and then click 3½ Floppy (A:).

3 Double-click Spring Break.

4 Click File on the menu bar and then click Save As. Type `Spring Break Cruise` in the File name text box.

5 Click the Save button in the Save As dialog box.

The presentation is saved on the floppy disk in drive A with the file name, Spring Break Cruise (Figure 4-2).

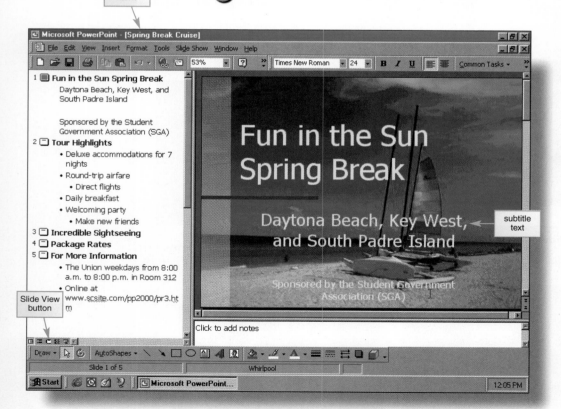

FIGURE 4-2

Editing the Title Slide

Because the Spring Break location options are changing, you must change the subtitle text in the Object Area placeholder on the title slide. Text that displays on a slide can be edited in the slide or outline panes. Perform the following steps to display the title slide in slide view and then revise the text.

TO CHANGE TEXT

1 Click the Slide View button located at the lower left of the PowerPoint window.

2 Triple-click the text in the Object Area placeholder, Daytona Beach, Key West, and South Padre Island, to select it.

3 Type Eastern and Western Caribbean in place of the highlighted text.

4 Click anywhere on the slide other than the Title Area or Object Area placeholders.

Slide 1 displays the updated Object Area text (Figure 4-3).

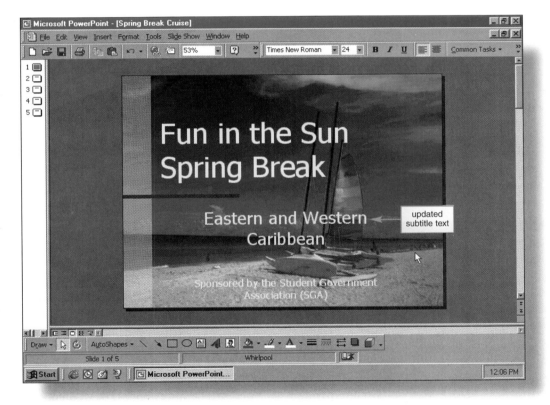

FIGURE 4-3

Changing the Background

The Student Government Association's Spring Break organizing team requests you change the background picture used in Project 3 to something more appropriate for a cruise. You examine various pictures and find one with a ship on the ocean. Perform the steps on the next page to insert this picture and change the slide background.

More About 2000

Backgrounds

Interesting backgrounds help add interest and individuality to your presentations. PowerPoint supplies a variety of backgrounds with various textures, patterns, and gradient styles and colors. In addition, the Internet is a source of unique backgrounds. To view some of these backgrounds, visit the PowerPoint 2000 Project 4 More About page (www.scsite.com/pp2000/more.htm) and click Backgrounds.

TO CHANGE THE BACKGROUND

1 Click View on the menu bar, point to Master, and then click Slide Master on the Master submenu.

2 Right-click Slide 1 anywhere except the slide master objects. Click Background on the shortcut menu.

3 Click the Background fill area box arrow. Click Fill Effects in the list.

4 Click the Select Picture button on the Picture tab in the Fill Effects dialog box. Click the Look in box arrow and then click 3½ Floppy (A:).

5 Double-click Ship in the list.

6 Click the OK button in the Fill Effects dialog box and then click the Apply to All button.

7 Click the Slide View button located at the lower left of the PowerPoint window.

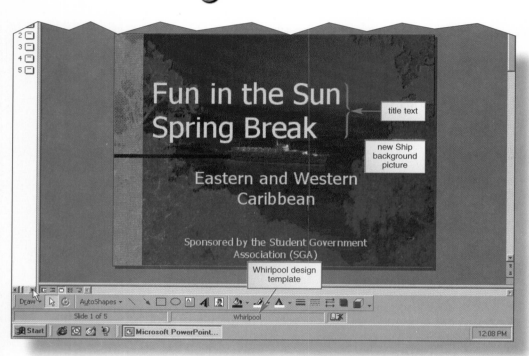

FIGURE 4-4

Slide 1 displays the new Ship background picture in slide view (Figure 4-4).

The Spring Break Cruise presentation maintains the same color scheme as the original Spring Break presentation because you are keeping the same design template, Whirlpool. A **color scheme** is a set of eight balanced colors you can apply to all slides, an individual slide, notes pages, or audience handouts. A color scheme consists of colors for a background, text and lines, shadows, title text, fills, accent, accent and hyperlink, and accent and followed hyperlink. Table 4-1 explains the components of a color scheme.

Table 4-1	Color Scheme Components
COMPONENT	DESCRIPTION
Background color	The background color is the fundamental color of a PowerPoint slide. For example, if your background color is white, you can place any other color on top of it, but the fundamental color remains white. The white background shows everywhere you do not add color or other objects. The background color on a slide works the same way.
Text and lines color	The text and lines color contrasts with the background color of the slide. Together with the background color, the text and lines color sets the tone for a presentation. For example, a gray background with a black text and lines color sets a dramatic tone. In contrast, a red background with a yellow text and lines color sets a vibrant tone.
Title text color	The title text color contrasts with the background color in a manner similar to the text and lines color. Title text displays in the Title Area placeholder on a slide.
Shadow color	The shadow color is applied when you color an object. This color usually is a darker shade of the background color.
Fill color	The fill color contrasts with both the background color and the text and lines color. The fill color is used for graphs and charts.
Accent colors	Accent colors are designed as colors for secondary features on a slide. Additionally, accent colors are used as colors on graphs.

Creating a WordArt Object

The background picture is changed to differentiate the Spring Break Cruise presentation from the Spring Break presentation created in Project 3. Another way to differentiate the two presentations is by altering the style of the heading. WordArt is used to create the graphical heading that displays on the title slide shown in Figure 4-1a on page PP 4.5.

Creating the Spring Break Cruise heading requires several steps. First, you must delete the heading currently located on the title slide. Next, you use the presentation name to create a WordArt object. Finally, you position and size the heading on the Spring Break Cruise title slide. The next several sections explain how to create the Spring Break Cruise heading object using WordArt.

Deleting the Slide Text

A slide heading is a standard object on a title slide. In this presentation, the slide heading will be replaced with an object created with WordArt. The Florida and Texas destinations will be changed to promote the Eastern and Western Caribbean islands. The following steps show how to delete the title text.

TO DELETE THE SLIDE TEXT

1. Triple-click the title text, Fun in the Sun Spring Break.
2. Double-click the move handle on the Standard toolbar.
3. Click the Cut button on the Standard toolbar.

The title text is deleted (Figure 4-5).

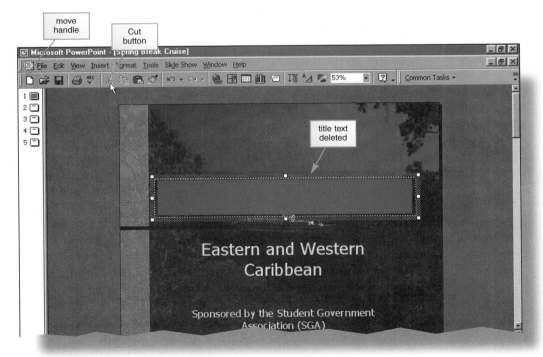

FIGURE 4-5

More About

WordArt Content

Text used in a different application can be copied to your PowerPoint slide and used in a WordArt object. Just select that text, copy it by pressing the CTRL+C keys, and then paste it inside PowerPoint's Edit WordArt Text dialog box by pressing the CTRL+V keys.

Other Ways

1. Highlight title text, on Edit menu click Cut, highlight first subtitle text paragraph, type new text
2. Highlight title text, press CTRL+X, highlight first subtitle text paragraph, type new text

Displaying the Rulers

To help you align objects, PowerPoint provides two **rulers**: a horizontal ruler and a vertical ruler. The **horizontal ruler** displays at the top of the slide window. The **vertical ruler** displays at the left side of the slide window. When the zoom percentage is less than 37 percent, **tick marks** display in one-half-inch segments. When the zoom percentage is 37 percent or greater, tick marks display in one-eighth-inch segments. Your percentages may vary based on your computer system. When you move the mouse pointer, a **pointer indicator** traces the position of the mouse pointer and displays its exact location on both rulers. Perform the following steps to display the horizontal and vertical rulers.

 To Display the Rulers

1 **Right-click anywhere on Slide 1 other than the Title Area and Object Area placeholders, and then point to Ruler on the shortcut menu.**

The shortcut menu displays (Figure 4-6).

2 **Click Ruler.**

Rulers display above and to the left of Slide 1.

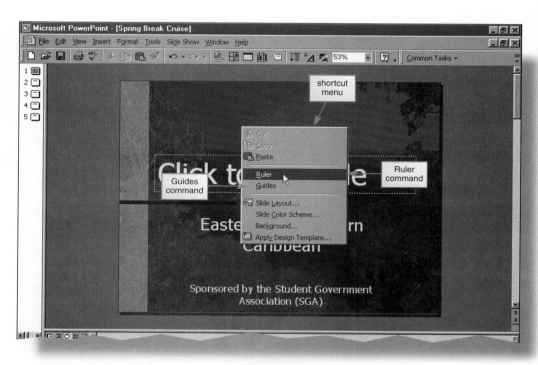

FIGURE 4-6

 Ways

1. On View menu click Ruler
2. Press ALT+V, press R

When the **Ruler command** is active, a check mark displays in front of the Ruler command on both the shortcut menu and the View menu. When you want to prohibit the rulers from displaying in the PowerPoint window, you **hide the rulers**. To hide the rulers, right-click anywhere in the PowerPoint window except on a placeholder, and then click Ruler.

Displaying the Guides

PowerPoint guides are used to align objects. The **guides** are two straight dotted lines, one horizontal and one vertical. When an object is close to a guide, its corner or its center (whichever is closer) *snaps*, or attaches itself, to the guide. You can move the guides to meet your alignment requirements. Because you are preparing the slide window to create the presentation heading, perform this step to display the guides.

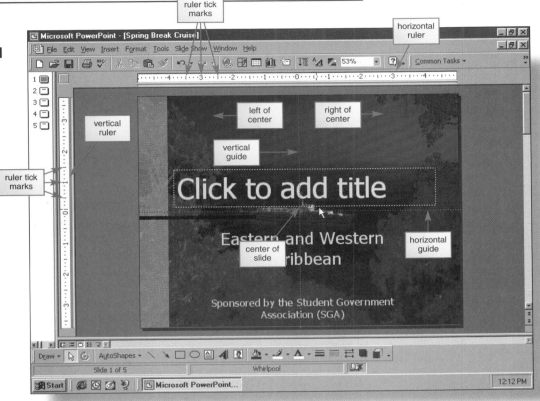

FIGURE 4-7

To Display the Guides

1 **Right-click anywhere on Slide 1 except in the Title Area or Object Area placeholders, and then click Guides on the shortcut menu.**

The horizontal and vertical guides intersect in the middle of the slide window and align with the 0-inch tick marks on the horizontal and vertical rulers (Figure 4-7).

On the shortcut menu displayed in Step 1, a check mark displays in front of the Ruler command because you activated it in the previous section. Recall that a check mark displays when a command is active, or turned on. In the same manner, when the Guides command is active, a check mark displays in front of the Guides command on both the shortcut menu and the View menu.

Positioning the Guides

The guides can be used to position the WordArt heading. You use the vertical and horizontal guides to help position the heading on the title slide. The center of a slide is 0.00 on both the vertical and the horizontal guides. Position a guide by dragging it to a new location. When you point to a guide and then press and hold the mouse button, PowerPoint displays a box containing the exact position of the guide on the slide in inches. An arrow displays under the guide position to indicate the vertical guide is either left or right of center. An arrow displays to the right of the guide position to indicate the horizontal guide is either above or below center. Perform the steps on the next page to position the guides.

1. On View menu click Guides
2. Press ALT+V, press G

Displaying Guides

At times you may want to display multiple vertical and horizontal guides on your slide. To display an additional guide, press and hold the CTRL key and then drag one of the guides. When the new guide displays, drag it to the position where you want to place an object.

To Position the Guides

1 **Drag the vertical guide to 3.92 inches left of center.**

The pointer indicator displays 3.92 inches left of center (Figure 4-8).

FIGURE 4-8

2 **Drag the horizontal guide to 0.83 inches above center.**

The pointer indicator displays 0.83 inches above center (Figure 4-9).

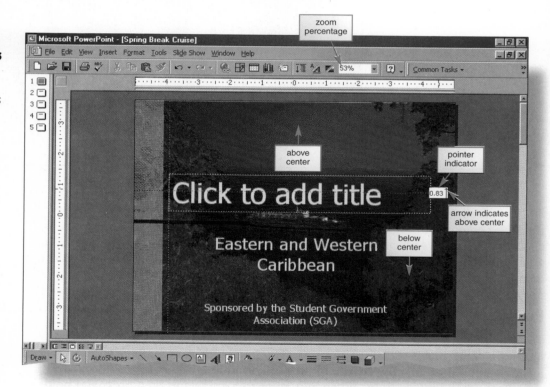

FIGURE 4-9

When you no longer want the guides to display on the screen or want to control the exact placement of objects, you can **hide the guides**. To hide the guides, right-click anywhere in the PowerPoint window except on a placeholder, and then click Guides.

Increasing the Zoom Percentage

Increasing the zoom percentage reduces the editing view of a slide in slide view, but it increases the editing view of individual objects. You increase the zoom percentage to make working with detailed objects or small objects easier. In this project, you increase the zoom percentage to 75 percent because it allows you to work easily with the Title Area object. The following steps summarize how to increase the zoom percentage.

TO INCREASE THE ZOOM PERCENTAGE

1 Click the Zoom box arrow on the Standard toolbar.

2 Click 75% in the list.

The zoom percentage changes to 75% (Figure 4-10). You may drag the vertical or horizontal scroll boxes to display the horizontal and vertical rulers on various areas of the screen.

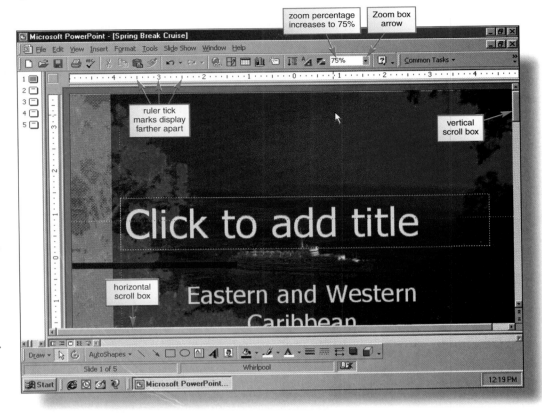

FIGURE 4-10

Adding Special Text Effects

The desired Spring Break Cruise heading contains letters that have been altered with special text effects. Using WordArt, first you will select a letter style for this text. Then you will type the name of the presentation and select a unique shape for their layout, although many other predefined shapes could be used. Buttons on the WordArt toolbar also allow you to rotate, slant, curve, and alter the shape of letters. WordArt also can be used in the other Microsoft Office applications. The next several sections explain how to create the text object shown on the title slide in Figure 4-1a on page PP 4.5.

Selecting a WordArt Style

PowerPoint supplies 30 predefined WordArt styles that vary in shape and color. Perform the steps on the next page to select a style for the Spring Break Cruise text.

More About

Backgrounds

Corporations spend thousands of dollars designing corporate logos. They often request several potential designs and then ask the public to evaluate the message of these logos. For example, do the logos illustrate concepts of strength, creativity, dominance, or youthfulness? BMW redesigned its logo in 1997 for the sixth time in its 80-year history. BMW states that their logo should be printed in black and white if it is on a color background, and the background should not be a medium-blue color because the corporate BMW color is blue. For more information, visit the PowerPoint 2000 Project 4 More About page (www.scsite.com/pp2000/more.htm) and click Logo.

To Select a WordArt Style

1 **Click the Insert WordArt button on the Drawing toolbar. When the WordArt Gallery dialog box displays, point to the WordArt style in row 1, column 4.**

The WordArt Gallery dialog box displays (Figure 4-11).

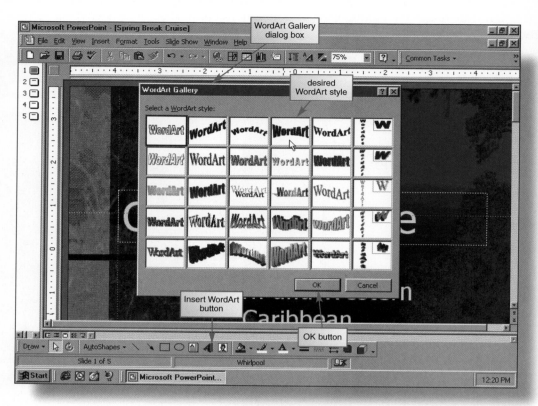

FIGURE 4-11

2 **Click the WordArt style in row 1, column 4. Click the OK button.**

The Edit WordArt Text dialog box displays (Figure 4-12). The default text, Your Text Here, inside the dialog box is highlighted.

FIGURE 4-12

Entering the WordArt Text

To create a text object, you must enter text in the Edit WordArt Text dialog box. By default, the words, Your Text Here, in the Edit WordArt Text dialog box are highlighted. When you type the text for your title object, it replaces the selected text. When you want to start a new line, press the ENTER key. Perform the following steps to enter the text for the Spring Break Cruise heading.

 To Enter the WordArt Text

1 **If necessary, select the text in the Edit WordArt Text dialog box. Type** Spring Break Cruise **in the box.**

The text displays in the Text text box in the Edit WordArt Text dialog box (Figure 4-13). The default font is Impact, and the font size is 36.

FIGURE 4-13

2 **Click the OK button. If necessary, display the WordArt toolbar by right-clicking a toolbar and then clicking WordArt.**

The Spring Break Cruise text displays (Figure 4-14). The WordArt toolbar displays in the same location and with the same shape as it displayed the last time it was used. You can move the WordArt toolbar by dragging its title bar.

FIGURE 4-14

The WordArt toolbar contains the buttons that allow you to change an object's appearance. For example, you can rotate the letters, change the character spacing and alignment, scale the size, and add different fill and line colors. Table 4-2 explains the purpose of each button on the WordArt toolbar.

Table 4-2	WordArt Toolbar Button Functions	
BUTTON	*BUTTON NAME*	*DESCRIPTION*
	Insert WordArt	Creates a WordArt object
Edit Te_xt...	WordArt Edit Text	Changes the text characters, font, and font size
	WordArt Gallery	Chooses a different WordArt style for the selected WordArt object
	Format WordArt	Formats the line, color, fill and pattern, size, position, and other properties of the selected object
	WordArt Shape	Modifies the text shape
	Free Rotate	Turns an object around its axis
	WordArt Same Letter Heights	Makes all letters the same height, regardless of case
	WordArt Vertical Text	Stacks the text in the selected WordArt object vertically — one letter on top of the other — for reading from top to bottom
	WordArt Alignment	Left-aligns, centers, right-aligns, word-aligns, letter-aligns, or stretch-aligns text
	WordArt Character Spacing	Displays options (Very Tight, Tight, Normal, Loose, Very Loose, Custom, Kern Character Pairs) for adjusting spacing between text

The next section explains how to shape the WordArt text.

Changing the WordArt Height and Width

WordArt objects actually are drawing objects, not text. Consequently, WordArt objects can be modified in various ways, including changing their height, width, line style, fill color, and shadows. Unlike text, however, they neither can display in outline view nor be spell checked. In this project, you will increase the height and width of the WordArt object. The Size tab in the Format WordArt dialog box contains two areas used to change an object's size. The first, the **Size and rotate area**, allows you to enlarge or reduce an object, and turn an object around its axis. The second, the **Scale area**, allows you to change an object's size while maintaining its height-to-width ratio, or **aspect ratio**. If you want to retain the object's original settings, you click the Reset button in the **Original size area**. Perform the following steps to change the height and width of the WordArt object.

Wrapping Text

You can add text to your slide by clicking the Text Box button on the Drawing toolbar and then typing the desired words. If you want the text to wrap to fit the contours of the text box automatically, select the text box, click Format on the menu bar, click Text Box, and then click the Text Box tab. Click Word wrap text in AutoShape.

To Change the WordArt Height and Width

1 **Click the Format WordArt button on the WordArt toolbar. Click the Size tab in the Format WordArt dialog box.**

The Size sheet displays in the Format WordArt dialog box (Figure 4-15).

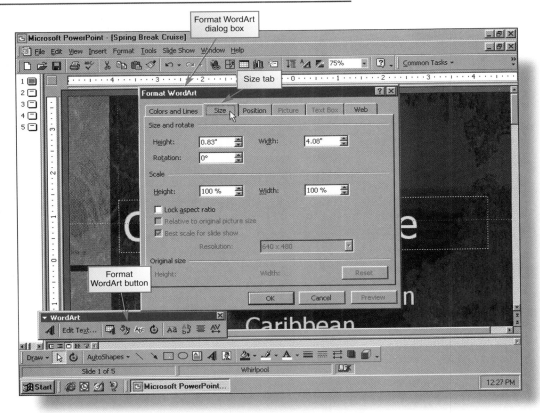

FIGURE 4-15

2 **Triple-click the Height text box in the Size and rotate area. Type 2.4 in the Height text box. Triple-click the Width text box in the Size and rotate area. Type 8.8 in the Width text box. Point to the OK button.**

The Height and Width text boxes display the new entries (Figure 4-16).

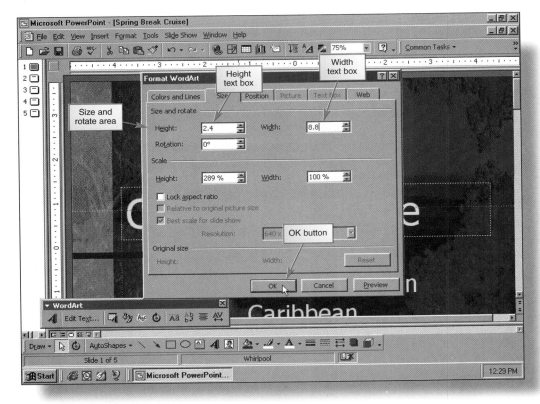

FIGURE 4-16

3 **Click the OK button.**

The WordArt text object displays over the Title Area placeholder (Figure 4-17).

FIGURE 4-17

4 **Drag the text object until the bottom edge snaps to the horizontal guide and the left edge snaps to the vertical guide. If necessary, you can make small adjustments in the position of the object by pressing the ARROW keys on the keyboard that correspond to the direction in which you want to move.**

The WordArt text object is positioned correctly (Figure 4-18).

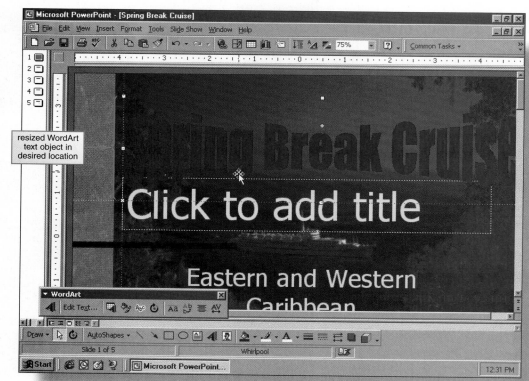

FIGURE 4-18

Changing the WordArt Fill Color

Now that the WordArt object is created, you want to lighten the font color to white. The Colors and Lines sheet in the Format WordArt dialog box contains an area to change the fill color. Perform the following steps to change the fill color.

Steps | **To Change the WordArt Fill Color**

1 **Click the Format WordArt button on the WordArt toolbar. Click the Colors and Lines tab in the Format WordArt dialog box. Point to the Color box arrow in the Fill area.**

The Colors and Lines sheet displays in the Format WordArt dialog box (Figure 4-19).

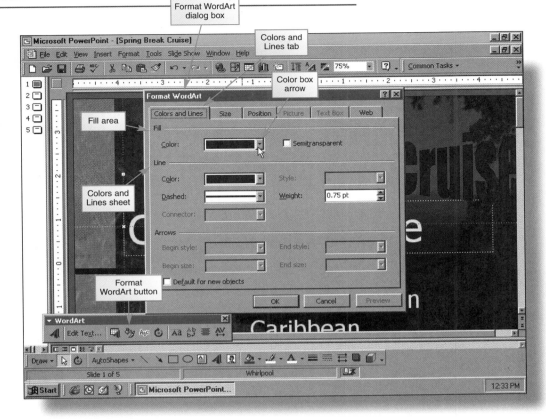

FIGURE 4-19

2 **Click the Color box arrow in the Fill area. Click the color white (row 1, column 2 under Automatic). Click the Weight box down arrow in the Line area once so that 0.5 pt displays.**

The color white displays in the Color box in the Fill area (Figure 4-20). White is the default Follow Text and Lines Scheme color for the Whirlpool template.

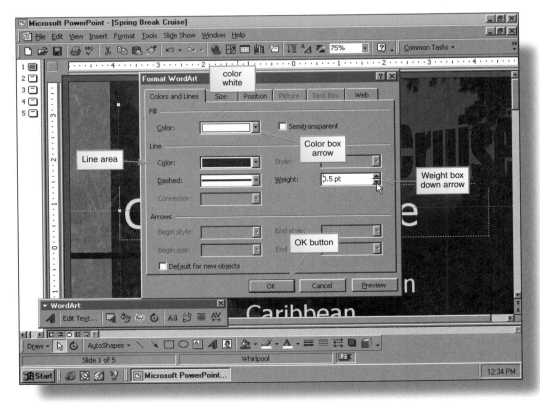

FIGURE 4-20

③ Click the OK button.

The WordArt text object displays with the color white and a .5 pt solid black border (Figure 4-21).

FIGURE 4-21

The WordArt text object is too large to fit in Slide 1 with the specified height and width. The most effective way to alter the object size is by scaling it. The next section describes how to scale a WordArt object.

Scaling a WordArt Object

The Spring Break Cruise text object is larger than the Spring Break Cruise title slide. To reduce the size of this object, you must scale it to 90 percent of its original size. Perform the following steps to scale the WordArt object.

 **To Scale the WordArt Object**

1 **Click the Format WordArt button on the WordArt toolbar. Click the Size tab in the Format WordArt dialog box.**

The Format WordArt dialog box displays.

2 **Click Lock aspect ratio in the Scale area, and then click the Height text box down arrow until 90% displays. Point to the OK button.**

The Height and Width text boxes both display 90% (Figure 4-22). When you change the percentage in the Height text box, the percentage in the Width text box also changes. In addition, the Height and Width text boxes in the Size and rotate area both change. The Lock aspect ratio check box is selected.

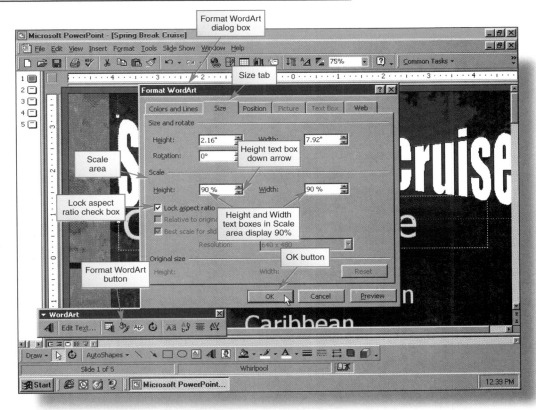

FIGURE 4-22

3 **Click the OK button.**

The WordArt object is reduced to 90 percent of its original size.

4 **Press the RIGHT ARROW key to center the WordArt object in the dark blue portion of the slide.**

The scaled WordArt object displays with the desired size in the correct location (Figure 4-23).

FIGURE 4-23

Other Ways

1. Right-click the WordArt object, click Format WordArt on shortcut menu, click Size tab, click Lock aspect ratio, double-click Height text box in Scale area, enter appropriate percent, click OK

2. Press ALT+O, press O, press ALT+A, press SPACEBAR, press ALT+H, enter appropriate percent, press ENTER

Hiding the Rulers and Guides

The rulers or guides are not needed when you modify the next slide, so you want to hide them. Recall that a check mark displays in front of the Ruler and Guides commands on the shortcut menu and View menu when the commands are active. Perform the following steps to remove the check mark and deactivate, or hide, the rulers and guides.

TO HIDE THE RULERS AND GUIDES

1 Right-click Slide 1 anywhere except the slide Title Area or Object Area placeholders.

2 Click Ruler on the shortcut menu.

3 Right-click Slide 1 anywhere except the slide Title Area or Object Area placeholders.

4 Click Guides on the shortcut menu.

The rulers and guides no longer display.

Resetting the Zoom Percentage

Zoom also is not needed. This setting can be modified so that PowerPoint determines the best size screen to display for the presentation.

TO RESET THE ZOOM PERCENTAGE

1 Click the Zoom box arrow.

2 Click Fit in the list.

The WordArt object displays as 57% (Figure 4-24). Your percentage may vary based on your computer system.

The changes to the title slide now are complete. The subtitle text was changed to reflect the purpose of the new presentation. The title text was deleted and replaced with a WordArt object. The next step is to edit Slide 2 to make it an interactive document.

FIGURE 4-24

Creating an Interactive Document

The next step in customizing the Spring Break Cruise presentation is to edit a slide so that it connects to two files with additional Spring Break Cruise information. You edit Slide 2 to contain two hyperlinks: one to a Microsoft Word document, Cruise Itinerary, and another to a Microsoft Excel spreadsheet, Cruise Pricing. Both of these files are stored on the Data Disk. Figure 4-25 illustrates the revised Slide 2, which contains two action buttons to reference additional Spring Break Cruise details. An **action button** is a built-in 3-D button that can perform specific tasks such as display the next slide, provide help, give information, and play a sound. In addition, the action button can activate a **hyperlink**, which is a shortcut that allows you to jump to another program, in this case Microsoft Word and Microsoft Excel, and load a specific document. A hyperlink also allows you to move to specific slides in a PowerPoint presentation or to an Internet address. In this slide, you will associate the hyperlink with an action button, but you also can use text or any object, including shapes, tables, or pictures. You specify which action you want PowerPoint to perform by using the **Action Settings** command on the Slide Show menu.

More *About*

Buttons

PowerPoint gives you 12 possible action buttons to use in your presentation. If you want to use less common buttons, shareware programs allow you to create custom buttons, which you can insert in your slide show. These unique buttons have various effects, such as three dimensions and pictures. To download a button customizing program, visit the PowerPoint 2000 Project 4 More About page (www.scsite.com/pp2000/more.htm) and click Buttons.

FIGURE 4-25

When you run the Spring Break Cruise presentation and click one of the action buttons in Slide 2, PowerPoint starts Microsoft Word or Excel and loads the designated file. For example, if you click the Itinerary action button, PowerPoint opens the Microsoft Word application and loads the Word document, Cruise Itinerary. Once you have finished viewing the Word document, you want to return to Slide 2. To do so, you will quit Word by clicking the Close button on the title bar, which will return you to the Spring Break Cruise slide show.

Editing Existing Text

Creating the slide shown in Figure 4-25 requires several steps. First, you edit the text in Slide 2 and add some additional text. After the text is edited, you display the guides. Then you add two action buttons and create hyperlinks to a Word document and an Excel spreadsheet. The final step is to scale the buttons and add color and shadows. The next several sections explain how to edit the text in Slide 2 in outline view.

TO EDIT EXISTING TEXT

1 Click the Outline View button at the lower left of the PowerPoint window.

2 Triple-click the first bulleted paragraph in Slide 2, Deluxe accommodations for 7 nights, to highlight it.

3 Type Exciting itineraries as the text.

4 Triple-click the fourth bulleted paragraph, Daily breakfast.

5 Type All meals as the text.

6 Triple-click the fifth and sixth bulleted paragraphs, Welcoming party and Make new friends.

7 Type Entertainment and then press the ENTER key.

8 Press the TAB key and then type Nightly shows as the text.

Slide 2 displays in outline view with the updated information (Figure 4-26).

Moving a Slide Bullet within Outline View

In the outline pane, the presentation appears as an outline of titles and text from each slide. Working in the outline view is a good way to develop the content of the presentation because you can see all of the titles and text of the entire presentation on the screen simultaneously. You can rearrange points within a slide, move entire slides from one position to another, and edit titles and text within a slide in outline view.

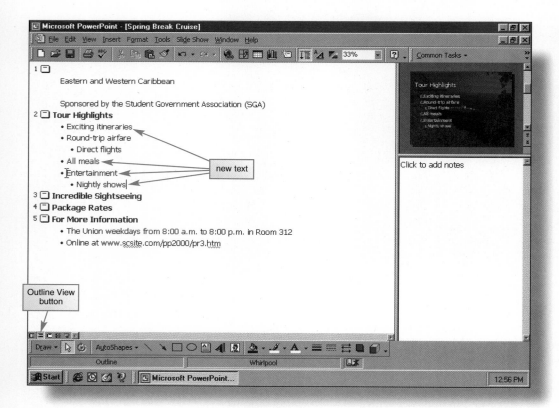

FIGURE 4-26

PROJECT 4

An important feature of the cruise pricing is that all meals are included. This aspect should be emphasized near the top of the bullet list, so you want to move the third paragraph, All meals, and make it the second bulleted item on the slide. Bullets can be moved in a presentation by dragging them to the selected location. Perform the following steps to move this paragraph.

To Move a Paragraph in Outline View

1 **Position the mouse to the left of the fourth bulleted paragraph, All meals.**

The mouse pointer becomes a four-headed arrow (Figure 4-27).

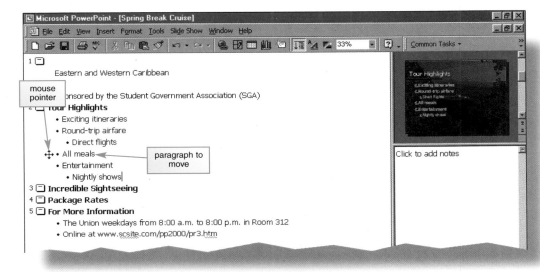

FIGURE 4-27

2 **Drag the third paragraph up directly under the first paragraph, Exciting itineraries.**

A move line helps position the text and the mouse pointer becomes a two-headed arrow (Figure 4-28).

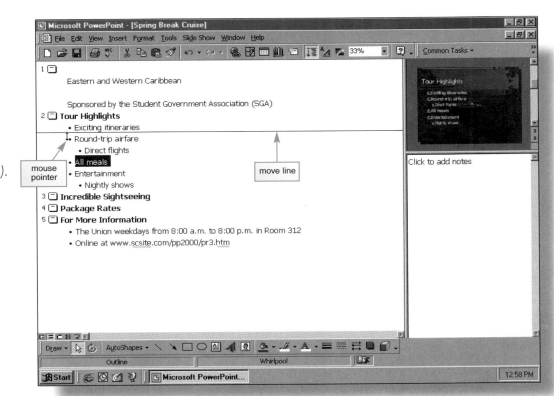

FIGURE 4-28

3 **Release the mouse button.**

Slide 2 displays in outline view with the newly edited and positioned text, All meals (Figure 4-29).

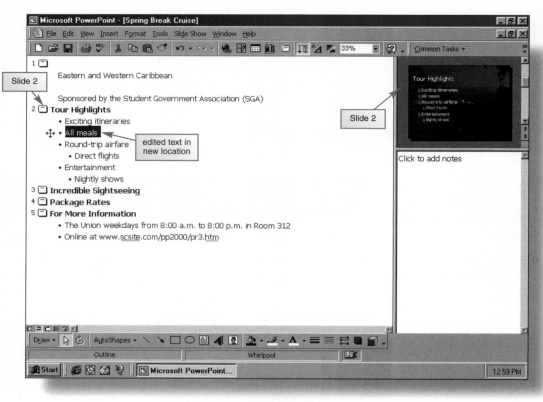

FIGURE 4-29

The text for Slide 2 is edited and rearranged. Perform the following steps to add action buttons and action settings to the slide.

Adding Action Buttons and Action Settings

You want to display additional information about the Spring Break cruise itinerary and pricing by opening files in Word and Excel without quitting PowerPoint. To obtain details on the cruise itineraries, you will click the left action button (Itinerary), and to obtain details on cruise pricing, you will click the right action button (Pricing). When you click a button, a chime sound will play. The next section describes how to create the action buttons and place them in Slide 2. These buttons are added in slide view.

More *About*

Action Buttons

Action buttons are a subset of PowerPoint's AutoShapes, which are convenient visuals designed to enhance your slides. Just click the AutoShapes button on the Drawing toolbar, select one of the categories of shapes on the menu, such as lines, connectors, basic shapes, flowchart elements, stars and banners, and callouts, click an AutoShape, and click the slide in the location where you want the AutoShape to appear. To add text to an AutoShape, just start typing.

To Add an Action Button and Action Settings

1 Click the Slide View button at the lower left of the PowerPoint window. Click Slide Show on the menu bar, point to Action Buttons, and then point to the first action button, Action Button: Custom, in the list.

The Action Buttons submenu displays 12 built-in 3-D buttons (Figure 4-30).

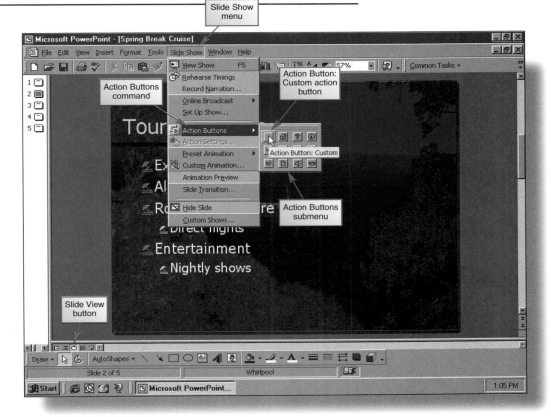

FIGURE 4-30

2 Click the Action Button: Custom action button (row 1, column 1) in the list. Click the bottom right of Slide 2.

The Action Settings dialog box displays (Figure 4-31) with the action button placed in Slide 2. None is the default Action on click.

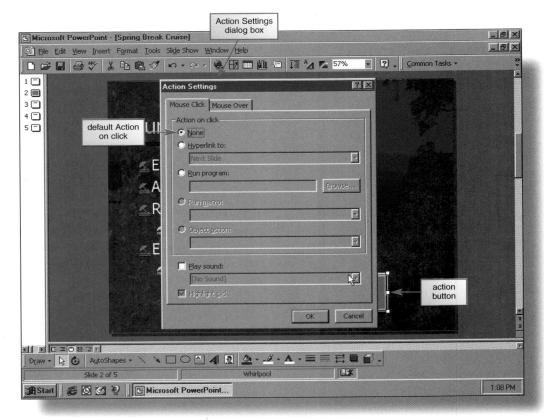

FIGURE 4-31

3 Click the Mouse Click tab. Click the Hyperlink to option button in the Action on click area. Click the Hyperlink to box arrow and then point to Other File in the list.

The list displays the possible locations in the slide show or elsewhere where a hyperlink can be established (Figure 4-32).

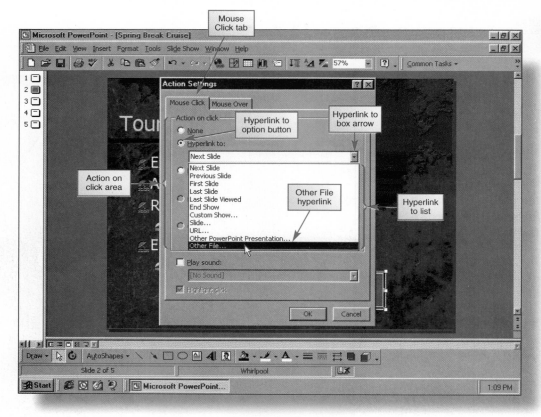

FIGURE 4-32

4 Click Other File. If necessary, click the Look in box arrow, click 3½ Floppy (A:), and then click Cruise Itinerary. Point to the OK button in the Hyperlink to Other File dialog box.

Cruise Itinerary is the Microsoft Word file you will link to the Itinerary action button (Figure 4-33). Your list of file names may vary.

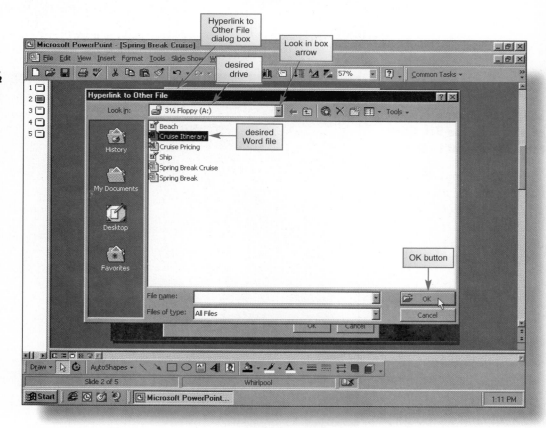

FIGURE 4-33

5 Click the OK button in the Hyperlink to Other File dialog box. Click the Play sound check box, click the Play sound box arrow, and then point to Chime.

The Hyperlink to box displays the Word document file name, Cruise Itinerary (Figure 4-34). A check mark displays in the Play sound check box. The Play sound list displays sounds that can play when you click the action button.

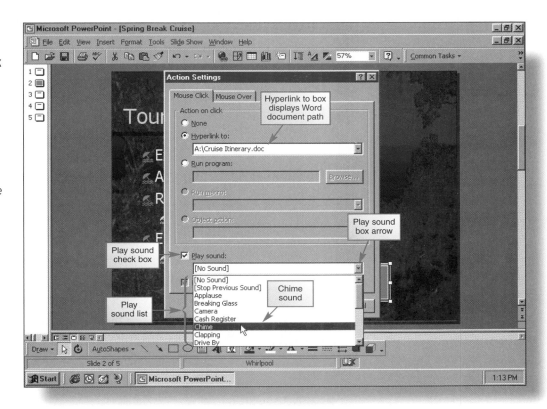

FIGURE 4-34

6 Click Chime. Click the OK button.

The action button is highlighted in Slide 2 (Figure 4-35).

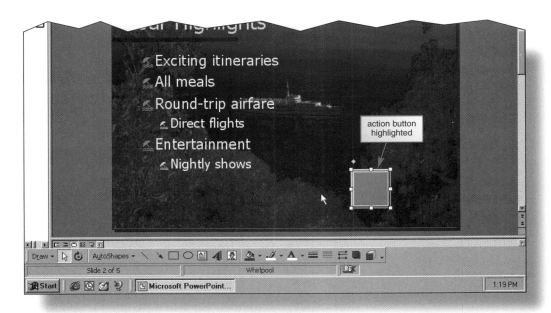

FIGURE 4-35

Now that you have created an action button and linked the Word document, Cruise Itinerary, you need to repeat the procedure for the Excel spreadsheet, Cruise Pricing. Perform the steps on the next page to create another action button and to hyperlink the Excel Cruise Pricing spreadsheet document to the PowerPoint presentation.

TO CREATE A SECOND ACTION BUTTON AND HYPERLINK

1 Click Slide Show on the menu bar, point to Action Buttons, and then click the Action Button: Custom action button (row 1, column 1) in the list.

2 Click to the right of the first action button in Slide 2.

3 Click Hyperlink to in the Action on click area in the Mouse Click sheet in the Action Settings dialog box.

4 Click the Hyperlink to box arrow and then click Other File.

5 Double-click Cruise Pricing in the list.

6 Click Play sound. Click the Play sound box arrow and then click Chime.

7 Click the OK button.

Slide 2 displays with the second action button for the Excel Pricing spreadsheet hyperlink (Figure 4-36). Later in this project you will make small adjustments to align the action button precisely.

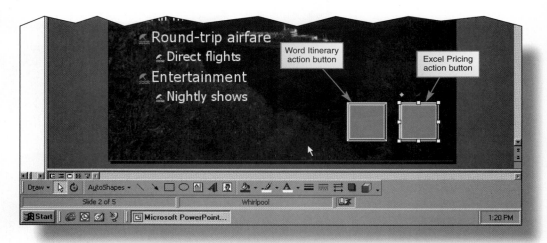

Word Itinerary action button

Excel Pricing action button

FIGURE 4-36

When you select a file from the Look in box, PowerPoint associates the file with a specific application, which is based on the file extension. For example, when you select the Cruise Itinerary file with the file extension **.doc**, PowerPoint recognizes the file as a Microsoft Word file. Additionally, when you select the Cruise Pricing file with the file extension **.xls**, PowerPoint recognizes the file as a Microsoft Excel file.

Displaying Guides and Positioning Action Buttons

Recall that the guides assist you in placing objects at specific locations on the slide. When an object is close to a guide, it snaps to the guide. In this project, you use the vertical and horizontal guides to help position the action buttons and captions in Slide 2. The center of a slide is 0.00 inches on both the vertical and the horizontal guides. You position a guide by dragging it to a new location. When you point to a guide and then press and hold the mouse button, PowerPoint displays a box containing the exact position of the guide on the slide in inches. An arrow displays under the guide position to indicate the vertical guide either left or right of center. An arrow displays to the right of the guide position to indicate the horizontal guide either above or below center. Perform the following steps to display the guides and position the action buttons.

Sounds

PowerPoint's sounds that play when you click an action button fit a variety of applications. You can, however, add custom sounds, such as a human voice, music, or sound effects, to your slide show. Many sites on the Internet provide these sound files, which have the file extension .wav, and allow you to download them free of charge. For an example of one of these sites, visit the PowerPoint 2000 Project 4 More About page (www.scsite.com/pp2000/more.htm) and click Sounds.

To Display the Guides and Position the Action Buttons

1 **Right-click Slide 2 anywhere except the Title Area or Object Area placeholders or the action buttons. Click Guides on the shortcut menu.**

The horizontal and vertical guides display where they were last positioned in Slide 2.

2 **Drag the vertical guide to 2.58 inches right of center.**

The vertical guide will be used to position the left side of the Microsoft Word action button (Figure 4-37).

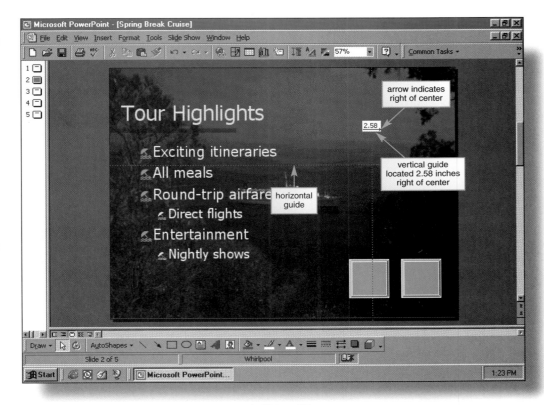

FIGURE 4-37

3 **Drag the horizontal guide to 2.50 inches below center.**

The horizontal guide will be used to position the top side of the Microsoft Word action button (Figure 4-38).

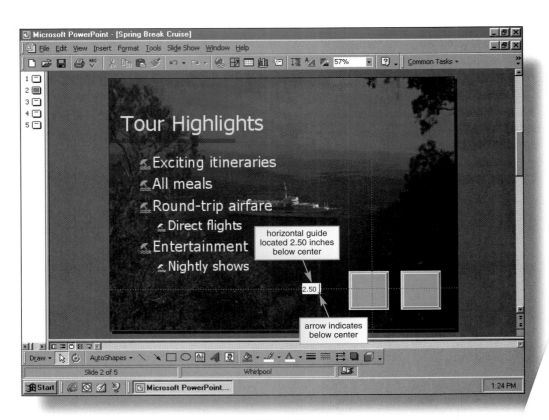

FIGURE 4-38

4 Drag the left action button for the Word document hyperlink until the top edge snaps to the horizontal guide and the left edge snaps to the vertical guide.

The top of the Word document action button aligns with the horizontal guide, and the left side of the button aligns with the vertical guide (Figure 4-39).

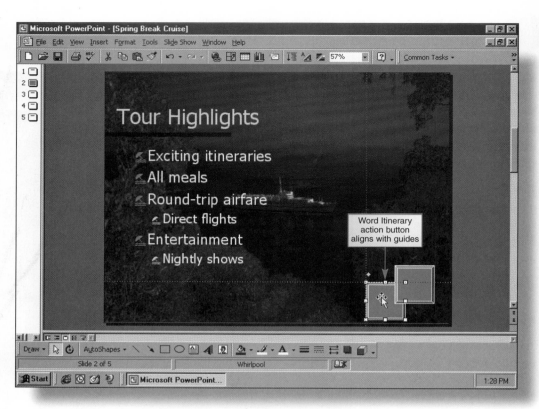

FIGURE 4-39

5 Drag the vertical guide to 4.00 inches right of center.

The vertical guide will be used to align the Excel action button (Figure 4-40).

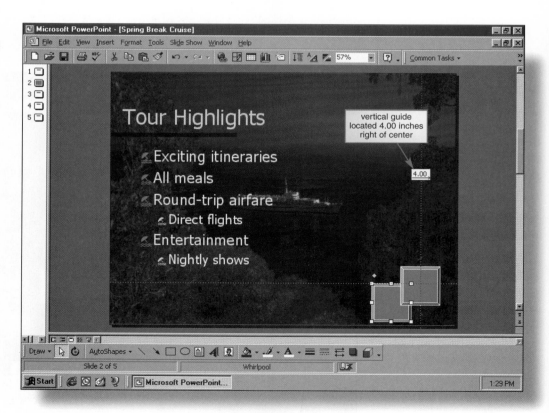

FIGURE 4-40

6 Drag the right action button for the Excel Pricing spreadsheet hyperlink until the top edge snaps to the horizontal guide and the left edge snaps to the vertical guide.

The top of the Excel Pricing spreadsheet action button aligns with the horizontal guide, and the left side of the button aligns with the vertical guide (Figure 4-41).

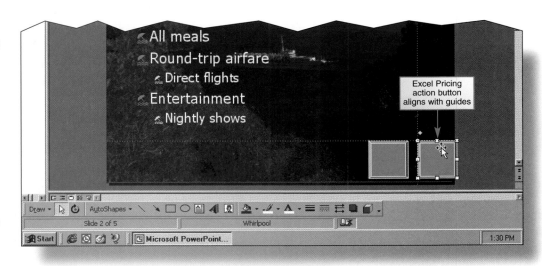

FIGURE 4-41

Other Ways

1. On View menu click Guides
2. Press ALT+V, press G

Scaling Objects

The action buttons in Slide 2 are too large in proportion to the screen. Perform the following steps to scale the two action buttons simultaneously.

TO SCALE ACTION BUTTONS

1 With the Pricing (right) action button still selected, press and hold the SHIFT key. Click the Itinerary (left) action button. Release the SHIFT key.

2 Right-click either action button and then click Format AutoShape on the shortcut menu.

3 If necessary, click the Size tab. Click Lock aspect ratio in the Scale area and then double-click the Height text box. Type 50 in the Height text box.

4 Click the OK button.

Both action buttons are resized to 50 percent of their original size (Figure 4-42).

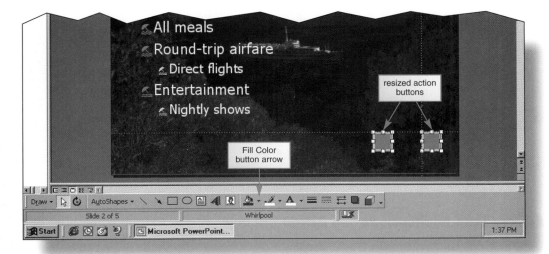

FIGURE 4-42

Adding Fill Color to the Action Buttons

To better identify the action buttons from the slide background, you can add fill color. Recall that fill color is the interior color of a selected object. Perform the following steps to add fill color to the action buttons in Slide 2.

 To Add Fill Color to the Action Buttons

1 **With the two action buttons still selected, click the Fill Color button arrow on the Drawing toolbar. Point to the color medium blue (row 1, column 7 under Automatic).**

The Fill Color list displays (Figure 4-43). Automatic is highlighted, indicating that lavender is the current default fill color based on the Whirlpool design template.

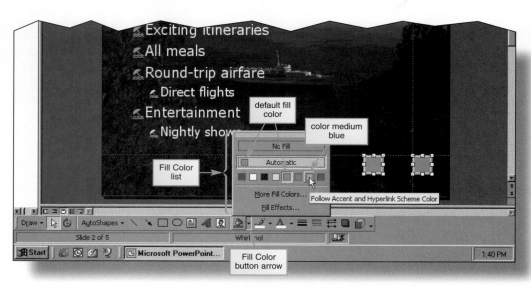

FIGURE 4-43

2 **Click the color medium blue (row 1, column 7 under Automatic).**

Both action buttons display filled with the color medium blue (Figure 4-44). Medium blue is the Follow Accent and Hyperlink Scheme Color in the Whirlpool design template color scheme.

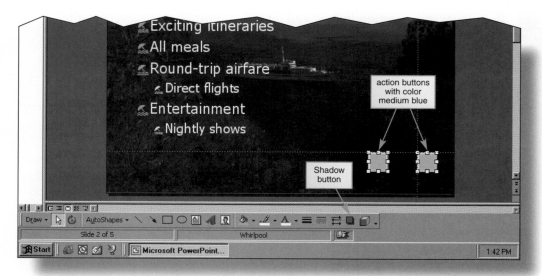

FIGURE 4-44

Adding Shadow Effects to the Action Buttons

To add depth to an object, you **shadow** it by clicking the Shadow button on the Drawing toolbar. Perform the following steps to add shadows to the two action buttons in Slide 2.

TO ADD SHADOWS TO THE ACTION BUTTONS

1 Click the Shadow button on the Drawing toolbar.

2 Click Shadow Style 17 (row 5, column 1) in the style list.

PowerPoint adds the shadow to the two action buttons (Figure 4-45).

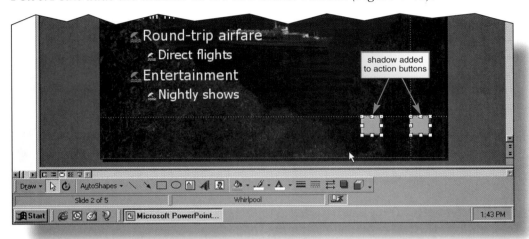

FIGURE 4-45

Adding Captions to the Action Buttons

The final components of Slide 2 that need to be added are the captions under the two action buttons. Perform the following steps to add captions to the action buttons in Slide 2.

TO ADD CAPTIONS TO THE ACTION BUTTONS

1 Click the Text Box button on the Drawing toolbar.

2 Click below the left action button. Type Itinerary as the caption.

3 Click the Text Box button on the Drawing toolbar.

4 Click below the right action button and then type Pricing as the caption.

The captions for the two action buttons display (Figure 4-46).

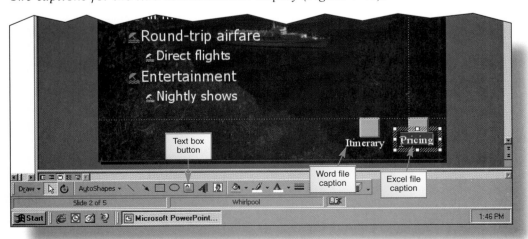

FIGURE 4-46

Formatting Text

To add visual appeal to the captions, you want to change the font to Arial, increase the font size to 28, and change the color to the same color as the title text. Perform the following steps to format the captions for the action buttons in Slide 2.

Steps **To Format Text**

1 **Double-click the Pricing caption text, click Edit on the menu bar, and then click Select All.**

2 **Right-click the text, Pricing, and then click Font on the shortcut menu. Click the Font box up arrow, and then click Arial in the Font list. Click the Size box down arrow and then click 28 in the list.**

Arial displays in the Font box, and the font size 28 displays in the Size box (Figure 4-47).

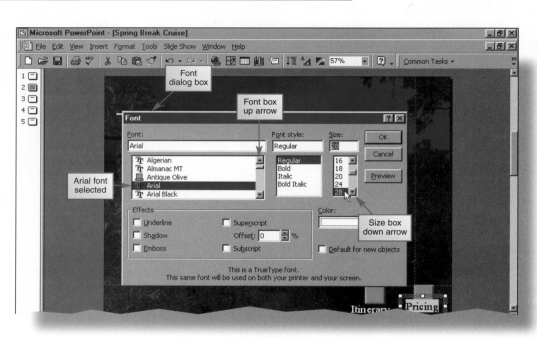

FIGURE 4-47

3 **Click the Color box arrow and then click the color aqua (row 1, column 4 under Automatic).**

The color aqua is the Follow Title Text Scheme Color in the Whirlpool design template color scheme (Figure 4-48). The color aqua displays in the Color box.

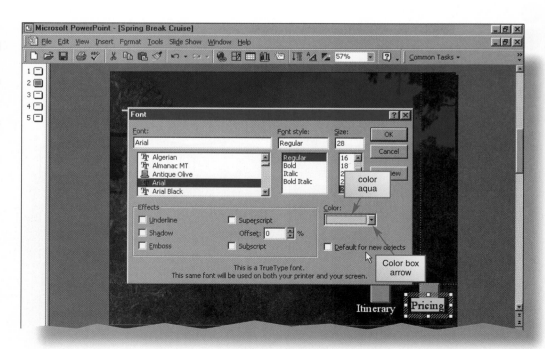

FIGURE 4-48

4 **Click the OK button and then click anywhere on a blank area of the slide.**

PowerPoint displays the Pricing caption with the 28-point Arial font and the color aqua (Figure 4-49).

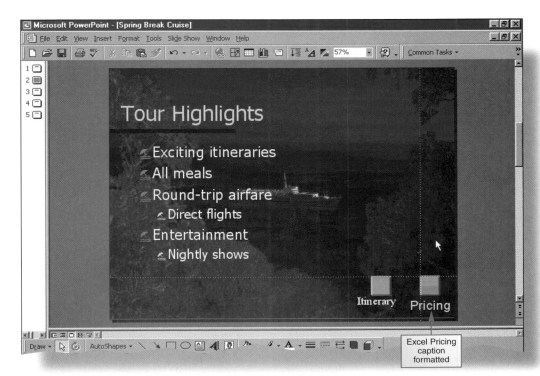

FIGURE 4-49

Now that you have formatted the Pricing caption text, you need to repeat the procedure to format the Itinerary caption text. Perform the following steps to format the Itinerary caption text.

TO FORMAT A SECOND CAPTION TEXT

1 Double-click the Itinerary caption, click Edit on the menu bar, and then click Select All.

2 Right-click the text and then click Font on the shortcut menu. When the Font dialog box displays, click the Font box up arrow, and then click Arial in the list.

3 Click the Size box down arrow and then click 28 in the list.

4 Click the Color box arrow and then click the color aqua (row 1, column 4 under Automatic).

5 Click the OK button and then click anywhere on a blank area of the slide.

Slide 2 is complete (Figure 4-50).

FIGURE 4-50

Now that the captions are added and formatted, you may need to make slight adjustments to their placements under the action buttons. If so, click a caption, click the border, and use the ARROW keys to position the text box as shown in Figure 4-50 on the previous page.

Because you do not need the guides when you modify the next slide, you want to hide them. Recall that a check mark displays in front of the Guides command on the shortcut menu and View menu when the commands are active. Perform the following steps to remove the check mark and deactivate, or hide, the guides.

TO HIDE THE GUIDES

1 Right-click Slide 1 anywhere except the Title Area or Object Area placeholders.

2 Click Guides on the shortcut menu.

The guides no longer display.

The next section explains how to change the organization chart.

Modifying an Organization Chart

Now that you have created aqua action buttons in Slide 2, you want the organization chart boxes in Slide 3 also to be the color aqua. The shadow effects and border style selected in Project 3 can remain. In addition, the Project 3 organization chart depicts the sightseeing excursions available for the three Florida and Texas Spring Break destinations. The organization chart in Project 4, shown in Figure 4-1g on page PP 4.5, displays the itineraries for the Eastern and Western Caribbean island cruises. Consequently, the structure of this organization chart needs to be changed. The next several sections explain how to modify the organization chart.

Changing the Box Color in an Organization Chart

First you will change the color of all the boxes to aqua and the text to red. Perform the following steps to modify the organization chart box and text colors.

TO CHANGE AN ORGANIZATION CHART BOX AND TEXT COLOR

1 Click the Next Slide button to display Slide 3.

2 Double-click an organization chart box to open the Microsoft Organization Chart application.

3 Click the Maximize button in the upper-right corner of the Microsoft Organization Chart window.

4 Click Edit on the menu bar, point to Select, and then click All on the submenu.

5 Click Boxes on the menu bar and then click Color.

6 Click the color aqua (row 2, column 3) and then click the OK button.

7 Click Text on the menu bar and then click Color.

8 Click the color red (row 1, column 9).

9 Click the OK button.

10 Click anywhere in the chart area except a box or line to deselect all.

The Microsoft Organization Chart applies the new color aqua to the boxes and color red to the text (Figure 4-51).

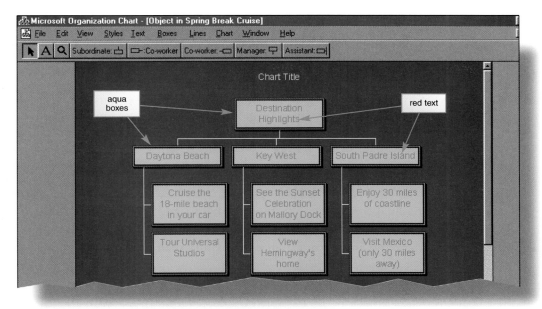

FIGURE 4-51

The organization chart in Project 3 has three branches (Daytona Beach, Key West, and South Padre Island). The Spring Break Cruise presentation only needs two branches (Eastern Caribbean and Western Caribbean). One branch of the organization chart needs to be deleted. The next section explains how to delete a branch.

Deleting a Branch of an Organization Chart

The South Padre Island branch of the organization chart can be removed because it is not needed. Only two branches display in the Spring Break Cruise presentation (Eastern Caribbean and Western Caribbean). The following steps describe how to eliminate a branch of the organization chart.

Other Ways

1. Select branch, press CTRL+B

TO DELETE A BRANCH OF AN ORGANIZATION CHART

1. Click the South Padre Island box.

2. Click Edit on the menu bar, point to Select, and then click Branch.

3. Press the DELETE key.

The South Padre Island branch is deleted, and only the Daytona Beach and Key West branches display (Figure 4-52).

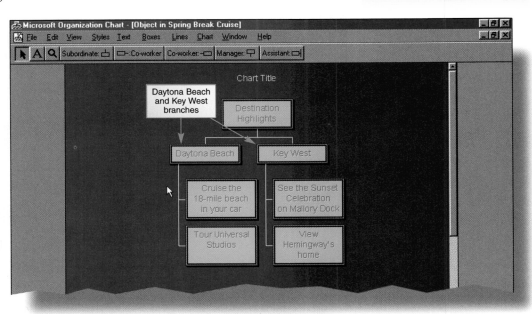

FIGURE 4-52

The text in the chart must be changed to reflect the Caribbean destinations. In the next sections, these editing changes are made.

Editing Text in an Organization Chart

The chart is reformatted for the new presentation. Now the text must be changed to reflect the new items. The two Level 2 subordinate boxes and the four Level 3 subordinate boxes must be changed by highlighting the existing text and then typing the new text. Perform the steps below to edit the text.

TO EDIT TEXT IN AN ORGANIZATION CHART

1 Click the root manager box, Destination Highlights, and type Islands as the first line of text.

2 Triple-click Highlights in the root manager box and then press the DELETE key.

3 Click the Daytona Beach subordinate box and then type Eastern Caribbean as the text.

4 Click the Key West subordinate box and then type Western Caribbean as the text.

5 Click the first box under Eastern Caribbean and then type St. Martin in the box.

6 Drag through each line of remaining text in the box and then press the DELETE key.

7 Repeat Steps 5 and 6 to insert the information in Figure 4-53.

The edited organization chart displays.

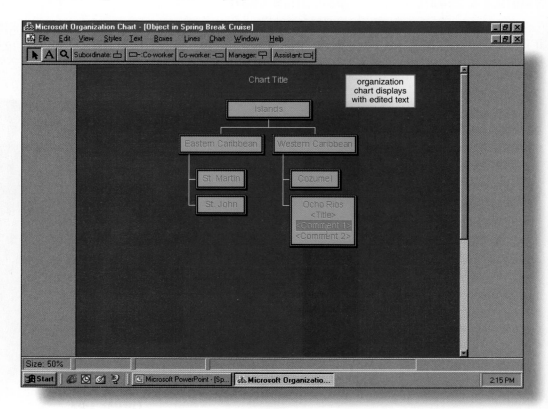

FIGURE 4-53

The seven boxes now reflect the new Caribbean destinations. Three additional subordinate boxes must be added to complete the organization chart. Perform the next steps to insert the remaining boxes.

Adding Co-worker Boxes

Co-workers boxes share the same manager. Three co-workers need to be added to the managers Eastern Caribbean and Western Caribbean. The two types of co-workers are the Left Co-worker, which branches to the left, and the Right Co-worker, which branches to the right. Level 3 of this organization chart has Right Co-worker boxes. Perform the following steps to add three Right Co-workers to Level 3.

 To Add Right Co-worker Boxes

1 **Click the Right Co-worker box tool button on the Microsoft Organization Chart window icon bar two times. Point to the St. John box.**

The Right Co-worker box tool button is recessed (Figure 4-54). The status bar displays the number of subordinate boxes Microsoft Organization Chart is creating, which is two. The mouse pointer changes shape to a Right Co-worker box.

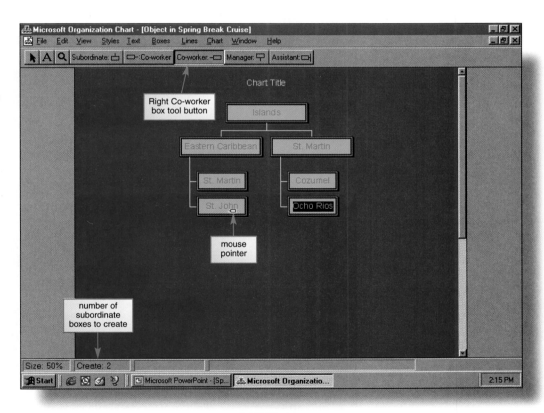

FIGURE 4-54

② **Click the St. John box and then type** St. Thomas **in the upper box and** Virgin Islands **in the lower box. Point to the Right Co-worker button.**

The new boxes and text display (Figure 4-55).

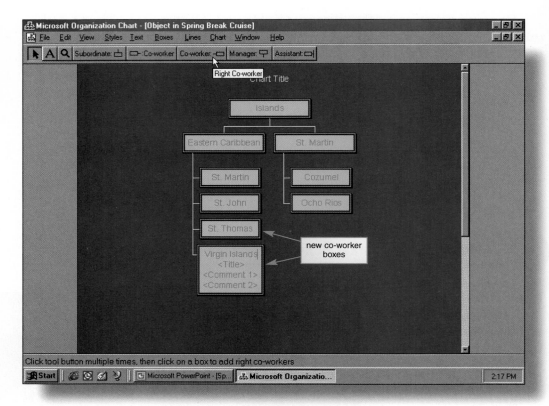

FIGURE 4-55

③ **Click the Right Co-worker box tool button, click the Ocho Rios box, and then type** Great Stirrup Cay **in the new box. Click anywhere in the chart area except on a line or box.**

The chart displays with the three new Level 3 Right Co-worker boxes (Figure 4-56).

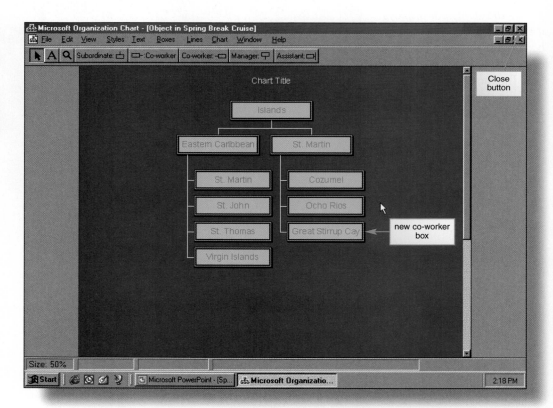

FIGURE 4-56

The organization chart changes now are complete. The text has been updated to reflect the topics of the Spring Break Cruise presentation. The color of the boxes has been changed to differentiate it from the original Spring Break presentation. The organization chart must be saved, and Slide 3 must be updated with the revised chart.

TO SAVE THE CHART AND RETURN TO THE PRESENTATION

1 Click the Close button on the Microsoft Organization Chart – [Object in Spring Break Cruise] title bar.

2 Click the Yes button.

Slide 3 displays the modified organization chart (Figure 4-57).

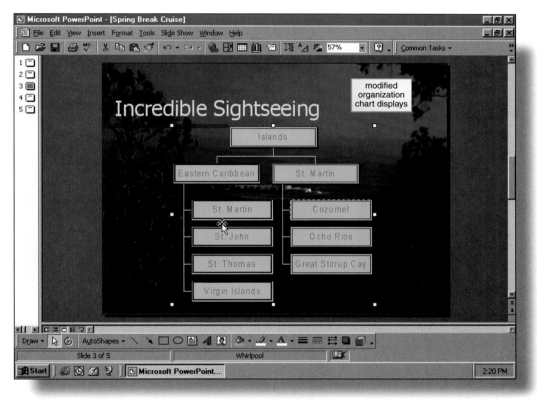

FIGURE 4-57

The organization chart has been updated in Slide 3 with the new colors for the boxes and text and the revised Spring Break Cruise information. The next step is to edit the Slide 4 PowerPoint table.

Editing a PowerPoint Table

The Package Rates slide, Slide 4, discusses the cost of the Florida and Texas travel packages. You want to change that slide to reflect the Eastern and Western Caribbean island prices for the cruises. The prices vary because of multiple departure cities, which is explained in the Excel spreadsheet, Cruise Pricing. The range of prices will be listed in Slide 4. In addition, the third row, South Padre Island, of the table is deleted because it is not needed. Finally, the background color of the slide is changed to better match the presentation's color scheme. The next sections explain how to modify Slide 4 by making these changes.

Other Ways

1. On Microsoft Organization Chart File menu click Update Spring Break Cruise, on Microsoft Organization Chart File menu click Exit and Return to Spring Break Cruise

2. In Microsoft Organization Chart – [Object in Spring Break Cruise] window, press ALT+F, press U, press ALT+F, press X

Editing the Table Text

All of the text in the table must be changed in Slide 4, while the slide title can remain the same. Recall text objects that display on a slide can be edited in slide view or outline view, and you must select text before editing it. Perform the following steps to display the title slide in slide view and then revise the Title Area text.

TO EDIT THE TABLE TEXT

1 Click the Next Slide button to display Slide 4.

2 Triple-click the words, Daytona Beach, in the first table cell, and then type `Eastern Caribbean` in place of the highlighted text.

3 Triple-click $529 in the next cell, and then type `$899 - $1,299` in place of the highlighted text.

4 Triple-click the words, Key West, in the next cell down, and then type `Western Caribbean` in place of the highlighted text.

5 Triple-click $669 in the next cell, and then type `$799 - $1,199` in place of the highlighted text.

Slide 4 displays two rows of updated table text (Figure 4-58).

FIGURE 4-58

More About

Modifying Tables

You can add rows or columns to a PowerPoint table. Just select the row above where you want to insert the new row or the column to the left of where you want to insert the new column. Then select the same number of rows or columns you want to insert. Right-click, and then click Insert Rows or Insert Columns on the shortcut menu. You can click the last cell of the last row of the table and then press the TAB key to add a row at the end of the table.

Deleting a Table Row

You need to delete the last row of the table because it is not needed. All text in the row should be highlighted, and then the entire row can be deleted. Perform the following steps to delete the last row of the table in Slide 4.

TO DELETE A TABLE ROW

1 Drag through the text, South Padre Island and $549, in the last row of the table.

2 Right-click anywhere in the selection.

3 Click Delete Rows on the shortcut menu.

Slide 4 displays the edited table with the last row deleted (Figure 4-59).

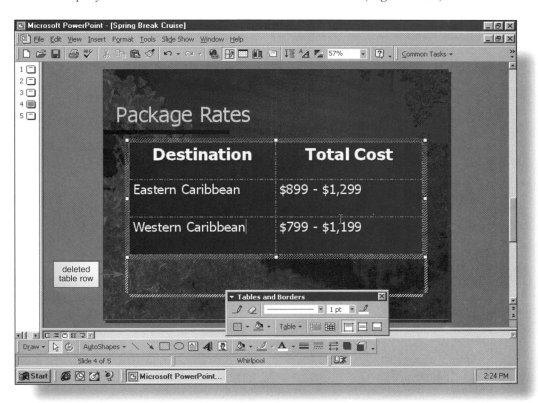

FIGURE 4-59

The final step is to change the table's background fill color. A medium blue color will complement the background picture.

Changing the Table Fill Color

To change the background fill color of the table in PowerPoint, you select the cells and then select a new fill color. Perform the following steps to change the fill color in the table in Slide 4.

TO CHANGE THE TABLE FILL COLOR

1 With the insertion point in the Western Caribbean cell, click Edit on the menu bar, and then click Select All. Right-click anywhere in the selection.

2 Click Borders and Fill on the shortcut menu.

3 Click the Fill tab.

More *About*

Fill Color

If you want to change the table background fill color to its original default color, select the entire table, click the Fill Color button arrow on the Tables and Borders toolbar, and then click Automatic.

4 Click the Fill color box arrow and then click the color medium blue (row 1, column 7 under Automatic). Click Semitransparent.

5 Click the OK button.

6 Click anywhere in Slide 4 except the table or the Title Area placeholder to deselect all the objects.

The fill color is changed to medium blue (Figure 4-60). The semitransparent color allows some of the slide background to show through.

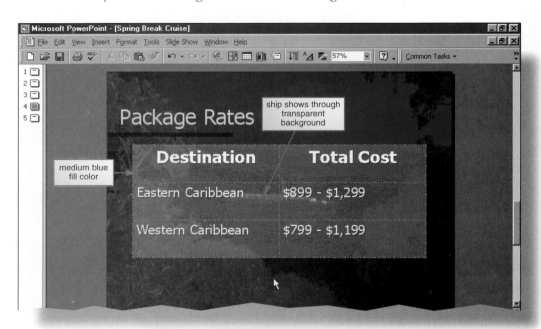

FIGURE 4-60

All the changes have been made to Slide 4. In the next section, a new hidden slide is created.

Hiding Slides

A **supporting slide** provides detailed information to supplement another slide in the presentation. For example, in a presentation to job applicants, a company recruiter displays a graph representing the corporation's current year's profits compared to the previous five years' profits. The supporting slide displays a graph contrasting the competitors' bottom lines.

When running a slide show, you may not always want to display the supporting slide. You would display it when time permits and when you want to show the audience more detail about a topic. You insert the supporting slide after the slide you anticipate may warrant more detail. Then, you use the Hide Slide command to hide the supporting slide. The **Hide Slide command** hides the supporting slide from the audience during the normal running of a slide show. When you want to display the supporting hidden slide, press the H key. No visible indicator displays to show that a hidden slide exists. You must be aware of the content of the presentation to know where the supporting slide is located.

Black Slides

At times you may want your audience to focus on the speaker or on other audience members. A black slide may be helpful to divert the attention away from the slide show and to these individuals. To create a black slide, click the New Slide button on the Standard toolbar, select the Blank AutoLayout, click Format on the menu bar, click Background, click the Background fill box arrow, and then click the color black.

Adding a New Slide

The first step in creating a hidden slide is adding a new slide. Perform the following steps to add a new slide.

TO ADD A NEW SLIDE

1 Click the New Slide button on the Standard toolbar.

2 When the New Slide dialog box displays, type 2 to select the Bulleted List AutoLayout.

3 Click the OK button.

The new Slide 5 displays the Bulleted List AutoLayout with the Ship background graphics (Figure 4-61). PowerPoint automatically renumbers the original Slide 5 as Slide 6.

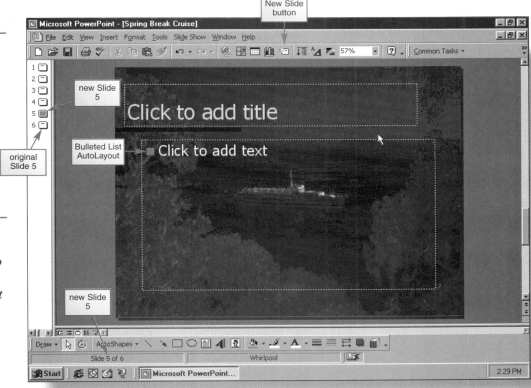

FIGURE 4-61

Adding a Slide Title

The title text for Slide 5 is Special Discounts. Perform the following steps to add a slide title to Slide 5.

TO ADD A SLIDE TITLE

1 Click the slide Title Area placeholder and type Special Discounts in the placeholder.

2 Click the Object Area placeholder.

The title, Special Discounts, displays in Slide 5 (Figure 4-62). The Object Area placeholder is selected.

FIGURE 4-62

Adding Text and Removing Bullets

In the next steps, a paragraph of text is inserted in the Title Area placeholder. Because only one paragraph will display, bullets are not needed. The bullet at the beginning of the line of text, therefore, is removed.

TO ADD SLIDE TEXT AND REMOVE BULLETS

1 Type Talk to the cruise sales representative for special discount information. as the information in the Object Area placeholder.

2 Right-click anywhere in the new paragraph of text. Click Bullets and Numbering on the shortcut menu.

3 Click the None bulleted list style and then click the OK button.

4 Click anywhere in Slide 5 except the Title Area or Object Area placeholders.

The new subtitle text displays in the Object Area placeholder with the bullet removed (Figure 4-63).

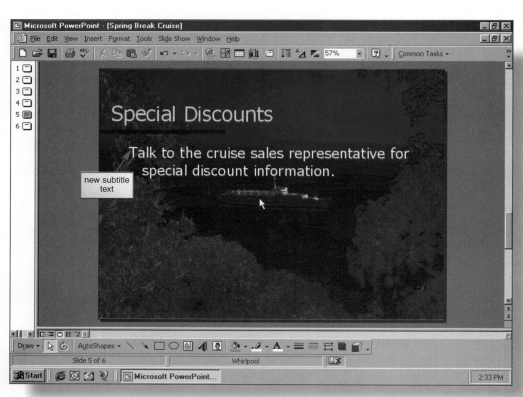

FIGURE 4-63

Persuasive Presentations

A relaxed and refreshed audience is more receptive to your presentation and ideas. Researchers suggest that audiences are more prone to feel relaxed and refreshed on Sundays, Mondays, and Tuesdays. Your viewers generally have less time to consider the major points of your presentation at the end of the week.

Hiding a Slide

Slide 5 supports the session information displayed in Slide 4. If time permits, or if the audience requires more information, you can display Slide 5. As the presenter, you decide whether to show Slide 5. You hide a slide in slide sorter view so you can see the **null sign**, which is a slashed square surrounding the slide number, to indicate the slide is hidden. Perform the following steps to hide Slide 5.

To Hide a Slide

1 **Click the Slide Sorter View button** at the lower left of the PowerPoint window. Right-click Slide 5 and then point to Hide Slide on the shortcut menu.

Slide 5 is selected in slide sorter view (Figure 4-64).

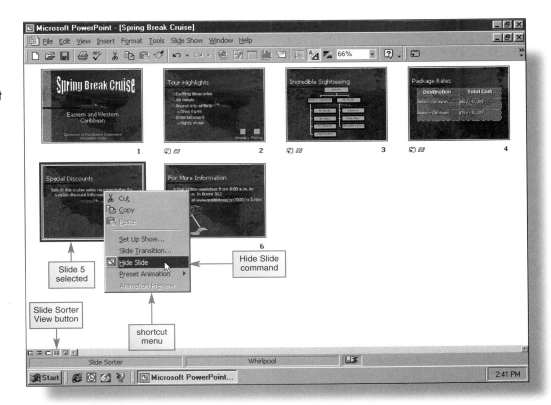

FIGURE 4-64

2 **Click Hide Slide.**

The null sign, a square with a slash, displays over the slide number to indicate Slide 5 is a hidden slide (Figure 4-65).

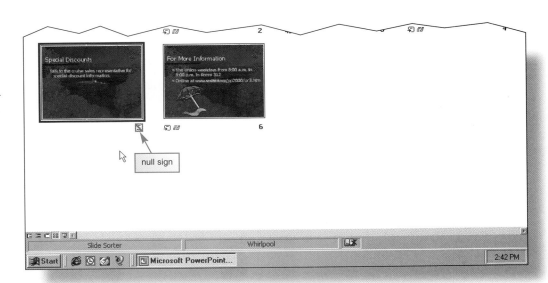

FIGURE 4-65

 Other Ways

1. Click Hide Slide button on Slide Sorter toolbar
2. On Slide Show menu click Hide Slide
3. Press ALT+D, press H

The Hide Slide button is a toggle — it either hides or displays a slide. It also applies or removes the null sign. When you no longer want to hide a slide, change views to slide sorter view, right-click the slide, and then click Hide Slide on the shortcut menu. This action removes the square with the null sign.

An alternative to hiding a slide in slide sorter view is to hide a slide in slide view, outline view, or normal view. In these views, however, no visible indication is given that a slide is hidden. To hide a slide in slide view or normal view, display the slide you want to hide, click Slide Show on the menu bar, and then click Hide Slide. To hide a slide in outline view, select the slide icon of the slide you want to hide, click Slide Show on the menu bar, and then click Hide Slide. An icon displays in front of the Hide Slide command on the Slide Show menu, and it is recessed when the slide is hidden. You also can choose not to hide a slide in slide view, normal view, and outline view by clicking Hide Slide on the Slide Show menu. The icon in front of the Hide Slide command no longer is recessed, and the slide then displays like all the other slides in the presentation.

When you run your presentation, the hidden slide does not display unless you press the H key when the slide preceding the hidden slide is displaying. For example, Slide 5 does not display unless you press the H key when Slide 4 displays in slide show view. You continue your presentation by clicking the mouse or pressing any of the keys associated with running a slide show. You skip the hidden slide by clicking the mouse and advancing to the next slide.

Changing the Order of Slides

The presentation changes nearly are complete. Next, the slides are rearranged to highlight the key points early in the presentation. Slides 4 and 5 are moved just after Slide 2. Perform the following steps to reposition Slides 4 and 5.

Steps To Change the Slide Order in a Presentation

1 With Slide 5 still selected, press and hold the CTRL key and then click Slide 4. Release the CTRL key.

2 Click Slide 4 or Slide 5 and drag the mouse pointer between Slides 2 and 3.

The move bar displays between Slides 2 and 3 (Figure 4-66). The mouse pointer changes to indicate the slide move.

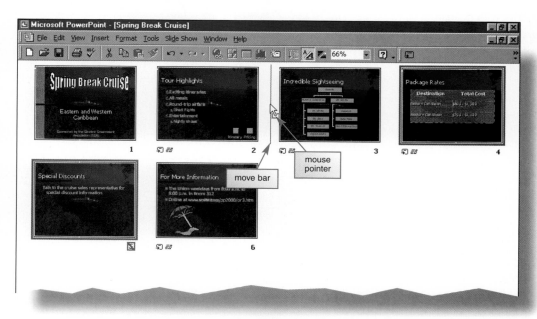

FIGURE 4-66

3 **Release the mouse button.**

The slide show is rearranged and the slides are renumbered automatically (Figure 4-67).

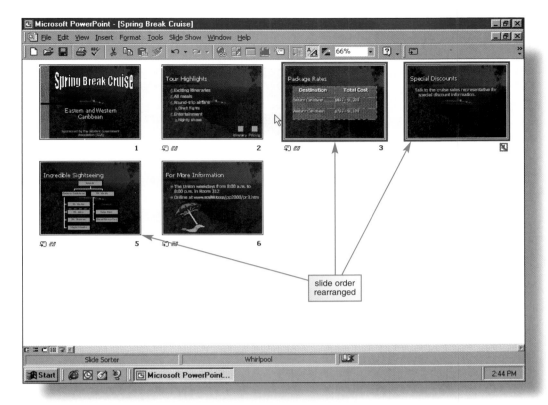

FIGURE 4-67

The final step for the Spring Break Cruise presentation is to create a summary slide. The following sections explain how to add this slide to the end of your presentation.

Adding a Summary Slide

The final step in the changes to the Spring Break Cruise presentation is to add a summary slide. A **summary slide** contains bulleted titles from selected slides. The summary slide can be used to summarize the main points of the presentation or as an agenda of topics. Because of this use, the summary slide displays automatically in front of the first selected slide.

In this presentation, only Slides 2, 3, and 5 will be included in the summary slide. The hidden slide, Slide 4, is not included because it is not presented during every presentation. Perform the steps on the next page to add a summary slide.

Other Ways

1. In outline pane, drag slide icon to new position

More About

Creating Slides Automatically

You can use your summary slide to create an agenda slide, which identifies the major presentation items for your audience. When you use an agenda slide, you click each bulleted item to jump to a particular slide, discuss the topic with your audience, and then jump back to your agenda slide. You create a hyperlink from each bulleted item on your summary slide to a corresponding custom show by clicking Action Settings on the Slide Show menu, clicking Hyperlink to, clicking Custom Shows, and then selecting a show. Click Show and return to the agenda slide after viewing the last slide in the custom show.

To Add a Summary Slide

1 **Click Slide 2. Press and hold the CTRL key and then click Slides 3 and 5. Release the CTRL key. Double-click the move handle on the Slide Sorter toolbar. Point to the Summary Slide button on the Slide Sorter toolbar.**

Three slides are selected (Figure 4-68).

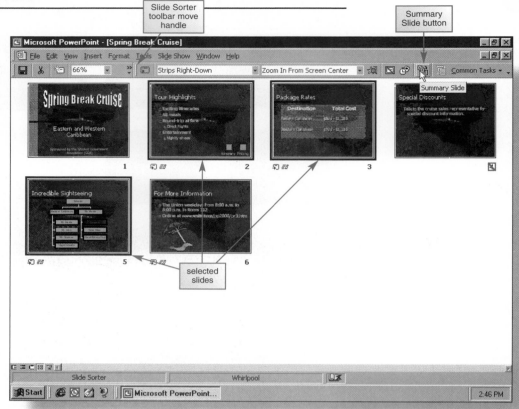

FIGURE 4-68

2 **Click the Summary Slide button.**

The summary slide is inserted as Slide 2 (Figure 4-69). The title text from Slides 2, 3, and 5 displays on this slide.

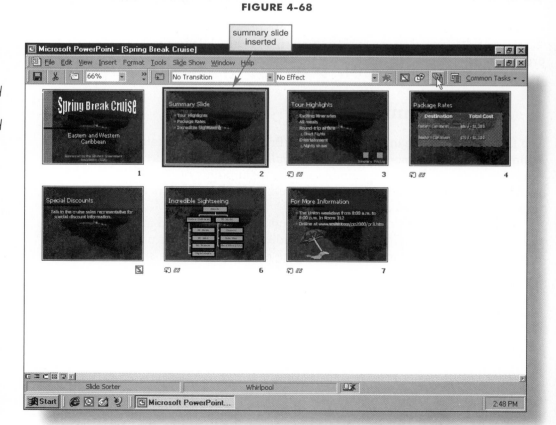

FIGURE 4-69

3 **Double-click Slide 2. Triple-click the Title Object placeholder, and then type** Cruise Summary **as the new title text.**

The summary slide displays in normal view, and the new title text displays (Figure 4-70).

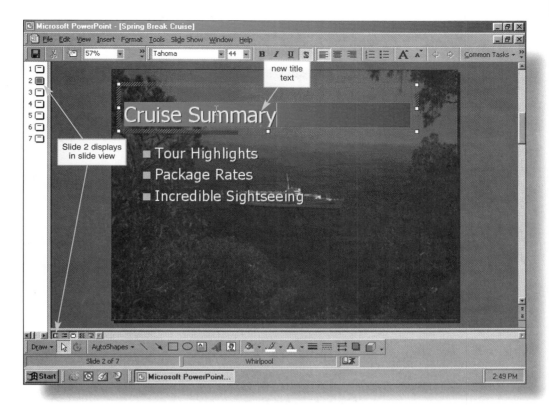

FIGURE 4-70

Deleting a Slide

The last steps in this project are to delete the last slide (Slide 7) and move the summary slide to the end of the presentation. Slide 7 is a slide from the original Spring Break presentation and is not necessary in this slide show. The summary slide ends the presentation conveniently, for it highlights the main topics that are discussed in the slide show. Perform the following steps to delete the last slide from within slide sorter view.

TO DELETE A SLIDE

1 Click the Slide 7 icon in the outline pane.

2 Press the DELETE key.

3 Click the OK button in the Microsoft PowerPoint dialog box.

Slide 7 is deleted from the presentation.

Repositioning the Summary Slide

The summary slide should be the last slide in the presentation before the black slide, which was added in Project 1. With the summary slide, the presenter can highlight the topics discussed previously and summarize them. This is an appropriate ending to the topics explained in the presentation, bringing closure to the sections.

You now are ready to reposition the summary slide to the end of the slide show as described in the steps on the next page.

To Reposition the Summary Slide

 Click the Slide 2 icon in the outline pane and drag it below Slide 6.

The ScreenTip, Cruise Summary, is the Slide 2 title text (Figure 4-71).

 Release the mouse button.

The summary slide now is Slide 6, and the slides in the presentation are renumbered to reflect this change.

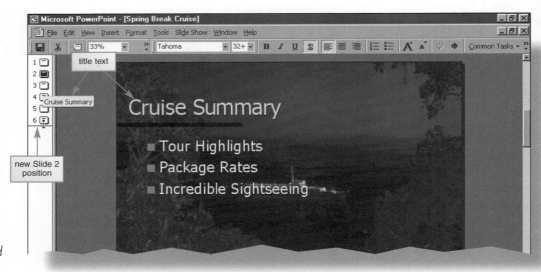

FIGURE 4-71

Applying Slide Transition Effects

Slide 6, the summary slide, was added to the presentation and therefore does not have slide transition effects applied. Recall from Project 3 that the Strips Right-Down slide transition effect was applied to all slides with bullets. The Zoom In From Screen Center preset animation effect also was applied. To keep Slide 6 consistent with the other bulleted slides in the presentation, apply these effects, as described in the following steps.

TO APPLY SLIDE TRANSITION AND TEXT PRESET ANIMATION EFFECTS

1 Click the Slide Sorter View button. If necessary, click Slide 6 to select it.

2 Click the Slide Transition Effects box arrow and then click Strips Right-Down in the list.

3 Click the Preset Animation box arrow and then click Zoom In From Screen Center in the list.

PowerPoint applies the Strips Right-Down slide transition and Zoom In From Screen Center preset animation effects to Slide 6 (Figure 4-72).

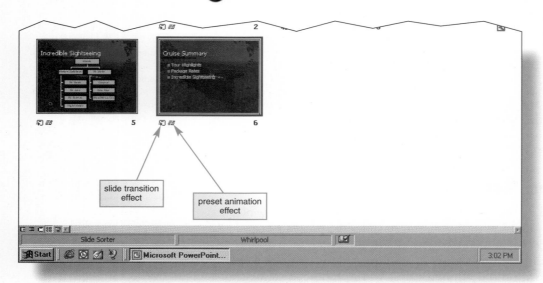

FIGURE 4-72

Save the Presentation

The presentation is complete. You now should save it again.

Running a Slide Show with a Hidden Slide and Interactive Documents

Running a slide show that contains hidden slides or interactive documents basically is the same as running any other slide show. You must, however, know where slides are hidden. When a slide contains interactive documents, you can activate them by clicking the action button that represents the document. The Cruise Itinerary document displays in Microsoft Word, and the Cruise Pricing spreadsheet displays in Microsoft Excel. When you are finished displaying the interactive document and want to return to the presentation, click the Close button on the title bar of the application. Perform the following steps to run the Spring Break Cruise presentation.

TO RUN A SLIDE SHOW WITH A HIDDEN SLIDE AND INTERACTIVE DOCUMENTS

(1) Go to Slide 1. Click the Slide Show button at the lower left of the PowerPoint window.

(2) Click Slide 1 to display Slide 2.

(3) When Slide 2 displays, click four times to display the bulleted list. Click the Itinerary action button. If necessary, maximize the Microsoft Word window when the document displays. Click the Close button on the Cruise Itinerary – Microsoft Word title bar to quit Word.

(4) In Slide 2, click the Pricing action button. If necessary, maximize the Microsoft Excel window when the spreadsheet displays. Click the Close button on the Microsoft Excel – Cruise Pricing title bar to quit Excel.

(5) Click Slide 2 to display Slide 3.

(6) Click Slide 3 to display the table. After viewing Slide 3, press the H key to display the hidden slide, Slide 4.

(7) Click the background of Slide 4 to display Slide 5.

(8) Click Slide 5 to display the organization chart. Click Slide 5 to display Slide 6.

(9) Click Slide 6 three times to display the bulleted summary list. Click Slide 6 again to display the black slide that ends the slide show. Click the black slide to return to the PowerPoint window.

(10) Double-click the move handle on the Standard toolbar. Click the Save button on the Standard toolbar.

(11) Click the Close button on the title bar.

Slide 1 displays in normal view, PowerPoint quits, and then control returns to the desktop.

More About

Presentation Guidelines

Graphic designers and speech coaches work together at the corporate level to help senior officials develop effective presentations. The individuals focus on aesthetically pleasing presentations and a fluent delivery. For specific examples of their advice, visit the PowerPoint 2000 Project 4 More About page (www.scsite.com/pp2000/more.htm) and click Guidelines.

CASE PERSPECTIVE SUMMARY

The revised Spring Break Cruise presentation should pique the students' interest once again in attending the Student Government Association's activity. Your slide show is a versatile method of marketing the cruise, for it contains an interactive slide that provides links to other slides with specific information on the itinerary and pricing for the Eastern and Western Caribbean islands that will be visited. The added slide can be hidden depending on time constraints, and the new WordArt object on the title slide adds visual interest. Running this presentation should result in another sold-out Spring Break Cruise trip for the SGA.

Project Summary

Project 4 customized the Spring Break presentation created in Project 3. The first step was to save the presentation with a new file name to preserve the Project 3 presentation. You then changed the presentation background by adding a new photograph. Next, you used WordArt to create a heading for the title slide. After creating the WordArt object, you added a special text effect to the letters. You repositioned the heading object on the title slide of the Spring Break Cruise presentation. Next, you created a slide containing hyperlinks to a Microsoft Word document and a Microsoft Excel spreadsheet highlighting additional information about the cruise options. Then, you altered a table, inserting a new background color and deleting a row. After completing changes to the table, you created a new slide and marked it hidden because you will display it during the slide show only if time permits or if the audience is interested in the material. Next, you created a summary slide that contains the titles of all selected slides. You repositioned the summary slide and added slide transition effects and preset animation to it. You ran the slide show to display the hidden slide and interactive documents. Finally, you closed the presentation and quit PowerPoint.

What You Should Know

Having completed this project, you now should be able to perform the following tasks:

▶ Add a New Slide *(PP 4.47)*
▶ Add a Slide Title *(PP 4.47)*
▶ Add a Summary Slide *(PP 4.52)*
▶ Add an Action Button and Action Settings *(PP 4.27)*
▶ Add Captions to the Action Buttons *(PP 4.35)*
▶ Add Fill Color to the Action Buttons *(PP 4.34)*
▶ Add Right Co-worker Boxes *(PP 4.41)*
▶ Add Shadows to the Action Buttons *(PP 4.35)*
▶ Add Slide Text and Remove Bullets *(PP 4.48)*
▶ Apply Slide Transition and Text Preset Animation Effects *(PP 4.54)*
▶ Change an Organization Chart Box and Text Color *(PP 4.38)*
▶ Change Text *(PP 4.7)*
▶ Change the Background *(PP 4.8)*
▶ Change the Slide Order in a Presentation *(PP 4.50)*
▶ Change the Table Fill Color *(PP 4.45)*
▶ Change the WordArt Fill Color *(PP 4.19)*
▶ Change the WordArt Height and Width *(PP 4.17)*
▶ Create a Second Action Button and Hyperlink *(PP 4.30)*
▶ Delete a Branch of an Organization Chart *(PP 4.39)*
▶ Delete and Modify the Slide Text *(PP 4.9)*
▶ Delete a Slide *(PP 4.53)*
▶ Delete a Table Row *(PP 4.45)*
▶ Display the Guides and Position the Action Buttons *(PP 4.31)*

▶ Display the Guides *(PP 4.11)*
▶ Display the Rulers *(PP 4.10)*
▶ Edit Existing Text *(PP 4.24)*
▶ Edit Text in an Organization Chart *(PP 4.40)*
▶ Edit the Table Text *(PP 4.44)*
▶ Enter the WordArt Text *(PP 4.15)*
▶ Format a Second Caption Text *(PP 4.37)*
▶ Format Text *(PP 4.36)*
▶ Hide a Slide *(PP 4.49)*
▶ Hide the Guides *(PP 4.38)*
▶ Hide the Rulers and Guides *(PP 4.22)*
▶ Increase the Zoom Percentage *(PP 4.13)*
▶ Move a Paragraph in Outline View *(PP 4.25)*
▶ Open a Presentation and Save It with a New File Name *(PP 4.6)*
▶ Position the Guides *(PP 4.12)*
▶ Reposition the Summary Slide *(PP 4.54)*
▶ Reset the Zoom Percentage *(PP 4.22)*
▶ Run a Slide Show with a Hidden Slide and Interactive Documents *(PP 4.55)*
▶ Save the Chart and Return to the Presentation *(PP 4.43)*
▶ Scale Action Buttons *(PP 4.33)*
▶ Scale the WordArt Object *(PP 4.21)*
▶ Select a WordArt Style *(PP 4.14)*

Apply Your Knowledge

Project Reinforcement at www.scsite.com/off2000/reinforce.htm

1 Changing a Background and Creating a WordArt Object

Instructions: Start PowerPoint. Open the Crocodile file on your Data Disk. See the inside back cover of this book for instructions for downloading the Data Disk or see your instructor for information on accessing the files required for this book. Perform the following tasks to modify the slide so it displays as shown in Figure 4-73.

1. Click File on the menu bar, and then click Save As. Save the presentation with the file name, Croc Update.
2. Apply the Bamboo design template.
3. Change the background by right-clicking the slide anywhere other than the Title Area or Object Area placeholders and clicking Background on the shortcut menu. Click the Background fill area box arrow and then click Fill Effects in the list. Click the Texture tab in the Fill Effects dialog box. Scroll down and double-click the Water Droplets texture (row 5, column 1).
4. Insert the crocodile clip art shown in Figure 4-73. Scale the crocodile clip art to 200% and drag it to the lower-right corner of the slide.
5. Right-click the crocodile clip art, point to Grouping on the shortcut menu, and then click Ungroup on the Grouping submenu. Click outside the object to deselect the ungrouped objects.
6. Click the green area above the crocodile's head and then press the DELETE key. Click the blue area below the crocodile's head and then press the DELETE key.
7. Regroup the crocodile by dragging the mouse pointer diagonally from the lower-right corner of the slide to above the crocodile's nose. Right-click the crocodile object, click Grouping on the shortcut menu, and then click Group.
8. Animate the crocodile object by right-clicking the object, clicking Custom Animation on the shortcut menu, and then clicking Crawl in the left Entry animation and sound box and From Right in the right Entry animation and sound box.

FIGURE 4-73

9. Click the Insert WordArt button on the Drawing toolbar. Click the WordArt style in row 4, column 4. Type Tales from the Swamp in the Edit WordArt Text dialog box. Scale the WordArt object to 175%.

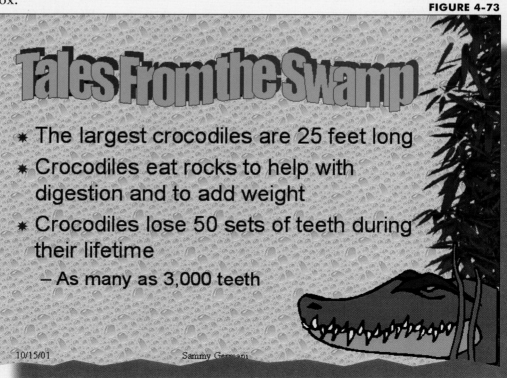

10. Add your name and today's date to the slide footer.
11. Save the Croc Update file again.
12. Print the slide using the Pure black and white option. Quit PowerPoint.

In the Lab

1 Creating a Title Slide Containing WordArt

Problem: Your local park district recently completed clearing a trail for mountain bikers. You have volunteered to help publicize the trail by creating a PowerPoint presentation to load on your school's intranet. The park board commissioners want to approve the title slide before you work on the entire project. The title slide contains a WordArt object and an AutoShape. You create the title slide shown in Figure 4-74.

Instructions: Start PowerPoint and perform the following tasks with a computer.

1. Open a blank presentation and then apply the Title Slide AutoLayout. Insert the Mountain Bike picture on the Data Disk for the background and then apply the Fireball design template. Type the subtitle text in the Object Area placeholder as shown in Figure 4-74.

2. Create the WordArt object by clicking the Insert WordArt button on the Drawing toolbar. In the WordArt Gallery dialog box, select the WordArt style in row 4, column 5. Type Come Play in the Dirt in the Edit WordArt Text dialog box. Scale the object to 160%. Display the guides and rulers. Drag the vertical guide to 4.58 inches left of center and the horizontal guide to 0.50 inches above center. Drag the WordArt object so that the left side of the object snaps to the vertical guide and the bottom of the object snaps to the horizontal guide. Hide the guides and rulers.

3. Click the AutoShapes menu button on the Drawing toolbar. Click Stars and Banners, and then click the Explosion 1 shape (row 1, column 1). Click the lower-left corner of the slide to insert the shape.

4. Scale the Explosion AutoShape to 250%. Type Now Open! in the shape. Change the font to 28-point Tahoma. Click the Free Rotate button on the Drawing toolbar, click one of the green handles on the perimeter of the shape, and rotate the shape to the left so it displays as shown in Figure 4-74.

5. Apply the Spiral animation effect to animate the shape automatically.

6. Save the presentation with the file name, Bike Trail. Print the title slide using the Pure black and white option. Quit PowerPoint.

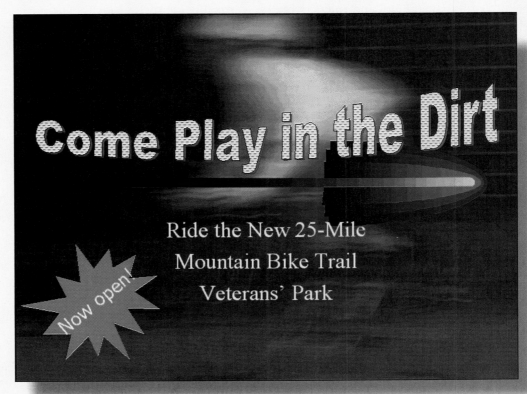

FIGURE 4-74

In the Lab

2 **Using the AutoContent Wizard**

Problem: Your Introduction to Business instructor, Professor John Fine, has required you to form a group to develop marketing materials for the Tutoring Center. Now he is asking for an oral status report of how the group is progressing and what specific tasks you have accomplished. You decide to create a PowerPoint slide show to accompany your group presentation. You use the AutoContent Wizard to help you develop the key ideas for the slides. You create the presentation shown in Figures 4-75a through 4-75d.

Instructions: Start PowerPoint and perform the following tasks with a computer.

1. Start PowerPoint by opening a new Office document. When the New Office Document dialog box displays, click the AutoContent Wizard icon. When the AutoContent Wizard displays, click the Next button to display the Presentation type panel. Click the Projects button. If necessary, click Reporting Progress or Status, and then click the Next button. If necessary, click On-screen presentation in the Presentation style panel, and then click the Next button. In the Presentation options panel, enter Tutoring Center in the Presentation title text box and BUS 205 in the Footer text box. If necessary, click Date last updated and Slide number. Click the Next button. When the Finish panel displays, click the Finish button.

2. Enter your name as the text in the second paragraph as shown in Figure 4-75a.

3. Click the Insert WordArt button on the Drawing toolbar, and then click the WordArt style in row 4, column 3. Click the OK button in the WordArt Gallery dialog box, and then type Marketing Status Report in the Text text box in the Edit WordArt Text dialog box. Click the OK button.

4. Click Format WordArt on the WordArt toolbar. If necessary, click the Size tab. Click Lock aspect ratio, scale the object to 125%, and then click the OK button.

5. Display the guides and rulers. Drag the vertical guide to 1.83 inches left of center and the horizontal guide to 0.58 inches below center. Drag the WordArt object so that the lower-left corner of the object snaps to the intersection of the guides. Hide the guides and rulers.

6. Click the Slide Sorter View button at the lower left of the PowerPoint window and then delete Slides 4 through 9.

7. Double-click Slide 2, which has the title text Status Summary. Enter the text shown in Figure 4-75b.

8. Click the Next Slide button to display Slide 3, Progress. Create the table shown in Figure 4-75c. Change the column headings to 36 point and change the fill color for those two cells to gold.

9. Click the Next Slide button to display Slide 4, Goals for Next Review. Enter the text shown in Figure 4-75d.

10. Click the Slide Sorter View button at the lower left of the PowerPoint window. Apply the Box Out slide transition effect and the Spiral preset animation effect to Slides 2, 3, and 4. Hide Slide 4.

11. Run the Status Report presentation. When the complete Slide 2 displays, right-click the slide, point to Pointer Options and then click Pen on the Pointer Options submenu. Click and make a check mark in front of the two round bullets, and then circle each group member's name.

12. Press the PAGE DOWN key two times to display Slide 3.

13. Type H and then press the PAGE DOWN key four times to display Slide 4, the hidden slide. Make a check mark in front of the four round bullets.

14. Press the PAGE DOWN key two times to end the presentation.

15. Save the presentation with the file name, Status Report. Print the slides using the Pure black and white option. Quit PowerPoint.

In the Lab

Tutoring Center

Marketing Status Report

Tamara Washington

10/15/01

BUS 205

(a) Slide 1

Project Overview

- **Team goal – to develop marketing materials for Tutoring Center**
- **Team members**
  - Liz Armstrong
  - Marcus Garcia
  - Tamara Washington

10/15/01   BUS 205   2

(b) Slide 2

Project Tasks and Status

Tasks	Status
Interview managers	Complete
Design layout	Complete
Create logo	Complete
Design background	Complete by end month
Develop content	In process
Test	Not started

10/15/01   BUS 205

(c) Slide 3

Group Goals

- **Improve communication skills**
  - Enhance interviewing abilities
  - Prepare written summaries
- **Develop group cohesiveness**
- **Learn task delegation**
- **Meet most deadlines**

10/15/01   BUS 205   4

(d) Slide 4

FIGURE 4-75

In the Lab

3 Linking PowerPoint Presentations

Problem: Gardening is the favorite pastime of millions of homeowners and apartment dwellers. From huge flower and vegetable gardens in the backyard to compact container gardens on a patio, people have found this hobby a means of relieving stress, getting exercise, and finding rewards. You have offered to create a PowerPoint presentation for the Hometown Gardening Club to help the members with their seminars throughout the community. You decide an interactive slide show would be the best vehicle to answer the home gardeners' questions. Develop the presentation shown in Figures 4-76a through 4-76f on pages PP 4.63 through 4.65.

Instructions Part 1: Perform the following tasks to create three presentations: one consisting of Figures 4-76a and 4-76b, one of Figure 4-76c, and one of Figure 4-76d.

1. Open a new presentation and apply the Bulleted List AutoLayout and the Nature design template. Change the background to the Stationery texture, which is in row 1, column 4 of the Fill Effects dialog box.

2. Create the bulleted list slides shown in Figures 4-76a and 4-76b. Apply the Uncover Down slide transition effect to both slides. Save the presentation with the file name, Gardening Do's and Don'ts. Print the presentation slides using the Pure black and white option. Close the presentation.

3. Open a new presentation, apply the Bulleted List AutoLayout, and then apply the Nature design template. Change the background to the Stationery texture. Create the slide shown in Figure 4-76c. Apply the Split Horizontal Out slide transition effect. Save the presentation with the file name, Fertilizing Guidelines. Print the presentation slide using the Pure black and white option. Close the presentation.

4. Open a new presentation, apply the Table AutoLayout, and then apply the Nature design template. Change the background to the Stationery texture. Create the slide shown in Figure 4-76d. Format the three table headings to 32-point Gill Sans MT. Fill the table with a transparent background that has the color gold (row 1, column 6 under Automatic). Apply the Box Out slide transition effect. Save the presentation with the file name, Conversion Table. Print the presentation slide using the Pure black and white option. Close the presentation.

In the Lab

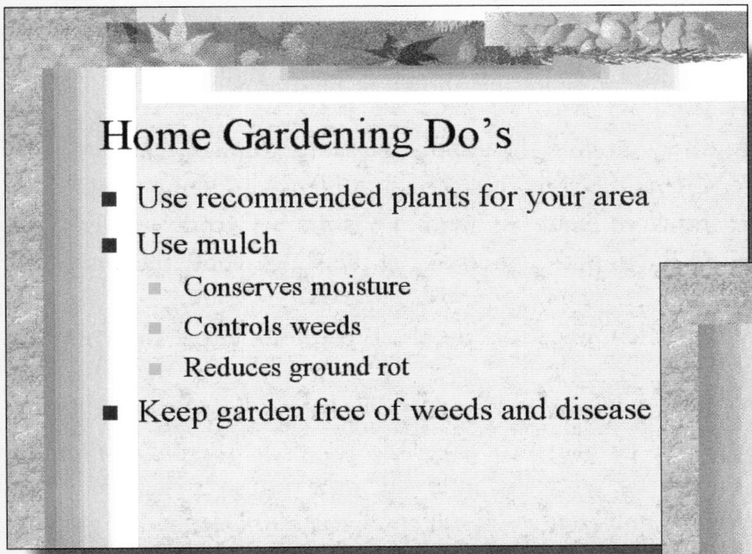

Home Gardening Do's

- Use recommended plants for your area
- Use mulch
  - Conserves moisture
  - Controls weeds
  - Reduces ground rot
- Keep garden free of weeds and disease

(a) Slide 1

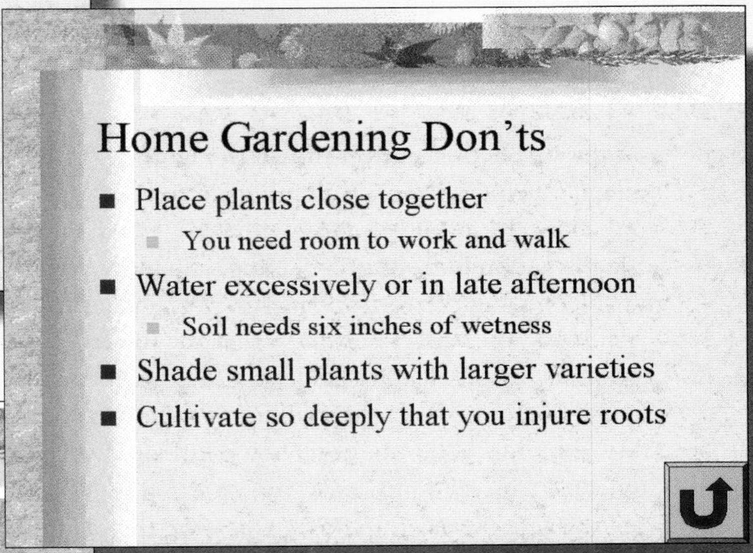

Home Gardening Don'ts

- Place plants close together
  - You need room to work and walk
- Water excessively or in late afternoon
  - Soil needs six inches of wetness
- Shade small plants with larger varieties
- Cultivate so deeply that you injure roots

(b) Slide 2

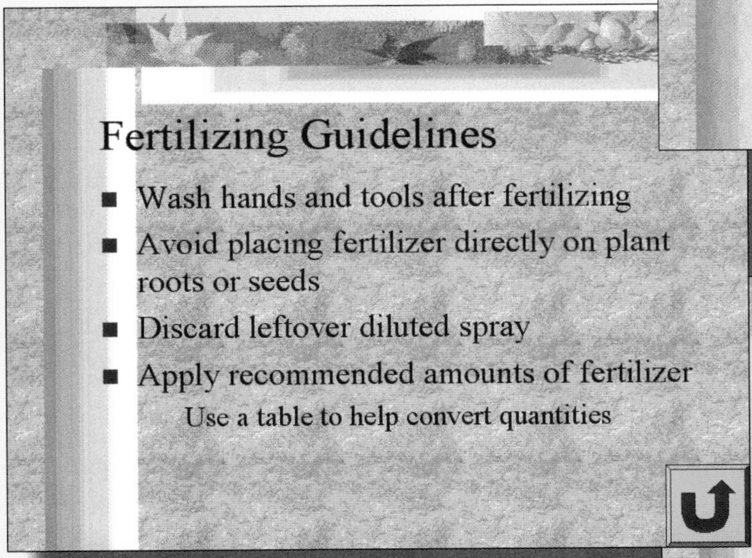

Fertilizing Guidelines

- Wash hands and tools after fertilizing
- Avoid placing fertilizer directly on plant roots or seeds
- Discard leftover diluted spray
- Apply recommended amounts of fertilizer
  Use a table to help convert quantities

(c) Slide 3

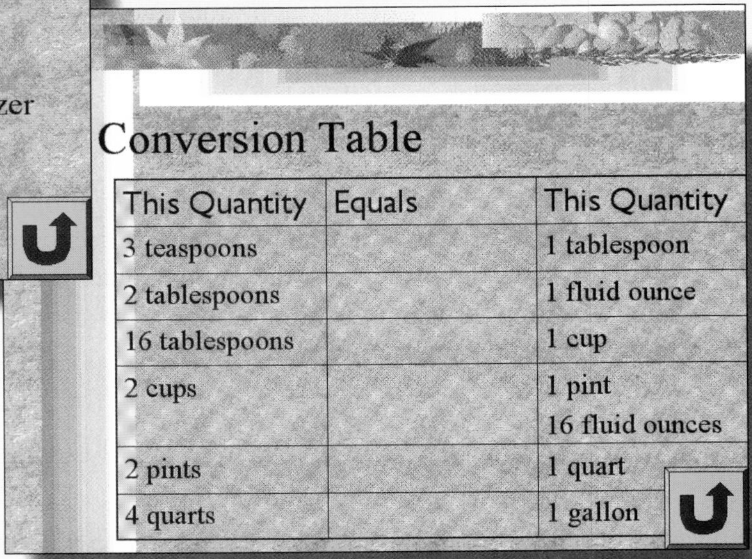

Conversion Table

This Quantity	Equals	This Quantity
3 teaspoons		1 tablespoon
2 tablespoons		1 fluid ounce
16 tablespoons		1 cup
2 cups		1 pint 16 fluid ounces
2 pints		1 quart
4 quarts		1 gallon

(d) Slide 4

FIGURE 4-76

(continued)

In the Lab

Linking PowerPoint Presentations *(continued)*

Instructions Part 2: Perform the following tasks to create the presentation shown in Figures 4-76e and 4-76f.

1. Open a new presentation, apply the Title Slide AutoLayout, and then apply the Nature design template. Change the background to the Stationery texture. Create the slide title shown in Figure 4-76e by typing the slide title text and subtitle text. Insert the clip art shown in Figure 4-76e that has the keywords, gardens, light bulbs. Scale the clip art to 125% and drag it to the upper-right corner of the slide. Apply the Dissolve animation effect to animate the flowers automatically.

2. Click the New Slide button and type 11 to apply the Title Only AutoLayout. Type the title text shown in Figure 4-76f.

3. Add the first action button shown in Figure 4-76f, which is in row 1, column 4 of the Action Buttons submenu. Hyperlink this action button to the first slide, Home Gardening Do's, of the Gardening Do's and Don'ts PowerPoint presentation created in Part 1. Play the Whoosh sound when the mouse is clicked.

4. Scale the action button to 75%, apply Shadow Style 2, and change the fill color to gold. Display the guides and rulers. Drag the vertical ruler to 0.42 inches left of center and the horizontal ruler to 0.25 inches above center. Drag the action button so that the lower-left corner snaps to the intersection of the guides. Type the caption Do s and Don ts under this action button, and then change the font to 20-point Gill Sans MT. Change the font color to navy blue. Use the ARROW keys to center the caption under the action button.

5. Add the middle action button shown in Figure 4-76f. Hyperlink this action button to the Fertilizing Guidelines PowerPoint presentation created in Part 1. Play the Whoosh sound when the mouse is clicked.

6. Scale the action button to 75%. Click the first action button, click the Format Painter button on the Standard toolbar, and then click the middle action button. Drag the horizontal ruler to 1.33 inches below center. Drag the second action button so that the lower-left corner snaps to the intersection of the guides. Type the caption Fertilizing Guidelines under this action button, click the caption under the first action button, click the Format Painter button, and then drag through the middle caption text. Use the ARROW keys to center the caption under the action button.

7. Add the bottom action button shown in Figure 4-76f. Hyperlink this action button to the Conversion Table PowerPoint presentation created in Part 1. Play the Whoosh sound when the mouse is clicked.

8. Scale the action button to 75%. Click the first action button, click the Format Painter button, and then click the third action button. Drag the horizontal ruler to 3.00 inches below center. Drag the action button so that the lower-left corner snaps to the intersection of the guides. Type the caption Conversion Table under this action button, click the caption under the first action button, click the Format Painter button, and then drag through the bottom caption text. Use the ARROW keys to center the caption under the action button. Hide the guides and rulers.

9. Apply the Split Vertical Out slide transition effect to Slide 2. Save the presentation with the file name, Bulbs to Blossoms.

10. Add the Return action button (row 3, column 1) to the lower-right corner of each of the three hyperlinked presentations, as shown in Figures 4-76b, 4-76c, and 4-76d. Hyperlink each button to Slide 2, Home Gardening Guide, of the Bulbs to Blossoms presentation. Change the buttons' fill color to gold. Save the three hyperlinked presentations.

In the Lab

11. Print the six presentation slides using the Pure black and white option.

12. Run the Bulbs to Blossoms slide show. Click the Do's and Don'ts action button to display the hyperlinked presentation. Display both slides. Click the hyperlink at the bottom of the second slide to jump to the Bulbs to Blossoms presentation. When the Home Gardening Guide presentation returns, click the Fertilizing Guidelines action button, read the new slide, and click the hyperlink at the bottom of the slide. Repeat this procedure for the Conversion Table action button. Click to display the black closing slide. End the slide shows and quit PowerPoint.

(e) Slide 5

(f) Slide 6

FIGURE 4-76d

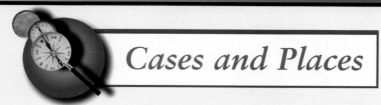

Cases and Places

The difficulty of these case studies varies:
▌ are the least difficult; ▌▌ are more difficult; and ▌▌▌ are the most difficult.

1 ▌ The marketing director of your local food pantry has asked you to help with a holiday food drive on campus. You decide to develop an interactive slide show to run in the cafeteria during the lunch and dinner rush. Prepare a short presentation aimed at encouraging students to bring canned goods and small cash donations to campus next week on Thursday and Friday. One slide should show an Excel worksheet explaining how one dollar can provide three dollars of food because local businesses have agreed to match the contributions. Other slides can feature a list of these participating businesses, statistics on how many people have come to the food pantry for assistance during the past three years, and volunteer opportunities. The title slide should give the dates and hours of the food drive and include WordArt for visual appeal. The final slide should give the address and telephone number of the food pantry.

2 ▌ Computer viruses and worm programs are a major concern in all facets of computing – from the corporate world to the home office. All computer users need to practice safe computing practices; these techniques include not opening or running any executable e-mail file attachment (.exe) sent from an unknown source, installing an anti-virus program on your computer (Norton or McAfee), and ensuring the anti-virus' auto protect feature is enabled (check the tray status area on the taskbar). Computer users should be alert for macro viruses, boot sector viruses, and worms. Macro viruses hide the virus code in the macro language of an application, such as Microsoft Word. When a user opens a document having an infected macro, the macro virus is loaded into memory. Certain actions, such as saving the document, activate the macro virus. Boot sector viruses replace the boot programs, which are used to start the computer systems, with modified, infected versions of the boot programs. When the infected boot programs are run, they load the viruses into the computers' memory. Once the viruses are in memory, they spread to floppy disks inserted into the computers. Unlike viruses, worm programs do not attach themselves to other programs. Instead, they copy themselves repeatedly in memory or on disk drives until no memory or disk space remains. The computers stop working when no memory or disk space exists. Some worm programs copy themselves to other computers on a network. Your school's computer lab supervisors have asked you to prepare a PowerPoint presentation explaining computer viruses and worms to students. Using the techniques introduced in this project, create an interactive short slide show using three buttons that correspond to the two virus types and the worm program. Include WordArt on the title slide, animated text, and slide transition effects.

Cases and Places

3 ▶▶ Swing dancing is popular on campus, but very few students know a variety of steps and how to blend them together smoothly. Four of your friends are expert ballroom dancers and have competed in local contests. They have decided to give dance lessons, and they want you to help with their publicity. You decide to create a slide show and want to start by designing a title slide that captures the spirit of swing dancing. Use PowerPoint and WordArt to create the title slide and a short slide show to present to your friends. Enhance the presentation by modifying the slide background and adding graphics, slide transition effects, and a summary slide.

4 ▶▶ Nearly two-thirds of colleges offer personal finance classes, but only one-fourth of the students actually enroll in one. Those who do enroll, however, are no more than nonenrollees to save regularly, comparison shop, or create a budget. Your local credit union realizes this problem that students have with saving routinely, and the managers want to encourage students to take advantage of the services offered at its on-campus branch. You have agreed to develop a persuasive PowerPoint slide show explaining how saving regularly builds a balance that helps with tuition payments. Add other slides featuring additional credit union services, such as certificates of deposit, credit cards with low interest, and vehicle loans. Visit local branches of credit unions or search the Internet to find information for the presentation.

5 ▶▶ Most prospective employees focus on salary and job responsibilities when they consider job offers. One area they often neglect, however, is benefit packages. Career counselors emphasize that these benefits can contribute significantly to salary levels and should be given serious consideration. Specifically, job hunters should investigate retirement plans, stock options, life insurance coverage, health coverage, tuition reimbursement, signing bonuses, and on-site fitness facilities. Visit your campus placement office or search the Internet to find the benefits packages offered by three companies to which you might consider sending a resume and cover letter. Using this information and the techniques introduced in the project, prepare an interactive presentation that compares these benefit packages. Enhance the presentation by modifying the slide background, adding graphics, using text preset animation effects, and applying slide transition effects. Include a hidden slide and a summary slide. Submit all files on a disk to your instructor.

Microsoft PowerPoint 2000

Importing Clips from the Microsoft Clip Gallery Live Web Site

C A S E   P E R S P E C T I V E

The two Spring Break trips to the Florida and Texas beaches and to the Caribbean islands have generated much interest and revenue for the Student Government Association. Now the SGA president, Marla Pervan, wants to add more special effects to your presentation. She suggests you revise the Spring Break presentation created in Project 3 by adding an animated sun and music that has the sound of waves in the background. You review the slide show and decide to add a winking sun and upbeat music to Slide 5. You look at Microsoft Clip Gallery 5.0, but you do not find any appropriate animated clips or music. Knowing that Internet access is built into the Microsoft Clip Gallery, you decide to browse the Microsoft Clip Gallery Live Web site for suitable animated clip art pictures and upbeat music for Slide 5.

Introduction

Although the Microsoft Clip Gallery has a wide variety of picture images, at times it does not have a file that fits your exact needs. Microsoft has created Clip Gallery Live, a source of additional pictures, sounds, and movie clips on the World Wide Web. To access this Web site easily, you click the Clips Online button in the Microsoft Clip Gallery dialog box, and then PowerPoint connects you directly to the Microsoft Clip Gallery Live start page (Figure 1a on the next page).

In this Integration Feature, you modify Slide 5 in the presentation created in Project 3 by adding music and an animated sun from the Web, as shown in Figures 1b and 1c on the next page.

Opening an Existing Presentation and Saving It with a New File Name

Because you are adding clips to the Spring Break presentation created in Project 3, the first step is to open the presentation. To ensure that the original Spring Break presentation remains intact, you save the presentation with a new name; Musical Spring Break. Then you connect to the World Wide Web and import the music and animated sun. The following pages illustrate these steps.

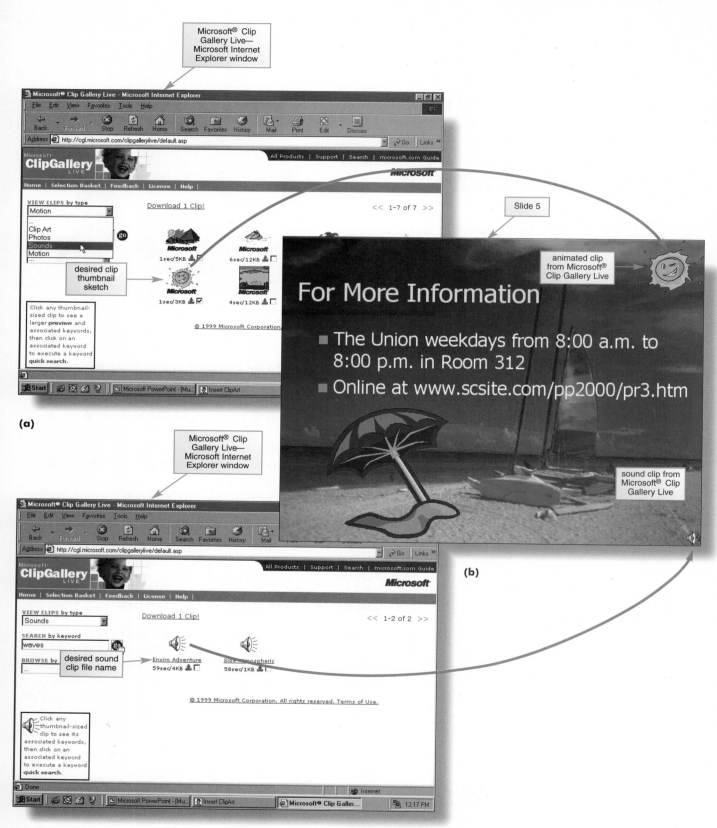

FIGURE 1

TO OPEN AN EXISTING PRESENTATION AND SAVE IT WITH A NEW FILE NAME

(1) Insert your Data Disk in drive A. Click the Start button on the taskbar. Click Open Office Document.

(2) If necessary, click the Look in box arrow and then click 3½ Floppy (A:).

(3) Double-click Spring Break.

(4) Click File on the menu bar and then click Save As. Type Musical Spring Break in the File name text box.

(5) Click the Save button in the Save As dialog box.

PowerPoint opens the Spring Break file and then saves it with a new file name, Musical Spring Break, on your floppy disk in drive A. The new file name displays on the title bar.

More About

Clip Gallery Live

The clips you download while working on your PowerPoint presentation can be used in other Microsoft Office applications. For example, the sun you import in this project can be part of a flyer created in Microsoft Word, and the music can play while users view a Microsoft Excel chart. The clips also can be used and reused in Microsoft Publisher, Microsoft FrontPage, Microsoft PhotoDraw, and Microsoft Works.

Moving to Another Slide

When creating or editing your presentation, you often want to display a slide other than the current one. Dragging the vertical scroll box up or down displays the slide indicator. Recall the slide indicator displays the slide number and title of the slide you are about to display. Once you see the number of the slide you wish to display, release the mouse button. Perform the following step to move to Slide 5 using the vertical scroll box.

TO MOVE TO ANOTHER SLIDE

(1) Drag the vertical scroll box down until Slide: 5 of 5 For More Information displays in the slide indicator.

Slide 5 displays (Figure 2).

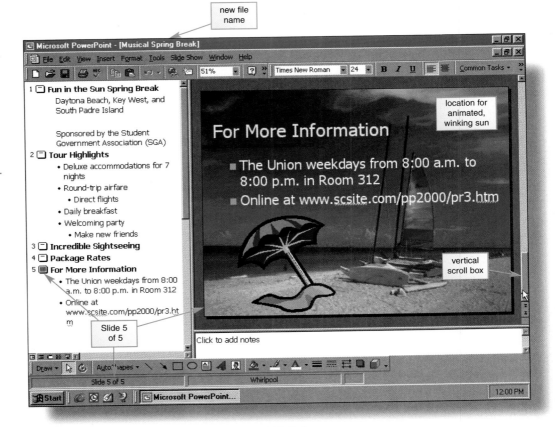

FIGURE 2

Importing Clip Art from Microsoft Clip Gallery Live on the World Wide Web

Recall from Project 2 that one source for additional clip art images is the World Wide Web. Many companies provide clip art images on the Web; some sites offer clips free of charge, and others charge a fee.

Microsoft maintains a Web site called Clip Gallery Live that contains clip art pictures, photographs, sounds, and videos. To use the Microsoft Clip Gallery Live Web site, you must have access to the World Wide Web through an **Internet service provider (ISP)**. Then you use **Web browser** software to find the Microsoft site. This project uses **Microsoft Internet Explorer** for the Web browser. If you do not have Internet access, your instructor will provide the two clips used in this project.

To simplify connecting to the Clip Gallery Live Web site, the Microsoft Clip Gallery dialog box contains a Clips Online button. Your sign-in process depends on your ISP and your computer configuration. For example, some ISPs require users to identify themselves with a name and password. Some schools bypass this window because of the school's Web connection setup. See your instructor for your school's requirements. If you are connecting to the Web at a location other than school, you must know the ISP's sign in requirements.

Connecting to the Microsoft Clip Gallery Live Site

You want to add music that contains the background sound of waves and insert an animated sun on Slide 5. Once you connect to the Web, the Microsoft Clip Gallery Live start page displays. A **start page** is a specially-designed page that serves as a starting point for a Web site. Microsoft updates this start page frequently to reflect seasons, holidays, new collections, artists, special offers, and events.

Perform the following steps to open Microsoft Clip Gallery, connect to the World Wide Web, and then display the Microsoft Clip Gallery Live start page.

More About 2000

The End-User License Agreement

When you view the Microsoft Clip Gallery Live start page for the first time, you may be asked to read the Microsoft End-User License Agreement (EULA). When you click the Accept button, you agree to abide by the copyright restrictions Microsoft imposes to protect the use of its software. Read the EULA to see what rights and restrictions you have to use clips found at this site. For more information, visit the PowerPoint 2000 More About Web page (www.scsite.com/pp2000/more.htm) and click EULA.

To Connect to the Microsoft Clip Gallery Live Site

1 **Click the Insert Clip Art button on the Drawing toolbar. Point to the Clips Online button on the Insert ClipArt toolbar.**

Microsoft Clip Gallery 5.0 opens and displays the Pictures sheet in the Insert ClipArt window (Figure 3).

2 **Click the Clips Online button. If necessary, click the OK button in the Connect to Web for More Clip Art, Photos, Sounds dialog box to browse for additional clips. Connect to the World Wide Web as required by your browser software and ISP. When the Microsoft Clip Gallery Live start page displays, if necessary maximize the screen and read the Microsoft End-User License Agreement for Microsoft Software and click the Accept button.**

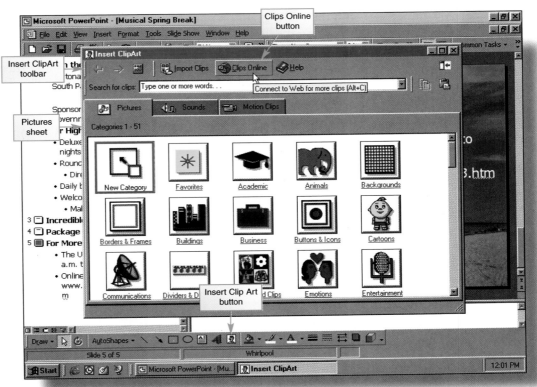

FIGURE 3

If you are using a modem, a dialog box displays that connects you to the Web via your ISP. If you are connected directly to the Web through a computer network, the dialog box does not display. Once connected to the Web, the Microsoft Clip Gallery Live start page displays the Microsoft End-User License Agreement. When you click the Accept button, the Microsoft End-User License Agreement area no longer displays. The site now displays information about Microsoft® Clip Gallery Live features and text boxes to locate specific types of clips.

Searching for and Downloading Microsoft Clip Gallery Live Clips

Microsoft Clip Gallery Live is similar to Microsoft Clip Gallery 5.0 in that you can search for clip art by keywords. You want to locate a motion clip animating the sun and music containing the sound of waves. You first will search Microsoft Clip Gallery Live for motion files with the keyword, sun. Then, you will search for sound files with the keyword, waves.

Accepting the EULA

When you accept the terms of the Microsoft End-User License Agreement, your computer sends a message to Clip Gallery Live stating that you agree to the licensing restrictions. Microsoft, in turn, sends a message, called a cookie, to your computer so that you will not be asked to accept the EULA each time you visit the Clip Gallery Live site. If you are using Internet Explorer 4.0 or later and are asked to accept the agreement each time you go to this site, your computer probably has been instructed not to accept cookies.

Finding Clips

You may enter a maximum of 36 characters or 6 keywords in the SEARCH by keyword text box. These keywords must be separated by spaces or by commas. Only clips matching all the keywords will display.

When you find a clip to add to your presentation, you can **download**, or copy, it instantly to the Microsoft Clip Gallery on your computer by clicking the Immediate Download icon under the desired clip. You also can select several clips individually and then download them simultaneously. In this project, you want to download motion and sound clips, so you will choose a motion file and then select the check box below the clip to add the file to the selection basket. The **selection basket** holds your selections temporarily until you are ready to add them to your computer. Then, you will add the sound clip to the selection basket. The downloaded clips will be added to the Microsoft Clip Gallery in the Downloaded Clips category. To remove a clip from the selection basket, clear the clip's check box.

Perform the following steps to search for clips in Microsoft Clip Gallery Live.

 To Search for and Download Microsoft Clip Gallery Live Clips

1 **Click the VIEW CLIPS by type arrow in the Microsoft® Clip Gallery Live window. Point to Motion in the list.**

The Selection Basket sheet displays (Figure 4). Microsoft groups the clips in four categories: Clip Art, Photos, Sounds, and Motion.

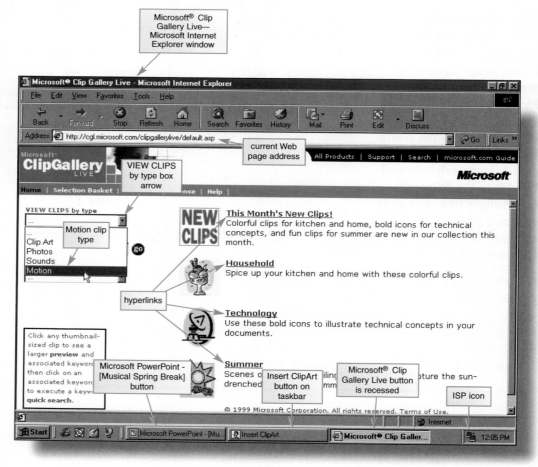

FIGURE 4

2 Click Motion. Click the SEARCH by keyword text box and type *sun* in the box. Point to the Go button (Figure 5).

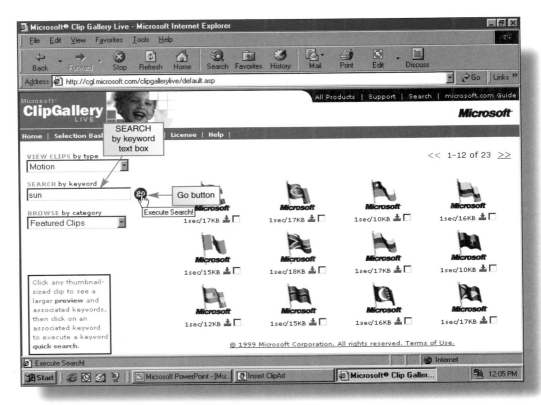

FIGURE 5

3 Click the Go button. When the search results display, click the check box below the winking sun clip. Click the VIEW CLIPS by type arrow. Point to Sounds in the list.

Clip Gallery Live executes the search and displays the results (Figure 6). When you click the check box associated with the thumbnail-sized clip, the motion clip is added to the selection basket, as indicated by the Download 1 Clip! hyperlink. The search status displays at the upper-right corner of the page and indicates the number of clips that match the search criteria. The numbers below the file name are the estimated download time and the clip's file size.

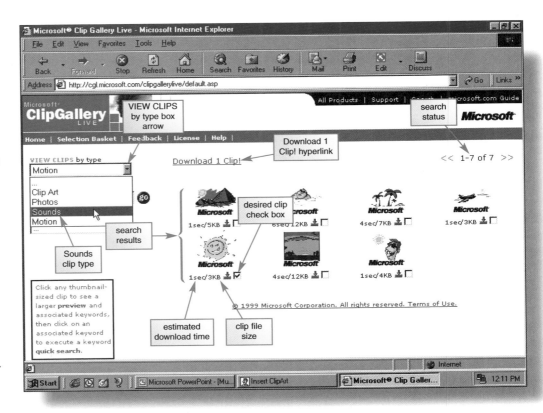

FIGURE 6

4 **Click Sounds. Click the SEARCH by keyword text box, select the text, and type** waves **in the box. Click the Go button.**

Clip Gallery Live executes the search. After a few moments, several thumbnail-sized sound clips with the keyword, waves, display (Figure 7). The speaker icons identify the sound clips. The hyperlink below each clip is its file name.

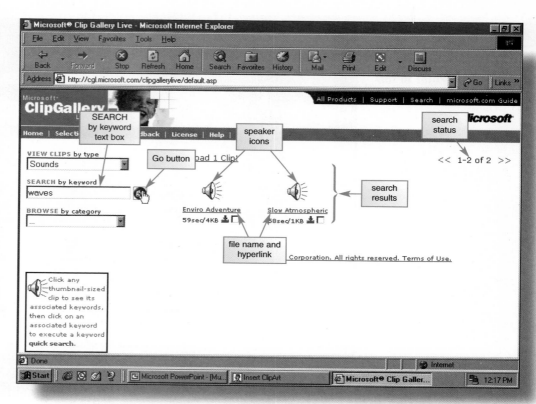

FIGURE 7

5 **Click the check box below the clip with the file name, Enviro Adventure. Point to the Download 2 Clips! hyperlink.**

When you click the check box, the sound clip is added to the selection basket, as indicated by the underlined Download 2 Clips! hyperlink (Figure 8).

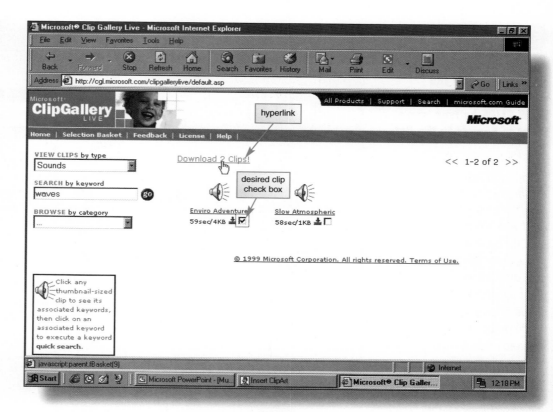

FIGURE 8

6 Click the Download 2 Clips! hyperlink. Point to the Download Now! hyperlink in the first instruction in the Selection Basket sheet.

The hyperlink displays with the font color red (Figure 9). Clicking the hyperlink will download the two clips stored temporarily in the selection basket.

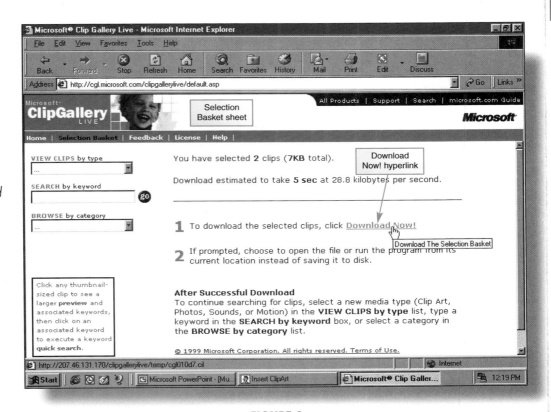

FIGURE 9

7 Click the Download Now! hyperlink. If necessary, click the Motion Clips tab in the Insert ClipArt window. Click the sun icon and then point to the Insert clip button.

When you click the sun icon, PowerPoint will insert the sun clip on Slide 5. Slide 5 will not be visible until you close the Insert ClipArt window (Figure 10).

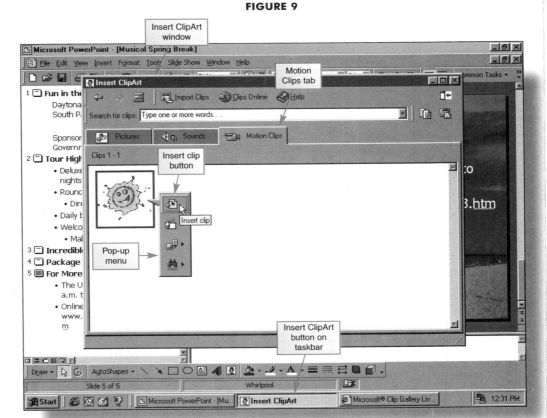

FIGURE 10

8 Click the Insert clip button on the Pop-up menu. Click the Sounds tab in the Insert ClipArt window. Click the ETHTRK01 icon and then click the Insert clip button on the Pop-up menu. Point to the Close button on the Insert ClipArt window title bar.

The Enviro Adventure clip, which has the file name ETHTRK01, displays on the Sounds sheet (Figure 11). When you click the Insert clip button, PowerPoint will insert this clip on Slide 5.

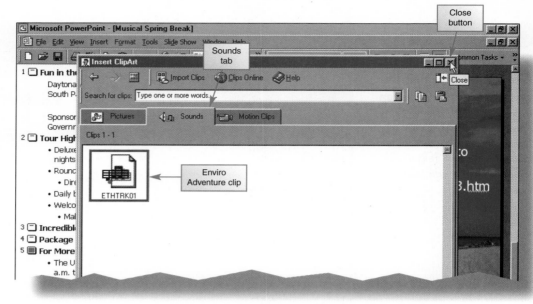

FIGURE 11

9 Click the Close button on the title bar. Click the Yes button in the Microsoft PowerPoint dialog box.

The animated sun and a speaker icon display on Slide 5 (Figure 12). You want the music to play automatically when your slide show displays Slide 5. Microsoft Clip Gallery Live still is open, and you still are connected to the ISP.

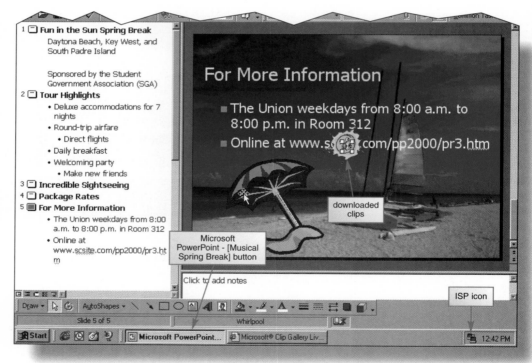

FIGURE 12

Quitting a Web Session

Once you have downloaded your clip art, you want to quit your Web session. Because Windows 98 displays buttons on the taskbar for each open application, you quickly can quit an application by right-clicking an application button and then clicking the Close button on the shortcut menu. Perform the following steps to quit your current Web session.

TO QUIT A WEB SESSION

(1) Right-click the Microsoft® Clip Gallery Live – Microsoft Internet Explorer button on the taskbar. If you are not using Microsoft Internet Explorer, right-click the button for your browser.

(2) Click Close on the shortcut menu.

(3) When the dialog box displays, click the Yes button to disconnect. If your ISP displays a different dialog box, terminate your connection to your ISP.

The browser software closes and the ISP connection is terminated.

Slide 5 displays with the two downloaded objects in the center of the screen. The speaker object represents the Enviro Adventure sound file.

Moving the Clips

You want to move the speaker icon to the lower-right corner of the slide and the sun to the upper-right corner. Perform the following steps to move the clips to these respective locations.

TO MOVE THE CLIPS

(1) Drag the speaker icon to the lower-right corner of Slide 5.

(2) Drag the sun object to the upper-right corner of Slide 5.

The clips display in the appropriate locations on Slide 5 (Figure 13).

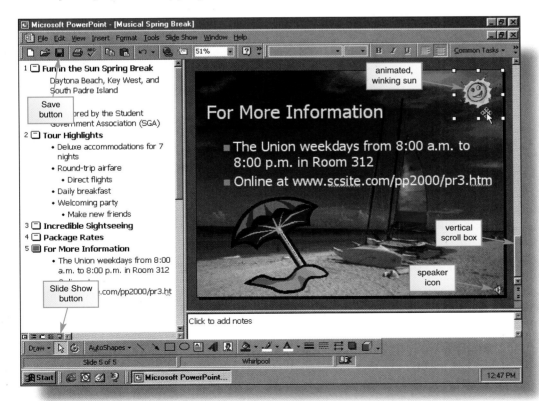

FIGURE 13

Saving the Presentation

The changes to the presentation are complete. Perform the following step to save the finished presentation on a floppy disk before running the slide show.

TO SAVE A PRESENTATION

1 Click the Save button on the Standard toolbar.

PowerPoint saves the presentation by saving the changes made to the presentation since the last save.

Running an Animated Slide Show

To verify that the presentation looks as expected, run the presentation in slide show view. Perform the following steps to run the revised Musical Spring Break slide show.

TO RUN AN ANIMATED SLIDE SHOW

1 Drag the vertical scroll box to display Slide: 1 of 5 Fun in the Sun Spring Break.

2 Click the Slide Show button at the lower left of the PowerPoint window. When Slide 1 displays in slide show view, click the slide anywhere except on the Pop-up menu buttons.

3 Continue clicking the slides to finish running the slide show and return to slide view.

The presentation displays the animated sun and plays the sound file in slide show view and returns to slide view when finished.

Now that the presentation is complete, the last step is to print the presentation slides.

Printing Presentation Slides

Perform the following steps to print the revised presentation.

TO PRINT PRESENTATION SLIDES

1 Click File on the menu bar and then click Print.

2 When the Print dialog box displays, click Pure black and white and then click the OK button.

Quitting PowerPoint

The changes to this presentation are saved. The last step is to quit PowerPoint. Perform the following steps to quit PowerPoint.

TO QUIT POWERPOINT

1 Click the Close button on the title bar.

2 If the Microsoft PowerPoint dialog box displays, click the Yes button to save changes made since the last save.

PowerPoint closes.

CASE PERSPECTIVE SUMMARY

The revised Spring Break presentation now has lively music and an animated, winking sun on Slide 5. These clips from the Microsoft Clip Gallery Live Web site enhance the slide show and should generate additional interest in this popular and profitable event for the Student Government Association.

Integration Feature Summary

This Integration Feature introduced importing sound and animation clips from Microsoft Clip Gallery Live on the World Wide Web to Microsoft Clip Gallery 5.0. You began by opening an existing presentation, Spring Break, and then saving the presentation with a new file name. Next, you accessed the Microsoft Clip Gallery Live start page on the World Wide Web by clicking the Clips Online button on the Insert ClipArt toolbar. Once connected to the Microsoft Clip Gallery Live start page, you searched for an animated sun and upbeat music with waves. Then you imported these clips to the Microsoft Clip Gallery by downloading the files from the Web page. You moved the clips to appropriate locations on Slide 5 and then quit the Web session by closing the browser software and disconnecting from the ISP. Finally, you saved the presentation, ran the presentation in slide show view to check for continuity, printed the presentation slides, and quit PowerPoint.

What You Should Know

Having completed this Integration Feature, you now should be able to perform the following tasks:

▶ Connect to the Microsoft Clip Gallery Live Site *(PPI 1.5)*
▶ Move the Clips *(PPI 1.11)*
▶ Move to Another Slide *(PPI 1.3)*
▶ Open an Existing Presentation and Save It with a New File Name *(PPI 1.3)*
▶ Print Presentation Slides *(PPI 1.12)*
▶ Quit a Web Session *(PPI 1.11)*
▶ Quit PowerPoint *(PPI 1.12)*
▶ Run an Animated Slide Show *(PPI 1.12)*
▶ Save a Presentation *(PPI 1.12)*
▶ Search for and Download Microsoft Clip Gallery Live Clips *(PPI 1.6)*

In the Lab

1 Importing Sound and Motion Clips

Problem: Dr. Mary Halen, the director of the Office of Financial Aid, realizes the importance of informing students of scholarship opportunities, and she wants to enhance the presentation you created in Project 2. Dr. Halen believes the sound of coins dropping into a drawer and an animated clip from the Microsoft Clip Gallery Live Web site would make the slide show even more impressive. She has asked you to find appropriate clips and to modify Slide 1 of the Searching for Scholarships presentation.

Instructions: Start PowerPoint and then perform the following steps with a computer.

1. Open the Searching for Scholarships presentation shown in Figures 2-1a through 2-1f on page PP 2.5 that you created in Project 2. (If you did not complete Project 2, see your instructor for a copy of the presentation.)
2. Save the Searching for Scholarships presentation with the new file name, Motion Scholarships.
3. Display Slide 1, click the Insert Clip Art button on the Drawing toolbar, and then click the Clips Online button on the Insert ClipArt toolbar.
4. Search for motion clips with the keyword, money. Then search for sound clips with the same keyword, money. Download the two clips, and have the sound play automatically.
5. Move the speaker icon to the lower-right corner of Slide 1, and move the money clip to the upper-right corner. Add today's date and your name to the footer.
6. Disconnect from the Web and save the file again.
7. Run the slide show. Print Slide 1. Quit PowerPoint.

2 Importing Motion and Multiple Sound Clips

Problem: The local park board commissioners are pleased that you have volunteered to publicize the new 25-mile mountain bike trail in Veterans' Park. They like the title slide you developed in the In the Lab 1 exercise in Project 4, but they would like you to add an animated bike rider and appropriate sound effects. You decide to search the Microsoft Clip Gallery Live Web site for the bike clips and for sounds of nature that reflect a relaxing outing.

Instructions: Start PowerPoint and then perform the following steps with a computer.

1. Open the Bike Trail presentation shown in Figure 4-74 on page PP 4.59 that you created in Project 4. (If you did not complete this exercise, see your instructor for a copy of the slide.)
2. Save the Bike Trail presentation with the new file name, Musical Biking.
3. Click the Insert Clip Art button on the Drawing toolbar, and then click the Clips Online button on the Insert ClipArt toolbar.
4. Search for a motion clip with the keyword, bike. Then search for sound clips with the keyword, nature, and select two sounds. Download these three clips.
5. If necessary, click the Motion Clips tab in the Insert ClipArt window. Click the bike rider icon, and then click the Insert clip button on the Pop-up menu.
6. Click the Microsoft PowerPoint – [Musical Biking] button on the taskbar. Scale the bike rider clip to 175%, and then apply the Crawl From Left entry animation effect. Move the bike rider clip to the lower-right corner of the slide.

In the Lab

7. Click the Insert ClipArt button on the taskbar. Click the Sounds tab. Click the first sound clip, click the Insert clip button on the Pop-up menu, and then click the Yes button in the Microsoft PowerPoint dialog box to play the first sound automatically. Move the speaker icon to the lower-left corner of Slide 1.

8. Click the Insert ClipArt button on the taskbar. Click the second sound clip, click the Insert clip button on the Pop-up menu, and then click the Yes button in the Microsoft PowerPoint dialog box to play the second sound automatically. Move this speaker icon beside the first speaker in the lower-left corner.

9. Add your name to the footer.

10. Disconnect from the Web and save the file again.

11. Run the slide show. Print Slide 1 using the Pure black and white option. Quit PowerPoint.

3 Modifying a Personal Presentation

Problem: In today's competitive job market, employers are searching for candidates with computer expertise. In addition to sending your cover letter and resume to potential employers, you decide to send a personalized PowerPoint presentation highlighting your computer skills, academic honors, and campus activities.

Instructions: Start PowerPoint and perform the following tasks with a computer.

1. Open the Supplemental Information presentation you created in the In the Lab 3 exercise in the Web Feature 1 project (page PPW 1.14). If you did not complete this exercise, perform Step 1 in that exercise.

2. Search the Microsoft Clip Gallery Live Web site for appropriate motion, picture, and sound clips. Add these clips to your presentation.

3. Save the presentation with the file name, Clip Information.

4. Run the slide show. Print the slides using the Pure black and white option. Quit PowerPoint.

Microsoft **PowerPoint 2000**

Microsoft PowerPoint 2000

P R O J E C T

5

Creating a Self-Running Presentation Using Animation Effects

O B J E C T I V E S

You will have mastered the material in this project when you can:

- Add a presentation within a presentation
- Insert animated clip art
- Apply animation effects
- Insert an Excel chart
- Build a PowerPoint chart or graph
- Add a table from Word
- Insert an AutoShape
- Rotate an AutoShape
- Customize a color scheme
- Omit background graphics from the master slide
- Set automatic slide timings
- Create a self-running presentation

Getting the Word Out Graphically

I n 1981, the modern movie, *Quest for Fire*, opened in theaters across America. Even without any dialogue, the movie conveyed a clear, compelling story about prehistoric humans who had no language to speak. Since the dawn of mankind, humans have relied on graphic images to communicate, even after the advent of spoken language. In today's global village, images play a vital role in promoting understanding between peoples of different languages.

Individuals long have used pictures, or graphics, as guides for building structures involving complex spatial relationships. Imagine trying to build the Pharaoh's pyramids without a plan drawn out on papyrus or a Boeing jet without engineering drawings.

Yet, in recent years, graphics, onscreen presentations, self-running presentations, online meetings, presentations on the Web, overhead transparencies, and 35mm slide shows have played an even greater role in the art of communication. People understand more easily when visual elements are combined. From sales presentations, to impressive slide shows in courtroom dramas, to disseminating information in kiosks, people turn to images to persuade others, to influence buying choices, or to adopt their points of view. PowerPoint is an outstanding example of the marriage of multimedia to help people present persuasive arguments or simply inform or entertain.

Information presented with images augments content. In this PowerPoint project, you will create a self-running presentation with animation effects. The presentation contains visual elements, an animated slide created in a separate PowerPoint presentation using the skills and tools you have learned previously, animated clip art, and other elements available from Excel and Word that combine so skillfully in the Office 2000 suite.

One popular method used for distributing information contained in self-running presentations is the kiosk. This freestanding, computerized information or reference center allows users to select various options to browse

through or find specific material. Typical kiosks are self-service structures equipped with computer hardware and software. Kiosk manufacturers offer a variety of designs appropriate for various locations. One such manufacturer is Kiosk Information Systems (KIS). It has introduced The Stealth, with its sleek form and logical engineering. Focusing on a certain market, KIS creates a custom product to match its location. Kiosks usually are positioned where they can reach the greatest number of people and generally are placed in public places such as shopping centers, hotels, airports, stadiums, tradeshows, and conventions where customers or visitors can obtain information on available services, product information, exhibit locations, and maps.

In a world increasingly dependent on images as well as language to communicate and inform, self-running presentations are a great way to communicate information without having someone available to run the slide show. With PowerPoint, you can set up your presentation to run unattended in a booth or kiosk. A self-running presentation restarts when it is finished. With their associated multimedia devices, animation, and sound, self-running presentations and kiosks are an entertaining combination for getting the word out.

Microsoft PowerPoint 2000

Creating a Self-Running Presentation Using Animation Effects

PROJECT 5

C A S E   P E R S P E C T I V E

The quest for a healthy, toned body has reached all segments of the population. Sales of home fitness products, particularly treadmills and free weights, have surged, and health club memberships have grown to record numbers.

The Fitness Center at your school has experienced an increase in the number of students coming to exercise. When they join the Fitness Center, they express an interest in maximizing their workout time due to their busy schedules and commitments. The Fitness Center director, Tiffani Olson, wants you to develop a PowerPoint presentation to run at a kiosk near the registration counter.

You discuss holistic exercise strategies with Tiffani and decide to focus on describing how students can optimize their weekly half-hour workouts by combining aerobic exercise using a treadmill and anaerobic exercise using free weights. You will enhance the presentation with a slide from one of Tiffani's previous presentations, charts created in Microsoft Excel and in PowerPoint, a table you import from Microsoft Word, and a diagram using AutoShapes that shows the benefits of exercise. You will time the presentation so that it runs for three minutes and repeats continuously.

Introduction

People have a thirst for information. From catching the breaking news on cable television to downloading our latest e-mail messages, individuals constantly are faced with keeping up with the day's events.

One method used for disseminating information is a **kiosk**. This freestanding, self-service structure is equipped with computer hardware and software and is used to provide information or reference materials to the public. Kiosks frequently are found in public places, such as shopping centers, hotels, museums, libraries, and airport terminals, where customers or visitors may have questions about community events, local hotels, and rental cars. Many kiosks have multimedia devices for playing sound and video clips. Some have a touch screen or keyboard that serves as an input device and allows users to select various options to browse through or find specific information. Advanced kiosks allow customers to place orders, make payments, and access the Internet.

In this project, you will create a slide show for Western College's Fitness Center. This show will run continuously on a computer near the registration counter, so present and potential members can view the brief three-minute presentation that gives them information on getting the most from a half-hour workout session. The presentation slides are shown in Figures 5-1a through 5-1g.

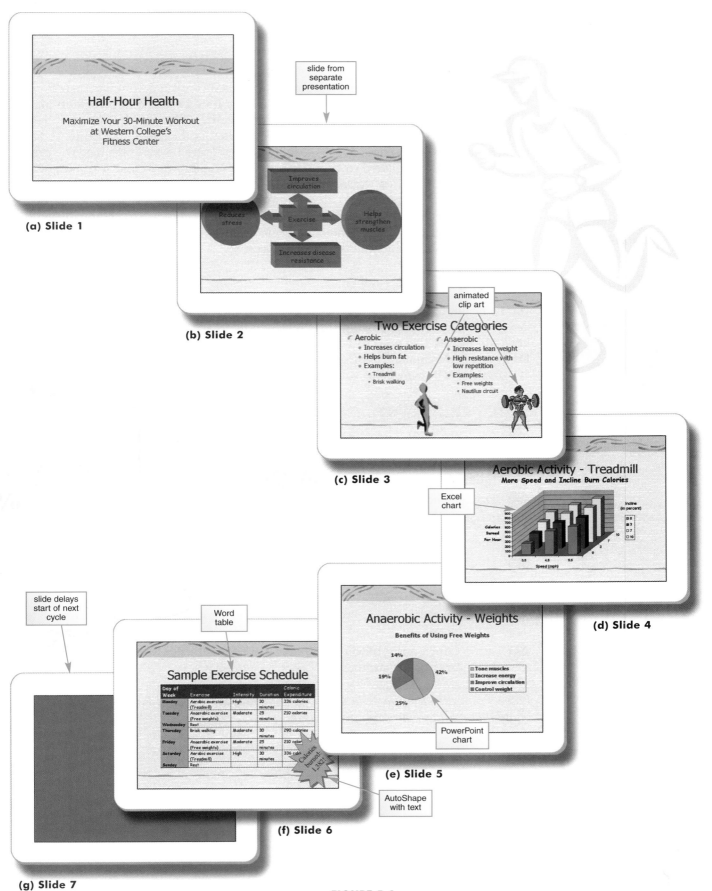

(a) Slide 1

slide from separate presentation

(b) Slide 2

animated clip art

(c) Slide 3

Excel chart

(d) Slide 4

slide delays start of next cycle

Word table

PowerPoint chart

(e) Slide 5

AutoShape with text

(f) Slide 6

(g) Slide 7

FIGURE 5-1

Project Five — Half-Hour Workout

The self-running three-minute presentation created in Project 5 contains several visual elements: an animated slide created in a separate PowerPoint presentation, animated clip art, an Excel chart, a PowerPoint chart, a Word table, and an AutoShape with text. After these objects are inserted in the slides, automatic slide timings are set so that these objects display after a desired period of time. The presentation then is designated to be a self-running presentation so that it restarts when it is finished. To separate the last slide from the beginning of the presentation, a completely blank purple slide is created and set to display for a specific period of time. As with other PowerPoint presentations, the first steps are to create a new presentation, select a design template, create a title slide, and save the presentation. The following steps illustrate these procedures.

Starting a New Presentation

To begin, create a new, blank presentation, choose an AutoLayout, and apply a design template. The following steps review how to accomplish these tasks. The toolbars and menus also need to be reset so they display exactly as shown in this book. For a detailed explanation of resetting the toolbars and menus, see Appendix C. Perform the following steps to start a new presentation.

TO START A NEW PRESENTATION

1. Click the Start button on the taskbar.

2. Click New Office Document on the Start menu. If necessary, click the General tab in the New Office Document dialog box.

3. Double-click the Blank Presentation icon.

4. Click the OK button when the New Slide dialog box displays to select the Title Slide AutoLayout.

5. Double-click the move handle on the left side of the Standard toolbar to display the toolbar in its entirety.

6. Double-click Default Design on the status bar. Double-click the Sumi Painting design template in the Presentation Designs list in the Apply Design Template dialog box.

7. If the Office Assistant displays, right-click the Office Assistant and then click Hide on the shortcut menu.

PowerPoint displays the Title Slide AutoLayout and the Sumi Painting design template on Slide 1 in normal view (Figure 5-2).

More About

Kiosks

Microsoft donated nearly $100,000 to develop the Microsoft Internet Discovery Kiosk, an interactive exhibit used to inform and educate users about the Internet's history, technology, uses, and future. The kiosk travels to museums and libraries throughout the United States and is designed to educate and entertain. To learn more about this multimedia kiosk and to read Microsoft Chairman and CEO Bill Gates' views on this innovative project, visit the PowerPoint 2000 Project 5 More About page (www.scsite.com/pp2000/more.htm) and click Kiosk.

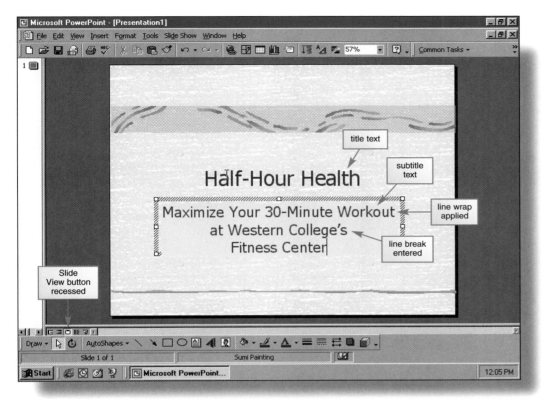

FIGURE 5-2

Creating the Title Slide in Slide View

The purpose of this presentation is to describe how students visiting Western College's Fitness Center can maximize their workout sessions. If they know the right techniques and understand how to vary their aerobic and anaerobic activities five times per week, they can obtain healthy results. The opening slide should introduce this concept. Perform the following steps to create a title slide in slide view.

TO CREATE A TITLE SLIDE IN SLIDE VIEW

1. Click the Slide View button located at the lower left of the PowerPoint window.

2. Click the Title Area placeholder to select it.

3. Type Half-Hour Health in the Title Area placeholder.

4. Press the CTRL+ENTER keys to move the insertion point to the Object Area placeholder.

5. Type Maximize Your 30-Minute Workout at Western College's and then press the SHIFT+ENTER keys.

6. Type Fitness Center but do not press the ENTER key.

The title text and subtitle text display in Slide 1 as shown in Figure 5-3 on the next page.

Formatting Tabs

You can use tabs to align text in the placeholders. To set or clear tab stops, select the text, display the ruler, and click the tab button at the left of the horizontal ruler to display the desired type of tab. Then click the ruler where you want to set the tab. You can drag any tab marker to a new position on the ruler. The space between all default tabs changes proportionately, so that if you move a default tab to one-half inch, all default tables become spaced one-half inch apart. To clear a tab, drag the tab marker off the ruler.

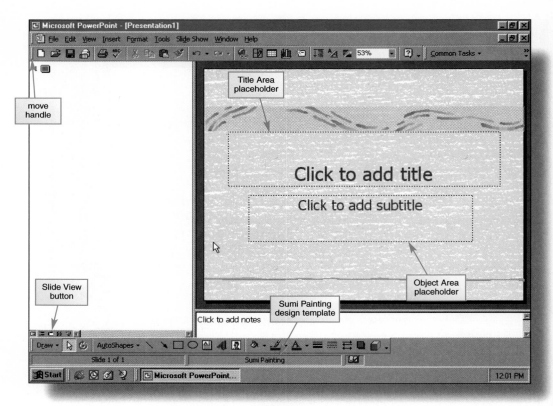

FIGURE 5-3

The first line of subtitle text in the Object Area placeholder uses PowerPoint's **line wrap** feature. PowerPoint line wraps text that exceeds the width of the placeholder so you can type words in a paragraph continually without pressing the ENTER key at the end of each line. PowerPoint positions the insertion point automatically at the beginning of the next line.

In this title slide, you want the words, Fitness Center, to display together on the last line of the Object Area placeholder. Sufficient space appears in the placeholder to display the word, Fitness, on the second line. You need to force that word to display on the third line, so you press the SHIFT and the ENTER keys simultaneously after you type the word, College's, to create a **line break**, which moves the insertion point to the beginning of the next line.

Although both the ENTER key and the SHIFT+ENTER keys advance the insertion point to the next line, these keystrokes produce different results. When you press the ENTER key, you create a new paragraph, which has specific attributes such as alignment and line spacing. The subtitle text in Slide 1 has the default font size of 32, line spacing of 38, and before paragraph line spacing of 8. When you press the ENTER key to insert a blank line into your slide or to create a new paragraph, you add 8 points of line spacing above this new paragraph. In contrast, when you press the SHIFT+ENTER keys, you do not create a new paragraph. The insertion point thus advances downward to a new line within the existing paragraph, and no additional line spacing is added above the new line.

Adding a Presentation within a Presentation

Tiffani has given many informative talks on campus and in the community regarding various fitness topics. She recently delivered a presentation at the local YMCA on the subject of using the computer to plug into online fitness resources. She used a PowerPoint presentation to accompany her speech, and she wants you to use one slide from that presentation in your Half-Hour Workout slide show.

Inserting a Slide from Another Presentation

Tiffani used the PowerPoint presentation with the file name Cyberfitness for her recent presentation. It contains four slides, and the second slide, shown in Figure 5-4, displays five animated graphical shapes that depict the benefits of keeping fit. The Cyberfitness file is on your Data Disk. The steps on the next page demonstrate how to insert Slide 2 from that file into your presentation.

The Favorites Folder

Each tab in the Insert Clip Art dialog box has a Favorites category where you can store new clips you import or commonly used clips. To add clips to the Favorites category when you are importing these files, select the Favorites category in the Clip Properties dialog box. To add existing clips to the Favorites category, click the clip, click the Add to category button on the Pop-up menu, click Favorites, and then click the Add button.

(a) Slide 1

desired
PowerPoint
slide to insert

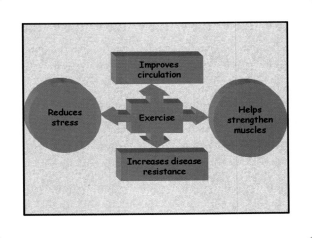

(b) Slide 2

(c) Slide 3

(d) Slide 4

FIGURE 5-4

To Insert a Slide from Another Presentation

1 **Insert your Data Disk into Drive A. Click Insert on the menu bar and then point to Slides from Files.**

The Insert menu displays (Figure 5-5). Slides from Files is highlighted.

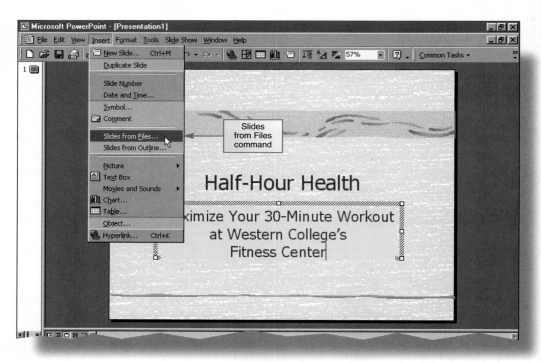

FIGURE 5-5

2 **Click Slides from Files. When the Slide Finder dialog box displays, if necessary click the Find Presentation tab, and then point to the Browse button.**

The Slide Finder dialog box displays (Figure 5-6). If you use several presentations on a regular basis, you can add them to your List of Favorites so you can find them easily.

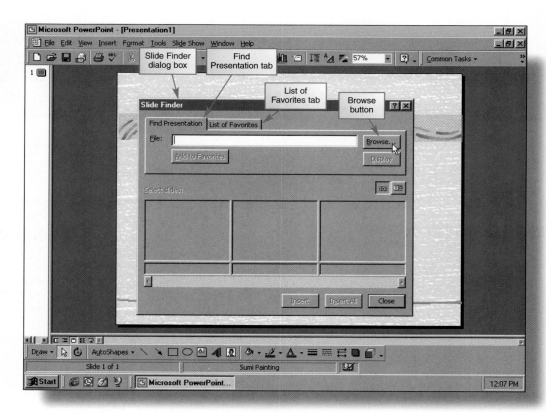

FIGURE 5-6

3 Click the Browse button. Click the Look in box arrow and then click 3½ Floppy (A:). Click Cyberfitness in the list. Point to the Open button.

The Browse dialog box displays (Figure 5-7). A list displays the files that PowerPoint can open. Your list may be different depending on your computer installation.

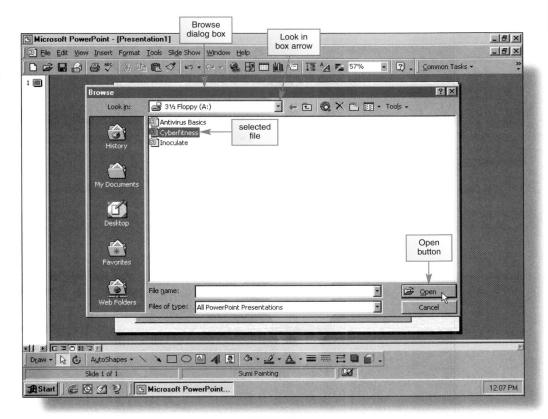

FIGURE 5-7

4 Click the Open button. Click the Slide 2 image in the Select slides area. Point to the Insert button.

The Slide Finder dialog box displays (Figure 5-8). The selected file, Cyberfitness, displays in the File text box. Slide 2 is the slide you want to insert in your presentation.

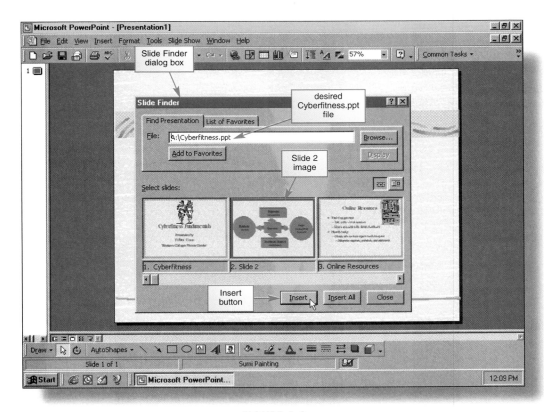

FIGURE 5-8

5 **Click the Insert button. Point to the Close button.**

PowerPoint inserts the Cyberfitness Slide 2 in your presentation (Figure 5-9). The Slide Finder dialog box remains open to allow you to insert additional slides.

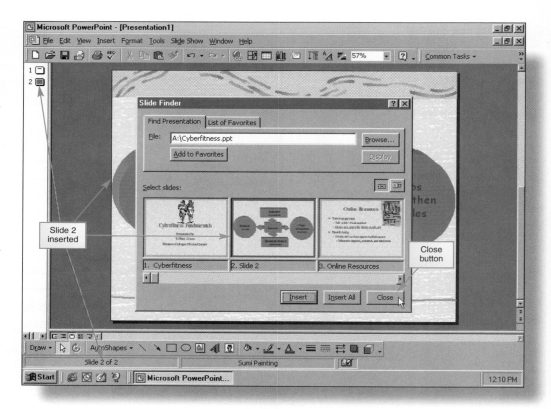

FIGURE 5-9

6 **Click the Close button.**

The Cyberfitness Slide 2 now is the second slide in your presentation (Figure 5-10).

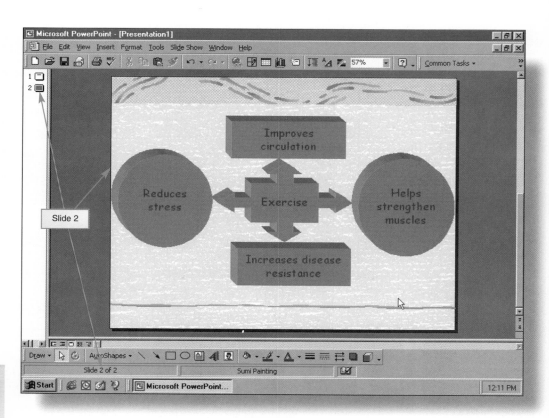

FIGURE 5-10

Other Ways

1. Press ALT+I, press F, press ALT+B, select desired file, press ALT+O, press ALT+S, select desired slide, press I, press ESC

If desired, you could have selected additional slides from Tiffani's Cyberfitness presentation or from other slide shows. If you believe you might want to use the Cyberfitness file at a later date, you can add that file to your Favorites folder so that it is readily accessible.

Creating a New Slide with Animated Clip Art

Your next step is to design a slide that describes the differences between aerobic and anaerobic exercise activities. The prefix, aero, means air, so an aerobic activity such as running, cycling, or brisk walking uses increased oxygen to help the circulatory system work efficiently and also to help burn fat. An anaerobic activity, in contrast, does not require additional air. Anaerobic activities like using free weights or using the Nautilus or Universal circuits increase lean weight, which helps tone the body.

Inserting a New Slide, Choosing a Layout, and Adding Text

The third slide you create will use the 2 Column Text slide layout and will have two animated clip art objects. Perform the following steps to add a new slide, choose a layout, and add text to the left Object Area placeholder.

TO ADD A SLIDE, CHOOSE A LAYOUT, AND ADD TEXT

1. Click the New Slide button on the Standard toolbar.

2. Double-click the 2 Column Text AutoLayout located in row one, column three.

3. Type Two Exercise Categories in the Title Area placeholder.

4. Press the CTRL+ENTER keys to move the insertion point to the left Object Area placeholder.

5. Type Aerobic in the left Object Area placeholder and then press the ENTER key.

6. Press the TAB key to demote the text. Type Increases circulation and then press the ENTER key.

7. Type Helps burn fat and then press the ENTER key.

8. Type Examples: and then press the ENTER key.

9. Press the TAB key. Type Treadmill and then press the ENTER key.

10. Type Brisk walking but do not press the ENTER key.

The text for the new slide displays in the left Object Area placeholder of the 2 Column Text AutoLayout (Figure 5-11 on the next page).

More About

Custom Shows

If you want to vary the slides and the slide order in your presentation, you can select particular slides and group them together to create a custom show. To create a new custom show, click Custom Shows on the Slide Show menu and then click New. Under Slides in presentation, hold down the CTRL key, select the desired slides, and then click Add. To change the slide order, select one slide and then click an arrow to move the slide location in the list. Next, type a name for the show in the Slide show name box and then click the OK button. To preview your show, select the custom show name in the Custom Shows dialog box, and then click Show.

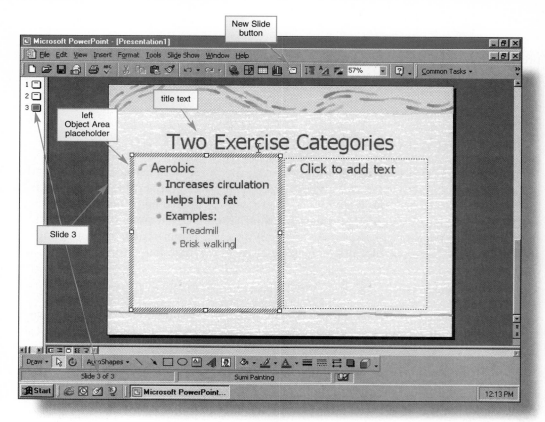

FIGURE 5-11

Now that the text is entered in the left Object Area placeholder, you need to add the text to the right Object Area placeholder. Perform the following steps to add this text.

TO ADD TEXT TO THE RIGHT PLACEHOLDER

1 Press the CTRL+ENTER keys to move the insertion point to the right Object Area placeholder.

2 Type Anaerobic in the right Object Area placeholder and then press the ENTER key.

3 Press the TAB key to demote the text. Type Increases lean weight and then press the ENTER key.

4 Type High resistance with low repetition and then press the ENTER key.

5 Type Examples: and then press the ENTER key.

6 Press the TAB key. Type Free weights and then press the ENTER key.

7 Type Nautilus circuit but do not press the ENTER key.

The text for the slide displays in the right Object Area placeholder (Figure 5-12).

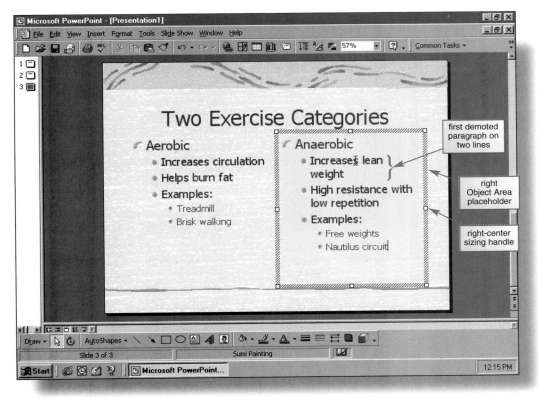

FIGURE 5-12

All text for the slide has been entered. Then next step is to add two animated clip art objects that will move when the slide show runs at the kiosk. You need sufficient space to display these objects, and you realize you can create additional space in the lower-right corner of the slide if the first demoted paragraph in the right Object Area placeholder displays on one line.

Increasing the Right Object Area Placeholder Width

If you increase the width of the right placeholder, the first demoted paragraph, Increases lean weight, will display on one line. Perform the following step to increase the width of the right Object Area placeholder.

TO INCREASE THE RIGHT OBJECT AREA PLACEHOLDER WIDTH

 Drag the right-center sizing handle on the right Object Area placeholder slightly to the right.

The mouse pointer becomes a two-headed arrow. The first demoted paragraph should display on one line (Figure 5-13 on the next page). If it displays on two lines, repeat this step until you achieve the desired results.

More About

Locating Clip Art

The entire Clip Art Gallery may not be installed on your computer system. If not, you may need to import specific clips into the Clip Gallery. To add these clips, click the Import Clips button on the Insert ClipArt toolbar, click the Look in box arrow in the Add clip to Clip Gallery dialog box, select the desired clips, click Let Clip Gallery find this clip in its current folder or volume, click the Import button, enter clip properties, and then click OK.

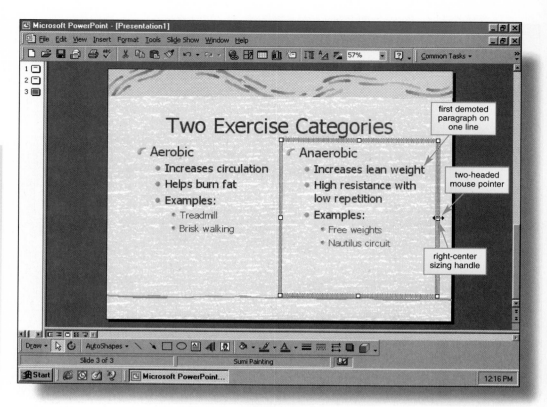

FIGURE 5-13

1. Right-click right Object Area Placeholder, click Format Placeholder, click Size tab, click Width box up arrow in Size and rotate area, click OK button

2. On Format menu click Placeholder, click Size tab, click Width box up arrow in Size and rotate area, click OK button

3. Press ALT+O, press O, press RIGHT ARROW key to select Size tab, press ALT+D, type 4.25, press ENTER

Additional space is added to the bottom of the slide to make room for the clip art you want to insert.

GIFs

GIF files are prevalent in PowerPoint presentations and on the World Wide Web. You can create GIF files by designing images in drawing software packages such as Adobe Photoshop and then saving the file in GIF format. For instructions on creating GIF files, visit the PowerPoint 2000 Project 5 More About page (www.scsite.com/pp2000/more.htm) and click GIF.

Inserting Animated Clip Art

One of the features of Office 2000 is the animated GIF files found in the Clip Art Gallery 5.0. PowerPoint GIF files are among the numerous file formats that PowerPoint recognizes. **GIF files**, or Graphics Interchange Format files, are identified by their .gif file extension and have been compressed to reduce their file size. They often have flat, one-color backgrounds, and a maximum of 256 colors can display in the entire graphic.

The 2 Column Text AutoLayout on this slide does not have placeholders for the two clip art objects. You must, consequently, insert each file, move these objects to the desired locations on the slide, and then size them. Perform the following steps to insert the two animated files on the slide. If the two clip art object do not display in the Microsoft Clip Gallery, see your instructor for copies of these files.

TO INSERT ANIMATED CLIP ART

1 Click the Insert Clip Art button on the Drawing toolbar.

2 Click the Motion Clips tab in the Insert ClipArt window.

3 Type people walking in the Search for clips text box and then press the ENTER key. If necessary, scroll to display the desired clip art, a blue figure facing to the right.

4 Click the desired clip art and then click Insert clip, the top button on the shortcut menu.

⑤ Type weight in the Search for clips text box and then press the ENTER key.

⑥ Click the desired cartoon clip art of a muscular weightlifter and then click Insert clip on the shortcut menu.

⑦ Click the Close button on the Insert ClipArt title bar.

The two clip art objects display in the center of the slide (Figure 5-14).

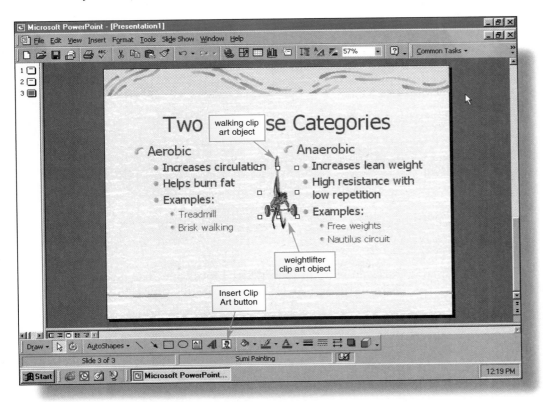

FIGURE 5-14

Moving the Animated Clip Art

Now that you have inserted the two clip art figures on the slide, you need to move these objects to new positions on the slide and then size them. The walking object should display below its present position, and the weightlifting object should display in the lower-right corner. Perform the following steps to move the animated clip art objects.

TO MOVE THE ANIMATED CLIP ART OBJECTS

① Click the weightlifting clip art object to select it and drag it to the lower-right corner of the slide. Center the plates on the barbell on the line that extends across the bottom of the slide.

② Click the walking clip art object and drag it downward. The figure's right big toe should just touch the line that extends across the bottom of the slide.

The two clip art objects display in their correct locations on the slide (Figure 5-15 on the next page).

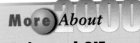

More About

Animated GIFs

The animated clip art figures available in the Microsoft Clip Gallery or the Microsoft Clip Gallery Live site add visual interest to your slides. The World Wide Web abounds with excellent sources of additional animated GIFs. To view a collection of these files, visit the PowerPoint 2000 Project 5 More About page (www.scsite.com/pp2000/more.htm) and click Animated GIFs.

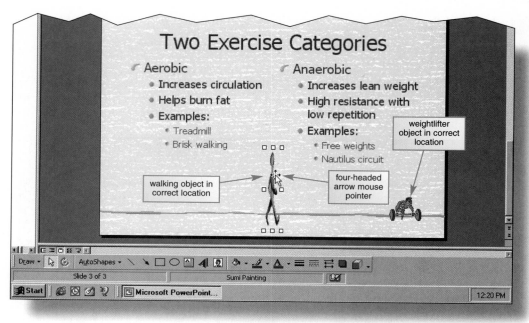

FIGURE 5-15

Sizing the Animated Clip Art

The two clip art figures now are in their desired locations. The next step is to enlarge these objects. Perform the following steps to size the animated clip art objects.

TO SIZE THE ANIMATED CLIP ART OBJECTS

1 Right-click the walking object, click Format Picture on the shortcut menu, and click the Size tab when the Format Picture dialog box displays.

2 With the Relative to original picture size check box selected, click Lock aspect ratio to remove the check. Triple-click the Width text box in the Size and rotate area and type 2.01 in the box.

3 Click the OK button.

4 Drag the walking object to re-center it in the area between the two bulleted lists.

5 Right-click the weightlifting object, click Format Picture on the shortcut menu, and click the Size tab when the Format Picture dialog box displays.

6 With the Lock aspect ratio and the Relative to original picture size check boxes selected, triple-click the Width text box in the Size and rotate area and type 1.95 in the box.

7 Click the OK button.

8 Drag the weightlifting object so that the plates on the barbell are once again centered on the line that extends across the bottom of the slide.

The two clip art objects are enlarged on the slide and restored to their correct locations (Figure 5-16). Lock aspect ratio maintains proportions, so when you deselect this check box, the walker gets wider but not taller. The Relative to original picture size check box keeps the object to scale.

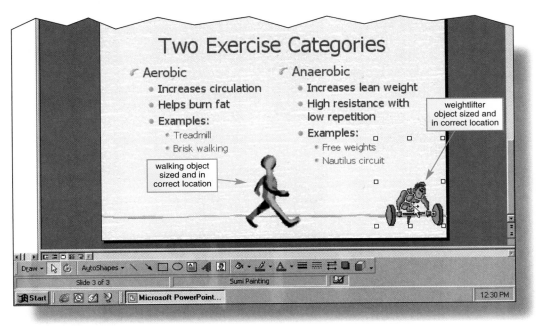

FIGURE 5-16

The third slide now is complete. The next slide will have another visual effect: an inserted chart created in Microsoft Excel.

Saving the Presentation

You now should save your presentation because you have done a substantial amount of work. The following steps summarize how to save a presentation.

TO SAVE A PRESENTATION

1. Click the Save button on the Standard toolbar.

2. Type Half-Hour Workout in the File name text box.

3. Click the Save in box arrow. Click 3½ Floppy (A:) in the Save in list.

4. Click the Save button in the Save As dialog box.

The presentation is saved on the floppy disk in drive A with the file name Half-Hour Workout. This file name displays on the title bar.

Inserting an Excel Chart

Aerobic activity helps strengthen the cardiovascular system and burn calories. These important benefits should be of interest to students at Western College, so you want to emphasize the aerobic qualities of a treadmill. A chart created in Microsoft Excel can depict how a treadmill's speed of 3.5, 4.5, or 5.5 miles per hour and incline ranging from 1 to 10 percent can affect the amount of calories burned. A **3-D Column chart** compares values across categories and across series. Similarly, the treadmill chart in Figure 5-17 illustrates the number of calories burned in relation to the amount of incline for the three speeds.

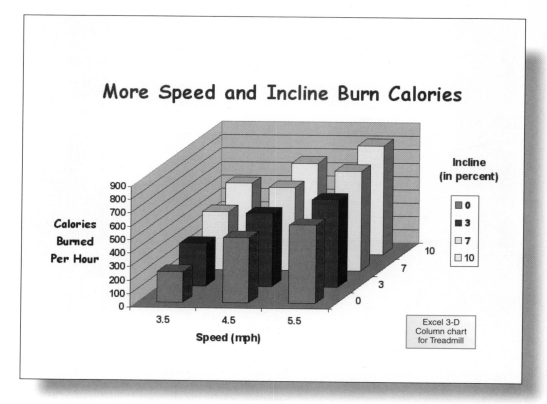

FIGURE 5-17

More *About*

Copyrights

Congress passed the Online Copyright Infringement Liability Limitation Act of 1998 to address the widespread practice of online copyright infringement. This law makes it difficult for Internet Service Providers to be found liable when its users download files illegally from the Internet. To learn about the legal cases and legislative process that led to this law, visit the PowerPoint 2000 Project 5 More About page (www.scsite.com/pp2000/more.htm) and click Copyright.

PowerPoint allows you to insert, or **embed,** many types of objects into a presentation. You inserted animated clip art into Slide 3, and you will import a Microsoft Word table into Slide 6. Other objects you can embed include video clips, Microsoft PhotoDraw pictures, and Adobe Acrobat documents. Perform the following steps to insert a new slide and to insert an Excel chart from your Data Disk.

Before you insert the Excel chart, you need to create a new slide and change the slide layout to the Object layout.

TO ADD A SLIDE, CHANGE THE SLIDE LAYOUT, AND TYPE THE TITLE TEXT

1️⃣ Click the New Slide button on the Standard toolbar to display Slide 4.

2️⃣ Type the number 16 to select the Object layout from the 24 available AutoLayouts. Then, click the OK button.

3️⃣ Type Aerobic Activity - Treadmill as the Slide 4 title text.

Slide 4 displays the title text and the placeholder for the Excel object (Figure 5-18). When the New Slide dialog box displays, you can type a number or double-click an AutoLayout to choose a particular layout style.

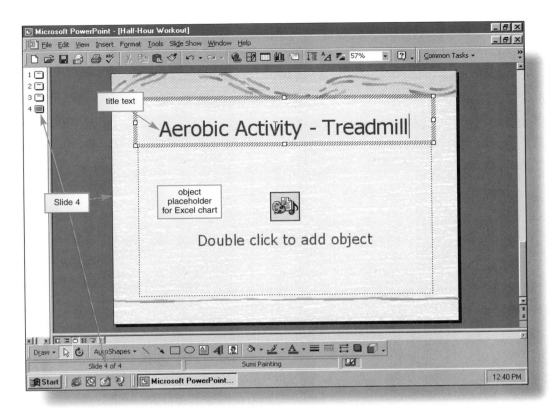

FIGURE 5-18

Slide 4 now displays the slide title and object placeholder for the Treadmill chart. The next section explains how to insert this Excel chart.

 To Insert an Excel Chart

1 **Double-click the object placeholder** in the middle of Slide 4. **Click Create from file. Point to the Browse button.**

The Insert Object dialog box displays (Figure 5-19). Drive A is the current drive. The Create from file option allows you to select an object cre- ated in another application or in PowerPoint.

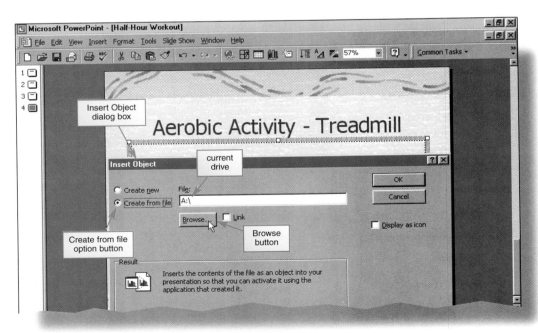

FIGURE 5-19

Other Ways

1. Move scroll bar downward to display Object layout, double-click Object layout

2 **Click the Browse button. When the Browse dialog box displays, click Treadmill. Point to the OK button.**

The Browse dialog box displays the files on the Data Disk (Figure 5-20). Treadmill is the Excel file you will insert into Slide 4.

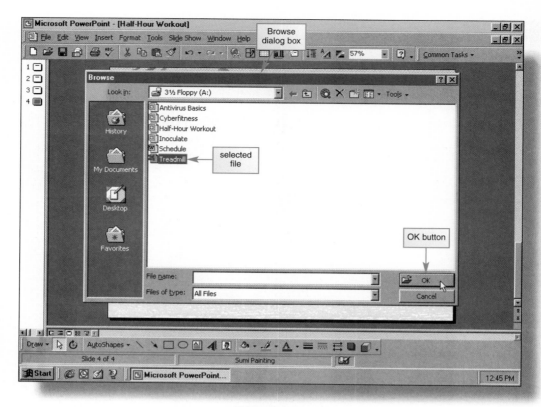

FIGURE 5-20

3 **Click the OK button. When the Insert Object dialog box displays, point to the OK button.**

The Insert Object dialog box now displays A:\Treadmill.xls in the File text box (Figure 5-21). The .xls extension indicates the file is a Microsoft Excel document.

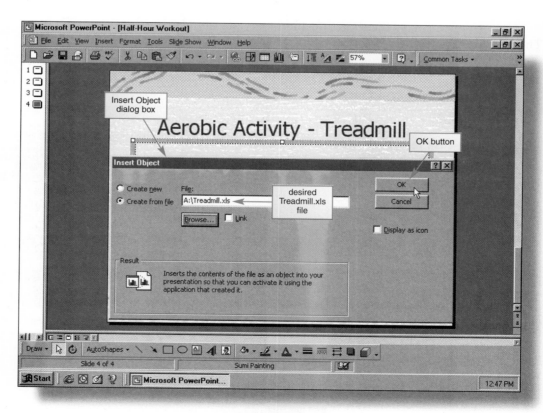

FIGURE 5-21

Click the OK button.

Slide 4 displays the Treadmill chart (Figure 5-22).

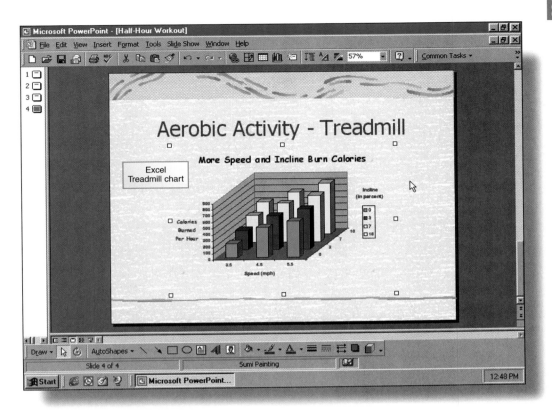

FIGURE 5-22

When you click the Create from file option button in the Insert Object dialog box, the dialog box changes. The File box replaces the Object type box. Another change to the dialog box is the addition of the **Link check box**. If the Link check box is selected, the object is inserted as a linked, instead of an embedded, object. Like an embedded object, a **linked object** also is created in another application; however, the linked object maintains a connection to its source. If the original object is changed, the linked object on the slide also changes. The linked object is stored in the **source file**, the file in which the object was created.

For example, the Excel chart you embedded into the slide is stored on the Data Disk. If you were to link rather than embed the Treadmill file, then every time the Treadmill file changed in Excel, the changes would display on the chart in Slide 4. Your PowerPoint presentation would store a representation of the original Treadmill file and information about its location. If you later moved or deleted the source file, the link would be broken, and the object would not be available. Consequently, if you make a presentation on a computer other than the one on which the presentation was created and the presentation contains a linked object, be certain to include a copy of the source files. The source files must be stored in the exact location as originally specified when you linked them to your presentation.

When you select a source file from the Browse dialog box, PowerPoint associates the file with a specific application, which is based on the file extension. For example, if you select a source file with the file extension **.doc**, PowerPoint recognizes the file as a Microsoft Word file. Additionally, if you select a source file with the file extension **.xls**, PowerPoint recognizes the file as a Microsoft Excel file.

1. On Insert menu click Object, click Create from file, enter file name, click OK button

More *About*

Editing an Embedded Excel Chart

If you need to edit an Excel chart you import into your slide, double-click the chart, use the Microsoft Excel tools and menus to modify the chart, and then click outside the chart to return to PowerPoint.

Scaling an Excel Chart

The Treadmill chart on Slide 4 is sized to fit the object placeholder, but sufficient space exists on the slide to enlarge the chart. Perform the following steps to scale the chart object.

TO SCALE THE EXCEL CHART

1 Right-click the selected Treadmill chart and then click Format Object on the shortcut menu.

2 If necessary, click the Size tab. Click the Height box up arrow in the Scale area until 110% displays.

3 Click the OK button.

4 Press the LEFT ARROW and UP ARROW keys to center the chart on the slide.

The Excel chart is scaled to 110 percent of its original size (Figure 5-23).

FIGURE 5-23

Slide 4 now is complete. The next slide also will have a chart; instead of importing this chart from the Data Disk, however, you will build this chart directly within your PowerPoint presentation using the supplementary application called **Microsoft Graph**.

Saving a Slide as a Graphic

Each slide can be saved in GIF format and then inserted as a picture in another program or on a Web page. To save a slide as a graphic, display the slide, click Save As on the File menu, and then click Windows Metafile or GIF Graphics Interchange Format in the Save as type box.

Building a PowerPoint Chart

The chart on Slide 4 shows the advantages of using a treadmill as a source of aerobic activity. The chart on the next slide, shown in Figure 5-24, will show four benefits of using free weights: toning muscles, increasing energy, improving circulation, and controlling weight. A **pie chart** clearly can depict the contribution of each of these four components to the total wellness benefit the students will receive by using free weights regularly. This chart type shows the relationship or proportion of parts to a whole. Each slice (or wedge) of the pie shows what percent that slice contributes to the total (100%).

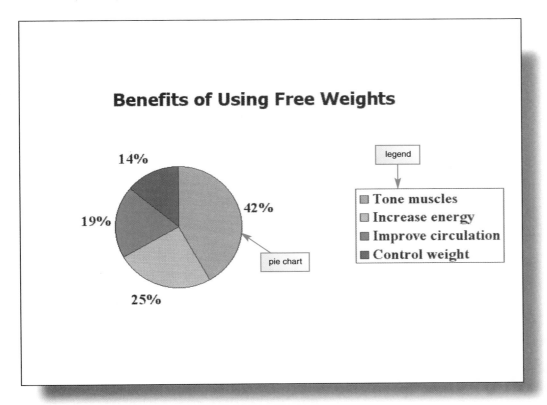

FIGURE 5-24

PowerPoint allows you to create a chart using Microsoft Graph within the application. The figures for the chart are entered in a corresponding **datasheet**, which is a rectangular grid containing columns (vertical) and rows (horizontal). Column letters display above the grid to identify particular **columns**, and row numbers display on the left side of the grid to identify particular **rows**. **Cells** are the intersections of rows and columns, and they are the locations for the chart data and text labels. For example, cell A1 is the intersection of column A and row 1. You enter numeric and text data in the **active cell**, which is the one cell surrounded by a heavy border.

Creating the chart shown in Figure 5-24 requires several steps: inserting a new slide and choosing the Chart AutoLayout, changing the chart type, replacing the sample data, and adding a chart title and data labels. The sections on the next page describe how to perform these actions.

Creating a New Slide, Choosing the Chart AutoLayout, and Typing the Title Text

Before you create the anaerobic benefits pie chart, you first must insert a new slide and then change the AutoLayout and add the slide title. The following steps describe these tasks.

TO ADD A SLIDE, CHANGE THE SLIDE LAYOUT, AND TYPE THE TITLE TEXT

1 Click the New Slide button on the Standard toolbar to display Slide 5.

2 Type the number 8 to select the Chart layout from the 24 available AutoLayouts. Then, click the OK button.

3 Type Anaerobic Activity - Weights as the Slide 5 title text.

Slide 5 displays the title text and the placeholder for the pie chart (Figure 5-25).

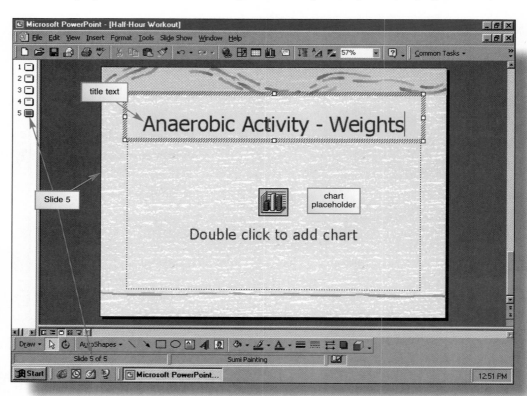

FIGURE 5-25

Slide 5 now displays the slide title and placeholder for the chart. The next section explains how to select a pie chart to depict the four benefits derived from using free weights.

Selecting a Different Chart Type

The default Micrograph Graph chart style is a 3-D column chart. This style is appropriate when comparing two or more items in specified intervals, such as in the Slide 4 chart depicting how various treadmill speeds and inclines affect the number of calories burned. In this free weight situation, however, you want to show how performing anaerobic activity affects the body in four ways.

Other **Ways**

1. Move scroll bar downward to display Chart layout, double-click Chart layout

More **About**

Chart Types

PowerPoint has a variety of 2-D, bubble, and 3-D chart types. For 2-D charts, you can change the chart type of either a group of data or the entire chart. For bubble charts, you can change only the type of the entire chart. For 3-D bar and column charts, you can change the data series to the cone, cylinder, or pyramid chart types. For most other 3-D charts, you change the entire chart when you change the chart type.

A pie chart is an appropriate chart style for the free weight example. The following steps describe how to change the chart type.

 Steps **To Select a Different Chart Type**

1 **Double-click the chart placeholder in the middle of Slide 5. Click Chart on the menu bar and then point to Chart Type.**

The sample datasheet and chart display (Figure 5-26).

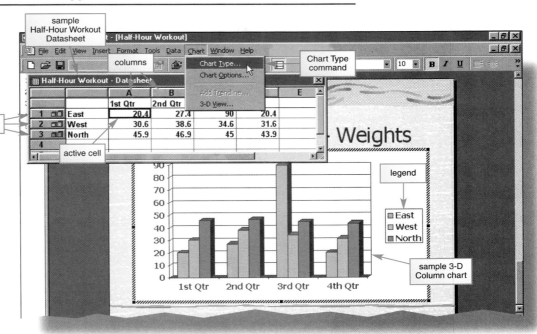

FIGURE 5-26

2 **Click Chart Type. When the Chart Type dialog box displays, click Pie in the Chart type list on the Standard Types sheet. Point to the Press and Hold to View Sample button.**

The Pie chart type is selected (Figure 5-27). You can view a sample of your chart before you actually change the chart type.

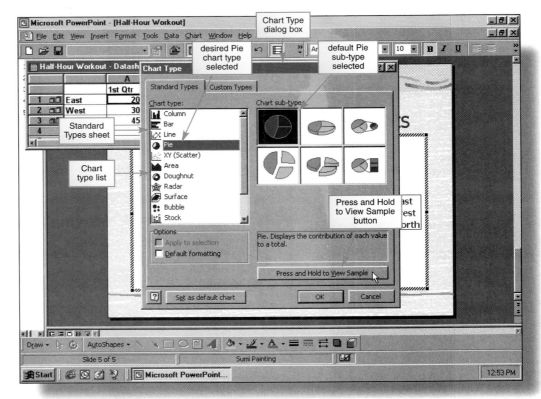

FIGURE 5-27

3 **Click the Press and Hold to View Sample button.**

The sample Pie chart displays (Figure 5-28).

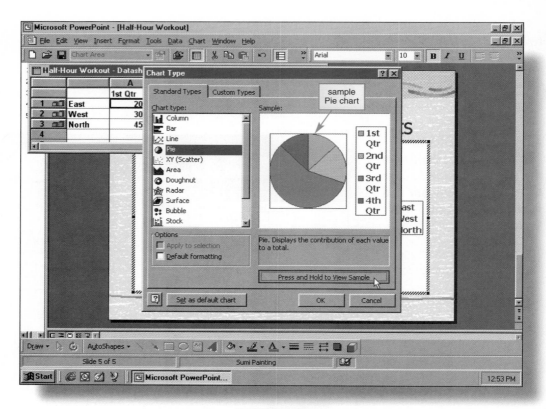

FIGURE 5-28

4 **Click the OK button.**

Microsoft Graph changes the chart type from a 3-D column chart to a pie chart (Figure 5-29).

Other **Ways**

1. Double-click chart place-holder, press ALT+C, press T, press P, press V, press SPACEBAR, press TAB, press ENTER

2. Double-click chart place-holder, right-click chart, click Chart Type on shortcut menu, click Pie, click Press and Hold to View Sample button, click OK button

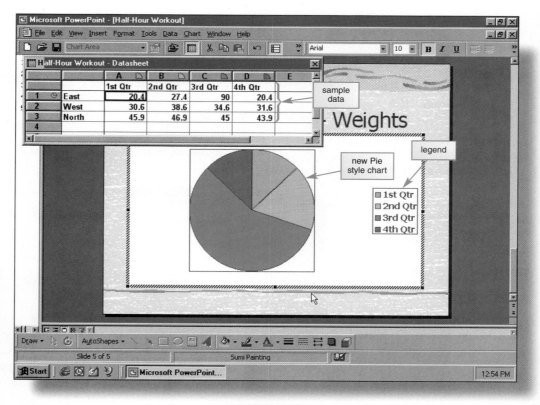

FIGURE 5-29

The sample data now is represented in a pie chart rather than the default column chart. Your next step is to replace the sample data with actual percentages.

Replacing the Sample Data

Microsoft Graph provides sample data to create the default chart. You need to change these figures to the numbers representing the amount of benefit students receive from using free weights. The following steps describe how to replace the sample data.

 To Replace the Sample Data

1 **Point to cell A1, which is the intersection of column A and row 1.**

Cell A1 is selected (Figure 5-30). The mouse pointer changes to a block plus sign.

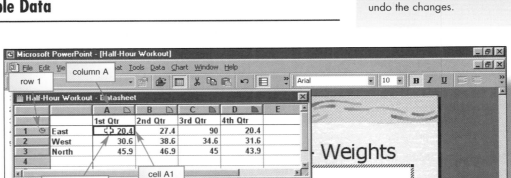

FIGURE 5-30

2 **Type** 42 **in cell A1 and press the RIGHT ARROW key. Type** 25 **in cell B1,** 19 **in cell C1, and** 14 **in cell D1. Point to the cell above cell A1 that contains the label, 1st Qtr.**

The four figures represent the percentage of benefits obtained by using free weights (Figure 5-31).

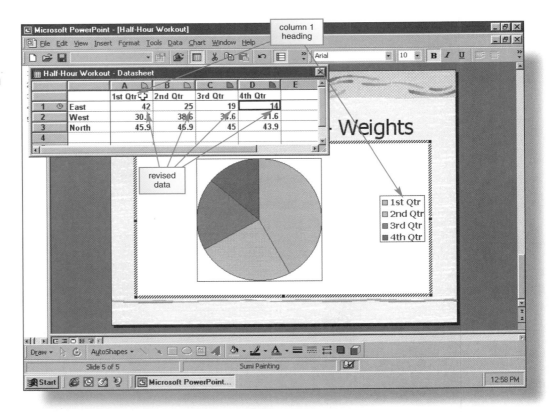

FIGURE 5-31

3 **Click the cell above cell A1 that contains the label, 1st Qtr. Type** Tone muscles **in this cell.**

Tone muscles is the corresponding label for the entry, 42, in cell A1 (Figure 5-32). Forty-two percent of the energy expended in using free weights goes toward toning the body.

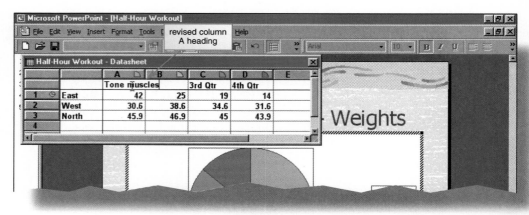

FIGURE 5-32

4 **Press the RIGHT ARROW key to advance to the cell above cell B1. Type** Increase energy **in this cell and press the RIGHT ARROW key.**

As you type these entries, the text displays in the datasheet and in the chart legend (Figure 5-33).

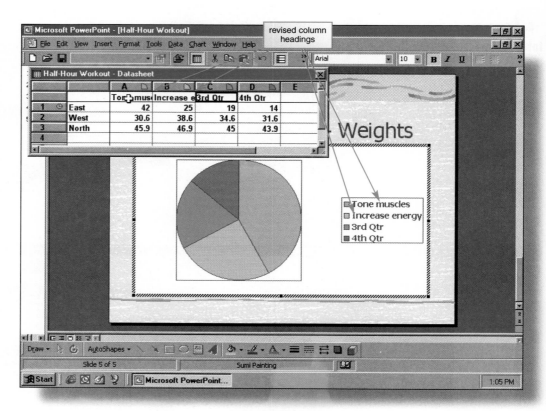

FIGURE 5-33

5 **Type** Improve circulation **in the cell above cell C1 and** Control weight **in the cell above cell D1.**

The data labels are entered, and they will display in their entirety when you modify the datasheet and chart (Figure 5-34).

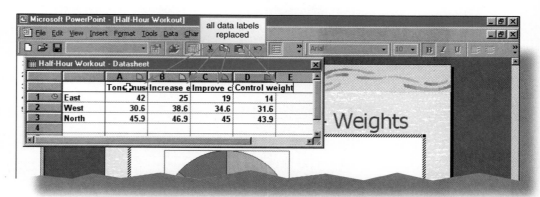

FIGURE 5-34

6 **Click the cell to the left of cell A1 that contains the label, East. Press and hold down the SHIFT key, and then click the cell to the left of cell A3 that contains the label, North.**

The three cells in the first column of the datasheet are selected (Figure 5-35).

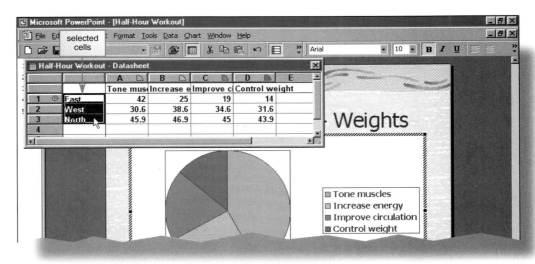

FIGURE 5-35

7 **Press the DELETE key.**

The entries in these three cells are deleted (Figure 5-36).

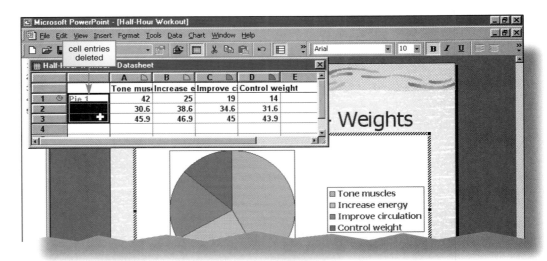

FIGURE 5-36

8 **Click cell A2. Press and hold the SHIFT key and then click cell D3.**

The eight cells in the range from A2 to D3 are selected (Figure 5-37).

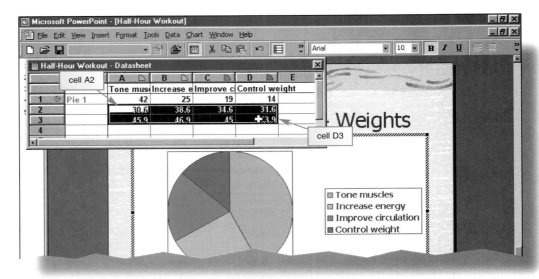

FIGURE 5-37

9 **Press the DELETE key. Point to the Close button on the datasheet.**

The entries in these eight cells are deleted (Figure 5-38).

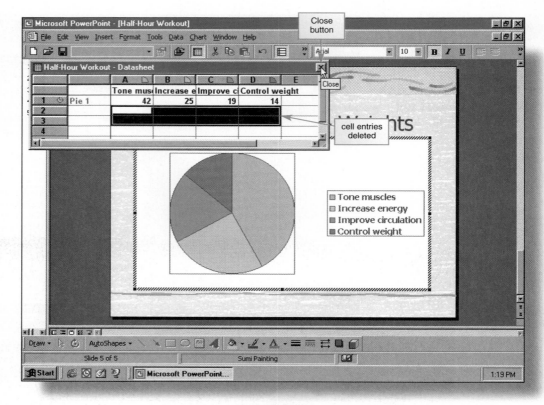

FIGURE 5-38

10 **Click the Close button.**

The datasheet closes and the revised chart and legend display (Figure 5-39).

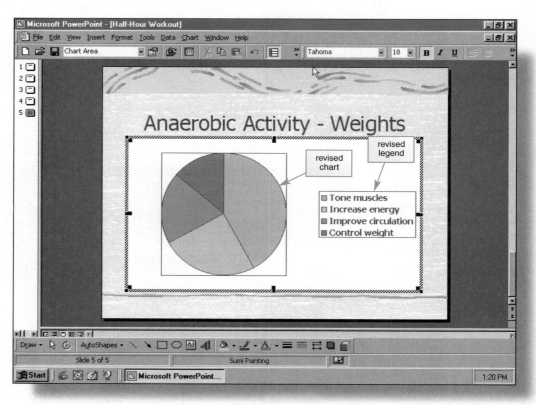

FIGURE 5-39

The free weight data has been entered in the Microsoft Graph datasheet. The four benefits – tone muscles, increase energy, improve circulation, and control weight – display in the **legend**, which identifies each slice in the chart. Microsoft Graph automatically selects the data in the first row of the datasheet as titles within the legend.

Adding a Chart Title and Data Labels

The slices of the free weight chart now display in correct proportions. Next, you will add a title above the chart and display the benefit percentage figures. The following steps describe how to add these elements to the slide.

 To Add a Chart Title and Data Labels

1 **Click Chart on the menu bar and then click Chart Options.**

The Chart Options dialog box displays (Figure 5-40). The three tabs – Titles, Legend, and Data Labels – allow you to display and format several chart elements.

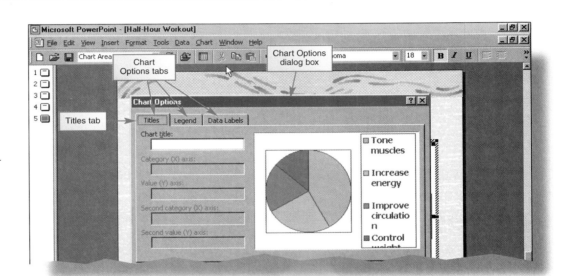

FIGURE 5-40

2 **If necessary, click the Titles tab. Click the Chart title text box and then type** Benefits of Using Free Weights **in the text box. Point to the Data Labels tab.**

The chart title displays in the chart preview box (Figure 5-41). The chart title helps viewers understand the purpose of the chart. The chart title can display on multiple lines if you press the ENTER key to start a new paragraph or the SHIFT+ENTER keys to insert a line break.

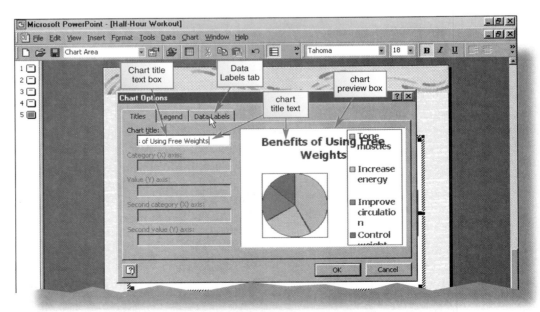

FIGURE 5-41

3 Click the Data Labels tab. Click Show percent in the Data labels area. Point to the OK button.

The benefit percentages display in the chart preview box (Figure 5-42). Various visuals can display on the chart, including the figures, the figures with a percent sign, and the data labels. You also can choose whether to display the chart legend.

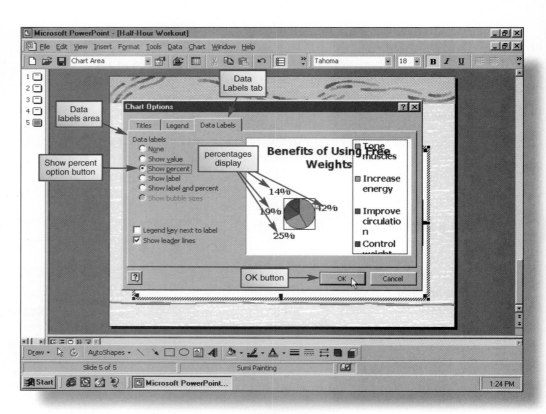

FIGURE 5-42

4 Click the OK button. Click the box surrounding the chart Plot Area.

Sizing handles display on the Plot Area box (Figure 5-43).

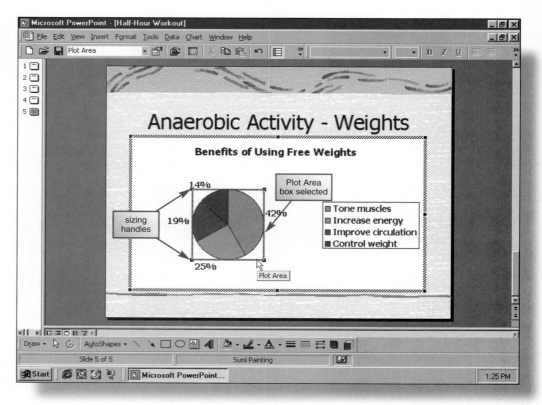

FIGURE 5-43

6 **Press the DELETE key.**

The Plot Area box is deleted (Figure 5-44).

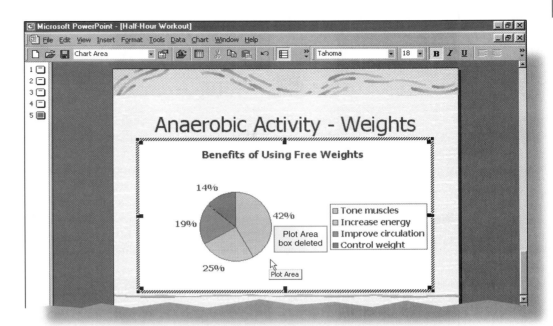

FIGURE 5-44

7 **Click outside the chart placeholder to return to PowerPoint (Figure 5-45).**

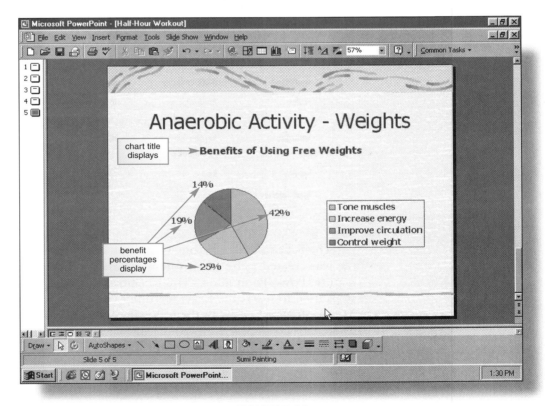

FIGURE 5-45

Other Ways

1. Select the chart placeholder, press ALT+C, press O, press TAB, type chart title text, press TAB four times, press D, press P, press ENTER

Slide 5 is complete. The next slide in the presentation describes how to vary aerobic and anaerobic workouts throughout the week.

Adding a Table from Word

Western College students now see the benefits of aerobic and anaerobic activity. Combining workouts using a treadmill and free weights should provide a good overall fitness plan. Fitness experts recommend varying aerobic and anaerobic workouts to achieve optimal results. By alternating these activities and resting two days during the week, students can benefit from a strong cardiovascular system and a toned body. In addition, they can burn 1,382 calories each week by exercising on the treadmill or by brisk walking for 30 minutes on three days and by working with free weights for 25 minutes on two days. Table 5-1 shows a sample weekly workout schedule that varies the aerobic and anaerobic activities.

More About

Editing an Embedded Word Table

If you need to edit a Word chart you import into your slide, double-click the table and use the Word tools and menus to format the table. For example, to change the width of the table, click the Table Properties command on the Table menu, click the Table tab, and then change the figure in the Preferred width text box. Then click the OK button.

Table 5-1	Sample Exercise Schedule			
DAY	*EXERCISE*	*INTENSITY*	*WORKOUT MINUTES*	*CALORIES BURNED*
Monday	Aerobic exercise (Treadmill)	High	30	336
Tuesday	Anaerobic exercise (Free weights)	Moderate	25	210
Wednesday	Rest			
Thursday	Brisk walking	Moderate	30	290
Friday	Anaerobic exercise (Free weights)	Moderate	25	210
Saturday	Aerobic exercise (Treadmill)	High	30	336
Sunday	Rest			
Total calories burned				1,382

The Schedule file on your Data Disk contains these elements of Table 5-1. This file was created using Microsoft Word and enhanced with Word's Table AutoFormat feature. PowerPoint allows you to embed this table into your presentation. The same steps used to insert the Excel treadmill chart into a slide are used to insert a Microsoft Word table. In the following sections, you will create a new slide and insert the Word table from your Data Disk.

Before you insert the Word table, you need to insert a new slide and change the slide layout to the Object layout.

TO ADD A SLIDE, CHANGE THE SLIDE LAYOUT, AND TYPE THE TITLE TEXT

1 Click the New Slide button on the Standard toolbar to display Slide 6.

2 Type the number 16 to select the Object layout from the 24 available AutoLayouts. Then, click the OK button.

3 Type Sample Exercise Schedule as the Slide 6 title text.

Slide 6 displays the title text and the placeholder for the Word object (Figure 5-46).

FIGURE 5-46

Other **Ways**

1. Move scroll bar downward
   to display Object layout,
   double-click Object layout

Slide 6 now displays the slide title and placeholder for the Schedule table. The next section explains how to insert this Word table, which has the file name Schedule.doc.

TO INSERT A WORD TABLE

(1) Double-click the object placeholder in the middle of Slide 6. Click Create from file.

(2) Click the Browse button. When the Browse dialog box displays, click Schedule.

(3) Click the OK button. When the Insert Object dialog box displays, click the OK button.

Slide 6 displays the Schedule table (Figure 5-47 on the next page).

Microsoft **PowerPoint 2000**

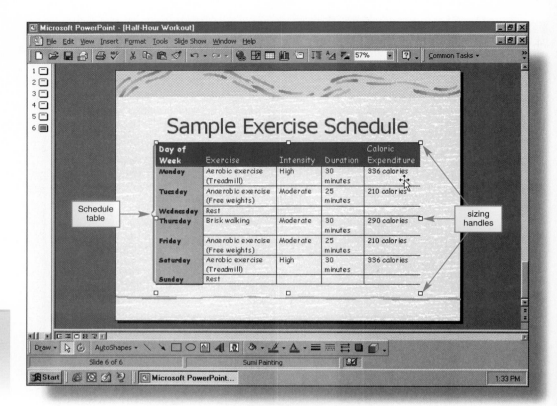

FIGURE 5-47

If you want to edit the Schedule table, double-click the table. This action starts Microsoft Word and opens the Schedule table as a Word document. Then make the desired changes or use the Word tools and menus to modify the table, save the table, and then click outside the table to exit Word and return to PowerPoint. These editing changes will appear in the Schedule table embedded into Slide 6. However, the source file in Word remains unchanged.

Inserting and Formatting an AutoShape

As shown in Schedule table on Slide 6, the workout sessions burn calories while they improve muscle tone and cardiovascular endurance. If the Western College students exercise regularly and with high or moderate intensity, they should burn 1,382 calories weekly. You believe students would be interested in this fact, so you want to add an AutoShape that calls attention to this caloric total. An **AutoShape** is a ready-made object, such as a line, star, banner, arrow, connector, or callout. These shapes can be sized, rotated, flipped, colored, and combined to add unique qualities to a presentation. Most of the shapes contain an **adjustment handle** that allows changes to the object, such as changing the size of the point of an arrow.

You click the AutoShapes menu button on the Drawing toolbar to select a category, such as Block Arrows or Flowchart. Then you choose the desired AutoShape and click the area of the slide where you want to insert the AutoShape. You then can add text by clicking the AutoShape and typing the desired information. You also can rotate the AutoShape by clicking the **Free Rotate button** on the Drawing toolbar, positioning the mouse pointer over an AutoShape's round handle, and dragging the AutoShape.

Figure 5-48 shows the AutoShape you want to create to accompany the Schedule chart. Creating this object requires several steps. First, you must choose the desired AutoShape and insert it onto the slide. Next, you add a shadow. You then add text and resize the AutoShape to accommodate this text. Finally, you rotate the AutoShape to cover the lower-right corner of the Schedule table. The next several sections explain how to create this AutoShape.

FIGURE 5-48

Inserting an AutoShape

PowerPoint has a variety of AutoShapes organized in the categories of Lines, Connectors, Basic Shapes, Block Arrows, Flowchart, Stars and Banners, Callouts, and Action Buttons. In addition, the More AutoShapes category displays AutoShapes in the Clip Gallery. The first step in creating the AutoShape object is to select the desired shape. Perform the steps on the next page to insert an AutoShape onto Slide 6.

Adding AutoShapes

Additional AutoShapes are located in the Clip Gallery. To add one of these shapes onto your slide, drag the desired AutoShape from the Clip Gallery to the desired location on your slide.

Steps   To Insert an AutoShape

1 **Click the AutoShapes menu button on the Drawing toolbar, point to Stars and Banners, and then point to the Explosion 2 AutoShape (row 1, column 2).**

The Stars and Banners style list displays (Figure 5-49). You may have to wait a few seconds for the full AutoShapes menu to display. The desired AutoShape, Explosion 2, is selected.

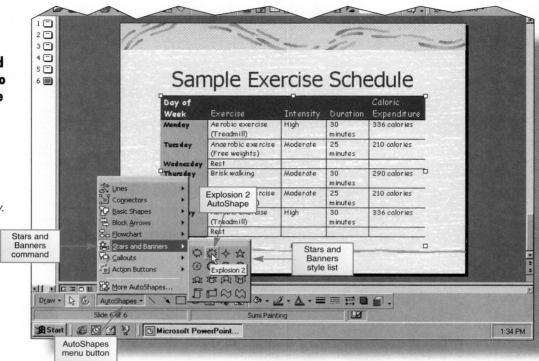

FIGURE 5-49

2 **Click the Explosion 2 AutoShape. Point to the lower-right corner of the Schedule table.**

The mouse pointer changes shape to a cross hair (Figure 5-50). You want the AutoShape to display at the bottom of the Caloric Expenditure column.

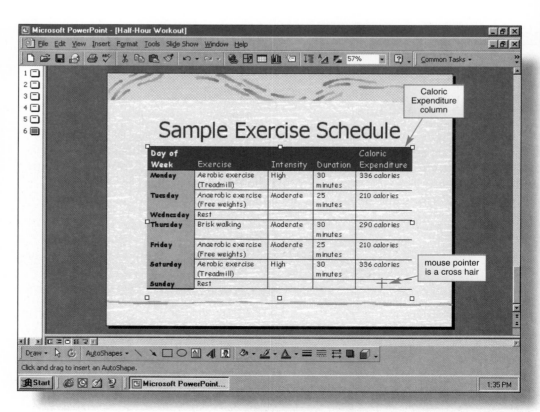

FIGURE 5-50

3 **Click the lower-right corner of the Schedule table.**

The Explosion 2 AutoShape displays at the end of the Caloric Expenditure column (Figure 5-51).

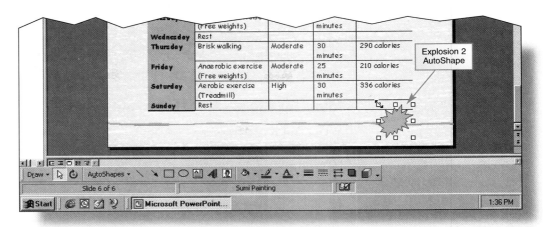

FIGURE 5-51

Now that the desired AutoShape displays on Slide 6, you want to add a shadow to give a three-dimensional appearance.

Adding a Shadow to an AutoShape

To add depth to the Explosion 2 AutoShape, you shadow it by clicking the Shadow button on the Drawing toolbar and selecting one of the 20 predefined shadow styles. Perform the following steps to add a shadow to the object.

TO ADD A SHADOW TO THE AUTOSHAPE

1 Click the Shadow button on the Drawing toolbar.

2 Click Shadow Style 6 (row 2, column 2) in the style list.

PowerPoint adds the shadow to the AutoShape (Figure 5-52).

More About

Changing AutoShapes

If you want to change the Explosion 2 AutoShape to another shape, select the AutoShape, click Draw on the Drawing toolbar, point to Change AutoShape, point to a category, and then click the desired shape.

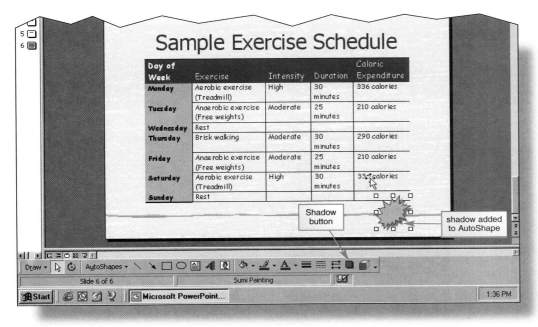

FIGURE 5-52

Once you add a shadow to an object, you can alter its appearance. If you click Shadow Settings in the Shadow list, PowerPoint displays the Shadow Settings toolbar. The buttons on this toolbar allow you to turn the shadow on or off, to nudge the shadow up, down, left, or right, and to change the shadow color.

Adding Text to an AutoShape

The AutoShape displays on Slide 6 in the correct location. The next step is to add text giving the total number of calories burned during the weekly workouts. The following steps describe how to add this information.

 To Add Text to an AutoShape

1 **With the AutoShape selected, type** Calories **and then press the** SHIFT+ENTER **keys. On the next line, type** burned: **and then press the** SHIFT+ENTER **keys. On the third line, type** 1,382! **as the text.**

The AutoShape text displays on three lines (Figure 5-53). You press the SHIFT+ENTER *keys to create a line break, which moves the insertion point to the beginning of the next line and does not create a new paragraph.*

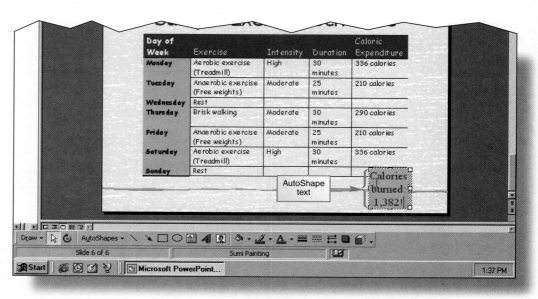

FIGURE 5-53

2 **Right-click the AutoShape, click Format AutoShape on the shortcut menu, and then click the Text Box tab when the Format AutoShape dialog box displays. Point to Resize AutoShape to fit text.**

The Text Box sheet in the Format AutoShape dialog box displays (Figure 5-54). The default text placement is in the center of the object, as indicated by the Text anchor point list box.

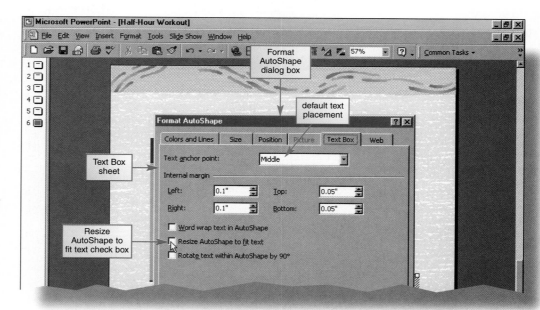

FIGURE 5-54

③ **Click Resize AutoShape to fit text, and then point to the OK button.**

PowerPoint will change the size of the AutoShape automatically based on the amount of text entered and the amount of desired internal margins (Figure 5-55). You can click the Preview button to see the resized AutoShape.

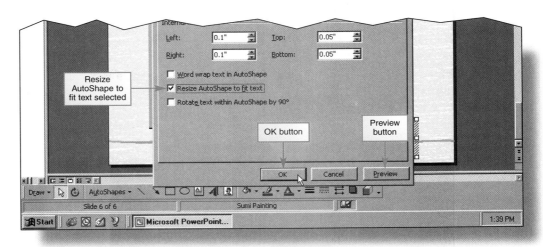

FIGURE 5-55

④ **Click the OK button.**

The AutoShape enlarges to accommodate the text box (Figure 5-56).

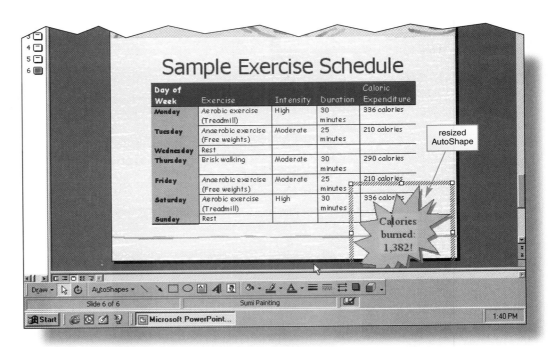

FIGURE 5-56

Text added to an AutoShape becomes part of the shape, which means that it increases font size if the AutoShape is enlarged or that it rotates or flips if the shape is rotated or flipped. If you do not want to attach text to the object, add text instead by using the Text Box tool on the Drawing toolbar and then placing the text on top of the object.

Rotating an AutoShape

The next step in creating the AutoShape is to rotate the object to add visual appeal to the slide. The **Free Rotate button** on the Drawing toolbar allows you to position the mouse pointer over one of the AutoShape's round handles and then visually turn the object to the desired degree.

Other Ways

1. Type desired text, on Format menu click AutoShape, click Text Box tab, click Resize AutoShape to fit text, click OK button

2. Type desired text, press ALT+O, press O, press CTRL+TAB to select Text Box tab, press TAB to select Resize AutoShape to fit text check box, press SPACEBAR, press ENTER

3. Click AutoShape object, drag a sizing handle until object is desired shape and size

To Rotate an AutoShape

1 **Click the Free Rotate button on the Drawing toolbar. Place the mouse pointer on the upper-right green round handles surrounding the AutoShape.**

The mouse pointer changes to a semicircular arrow when it is near one of the four green round handles (Figure 5-57).

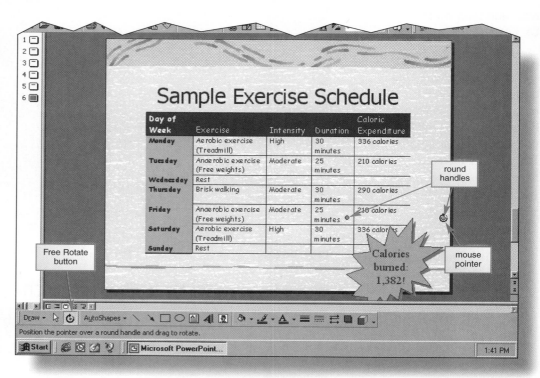

FIGURE 5-57

2 **Click the round handle and drag it to the left until it is at the top of the AutoShape.**

The mouse pointer changes to a full circle when you click the round handle (Figure 5-58). The AutoShape is rotated to the desired degree.

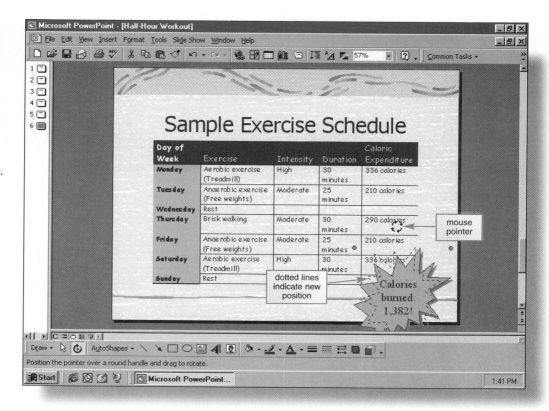

FIGURE 5-58

3 **Press the ARROW keys to move the AutoShape's shadow to the edges of the slide.**

The AutoShape fits nicely in the lower-right corner of the slide and emphasizes the total of the Caloric Expenditure column (Figure 5-59).

FIGURE 5-59

The Free Rotate button allows you to visually turn the AutoShape to a desired degree. You also can apply other effects to an AutoShape object. For example, you flip a shape vertically or horizontally by clicking the Draw button on the Drawing toolbar, pointing to Rotate or Flip, and then selecting the desired effect. You also can change the font color, the fill color, and the line color and style. Indeed, these effects allow you to personalize your presentation and enhance its visual appeal.

Animating the AutoShape Object

The final step in creating Slide 6 is to animate the AutoShape object. Perform the following step to animate this object.

TO ANIMATE THE AUTOSHAPE

1 Click Slide Show on the menu bar, point to Preset Animation, and then click Dissolve on the Preset Animation submenu.

PowerPoint applies the Dissolve animation effect to the AutoShape.

Slide 6 now is complete. The next step in creating the Half-Hour Health presentation is to create a completely solid slide as a final slide to separate the end of the presentation from the beginning as the slide show loops at the kiosk.

Omitting Background Graphics and Changing the Background Color

You can instruct PowerPoint to conclude a slide show gracefully with a black slide by clicking the End with black slide check box in the Options dialog box. When you run your slide show, this black slide displays with the message, End of slide show, click to exit. When the user clicks this slide, the presentation ends and the PowerPoint window returns.

The presentation in this project, however, will run continuously until a user clicks the ESC key. You will not, consequently, select the End with black slide option. An alternate method is to insert another slide and remove the background graphics. The steps on the next page describe how to create this final blank slide of your presentation and change the background color.

More About

Rotating AutoShapes

Once you insert and format an AutoShape, you easily can rotate it 90 degrees to the left or the right. To turn the AutoShape, select the object, click Draw on the Drawing toolbar, point to Rotate or Flip, and the click Rotate Left or Rotate Right.

To Omit Background Graphics and Change the Background Color

1 **Click the New Slide button on the Standard toolbar, type** 12 **to select the Blank AutoLayout, and then click the OK button.**

Slide 7 displays (Figure 5-60).

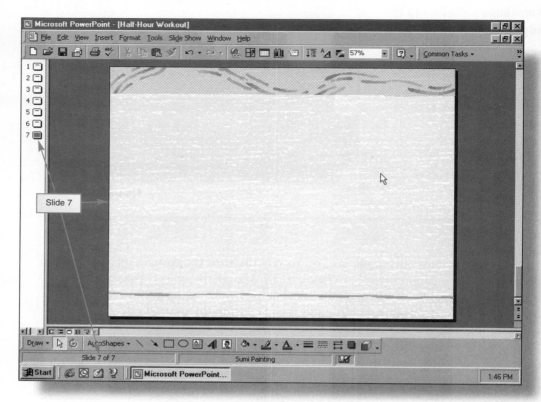

FIGURE 5-60

2 **Right-click Slide 7, click Background on the shortcut menu, and then point to Omit background graphics from master.**

The Background dialog box displays (Figure 5-61). The Sumi Painting design template has a number of background graphics, including the purple swirls at the top of the slide and the horizontal line near the bottom. You do not want these graphics to display on your last slide.

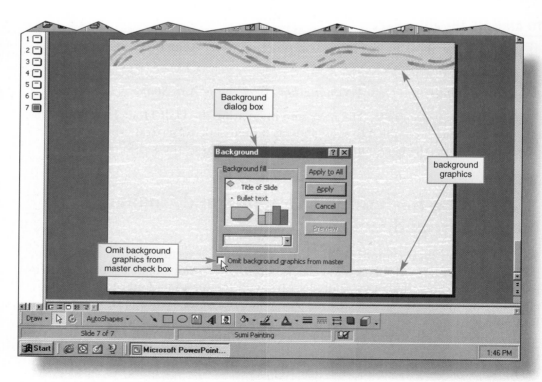

FIGURE 5-61

3 Click Omit background graphics from master. Point to the Background fill box arrow.

The background graphics will be removed from Slide 7 after you click the Apply button (Figure 5-62).

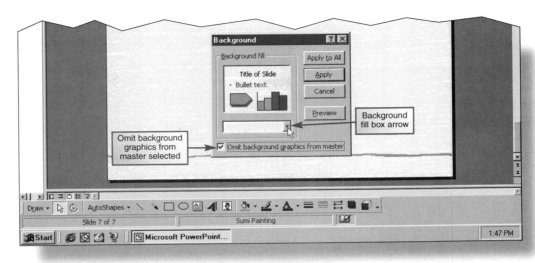

FIGURE 5-62

4 Click the Background fill box arrow. Point to the color medium purple (color 3 in the row).

The color medium purple is the default shadows color in the Sumi Painting design template color scheme (Figure 5-63).

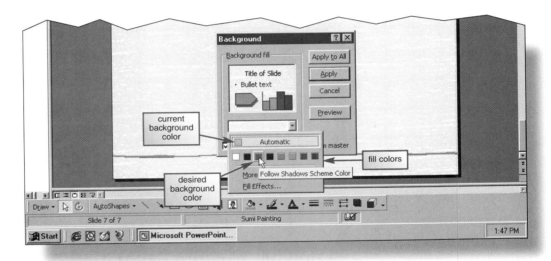

FIGURE 5-63

5 Click the color medium purple. Point to the Apply button.

The color medium purple displays in the Background Fill area (Figure 5-64). When you click the Apply button, the medium purple color is displayed on only the current slide. You would click the Apply to All button if you wanted to change the background color on all slides. You can test your color selection by clicking the Preview button.

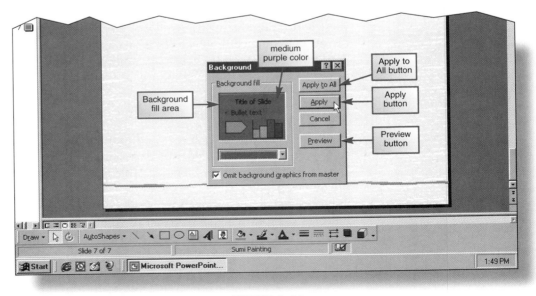

FIGURE 5-64

6 **Click the Apply button.**

Slide 7 displays with only a medium purple background (Figure 5-65).

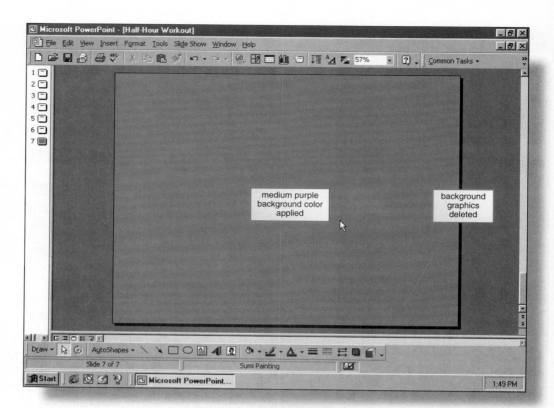

FIGURE 5-65

Each slide in the presentation now contains all the desired visual elements. The next step is to set the order in which the text and objects display on the slides.

Applying Custom Animation

The first six slides in the Half-Hour Workout slide show contain numerous bulleted lists and text objects. To add visual interest to your presentation, you want some of these slide components to display in a specific order. You will use custom animation to set the sequence in which these elements display on each slide. You also need to determine how quickly these objects display on the slide. The following steps describe how to apply custom animation to the presentation.

Setting the Animation Order

PowerPoint gives each text and graphic object on the slide a unique name. For example, title text is called a title object, a bulleted list is called a text object, clip art is called a picture, and a chart or table is called an object or a chart. You can view the names of these slide elements in a list in the Custom Animation dialog box, and you can change the order in which they display on the slide and when they display. Perform the following steps to set the animation order of the objects on Slide 3.

Steps **To Set the Animation Order**

1 Drag the vertical scroll box to display Slide 3. Click Slide Show on the menu bar and then click Custom Animation. When the Custom Animation dialog box displays, point to Text 2 in the Check to animate slide objects list.

The Custom Animation dialog box displays (Figure 5-66). Text 2 and Text 3 are the names of the two bulleted lists. Picture frame 4 is the name of the walking figure animated clip art object; Picture frame 5 is the name of the weightlifting animated clip art object.

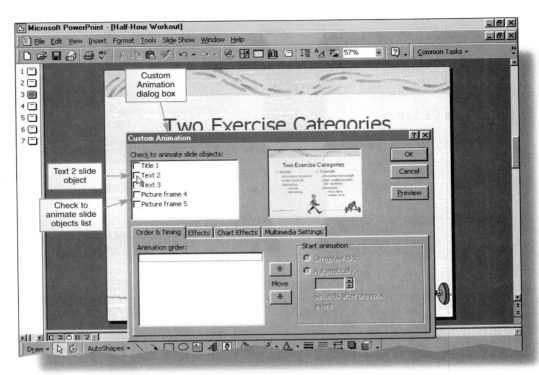

FIGURE 5-66

2 Click Text 2 in the Check to animate slide objects list. Then click Picture frame 4 in the Check to animate slide objects list, Text 3, and Picture frame 5. Point to the Preview button.

Four of the five objects on Slide 3 are animated (Figure 5-67). Their order of appearance displays in the Animation order list.

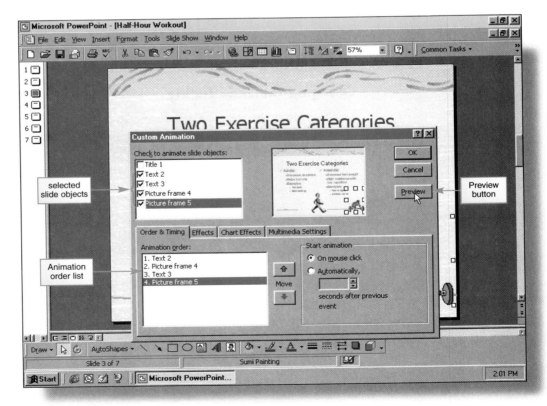

FIGURE 5-67

Click the Preview button. Point to the OK button.

Clicking the Preview button allows you to view the animation order (Figure 5-68).

4 **Click the OK button.**

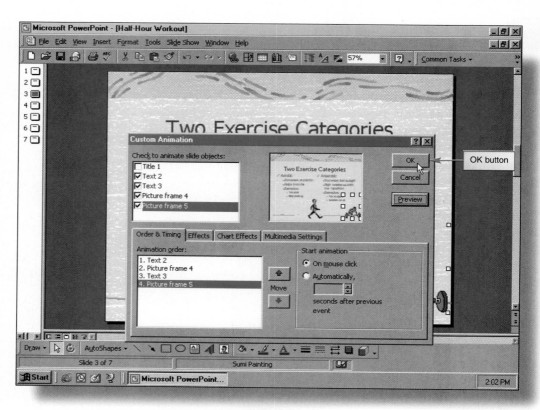

FIGURE 5-68

Using NetMeeting

As you complete your presentation, you may want collaborate with and receive feedback from other people simultaneously. Microsoft has integrated its Office and Net-Meeting programs so a number of people can view a presentation and share the contents of a file. You can schedule the meeting in advance by using Microsoft Outlook or start an impromptu online meeting from within your active PowerPoint presentation. If your colleagues are available and they decide to accept your invitation, the online meeting begins. They can use such tools as a whiteboard, video, and audio to present their opinions and comments. To learn more about using NetMeeting, visit the PowerPoint 2000 Project 5 More About page (www.scsite.com/pp2000/more.htm) and click NetMeeting.

The animation order for the Slide 3 objects is correct. The next custom animation changes you want to make are to determine when the two charts and the table display on the slides.

Changing the Slide Timing

Now that the order in which the slide elements display is correct, you need to determine when these elements display. The Custom Animation dialog box also is used to create these timings. Perform the following steps to set the timing for the Slide 4 treadmill chart so that it displays three seconds after the title text displays.

Steps | **To Change the Slide Timing**

1 **Click the Next Slide button to display Slide 4. Click Slide Show on the menu bar and then click Custom Animation. When the Custom Animation dialog box displays, click Object 2 in the Check to animate slide objects list. Point to Automatically in the Start animation area.**

Object 2, the treadmill chart, is selected (Figure 5-69). You can specify whether you want it to display when you click the mouse or when a particular number of seconds has elapsed.

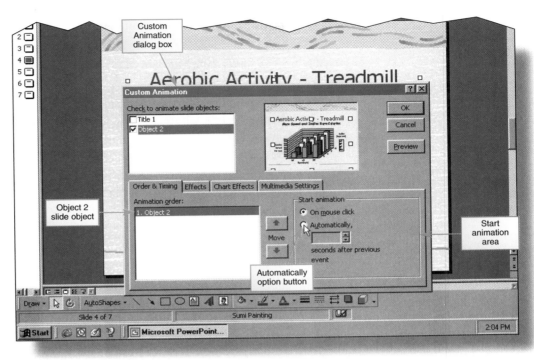

FIGURE 5-69

2 **Click Automatically. Type** :03 **in the seconds after previous event text box. Point to the OK button.**

When you run the slide show, the treadmill chart will display three seconds after the slide displays with the title text (Figure 5-70).

3 **Click the OK button.**

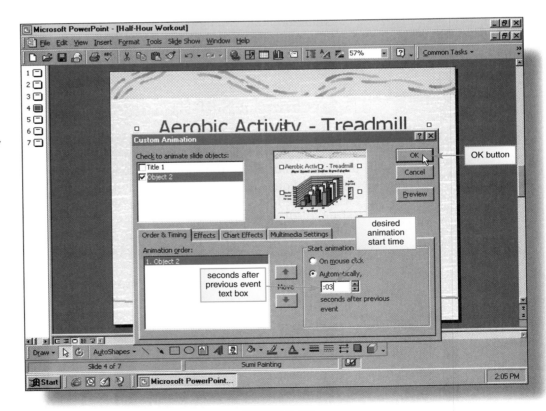

FIGURE 5-70

The Slide 4 timing is set. You need to repeat these steps to set the timings for the free weights benefits chart on Slide 5 and the schedule chart on Slide 6. You also need to set the timing for the AutoShape on Slide 6 so that it displays 10 seconds after the chart displays. The following steps describe how to add these timings.

TO CHANGE THE SLIDE TIMINGS FOR SLIDES 5 AND 6

1 Click the Next Slide button to display Slide 5. Click Slide Show on the menu bar, and then click Custom Animation. When the Custom Animation dialog box displays, click Chart 2 in the Check to animate slide objects list.

2 Click Automatically in the Start animation area. Type :03 in the seconds after previous event text box. Click the OK button.

3 Click the Next Slide button to display Slide 6. Click Slide Show on the menu bar, and then click Custom Animation. When the Custom Animation dialog box displays, click Object 2 in the Check to animate slide objects list.

4 Click Automatically in the Start animation area. Type :03 in the seconds after previous event text box.

5 Click the Move up button to move Object 2 to the top of the Animation order list.

6 Click Text 3 in the Animation order list. Click Automatically in the Start animation area and type :10 in the seconds after previous event text box. Click the OK button.

The free weights benefits chart and workout schedule table will display three seconds after Slide 5 and Slide 6 display during the presentation. The AutoShape will display 10 seconds later on Slide 6.

Animation and timing have been added to the graphical objects in your slide show. You now are ready to make this slide show run automatically without user intervention.

Creating a Self-Running Presentation

The Half-Hour Workout presentation is designed to run unattended at a kiosk located near the registration counter at the Fitness Center. When the last slide in the presentation displays, the slide show **loops**, or restarts, at Slide 1.

PowerPoint has the option of running continuously until a user presses the ESC key. The following steps explain how to set the controls so the slide show runs automatically without user intervention.

More About

Using NetShow

Instead of discussing your PowerPoint presentation using NetMeeting in real time, you may want to broadcast the file over the Internet or on an intranet. Using this method, your colleagues can view the slide show on demand at their own convenience. If you want to broadcast this presentation to more than 15 people, you will need a NetShow server. In addition, a NetShow server on a LAN or a third-party NetShow service provider is required if you will be using live video. To learn more about NetShow, visit the PowerPoint 2000 Project 5 More About page (www.scsite.com/pp2000/more.htm) and click NetShow.

To Create a Self-Running Presentation

1 **Click Slide Show on the menu bar and then point to Set Up Show.**

The Set Up Show options let you decide how much control, if any, you will give to your audience (Figure 5-71).

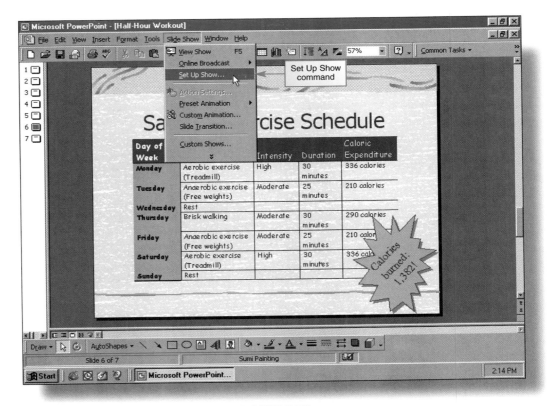

FIGURE 5-71

2 **Click Set Up Show. Point to Browsed at a kiosk (full screen).**

The Set Up Show dialog box displays (Figure 5-72). The default show type is Presented by a speaker (full screen). The Set Up Show dialog box is used to specify the show type, which slides to display, and how to advance slides.

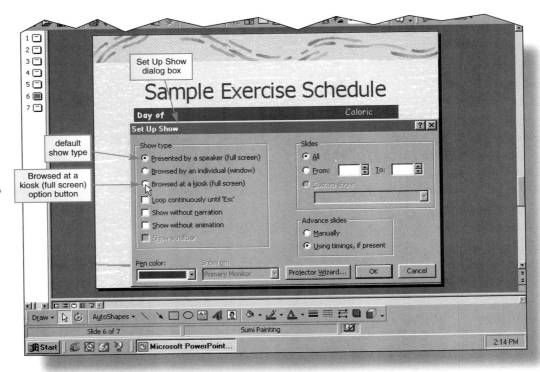

FIGURE 5-72

3 **Click Browsed at a kiosk (full screen). Point to the OK button.**

A check appears in the Loop continuously until 'Esc' check box, and this text is dimmed (Figure 5-73). The slides will advance automatically based on the timings you specify.

4 **Click the OK button.**

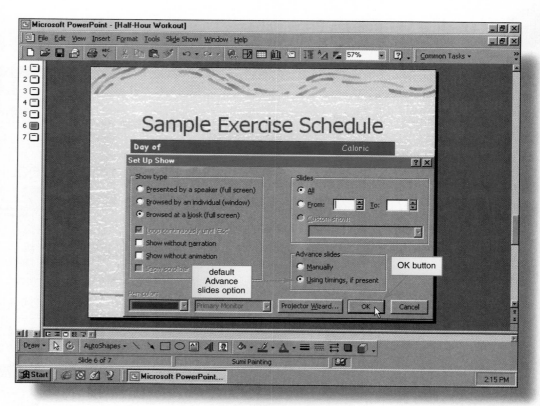

FIGURE 5-73

This slide show will run by itself without user intervention. You alternately could have designed the slide show to allow a user to advance through slides manually by clicking action buttons, which are associated with hyperlinks. Standard mouse clicks are ignored in both show types.

Setting Timings for the Slide Show

The slide show is designed to loop continuously at a kiosk for three minutes, so no user will move through the slides manually. You must, consequently, determine the length of time each slide will display on the screen. You can set these times in two ways. One method is to use PowerPoint's **rehearsal** feature, which allows you to advance through the slides at your own pace, and the amount of time you view each slide is recorded. The other method is to manually set each slide's display time. You will use this second technique in the following steps.

To Set Slide Show Timings Manually

1 **Click the Slide Sorter View button. Right-click Slide 1 and then point to Slide Transition.**

Slide 1 is selected (Figure 5-74).

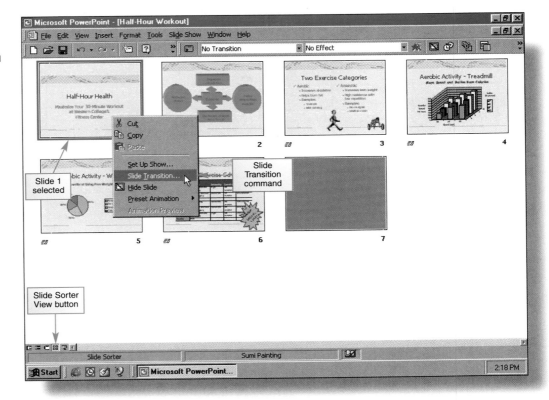

FIGURE 5-74

2 **Click Slide Transition. Point to On mouse click.**

The Slide Transition dialog box displays (Figure 5-75). The On mouse click Advance option is selected. A speaker generally uses this default setting to advance through the slides in a presentation.

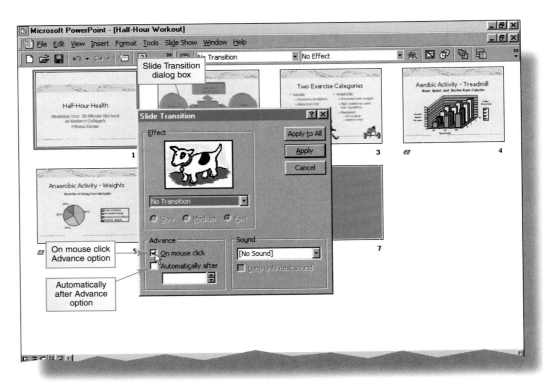

FIGURE 5-75

3 **Click On mouse click to deselect it. Point to Automatically after.**

In this slide show, you want to advance the slide automatically after it has displayed for a designated period of time (Figure 5-76).

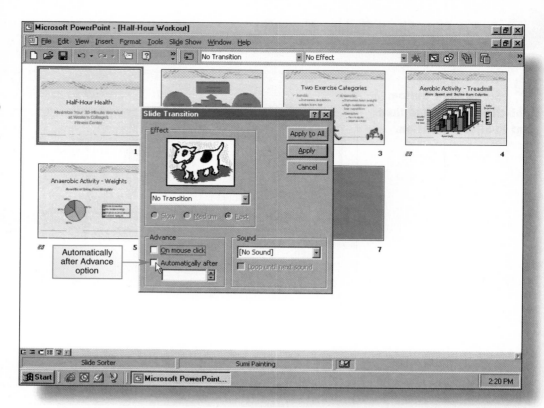

FIGURE 5-76

4 **Click Automatically after and then point to the Automatically after text box up arrow.**

You specify the length of time in the Automatically after text box that you want to slide to display (Figure 5-77).

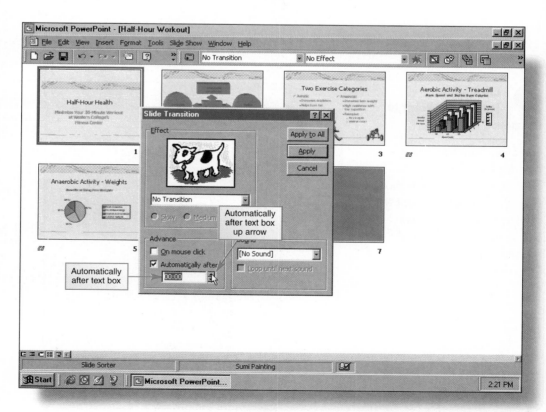

FIGURE 5-77

5 **Click the Automatically after text box up arrow 10 times. Point to the Apply button.**

The Automatically after text box displays 00:10 seconds (Figure 5-78). Another method of entering the time is to type the specific number of minutes and seconds in the text box.

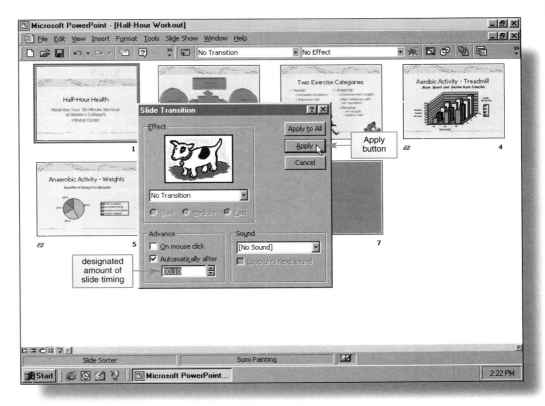

FIGURE 5-78

6 **Click the Apply button.**

The designated slide timing, :10, displays below Slide 1 (Figure 5-79).

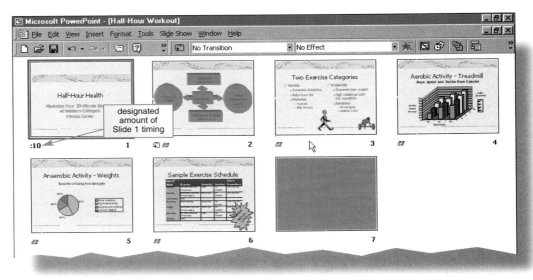

FIGURE 5-79

The timing for Slide 1 is complete. Now you need to repeat this procedure for the other slides in the Half-Hour Workout presentation. Perform the steps on the next page to set these timings.

Other Ways

1. On Slide Show menu click Slide Transition, click Automatically after, click Automatically after text box up arrow, click Apply button

2. Press ALT+D, press T, press ALT+C, press SPACEBAR, type desired time, press ENTER

TO SET SLIDE TIMINGS FOR THE REMAINING SLIDES

1 Right-click Slide 2 and then click Slide Transition. Click On mouse click. Click Automatically after and then type :30 in the text box. Click the Apply button.

2 Right-click Slide 3 and then click Slide Transition. Click On mouse click. Click Automatically after and then type 1:00 in the text box. Click the Apply button.

3 Click Slide 4, press and hold the SHIFT key, and then click Slide 7. Right-click one of the selected slides and then click Slide Transition. Click On mouse click. Click Automatically after and then type :20 in the text box. Click the Apply button.

Each slide's timing displays in the lower-left corner (Figure 5-80).

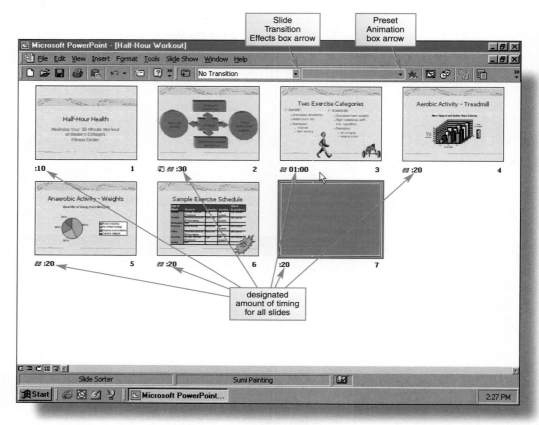

FIGURE 5-80

The Half-Hour Workout slide timing is complete. The presentation will run for three minutes at the kiosk in the Fitness Center.

More *About*

Self-Running Presentations

A self-running presentation restarts when it is finished and also when it has been idle on a manually advanced slide for longer than five minutes.

Adding Slide Transition and Text Preset Animation Effects

The final step in preparing the Half-Hour Workout presentation is to add slide transition and text preset animation effects. Perform the following steps to add the slide transition and text preset animation effects.

TO ADD SLIDE TRANSITION AND TEXT PRESET ANIMATION EFFECTS

1 With Slide 7 selected in Slide Sorter View, press and hold down the SHIFT key and then click Slide 1. Release the SHIFT key.

2 Click the Slide Transition Effects box arrow. Scroll down and then click Uncover Down.

3 Click the Preset Animation box arrow. Scroll down and then click Dissolve.

The presentation displays in Slide Sorter View (Figure 5-81). Slide transition effects and preset animation effects are applied to all slides in the presentation.

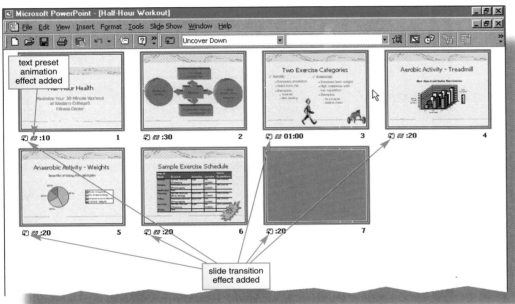

FIGURE 5-81

More About

Quick Reference

For a table that lists how to complete the tasks covered in this book using the mouse, menu, shortcut menu, and keyboard, see the PowerPoint Quick Reference Summary at the back of this book or visit the Office 2000 Web page (www.scsite.com/off2000/qr.htm), and then click Microsoft PowerPoint 2000.

Saving the Presentation

The presentation is complete. You now should save it again.

Starting the Self-Running Presentation

Starting a self-running slide show basically is the same as starting any other slide show. Perform the following steps to run the presentation.

TO START THE SELF-RUNNING PRESENTATION

1 Click Slide 1 and click the Slide Show button.

2 When all the slides have displayed, press the ESC key to stop the presentation.

The presentation will run for three minutes, and then it will loop back to the beginning and start automatically.

Printing Slides as Handouts

Perform the steps on the next page to print the presentation slides as handouts, four slides per page.

Other Ways

1. In Slide View or Slide Sorter View, select slide to add transitions, right-click selected slide, click Slide Transition on shortcut menu, click Effect box arrow, choose desired transition, click Apply button
2. Select slide to add transitions, on Slide Show menu click Slide Transition, click Effect box arrow, choose desired transition, click Apply button

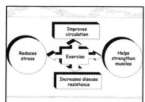
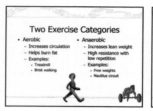

TO PRINT SLIDES AS HANDOUTS

1 Ready the printer according to the printer manufacturer's instructions.

2 Click File on the menu bar and then click Print on the File menu.

3 Click the Print what box arrow and then click Handouts in the list.

4 Click the Slides per page box arrow in the Handouts area and then click 4 in the list.

5 Click Pure black and white and then click the OK button.

The handouts print as shown in Figure 5-82.

The Half-Hour Fitness presentation now is complete. If you made any changes to your presentation since your last save, you now should save it again before quitting PowerPoint.

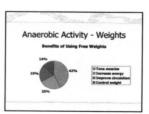

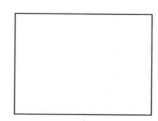

FIGURE 5-82

CASE PERSPECTIVE SUMMARY

The Half-Hour Fitness slide show should help Western College's students understand how to optimize their workouts. When they register at the Fitness Center, they can view your presentation at a kiosk and learn why exercise is important and how aerobic and anaerobic activities are beneficial. Your charts depicting use of the treadmill and free weights and your table showing how to vary the workouts explain these basic exercise principles. As director of the Fitness Center, Tiffani Olson should find your presentation beneficial for promoting the Center's holistic wellness philosophy.

Project Summary

Project 5 presented the principles of creating a self-running presentation that can run at a kiosk. You began the project by starting a new presentation and then inserting an animated slide from another presentation. Next, you embedded animated clip art, an Excel chart, a PowerPoint chart, and a Word table. You then inserted and formatted an AutoShape. Next, you created an ending slide with a purple background to separate the end of your presentation from the beginning when the slide show loops. You used custom animation effects to stagger the display of various slide objects. You then set automatic slide timings to display each slide for a designated period of time and added slide transition effects. Finally, you printed your presentation slides as handouts with four slides displaying on each page.

What You Should Know

Having completed this project, you now should be able to perform the following tasks:

- Add a Chart Title and Data Labels *(PP 5.33)*
- Add a Slide, Choose a Layout, and Add Text *(PP 5.13, PP 5.20, PP 5.26, PP 5.36)*
- Add a Shadow to an AutoShape *(PP 5.41)*
- Add Slide Transition and Text Preset Animation Effects *(PP 5.59)*
- Add Text to an AutoShape *(PP 5.42)*
- Add Text to the Right Placeholder *(PP 5.14)*
- Animate an AutoShape *(PP 5.45)*
- Change the Background Color *(PP 5.46)*
- Change the Slide Timing *(PP 5.51, 5.52)*
- Create a Self-Running Presentation *(PP 5.53)*
- Create a Title Slide in Slide View *(PP 5.7)*
- Increase the Right Object Area Placeholder Width *(PP 5.15)*
- Insert a Slide from Another Presentation *(PP 5.10)*
- Insert a Word Table *(PP 5.37)*
- Insert an AutoShape *(PP 5.40)*
- Insert an Excel Chart *(PP 5.21)*
- Insert Animated Clip Art *(PP 5.16)*
- Move Animated Clip Art Objects *(PP 5.17)*
- Omit Background Graphics and Change the Background *(PP 5.46)*
- Print Slides as Handouts *(PP 5.60)*
- Replace Sample Data in a Datasheet *(PP 5.29)*
- Rotate an AutoShape *(PP 5.44)*
- Save a Presentation *(PP 5.19)*
- Scale an Excel Chart *(PP 5.24)*
- Select a Different Chart Type *(PP 5.27)*
- Set Slide Show Timings Manually *(PP 5.55)*
- Set Slide Timings for the Remaining Slides *(PP 5.58)*
- Set the Animation Order *(PP 5.49)*
- Size the Animated Clip Art Objects *(PP 5.18)*
- Start a New Presentation *(PP 5.6)*
- Start the Self-Running Presentation *(PP 5.59)*

Apply Your Knowledge

Project Reinforcement at www.scsite.com/off2000/reinforce.htm

1 Changing the Color Scheme, Removing an Object from the Slide Master, Adding Animated Clip Art, and Inserting a Presentation

Instructions: Start PowerPoint. Open the Antivirus Basics file on your Data Disk. See the inside back cover of this book for instructions for downloading the Data Disk or see your instructor for information on accessing the files required for this book. Perform the following tasks to modify the slides to look like Figures 5-83a through 5-83f.

1. Click File on the menu bar, and then click Save As. Save the presentation with the file name, Antivirus Policy.
2. Apply the Lock And Key design template.
3. Change the slide color scheme. To make this change, click Format on the menu bar, click Slide Color Scheme, and then click the Custom tab in the Color Scheme dialog box. Next, change the Background color to red and the Title text color to dark blue. Click the Apply to All button.
4. Display Slide 2. Delete the key from the slide master by changing to slide master view, clicking the key object, and then pressing the DELETE key. Click the Slide View button.
5. On Slide 4, insert the animated question mark clip art image shown in Figure 5-83d. Scale the clip art to 285%. Drag the image under the text and center it on the slide.
6. Insert the PowerPoint file, Inoculate, after Slide 4. This file is on your Data Disk.
7. Introduce the subtitle text in the Object Area placeholder on each slide all at once grouped by 2nd level paragraphs.
8. Add a summary slide from Slides 2, 3, and 4, and reposition it after Slide 5. Change the title text to Mini-mizing the Virus Threat, as shown in Figure 5-83f. Insert the animated computer clip art image shown in Figure 5-83f. Scale the clip art to 400%. Drag the image to the lower-right corner of the slide.
9. Apply the Dissolve animation effect to the clip art images on Slides 4 and 6. Move each image to the top of the Animation order list, and start the animation automatically 2 seconds after the previous event.
10. Add your name and the slide number to the slide footer.
11. Apply the Split Vertical Out slide transition effect to all slides except Slide 1. Apply the Split Horizontal In preset animation effect to all text.
12. Save the Antivirus Policy file again.
13. Print the slides using the Pure black and white option. Quit PowerPoint.

Apply Your Knowledge

Project Reinforcement at www.scsite.com/off2000/reinforce.htm

(a) Slide 1

Security Rules

- Check floppy disks on standalone machine
  - Includes
    - Floppies purchased from shareware sources
    - Floppies brought from home
- Report viruses to Technical Services
- Check downloaded software

Charles Johnson

(b) Slide 2

Security Procedures

- Save downloaded files on second hard drive
- Check downloaded software before installing on your computer
- Use current versions of antivirus programs and updates to the virus signature files
- Back up your files regularly

Charles Johnson

(c) Slide 3

Security Education

- Distinguish between actual and hoax viruses
- Determine the type of infection
- Distribute and discuss rules and procedures
  - Apply disciplinary action for violations

Charles Johnson

(d) Slide 4

Inoculate Your Computer

Protect your system from viruses

Charles Johnson

(e) Slide 5

Minimizing the Virus Threat

- Security Rules
- Security Procedures
- Security Education

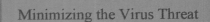

Charles Johnson

(f) Slide 6

FIGURE 5-83

In the Lab

1 Inserting Animated Clip Art, Applying Animation Effects, and Importing Word and Excel Files

Problem: In an effort to be more helpful to students, the Student Career Center (SCC) has asked to meet with various student representatives. One of the ideas adopted by the SCC is to highlight different careers every few days as part of their information kiosk. As a work-study student, you have been asked to create several of the kiosk presentations. Your first presentation is about careers in Computer Information Systems. To make the display interesting, you add clip art, a slide with a Microsoft Excel chart, and a slide with a Microsoft Word table. You create the presentation shown in Figures 5-84a through 5-84g.

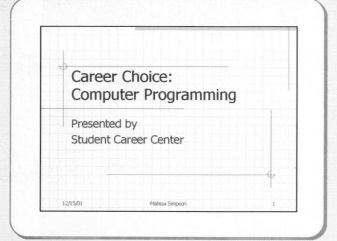

(a) Slide 1

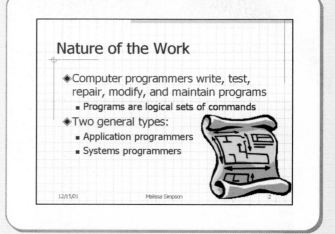

(b) Slide 2

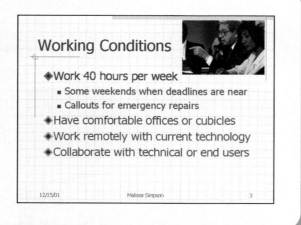

(c) Slide 3

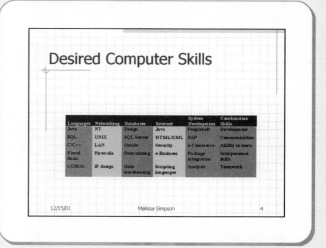

(d) Slide 4

FIGURE 5-84

In the Lab

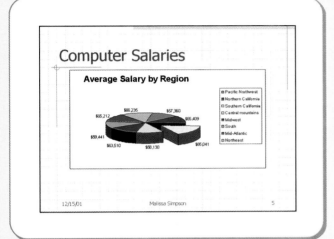

(e) Slide 5

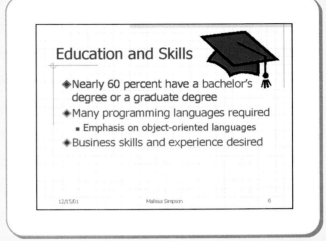

(f) Slide 6

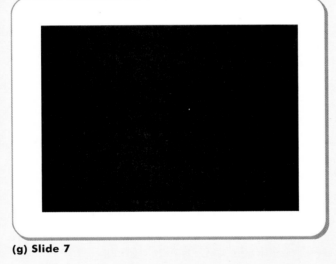

(g) Slide 7

FIGURE 5-84

Instructions: Start PowerPoint and perform the following tasks with a computer. If the designated clip art images do not display in your Microsoft Clip Gallery, see your instructor for copies of these files or substitute similar objects.

1. Open a new presentation and apply the Title Slide AutoLayout and the Blueprint design template.
2. Create the title slide shown in Figure 5-84a. Apply the Peek From Left Entry animation effect to the subtitle text.
3. Insert a new slide and apply the Bulleted List AutoLayout. Type the title text and bulleted text shown in Figure 5-84b.
4. Insert the animated clip art shown in Figure 5-84b that has the keyword, layouts. Scale the clip art to 205% and drag it to the lower-right corner of the slide.

(continued)

In the Lab

Inserting Animated Clip Art, Applying Animation Effects, and Importing Word and Excel Files *(continued)*

5. Apply the Fly From Bottom-Right Entry animation effect to the clip art. Start the animation automatically, 00:02 seconds after the previous event.

6. Apply the Peek From Left Entry animation effect to the Slide 2 bulleted list. Introduce this text all at once grouped by 2nd level paragraphs.

7. Insert a new slide, apply the Bulleted List AutoLayout, and create Slide 3 as shown in Figure 5-84c. Insert the animated clip art that has the keywords, business, communication. Scale the clip art to 140% and drag it to the upper-right corner of the slide.

8. Apply the Fly From Top-Right Entry animation effect to the animated clip art. Start the animation automatically, 00:02 seconds after the previous event.

9. Apply the Peek From Left Entry animation effect to the Slide 3 bulleted list. Introduce this text all at once grouped by 2nd level paragraphs.

10. Insert a new slide and apply the Object AutoLayout. Type the Slide 4 title text shown in Figure 5-84d. Insert the Employment Table file on your Data Disk. Apply the Split Vertical In Entry animation effect to this table, which is Object 2.

11. Insert a new slide and apply the Chart AutoLayout. Type the Slide 5 title text shown in Figure 5-84e. Insert the Programming Salaries file on your Data Disk. Apply the Split Vertical In Entry animation effect to this chart, which is Object 4.

12. Insert a new slide and apply the Bulleted List AutoLayout. Enter the Slide 6 text shown in Figure 5-84f. Insert the animated clip art that has the keyword, mortarboards. Scale the clip art to 145% and drag it to the upper-right corner of the slide.

13. Apply the Fly From Top-Right Entry animation effect to the animated clip art. Start the animation automatically, 00:02 seconds after the previous event.

14. Apply the Peek From Left Entry animation effect to the Slide 6 bulleted list. Introduce this text all at once grouped by 2nd level paragraphs.

15. Insert a new slide and apply the Blank AutoLayout. Change the background fill color to black. Omit the background graphics from the master.

16. Apply the Wipe Down slide transition effect to Slides 2 through 7.

17. Set the slide timings to 10 seconds for Slide 1 and 15 seconds for Slides 2 through 7.

18. Set the show type as Browsed at a kiosk.

19. Add your name, today's date, and the slide number to the slide footer.

20. Save the presentation with the file name, Programming Career. Print the slides using the Pure black and white option. Quit PowerPoint.

In the Lab

2 Inserting Animated Clip Art, Applying Animation Effects, Changing the Slide Background, and Creating a Chart

Problem: You are enrolled in a business seminar course called the Modern Entrepreneur. The main requirement for the course is to present a business plan on a legitimate business venture. The plan and the presentation are a "pitch" for funding, such as a small business loan. You are interested in owning and operating an Internet Service Provider (ISP), so you decide to make a presentation on launching an ISP called the New Millennium Internet Access (NMIA). To make the presentation persuasive, you add a Microsoft Excel chart showing five-year projected income. In addition, you add some clip art and change the design template background color. You create the presentation shown in Figures 5-85a through 5-85f.

(a) Slide 1

(b) Slide 2

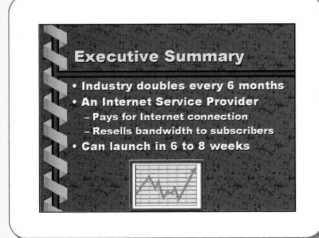

(c) Slide 3

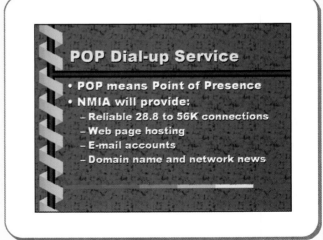

(d) Slide 4

FIGURE 5-85 *(continued)*

(continued)

In the Lab

Inserting Animated Clip Art, Applying Animation Effects, Changing the Slide Background, and Creating a Chart *(continued)*

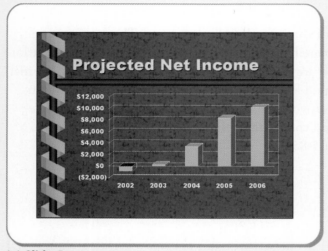

(e) Slide 5

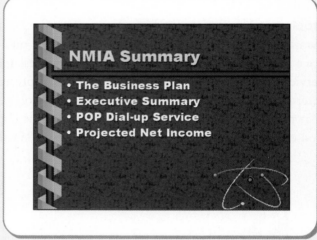

(f) Slide 6

FIGURE 5-85 *(continued)*

Instructions: Start PowerPoint and perform the following tasks with a computer. If the designated clip art images do not display in your Microsoft Clip Gallery, see your instructor for copies of these files or substitute similar objects.

1. Open a new presentation and apply the Title Slide AutoLayout and the High Voltage design template.
2. Create the title slide shown in Figure 5-85a. Use your name instead of the name Sandra Linden. Apply the Spiral animation effect to the Slide 1 subtitle text. Start the animation automatically, 00:03 seconds after the previous event.
3. Change the background by right-clicking anywhere on Slide 1 except the slide master objects, clicking Background on the shortcut menu, and then clicking the Background fill area box arrow. Click Fill Effects in the list and then click the Texture tab. Click the Purple mesh texture in row 3, column 3, and then click the OK button. To apply the change to all slides, click the Apply to All button.
4. Display the rulers and guides. Drag the vertical guide to 3.17 inches left of center and the horizontal guide 1.67 inches below center.
5. Insert the animated clip art shown in Figure 5-85a that has the keywords, technology, borders. Drag the clip art object so its upper-left corner snaps to the intersection of the guides. Apply the Fly From Left Entry animation effect to the clip art. Start the animation automatically, 00:03 seconds after the previous event.
6. Insert a new slide and apply the Clip Art & Text AutoLayout. Type the Slide 2 title text and bulleted text shown in Figure 5-85b. Insert the clip art that has the keywords, earth, technology. Apply the Fly From Top-Left Entry animation effect to the clip art, Object 3.
7. Apply the Spiral animation effect to the Slide 2 subtitle text, Text 2. Introduce this text all at once grouped by 2nd level paragraphs.

In the Lab

8. Insert a new slide and apply the Bulleted List AutoLayout. Type the Slide 3 title text and bulleted text shown in Figure 5-85c. Drag the vertical guide to 1.50 inches left of center. Insert the animated clip art that has the keywords, charts, increases. Scale it to 233% and drag it so that its upper-left corner snaps to the intersection of the guides.

9. Apply the Fly From Bottom Entry animation effect to the clip art, Picture frame 3.

10. Apply the Spiral animation effect to the Slide 3 subtitle text, Text 2. Introduce this text all at once grouped by 2nd level paragraphs.

11. Insert a new slide and apply the Bulleted List AutoLayout. Type the Slide 4 title text and bulleted list shown in Figure 5-85d.

12. Drag the vertical guide to 3.92 inches left of center and the horizontal guide to 2.67 inches below center. Insert the animated clip art shown in Figure 5-85d that has the keywords, web dividers, lines. Scale the clip art to 153%. Align the top-left corner of the clip art with the intersection of the guides.

13. Apply the Spiral animation effect to the Slide 3 subtitle text, Text 2. Introduce this text all at once grouped by 2nd level paragraphs.

14. Hide the rulers and guides.

15. Insert a new slide and apply the Chart AutoLayout. Type the Slide 5 title text shown in Figure 5-85e. Create the 3-D Column chart shown in Slide 5 by using the data in Table 5-2.

Table 5-2	Projected Net Income
YEAR	NET INCOME
2002	$-867
2003	$253
2004	$3,421
2005	$8,342
2006	$10,234

16. Add a summary slide from Slides 2, 3, 4, and 5, and reposition it after Slide 5. Change the title text to NMIA Summary, as shown in Figure 5-85f. Insert the animated clip art image that has the keywords, atoms, technology. Scale the clip art to 187%. Drag the image to the lower-right corner of the slide. Apply the Spiral animation effect to the Slide 6 subtitle text, Text 2.

17. Apply the Box Out slide transition effect to Slides 2 through 6.

18. Save the presentation with the file name, Business Plan. Print the slides using the Pure black and white option. Quit PowerPoint.

In the Lab

3 Using AutoShapes and Adding a Presentation within a Presentation

Problem: Your Aunt Julia owns the Melting Pot, which is a specialty food and kitchen utensils store. She offers numerous cooking classes with topics ranging from economy family meals to formal business dinner parties. She often is asked how to present food for buffet style dinners, so she has asked you to create a presentation on planning a buffet style dinner party. She has created an outline of the course and has assembled some graphics for you to use in the presentation.

Instructions Part 1: Start PowerPoint and perform the following tasks with a computer to create the presentation consisting of Figures 5-86a through 5-86e. If the designated clip art images do not display in your Microsoft Clip Gallery, see your instructor for copies of these files or substitute similar objects.

1. Open a new presentation and apply the Title Slide AutoLayout and the Citrus design template.
2. Create the title slide shown in Figure 5-86a. Add your name and today's date to this slide.
3. Insert a new slide and apply the Text & Clip Art slide layout. Type the Slide 2 title text and bulleted list shown in Figure 5-86b. Insert the clip art that has the keywords, meals, fried chicken.
4. Insert a new slide and apply the Object layout design. Type the Slide 3 title text shown in Figure 5-86c. Insert the Party Timetable file on your Data Disk. Apply the Split Vertical Out Entry animation effect to this table, which is Object 2. Start the animation automatically, 00:03 seconds after the previous event.
5. Insert a new slide and apply the Bulleted list slide layout. Enter the Slide 4 title text and bulleted text shown in Figure 5-86d.
6. Insert a new slide and apply the 2 Column Text slide layout. Enter the Slide 5 title text and bulleted text shown as Figure 5-86e.
7. Apply the Split Horizontal Out Entry animation effect to the Slide 1, 2, 4, and 5 subtitle text. Start the Slide 1 animation automatically.
8. Apply the Blinds Vertical Out slide transition effect to Slides 2 through 5.
9. Save the presentation with the file name, Buffet Dinner.

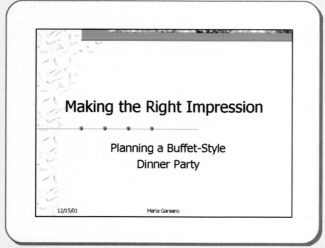

(a) Slide 1

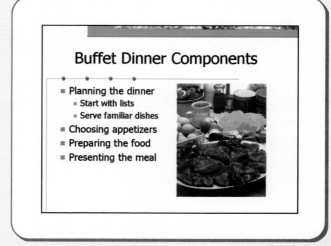

(b) Slide 2

FIGURE 5-86

In the Lab

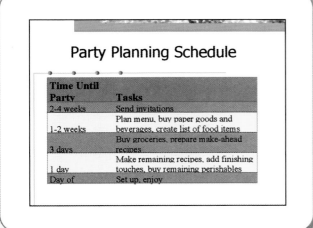

(c) Slide 3

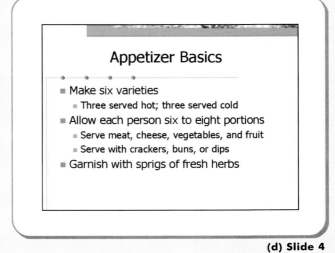

(d) Slide 4

(e) Slide 5

(f) Slide 6

FIGURE 5-86 *(continued)*

Instructions Part 2: Perform the following tasks to create the presentation shown in Figure 5-86f and to insert this slide in the presentation created in Part 1. If the designated clip art images do not display in your Microsoft Clip Gallery, see your instructor for copies of these files or substitute similar objects.

1. Open a new presentation, apply the Blank AutoLayout, and then apply the Citrus design template.
2. Create the slide shown in Figure 5-86f.
3. Insert a bent arrow from the Auto Shapes, Block Arrows.
4. If the fill color is not already green, change the fill color to green.
5. Use the Draw, Rotate or Flip command to Flip Vertical. Rotate the arrow so it appears as shown in Figure 5-86f.
6. Insert the clip art that has the keywords dining, food, place settings.

(continued)

In the Lab

Using AutoShapes and Adding a Presentation within a Presentation *(continued)*

7. Select the clip art image. Ungroup the image. Click the mouse anywhere off the image.
8. Select the fork by dragging the mouse over the fork. After the sizing handles appear, click the draw button and group the image. Drag the fork to the left away from the plate.
9. Select the knife and spoon by dragging the mouse over the mouse and spoon. After the sizing handles appear, click the draw button and group the image.
10. Drag the knife and spoon next to the fork.
11. Hold the shift key down and click the fork so the fork, knife, and spoon are selected. Click the Draw button and group the two images into one.
12. Rotate the fork, knife, and spoon as one image 90 degrees to the right.
13. Insert a text box above the plate as shown in Figure 5-86f. Enter the description, 1. Plates.
14. Insert a down arrow from the Auto Shapes, Block Arrows. Change the fill color to green and place the arrow on the lower-right side of the plate, as shown in Figure 5-86f.
15. Insert the clip art dinner, food, meat, seafood, which contains a lobster, beneath the plate.
16. Insert a text box below the lobster and enter the description, 2. Main Course.
17. Insert a bent arrow from the Auto Shapes, Block Arrows. Use the Draw, Rotate or Flip command to Flip Vertical, then flip Horizontal. Rotate the arrow to so it appears as Figure 5-86f.
18. Add the remaining clip art, text box descriptions, arrows and shown in Figure 5-86f.
19. Use Table 5-3 to set the animation order and timing.
20. Save the second presentation with the file name, Buffet Table. Close this presentation.
21. Add the Buffet Table presentation slide to your Buffet Dinner presentation after Slide 5.
22. Apply the Blinds Vertical slide transition effect to Slide 6.
23. Save the Buffet Dinner presentation again. Print the slides using the Pure black and white option. Quit PowerPoint.

Table 5-3 Buffet Table Automation		
ORDER AND TIMING	START AUTOMATION	EFFECT
Bent Arrow	Automatically, 1 second	Fly From Top-Right
Dinner Plate	Automatically, 1 second	Fly From Top-Right
Textbox (1. Plates)	Automatically, 1 second	Fly From Top-Right
Down Arrow	Automatically, 1 second	Fly From Top-Right
Lobster Dinner	Automatically, 5 seconds	Fly From Right
Textbox (2. Main Course)	Automatically, 1 second	Fly From Right
Bent Arrow	Automatically, 1 second	Fly From Right
Shrimp on plate	Automatically, 5 seconds	Fly From Bottom
Textbox (3. Cold Food)	Automatically, 1 second	Fly From Bottom
Left Arrow	Automatically, 1 second	Fly From Right
Salads	Automatically, 5 seconds	Fly From Left
Textbox (4. Salads)	Automatically, 1 second	Fly From Left
Bent Arrow	Automatically, 1 second	Fly From Bottom
Bread basket	Automatically, 5 seconds	Fly From Left
Textbox (5. Breads)	Automatically, 1 second	Fly From Left
Bent Arrow	Automatically, 1 second	Fly From Bottom-Left
Flatware	Automatically, 5 seconds	Fly From Top
Textbox (6. Flatware)	Automatically, 1 second	Fly From Top
Right Arrow	Automatically, 1 second	Fly From Left
Beverages	Automatically, 5 seconds	Fly From Top
Textbox (7. Beverages)	Automatically, 1 second	Fly From Top
Bent Arrow	Automatically, 1 second	Fly From Left

Cases and Places

1 ▶ E-commerce is growing quickly as the number of Internet users increases. Shopping Web sites are sprouting overnight. Technology allows the average person at home to sell things over the Web. Most of the technology needed today requires Common Gateway Interfaces (CGI), Java, JavaScript, and VBScript. One technique used for tracking a shopper's visit to a Web site is to use cookies. A cookie is a mechanism used to store and retrieve data on the client's (user's) computer. In other words, it is a variable that holds data, and that data is stored on the disk in a special file. Cookie items make it easy for Web sites to keep track of user preferences because the data is stored on the user's computer, not on the Web server. Cookies set aside a small amount of disk space to save the data. The cookie then can be sent to the Web site as needed. The browser will not transfer a cookie's data to any Web site other than the one that requested it. This feature is important for security reasons. Cookies can keep track of frames, shopping cart selections, a user name for a Web site, a password for a Web site, and an account number for a Web site. Any personal data that is needed can be stored in a cookie. The only restriction is that a cookie cannot exceed 4,000 characters. Cookies cannot do certain things: they cannot read e-mail addresses, but they can save one if requested. Cookies cannot gather other sensitive data. If a server does not allow the use of CGI scripts, Web page developers can create cookies in JavaScript, VBScript, or Java. The basic logic requires these programmers to use three functions: a function that reads the cookie (if present), a function that stores the cookie, and a function that deletes the cookie. Most Web developers call these functions getCookie, setCookie, and delCookie. You have enrolled in a Web design course, and part of your coursework is to create a presentation on some aspect of Web page development. You have chosen to describe cookies. Using the techniques introduced in this project, create a short slide show explaining cookies. Include a Word Table, and modify a clip art image to display an animated object. Add the necessary slide transition effects. Submit all files on a disk to your instructor.

2 ▶ The Magnuson-Moss Warranty-Federal Trade Commission Improvement Act, better know as the Lemon Law, was enacted to give consumers rights in dealing with automobiles having persistent problems that are not rectified. The law protects any consumer of a product with a written warranty. The manufacturer must make a reasonable number of attempts to repair a defective product. After such repairs fail to correct the situation, the consumer may elect to collect a refund or ask for a replacement of the product. The Lemon Law also prohibits a warrantor from excluding or modifying warranties under the Uniform Commercial Code (UCC). The UCC or TARR BABY code, as it has been called, has been enacted in all 50 states and covers tender, acceptance, rejection, and revocation. The tender provision entitles a buyer to reject any goods that fail in any respect to conform to the contract. Acceptance covers the new car buyer who accepts the product in good faith and believes that the manufacturer will repair any problems. A new car buyer may discover defects in the car within a reasonable time to reject the vehicle. This period is inexact. Revocation protects the consumer who has used the new car for a lengthy period of time. This describes the typical lemon car, and the UCC provides that a buyer may revoke his acceptance of goods. Each state has different provisions regarding this law, so consumers must research their state's provisions. Using the techniques introduced in this project, create a short slide show describing your state's Lemon Law. Include a Word table, and modify a clip art image to display an animated object. Add the necessary slide transition effects. Submit all files on a disk to your instructor.

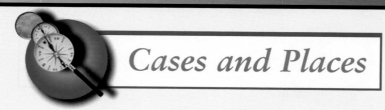

Cases and Places

3 ▶▶ Day trading has been defined as a way to buy and sell stocks during the day based on daily price movement. Day trading has changed the traditional market that exists in a central location on the trading floor. Today's brokers and traders find each other electronically. Because of the Internet, anyone, anywhere has immediate access to the stock market. Day trading is very short-term and can involve as little as a few minutes of time. A change of a few points on 1,000 shares of a stock can translate into as much as $200 or more in a short time. These kinds of changes are attributed to growth in the market with new stocks that often increase value from 20% to 100% in one day. The goal is to be profitable, and the smart trader realizes that the opposite also can be true with massive losses in one day. Many people believe that day trading is gambling, assuming that one randomly picks stocks to "play" and does not do any research on the companies. Day trading is serious business and requires training, experience, and capital to get started. Successful day traders must have discipline and be able to learn and apply rules, strategies, and techniques. Learn some of the few simple trading strategies: have patience, do not follow the crowd, watch the stock price, don't let your emotions rule your day. Don't get greedy. Do not trade during that last hour of the day in the S&P futures market or place orders for the opening bell. If you do not like what you are holding, get out. Learn the jargon, so you will not make mistakes because you do not understand the language. Using the techniques introduced in this project, create a short slide show describing day trading principles. Include a Word table and animate two clip art objects. Add slide transition effects. Submit all files on a disk to your instructor.

4 ▶▶ You are a mass communication major and are enrolling in the Senior Seminar course. Your assignment is to tour a major newspaper, magazine, or book publisher to find out the process of putting together a daily newspaper, monthly magazine, or a book. You decide to visit a book publisher and to develop a slide show on how a book is made. Your show should discuss submitting a manuscript to an editor, who decides if the book is publishable. Subsequent slides should discuss the editing process, the illustrating and layout phases, and finally printing the book. One slide should use the Microsoft Draw feature to ungroup parts of a clip art object and reassemble it in the slide as animation. Enhance the presentation by modifying the slide background, placing additional clip art graphics, using text preset animation effects, and applying slide transition and animation effects to the text and the graphics. Submit all files on a disk to your instructor.

5 ▶▶▶ You have been elected president of the campus Computer Club. Your faculty advisor, who knows you are savvy about computers, suggests you do a presentation on building a computer. You decide this presentation could be a good introduction to a semester-long project, in which the club buys and assembles parts for a computer. Using the techniques introduced in this project, create a slide show describing how to build a PC. Research what components are required to build a computer and the sequence of steps used in the assembling process. List several popular places to purchase parts. Include a Word table describing CMOS settings, and modify at least two clip art images to show animated objects. Add slide transition effects. Submit all files on a disk to your instructor.

Microsoft **PowerPoint 2000**

Microsoft PowerPoint 2000

P R O J E C T

6

Using Visual Basic for Applications (VBA) with PowerPoint

You will have mastered the material in this project when you can:

O B J E C T I V E S

- Create a toolbar
- Customize a toolbar by adding a button
- Use the macro recorder to create a macro
- Customize a menu by adding a command
- Open a presentation and print it by executing a macro
- Understand Visual Basic for Applications code
- Add controls, such as command buttons, option buttons, and check boxes to a form
- Assign properties to controls
- Create a form to automate data entry
- Write a procedure to automate data entry
- Create a user interface
- Use the Visual Basic Editor to enter a procedure
- Export an outline to Microsoft Word

Make a Point

Electronic Portfolios
Do the Job

After taking classes for years and studying for exams for hours on end, you decide it is time to get serious and hunt for a job in your major field of study.

But where do you begin? Your college's placement center is a good start. So are two types of pages: the help wanted pages in your local paper and the Web pages on career sites.

When you peruse these ads, you will see that computer skills are in great demand. The U.S. Department of Labor predicts that soon most employees will need basic computer skills to land a job and then require additional specialized training to advance.

Many employers are seeking candidates with more than just a basic knowledge of computers; they desire individuals proficient in the latest versions of software, especially in

Microsoft Word, Microsoft Excel, and Microsoft PowerPoint. When you write your cover letter and resume, you need to emphasize your competency in these programs.

After you receive a call to schedule an interview, you must prepare for presenting yourself in the most persuasive manner. Career books and Web sites abound with advice on what questions to expect, what questions to ask, and what clothes to wear. In the typical 30-minute interview, you will be judged on your communications skills, leadership ability, maturity, and intelligence.

No doubt you also will be asked questions about your computer expertise. While you can list these skills on your resume and discuss them with the interviewer, nothing is more persuasive than actually demonstrating your proficiency. One of the most influential methods of showing this technological knowledge is with an electronic portfolio.

The portfolio concept is not new; artists, architects, and journalists routinely bring three-ring notebooks, scrapbooks, and folders to interviews to showcase their actual drawings and writings. But today's technology-savvy students have transformed these tangible notebooks to electronic notebooks.

Job hunters today are using Microsoft PowerPoint to display their projects, describe their experiences, and demonstrate their skills. For example, elementary education majors can import photographs taken during their student teaching experiences. Computer science majors can include flowcharts, documentation, and hypertext links to projects published to class Web pages. Music majors can import video clips of their performances. These interviewees can give interviewers copies of their presentations on a floppy disk to peruse at their convenience and to share with other employees at the worksite.

In this project, you will create an electronic portfolio for Benito Kovich, a student seeking a job in the fields of management or information systems. This presentation highlights his skills and experiences by including clip art, a photoraph, and a video clip. Benito can customize this portfolio for each interview by using Visual Basic for Applications, a programming language that extends PowerPoint's capabilities.

Recruiters state that interviewees who display eye-catching, professional looking electronic portfolios often have a definite edge over the typical interviewee. By applying the concepts you learn in this project, carefully developing your portfolio, and planning for the interview, you will be on your way to interviewing success.

Microsoft PowerPoint 2000

Using Visual Basic for Applications (VBA) with PowerPoint

PROJECT
6

CASE PERSPECTIVE

When students apply for a job and then receive an invitation to interview, they focus their efforts on presenting themselves in the best light.

Some candidates develop electronic career portfolios using PowerPoint to show on notebook computers during the interviews. Your neighbor, Benito Kovich, has asked you to help him develop a slide show for several interviews. Benito is majoring in management and minoring in information technology, and he has secured job interviews in both fields. He wants to tailor his slide show for each prospective employer.

You examine the information Benito wants to emphasize in the slide show and decide the best method for him to customize each presentation is to use a form you develop using Visual Basic for Applications. Benito's responses on the form will create a unique slide show for each interview. You also will create a toolbar and add buttons and then add a command to the File menu to simplify the related tasks he must perform: saving the presentation as a Web page, using the Pack and Go Wizard, printing a handout of his slides, and displaying the form.

Introduction

Before a computer can take an action and produce a desired result, it must have a step-by-step description of the task to be accomplished. This series of precise instructions is called a **procedure,** which also is called a **program** or **code.** The process of writing a procedure is called **computer programming.** Every PowerPoint command on a menu and button on a toolbar has a corresponding procedure that executes when you click the command or button. When the computer **executes** a procedure, it carries out the step-by-step instructions. In a Windows environment, the instructions associated with a task are executed when an **event** takes place, such as clicking a button, an option button, or a check box.

Because a command or button does not exist for every possible task, Microsoft has included a powerful programming language called **Visual Basic for Applications (VBA).** This language allows you to customize and extend PowerPoint's capabilities.

In this project, you will learn how create macros using a code generator called a **macro recorder.** A **macro** is a procedure composed of VBA code that automates multi-step tasks. By simply executing a macro, the user can perform tasks that would otherwise require many keystrokes. You also will add buttons to toolbars. You will add a command to a menu and associate it with a print macro. Finally, you will learn the basics of VBA.

The slide show you create in this project will help Benito Kovich in his job search. As he goes to each interview, he will open the BK Career Portfolio file on his notebook computer and then open a form. He will make selections on the form to indicate whether the position is in management or information systems, the company name, the type of clip art, and slide order. He then can decide to run the presentation immediately or later. VBA will create the presentation corresponding to his selections. Two possible slide shows are shown in Figures 6-1a through 6-1h.

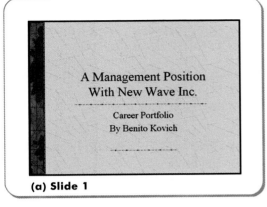

(a) Slide 1

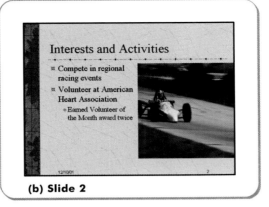

(b) Slide 2

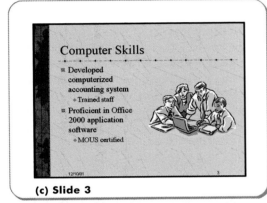

(c) Slide 3

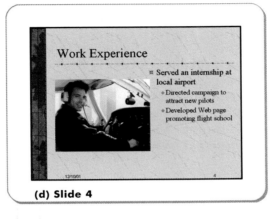

(d) Slide 4

Slide Presentation No. 1

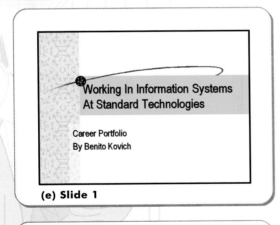

(e) Slide 1

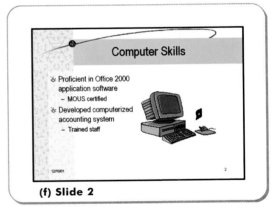

(f) Slide 2

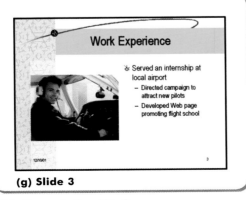

(g) Slide 3

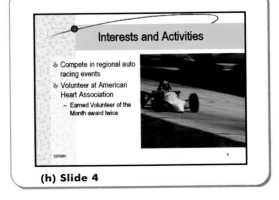

(h) Slide 4

Slide Presentation No. 2

FIGURE 6-1

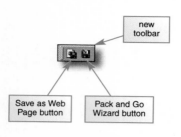

FIGURE 6-2

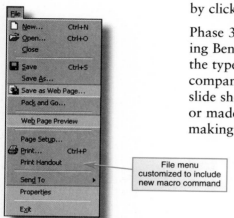

FIGURE 6-3

Project Six — Creating an Electronic Portfolio

When you meet with Benito, you identify the following project requirements for his electronic portfolio:

Needs: The portfolio requires an easy-to-use interface. This interface will be implemented in three phases:

Phase 1 – Create a toolbar and add two buttons (Save as Web Page and Pack and Go) that normally do not display on any toolbar (Figure 6-2).

Phase 2 – Use the macro recorder to create a macro that prints handouts that display four slides per page vertically using the Pure black and white option. Assign the macro to a command on the File menu (Figure 6-3) so Benito can execute the macro by clicking the command.

Phase 3 – Add a button to the toolbar created in Phase 1 that displays a form allowing Benito to design his custom presentation (Figure 6-4). This form lets Benito select the type of position for which he is applying (management or computer), enter the company name, select clip art, change the slide order, and select whether to run the slide show immediately or later. The VBA code verifies that Benito has entered data or made a choice in each part of the form. If he has not, he is prompted to continue making choices on the form.

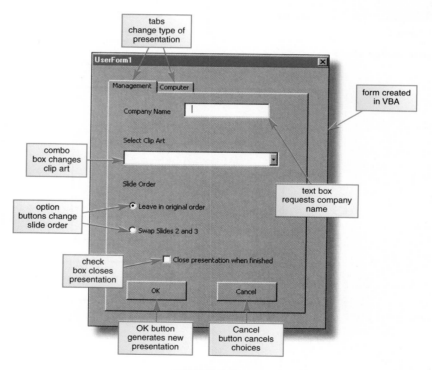

FIGURE 6-4

Source of Data: While meeting with Benito, you develop a preliminary presentation that he will complete by making appropriate selections on a form. This slide show shown in Figures 6-5a through 6-5d is available to you on the Data Disk under the file name BK Career Portfolio.

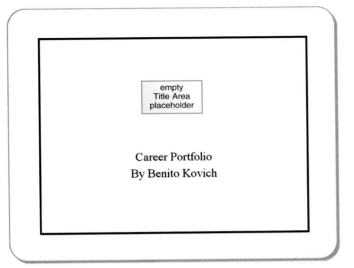

(a) Slide 1

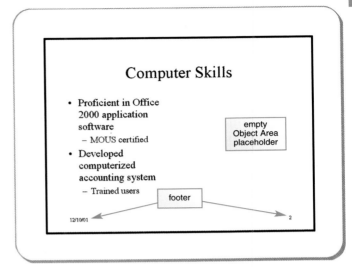

(b) Slide 2

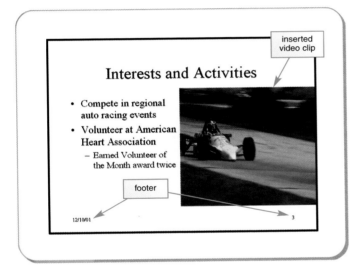

(c) Slide 3

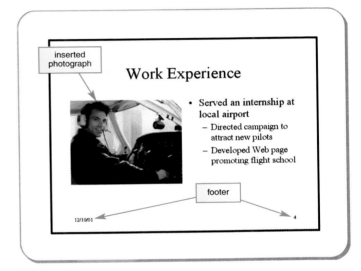

(d) Slide 4

FIGURE 6-5

Opening a Presentation and Saving it with a New File Name

To begin, start PowerPoint and open the BK Career Portfolio file on the Data Disk. Then reset the toolbars and menus so they display exactly as shown in this book. Perform the following steps.

TO OPEN A PRESENTATION AND SAVE IT WITH A NEW FILE NAME

1 Insert your Data Disk into Drive A. See the inside back cover of this book for directions for downloading the Data Disk.

2 Click the Start button on the taskbar and then click Open Office Document.

3 When the Open Office Document dialog box displays, click the Look in box arrow and then click 3½ Floppy (A:). Double-click BK Career Portfolio in the list.

4 When the BK Career Portfolio presentation displays, click View on the menu bar, click Toolbars, and then click Customize.

(5) When the Customize dialog box displays, click the Options tab, make sure the top three check boxes in the Personalized Menus and Toolbars area have check marks, click the Reset my usage data button, and then click the Yes button.

(6) Click the Toolbars tab. Click Standard in the toolbars list, click the Reset button, and then click the OK button. Click Formatting, click the Reset button, and then click the OK button. Click Drawing, click the Reset button, and then click the OK button. Click Menu Bar, click the Reset button, and then click the OK button. Click the Close button.

(7) Click File on the menu bar and then click Save As. Type `Electronic Portfolio` in the File name text box.

(8) Click the Save button in the Save As dialog box.

The presentation is saved on the floppy disk in drive A with the file name, Electronic Portfolio (Figure 6-6).

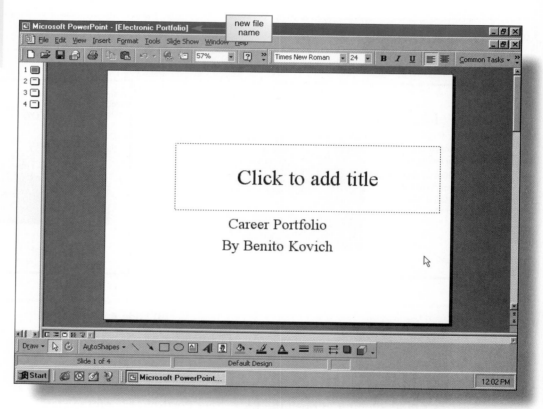

FIGURE 6-6

The Electronic Portfolio presentation is composed of four slides (Figure 6-5 on the previous page). The first is a title slide with an empty Title Area placeholder and Benito's identifying information in the Object Area placeholder. Benito will enter the company name in the Visual Basic form you will create in Phase 3 of this project, and this name will be inserted automatically in the Title Area placeholder.

Slide 2 describes Benito's computer expertise, and it uses the Text & Clip Art AutoLayout. The Object Area placeholder is empty, but it will contain one of four possible clip art files based on the selection Benito makes in the Visual Basic form. If he wants the presentation to have an information technology theme, he will select either an airplane dropping floppy diskettes or an animated computer. If he wants a management theme, he will select either clip art of people having a discussion or an animated man making a presentation.

Slide 3 highlights Benito's interests and activities. He actively competes in auto races, and you accompanied him to a local racecourse to shoot some video to insert in this presentation. In addition, Benito spends some of his spare time volunteering at the local American Heart Association. He wants to emphasize this activity and the awards he received for his efforts.

Slide 4 emphasizes Benito's work experience at the local airport. One of the most valuable experiences in his college career has been this internship, so he wants potential employers to understand his accomplishments during this full-year project. One of his activities was developing an advertising campaign to attract regional pilots to the airport to rent hangar space and buy fuel for their planes. Another achievement was developing a Web page to encourage students to take flying lessons. Benito supplied you with a photo of himself at the controls of one of the airplanes. You scanned this photo to create a digitized file that you inserted in the presentation.

Slides 2, 3, and 4 have a footer that contains the current date and the slide number. In addition, as seen in Figure 6-7, they use the Split Horizontal Out slide transition and the Split Vertical In preset animation effect. Slide 1 automatically advances in 10 seconds or when you click the mouse, and Slides 2, 3, and 4 advance 15 seconds after they display or when you click the mouse.

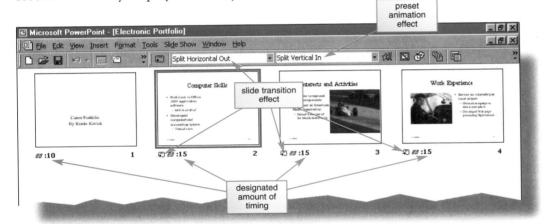

FIGURE 6-7

Phase 1 — Creating a Toolbar and Adding Two Buttons

The first phase of this project creates a toolbar that displays in the lower-right corner of the screen beside the Drawing toolbar. Although PowerPoint provides more than a dozen toolbars for a variety of purposes, a custom toolbar allows you to display the buttons specific to your needs.

Creating and Customizing a Toolbar

One of the buttons you will add to the custom toolbar is the Save as Web Page button. Although a user can save a file as a Web page by clicking the Save as Web Page command on the File menu, he also can click a button when he wants to make his presentation available for potential employers to view on the Internet. The second button you will add to the custom toolbar in this phase of the project will launch the Pack and Go Wizard. A user can click this button when he wants to compress his presentation files onto floppy disks. He then can transport his presentation on floppy disks to show on a computer at the interviewing site, rather than viewing

More *About*

Renaming ScreenTips

Once you have added a button to a toolbar, you can change its ScreenTip. To make this change, click Customize on the Tools menu, right-click the button, type the new name in the Name text box, and then press the ENTER key. You will see the name change when you view the ScreenTip.

it on his notebook computer. You will learn more about using the Pack and Go Wizard in the Web Feature that follows this project.

You can customize toolbars and menus by adding buttons and commands, deleting buttons and commands, and changing the function of buttons and commands. Once you add a button to a toolbar or a command to a menu, you can assign a macro to the button or command. You customize a toolbar or menu by invoking the **Customize command** on the Tools menu. The key to understanding how to customize a toolbar or menu is to recognize that when you have the Customize dialog box open, PowerPoint's toolbars and menus are in Edit mode. Edit mode allows you to modify the toolbars and menus.

Perform the following steps to create a custom toolbar and add two buttons.

Steps **To Create a Custom Toolbar and Add Two Buttons**

1 **Click Tools on the menu bar and then point to Customize.**

The Tools menu displays (Figure 6-8).

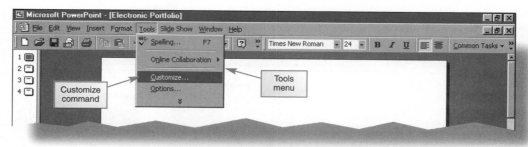

FIGURE 6-8

2 **Click Customize. When the Customize dialog box displays, if necessary, click the Toolbars tab, and then point to the New button.**

The Toolbars sheet in the Customize dialog displays as shown in Figure 6-9. The entire Standard and Formatting toolbars display.

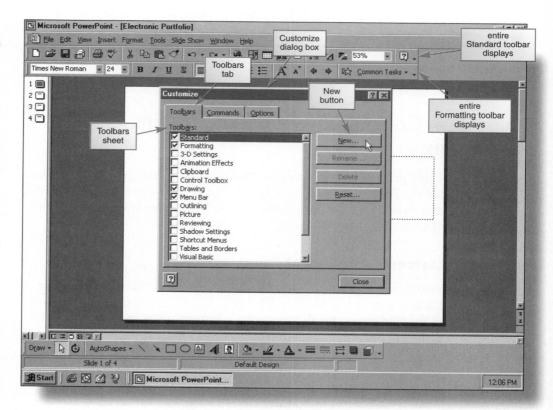

FIGURE 6-9

③ **Click the New button. When the New Toolbar dialog box displays, type** Using Presentation **in the Toolbar name text box and then point to the OK button (Figure 6-10).**

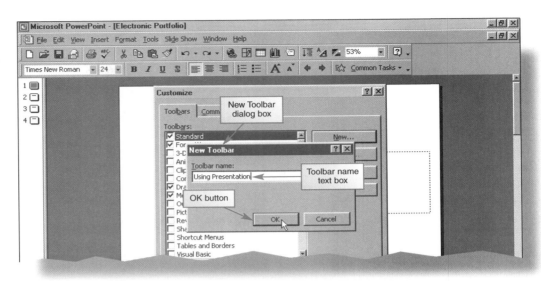

FIGURE 6-10

④ **Click the OK button. Click the toolbar and drag it to the bottom-right corner of the screen beside the Drawing toolbar.**

The Using Presentation toolbar displays in the desired location (Figure 6-11). The toolbar title does not display.

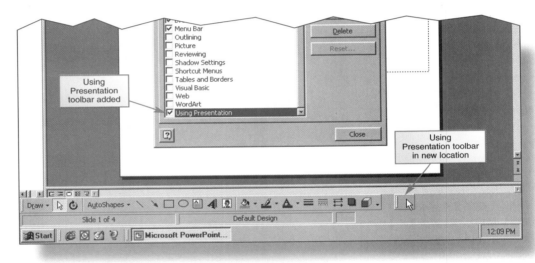

FIGURE 6-11

⑤ **Click the Commands tab in the Customize dialog box. Scroll down in the Commands list and then click Save as Web Page.**

You can select buttons from several categories, and each category has a variety of commands (Figure 6-12). File is the default category. Some commands have images associated with them.

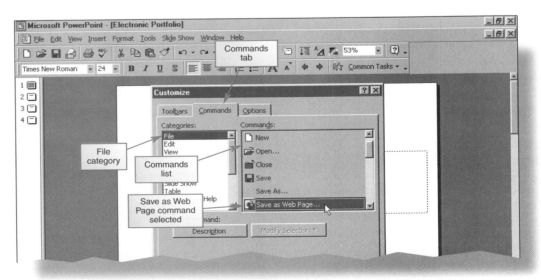

FIGURE 6-12

6 Drag the Save as Web Page command from the Commands list to the new Using Presentation toolbar.

The Save as Web Page button displays with an image on the Using Presentation toolbar (Figure 6-13). The heavy border surrounding the button indicates PowerPoint is in Edit mode.

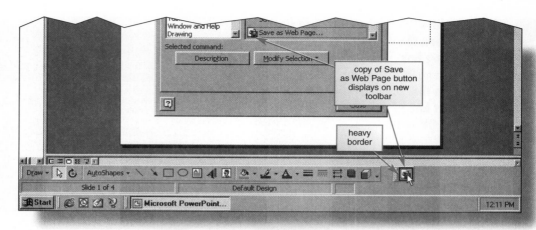

FIGURE 6-13

7 Scroll down in the Commands list and then click Pack and Go. Drag the Pack and Go command from the Commands list to the right of the Save as Web Page button on the Using Presentation toolbar. Point to the Modify Selection menu button.

The Pack and Go button displays on the Using Presentation toolbar with its name displaying on the face of the button (Figure 6-14). A heavy border surrounds the button, indicating that PowerPoint is in Edit mode.

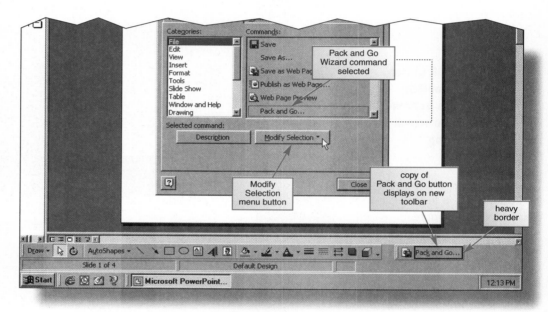

FIGURE 6-14

8 Click the Modify Selection menu button and then point to Change Button Image. When the Change Button Image palette displays, point to the button with a blue arrow pointing toward a floppy disk (row 1, column 6).

PowerPoint displays a palette of button images from which to choose (Figure 6-15).

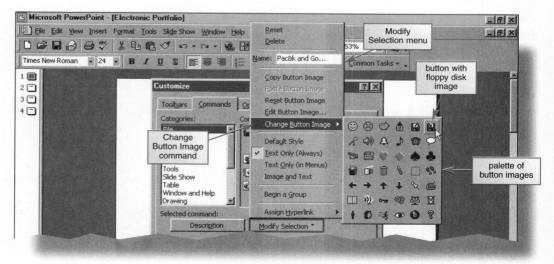

FIGURE 6-15

9 **Click the button with the floppy disk image. Point to the Modify Selection menu button.**

The Pack and Go button displays on the toolbar with the floppy disk image and the text, Pack and Go (Figure 6-16).

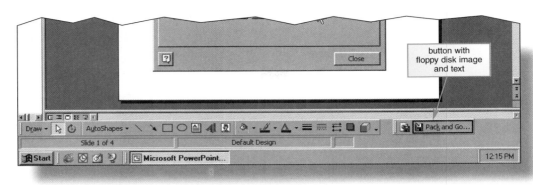

FIGURE 6-16

10 **Click the Modify Selection menu button and then point to Default Style.**

The default style includes only the image, not text (Figure 6-17).

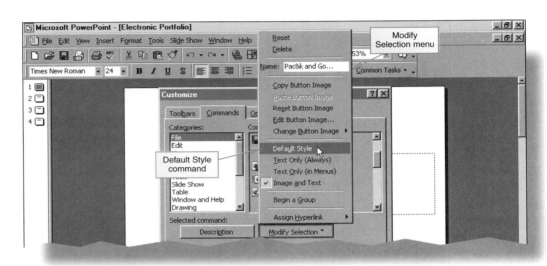

FIGURE 6-17

11 **Click Default Style. Point to the Close button.**

The Pack and Go button image displays with the floppy disk only (Figure 6-18).

12 **Click the Close button.**

PowerPoint exits Edit mode.

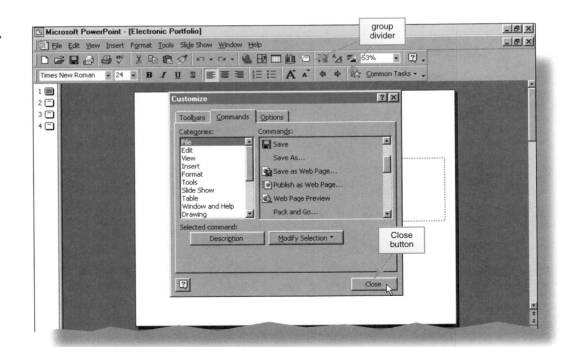

FIGURE 6-18

The previous steps illustrate how a toolbar is created easily and how buttons are added. PowerPoint includes a complete repertoire of commands for editing buttons on a toolbar as shown on the Modify Selection menu in Figure 6-17. Table 6-1 briefly describes each of the commands on this menu.

Table 6-1 Summary of Commands on the Modify Selection Menu	
COMMAND	DESCRIPTION
Reset	Changes the image on the selected button to the original image and disassociates the macro with the button
Delete	Deletes the selected button
Name box	Changes the ScreenTip for a button and changes the command name for a command on a menu
Copy Button Image	Copies the button image to Office Clipboard
Paste Button Image	Pastes the button image on Office Clipboard onto selected button
Reset Button Image	Changes the button image back to the original image
Edit Button Image	Allows you to edit the button image
Change Button Image	Allows you to choose a new button image
Default Style; Text Only (Always); Text Only (in Menus); Image and Text	Allows you to choose one of the four styles to indicate how the button should display
Begin a Group	Groups buttons by drawing a vertical line (divider) on the toolbar (see the group dividing lines in Figure 6-18)
Assign Hyperlink	Assigns a hyperlink to a Web page or document
Assign Macro	Assigns a macro to the button

You can add as many buttons as you want to a toolbar. You also can change any button's function. For example, when in edit mode with the Customize dialog box displaying, you can right-click the Save button on the Standard toolbar and assign it a macro or hyperlink. The next time you click the Save button, the macro will execute or PowerPoint will launch the application associated with the hyperlink, rather than save the presentation.

You reset the toolbars to their installation default by clicking the Toolbars tab in the Customize dialog box, selecting the toolbar in the Toolbars list, and clicking the Reset button. Because it is so easy to change the buttons on a toolbar, each project in this book begins by resetting the toolbars.

Saving the Presentation

The changes to Phase 1 of the presentation are complete. Perform the following step to save the presentation before recording a macro in Phase 2 of this project.

TO SAVE A PRESENTATION

 Click the Save button on the Standard toolbar.

PowerPoint saves the presentation by saving the changes made to the presentation since the last save.

Phase 2 — Recording a Macro and Assigning It to a Menu Command

The second phase of the project creates a macro to print a handout displaying four slides per page vertically using the Pure black and white option. The default PowerPoint print setting is Slides, with one slide printing on each sheet of paper. When the Print what setting is changed to handouts, the default setting is six slides per page in a horizontal order, meaning Slides 1 and 2 display at the top of the page, and Slides 3 and 4 display below. The user can distribute a one-page handout, shown in Figure 6-19, of the four slides in the presentation printed using the Pure black and white option and displayed vertically, meaning Slides 1 and 3 display on the top, and Slides 2 and 4 display below.

The planned macro will change the output from slides to handouts and will change the slide order on the handout from horizontal to vertical. The handout will print using the Pure black and white option instead of grayscale or other default setting on your system, so all shades of gray will change to either black or white. The macro then will reset the Print dialog box to its original settings.

With the macro, a user can print a one-page handout by executing a single command, rather than performing the several steps otherwise required. He can click the Print button on the Standard toolbar and change the settings in the Print dialog box to print these handouts, or he can execute the macro to print the handout. Once the macro is created, it will be assigned to a command on the File menu.

Recording a Macro

PowerPoint has a macro recorder that creates a macro automatically based on a series of actions you perform while it is recording. Like a tape recorder, the macro recorder records everything you do to a presentation over a period of time. The macro recorder can be turned on, during which time it records your activities, and then turned off to stop the recording. Once the macro is recorded, it can be **played back** or **executed** as often as you want.

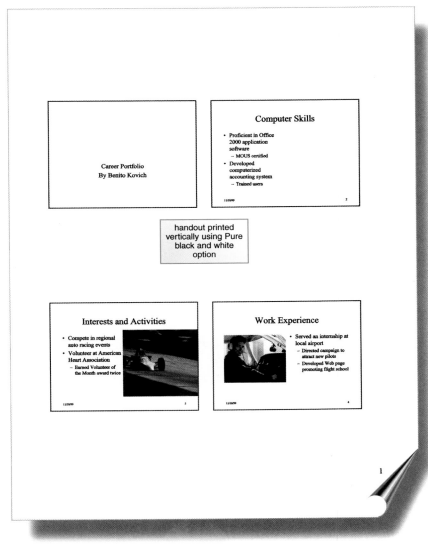

FIGURE 6-19

More About

Deleting Macros

Once you create a macro, you may decide you no longer need these steps. To delete a Macro, point to Macro on the Tools menu and then click Macros. Click the name of the macro in the Macro name box that you want to delete. Then click the Delete button.

It is easy to create a macro. All you have to do is turn on the macro recorder and carry out these steps:

1. Start the macro recorder.
2. Change the output settings from slides to handouts, the slides per page from six to four, the slide order on the handout from horizontal to vertical, and the print option from Grayscale (or default print setting on your computer) to Pure black and white.
3. Print the handout.
4. Restore the output settings from four slides per page to six, from vertical to horizontal slide order, from handouts to slides, and from Pure black and white to Grayscale (or the default print setting on your computer).
5. Stop the macro recorder.

What is impressive about the macro recorder is that you actually step through the task as you create the macro. You will see exactly what the macro will do before you use it.

When you first create the macro, you must name it. The name is used to reference the macro when you want to execute it. The name PrintHandout will be used for the macro. **Macro names** can be up to 255 characters long; they can contain numbers, letters, and underscores; they cannot contain spaces and other punctuation. Perform the following steps to record the macro.

 Steps To Record a Macro to Print Handouts in Vertical Slide Order in Pure Black and White

1 **Click Tools on the menu bar, point to Macro, and then point to Record New Macro on the Macro submenu.**

The Tools menu and Macro submenu display (Figure 6-20).

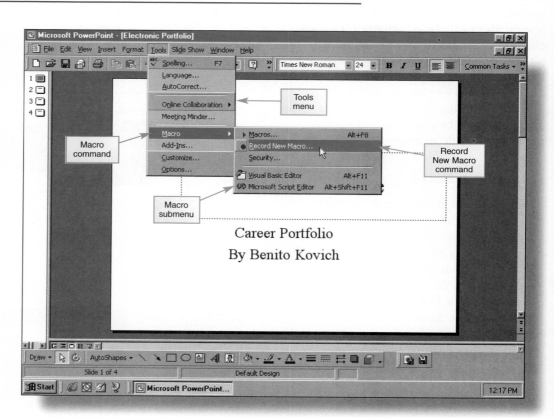

FIGURE 6-20

2 **Click Record New Macro. When the Record Macro dialog box displays, type** PrintHandout **in the Macro name text box. Type** Macro prints pure black and white handouts in vertical slide order **in the Description text box. Make sure the Store macro in box displays Electronic Portfolio. Point to the OK button.**

The Record Macro dialog box displays as shown in Figure 6-21.

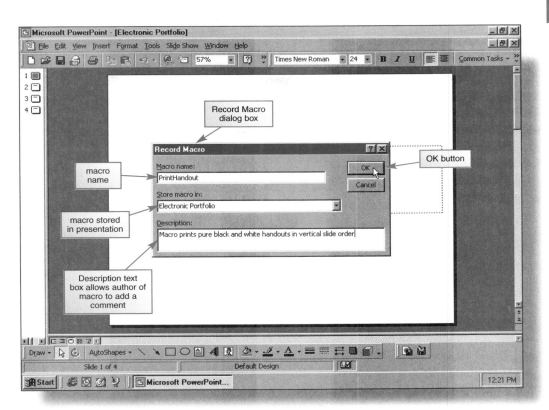

FIGURE 6-21

3 **Click the OK button. Click File on the menu bar and then point to Print.**

The Stop Recording toolbar and the File menu display (Figure 6-22). Any task you perform after the Stop Recording toolbar displays will be part of the macro. When you are finished recording the macro, you will click the Stop Recording button on the Stop Recording toolbar to end the recording.

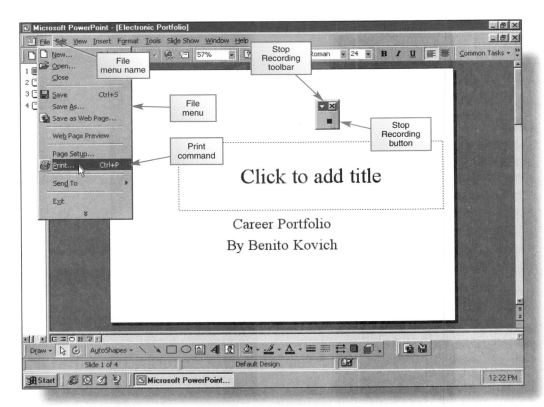

FIGURE 6-22

④ Click Print. When the Print dialog box displays, click the Print what box arrow and click Handouts, click the Slides per page box arrow in the Handouts area and click 4, click Vertical order in the Handouts area, click Pure black and white, and then point to the OK button.

The Print dialog box displays as shown in Figure 6-23.

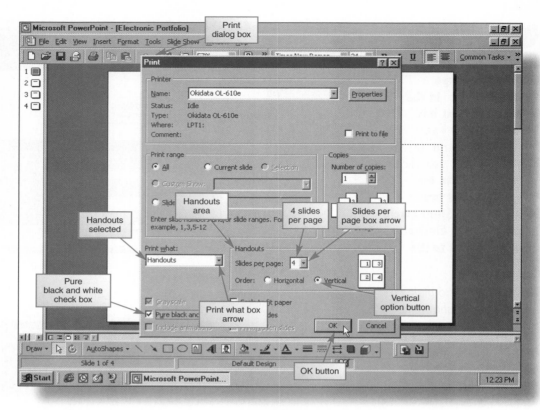

FIGURE 6-23

⑤ Click the OK button. Click File on the menu bar and then click Print. When the Print dialog box displays, click Pure black and white, click the Slides per page box arrow in the Handouts area and click 6, click Horizontal order in the Handouts area, click the Print what box arrow and click Slides, and then point to the OK button.

The Print dialog box displays as shown in Figure 6-24. The Pure black and white check box is no longer checked, restoring your computer to its default print setting. The printout resembles the handout shown in Figure 6-19 on page PP 6.15.

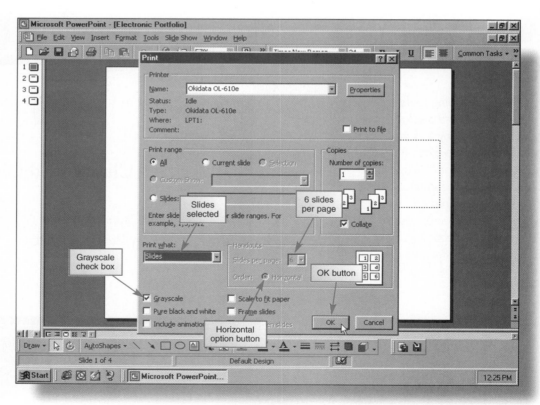

FIGURE 6-24

6 **Click the OK button. Point to the Stop Recording button.**

The four slides in the presentation print in the Pure black and white or your computer's default print option (Figure 6-25).

7 **Click the Stop Recording button.**

PowerPoint stops recording the printing activities and hides the Stop Recording toolbar.

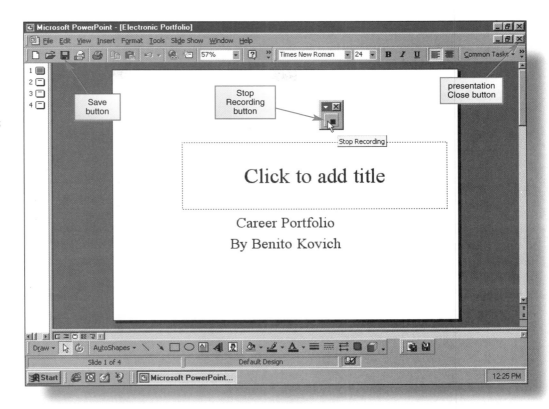

FIGURE 6-25

If you recorded the wrong actions, delete the macro and record it again. You delete a macro by clicking Tools on the menu bar, pointing to Macro on the Tools menu, and then clicking Macros on the Macro submenu. When the Macro dialog box displays, click the name of the macro (PrintHandout), and then click the Delete button. Then record the macro again.

Customizing a Menu

As you use PowerPoint to create presentations and print handouts, you may find yourself repeating many steps. You may find it convenient to simplify these repetitive processes by adding a button to a toolbar or a command to a menu that you can click to perform these tasks automatically. PowerPoint allows you to add commands to a button or to a menu. The steps on the next page show how to add a command to the File menu to execute the PrintHandout macro.

Other Ways

1. Click Record Macro button on Visual Basic toolbar
2. Press ALT+T, press M, press R

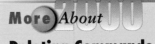

More About

Deleting Commands

If you no longer need a command you added to a menu, you can delete this command. To perform this action, click Customize on the Tools menu, click the menu that contains the command you want to delete, and then drag the desired command off the menu.

Steps **To Add a Command to a Menu, Assign the Command to a Macro, and Invoke the Command**

---

1 **Click Tools on the menu bar and then click Customize. When the Customize dialog box opens, if necessary, click the Commands tab. Scroll down in the Categories box and then click Macros. Click File on the menu bar to display the File menu.**

The Customize dialog box and File menu display as shown in Figure 6-26.

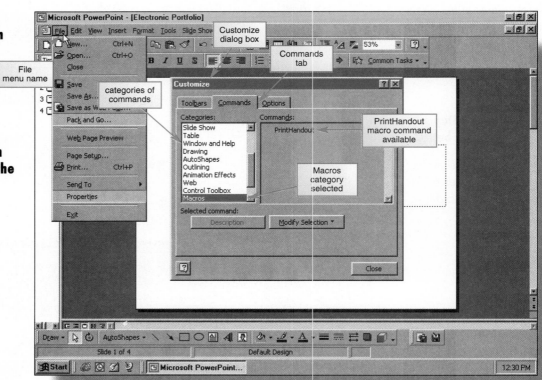

FIGURE 6-26

2 **Drag the PrintHandout entry from the Commands list in the Customize dialog box immediately below the Print command on the File menu.**

PowerPoint adds PrintHandout to the File menu (Figure 6-27). A heavy border surrounds PrintHandout on the File menu, indicating it is in the edit mode.

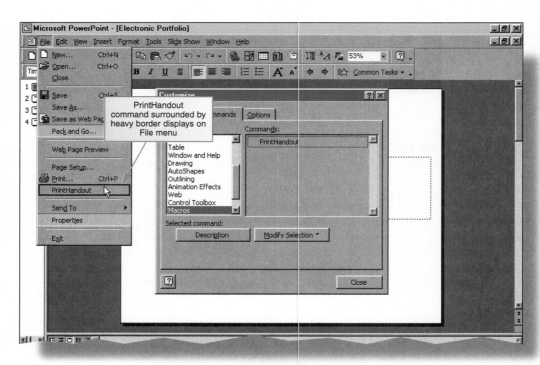

FIGURE 6-27

3 Right-click **PrintHandout in the File menu and then click the Name text box on the shortcut menu. Type** Print Handout **as the new name of this command. Point to the Close button at the bottom of the Customize dialog box.**

The shortcut menu displays (Figure 6-28).

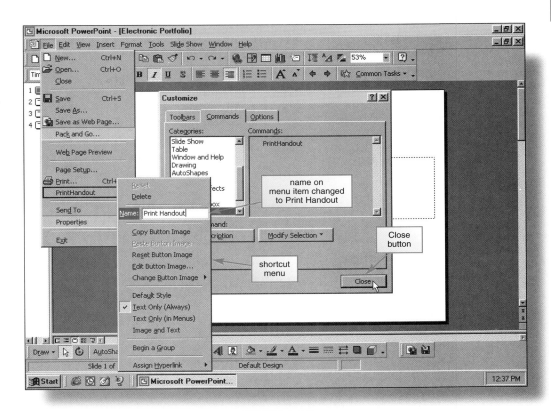

FIGURE 6-28

4 Click the Close **button. Click File on the menu bar and then point to Print Handout.**

PowerPoint exits the edit mode. The File menu displays with the new command, Print Handout, on the menu (Figure 6-29).

5 Click Print Handout **on the File menu.**

After several seconds, the handout prints as shown in Figure 6-19 on page PP 6.15.

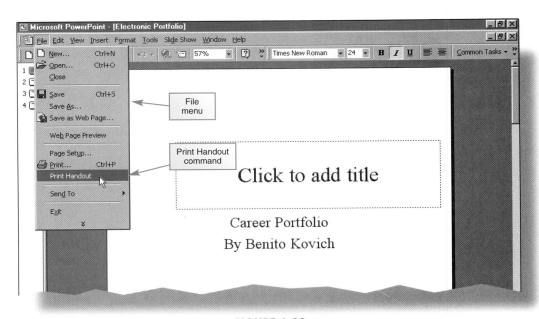

FIGURE 6-29

Other Ways

1. Right-click toolbar, click Customize on shortcut menu, click Commands tab

2. On View menu point to Toolbars, click Customize on Toolbars submenu, click Commands tab

You have the same customization capabilities with menus as you do with toolbars. All of the commands described in Table 6-1 on page PP 6.14 apply to menus as well. Any command specific to buttons pertains to editing the button on the left side of a command on a menu.

An alternative to adding a command to a menu is to add a new menu name to the menu bar and add commands to its menu. You can add a new menu name to the menu bar by selecting New Menu in the Categories list of the Customize dialog box and dragging New Menu from the Commands list to the menu bar.

Now that you have added the toolbar and macro to the presentation, you want to save the file and then close the presentation. Perform the following steps.

TO SAVE THE PRESENTATION AND CLOSE THE PRESENTATION

 Click the Save button on the Standard toolbar.

 Click the presentation's Close button on the right side of the menu bar to close the presentation and leave PowerPoint open.

PowerPoint saves the Electronic Portfolio presentation on drive A and then closes the presentation.

Opening a Presentation Containing a Macro and Executing the Macro

A **computer virus** is a potentially damaging computer program designed to affect your computer negatively by infecting it and altering the way it works without your knowledge or permission. Currently, more than 13,000 known computer viruses exist, and an estimated six new viruses are discovered each day. The increased use of networks, the Internet, and e-mail has accelerated the spread of computer viruses.

To combat this evil, most computer users run antivirus programs that search for viruses and destroy them before they ever have a chance to infect the computer. Macros are a known carrier of viruses because people easily can add code to them. For this reason, each time you open a presentation with a macro associated with it, PowerPoint displays a Microsoft PowerPoint dialog box warning that a macro is attached and that macros can contain viruses. Table 6-2 summarizes the buttons users can use to continue the process of opening a presentation with macros.

Table 6-2	Buttons in the Microsoft PowerPoint Dialog Box When Opening a Presentation with Macros
BUTTONS	**DESCRIPTION**
Disable Macros	Macros are unavailable to the user
Enable Macros	Macros are available to the user to execute
More Info	Opens the Microsoft PowerPoint Help window and displays information on viruses and macros

If you are confident of the source (author) of the presentation and macros, click the Enable Macros button. If you are uncertain about the reliability of the source, then click the Disable Macros button. For more information on this topic, click the More Info button.

The following steps open the Electronic Portfolio presentation to illustrate the Microsoft PowerPoint dialog box that displays when a presentation contains a macro. The steps then show how to execute the recorded macro, PrintHandout.

To Open a Presentation with a Macro and Execute the Macro

1 **With PowerPoint active, click File on the menu bar and then click Open. When the Open dialog box displays, click the Look in box arrow, and if necessary click 3½ Floppy (A:). Double-click the file name Electronic Portfolio. Point to the Enable Macros button.**

PowerPoint displays the dialog box shown in Figure 6-30.

2 **Click the Enable Macros button. When Slide 1 of the Electronic Portfolio displays, click File on the menu bar and then click Print Handout.**

PowerPoint opens the Electronic Portfolio presentation, executes the macro, and then prints the handout and the four slides shown in Figures 6-5 and 6-19 on pages PP 6.7 and PP 6.15.

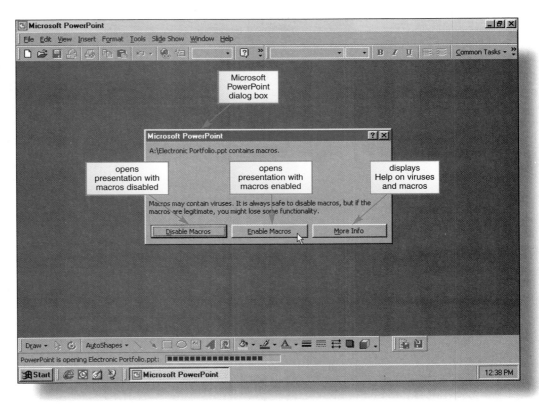

FIGURE 6-30

If you are running antivirus software, you may want to turn off the security warning shown in Figure 6-30. You can turn off the security warning by clicking Tools on the menu bar, pointing to Macro, and then clicking Security on the Macro submenu. When the Security dialog box displays, click the Low button. Then the next time you open a workbook with an attached macro, PowerPoint will open the workbook immediately, rather than display the dialog box shown in Figure 6-30.

Viewing a Macro's VBA Code

As described earlier, a macro is composed of VBA code, which is created automatically by the macro recorder. You can view the VBA code through the Visual Basic Editor. The **Visual Basic Editor** is used by all Office applications to enter, modify, and view VBA code.

Other Ways

1. Click Run Macro button on Visual Basic toolbar
2. On Tools menu point to Macro, click Macros on Macro submenu, double-click macro name
3. Press ALT+F8, double-click macro name

To View a Macro's VBA Code

1 **Click Tools on the menu bar. Point to Macro on the Tools menu and then point to Macros on the Macro submenu.**

The Tools menu and Macro submenu display (Figure 6-31).

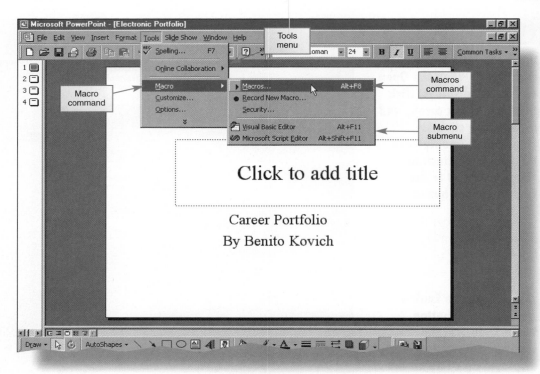

FIGURE 6-31

2 **Click Macros. When the Macro dialog box displays, if necessary click PrintHandout in the list, and then point to the Edit button.**

The Macro dialog box displays as shown in Figure 6-32.

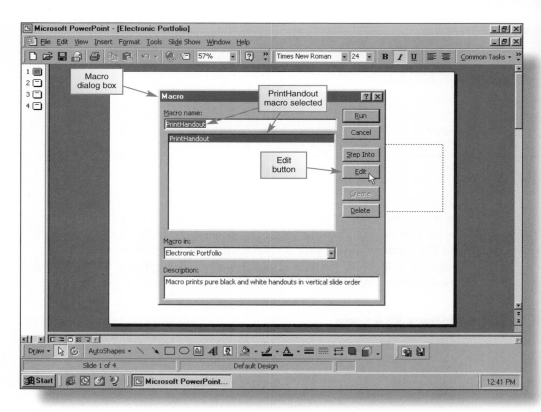

FIGURE 6-32

③ Click the Edit button.

The Visual Basic Editor starts and displays the VBA code in the macro PrintHandout (Figure 6-33).

④ Scroll through the VBA code. When you are finished, click the Close button on the right side of the title bar.

The Visual Basic Editor closes and Slide 1 in the Electronic Portfolio presentation displays.

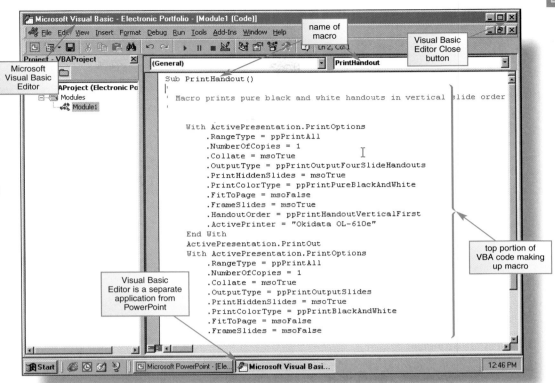

FIGURE 6-33

This set of instructions, beginning with line 1 in Figure 6-33 and continuing sequentially to the last line, executes when you invoke the macro. By scrolling through the VBA code, you can see that the macro recorder generates a lot of instructions. In this case 32 lines of code are generated to print the handout vertically using the Pure black and white option.

Phase 3 — Creating a Form to Customize the Presentation

Now that you have added a toolbar and buttons and have recorded a macro to print handouts, you are ready to develop a form that allows the user to design custom presentations for each of his interviews. This form is called a **user interface** because it allows the user to input data, and then it displays results. This user interface and the step-by-step procedure for its implementation are called an **application**. Thus, Microsoft created the name Visual Basic for Applications (VBA) for its programming language used to customize PowerPoint and other Office 2000 programs.

Applications are built using the three-step process shown in Figure 6-34: (1) create the user interface; (2) set the control properties; and (3) write the VBA code.

Other Ways

1. Click Visual Basic Editor button on Visual Basic toolbar.

More About

VBA

Microsoft publishes a comprehensive book that describes how to write code using Visual Basic for Applications. Microsoft Office 2000/Visual Basic Programmer's Guide teaches readers how to customize and adapt tools for specific needs, including how to create custom commands, menus, dialog boxes, messages, and buttons, as well as how to show custom Help for all these elements. To learn more about this book, visit the PowerPoint 2000 Project 6 More About page (www.scsite.com/pp2000/more.htm) and click Microsoft Press.

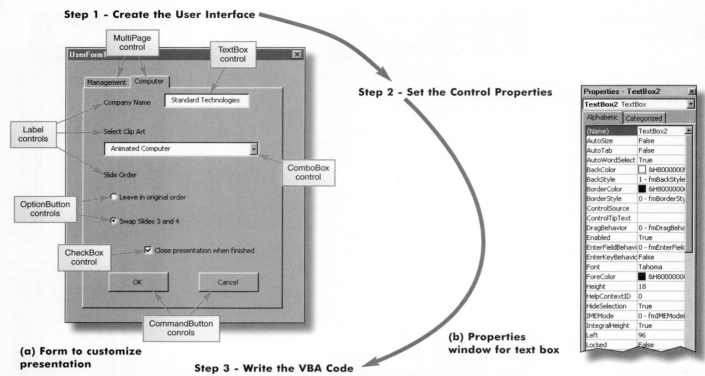

Step 1 - Create the User Interface

MultiPage control

TextBox control

Step 2 - Set the Control Properties

Label controls

ComboBox control

OptionButton controls

CheckBox control

CommandButton conrols

(a) Form to customize presentation

(b) Properties window for text box

Step 3 - Write the VBA Code

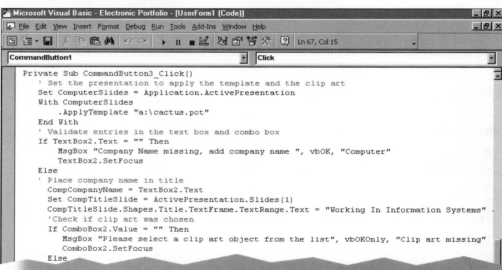

```
Private Sub CommandButton3_Click()
    ' Set the presentation to apply the template and the clip art
    Set ComputerSlides = Application.ActivePresentation
    With ComputerSlides
        .ApplyTemplate "a:\cactus.pot"
    End With
    ' Validate entries in the text box and combo box
    If TextBox2.Text = "" Then
        MsgBox "Company Name missing, add company name ", vbOK, "Computer"
        TextBox2.SetFocus
    Else
    ' Place company name in title
        CompCompanyName = TextBox2.Text
        Set CompTitleSlide = ActivePresentation.Slides(1)
        CompTitleSlide.Shapes.Title.TextFrame.TextRange.Text = "Working In Information Systems"
        'Check if clip art was chosen
        If ComboBox2.Value = "" Then
            MsgBox "Please select a clip art object from the list", vbOKOnly, "Clip art missing"
            ComboBox2.SetFocus
        Else
```

(c) VBA code associated with text box

FIGURE 6-34

Step 1 – Create the User Interface

The form shown Figure 6-34a presents the application's user interface. This interface allows the user to specify which information should be in the presentation and to cancel the procedure if required. The form contains controls and two command buttons. At the top of the form are two tabs: one for a management position, and the other for a computer-based job in the information systems field. If the user clicks the Management tab, the user will select options on a sheet pertaining to a slide show focusing on management skills. If the user clicks the Computer tab, the user will select options on another sheet regarding a computer presentation.

The first element on both sheets is a text box control, where the user will enter the name of the company where the user is interviewing. Next is the combo box containing the description of two clip art files – one animated, and one not animated. Below the clip art combo box is a Slide Order area where the user can click an option button to leave the slides in their original order or to switch the order to emphasize a specific strength. The Close presentation when finished check box allows the user to close the custom presentation after the user has completed making selections on the user form. If the user does not select this check box, the VBA procedure will assemble the custom slide show automatically and display it on his screen. The two command buttons at the bottom of the form – the OK button and the Cancel button – are standard buttons found on most forms. The OK button executes the VBA procedure; the Cancel button prevents the VBA code from executing. When the user clicks either button, the procedure hides the user form and unloads it from memory.

Creating the interface consists of sizing and locating the form and then adding each of the controls to the form and adjusting their sizes and positions. When you begin to create a user interface, you position the controls as close as you can to their final locations on the form, and then after setting the properties you finalize their positions. When you perform the following steps, therefore, do not attempt to position the controls exactly in the locations shown in Figure 6-34a.

The Standard toolbar (Figure 6-35) displays when you use VBA. Alternately, you can right-click a toolbar and then click Standard on the shortcut menu to display it.

> **More About**
>
> **Docking Toolbars**
> A toolbar becomes docked when you drag it to the edge of a program window. When you move a docked toolbar, this action may affect the location and size of other toolbars on the same row.

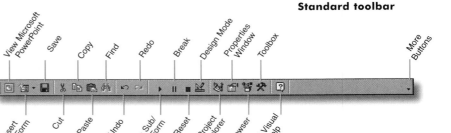

FIGURE 6-35

Opening the Visual Basic IDE and a New Form

Before you begin creating the interface, however, you need to start the **Visual Basic integrated development environment (IDE)**, which contains nine different windows and four toolbars. The windows can be **docked**, or anchored to other windows that are dockable, and the four toolbars can be docked or float in their own windows. Perform the following steps to open the Visual Basic IDE and open a new form.

 ## To Open the Visual Basic IDE and a New Form

1 **With the Electronic Portfolio still open, click Tools on the menu bar, point to Macro, and then point to Visual Basic Editor.**

The Macro submenu displays (Figure 6-36).

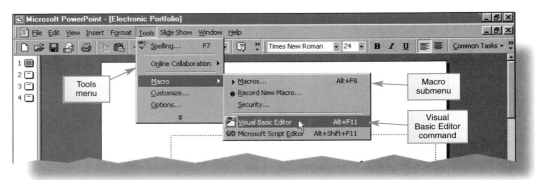

FIGURE 6-36

2 **Click Visual Basic Editor. Click Insert on the menu bar and then point to UserForm.**

The Visual Basic Editor opens and displays a Project Explorer window and a Properties window (Figure 6-37). The Insert menu displays.

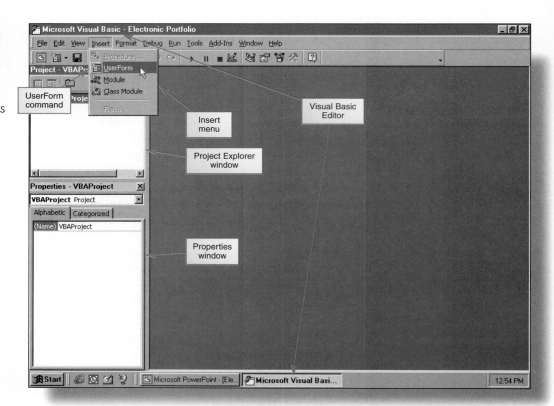

FIGURE 6-37

3 **Click UserForm.**

A new form, UserForm1, opens and the Toolbox displays (Figure 6-38). If the Toolbox does not display, click the Toolbox button.

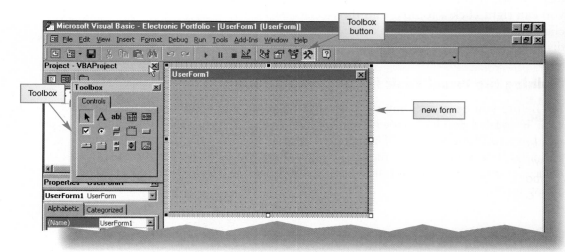

FIGURE 6-38

Changing the Form Size and Arranging the Toolbox Position

You can resize a form in design mode by changing the values of its **Height** and **Width properties** in the Properties window, and you can change a form's location on the screen by changing the values of its **Top** and **Left properties**. You also can resize a form by dragging its borders and change its location by dragging and dropping. Perform the following steps to set the size of the form by dragging its borders and set the location by dragging and dropping.

Steps To Change the Form Size and Arrange the Toolbox Position

1 **Point to the form's lower-right corner. Without releasing the mouse button, drag its corner down and to the right.**

Dragging a corner of the form moves the two adjacent borders at the same time (Figure 6-39). The mouse pointer displays as a two-headed arrow.

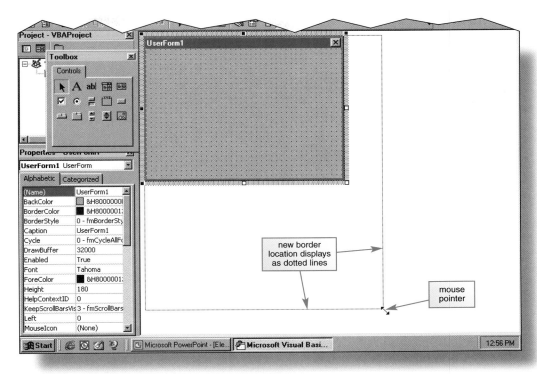

FIGURE 6-39

2 **Release the mouse button. Click Toolbox title bar and drag it to the lower-right corner of the screen.**

The form's size displays as shown in Figure 6-40. The Toolbox displays in the lower-right corner.

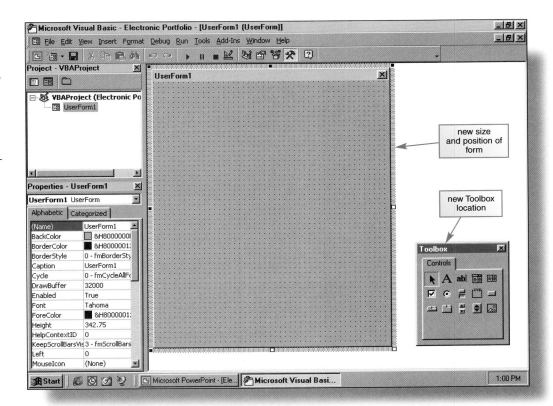

FIGURE 6-40

VBA Sites

Several Web sites collect and organize links to other sites. Some of these sites contain links to Visual Basic sites that offer information on coding, magazines, games, and tips. To view one of these sites, visit the PowerPoint 2000 Project 6 More About page (www.scsite.com/pp2000/more.htm) and click VBA Sites.

Adding Controls

Graphical images, or objects, in Windows applications include buttons, check boxes, tabs, and text boxes. In Visual Basic, these objects are called **controls**. The form will contain seven types of controls (see Figure 6-34a on page PP 6.26). These controls and their functions are described as follows.

Table 6-3   VBA Controls Used in the Form

CONTROL	DESCRIPTION
MultiPage	Creates tabbed forms.
Label	Displays text on a form. At run time, the person using the application cannot change the text on a label, such as the words, Company Name.
TextBox	Displays text on a form, but the person using the application can change its contents at run time. It frequently serves as a way for the user to supply information to the application, such as the specific name of the company where the interview is being held.
ComboBox	Presents a list of choices. When an item is selected from the list, the item displays in a highlighted color.
OptionButton	Presents a set of choices. Option buttons are placed in groups that allow the user to make only one selection within the group.
CheckBox	Turns options on or off. Clicking an empty check box places a check mark in the check box to indicate the option is selected. Clicking a selected check box removes the check mark to indicate the option is not selected.
CommandButton	Represents a button that initiates an action when clicked.

Controls are added to a form using tools in the **Toolbox**. To use a tool, you click its respective button in the Toolbox. Table 6-4 identifies the Toolbox buttons. Many of these buttons allow you to add controls that you have worked with previously in PowerPoint, such as text boxes, check boxes, and list boxes.

Table 6-4   Summary of Buttons in the Toolbox

BUTTON	NAME	FUNCTION
	Select Objects	Draws a rectangle around the controls you want to select
	Label	Adds text that a user cannot change
	TextBox	Holds text that a user can either enter or change
	ComboBox	Adds a custom edit box, list box, or combo box on a menu bar, toolbar, menu, submenu, or shortcut menu
	ListBox	Displays a list of items from which a user can choose. The list can be scrolled if it has more items than can be displayed at one time.
	CheckBox	Creates a box that a user can choose to indicate one of two choices, such as true or false, or to display multiple choices when the user can select more than one preference
	OptionButton	Displays multiple choices when a user can select only one option
	Toggle Button	Creates a button that toggles on and off

Table 6-4   Summary of Buttons in the Toolbox *(continued)*

BUTTON	NAME	FUNCTION
	Frame	Creates a graphical or functional grouping for controls with closely related contents
	CommandButton	Creates a button a user chooses to carry out a command
	TabStrip	Contains a collection of one or more tabs
	MultiPage	Contains a collection of one or more pages
	ScrollBar	Adds a ScrollBar control
	SpinButton	Adds a SpinButton control
	Image	Adds an Image control

More About

VBA Technology

The Microsoft Visual Basic for Applications Home Page gives information geared toward independent software vendors and corporate developers. The site includes VBA news and related topics that help programmers customize their applications. To view this page, visit the PowerPoint 2000 Project 6 More About page (www.scsite.com/ pp2000/more.htm) and click VBA Technology.

ADDING A MULTIPAGE CONTROL The first step in building the form is to add a MultiPage control. This control will create two separate pages, or sheets, that both allow the user to input the company name, choose clip art, select the slide order, and decide whether to run the presentation immediately or later. The selections on one page are appropriate for management interviews, and those on the other page will be tailored for computer positions. Perform the following steps to add this first control.

 To Add a MultiPage Control to a Form and Increase Its Size

1 Click the MultiPage button in the Toolbox. Position the mouse pointer in the upper-left corner of the form.

The MultiPage button in the Toolbox is recessed, and the mouse pointer displays as a cross hair and a copy of the MultiPage button when it is on the form (Figure 6-41). The upper-left corner of the MultiPage control will be positioned in this location.

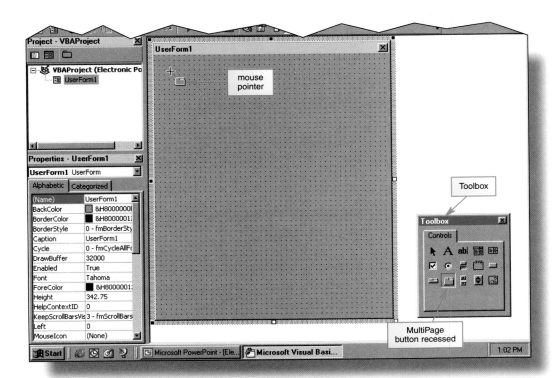

FIGURE 6-41

② Click the mouse button. Point to the lower-right sizing handle.

The MultiPage control displays on the form with two default tabs, Page1 and Page2 (Figure 6-42). A selection rectangle and sizing handles display around the MultiPage control.

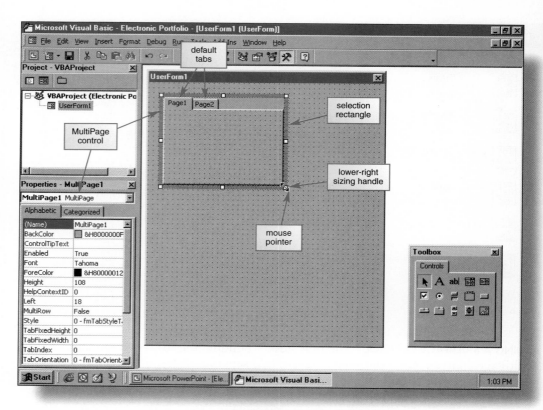

FIGURE 6-42

③ Drag the sizing handle down and to the right.

The form size increases (Figure 6-43). Additional controls now can fit on the form.

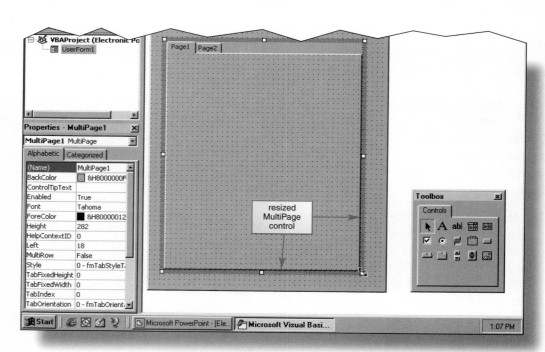

FIGURE 6-43

ADDING LABEL CONTROLS The next steps are to add the three Label controls shown in Figure 6-34a on page PP 6.26. Perform the following steps to add these controls to the form.

Steps To Add Label Controls to a Form

1 Click the Label button in the Toolbox. Position the mouse pointer in the upper-left corner of the form.

The Label button in the Toolbox is recessed, and the mouse pointer changes to a cross hair and a copy of the Label button when it is on the form (Figure 6-44). The upper-left corner of the Label control will be positioned in this location.

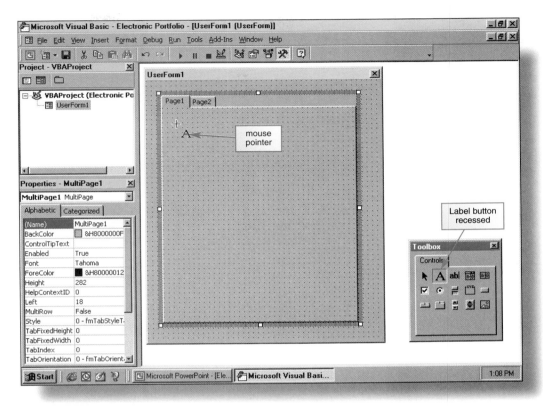

FIGURE 6-44

2 Click the mouse button.

The label displays on the form with the default caption, Label1 (Figure 6-45). The label is surrounded by a selection rectangle and sizing handles.

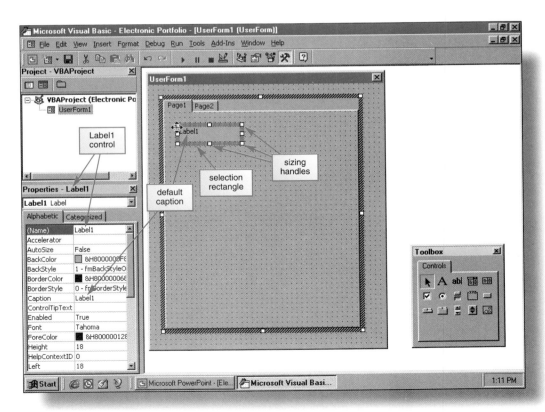

FIGURE 6-45

3 Repeat Steps 1 and 2 to draw a second Label control, Label2, and a third Label control, Label3, on the form as shown in Figure 6-46. Then click any blank area on the form.

The three Label controls display on the form (Figure 6-46).

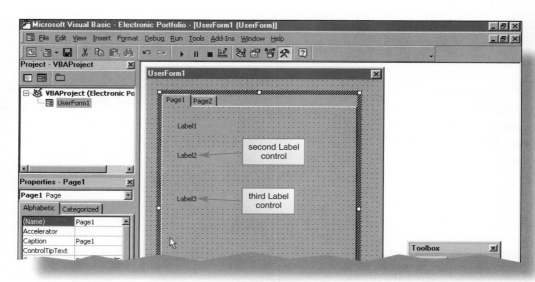

FIGURE 6-46

Now that the labels have been added to the form, the next step is to add the TextBox control beside the first Label control.

ADDING A TEXTBOX CONTROL The user will enter the name of the company where the interview is scheduled in a text box located to the right of the Label1 control. Perform the following steps to use the Toolbox to add a TextBox control to the form.

 To Add a TextBox Control to a Form

1 Click the TextBox button in the Toolbox. Position the mouse pointer in the upper-right corner of the form beside the Label1 control (Figure 6-47).

The TextBox button in the Toolbox is recessed, and the mouse pointer changes to a cross hair and a copy of the TextBox button when it is on the form (Figure 6-47). The upper-left corner of the TextBox control will be positioned in this location.

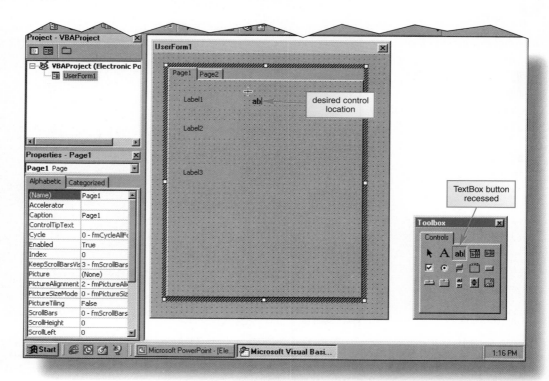

FIGURE 6-47

2 Click the mouse button.

The TextBox control is added to the form (Figure 6-48).

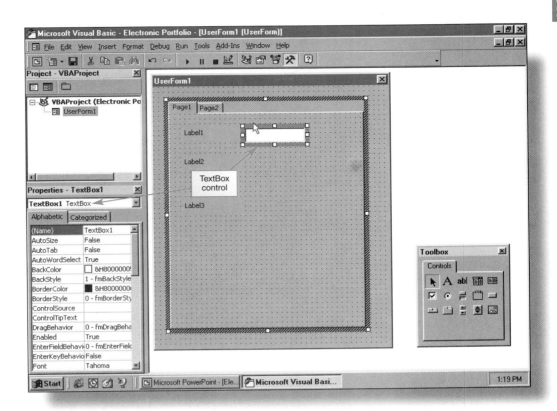

FIGURE 6-48

ADDING A COMBOBOX CONTROL The user will select one of two clip art images to insert on the second slide in the slide show. You need to add a ComboBox control to the form to display descriptions of these files. Perform the following steps to use the Toolbox to add a ComboBox control to the form.

 ## To Add a ComboBox Control to a Form

1 Click the ComboBox button in the Toolbox. Position the mouse pointer below the Label2 control.

The ComboBox button in the Toolbox is recessed, and the mouse pointer changes to a cross hair and a copy of the ComboBox button when it is on the form (Figure 6-49). The upper-left corner of the ComboBox control will be positioned in this location.

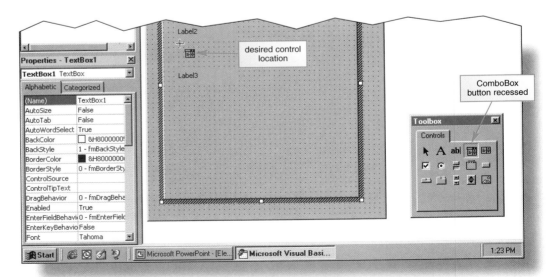

FIGURE 6-49

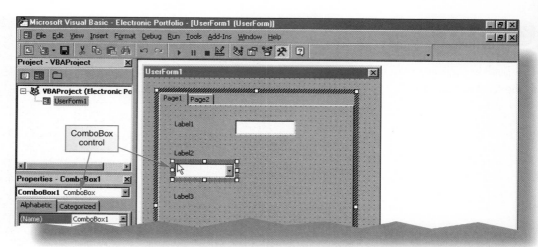

② Click the mouse button.

The ComboBox control is added to the form (Figure 6-50).

FIGURE 6-50

ADDING OPTIONBUTTON CONTROLS   The user will determine the order in which the slides display. He can choose to leave the slides in the order they display in the Electronic Portfolio file, or he can select an alternative. He can opt to display the current Slide 3 display before Slide 2 in the management presentation and to display the current Slide 4 before Slide 3 in the computer presentation. He will make this selection by clicking an option button. Perform the following steps to use the Toolbox to add two OptionButton controls to the form.

 To Add OptionButton Controls to a Form

① Click the OptionButton button in the Toolbox. Position the mouse pointer below the Label3 control.

The OptionButton button in the Toolbox is recessed, and the mouse pointer changes to a cross hair and a copy of the OptionButton button when it is on the form (Figure 6-51). The upper-left corner of the OptionButton control will be positioned in this location.

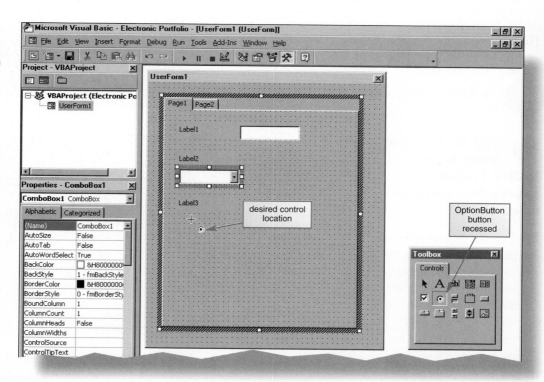

FIGURE 6-51

2 Click the mouse button.

The first Option Button control, OptionButton1, is added to the form (Figure 6-52).

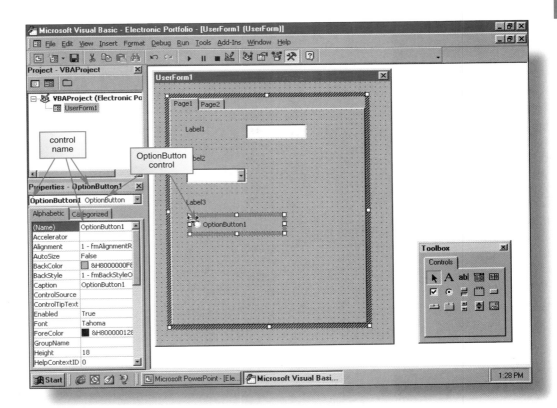

FIGURE 6-52

3 Repeat Steps 1 and 2 to add a second OptionButton control, OptionButton2, to the form below the first OptionButton control (Figure 6-53).

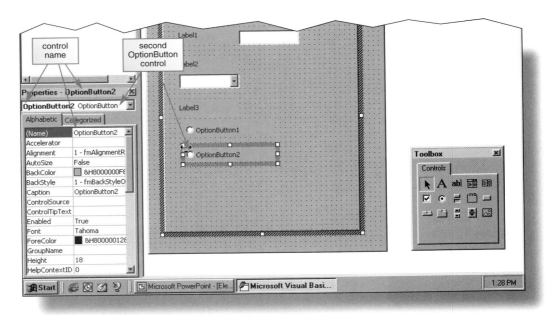

FIGURE 6-53

ADDING A CHECKBOX CONTROL The user can choose to have his slide show display immediately after he makes his selections on this form, or he can decide to save the presentation and open it later. The presentation will run immediately unless he clicks the Close presentation when finished check box. Perform the steps on the next page to use the Toolbox to add this CheckBox control to the form.

To Add a CheckBox Control to a Form

 Click the CheckBox button in the Toolbox. Position the mouse pointer below the second OptionButton control.

The CheckBox button in the Toolbox is recessed, and the mouse pointer changes to a cross hair and a copy of the CheckBox button when it is on the form (Figure 6-54). The upper-left corner of the CheckBox control will be positioned in this location.

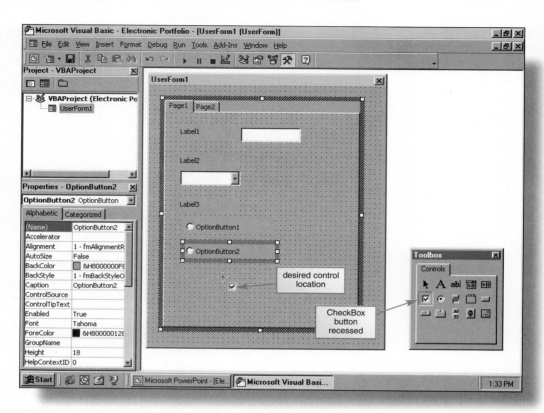

FIGURE 6-54

 Click the mouse button.

The Check Box control, CheckBox1, is added to the form (Figure 6-55).

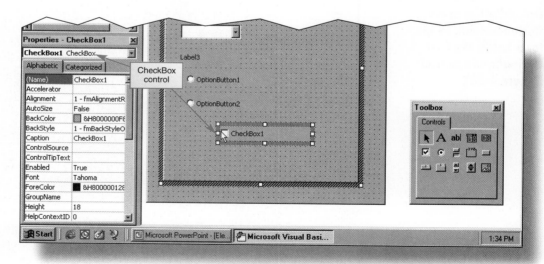

FIGURE 6-55

ADDING COMMANDBUTTON CONTROLS When the user finishes making selections on the form, then the user can click the OK button to assemble the presentation. If the user wants to exit the Visual Basic program, the user can click the Cancel button. The OK and Cancel buttons are created using CommandButton controls. Perform the following steps to add two CommandButton controls to the form.

To Add CommandButton Controls to a Form

1 **Click the CommandButton button in the Toolbox. Position the mouse pointer in the lower-left corner of the form.**

The CommandButton button in the Toolbox is recessed, and the mouse pointer changes to a cross hair and a copy of the CommandButton button when it is on the form (Figure 6-56). The upper-left corner of the first CommandButton control will be positioned in this location.

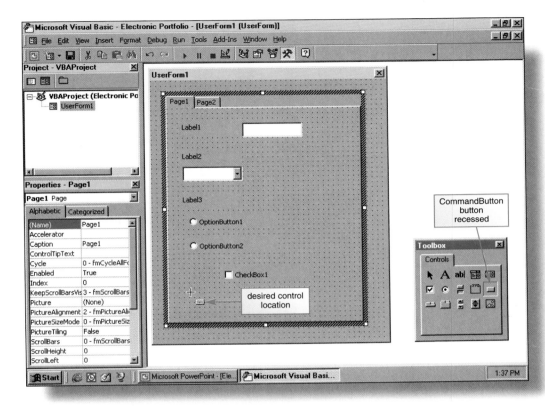

FIGURE 6-56

2 **Click the mouse button.**

The CommandButton1 control is added to the form (Figure 6-57).

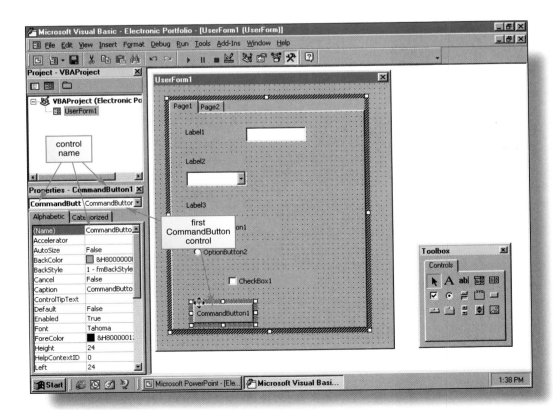

FIGURE 6-57

③ **Repeat Steps 1 and 2 to add a second CommandButton control, CommandButton2, to lower-right corner of the form beside the left CommandButton (Figure 6-58).**

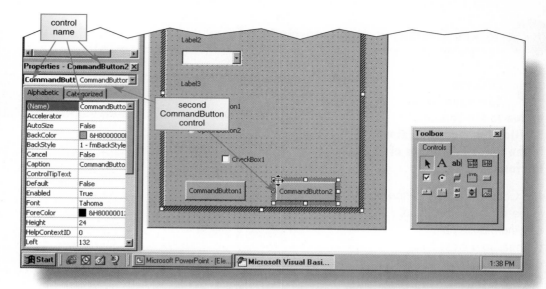

FIGURE 6-58

Step 2 – Set the Control Properties

Controls have many different **properties** (Figure 6-58), such as caption (the text on the face of the button), background color, foreground color, height, width, and font. Once you add a control to a form, you can change any of the properties to improve its appearance and modify how it works.

SETTING THE CAPTION PROPERTIES   The controls on the form are not very informative because they do not state their functions. You want to provide meaningful descriptions of the choices the user can make when using the form. These descriptions are called captions. The following steps change the caption properties.

 To Set the Caption Properties

① **Click the Page1 tab. With the Page1 control selected, click Caption in the Properties window.**

The Properties window for the Page1 control displays (Figure 6-59). The default Caption property is Page1.

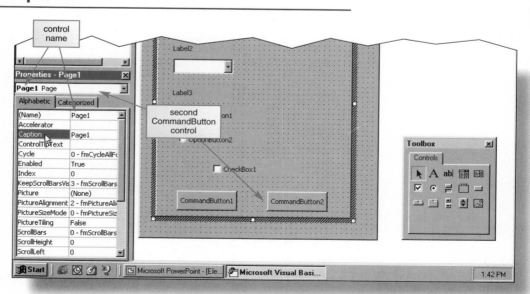

FIGURE 6-59

2 Triple-click the current caption, Page1, to select it, type Management as the new caption, and then press the ENTER key.

Management is the new caption for the Page1 tab (Figure 6-60). The new caption displays on the form.

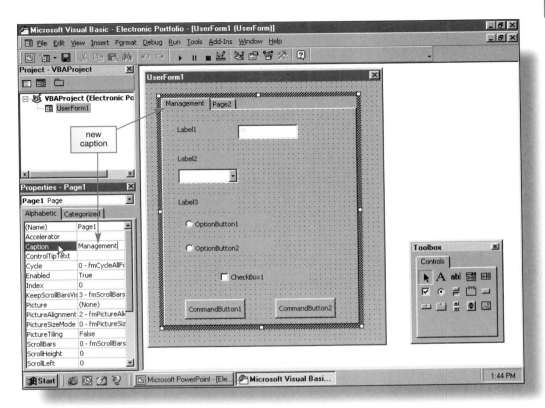

FIGURE 6-60

3 Click the Label1 control on the form. With Caption still selected in the Properties window, triple-click the current caption, Label1, in the Properties window, type Company Name as the caption, and then press the ENTER key.

The Properties window for the Label1 control displays (Figure 6-61). You change the default Caption property, Label1, to Company Name. The new name will display when you click another property or control.

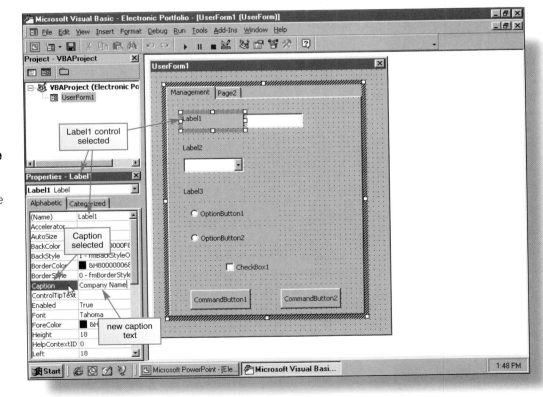

FIGURE 6-61

4 **Change the captions for the remainder of the controls on the Management sheet using Table 6-5.**

The captions for the Management sheet display (Figure 6-62).

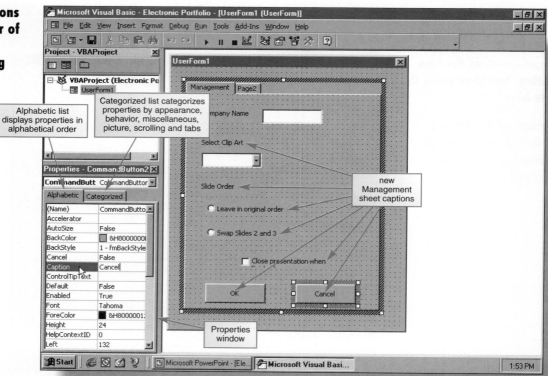

FIGURE 6-62

Table 6-5	New Management Sheet Captions
DEFAULT CAPTION	*NEW CAPTION*
Label2	Select Clip Art
Label3	Slide Order
OptionButton1	Leave in original order
OptionButton2	Swap Slides 2 and 3
CheckBox1	Close presentation when finished
CommandButton1	OK
CommandButton2	Cancel

The Properties window in Figure 6-62 has two tabs, Alphabetic and Categorized. The **Alphabetic list** displays the properties in alphabetical order. The **Categorized list** displays the properties in categories, such as appearance, behavior, font, and miscellaneous.

FINE TUNING THE USER INTERFACE After setting the properties for all the controls, you can fine tune the size and location of the controls in the form. You can reposition a control in the following ways:

1. Drag the control to its new location.
2. Select the control and use the arrow keys to reposition it.
3. Select the control and set the control's Top and Left properties in the Property window.

To use the third technique, you need to know the distance the control is from the top of the form and the left edge of the form in points. Recall that a point is equal to 1/72 of an inch. Thus, if the Top property of a control is 216, then the control is 3 inches (216 / 72) from the top of the form.

Controls also may require resizing. You need to increase the width of the CheckBox1 control so the caption fits on one line. You can resize a control in two ways:

1. Drag the sizing handles.
2. Select the control and set the control's Height and Width properties in the Properties window.

As with the Top and Left properties, the Height and Width properties are measured in points. Table 6-6 lists the exact points for the Top, Left, Height, and Width properties of each of the controls in the form.

The following steps resize and reposition the controls in the form using the values in Table 6-6.

Table 6-6	Exact Locations of Controls in the Form			
CONTROL	TOP	LEFT	HEIGHT	WIDTH
Label1	18	18	18	57
TextBox1	12	90	18	102
Label2	54	18	18	51
ComboBox1	72	18	18	186
Label3	108	18	18	41
OptionButton1	132	24	18	103
OptionButton2	162	24	18	103
CheckBox1	198	66	18	138
CommandButton1	234	24	24	72
CommandButton2	234	132	24	72

Steps To Resize and Reposition the Controls on a Form

1 **Click the Label1 control. Change its Top, Left, Height, and Width properties in the Properties window to those listed in Table 6-6.**

The Label1 control Properties window displays as shown in Figure 6-63.

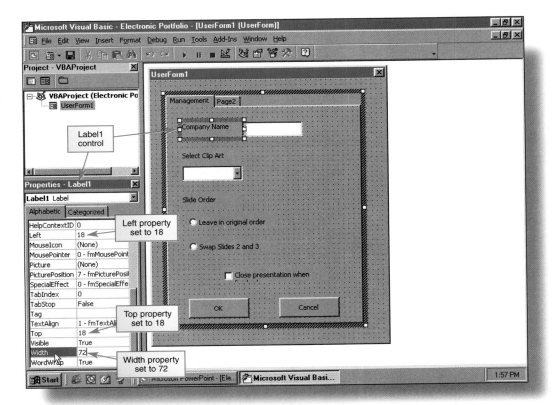

FIGURE 6-63

2 **One at a time, select the remaining controls and change their Top, Left, Height, and Width properties to those listed in Table 6-6.**

The form displays with the resized and repositioned controls (Figure 6-64).

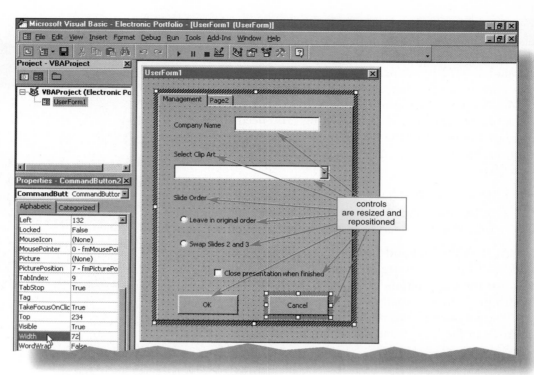

FIGURE 6-64

COPYING CONTROLS FROM ONE SHEET TO ANOTHER   Now that you have added all the controls, changed their captions, and set their locations on the Page1 sheet, you want to copy these controls to the Page2 sheet. Perform the following steps to copy the controls from the Page1 sheet to the Page2 sheet.

 To Copy Controls From One Sheet to Another

1 **Right-click a blank area of the Page1 sheet and then point to Select All on the shortcut menu (Figure 6-65).**

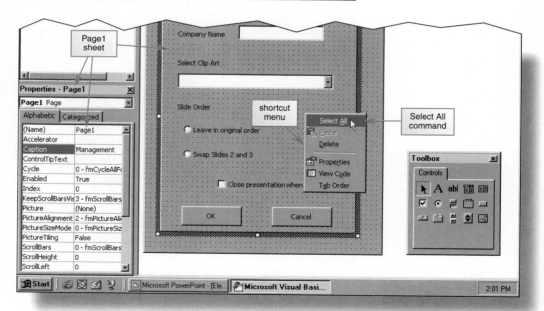

FIGURE 6-65

2 Click Select All. Point to the Copy button on the Standard toolbar.

All controls on the Page1 sheet are selected (Figure 6-66).

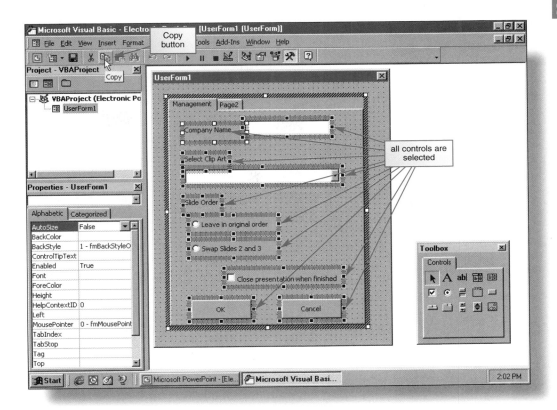

FIGURE 6-66

3 Click the Copy button. Click the Page2 tab on the form. Right-click the Page2 sheet and then point to Paste on the shortcut menu (Figure 6-67).

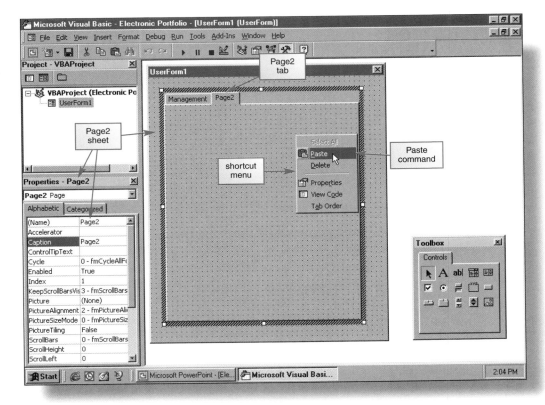

FIGURE 6-67

4 **Click Paste. Point to the Page2 tab on the form.**

The controls are added to the Page2 sheet (Figure 6-68).

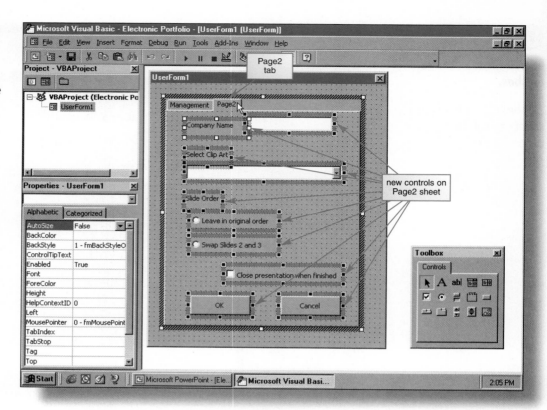

FIGURE 6-68

5 **Click the Page2 tab. Click Caption in the Properties window, type Computer as the new Page2 caption, and then press the ENTER key.**

The caption for the Computer sheet displays (Figure 6-69).

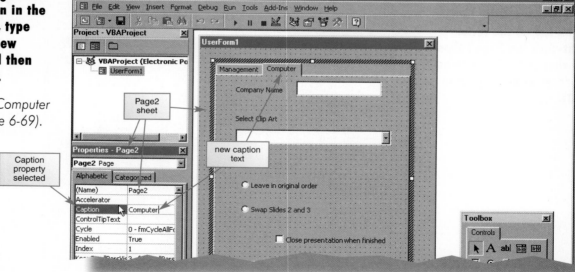

FIGURE 6-69

You want all controls on the Computer sheet are identical to those on the Management sheet except for the second option button. The user can choose to swap Slides 3 and 4 in the slide show if he is interviewing for a computer position. Perform the following steps to change the caption of the second option button on the Computer sheet, which has the control name OptionButton4.

TO CHANGE THE OPTIONBUTTON4 CAPTION

① Click the OptionButton4 control. Click Caption in the OptionButton4 Properties window.

② Type Swap Slides 3 and 4 as the caption.

③ Press the ENTER key.

OptionButton4 displays on the form with the new caption (Figure 6-70).

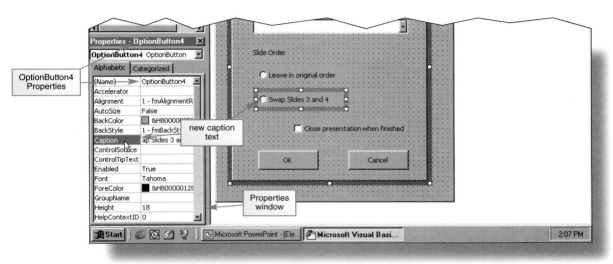

FIGURE 6-70

Saving the Form

The form is complete. Perform the following step to save your work before writing the VBA code.

TO SAVE A PRESENTATION

① Click the Save button on the Standard toolbar.

PowerPoint saves the presentation by saving the changes made since the last save.

Step 3 – Write the VBA Code

You have created the interface and set the properties of the controls for this project. The next step is to write and then enter the procedure that will execute when you click the Create Presentation button on the Using Presentation toolbar. You will create this button near the end of this project. Clicking this button is the event that triggers execution of the procedure that assembles the custom presentation. As mentioned earlier, Visual Basic for Applications (VBA) is a powerful programming language that you can use to automate many activities described thus far in this book. The code for this project will include events and modules. A **module** is a collection of code that performs a specific task. Modules often serve as the smaller components in a program. They may, however, function independently as a macro.

The user will generate the **events** in this program by clicking buttons and boxes and by entering text in the boxes on the form. Recall that a macro consists of VBA statements associated with a menu command or button. To begin the process, you will write a module of VBA code to serve as a macro that displays a form when a user clicks the Create Presentation button.

VBA Partners

More than 100 companies using VBA are profiled in the Microsoft VBA site. They represent a variety of industries, including manufacturing, healthcare, and engineering. To learn how these companies have applied VBA, visit the PowerPoint 2000 Project 6 More About page (www.scsite.com/pp2000/more.htm) and click VBA Companies.

Editor Options

You can customize the appearance of your VBA code on the Editor Format tab sheet in the Options dialog box, accessed on the Tools menu. You can specify the foreground and background colors used for different types of text, such as Comment Text or Keyword Text.

PLANNING A PROCEDURE When you trigger the event that executes a procedure, PowerPoint steps through the Visual Basic statements one at a time, beginning at the top of the procedure. Thus, when you plan a procedure, remember that the order in which you place the statements in the procedure is important because this order determines the sequence of execution.

Once you know what you want the procedure to do, write the VBA code on paper in a format similar to Table 6-7. Then, before entering the procedure into the computer, test it by putting yourself in the position of PowerPoint and stepping through the instructions one at a time. As you do so, think about how it affects the slide show. Testing a procedure on paper before entering it is called **desk checking** and is an important part of the development process.

Adding comments before a procedure will help you remember its purpose at a later date. In Table 6-7, the first seven lines are comments. **Comments** begin with the word Rem or an apostrophe ('). These comments contain overall documentation and are placed before the procedure, above the Sub statement. Comments have no effect on the execution of a procedure; they simply provide information about the procedure, such as name, creation date, and function.

Table 6-7	Create Presentation Procedure	
LINE	*VBA CODE*	
1	' Create Presentation Procedure	Author: Mary Lynn Tranita
2	' Date Created: 12/1/2001	
3	' Run from: Electronic Portfolio by clicking Create Presentation button	
4	' Function: When executed, this procedure accepts data that causes	
5	'	PowerPoint to build a custom presentation that adds
6	'	the company name, selects clip art, and runs the slide show.
7	'	
8	Sub CreatePresentationCareer()	
9	UserForm1.InitializeForm	
10	UserForm1.Show	
11	End Sub	

A procedure begins with a **Sub statement** and ends with an **End Sub statement** (lines 8 and 11 in Table 6-7). The Sub statement begins with the name of the procedure. The parentheses following the procedure name indicate that arguments can be passed from one procedure to another. Passing arguments is beyond the scope of this project, but the parentheses still are required. The End Sub statement signifies the end of the procedure and returns PowerPoint to Ready mode.

The first executable statement in Table 6-7 is line 9, which calls the InitializeForm procedure for the form, indicated by the object name, UserForm1. Line 10 issues the command to show or display the form in the PowerPoint slide view window. Line 11 is the end of the procedure. Every procedure must conclude with an End Sub statement.

To enter a procedure, you use the Visual Basic Editor. To open the Visual Basic Editor, you can click the **View Code button** on the Project Explorer toolbar or click the Insert UserForm button arrow on the Standard toolbar and then click Module in the Insert UserForm list.

The Visual Basic Editor is a full-screen editor, which allows you to enter a procedure by typing the lines of VBA code as if you were using word processing software. At the end of a line, you press the ENTER key to move to the next line. If you make a mistake in a statement, you can use the arrow keys and the DELETE or BACKSPACE keys to correct it. You also can move the insertion point to previous lines to make corrections.

USING THE VISUAL BASIC EDITOR TO ENTER A PROCEDURE The following steps open the Visual Basic Editor and create the procedure for the Create Presentation module.

 To Enter the Create Presentation Career Procedure

1 **Click the Insert Module button arrow on the Standard toolbar and then point to Module.**

The Insert Module list displays (Figure 6-71).

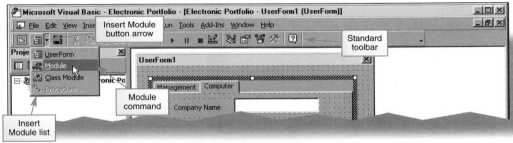

FIGURE 6-71

2 **Click Module in the Insert Module list. When the Visual Basic Editor opens, type the seven comment statements (lines 1 through 7) in Table 6-7. Be certain to enter an apostrophe at the beginning of each comment line. Click the Properties window Close button.**

PowerPoint starts the Visual Basic Editor and opens the Microsoft Visual Basic window (Figure 6-72). The comment lines display in green.

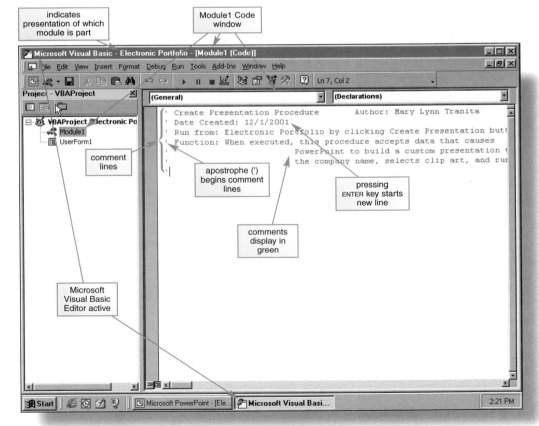

FIGURE 6-72

3 **Press the ENTER key to position the insertion point on the next line. Enter lines 8 through 10 in Table 6-7. Do not enter the End Sub statement (line 11). For clarity, indent all lines between the Sub statement and End Sub statement by three spaces. Point to the Close Window button on the right side of the menu bar.**

The Create Presentation Career procedure is complete (Figure 6-73). You do not need to enter the End Sub statement in line 11 of Table 6-7 because the Visual Basic Editor displays that line automatically.

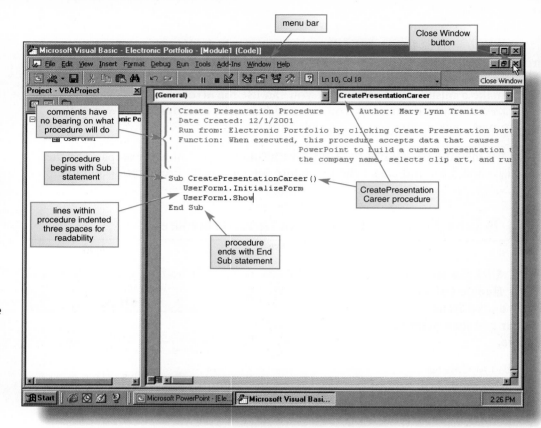

FIGURE 6-73

4 **Click the Close Window button.**

The Module1 Code window closes, and the UserForm window displays the form.

Other Ways

1. On Insert menu click Module
2. Press ALT+I, press M

Variables

When variables are initialized, a numeric variable is initialized to zero, a variable-length string is initialized to a zero-length string (" "), which also is called a null string, and a fixed-length string is filled with zeros.

More About Visual Basic for Applications

Visual Basic for Applications uses many more statements than those presented here. Even this simple procedure, however, should help you understand the basic makeup of a Visual Basic statement. Lines 9 and 10 in the procedure shown in Figure 6-73 includes a period. The entry on the left side of the period tells PowerPoint which object you want to affect.

An **object** is a real-world thing. Your textbook, your car, your pets, your friends are objects. Visual Basic makes use of objects in its association with applications. This technique is described as object-oriented (OO). When it refers to programming it is called **OOP** (Object-Oriented Programming). The development of OOP provides a way to represent the world in conceptual terms that everyone understands. People relate to their everyday objects and easily can understand that these objects can have properties and behaviors.

An object is described by its properties. **Properties** are attributes that help us differentiate one object from another. For example, your car has a color, a certain body style, and a certain type of interior. These properties can be used to describe the car. The Visual Basic programming language has specific rules, or **syntax**. In Visual Basic syntax, you separate an object and its property with a period. For example, *car.color* specifies a car object and the property color. You would write the statement *car.color = "red"* to set the value of the color property to red.

An object also has certain behaviors, or methods. A **method** is a function or action you want the object to perform, or an action that will be performed on an object. You can write your own functions, or you can use the built-in methods supplied with Visual Basic. Methods associated with car, pet, and friend objects might be drive, feed, and talk, respectively. The drive method would be written as *car.drive*, just as in the statement UserForm1.Show, where UserForm1 is the object, and Show is the method.

The following example shows that you can change an object's property value during execution of a procedure. Similar statements often are used to clear the properties of controls or to set them to initial values. This process is called **initialization**. The object in this case is a text box control.

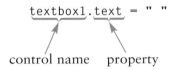

```
textbox1.text = " "
```
control name   property

More About

VBA Help

Microsoft offers a variety of VBA help on its Web site. Topics include understanding VBA syntax, setting References, using Object Variables, and writing efficient code. To view this site, visit the PowerPoint 2000 Project 6 More About page (www.scsite.com/pp2000/more.htm) and click VBA Help.

WRITING THE INITIALIZING VARIABLES PROCEDURE   Whenever you need to work with an object's properties or methods in more than one line of code, you can use the With statement to eliminate some coding. The With statement accepts an object as a parameter and is followed by several lines of code that pertain to this object. You therefore do not need to retype the object name in these lines. Table 6-8 describes the

Table 6-8	With Statement Format

General Form:	`With object`
	`        Visual Basic code`
	`End With`

Comment:	where object is any valid Visual Basic or user-defined object

Example:	`With textbox1`
	`        .text = ""`
	`End With`

general form of the With statement.

The next step is to write the procedure to initialize some of the control properties. Recall from Step 2 of this project how you added the controls to the form and set some of their properties. With respect to VBA, PowerPoint has two modes: design mode and run mode. In **design mode**, you can resize controls, assign properties to controls, and enter VBA code. In **run mode**, all controls are active. That is, if you click a control, it triggers the event, and PowerPoint executes the procedure associated with the control.

The initialize procedure in Table 6-9 sets some controls during run mode. If the With statement were not used in Table 6-9, then each statement would have to be preceded by the specific object name. The Initialize Form procedure ensures the text boxes are clear, adds the description of the clip art choices to the combo boxes, sets the initial values for the option buttons, and clears the check boxes.

The **With statements** in lines 3, 6, 10, 14, 18, 21, 24, and 27 provide a shortcut to some of the complicated syntax sometimes used in VBA. Lines 4 and 7 clear the text boxes. The text properties are assigned a null value. Lines 11, 12, 15, and 16 add the clip art choices to the combo boxes. The Management sheet is assigned "Meeting" and "Training" clip art choices. The Computer sheet is assigned "Parachutes" and "Animated Computer" clip art choices. Lines 18 through 23 set the Slide Order option buttons to their default values. By setting the values of Option Buttons 1 and 3 to True, the default slide order value for each sheet is Leave in Original Order. Lines 24 through 29 clear the check boxes. The check box values are set to False. Each With statement must end with an End With statement as indicated in lines 5, 8, 13, 17, 20, 23, 26, and 29. To complete the section of code for the InitializeForm procedure, an End Sub statement closes the procedure at line 30.

CommandButton Click Events

You can allow a user to press the ENTER key during run time as a substitute method for clicking a command button by changing the CommandButton control's Default property. Only one command button on a form can be the default command button. When Default is set to True for one command button, it automatically is set to False for all other command buttons on the form.

Table 6-9 Initialize Form Procedure

LINE	VBA CODE
1	`Sub InitializeForm()`
2	`' Clear text boxes`
3	`With textbox1`
4	`    .Text = ""`
5	`End With`
6	`With textbox2`
7	`    .Text = ""`
8	`End With`
9	`' Add items to combo box`
10	`With ComboBox1`
11	`    .AddItem "Meeting"`
12	`    .AddItem "Training"`
13	`End With`
14	`With ComboBox2`
15	`    .AddItem "Parachutes"`
16	`    .AddItem "Animated Computer"`
17	`End With`
18	`With OptionButton1`
19	`    .Value = True`
20	`End With`
21	`With OptionButton3`
22	`    .Value = True`
23	`End With`
24	`With CheckBox1`
25	`    .Value = False`
26	`End With`
27	`With CheckBox2`
28	`    .Value = False`
29	`End With`
30	`End Sub`

Steps **To Enter the InitializeForm Procedure**

1 **Click the View Code Button on the Project Explorer toolbar. Point to the Project Explorer Close button on the Project Explorer toolbar.**

UserForm1 is selected in the Project Explorer window (Figure 6-74).

FIGURE 6-74

2 **Click the Project Explorer Close button. When the UserForm1 Code window displays in its entirety, enter lines 1 through 29 of the VBA code shown in Table 6-9.**

The InitializeForm procedure displays as shown in Figure 6-75. You do not need to enter line 30 in Table 6-9 because the Visual Basic Editor displays that line automatically.

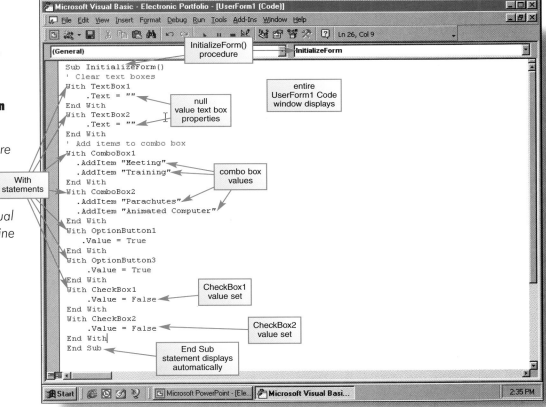

FIGURE 6-75

WRITING THE COMMANDBUTTON1 PROCEDURE The next step is to write the code for the CommandButton1 procedure shown in Table 6-10. The CommandButton1 procedure is activated when the user clicks the OK button on the form for the Management style presentation. The code for this procedure is associated with the Click event; the spaces preceding the lines are used for visual clarity.

Table 6-10 CommandButton1 Procedure

LINE	VBA CODE
1	` Set the presentation to apply the template and clip art
2	Set MgmtSlides = Application.ActivePresentation
3	With MgmtSlides
4	.ApplyTemplate "a:\expedition.pot"
5	End With
6	` Validate entries in text box and combo box
7	If TextBox1.Text = "" Then
8	MsgBox "Company Name missing, please add company name ", vbOK, "Management"
9	TextBox1.SetFocus
10	Else
11	` Place company name in title
12	MgmtCompanyName = textbox1.Text
13	Set mgmtTitleSlide = ActivePresentation.Slides(1)
14	mgmtTitleSlide.Shapes.Title.TextFrame.TextRange.Text = "A Management Position" & vbCr & "With " & MgmtCompanyName
15	` Check if clip art was chosen
16	If ComboBox1.Value = "" Then
17	MsgBox "Please select a clip art object from the list", vbOKOnly, "Clip art missing"
18	ComboBox1.SetFocus
19	Else
20	` Place selected clip art in slide
21	Select Case ComboBox1.Value
22	Case "Meeting" 'first
23	Set MgmtClipartSlide = Application.ActivePresentation.Slides(2)
24	With MgmtClipartSlide
25	.Shapes.AddPicture "a:\meeting.wmf", True, True, 375, 150, 300, 350
26	End With
27	Case "Training" 'second
28	Set MgmtClipartSlide = Application.ActivePresentation.Slides(2)
29	With MgmtClipartSlide
30	.Shapes.AddPicture "a:\training.gif", True, True, 375, 150, 300, 350
31	End With
32	End Select
33	` Check if slides should be swapped; if so, swap them
34	If OptionButton2.Value = True Then
35	ActivePresentation.Slides.Range(Array(3)).Cut
36	ActivePresentation.Slides.Paste 2
37	End If
38	` wrap up, reset combo boxes for next time,

Table 6-10	CommandButton1 Procedure *(continued)*
LINE	**VBA CODE**
39	' close form and run presentation
40	ResetComboxes
41	UserForm1.Hide
42	Unload UserForm1
43	' Start slide show
44	If CheckBox1.Value = True Then
45	Set MgmtSlides = Application.ActivePresentation
46	With MgmtSlides.SlideShowSettings
47	.RangeType = ppShowNamedSlideShow
48	.Run
49	End With
50	End If
51	End If
52	End If

Line 2 sets the presentation object to MgmtSlides. Using the With statement in line 3, the assignment statement in line 4 assigns the Expedition design template file to the presentation using the ApplyTemplate method. Lines 7 through 14 verify that the Company Name text box (TextBox1) is not blank using an If-Then-Else statement (see Table 6-10). If it is blank, a message will display (line 8) notifying the user an entry must be made, and the insertion point will be placed back in the text box by the **SetFocus** method (line 9). The SetFocus method is used to set the insertion point or mouse pointer on or in a control. To set focus to a control, write the control name, a period, and the SetFocus method.

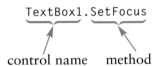

TextBox1.SetFocus

control name   method

If the Company Name text box has a name entered, line 12 assigns the name (in textbox1.text) to the slide. The first slide (line 13) is designated as the title slide, and the contents of the title slide are constructed in line 14. The procedure then verifies that a clip art item has been selected from the Select Clip Art combo box (ComboBox1) in lines 16 through 18. If the ComboBox1 value is blank, a message displays notifying the user to select a clip art item (line 17) and places the focus back on the combo box (line 18). If a clip art item has been selected, the Select Case statements (see Table 6-10) in lines 22 through 33 assign the selected clip art item to the slide. Depending on the selected clip art, in the Management style presentation, lines 23 or 28 assign Slide 2 as the slide to have clip art. Lines 25 or 30 then add the picture to Slide 2 with the appropriate settings.

Color Schemes

If you develop a color scheme for one slide that you want to use on another slide, click the Slide Sorter View button on the View button bar, click the Format Painter button on the Standard toolbar, and click the slide to which you want to apply the color scheme. You also can use this technique to copy a color scheme from one presentation to another. With both presentations open, click Arrange All on the Window menu, click Arrange All, and then follow the above steps.

Next, the values of the option buttons are examined. In the Management style presentation, the user can indicate to swap Slides 2 and 3. If the Leave in original order option button has been selected, nothing happens; otherwise lines 35 and 36 swap the slides. To swap the slides, the VBA code uses the Cut and Paste technique. The last steps in the procedure (lines 40 through 52) reset the combo boxes, hide and unload the form, and examine the check box value to determine if the slide show should run immediately or later.

Line 40 calls a subroutine, which will be written later, that resets the values in the combo boxes back to blank. Line 41 hides the form with the Hide method (UserForm1.Hide). Line 42 **unloads** the form, which removes it from the desktop during run time. If CheckBox1 has been checked, the active presentation is assigned to the MgmtSlides object (line 45), the RangeType property is set to the built-in PowerPoint constant for the named slide show, and the Run method used in line 48 launches the PowerPoint presentation.

If-Then-Else Statement   The If-Then-Else statement represents a two-way decision with an action specified for each of the two alternatives. The computer never executes both the true and false alternatives. It selects one or the other alternative based on the result of a test or condition. The general form of the If-Then-Else statement is shown in Table 6-11. You place the Visual Basic code to be executed if the result of the conditional test is True after the Then keyword.

Table 6-11	If-Then-Else Statement Format

General form:	`If condition Then`
	`        Visual Basic statements to execute if condition is true`
	`Else`
	`        Visual Basic statements to execute if condition is false`
	`End If`

Comment:	The condition is a statement that compares values. If the result of the comparison statement is true, Visual Basic executes the statements after the Then statement. If the result of the comparison statement is false, Visual Basic executes the statements after the Else statement.

Example:	`If textbox1.Text = "" Then`
	`        MsgBox "Company Name missing.", vbOK, "Management"`
	`        textbox1.SetFocus`
	`Else`
	`        MgmtCompanyName = textbox1.Text`
	`End If`

A **condition** is any expression that evaluates to True or False. In the example in Table 6-11, Visual Basic evaluates the condition, *TextBox1.text* = " ", by comparing the value in the text property of TextBox1 with a blank value, indicated by the empty double quotes. If the user has not entered the Company Name, the text property is blank, so the condition evaluates to True and the "Company Name missing" message displays. If the user had entered a Company Name, the value of the text property would not be blank, and the condition would evaluate to False. Visual Basic then would execute the Else statement, which assigns the entered name to the MgmtCompanyName object on the form. When writing an If statement, leave a space between the word If and the condition so Visual Basic does not interpret the If statement incorrectly. Table 6-12 shows the comparison operators and their meanings.

More About

Designing Templates

You can change the pre-designed formats and color schemes that are part of a design template, or you can create a new template to fit your specific needs. To design a template, open an existing presentation and make the desired changes, or click the New button on the Standard toolbar to start with a blank presentation. On the File menu click Save As, type a name for your design template in the File name text box, and then click Design Template in the Save as type box. You can save this new design template with the other design templates in the Presentation Designs folder, or you can save it in one of your own folders.

Table 6-12	Comparison Operators	
OPERATOR	EXAMPLE	RESULTS
=	a = b	True if a equals b
<>	a <> b	True if a does not equal b
>	a > b	True if a is greater than b
<	a < b	True if a is less than b
>=	a >= b	True if a is greater than or equal to b
<=	a <= b	True if a is less than or equal to b

The If-Then-Else statements in lines 7 and 16 verify the user entered a value in the Company Name text box and selected a clip art item from the Clip Art combo box. The If-Then statements in line 34 and 44 execute code based on the values of the Slide Order option buttons and the Close presentation when finished check box.

The Select Case statements (lines 21 through 32) are used to streamline the use of multiple If-Then-Else statements. The value of the combo box is examined, and the appropriate clip art item is assigned to Slide 2. The Set statement in line 23 defines the shape object name, MgmtClipartSlide. Using the With statement described earlier, the Shapes.AddPicture property in line 25 assigns the clip art and sets the clip art dimensions. Table 6-13 describes the general form of the Select Case statement.

Table 6-13	Select Case Statement Format

General form:	`Select Case testexpression`
	`        Case expression1`
	`                Visual Basic statements`
	`        Case expression2`
	`                Visual Basic statements`
	`End Select`

Comments:	The Select Case statement begins the case structure. testexpression is the name of a valid Visual Basic expression or variable. If testexpression matches the expression associated with a Case clause, the Visual Basic statements following that Case clause are executed. End Select ends the Select Case structure.

Example:	`Select Case ComboBox2.Value`
	`        Case "Parachutes"    'first`
	`          Set CompClipartSlide = Application.ActivePresentation.Slides(2)`
	`          With CompClipartSlide`
	`            .Shapes.AddPicture "a:\parachutes.wmf", True, True, 375, 150, 300, 350`
	`          End With`
	`        Case "Animated Computer"    'Second`
	`          Set CompClipartSlide = Application.ActivePresentation.Slides(2)`
	`          With CompClipartSlide`
	`            .Shapes.AddPicture "a:\anicomp1.gif", True, True, 375, 150, 300, 300`
	`          End With`
	`End Select`

The If-Then statement in line 34 checks the value of the option button. If OptionButton2 is selected, then lines 35 and 36 swap Slide 2 and Slide 3. If OptionButton1 is selected, then the original sequence of the slides is left intact. Lines 40 through 42 perform the finishing tasks. The combo boxes are reset for next time the procedure is executed, and the form is hidden and unloaded. Lines 44 through 50 contain the final If-Then statement that examines the value in the check box to see if the presentation should be run or closed upon finishing. The Set statement on line 45 assigns the active presentation to the MgmtSlides object. Recall that the With statement allows you to simplify using the current object. Consequently, the With statement on line 46 allows you to use the object name, Application.ActivePresentation, without typing this entire object name on lines 47 and 48. The RangeType property of the SlideShowSettings is set on line 47. ppShowNamed SlideShow is a built-in PowerPoint VBA constant that indicates all slides in the presentation. Finally, the slide show is run by the .Run method on line 48. The final End If statements close all the If-Then and If-Then-Else statements because every If statement needs a corresponding End If statement.

Steps To Enter the CommandButton1 Procedure

1 Click the Object box arrow at the top of the Code window, and then point to CommandButton1 in the Object list (Figure 6-76).

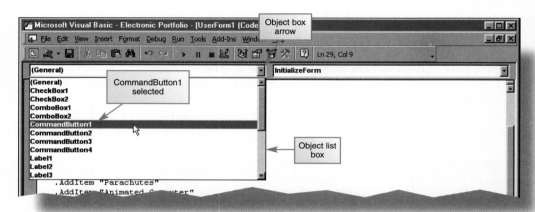

FIGURE 6-76

2 Click CommandButton1. Make sure Click is in the Procedure box.

The Visual Basic Editor displays the Sub and End Sub statements for the Command-Button1 procedure and positions the insertion point between the two statements (Figure 6-77).

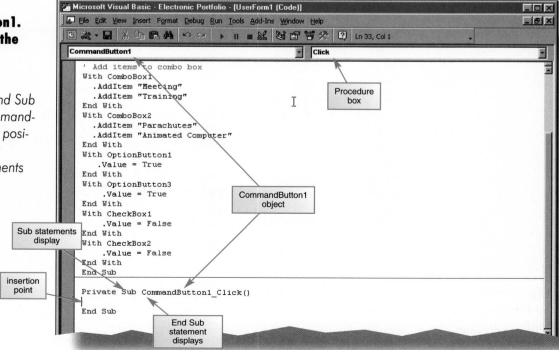

FIGURE 6-77

3 **Enter the VBA code shown in lines 1 through 52 in Table 6-10.**

The CommandButton1_Click() procedure displays as shown in Figure 6-78. You do not need to enter the End Sub statement in line 53 of Table 6-10 because the Visual BasicEditor displays that line automatically.

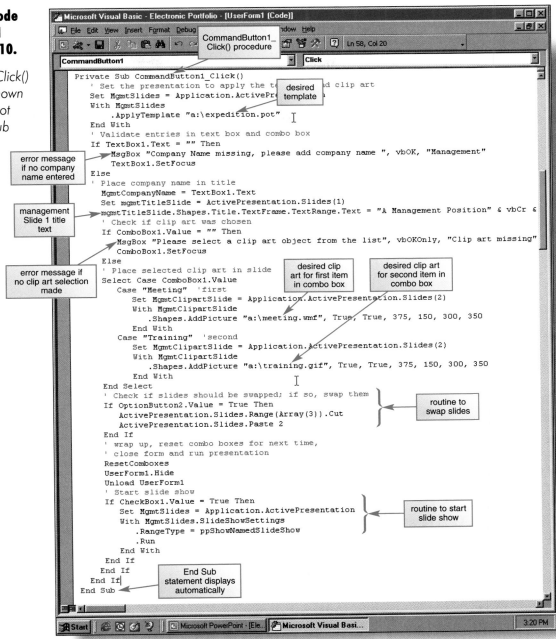

FIGURE 6-78

WRITING THE COMMANDBUTTON2 PROCEDURE   The next step is to write the CommandButton2 procedure. This procedure is executed if the user clicks the Cancel button. The procedure calls a subroutine (ResetComboxes) that clears the text value of the combo boxes, closes the presentation, and hides and unloads the form.

Table 6-14	CommandButton2 Procedure	
LINE	*VBA CODE*	
1	' Close the application presentation	
2	' without saving	
3	ResetComboxes	
4	With Application.ActivePresentation	
5	.Close	
6	End With	
7	UserForm1.Hide	
8	Unload UserForm1	

Line 3 calls the subroutine to clear the combo boxes. Lines 4 though 6 close the current active presentation. Line 7 hides the form (UserForm1), and line 8 unloads the form.

To Enter the CommandButton2 Procedure

1   **Click the Object box arrow at the top of the Code window, and then click CommandButton2 in the Object list. Make sure Click is in the Procedure box.**

The Visual Basic Editor displays the Sub and End Sub statements for the Command-Button2 procedure and positions the insertion point between the two statements (Figure 6-79).

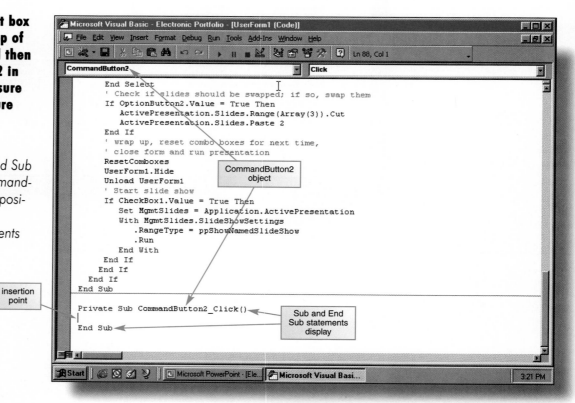

FIGURE 6-79

② Enter the VBA code shown in Table 6-14.

The CommandButton2_Click() procedure displays as shown in Figure 6-80.

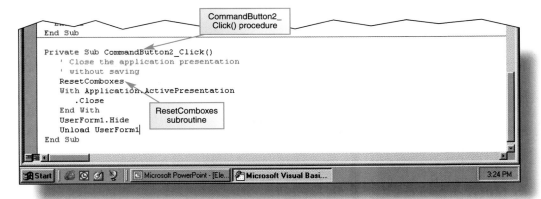

```
        End Sub

Private Sub CommandButton2_Click()
    ' Close the application presentation
    ' without saving
    ResetComboxes
    With Application.ActivePresentation
        .Close
    End With
    UserForm1.Hide
    Unload UserForm1
End Sub
```

CommandButton2_Click() procedure
ResetComboxes subroutine

Start | Microsoft PowerPoint - [Ele.. | Microsoft Visual Basi... | 3:24 PM

FIGURE 6-80

WRITING THE COMMANDBUTTON3 PROCEDURE The next step is to write the CommandButton3 procedure. The code for the CommandButton3 button control almost is identical to the code for the CommandButton1 control button in Table 6-10. The difference between the two procedures is that CommandButton1 sets the presentation clip art, design template, and control properties for the Management slides, while CommandButton3 sets the presentation clip art, design template, and control properties for the Computer slides.

Table 6-15 CommandButton3 Procedure

LINE	VBA CODE
1	' Set the presentation to apply the template and the clip art
2	Set ComputerSlides = Application.ActivePresentation
3	With ComputerSlides
4	.ApplyTemplate "a:\cactus.pot"
5	End With
6	' Validate entries in the text box and combo box
7	If textbox2.Text = "" Then
8	MsgBox "Company Name missing, add company name ", vbOK, "Computer"
9	textbox2.SetFocus
10	Else
11	' Place company name in title
12	CompCompanyName = textbox2.Text
13	Set CompTitleSlide = ActivePresentation.Slides(1)
14	CompTitleSlide.Shapes.Title.TextFrame.TextRange.Text = "Working In Information Systems" & vbCr & "At " & CompCompanyName
15	'Check if clip art was chosen
16	If ComboBox2.Value = "" Then
17	MsgBox "Please select a clip art object from the list", vbOKOnly, "Clip art missing"
18	ComboBox2.SetFocus
19	Else

(continued)

Table 6-15 CommandButton3 Procedure *(continued)*

LINE	VBA CODE
20	' Place selected clip art in slide
21	Select Case ComboBox2.Value
22	Case "Parachutes" 'first
23	Set CompClipartSlide = Application.ActivePresentation.Slides(2)
24	With CompClipartSlide
25	.Shapes.AddPicture "a:\parachutes.wmf", True, True, 375, 150, 300, 350
26	End With
27	Case "Animated Computer" 'Second
28	Set CompClipartSlide = Application.ActivePresentation.Slides(2)
29	With CompClipartSlide
30	.Shapes.AddPicture "a:\anicomp1.gif", True, True, 375, 150, 300, 300
31	End With
32	End Select
33	' Check if slides should be swapped; if so, swap them
34	If OptionButton4.Value = True Then
35	ActivePresentation.Slides.Range(Array(4)).Cut
36	ActivePresentation.Slides.Paste 3
37	End If
38	' wrap up, reset combo boxes for next time
39	' close form, and run presentation
40	ResetComboxes
41	UserForm1.Hide
42	Unload UserForm1
43	' Start slide show
44	If CheckBox2.Value = True Then
45	Set CompSlides = Application.ActivePresentation
46	With CompSlides.SlideShowSettings
47	.RangeType = ppShowNamedSlideShow
48	.Run
49	End With
50	End If
51	End If
52	End If

As indicated earlier, the code for CommandButton3 is nearly identical to the code for CommandButton1. Line 4 assigns a different template file. Although the first slide is designated as the title slide, a different title is assembled at line 14. The clip art pictures assigned to Slide 2 are different based on the Select Case statements in lines 21 through 32. In addition, lines 35 and 36 swap Slides 3 and 4, instead of Slides 2 and 3 that were changed in the CommandButton1 procedure.

Steps ## To Enter the CommandButton3 Procedure

1 **Click the Object box arrow at the top of the Code window, and then click CommandButton3 in the Object list. Make sure Click is in the Procedure box.**

The Visual Basic Editor displays the Sub and End Sub statements for the CommandButton3 procedure and positions the insertion point between the two statements.

2 **Enter the VBA code shown in Table 6-15 on the previous page.**

The CommandButton3_Click() procedure displays as shown in Figure 6-81.

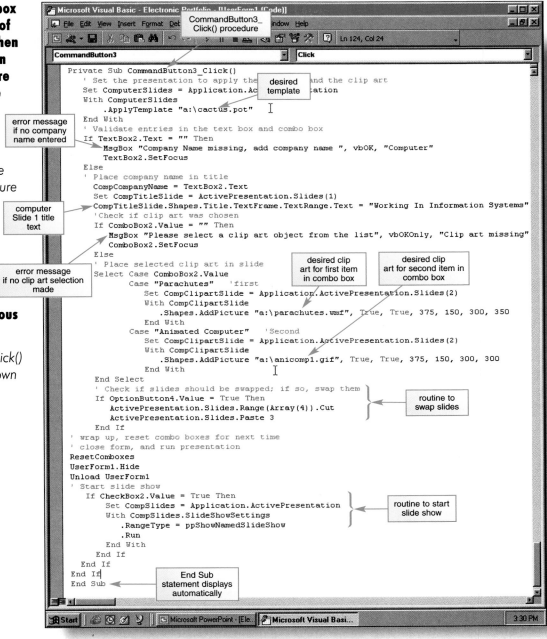

FIGURE 6-81

WRITING THE COMMANDBUTTON4 PROCEDURE Next, the code for CommandButton4 must be written. The code for this command control is identical to the code for CommandButton2. In the event a user does not want to change the presentation, he can click the Cancel button.

Table 6-16 CommandButton4 Procedure	
LINE	VBA CODE
1	' Close the application presentation
2	' without saving
3	ResetComboxes
4	With Application.ActivePresentation
5	.Close
6	End With
7	UserForm1.Hide
8	Unload UserForm1

 To Enter the CommandButton4 Procedure

 Click the Object box arrow at the top of the Code window, and then click CommandButton4 in the Object list. Make sure Click is in the Procedure box.

The Visual Basic Editor displays the Sub and End Sub statements for the CommandButton4 procedure and positions the insertion point between the two statements.

 Enter the VBA code shown in Table 6-16.

The CommandButton4_Click() procedure displays as shown in Figure 6-82.

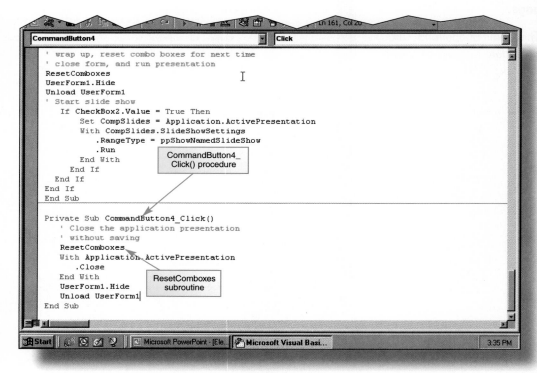

FIGURE 6-82

WRITING THE RESET COMBO BOXES PROCEDURE The final procedure that must be entered is the code that resets the combo boxes values. The Clear method is used to clear the values that were last selected.

Table 6-17	Reset Combo Boxes Procedure
LINE	VBA CODE
1	Sub ResetComboxes()
2	With ComboBox1
3	.Clear
4	End With
5	With ComboBox2
6	.Clear
7	End With

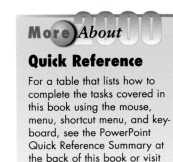

More About

Quick Reference

For a table that lists how to complete the tasks covered in this book using the mouse, menu, shortcut menu, and keyboard, see the PowerPoint Quick Reference Summary at the back of this book or visit the Office 2000 Web page (www.scsite.com/off2000/qr.htm), and then click Microsoft PowerPoint 2000.

For both combo boxes, the Clear method is used in lines 3 and 6.

Steps To Enter the ResetComboxes Procedure

1 **Click the Object box arrow at the top of the window and scroll up and click General. Make sure Declarations is in the Procedure box.**

The Visual Basic Editor positions the insertion point at the top of the UserForm1 Code window (Figure 6-83).

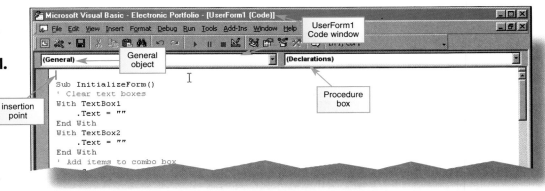

FIGURE 6-83

2 **Enter the VBA code shown in lines 1 through 7 of Table 6-17.**

The code for the ResetComboxes() procedure displays as shown in Figure 6-84. You do not need to enter line 8 of Table 6-17 because the Visual Basic Editor inserts that statement automatically.

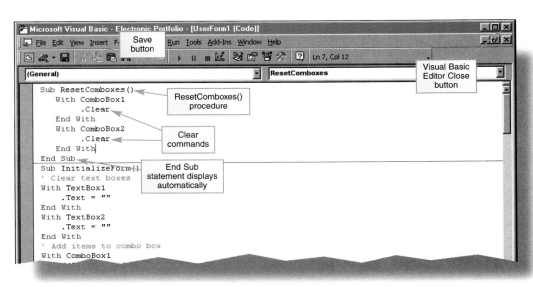

FIGURE 6-84

The VBA code is complete. The next step is to close the Visual Basic Editor and save the presentation. Before closing the Visual Basic Editor, you should verify your code by comparing it to Figures 6-72 through 6-84 on pages 6.49 through 6.65.

TO SAVE THE VISUAL BASIC CODE, CLOSE THE VISUAL BASIC EDITOR, AND SAVE THE PRESENTATION

1 Click the Save button on the Standard toolbar.

2 Click the Close button on the right side of the Visual Basic Editor title bar.

3 When the PowerPoint window displays, click the Save button on the Standard toolbar to save the presentation using the file name, Electronic Portfolio.

Adding a Button to Run the Form

The third button you will add to the custom Using Presentations toolbar is the Create Presentation button. When the user wants to create his custom presentation, he will click this button and the make his selections on the form. Perform the following steps to add this button.

TO ADD THE CREATE PRESENTATION BUTTON

1 Click Tools on the menu bar and then click Customize.

2 When the Customize dialog box opens, if necessary, click the Commands tab. Scroll down in the Categories box and then click Macros. Click CreatePresentationCareer in the Commands box.

3 Drag the CreatePresentationCareer entry from the Commands list in the Customize dialog box to the right of the Pack and Go button on the Using Presentation toolbar.

4 Click the Modify Selection menu button and then point to Change Button Image on the submenu. When the Change Button Image palette displays, click the button with a key (row 6, column 3).

5 Click the Modify Selection menu button and then click Name on the shortcut menu. Type Create Presentation as the new name of this button.

6 Click Default Style on the submenu.

7 Click the Close button.

The Create Presentation button displays with a key image (Figure 6-85 on the next page).

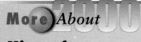

Microsoft Certification

The Microsoft Office User Specialist (MOUS) Certification program provides an opportunity for you to obtain a valuable industry credential – proof that you have the PowerPoint 2000 skills required by employers. For more information, see Appendix D or visit the Shelly Cashman Series MOUS Web page at www.scsite.com/off2000/cert.htm.

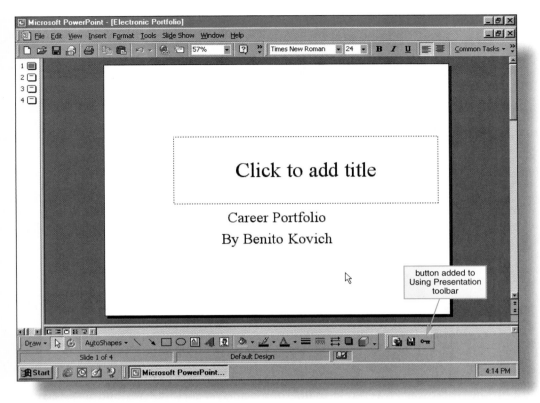

FIGURE 6-85

Saving the Presentation

The changes to the presentation are complete. Perform the following step to save the finished presentation before testing the controls.

TO SAVE A PRESENTATION

 Click the Save button on the Standard toolbar.

PowerPoint saves the presentation by saving the changes made to the presentation since the last save.

Testing the Controls

The final step is to test the controls in the form. Use the following data: Computer interview type; Company Name: Standard Technologies; computer clip art; Swap Slides 3 and 4, and Close presentation at finish.

TO TEST THE CONTROLS IN THE FORM

1 Click the Create Presentation button on the Using Presentation toolbar.

2 When the form displays, click the Computer tab. Type `Standard Technologies` as the Company Name.

3 Click the Select Clip Art arrow and click the Animated Computer clip art.

4 Click Swap Slides 3 and 4.

5 Click Close presentation when finished.

6 Click the OK button.

7 Click File on the menu bar and then click Print Handout to print the four slides and a handout.

The Electronic Portfolio presentation will display automatically (Figures 6-1e - 6-1f on page PP 6.5). The company name, Standard Technologies, displays on Slide 1. The animated computer clip art displays on Slide 2. The slide with the pilot photographs displays as Slide 3. The slide with the race car displays as Slide 4.

If the slides do not display as indicated here, then click Tools on the menu bar, point to Macro, and then click Visual Basic Editor. Click the View Code button on the Project Explorer toolbar, and then check the controls' properties and VBA code. Save the presentation again and repeat steps 1 through 7 above.

Quitting PowerPoint

The project is complete. To quit PowerPoint, follow the steps below.

TO QUIT POWERPOINT

1 Click the Close button on the title bar.

2 If the Microsoft PowerPoint dialog box displays, click the Yes button to save changes made since the last save.

PowerPoint quits.

CASE PERSPECTIVE SUMMARY

The Electronic Portfolio slide show should assist Benito with his job search. The form you developed using Visual Basic for Applications allows him to create a unique presentation for each interview. He can add the name of the company to the title slide, choose appropriate clip art, change the slide order, and run his presentation immediately or later. In addition, the buttons on the Using Presentation toolbar you created and the new command on the File menu easily allow him to save the presentation as a Web page, to use the Pack and Go Wizard to transport this file, and to print a handout for the interviewer. Benito's extraordinary and professional custom presentation should impress interviewers and help him land the best job possible.

Project Summary

Project 6 presented the principles of customizing a presentation. In Phase 1, you learned how to create a toolbar and add two buttons, Save as a Web Page and the Pack and Go Wizard. In Phase 2, you learned how to use the macro recorder to create a macro that prints handouts displaying four slides per page and assign this macro to a command on the File menu. In Phase 3, you learned how to create a form composed of Label controls, TextBox controls, ComboBox controls, OptionButton controls, CheckBox controls, and CommandButton controls. You were introduced to Visual Basic for Applications and the concept of object-oriented programming. You worked with objects that had properties and behaviors, or methods. In this phase, you also learned how to write VBA code that included looping and decision making by writing With statements, If-Then-Else statements, and Select Case Value statements.

What You Should Know

Having completed this project, you now should be able to perform the following tasks:

▶ Add a CheckBox Control to a Form *(PP 6.38)*

▶ Add a ComboBox Control to a Form *(PP 6.35)*

▶ Add a Command to a Menu, Assign the Command a Macro, and Invoke the Command *(PP 6.20)*

▶ Add a MultiPage Control to a Form and Increase Its Size *(PP 6.31)*

▶ Add a TextBox Control to a Form *(PP 6.34)*

▶ Add CommandButton Controls to a Form *(PP 6.39)*

▶ Add Label Controls to a Form *(PP 6.33)*

▶ Add OptionButton Controls to a Form *(PP 6.36)*

▶ Add the Create Presentation Button *(PP 6.66)*

▶ Change the Form Size and Arrange the Toolbox Position *(PP 6.29)*

▶ Change the OptionButton4 Caption *(PP 6.47)*

▶ Copy Controls from One Sheet to Another *(PP 6.44)*

▶ Create a Custom Toolbar and Add Two Buttons *(PP 6.10)*

▶ Enter the CommandButton1 Procedure *(PP 6.58)*

▶ Enter the CommandButton2 Procedure *(PP 6.60)*

▶ Enter the CommandButton3 Procedure *(PP 6.63)*

▶ Enter the CommandButton4 Procedure *(PP 6.64)*

▶ Enter the Create Presentation Career Procedure *(PP 6.49)*

▶ Enter the InitializeForm Procedure *(PP 6.53)*

▶ Enter the ResetComboboxes Procedure *(PP 6.65)*

▶ Open a Presentation and Save it with a New File Name *(PP 6.7)*

▶ Open a Presentation with a Macro and Execute the Macro *(PP 6.23)*

▶ Open the Visual Basic IDE and a New Form *(PP 6.27)*

▶ Quit PowerPoint *(PP 6.68)*

▶ Record a Macro to Print Handouts in Vertical Slide Order in Pure Black and White *(PP 6.16)*

▶ Resize and Reposition the Controls on a Form *(PP 6.43)*

▶ Save a Presentation *(PP 6.14, PP 6.22, PP 6.47)*

▶ Save the Visual Basic Code, Close the Visual Basic Editor, and Save the Presentation *(PP 6.66)*

▶ Set the Caption Properties *(PP 6.40)*

▶ Test the Controls in the Form *(PP 6.67)*

▶ View a Macro's VBA Code *(PP 6.24)*

Apply Your Knowledge

➕ Project Reinforcement at www.scsite.com/off2000/reinforce.htm

1 Creating a Macro and Customizing a Menu and Toolbar

Instructions: Start PowerPoint and perform the following tasks.

1. Open the Snow file from your Data Disk. If you do not have a copy of the Data Disk, then see the inside back cover of this book.
2. Click File on the menu bar and then click Save As. Save the presentation with the file name, Ski Vacation.
3. Reset the toolbars to their installation settings (see Step 6 on page PP 6.8).
4. Add a footer with your name, today's date, and the slide number to all slides.
5. Use the Record New Macro command to create a macro that exports the presentation outline to Microsoft Word. Call the macro ExportWord. Change the name of the author in the Description box to your name. Make sure the Store macro in box displays Ski Vacation. Click the OK button. When the Stop Recording toolbar displays, do the following:

   (a) Click File on the menu bar and then click Save As; (b) When the Save As dialog box displays, type Snow Outline in the File name box; (c) Click the Save as type box arrow and click Outline/RTF in the Save as type list; (d) Be certain the Save in box location is 3½ Floppy (A:); (e) click the Save button; and (f) click the Stop Recording button on the Stop Recording toolbar.

6. Add a button to the Standard toolbar (Figure 6-86a) and a command to the File menu (Figure 6-86b) to run the macro. Use the image of a floppy disk with an arrow pointing up (row 1, column 5) and the Default Style for the button and the Export to Word command on the file menu.
7. View the ExportWord's VBA code. When the Visual Basic Editor displays the macro, click File on the menu bar, click Print, and then click the OK button. Close the Visual Basic Editor.
8. Run the macro as follows: (a) click the button you added to the Standard toolbar; (b) on the File menu, click the Export to Word command.
9. Save the Ski Vacation file again.
10. Reset the toolbars to their installation settings (see Step 6 on page PP 6.8). Hand in the macro and outline printouts to your instructor. Quit PowerPoint.

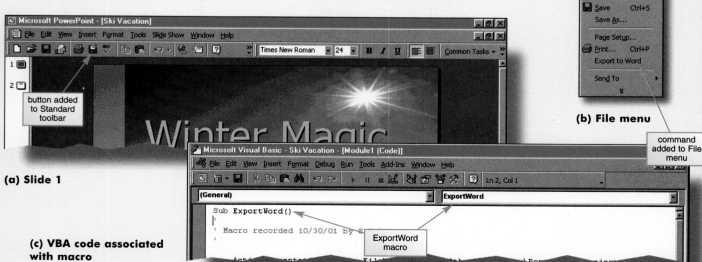

(a) Slide 1

(b) File menu

(c) VBA code associated with macro

FIGURE 6-86

In the Lab

1 Producing a Web Page Automatically

Problem: Your job at Z-Net is to create and post Web pages. The company owner has decided to display a Web page listing birth announcements for customers. Because the owner does not want to burden you with this task frequently, he wants you to design a process that the receptionist can use to complete this assignment. You decide to create a basic, one slide presentation. The receptionist's task will be to add the data to a basic slide (Figure 6-87a on the next page) and then save the presentation as a Web page. To streamline the process, you create a macro toolbar and place three buttons on it. The first button will run a macro that sets the background to pink for a female, the second button will set the background to blue for a male, and the third button will save the presentation as an HTML file. Figure 6-87b on the next page shows a presentation for a female.

Instructions: Start PowerPoint and perform the following tasks with a computer.

1. Open the Announce presentation on the Data Disk. If you do not have a copy of the Data Disk, then see the inside back cover of this book.
2. Reset the toolbars to their installation settings (see Step 6 on page PP 6.8).
3. Create a toolbar and name it Baby. Place the toolbar next to the Drawing toolbar.
4. Use the Record New Macro command to create a macro generates the female slide. Call the macro BabyGirl, change the name of the author in the Description box to your name, and store the macro in the Announce Update file.
5. With the Stop Recording toolbar on the screen, do the following: (a) On the Format menu, click Background, click the Background fill box arrow, click Fill Effects on the menu, click the Texture tab in the Fill Effects dialog box, double click the Pink tissue paper texture (row 3, column 2), and then click the Apply button; (b) Select the title text and change the font to Script MT (or a similar script font); and (c) Click the Stop Recording button on the Stop Recording toolbar. Click the slide anywhere except a placeholder.
6. Add a button to the Baby toolbar (Figure 6-87a) and a command to the Edit menu (Figure 6-87b and 6-87c on the next page). Assign the button and command the BabyGirl macro. Change the button image to a diamond (row 3, column 4) and use the Default Style.
7. Use the Record New Macro command to create a second macro that generates the male slide. Call the macro BabyBoy, change the name of the author in the Description box to your name, and store the macro in the Announce Update file.
8. With the Stop Recording toolbar on the screen, do the following: (a) On the Format menu, click Background, click the Background fill box arrow, click Fill Effects on the menu, double click the Blue tissue paper texture (row 3, column 1), and then click the Apply button; (b) Select the title text and change the font to Arial and the style to Bold with no Italics; and (c) Click the Stop Recording button on the Stop Recording toolbar.
9. Add a button to the Baby toolbar (Figure 6-87b) and a command to the Edit menu (Figure 6-87c). Assign the button and command the BabyBoy macro. Modify the button image to a heart (row 3, column 3) and use the Default Style.
10. Add the Save as Web Page command to the Baby toolbar. Change the button image to the Default Style.
11. Save the presentation using the file name, Announce Update.

(continued)

In the Lab

Producing a Web Page Automatically *(continued)*

12. Modify the slide as by replacing the XX in the title text to your last name. Enter your first name after the Announces the birth of: paragraph. Enter today's date for the date of birth. Enter the current time for the time of birth. Enter your estimated weight and length at birth.

13. If you are a male, execute the BabyBoy macro; if you are a girl, execute the BabyGirl macro.

14. Click the Save as Web Page button on your Baby toolbar. Save the file as Announce Web.

15. Save the presentation with the file name, Announce xx Baby, replacing the XX with your last name.

16. Print the presentation, print the macro code, and print the Web page. Quit PowerPoint

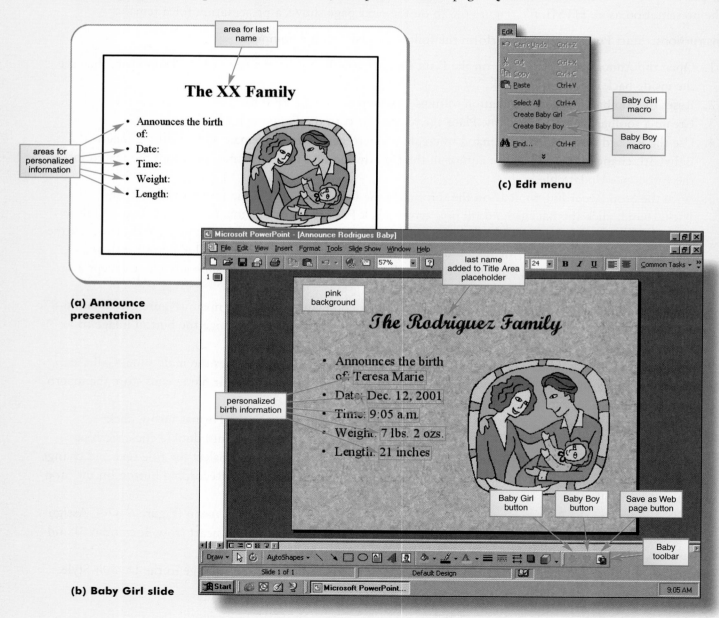

FIGURE 6-87

In the Lab

2 Creating a Summary Slide Automatically

Problem: While talking with one of your colleagues about PowerPoint's features, you discuss how some toolbar buttons do not record as part of a macro. For example, the Insert Summary Slide button on the Slide Sorter toolbar will not record as part of a macro. Using your knowledge of how slides are treated as objects and searching through the Visual Basic help screens, you discover a method of writing a Visual Basic module that creates a new blank slide at the end of the slide sequence and reads the title text of Slides 2 through the end of the slides. By incorporating the count method and using Visual Basic For/Next statements, you can solve the problem. The completed summary slide is shown in Figure 6-88b on page PP 6.75.

Instructions: Start PowerPoint and perform the following tasks with a computer.

1. Open the Studying presentation you created in Project 1. If you did not create that presentation, see your instructor for a copy of that file.
2. Open the Visual Basic Editor and insert a new module.
3. In the General Declarations window, enter the code from the following table to declare the variables used in the module.

Table 6-18	General Declarations
LINE	*VBA CODE*
1	Dim mySlide As Integer
2	Dim SumText As String
3	Dim SummarySlideLines(4) As String

4. Start a new subroutine for a module called SummarySlide(). Type Sub Summary_Slide() and press the ENTER key. The End Sub statement should display automatically.
5. Enter the code in Table 6-19 to determine the total number of slides in the presentation.

Table 6-19	Determine Slide Count Procedure
LINE	*VBA CODE*
1	Sub SummarySlide()
2	Dim SlideCount as Integer
3	With ActivePresentation.Slides
4	'Determine the number of total slides
5	SlideCount = .Count + 1
6	End With

6. Enter the code from Table 6-20 to collect the titles from every slide.

(continued)

In the Lab

Creating a Summary Slide Automatically Table 6-20 Collect Titles Procedure *(continued)*

Table 6-20	Collect Titles Procedure
LINE	VBA CODE
1	For mySlide = 2 To SlideCount - 1
2	'Collect the titles from every slide
3	Set myPresentation = ActivePresentation.Slides(mySlide)
4	SummarySlideLines(mySlide) = myPresentation.Shapes.Title.TextFrame.TextRange.Text
5	Next mySlide

7. Add the code from Table 6-21 to add a slide at the end of the presentation and insert the title for this slide.

Table 6-21	Add Summary Slide Procedure
LINE	VBA CODE
1	'Add the summary slide
2	Set SumSlide = ActivePresentation.Slides.Add(SlideCount, ppLayoutText).Shapes
3	'Insert the title for the summary slide
4	SumSlide.Title.TextFrame.TextRange.Text = "In Conclusion"

8. Use the code from Table 6-22 to use a For Next loop to collect the slide titles into one long string of text. Insert a carriage return at the end of each title so the titles will display on separate lines in the slide.

Table 6-22	Collect Slide Titles Procedure
LINE	VBA CODE
1	'Collect the Slide titles into one long string of text
2	'inserting a carriage return at the end of each title
3	'so the titles will display on separate lines
4	For mySlide = 2 To SlideCount - 1
5	SumText = SumText & SummarySlideLines(mySlide) & Chr(13)
6	Next mySlide

9. Insert the SumText into the Object Area placeholder using the code in Table 6-23.

Table 6-23	Insert Summary Text Procedure
LINE	VBA CODE
1	'Now insert the titles in the Text list placeholder of the slide
2	SumSlide.Placeholders(2).TextFrame.TextRange.Text = SumText
3	End Sub

In the Lab

10. Add the Summary_Slide() module to the Common Tasks menu on the Formatting toolbar (Figure 6-88c).
11. Save the Visual Basic code, and then save the presentation using the file name, Studying Update.
12. Execute the Visual Basic code. Print the Visual Basic code and the slides using the Pure black and white option. Quit PowerPoint.

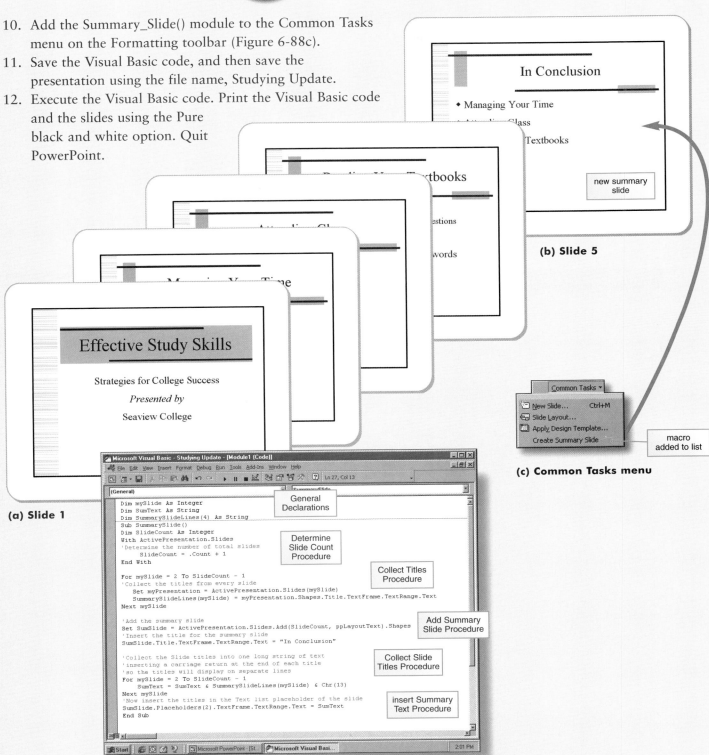

In Conclusion

◆ Managing Your Time
◆ Attending Class
◆ Reading Your Textbooks

new summary slide

(b) Slide 5

Effective Study Skills

Strategies for College Success

Presented by

Seaview College

(a) Slide 1

Common Tasks ▾

New Slide...   Ctrl+M
Slide Layout...
Apply Design Template...
Create Summary Slide

macro added to list

(c) Common Tasks menu

Microsoft Visual Basic - Studying Update - [Module1 [Code]]
File Edit View Insert Format Debug Run Tools Add-Ins Window Help

(General)   Summary_Slide

```
Dim mySlide As Integer
Dim SumText As String
Dim SummarySlideLines(4) As String
Sub SummarySlide()
Dim SlideCount As Integer
With ActivePresentation.Slides
'Determine the number of total slides
    SlideCount = .Count + 1
End With

For mySlide = 2 To SlideCount - 1
'Collect the titles from every slide
    Set myPresentation = ActivePresentation.Slides(mySlide)
    SummarySlideLines(mySlide) = myPresentation.Shapes.Title.TextFrame.TextRange.Text
Next mySlide

'Add the summary slide
Set SumSlide = ActivePresentation.Slides.Add(SlideCount, ppLayoutText).Shapes
'Insert the title for the summary slide
SumSlide.Title.TextFrame.TextRange.Text = "In Conclusion"

'Collect the Slide titles into one long string of text
'inserting a carriage return at the end of each title
'so the titles will display on separate lines
For mySlide = 2 To SlideCount - 1
    SumText = SumText & SummarySlideLines(mySlide) & Chr(13)
Next mySlide
'Now insert the titles in the Text list placeholder of the slide
SumSlide.Placeholders(2).TextFrame.TextRange.Text = SumText
End Sub
```

General Declarations

Determine Slide Count Procedure

Collect Titles Procedure

Add Summary Slide Procedure

Collect Slide Titles Procedure

insert Summary Text Procedure

Start   Microsoft PowerPoint - [St...   Microsoft Visual Basi...   2:01 PM

(d) Module1 VBA code

FIGURE 6-88

In the Lab

3 Automating a Monthly Payment Calculation

Problem: Your neighbor is a real estate broker who gives weekly presentations to community groups on house buying techniques. One of the topics she discusses is the cost of the loan. Many people have asked her during the presentations what the monthly payment would be on a certain loan amount. She says she could help her audience if she could display a form in her presentation, enter figures, and get a monthly payment. You agree to help her with this project.

Instructions: Start PowerPoint and perform the following tasks with a computer.

1. Open the Home Buying Basics presentation on the Data Disk. If you do not have a copy of the Data Disk, then see the inside back cover of this book.
2. Create the form shown in Figure 6-89a. Use the following table to set the control properties.

Table 6-24	Exact Locations of Controls in the Form	
CONTROL	*PROPERTY*	*VALUE*
Label1	Caption	Loan Amount
	Left	12
	Top	12
	Width	72
Label2	Caption	Interest in Percent
	Left	12
	Top	42
	Width	72
Label3	Caption	Number of Years
	Left	12
	Top	72
	Width	72
Label4	Caption	Monthly Payment
	Left	12
	Top	102
	Width	72
Label5	Caption	Blank
	Left	96
	Top	102
	Width	72
	Special Effect	2 frmSpecialEffectSunken

Table 6-24	Exact Locations of Controls in the Form	
CONTROL	*PROPERTY*	*VALUE*
TextBox1	Left	96
	Top	12
	Width	72
TextBox2	Left	96
	Top	42
	Width	72
TextBox3	Left	96
	Top	72
	Width	72
CommandButton1	Caption	Calculate
	Left	18
	Top	132
	Width	54
CommandButton2	Caption	Clear
	Left	90
	Top	132
	Width	54
CommandButton3	Caption	Close
	Left	162
	Top	132
	Width	54

3. Write the code for the Calculate command button using Table 6-25.

In the Lab

Table 6-25 Verify Values and Calculate Payment Procedure

LINE	VBA CODE
1	'Validate the text box fields
2	'If OK, then calculate mortgage
3	If TextBox1.Text = "" Then
4	MsgBox "Please enter a loan amount", vbOKOnly, "Loan Amount"
5	TextBox1.SetFocus
6	ElseIf TextBox2.Text = "" Then
7	MsgBox "Please enter an interest rate", vbOKOnly, "Interest Rate"
8	TextBox2.SetFocus
9	ElseIf TextBox3.Text = "" Then
10	MsgBox "Please enter the number of years for the loan", vbOKOnly, "Years"
11	TextBox3.SetFocus
12	Else
13	Label5.Caption = FormatCurrency(Pmt(TextBox2.Text / 1200, TextBox3.Text * 12, -TextBox1.Text, 0, 0), 2)
14	End If

4. Write the code for the Clear command button using Table 6-26.

Table 6-26 Clear Procedure

LINE	VBA CODE
1	'Clear all text boxes and monthly payment
2	'Set insertion point in first textbox
3	TextBox1.Text = ""
4	TextBox1.SetFocus
5	TextBox2.Text = ""
6	TextBox3.Text = ""
7	Label5.Caption = ""

5. Write the code for the Close Button Procedure using Table 6-27.

Table 6-27 Close Button Procedure

LINE	VBA CODE
1	UserForm1.Hide
2	Unload UserForm1

In the Lab

Table 6-28	Display Mortgage Form Procedure
LINE	*VBA CODE*
1	Sub DisplayMortForm()
2	UserForm1.Show
3	End Sub

6. Insert a module, and use the code in Table 6-28 to enter the code for displaying the form.

7. Add the module to the pop-up menu for the slide show by using the Customize command on the tools menu.

8. Click the Toolbars tab and click Shortcut Menus in the Customize dialog box. Click the Commands tab and select Macros in the Categories list. Click the DisplayMortForm macro in the Commands list and drag it to the SlideShow menu on the Shortcut Menus bar.

9. Click the SlideShow menu button on the Shortcut Menus bar. When the drop down menu displays, drag the DisplayMortForm command to the Slide Show command and place it below the Go command.

10. Save the presentation as House Buying Update. Print the form and the Visual Basic code. Close the Visual Basic Editor and quit PowerPoint.

In the Lab

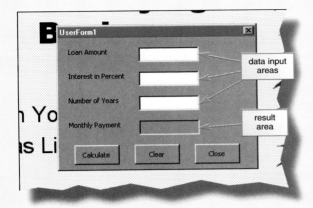

(a) Payment form

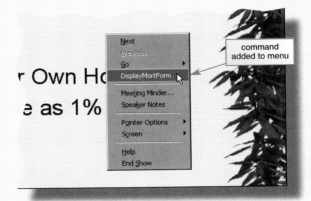

(b) Popup menu

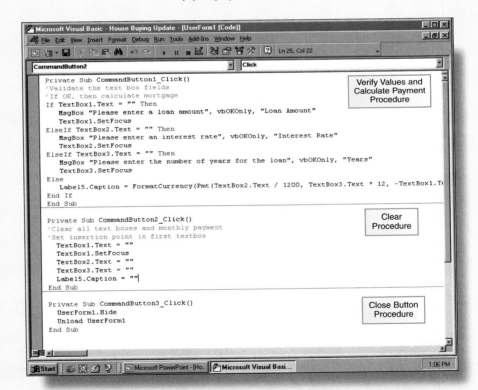

(c) UserForm1 VBA code

(d) Module1 VBA code

FIGURE 6-89

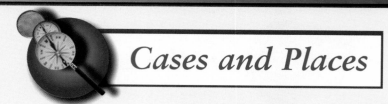

Cases and Places

The difficulty of these case studies varies:
▶ are the least difficult; ▶▶ are more difficult; and ▶▶▶ are the most difficult.

1 ▶ Open the Investing presentation from the Data Disk. Create a macro that prints the Notes Pages using the Pure black and white, Scale to fit paper, and Frame slides options. In addition, the macro should print the outline using the Pure black and white and the Scale to fit paper options. Then create another macro that exports the presentation outline to Microsoft Word. Call the macro ExportWord. Execute the macros, print the macros, and hand in the printouts to your instructor.

2 ▶▶ Open the Electronic Portfolio presentation you created in this project. You would like to share the layout of your form with various colleagues to obtain their feedback. Using the Visual Basic Editor, write a new module that prints the form. Save the module as PrintThisForm. Using the Customize command on the Tools menu, find your module in the Macro commands. Drag the PrintThisForm entry to the right of the Create Presentation button on the Using Presentation toolbar you created in the project. Modify this new button using the open pages image (row 6, column 1) on the Change Button Image palette. Name the button Print Form and then set the new button to the Default Style. Execute and print the macro. Hand in the printouts to your instructor.

3 ▶▶ Open the Home presentation from the Data Disk. Add a form that allows the user to select one of five templates from a combo box. Because slides two and four have clip art, you want the user to be able to select one of five clip art images for Slide 2 and one of five clip art images for Slide 4. The same five images may be used. Your Visual Basic code should warn the user if the same image has been selected for both slides. Write the Visual Basic module that executes this form. Name the module AddTemplates_ClipArt, and add that module to your Formatting toolbar. Print the form, the Visual Basic code, and the presentation. Hand in the printouts to your instructor.

4 ▶▶ Using Microsoft Internet Explorer, go to the Microsoft Office Developer's Web site http://msdn. microsoft.com/officedev/. Scroll down the page and enter Visual Basic for Applications in the Search text box. Click the Search button. Print and read three of the articles and then write a one-page summary of the articles. Hand in the article printouts and your summary to your instructor.

5 ▶▶▶ Open the Spring Break presentation you created in Project 3. If you did not complete this project, see your instructor for a copy of the file. Create a new toolbar named Vacations. Record a macro that prints handouts and notes. Place this macro on the new toolbar, and change the text of the button to an appropriate image. Next, add a button to your toolbar to execute the Pack and Go Wizard. Using Visual Basic Help, create a form that allows the user to modify the vacation slides to present either summer or winter vacations. Use the WinterChart.doc and the WinterTable.doc from your Data Disk for Slides 3 and 4 respectively when the winter vacation is chosen. Give the user the option to change templates depending on the season. Execute the print macro, and then display the form. Change the summer vacation presentation to a winter vacation presentation. Print slides, the Visual Basic code, and the form, and submit the handouts to your instructor.

Microsoft PowerPoint 2000

Distributing Presentations to Remote Audiences

C A S E   P E R S P E C T I V E

Job-hunting experts claim that searching for a full-time job is a full-time job in itself. Every day many students visit the Valley View College Placement Office to learn how to begin their job search. Jessica Cantero, the placement director, conducts several monthly seminars using a PowerPoint presentation with her talk on writing resumes.

Students attending Valley View's remote campuses have asked Jessica to deliver this speech. Jessica wants to put her PowerPoint presentation on floppy disks to take to these locations. She is not certain if PowerPoint is installed on computers where she will speak, so she needs to include the PowerPoint Viewer to ensure her slide show will run properly. Jessica has asked you to transfer her presentation and the Viewer onto floppy disks. You agree to use the Pack and Go Wizard, which optionally includes the Viewer, to compress the files.

In addition, Jessica had her network administrator transfer the Resumes With Results file to the College's Web server so she can collaborate with her cohorts about the content. Jessica wants you to develop subscriptions for the presentation to notify her when colleagues submit comments.

Introduction

PowerPoint file sizes often are much larger than those produced by other Microsoft Office programs such as Word and Excel. Presentations with embedded pictures and video, such as the one you created in Project 6, easily can grow beyond the 1.44 MB capacity of floppy disks. The large file size may present difficulties if you need to transport your presentation to show on another computer.

One solution to this file size limitation is using the **Pack and Go Wizard**. This program, which also is used in Microsoft Publisher, compresses and saves all the components of your presentation so it can be delivered on a computer other than the one on which it was created. Linked documents and multimedia files are included in this packaged file. The Wizard can embed any TrueType font that is included in Windows; however, it cannot embed other TrueType fonts that have built-in copyright restrictions.

If the destination computer does not have Microsoft PowerPoint installed, the Pack and Go Wizard can pack the **PowerPoint Viewer** along with the presentation. The Viewer is a program, PPview32.exe, that allows you to run, but not edit, a PowerPoint presentation created in PowerPoint for Windows or PowerPoint for the Macintosh. It is available on the Microsoft Office CD-ROMs and on the Microsoft Office Update Web site, http://officeupdate.microsoft.com/, which is a source for viewer updates and for additional information. You can distribute the Viewer freely and install it on computers that do not have Microsoft Office installed. It supports all features from PowerPoint 97 and PowerPoint 95; however, it does not support some PowerPoint 2000 features, such as picture bullets, automatic numbering, and animated GIF files.

Part 1: Saving the Presentation Using the Pack and Go Wizard

The resume slide show consists of five slides that provide general guidelines, specific strategies for listing education and work experience, and considerations for writing electronic resumes (Figure 1). The presentation uses clip art, slide transitions, and preset animation to add visual interest.

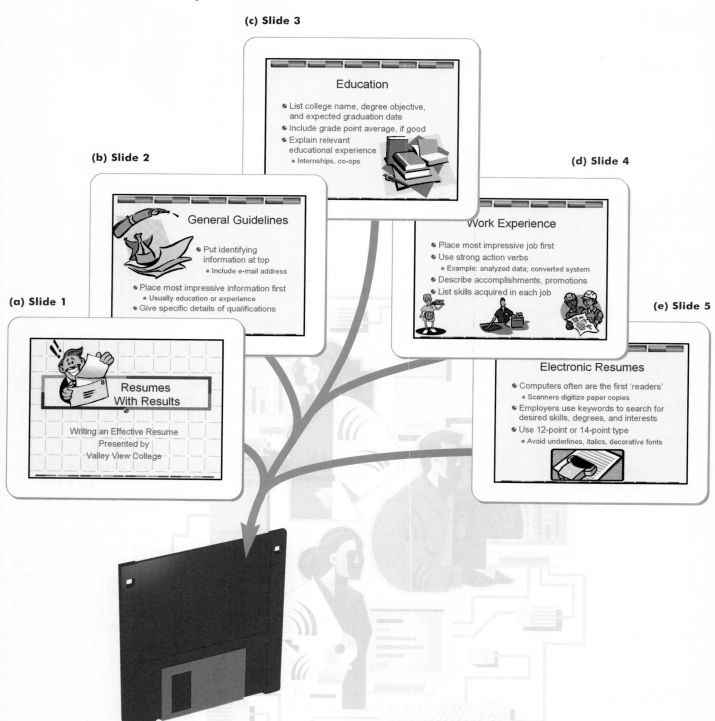

(c) Slide 3

(b) Slide 2

(d) Slide 4

(a) Slide 1

(e) Slide 5

FIGURE 1

The Pack and Go Wizard will compress your presentation and package it with the PowerPoint Viewer so you can show it on another computer. As you proceed through the Wizard, PowerPoint will prompt you to select the presentation file, a destination drive, linking and embedding options, and whether to add the Viewer.

The Resumes With Results file size is 156 KB; the Pack and Go Wizard will create a compressed file with the file name pres0.ppz with a file size of 66 KB. If you add the Viewer to the package, the file increases to more than 2,700 KB, which is too large to fit onto one floppy disk. In addition, the Wizard creates another file, pngsetup.exe, which is needed to unpack, or extract, the Viewer and presentation file and copy them onto a remote computer. The pngsetup file is 55 KB. You consequently will need at least two additional floppy disks to run the Pack and Go Wizard and save the compressed files to drive A. The Wizard truncates the presentation file name to Resume~1 because it supports file names with a maximum of eight characters and cannot include spaces. Perform the following steps to use the Pack and Go Wizard and add the PowerPoint Viewer.

More About

the Projector Wizard

When you show your presentation on another computer at a remote site, you may need to set the screen resolution according to the projection system you are using. The Projector Wizard helps you optimize viewing the slide show. To run the Projector Wizard, click Set Up Show on the Slide Show menu and follow the prompts to set up the presentation for the particular monitor or projection system you are using. If you are running Microsoft Windows 98 or 2000, you can run your slide show on one monitor and view your slides, notes, and the presentation outlines on another monitor.

 To Save the Presentation Using the Pack and Go Wizard

1 **Start PowerPoint and then open the Resumes With Results file on the Data Disk. Reset your toolbars as described in Appendix C. Click File on the menu bar and then point to Pack and Go.**

PowerPoint opens and displays the presentation in slide view (Figure 2). The File menu displays. Depending on your computer system installation, you may be prompted to install the Pack and Go Wizard. If this message occurs, see your instructor.

2 **Click Pack and Go. When the Pack and Go Wizard dialog box displays, point to the Next button.**

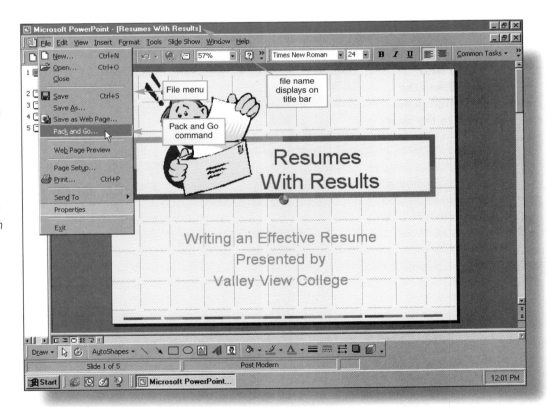

FIGURE 2

PowerPoint displays the Start panel, describing the function of the Pack and Go Wizard. You can click the Help button if you desire further explanations from the Office Assistant or the Cancel button to exit the Pack and Go Wizard.

③ **Click the Next button. When the Pick files to pack panel displays, point to the Next button.**

The Active presentation check box is selected (Figure 3). You can choose to package the Resumes With Results file with one or more other PowerPoint files. You can click the Back button to review previous panels.

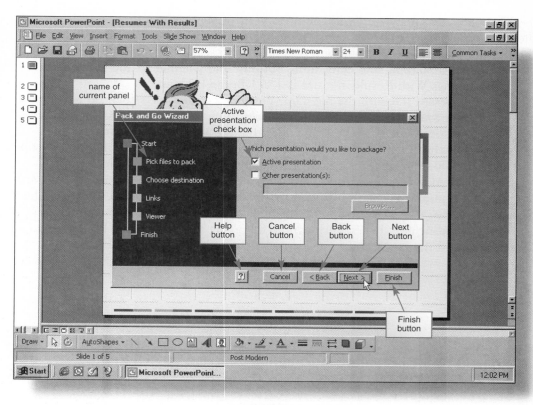

FIGURE 3

④ **Click the Next button. When the Choose destination panel displays, point to the Next button.**

PowerPoint defaults to saving the packed file on the floppy disk in drive A (Figure 4). You could select an alternate destination, such as your hard drive, a Zip drive, or to another computer on your network.

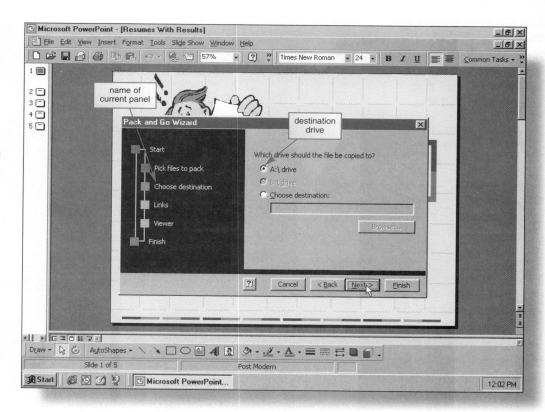

FIGURE 4

5 **Click the Next button. When the Links panel displays, click Include linked files to deselect the option. Point to the Next button.**

The Resumes With Results presentation does not contain any linked files, so you do not need to select this option (Figure 5). If the presentation had linked files, such as embedded Excel charts and Word tables, you would need to include these files in the package. The presentation uses the TrueType Arial font, but this standard font is found on most computers. Embedding fonts ensures the text displays correctly if the font is not installed on the destination computer.

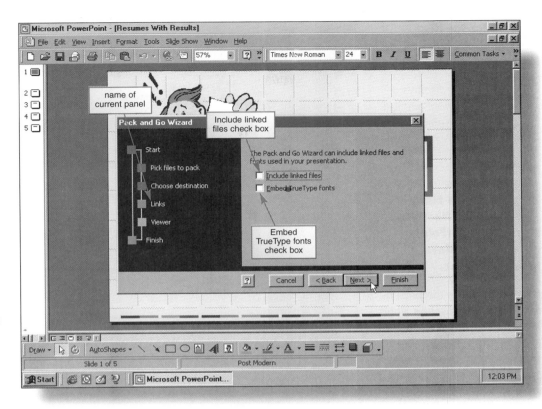

FIGURE 5

6 **Click the Next button. When the Viewer panel displays, click Viewer for Windows 95 or NT. Point to the Next button.**

The Viewer will run the presentation if the application is not installed (Figure 6). You want to include the PowerPoint Viewer because you are uncertain whether PowerPoint is installed on computers at the remote campuses.

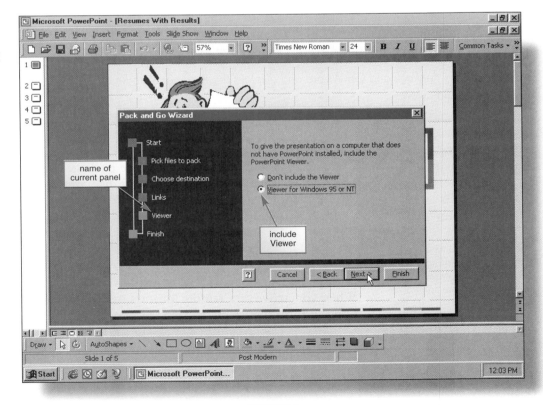

FIGURE 6

7 Click the Next button. Point to the Finish button.

The Finish panel displays a message that PowerPoint will compress the Resumes With Results presentation to drive A (Figure 7).

8 Click the Finish button. When the Microsoft PowerPoint dialog box displays, point to the OK button.

PowerPoint packs the presentation files and displays status messages of which files are being added to the package. When the packing process is completed, PowerPoint displays the message that the Pack and Go Wizard has packed the presentation successfully.

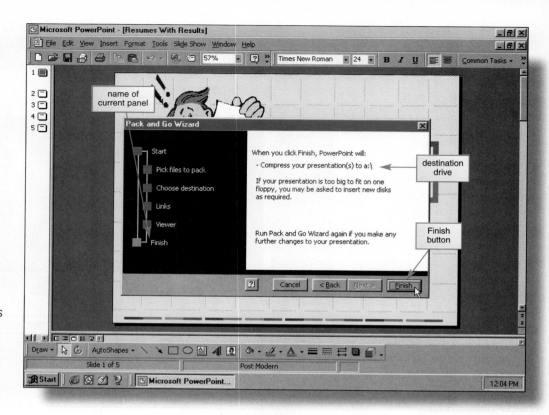

FIGURE 7

9 Click the OK button in the Microsoft PowerPoint dialog box.

PowerPoint closes the Pack and Go Wizard and displays the Resumes With Results presentation in slide view.

The Pack and Go Wizard saves the package containing the presentation and Viewer as pres0.ppz on the first floppy disk, pres0.pp1 on the second disk, and pres0.pp2 on the third disk. You now are ready to transport the presentation to a remote site.

Unpacking a Presentation

When you arrive at a remote location, you will need to open the packed presentation. Perform the following steps to unpack the presentation.

TO UNPACK A PRESENTATION

1. Insert your first floppy disk of packed files in drive A. Right-click the Start button on the taskbar and then click Open on the shortcut menu.

2. Click the Up button on the Standard Buttons toolbar three times so that the My Computer window displays. Double-click 3½ Floppy (A:).

3. When the 3½ Floppy (A): window opens, double-click pngsetup.

4. When the Pack and Go Setup dialog box displays, enter C:\RESUME in the Destination Folder text box and then click the OK button. Click the OK button when asked to create this directory. When prompted, insert the second disk and click the OK button. Then insert the third disk when prompted and click the OK button.

5. When the Pack and Go Setup dialog box displays the message that the presentation has been installed successfully in C:\RESUME directory, click the Yes button to run the slide show now.

PowerPoint unpacks the Resumes With Results presentation and runs the slide show.

You can create a **playlist** to use with the Viewer if you have multiple presentations you want to show sequentially. To create this list, open Notepad or a new document in Microsoft Word. Next, type the file names, including the .ppt file extensions, of the desired presentations on separate lines. Save this file with the extension .lst. When you are ready to start running the presentations, start the Viewer, PPview32.exe, enter the file name of the document that contains the playlist, and then click Show.

Part 1 of this project is complete. You now should close the Resumes With Results presentation. Perform the following steps to close the presentation but leave PowerPoint running.

TO CLOSE THE PRESENTATION

1. Click File on the menu bar and then click Close on the File menu.

PowerPoint closes the Resumes With Results presentation.

Part 2: Discussing and Subscribing to a Publication

Sending and receiving e-mail messages constitutes a major portion of the day for many students and business workers. An estimated 25 million e-mail users send 15 billion messages each year. If you want a colleague to review your PowerPoint presentation or Word document draft, you can send the document as an attachment to an e-mail message and then ask the recipient to respond with comments. Another method for soliciting comments on a document, Web folder, or discussion is a **subscription**, which automatically notifies participants by e-mail when a specified document had been modified, moved, or deleted.

The first step in beginning a subscription is to save the file on a Web server. A **Web server** is a computer that delivers requested Web pages. Your network administrator needs to **upload** your Resumes With Results file to your Web server. A file is uploaded when it is copied from a local computer to a remote computer. Before uploading the file, the network administrator has to install the **Office Server Extensions (OSE)** on the server to enable you to participate in Office's Web discussion and subscription features. The OSE are a set of technologies that provide

More About

Playlists

Playlist (.lst) files are supported in the PowerPoint Viewer, not in the PowerPoint application. If you open a Playlist file in PowerPoint by clicking the File command and then clicking Open, PowerPoint opens the file as text within as an outline. If you want to run a series of presentations as slide shows in PowerPoint, you can use a batch file. The result is very similar to a playlist; the presentations play in order. The only difference is that you will see your desktop for a moment between presentations. The Microsoft Web site has detailed directions on how to create this batch file. For more information, visit the PowerPoint 2000 Web Feature 2 More About page (www.scsite.com/pp2000/more.htm) and click Playlist.

Other Ways

1. Press ALT+F, press C

More About

OSE

When network administrators install the Web Discussions feature they install the Office Service Extensions (OSE). These files enable subscriptions and discussions to occur. The OSE have their own Setup program and an OSE Configuration Wizard that guides installation on a Web server by configuring database, security, and e-mail server settings. For more information, visit the PowerPoint 2000 Web Feature 2 More About page (www.scsite.com/pp2000/more.htm) and click OSE.

publishing, collaboration, and searching capabilities for Office 2000 documents and Web pages. The administrator places your file in the College's **Web folder**, which is an area on a Web server where the document is stored.

Now you are ready to ask your colleagues to review the presentation. Each of these individuals will join a **Web discussion**, which is a new Office 2000 feature that allows users to collaborate by inserting comments on files accessible from a Web server. They will make their comments using the **Discussions toolbar** (Figure 8), which contains buttons that allow you to add, navigate through, edit, and reply to comments, to subscribe to a document, and to view or hide the Discussions window. This toolbar displays only when you start a Web discussion; it cannot be displayed from the Toolbars option in the View menu or from a shortcut menu. The participants' comments will be **threaded** so the original comments and all related replies display together. These discussion comments are stored in a database on the server, so the original Resumes With Results presentation is not altered.

You will start a discussion and then read the comments by subscribing to the Resumes With Results file at Valley View College. Ask your instructor for the location of that file on your Web server.

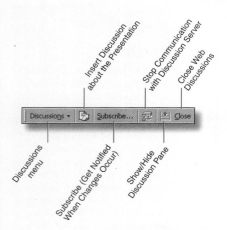

Discussions toolbar

FIGURE 8

Opening a File in a Web Folder

To comment on a presentation, you first must **download** a copy of it from the Web server where it is stored. A file is downloaded when it is copied from a remote computer to a local computer. Perform the following steps to open the Valley View College Web folder and then download the Resumes with Results file.

 To Open a File in a Web Folder

1 **With PowerPoint open, click File on the menu bar and then click Open on the File menu. When the Open dialog box displays, click Web Folders in the Places bar of the Open dialog box, click Valley View College in the Web Folders list, and then point to the Open button.**

PowerPoint opens the Web Folders folder (Figure 9). You will need to ask your instructor to verify the location of the Resumes With Results file on your network. You also may be able to use your browser to view the list of files in a Web folder.

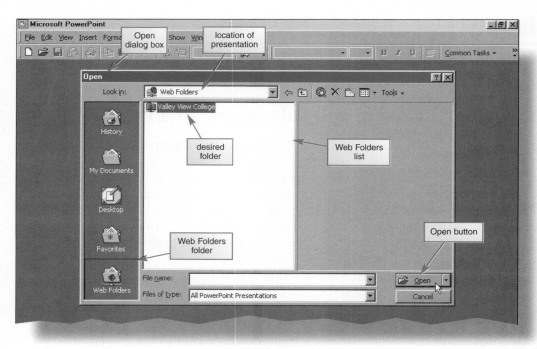

FIGURE 9

Click the Open button. When the Open dialog box displays again, point to the Open button.

The Valley View College folder opens and displays the one document, Resumes With Results, it contains (Figure 10). Your list of file names may vary if your network administrator has added other files to the folder.

 Click the Open button.

As the Resumes With Results presentation downloads from the Web server to your computer, Office 2000 displays a Transferring File progress meter. Slide 1 of the presentation displays in slide view.

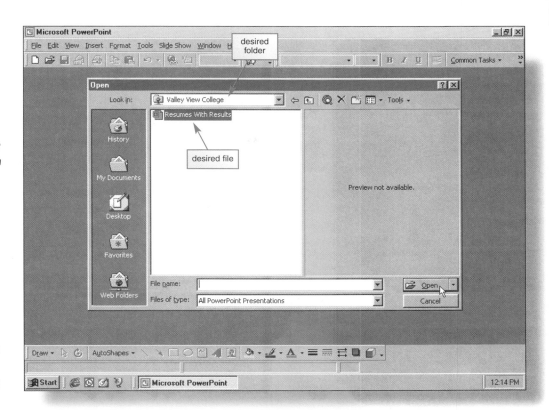

FIGURE 10

You are able to scroll through the slides in the presentation and run the slide show. Although you cannot alter the slide show, you can comment on the presentation and view comments your cohorts have made about the slides.

Starting Web Discussions

Microsoft added the Office 2000 Web discussions tool as a means of allowing Office users to view presentations and then make comments. A discussion database on the server stores the comments along with pointers to the locations where the comments belong in the document. This technology is designed to help teams work efficiently and effectively. Perform the steps on the next page to discuss the content of the presentation.

More About

Newsgroup Discussions

Along with subscribing to presentations, you also can subscribe to newsgroups, which are online discussions on a wide variety of topics. When you subscribe, you can read and post comments on the topic of conversation. You can find newsgroups that interest you by searching for them through the Deja.com site. Together, newsgroups make up Usenet, a part of the Internet. For more information, visit the PowerPoint 2000 Web Feature 2 More About page (www.scsite.com/ pp2000/more.htm) and click Discussions.

To Start a Web Discussion

1 **Click Tools on the Menu bar, point to Online Collaboration, and then point to Web Discussions (Figure 11).**

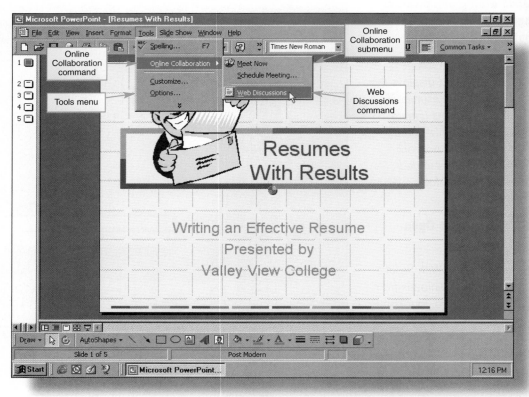

FIGURE 11

2 **Click Web Discussions. When the Discussions toolbar displays, click the Discussions menu button and then point to Discussion Options.**

The Discussions toolbar displays above the Drawing toolbar (Figure 12). Depending upon your computer's configuration, you may be prompted to enter the name of your Web discussion server in a separate dialog box.

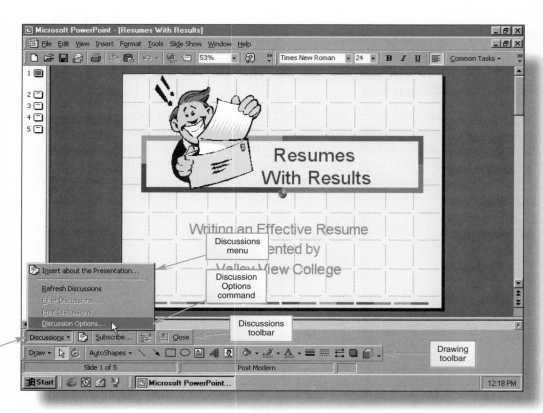

FIGURE 12

Click Discussion Options. When the Discussion Options dialog box displays, point to the OK button.

The Discussion Options dialog box allows you to select the server for the discussion group in which you are participating (Figure 13). Ask your instructor for the name of your discussion server. The selected check boxes indicate the types of information the collaborators will see in the discussion pane when they participate in the discussion.

④ Click the OK button.

The Discussion Options dialog box closes.

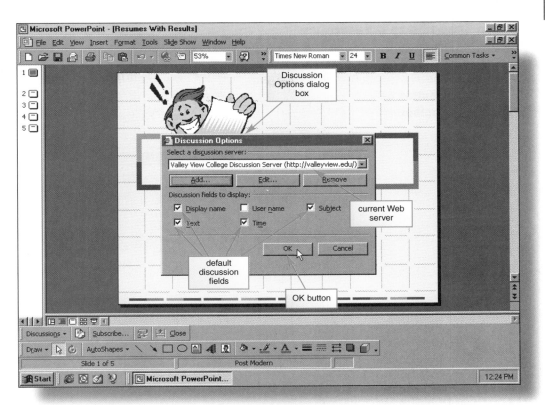

FIGURE 13

At this point, you can use the buttons on the Discussions toolbar to participate in the discussion. For example, you can initiate a discussion about the entire document, such as asking collaborators if the design template should be changed, if the title text color should be a darker shade of blue, or if the presentation needs additional content. You click the **Insert Discussion about the Presentation** button to start this type of discussion.

The **Print Discussions** command on the Discussions menu allows you to print all comments on the discussion. If participants have made many comments, you may want to use the **Filter Discussion** command, also on the Discussions menu, to view discussion items that were created by specific participants or on particular dates.

Subscribing to a Publication

Now that you have started a discussion regarding the Resumes With Results presentation, you want your colleagues to view the slide show and provide additional feedback. When they have posted a comment, you want to be aware that the comments database has been updated. Office 2000's subscription feature will notify subscribers to folders or documents via e-mail when a discussion item is inserted, edited, or deleted, when a new document is added, or when a document is modified, deleted or moved. You can choose to be notified of these changes instantly, daily, or weekly.

The steps on the next page describe how you subscribe to the Resumes With Results publication. You may ask your instructor if your network is configured so that you may alternately enter your e-mail address and participate in a discussion with your classmates.

More About 2000

Managing Homework Assignments Using Subscriptions

Many businesses subscribe to a publication to save time and resources. The same subscription techniques are used in education to allow students to receive and submit homework assignments and to participate in threaded discussions about documents. The Microsoft Web site offers information on how teachers are using this feature, including directions on creating a Web folder, assigning folder permissions, subscribing to a folder, instructing students how to subscribe to a folder, creating a Web discussion, submitting assignments to Web folders, and round tripping a document for editing. For more information, visit the PowerPoint 2000 Web Feature 2 More About page (www.scsite.com/pp2000/more.htm) and click Homework.

To Subscribe to a Publication

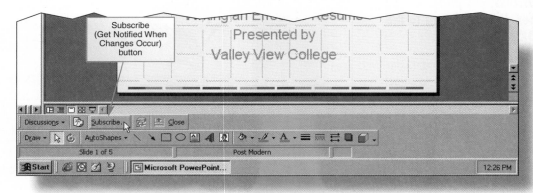

1 Point to the Subscribe button on the Discussions toolbar (Figure 14).

FIGURE 14

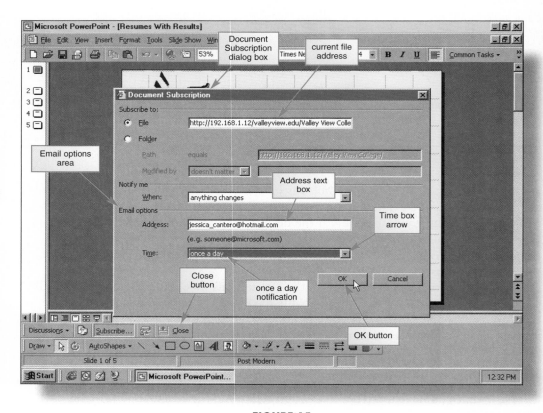

2 Click the Subscribe button. When the Document Subscription dialog box displays, type jessica_cantero@ hotmail.com in the Address text box in the Email options area. Click the Time box arrow in the Email options area and then click once a day. Point to the OK button.

The Web address displayed in the dialog box is the location of the Resumes With Results file on the network server (Figure 15). You may select another file or folder to subscribe to. The default setting is to be notified when anything changes, but you have the options of being notified immediately or weekly whenever the document is edited, moved, or deleted.

FIGURE 15

3 Click the OK button.

In a few seconds, PowerPoint notifies you that the subscription has begun.

You will receive an e-mail message daily notifying you if anyone has commented on your presentation. When you receive this message, you also have the option of unsubscribing at that time. If you choose to unsubscribe, you will click a link in the message, which will launch your default Internet browser, open a form, and permit you to confirm that you want to cancel your subscription to the presentation.

Ending the Discussion

When you have completed making comments and subscribing, you close the Discussions toolbar.

TO CLOSE A DISCUSSION

 Click the Close button on Discussions toolbar.

The PowerPoint window is restored to its full size. At this point you can work on another PowerPoint presentation or quit PowerPoint.

More About

E-Mail

Learn e-mail terminology and techniques by surfing to the PowerPoint 2000 Web Feature 2 More About page (www.scsite.com/pp2000/more.htm) and clicking E-mail.

Other Ways

1. On Tools menu point to Online Collaboration, click Web discussions

CASE PERSPECTIVE SUMMARY

Jessica Cantero can now show her Resumes With Results presentation to students attending Valley View College's satellite campuses. By using the Pack and Go Wizard, she can transport her presentation file and a copy of the PowerPoint Viewer to these sites. In addition, she can share her slide show with teachers and administrators at neighboring colleges and solicit ways to improve its content. By subscribing to this presentation, Jessica is notified daily when her colleagues submit comments.

Web Feature Summary

This Web Feature demonstrated two methods of sharing a presentation with others. In Part 1, you learned to use the Pack and Go Wizard to condense files and include the PowerPoint Viewer. In Part 2, you learned to download a file from a server, set discussion options, and subscribe to a publication so that you are notified when your associates provide comments.

What You Should Know

Having completed this Web Feature, you now should be able to perform the following tasks:

▶ Close a Discussion *(PPW 2.13)*
▶ Close a Presentation *(PPW 2.7)*
▶ Open a File in a Web Folder *(PPW 2.8)*
▶ Save a Presentation Using the Pack and Go Wizard *(PPW 2.3)*
▶ Start a Web Discussion *(PPW 2.10)*
▶ Subscribe to a Publication *(PPW 2.12)*
▶ Unpack a Presentation *(PPW 2.7)*

In the Lab

1 Saving a Presentation Using the Pack and Go Wizard

Problem: Tiffani Olson, the director of the Western College Fitness Center, wants to show the presentation you created for her in Project 5 in the cafeteria at each of the College's satellite campuses. She knows that the cafeterias are equipped with computers that have Office 2000 installed, so she would like for you to use the Pack and Go Wizard to transfer the presentation to floppy disks.

Instructions: Start PowerPoint and then perform the following steps with a computer.

1. Open the Half-Hour Workout presentation shown in Figures 5-1a through 5-1g on page PP 5.5. (If you did not complete Project 5, see your instructor for a copy of the presentation.)
2. Save the Presentation using the Pack and Go Wizard. Include the linked files, but do not embed TrueType fonts. Do not include the Viewer.
3. Hand in the floppy disks containing the presentation to your instructor. Quit PowerPoint.

2 Saving a Presentation with a Viewer Using the Pack and Go Wizard

Problem: Your friend Benito Kovich is extremely satisfied with the electronic portfolio you created for him in Project 6 using Visual Basic for Applications. He has shown the slide show successfully on several job interviews using his notebook computer. He informs you that most of the sites where he has interviewed had computers available, so in the future he would like to transport the slide show on floppy disks and install it on the companies' computers instead of taking his notebook to the interviews. You agree to help him by using the Pack and Go Wizard to transfer the presentation to floppy disks.

Instructions: Start PowerPoint and then perform the following steps with a computer.

1. Open the Electronic Portfolio presentation you created in Project 6. (If you did not complete Project 6, see your instructor for a copy of the presentation.)
2. Save the Presentation using the Pack and Go Wizard. Include the linked files, but do not embed TrueType fonts. Include the Viewer.
3. Hand in the floppy disks containing the presentation to your instructor. Quit PowerPoint.

3 Discussing and Subscribing to a Presentation

Problem: After seeing Benito Kovich's customized presentation in Project 6, you decide to create a similar presentation highlighting your academic achievements, extra-curricular activities, and employment history. You create the slide show and decide to solicit comments regarding the presentation from your professors, club advisers, former employers, and alumni. You ask your network administrator or instructor to upload this file to a folder on your school's Web server.

Instructions: Start PowerPoint and perform the following tasks with a computer.

1. Open your presentation from the folder on your school's Web server.
2. Start a Web discussion. Display the User name, Subject, Text, and Time discussion fields.
3. Subscribe to the presentation. Use your e-mail address, and request notification when a change occurs in any part of the discussion.
4. After your professional and personal associates have comented on your presentation, print their comments and hand them in to your instructor. Quit PowerPoint.

APPENDIX A

Microsoft PowerPoint 2000 Help System

Using the PowerPoint Help System

This appendix demonstrates how you can use the Microsoft PowerPoint Help system to answer your questions. At any time while you are using PowerPoint, you can interact with its Help system to display information on any topic associated with PowerPoint. It is a complete reference manual at your fingertips.

The two primary forms of Help are the Office Assistant and Microsoft PowerPoint Help window. The one you use will depend on your preference. As shown in Figure A-1, you access either form of Help in Microsoft PowerPoint by pressing the F1 key, clicking Microsoft PowerPoint Help on the Help menu, or clicking the Microsoft PowerPoint Help button on the Standard toolbar. PowerPoint responds in one of two ways:

1. If the Office Assistant is turned on, then the Office Assistant displays with a balloon (lower-right side in Figure A-1).
2. If the Office Assistant is turned off, then the Microsoft PowerPoint Help window displays (lower-left side in Figure A-1).

Table A-1 on the next page summarizes the nine categories of Help available to you. Because of the way the PowerPoint Help system works, please review the rightmost column of Table A-1 if you have difficulties activating the desired category of Help.

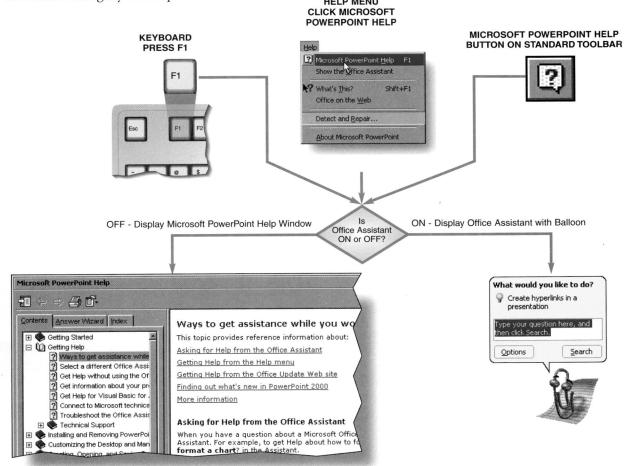

FIGURE A-1

Table A-1   PowerPoint Help System

TYPE	DESCRIPTION	HOW TO ACTIVATE	TURNING THE OFFICE ASSISTANT ON AND OFF
Answer Wizard	Similar to the Office Assistant in that it answers questions that you type in your own words.	Click the Microsoft PowerPoint Help button on the Standard toolbar. If necessary, maximize the Help window by double-clicking its title bar. Click the Answer Wizard tab.	If the Office Assistant displays, right-click it, click Options on the shortcut menu, click Use the Office Assistant to remove the check mark, click the OK button.
Contents sheet	Groups Help topics by general categories. Use when you know only the general category of the topic in question.	Click the Microsoft PowerPoint Help button on the Standard toolbar. If necessary, maximize the Help window by double-clicking its title bar. Click the Contents tab.	If the Office Assistant displays, right-click it, click Options, click Use the Office Assistant to remove the check mark, click the OK button.
Detect and Repair	Automatically finds and fixes errors in the application.	Click Detect and Repair on the Help menu.	
Hardware and Software Information	Shows Product ID and allows access to system information and technical support information.	Click About Microsoft PowerPoint on the Help menu and then click the appropriate button.	
Help for WordPerfect Users	Used to assist WordPerfect users who are learning Microsoft PowerPoint.	Click WordPerfect Help on the Help menu.	
Index sheet	Similar to an index in a book; use when you know exactly what you want.	Click the Microsoft PowerPoint Help button on the Standard toolbar. If necessary, maximize the Help window by double-clicking its title bar. Click the Index tab.	If the Office Assistant displays, right-click it, click Options, click Use the Office Assistant to remove the check mark, click the OK button.
Office Assistant	Answers questions that you type in your own words, offers tips, and provides Help for a variety of PowerPoint features.	Click the Microsoft PowerPoint Help button on the Standard toolbar or double-click the Office Assistant icon. Some dialog boxes also include the Microsoft PowerPoint Help button.	If the Office Assistant does not display, click Show the Office Assistant on the Help menu.
Office on the Web	Used to access technical resources and download free product enhancements on the Web.	Click Office on the Web on the Help menu.	
Question Mark button and What's This? command	Used to identify unfamiliar items on the screen.	In a dialog box, click the Question Mark button and then click an item in the dialog box. Click What's This? on the Help menu, and then click an item on the screen.	

The best way to familiarize yourself with the PowerPoint Help system is to use it. The next several pages show examples of how to use the Help system. Following the examples is a set of exercises titled Use Help that will sharpen your PowerPoint Help system skills.

The Office Assistant

The **Office Assistant** is an icon that displays in the PowerPoint window (lower-right side of Figure A-1 on the previous page). It has dual functions. First, it will respond with a list of topics that relate to the entry you make in the What would you like to do? text box at the bottom of the balloon. This entry can be in the form of a word, phrase, or written question. For example, if you want to learn more about saving a file, you can type, save, save a file, how do I save a file, or anything similar in the text box. The Office Assistant responds by displaying a list of topics from which you can choose. Once you choose a topic, it displays the corresponding information.

Second, the Office Assistant monitors your work and accumulates tips during a session on how you might do your work better. You can view the tips at any time. The accumulated tips display when you activate the Office Assistant balloon. Also, if at any time you see a light bulb above the Office Assistant, click it to display the most recent tip.

You may or may not want the Office Assistant to display on the screen at all times. You can hide it, and then show it at a later time. You may prefer not to use the Office Assistant at all. In this case, you use the Microsoft PowerPoint Help window (lower-left side of Figure A-1 on page PP A.1). Thus, not only do you need to know how to show and hide the Office Assistant, but you also need to know how to turn the Office Assistant on and off.

Showing and Hiding the Office Assistant

When PowerPoint is first installed, the Office Assistant displays in the PowerPoint window. You can move it to any location on the screen. You can click it to display the Office Assistant balloon, which allows you to request Help. If the Office Assistant is on the screen and you want to hide it, you click the **Hide the Office Assistant command** on the Help menu. You also can right-click the Office Assistant to display its shortcut menu and then click the **Hide command** to hide it. When the Office Assistant is hidden, then the **Show the Office Assistant command** replaces the Hide the Office Assistant command on the Help menu. Thus, you can show or hide the Office Assistant at any time.

Turning the Office Assistant On and Off

The fact that the Office Assistant is hidden does not mean it is turned off. To turn the Office Assistant off, it must be displaying in the PowerPoint window. You right-click it to display its shortcut menu (right side of Figure A-2). Next, click Options on the shortcut menu. Invoking the **Options command** causes the Office Assistant dialog box to display (left side of Figure A-2).

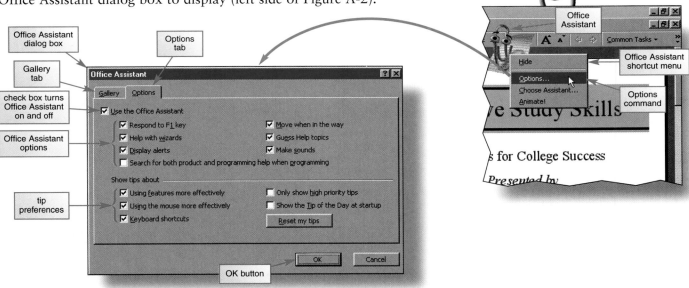

FIGURE A-2

The top check box in the Options sheet determines whether the Office Assistant is on or off. To turn the Office Assistant off, remove the check mark from the **Use the Office Assistant check box** and then click the OK button. As shown in Figure A-1 on page PP A.1, if the Office Assistant is off when you invoke Help, then the Microsoft PowerPoint Help window displays instead of the Office Assistant. To turn the Office Assistant on at a later date, click the Show the Office Assistant command on the Help menu.

Through the Options command on the Office Assistant shortcut menu, you can change the look and feel of the Office Assistant. For example, you can hide the Office Assistant, turn the Office Assistant off, change the way it works, choose a different Office Assistant icon, or view an animation of the current one. These options also are available by clicking the Options button that displays in the Office Assistant balloon (Figure A-3 on the next page).

The Gallery sheet (Figure A-2) in the Office Assistant dialog box allows you to change the appearance of the Office Assistant. The default is the paper clip (Clippit). You can change it to a bouncing red happy face (The Dot), a robot (F1), a professor (The Genius), the Microsoft Office logo (Office Logo), the earth (Mother Nature), a cat (Links), or a dog (Rocky).

Using the Office Assistant

As indicated earlier, the Office Assistant allows you to enter a word, phrase, or question and then it responds by displaying a list of topics from which you can choose to display Help. The following steps show how to use the Office Assistant to obtain Help on saving a presentation to a World Wide Web server.

Steps **To Use the Office Assistant**

1 If the Office Assistant is not turned on, click Help on the menu bar and then click Show the Office Assistant. Click the Office Assistant. When the Office Assistant balloon displays, type saving a presentation in the text box. Point to the Search button.

The Office Assistant balloon displays (Figure A-3).

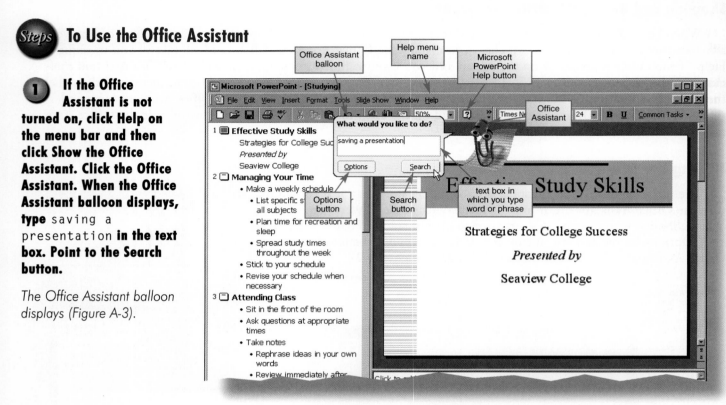

FIGURE A-3

2 Click the Search button. When the Office Assistant balloon redisplays, point to the topic, Save a copy of a presentation to a Web server in PowerPoint (Figure A-4).

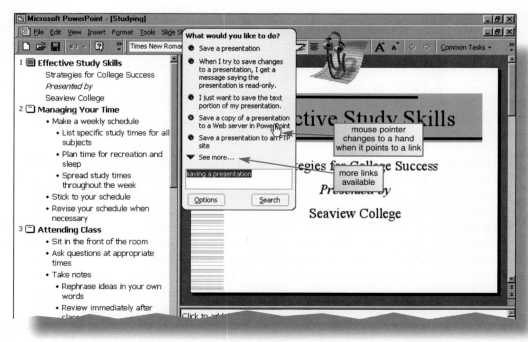

FIGURE A-4

③ Click the topic, Save a copy of a presentation to a Web server in PowerPoint. Double-click the Microsoft PowerPoint Help window title bar to maximize it. If necessary, move or hide the Office Assistant so you can view all of the text in the Microsoft PowerPoint Help window.

The Microsoft PowerPoint Help window displays with information on how to save a presentation to a Web server (Figure A-5).

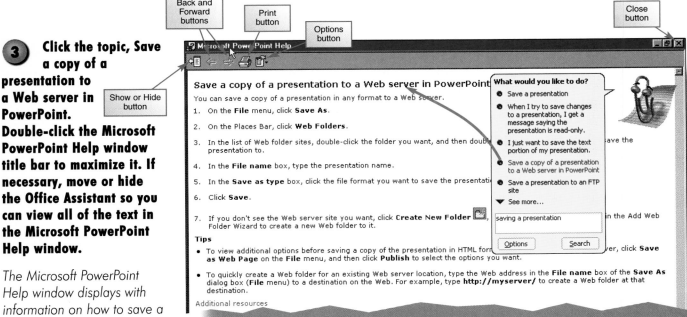

FIGURE A-5

Other Ways

1. If Office Assistant is turned on, on Help menu click Microsoft PowerPoint Help, or click Microsoft PowerPoint Help button on Standard toolbar to display Office Assistant balloon

When the Microsoft PowerPoint Help window displays, you can choose to read it or print it. To print the information, click the Print button on the Microsoft PowerPoint Help toolbar. Table A-2 lists the function of each button on the toolbar in the Microsoft PowerPoint Help window. To close the Microsoft PowerPoint Help window shown in Figure A-5, click the Close button on the title bar.

The Microsoft PowerPoint Help Window

If the Office Assistant is turned off and you click the Microsoft PowerPoint Help button on the Standard toolbar, the **Microsoft PowerPoint Help window** displays (Figure A-6 on the next page). This window contains three tabs on the left side: Contents, Answer Wizard, and Index. Each tab displays a sheet with powerful look-up capabilities. Use the Contents sheet as you would a table of contents at the front of a book to look up Help. The Answer Wizard sheet answers your queries the same as the Office Assistant. You use the Index sheet in the same fashion as an index in a book.

Click the tabs to move from sheet to sheet. The five buttons on the toolbar, Show or Hide, Back, Forward, Print, and Options also are described in Table A-2.

Besides clicking the Microsoft PowerPoint Help button on the Standard toolbar, you also can click the Microsoft PowerPoint Help command on the Help menu or press the F1 key to display the Microsoft PowerPoint Help window to gain access to the three sheets. To close the Microsoft PowerPoint Help window, click the Close button in the upper-right corner on the title bar.

Table A-2	Microsoft PowerPoint Help Window Buttons	
BUTTON	**NAME**	**FUNCTION**
or	Show or Hide	Displays or hides the Contents, Answer Wizard, Index tabs
	Back	Displays the previous Help topic
	Forward	Displays the next Help topic
	Print	Prints the current Help topic
	Options	Displays a list of commands

Using the Contents Sheet

The **Contents sheet** is useful for displaying Help when you know the general category of the topic in question, but not the specifics. The following steps show how to use the Contents sheet to obtain information on working on presentations on intranets and the Internet.

TO OBTAIN HELP USING THE CONTENTS SHEET

1 With the Office Assistant turned off, click the Microsoft PowerPoint Help button on the Standard toolbar (Figure A-3 on page PP A.4).

2 When the Microsoft PowerPoint Help window displays, double-click the title bar to maximize the window. If necessary, click the Show button to display the tabs.

3 Click the Contents tab.

4 Double-click the Working with Presentations on Intranets and the Internet book on the left side of the window.

5 Double-click the Publishing to the Web book below the Opening and Finding Presentations book.

6 Click the Publish a presentation or HTML file to the Web book.

PowerPoint displays Help on the subtopic, Publish a presentation or HTML file to the Web (Figure A-6).

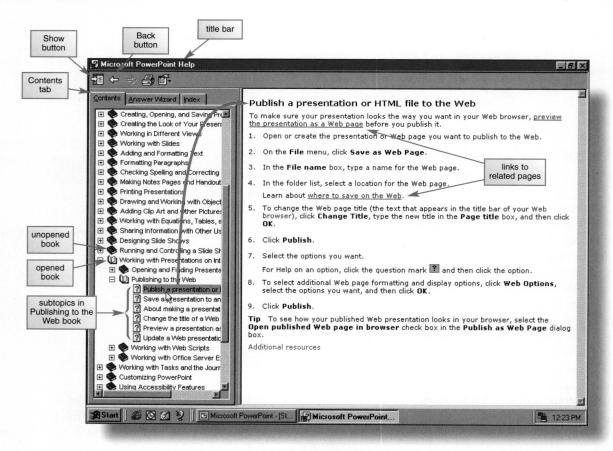

FIGURE A-6

Once the information on the subtopic displays, you can scroll through and read it or you can click the Print button to obtain a hard copy. If you decide to click another subtopic on the left or a link on the right, you can get back to the Help page shown in Figure A-6 by clicking the Back button as many times as necessary.

Each topic in the Contents list is preceded by a book icon or question mark icon. A **book icon** indicates subtopics are available. A **question mark icon** means information on the topic will display if you double-click the title. The book icon opens when you double-click the book (or its title) or click the plus sign (+) to the left of the book icon.

Using the Answer Wizard Sheet

The **Answer Wizard sheet** works like the Office Assistant in that you enter a word, phrase, or question and it responds with topics from which you can choose to display Help. The following steps show how to use the Answer Wizard sheet to obtain Help about discussions in a PowerPoint presentation.

TO OBTAIN HELP USING THE ANSWER WIZARD SHEET

1 With the Office Assistant turned off, click the Microsoft PowerPoint Help button on the Standard toolbar (Figure A-3 on page PP A.4).

2 When the Microsoft PowerPoint Help window displays, double-click the title bar to maximize the window. If necessary, click the Show button to display the tabs.

3 Click the Answer Wizard tab. Type what are discussions in the What would you like to do? text box on the left side of the window. Click the Search button.

4 When a list of topics displays in the Select topic to display list box, click About discussions in PowerPoint.

PowerPoint displays Help about discussions (Figure A-7).

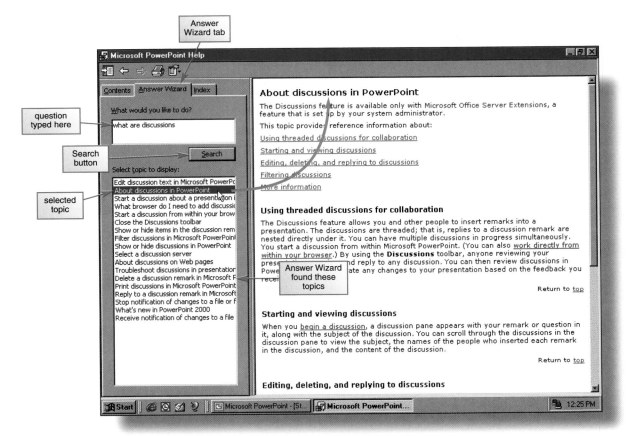

FIGURE A-7

If the topic, About discussions in PowerPoint, does not include the information you are searching for, click another topic in the list. Continue to click topics until you find the desired information.

Using the Index Sheet

The third sheet in the Microsoft PowerPoint Help window is the Index sheet. Use the **Index sheet** to display Help when you know the keyword or the first few letters of the keyword you want to look up. The following steps show how to use the Index sheet to obtain Help on making PowerPoint more accessible for users with disabilities.

TO OBTAIN HELP USING THE INDEX SHEET

1 With the Office Assistant turned off, click the Microsoft PowerPoint Help button on the Standard toolbar (Figure A-3 on page PP A.4).

2 When the Microsoft PowerPoint Help window displays, double-click the title bar to maximize the window. If necessary, click the Show button to display the tabs.

3 Click the Index tab. Type disability in the Type keywords text box on the left side of the window. Click the Search button.

PowerPoint highlights the first topic (Make PowerPoint more accessible) on the left side of the window and displays information about a variety of techniques that can help people with disabilities use PowerPoint effectively on the right side of the window (Figure A-8).

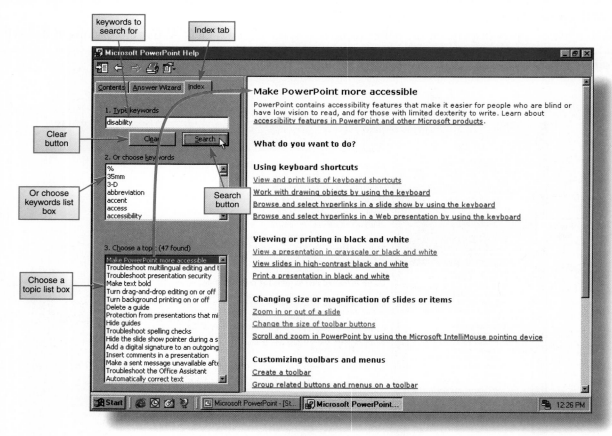

FIGURE A-8

In the Choose a topic list box on the left side of the window, you can click another topic to display additional Help.

An alternative to typing a keyword in the Type keywords text box is to scroll through the Or choose keywords list box (the middle list box on the left side of the window). When you locate the keyword you are searching for, double-click it to display Help on the topic. Also in the Or choose keywords list box, the PowerPoint Help system displays other topics that relate to the new keyword. As you begin typing a new keyword in the Type keywords text box, PowerPoint jumps to that point in the middle list box. To begin a new search, click the Clear button.

What's This? Command and Question Mark Button • PP A.9

APPENDIX A

What's This? Command and Question Mark Button

Use the What's This? command on the Help menu or the Question Mark button in a dialog box when you are not certain what an object on the screen is or what it does.

What's This? Command

You use the **What's This? command** on the Help menu to display a detailed Screen-Tip. When you invoke this command, the mouse pointer changes to an arrow with a question mark. You then click any object on the screen, such as a button, to display the Screen-Tip. For example, after you click the What's This? command on the Help menu and then click the Increase Font Size button on the Formatting toolbar, a description of the Increase Font Size button displays (Figure A-9). You can print the ScreenTip by right-clicking it and clicking Print Topic on the shortcut menu.

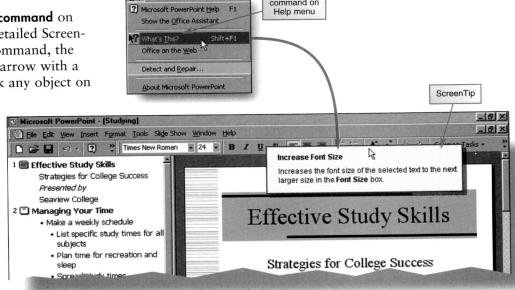

FIGURE A-9

Question Mark Button

Similar to the What's This? command, the **Question Mark button** displays a ScreenTip. You use the Question Mark button with dialog boxes. It is located in the upper-right corner on the title bar of dialog boxes, next to the Close button. For example, in Figure A-10, the Options dialog box displays on the screen. If you click the Question Mark button, and then click the Style Options button, an explanation of the style options displays. You can print the ScreenTip by right-clicking it and clicking Print Topic on the shortcut menu.

If a dialog box does not include a Question Mark button, press the SHIFT+F1 keys. This combination of keys will change the mouse pointer to an arrow with a question mark. You then can click any object in the dialog box to display the ScreenTip.

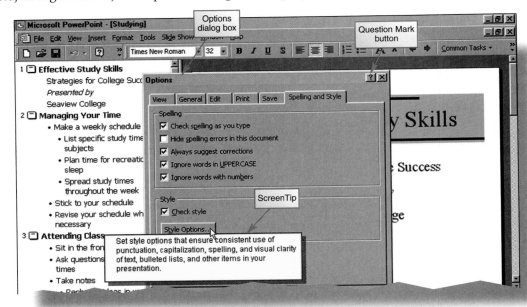

FIGURE A-10

Office on the Web Command

The **Office on the Web command** on the Help menu displays a Microsoft Web page containing up-to-date information on a variety of Office-related topics. To use this command, you must be connected to the Internet. Once the page displays, you can click the PowerPoint link on the left side of the window and then click the Assistance link (Figure A-11). The PowerPoint Assistance Web page contains several links such as Knowledge Base Articles about PowerPoint and PowerPoint Newsgroups.

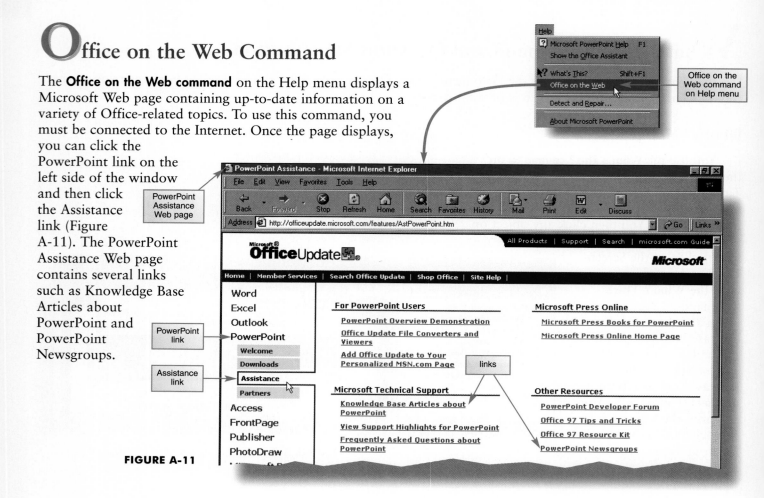

FIGURE A-11

Other Help Commands

Two additional commands available on the Help menu are Detect and Repair and About Microsoft PowerPoint.

Detect and Repair Command

Use the **Detect and Repair command** on the Help menu if PowerPoint is not running properly or if it is generating errors. When you invoke this command, the Detect and Repair dialog box displays. Click the Start button in the dialog box to initiate the detect and repair process.

About Microsoft PowerPoint Command

The **About Microsoft PowerPoint command** on the Help menu displays the About Microsoft PowerPoint dialog box. The dialog box lists the owner of the software and the product identification. You need to know the product identification if you call Microsoft for assistance. The two buttons below the OK button are the System Info button and the Tech Support button. The **System Info button** displays system information, including hardware resources, components, software environment, and applications. The **Tech Support button** displays technical assistance information.

Use Help

1 Using the Office Assistant

Instructions: Perform the following tasks using the PowerPoint Help system.

1. If the Office Assistant is turned on, click it to display the Office Assistant balloon. If the Office Assistant is not turned on, click Help on the menu bar, and then click Show the Office Assistant.
2. Right-click the Office Assistant and then click Options on the shortcut menu. Click the Gallery tab in the Office Assistant dialog box and then click the Next button. Click the Options tab in the Office Assistant dialog box and review the different options for the Office Assistant. Click the Question Mark button and then display ScreenTips for the first two check boxes (Use the Office Assistant and Respond to F1 key). Right-click the ScreenTips to print them. Give them to your instructor. Close the Office Assistant dialog box.
3. Click the Office Assistant and then type modify bullets in the What would you like to do? text box at the bottom of the balloon. Click the Search button.
4. Click, Troubleshoot working with bullets. If necessary, double-click the title bar to maximize the Microsoft PowerPoint Help window. Read and print the information. One at a time, click the links to learn about various ways to use bullets and numbers. Print the information. Hand in the printouts to your instructor. Use the Back and Forward buttons to return to the original page.
5. Click the Close button in the Microsoft PowerPoint Help window.
6. Click the Office Assistant. If it is not turned on, click Show the Office Assistant. Search for the topic, using Shortcut keys. Click the Use keyboard shortcuts link. Maximize the window and then click the Keys for sending e-mail link. Read and print the information. Close the Microsoft PowerPoint Help window.

2 Expanding on the PowerPoint Help System Basics

Instructions: Use the PowerPoint Help system to understand the topics better and answer the questions below.

1. Right-click the Office Assistant. If it is not turned on, click Show the Office Assistant on the Help menu. When the shortcut menu displays, click Options. Click Use the Office Assistant to remove the check mark, and then click the OK button.
2. Click the Microsoft PowerPoint Help button on the Standard toolbar. Maximize the Microsoft PowerPoint Help window. If the tabs are hidden on the left side, click the Show button. Click the Index tab. Type slide in the Type keywords text box. Click the Search button. Click Zoom in or out on a slide. Print the information. Click the Hide and then Show buttons. Close the Microsoft PowerPoint Help window. Hand in the printouts to your instructor.
3. Press the F1 key. Maximize the Microsoft PowerPoint Help window. Click the Answer Wizard tab. Type change a chart in the What would you like to do? text box, and then click the Search button. Click Move a file. Read through the information that displays. Print the information. Click the How to select multiple files link. Read and print this information.
4. Click the Contents tab. Click the plus sign (+) to the left of the Running and Controlling a Slide Show book. One at a time, click Hide the slide show pointer during a slide show, Create a list of action items during a slide show, and Slide show controls. Read and print each topic. Close the Microsoft PowerPoint Help window. Hand in the printouts to your instructor.
5. Click Help on the menu bar and then click What s This? Click the Text Shadow button on the Standard toolbar. Right-click the ScreenTip and click Print Topic on the shortcut menu. Click the Meeting Minder command on the Tools menu. When the Meeting Minder dialog box displays, click the Question Mark button on the title bar. Click the Schedule button. Right-click the ScreenTip and click Print Topic. Hand in the printouts to your instructor.

APPENDIX B
Publishing Office Web Pages to a Web Server

With a Microsoft Office 2000 program, such as Word, Excel, Access, or PowerPoint, you use the Save as Web Page command on the File menu to save the Web page to a Web server using one of two techniques: Web folders or File Transfer Protocol. A **Web folder** is an Office 2000 shortcut to a Web server. **File Transfer Protocol (FTP)** is an Internet standard that allows computers to exchange files with other computers on the Internet.

You should contact your network system administrator or technical support staff at your ISP to determine if their Web server supports Web folders, FTP, or both, and to obtain necessary permissions to access the Web server. If you decide to publish Web pages using a Web folder, you must have the Office Server Extensions (OSE) installed on your computer. OSE comes with the Standard, Professional, and Premium editions of Office 2000.

Using Web Folders to Publish Office Web Pages

If you are granted permission to create a Web folder (shortcut) on your computer, you must obtain the URL of the Web server, and a user name and possibly a password that allows you to access the Web server. You also must decide on a name for the Web folder. Table B-1 explains how to create a Web folder.

Office adds the name of the Web folder to the list of current Web folders. You can save to this folder, open files in the folder, rename the folder, or perform any operations you would to a folder on your hard disk. You can use your Office program or Windows Explorer to access this folder. Table B-2 explains how to save to a Web folder.

Using FTP to Publish Office Web Pages

When publishing a Web page using FTP, you first add the FTP location to your computer and then you can save to it. An **FTP location**, also called an **FTP site**, is a collection of files that resides on an FTP server. In this case, the FTP server is the Web server.

To add an FTP location, you must obtain the name of the FTP site, which usually is the address (URL) of the FTP server, and a user name and a password that allows you to access the FTP server. You save and open the Web pages on the Web server using the name of the FTP site. Table B-3 explains how to add an FTP site.

Office adds the name of the FTP site to the FTP locations in the Save As and Open dialog boxes. You can open and save files on this FTP location. Table B-4 explains how to save using an FTP location.

Table B-1   Creating a Web Folder

1. Click File on the menu bar and then click Save As; or click File on the menu bar and then click Open.
2. When the Save As dialog box or the Open dialog box displays, click the Web Folders shortcut on the Places Bar along the left side of the dialog box.
3. Click the Create New Folder button.
4. When the first dialog box of the Add Web Folder wizard displays, type the URL of the Web server and then click the Next button.
5. When the Enter Network Password dialog box displays, type the user name and, if necessary, the password in the respective text boxes and then click the OK button.
6. When the last dialog box of the Add Web Folder wizard displays, type the name you would like to use for the Web folder. Click the Finish button.
7. Close the Save As or the Open dialog box.

Table B-2   Saving to a Web Folder

1. Click File on the menu bar and then click Save As.
2. When the Save As dialog box displays, type the Web page file name in the File name text box. Do not press the ENTER key.
3. Click Web Folders shortcut on the Places Bar along the left side of the dialog box.
4. Double-click the Web folder name in the Save in list.
5. When the Enter Network Password dialog box displays, type the user name and password in the respective text boxes and then click the OK button.
6. Click the Save button in the Save As dialog box.

Table B-3   Adding an FTP Location

1. Click File on the menu bar and then click Save As; or click File on the menu bar and then click Open.
2. In the Save As dialog box, click the Save in box arrow and then click Add/Modify FTP Locations in the Save in list; or in the Open dialog box, click the Look in box arrow and then click Add/Modify FTP Locations in the Look in list.
3. When the Add/Modify FTP Locations dialog box displays, type the name of the FTP site in the Name of FTP site text box. If the site allows anonymous logon, click Anonymous in the Log on as area; if you have a user name for the site, click User in the Log on as area and then enter the user name. Enter the password in the Password text box. Click the OK button.
4. Close the Save As or the Open dialog box.

Table B-4   Saving to an FTP Location

1. Click File on the menu bar and then click Save As.
2. When the Save As dialog box displays, type the Web page file name in the File name text box. Do not press the ENTER key.
3. Click the Save in box arrow and then click FTP Locations.
4. Double-click the name of the FTP site you want to save to.
5. When the FTP Log On dialog box displays, enter your user name and password and then click the OK button.
6. Click the Save button in the Save As dialog box.

APPENDIX C

Resetting the PowerPoint Menus and Toolbars

When you first install Microsoft PowerPoint 2000, the Standard and Formatting toolbars display on one row. As you use the buttons on the toolbars and commands on the menus, PowerPoint personalizes the toolbars and the menus based on their usage. Each time you start PowerPoint, the toolbars and menus display in the same settings as the last time you used the application. The following steps show how to reset the menus and toolbars to their installation settings.

 To Reset My Usage Data and Toolbar Buttons

1 **Click View on the menu bar and then point to Toolbars. Point to Customize on the Toolbars submenu.**

The View menu and Toolbars submenu display (Figure C-1).

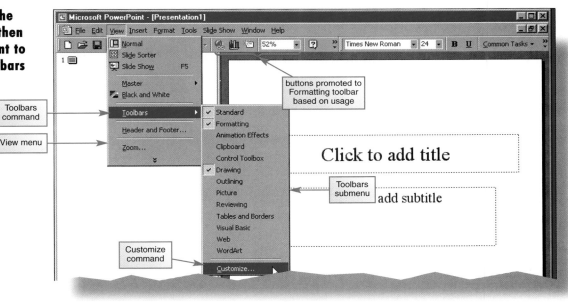

FIGURE C-1

2 **Click Customize. When the Customize dialog box displays, click the Options tab. Make sure the three check boxes in the Personalized Menus and Toolbars area have check marks and then point to the Reset my usage data button.**

The Customize dialog box displays (Figure C-2).

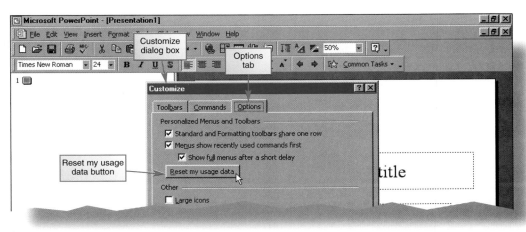

FIGURE C-2

3 Click the Reset my usage data button. When the Microsoft PowerPoint dialog box displays explaining the function of the Reset my usage data button, click the Yes button. In the Customize dialog box, click the Toolbars tab.

The Toolbars sheet displays (Figure C-3).

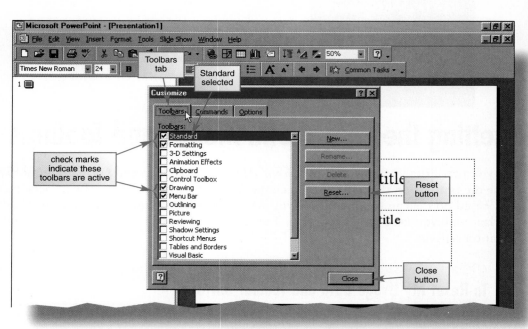

FIGURE C-3

4 Click Standard in the Toolbars list and then click the Reset button. When the Reset Toolbar dialog box displays, click the OK button. Click Formatting in the Toolbars list and then click the Reset button. Click Drawing in the Toolbars list and then click the Reset button. When the Reset Toolbar dialog box displays, click the OK button.

5 Click the Close button in the Customize dialog box.

The toolbars display (Figure C-4).

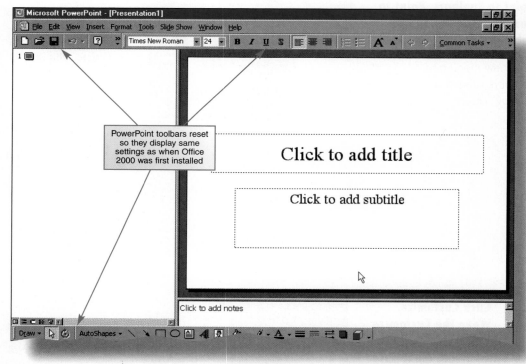

FIGURE C-4

Steps 3 and 4 display or remove any buttons that were added or deleted through the use of the Add or Remove Buttons button on the More Buttons menu.

You can turn off both the toolbars sharing a single row and the short menus by removing the check marks from the two top check boxes in the Options sheet in the Customize dialog box (Figure C-2 on the previous page). If you remove these check marks, PowerPoint will display the toolbars on two separate rows below the menu bar and will show only full menus.

APPENDIX D

Microsoft Office User Specialist Certification Program

The Microsoft Office User Specialist (MOUS) Certification Program provides a framework for measuring your proficiency with the Microsoft Office 2000 applications, such as Word 2000, Excel 2000, Access 2000, and PowerPoint 2000. Three levels of certification are available—Master, Expert, and Core. The three levels of certification are described in Table D-1.

Table D-1	Three Levels of MOUS Certification		
LEVEL	*DESCRIPTION*	*REQUIREMENTS*	*CREDENTIAL AWARDED*
Master	Indicates that you have a comprehensive understanding of Microsoft Office 2000	Pass all FIVE of the required exams: Microsoft Word 2000 Expert Microsoft Excel 2000 Expert Microsoft PowerPoint 2000 Core Microsoft Access 2000 Core Microsoft Outlook 2000 Core	Candidates will be awarded one certificate for passing all five of the required Microsoft Office 2000 exams: Microsoft Office User Specialist: Microsoft Office 2000 Master
Expert	Indicates that you have a comprehensive understanding of the advanced features in a specific Microsoft Office 2000 application	Pass any ONE of the Expert exams: Microsoft Word 2000 Expert Microsoft Excel 2000 Expert	Candidates will be awarded one certificate for each of the Expert exams they have passed: Microsoft Office User Specialist: Microsoft Word 2000 Expert Microsoft Office User Specialist: Microsoft Excel 2000 Expert
Core	Indicates that you have a comprehensive understanding of the core features in a specific Microsoft Office 2000 application	Pass any ONE of the Core exams: Microsoft Word 2000 Core Microsoft Excel 2000 Core Microsoft PowerPoint 2000 Core Microsoft Access 2000 Core Microsoft Outlook 2000 Core	Candidates will be awarded one certificate for each of the Core exams they have passed: Microsoft Office User Specialist: Microsoft Word 2000 Microsoft Office User Specialist: Microsoft Excel 2000 Microsoft Office User Specialist: Microsoft PowerPoint 2000 Microsoft Office User Specialist: Microsoft Access 2000 Microsoft Office User Specialist: Microsoft Outlook 2000

Why Should You Get Certified?

Being a Microsoft Office User Specialist provides a valuable industry credential—proof that you have the Office 2000 applications skills required by employers. By passing one or more MOUS certification exams, you demonstrate your proficiency in a given Office application to employers. With nearly 80 million copies of Office in use around the world, Microsoft is targeting Office certification to a wide variety of companies. These companies include temporary employment agencies that want to prove the expertise of their workers, large corporations looking for a way to measure the skill set of employees, and training companies and educational institutions seeking Microsoft Office teachers with appropriate credentials.

The MOUS Exams

You pay $50 to $100 each time you take an exam, whether you pass or fail. The fee varies among testing centers. The Expert exams, which you can take up to 60 minutes to complete, consist of between 40 and 60 tasks that you perform online. The tasks require you to use the application just as you would in doing your job. The Core exams contain fewer tasks, and you will have slightly less time to complete them. The tasks you will perform differ on the two types of exams.

How Can You Prepare for the MOUS Exams?

The Shelly Cashman Series® offers several Microsoft-approved textbooks that cover the required objectives on the MOUS exams. For a listing of the textbooks, visit the Shelly Cashman Series MOUS Web page at www.scsite.com/off2000/cert.htm and click the Shelly Cashman Series Office 2000 Microsoft-Approved MOUS Textbooks link (Figure D-1). After using any of the books listed in an instructor-led course, you will be prepared to take the MOUS exam indicated.

How to Find an Authorized Testing Center

You can locate a testing center by calling 1-800-933-4493 in North America or visiting the Shelly Cashman Series MOUS Web page at www.scsite.com/off2000/cert.htm and then clicking the Locate an Authorized Testing Center Near You link (Figure D-1). At this Web page, you can look for testing centers around the world.

Shelly Cashman Series MOUS Web Page

The Shelly Cashman Series MOUS Web page (Figure D-1) has more than fifteen Web pages you can visit to obtain additional information on the MOUS Certification Program. The Web page (www.scsite.com/off2000/cert.htm) includes links to general information on certification, choosing an application for certification, preparing for the certification exam, and taking and passing the certification exam.

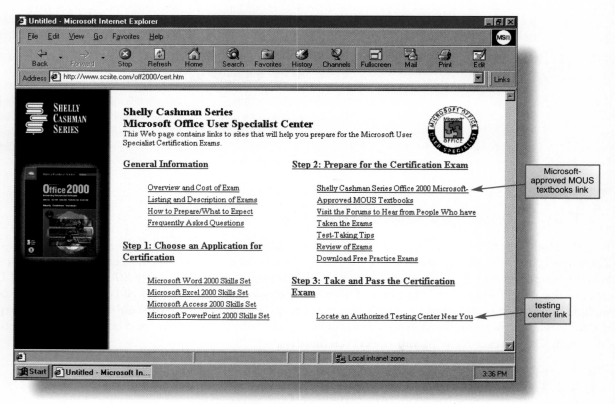

FIGURE D-1

Microsoft PowerPoint 2000 Specialist Certification Map

This book has been approved by Microsoft as courseware for the Microsoft Office User Specialist (MOUS) program. After completing the projects and exercises in this book, students will be prepared to take the Core level Microsoft Office User Specialist Exam for Microsoft PowerPoint 2000. Table D-2 lists the skill sets, activities, and page number where the activity is discussed in the book for the Core level Microsoft Office User Specialist Exam for Microsoft PowerPoint 2000. You should be familiar with each of the activities if you plan to take the Microsoft PowerPoint 2000 Core examination. Table D-3 on the next page lists the skill sets, activities, and page number where the activity is discussed in the book for the Expert level Microsoft Office User Specialist Exam for Microsoft PowerPoint 2000.

Table D-2 Microsoft PowerPoint 2000 MOUS Core Skill Sets, Activities, and Map

SKILL SETS	ACTIVITIES	PAGE NUMBERS
Creating a presentation	Delete slides	PP 4.53
	Create a specified type of slide	PP 1.33, PP 1.40-42, PP 2.7, PP 2.11, PP 2.13, PP 2.15, PP 2.18
	Create a presentation from a template and/or a Wizard	PP 1.8, PP 2.7, PPW 1.1
	Navigate among different views (slide, outline, sorter, tri-pane)	PP 1.13, PP 2.8, PP 2.20, PP 2.21, PP 2.46
	Create a new presentation from existing slides	PP 4.6
	Copy a slide from one presentation into another	PP 3.8
	Insert headers and footers	PP 2.35
	Create a blank presentation	PP 1.10, PP 2.6, PP 3.7
	Create a presentation using the AutoContent Wizard	PP 1.8
	Send a presentation via e-mail	PP 2.55
Modifying a presentation	Change the order of slides using Slide Sorter view	PP 4.50-51
	Find and replace text	PP 1.57, PPW 1.10, PP 4.7, PP 4.24
	Change the layout for one or more slides	PP 2.22, PP 2.27-28
	Change slide layout (modify the Slide Master)	PP 1.57-63, PP 2.42, PP 3.14-18, PP 4.8
	Modify slide sequence in the outline pane	PP 2.10, PP 4.25-26, PP 4.49, PP 4.54
	Apply a design template	PP 1.18, PP 2.7, PP 3.9
Working with text	Check spelling	PP 1.54
	Change and replace text fonts (individual slide and entire presentation)	PP 1.24, PP 1.27, PP 2.47, PP 3.10
	Enter text in tri-pane view	PP 1.21, PP 1.23, PP 1.35, PP 1.37-42, PP 2.11-12 PP 2.14-19
	Import text from Word	PP 3.7-8
	Change the text alignment	PP 1.59
	Create a text box for entering text	PP 4.35, PP 4.37
	Use the Wrap text in AutoShape feature	PP 4.59
	Use the Office Clipboard	PP 3.34
	Use the Format Painter	PP 4.64

Table D-2 Microsoft PowerPoint 2000 MOUS Core Skill Sets, Activities, and Map

SKILL SETS	ACTIVITIES	PAGE NUMBERS
Working with text (con't)	Promote and Demote text in slide and outline panes	PP 1.37-41, PP 2.11, PP 2.14-19
Working with visual elements	Add a picture from the ClipArt Gallery	PP 2.24, PP 2.27-30, PP 3.16-18, PP 3.52, PP 4.8
	Add and group shapes using WordArt or the Drawing toolbar	PP 3.53-58, PP 4.13-21
	Apply formatting	PP 1.25, PP 1.27, PP 2.47, PP 3.14, PP 3.45-49, PP 4.34-38
	Place text inside a shape using a text box	PP 4.35
	Scale and size an object including clip art	PP 2.32, PP 3.39, PP 3.53, PP 4.21, PP 4.33
	Create tables within PowerPoint	PP 3.41-49
	Rotate and fill an object	PP 4.19-20, PP 4.34
Customizing a presentation	Add AutoNumber bullets	PP 3.18
	Add speaker notes	PPW 1.4
	Add graphical bullets	PP 3.19-21
	Add slide transitions	PP 2.38, PP 3.58, PP 4.54
	Animate text and objects	PP 2.50-51, PP 3.58, PP 4.54
Creating output	Preview presentation in black and white	PP 1.63
	Print slides in a variety of formats	PP 1.64, PP 2.51, PP 2.54
	Print audience handouts	PP 1.64, PP 2.5, PP 3.59
	Print speaker notes in a specified format	PP 3.55
Delivering a presentation	Start a slide show on any slide	PP 1.46, PP 1.48, PP 2.49
	Use on-screen navigation tools	PP 1.48, PP 2.50, PP 3.40 PP 3.41, PP 4.38, PP 4.44
	Print a slide as an overhead transparency	PP 1.67
	Use the pen during a presentation	PP 4.60
Managing files	Save changes to a presentation	PP 1.51, PP 1.65, PP 1.69, PP 2.35, PP 2.49, PP 2.57, PPW 1.4, PP 3.12, PP 4.6
	Save as a new presentation	PP 1.28, PP 2.19
	Publish a presentation to the Web	PPW 1.3
	Use Office Assistant	PP 1.67
	Insert hyperlink	PP 2.35, PP 4.27-30

Table D-3   Microsoft PowerPoint 2000 MOUS Expert Skill Sets, Activities, and Map

SKILL SETS	ACTIVITIES	PAGE NUMBERS
Creating a presentation	Automatically create a summary slide	PP 4.52-53
	Automatically create slides from a summary slide	PP 4.51
	Design a template	PP 2.11, PP 6.56
	Format presentations for the Web	PPW 1.3
Modifying a presentation	Change tab formatting	PP 5.7
	Use the Wrap text in AutoShape feature	PP 4.16, PP 5.42
	Apply a template from another presentation	PP 3.9
	Customize a color scheme	PP 4.8, PP 6.55
	Apply animation effects	PP 2.37, PP 2.46-48, PP 3.58, PP 4.54, PP 5.45, PP 5.59
	Create a custom background	PP 3.12-18, PP 4.8, PP 5.45-48
	Add animated GIFs	PPI 2.8, PP 5.16-17, PP 6.52
	Add links to slides within the presentation	PP 4.64
	Customize clip art and other objects (resize, scale, etc.)	PP 2.33, PP 3.39, PP 3.53, PP 3.54-58, PP 5.18
	Add a presentation within a presentation	PP 5.9-13
	Add an action button	PP 4.27-30
	Hide slides	PP 4.49
	Set automatic slide timings	PP 5.54-58
Working with visual elements	Add textured backgrounds	PP 4.58
	Apply diagonal borders	PP 5.33
Using data from other sources	Export an outline to Word	PP 2.51, PP 6.70
	Add a table (from Word)	PP 5.36-38
	Insert an Excel chart	PP 5.19-33
	Add sound	PP 4.27-30, PPI 2.6-8
	Add video	PPI 2.1, PP 6.9
Creating output	Save slide as a graphic	PP 5.24
	Generate meeting notes	PP 5.60
	Change output format (Page setup)	PP 2.51, PP 3.59, PP 5.19, PP 6.16-19
	Export to 35mm slides	PP 4.53
Delivering a presentation	Save presentation for use on another computer (Pack 'N Go)	PPW 1.8, PP 6.12-13, PPW 2.2-6
	Electronically incorporate meeting feedback	PP 5.50
	Use presentations on demand	PP 5.48, PP 5.52
Managing files	Save embedded fonts in presentation	PPW 2.5
	Save HTML to a specific target browser	PPW 1.6
Working with PowerPoint	Customize the toolbar	PP 2.22, PP 6.9-14, PP 6.66
	Create a toolbar	PP 6.9-11
Collaborating with workgroups	Subscribe to a presentation	PPW 2.12
	View a presentation on the Web	PPW 1.6, PPW 2.6
	Use Net Meeting to schedule a broadcast	PP 5.50
	Use NetShow to deliver a broadcast	PP 5.52
Working with charts and tables	Build a chart or graph	PP 5.25-35
	Modify charts or graphs	PP 5.29-35
	Build an organization chart	PP 3.22-40
	Modify an organization chart	PP 4.38-43
	Modify PowerPoint tables	PP 4.44-46

Index

Microsoft PowerPoint 2000

Microsoft PowerPoint 2000 Quick Reference Summary

In Microsoft PowerPoint 2000, you can accomplish a task in a number of ways. The following table provides a quick reference to each task presented in this textbook. You can invoke the commands listed in the MENU BAR and SHORTCUT MENU columns using either the mouse or keyboard.

Microsoft PowerPoint 2000 Quick Reference Summary

TASK	PAGE NUMBER	MOUSE	MENU BAR	SHORTCUT MENU	KEYBOARD SHORTCUT
Action Button, Add	PP 4.27	AutoShapes button on Drawing toolbar | Action Buttons	Slide Show | Action Buttons		ALT+D | I
Action Button, Add Caption (Text Box)	PP 4.35	Text Box button on Drawing toolbar	Insert | Text Box		ALT+I | X
Action Button, Fill Color	PP 4.34	Fill Color button on Drawing toolbar	Format | AutoShape | Colors and Lines tab	Format AutoShape | Colors and Lines tab	ALT+O | O | Colors and Lines tab
Action Button, Scale	PP 4.33	Drag sizing handle	Format | AutoShape | Size tab	Format AutoShape | Size tab	ALT+O | O | Size tab
Action Button, Shadow	PP 4.35	Shadow button on Drawing toolbar			
Animate Text	PP 2.48	Custom Animation button on Animation Effects toolbar	Slide Show | Custom Animation | Effects tab	Custom Animation | Effects tab	ALT+D | M
Animation Order, Set	PP 5.49	Animation Effects button on Formatting toolbar | Custom Animation button	Slide Show | Custom Animation	Custom Animation	ALT+D | M
Apply Design Template	PP 1.18	Apply Design Template button on Standard toolbar; Apply Design Template on Common Tasks button menu on Formatting toolbar	Format | Apply Design Template	Apply Design Template	ALT+O | Y
AutoShape, Add Shadow	PP 5.41	Shadow button on Drawing toolbar			
AutoShape, Add Text	PP 5.42	Drag sizing handle	Format | AutoShape | Text Box tab | Resize AutoShape to fit text	Format AutoShape | Text Box tab | Resize AutoShape to fit text	ALT+O | O | CTRL+TAB | TAB | SPACEBAR
AutoShape, Insert	PP 5.40	AutoShapes menu button on Drawing toolbar			ALT+U
AutoShape, Rotate	PP 5.44	Free Rotate button on Drawing toolbar; Draw button on Drawing toolbar | Rotate or Flip | Free Rotate	Format | AutoShape | Size tab | Rotation text box		ALT+R | P | T; ALT+O | O | CTRL+TAB
Bullets, Remove	PP 4.48	Bullets button on Formatting toolbar	Format | Bullets and Numbering | Bulleted tab | None	Bullets and Numbering | Bulleted tab | None	ALT+O | B | SPACEBAR

(continued)

MICROSOFT POWERPOINT 2000 QUICK REFERENCE SUMMARY

Microsoft PowerPoint 2000 Quick Reference Summary *(continued)*

TASK	PAGE NUMBER	MOUSE	MENU BAR	SHORTCUT MENU	KEYBOARD SHORTCUT
Change Design Templates	PP 3.9	Double-click design template name on status bar; Apply Design Template button on Standard toolbar	Format | Apply Design Template	Apply Design Template	ALT+O | Y
Change Font	PP 3.10	Font box arrow on Formatting toolbar	Format | Font	Font	ALT+O | F
Change Font Color	PP 1.24	Font Color button arrow on Drawing toolbar | color sample	Format | Font	Font | Color	ALT+O | F | ALT+C | DOWN ARROW
Change Slide Layout	PP 2.22	Slide Layout on Common Tasks button menu on Formatting toolbar	Format | Slide Layout	Slide Layout	ALT+O | L | RIGHT ARROW
Change Slide Order	PP 4.50, PP 4.54	Drag			
Change Slide Timing	PP 5.51		Slide Show | Custom Animation	Custom Animation	ALT+D | M
Chart, Add Title and Data Labels	PP 5.33		Chart | Chart Options | Titles or Data Labels tab	Chart Options	ALT+C | O
Chart, Insert Excel	PP 5.21		Insert | Object | Create from file		ALT+I | O | ALT+F
Chart, Select Different Type	PP 5.27		Chart | Chart Type	Chart Type	ALT+C | T
Check Spelling	PP 1.55	Spelling button on Standard toolbar	Tools | Spelling		F7
Choose a Design Template	PP 1.18	Common Tasks button on Formatting toolbar | Apply Design Template	Format | Apply Design Template	Apply Design Template	ALT+C | Y
Clip Art, Animate	PP 2.47		Slide Show | Preset Animation		ALT+D | P
Clip Art, Change Size	PP 2.33	Format Picture button on Picture toolbar | Size tab	Format | Picture | Size tab	Format Picture | Size tab	ALT+O | I | Size tab
Clip Art, Insert	PP 2.25	Insert Clip Art button on Drawing toolbar	Insert | Picture | Clip Art		ALT+I | P | C
Clip Art, Move	PP 2.32	Drag			
Clip Art, Ungroup	PP 3.54	Draw button on Drawing toolbar | Ungroup		Grouping | Ungroup	SHIFT+F10 | G | U
Connect to Microsoft Clip Gallery Live Site	PPI 1.4	Insert Clip Art button on Drawing toolbar | Clips Online button on Insert ClipArt toolbar	Insert | Picture | Clip Art | Clips Online button on Insert ClipArt toolbar		ALT+I | P | C | ALT+C
Control, Add to Form	PP 6.31	Double-click Control in Toolbox			
Create a Table	PP 3.41	Insert Table button on Standard toolbar	Insert | Table		ALT+I | B
Custom Background, Insert Picture	PP 3.16		Format | Background	Background	ALT+O | K
Decrease Font Size	PP 1.25	Decrease Font Size button on Formatting toolbar	Format | Font	Font | Size	CTRL+SHIFT+<

Microsoft PowerPoint 2000 Quick Reference Summary *(continued)*

TASK	PAGE NUMBER	MOUSE	MENU BAR	SHORTCUT MENU	KEYBOARD SHORTCUT
Delete an Object	PP 3.56	Select object | Cut button on Standard toolbar	Edit | Clear or Edit | Cut	Cut	ALT+E | A or DELETE or CTRL+X
Delete Slide	PP 4.53	Click slide icon, press DELETE	Edit | Delete Slide		ALT+E | D
Delete Text	PP 4.9	Cut button on Standard toolbar	Edit | Cut	Cut	CTRL+X
Demote a Paragraph	PP 1.34	Demote button on Formatting toolbar			TAB or ALT+SHIFT+ RIGHT ARROW
Deselect a Clip Art Object	PP 3.55	Click outside clip art object area			
Discussions, Close	PPW 2.13	Close button on Discussions toolbar	Tools | Online Collaboration | Web Discussions		ALT+T | N | W
Discussions, Start	PPW 2.10	Discussions menu button on Discussions toolbar; Discussion Options	Tools | Online Collaboration | Web Discussions | Discussions menu button | Discussion Options		ALT+T | N | W
Display Guides	PP 4.11		View | Guides	Guides	ALT+V | G
Display Rulers	PP 4.10		View | Ruler	Ruler	ALT+V | R
Edit Web Page Through Browser	PPW 1.9	Edit button on Internet Explorer Standard Buttons toolbar			
E-mail from PowerPoint	PP 2.56	E-mail button on Standard toolbar	File | Send To | Mail Recipient		ALT+F | D | A
Export Outline to Microsoft Word	PP 6.70	Save button on Standard toolbar | Save as type | Outline/RTF	File | Save As | Save as type | Outline/RTF		ALT+F | A | ALT+T
Graphical Bullets, Add	PP 3.19	Bullets button on Formatting toolbar	Format | Bullets and Numbering | Bulleted tab | Character	Bullets and Numbering | Bulleted tab | Character	ALT+O | B | ALT+H
Group Objects	PP 3.57	Drag through objects | Draw button on Drawing toolbar | Group		Grouping | Group	
Header and Footer, Add to Page	PP 2.36		View | Header and Footer | Notes and Handouts tab		ALT+V | H
Header and Footer, Add to Slide	PP 1.75		View | Header and Footer | Slide tab		ALT+V | H
Help	PP 1.67	Microsoft PowerPoint Help button on Standard toolbar	Help		F1
Hide Guides	PP 4.38		View | Guides	Guides	ALT+V | G
Hide Rulers	PP 4.22		View | Ruler	Ruler	ALT+V | R
Hide Slide	PP 4.49	Hide Slide button on Slide Sorter toolbar	Slide Show | Hide Slide	Hide Slide	ALT+D | H
Increase Font Size	PP 1.25	Increase Font Size button on Formatting toolbar	Format | Font	Font | Size	CTRL+SHIFT+>
Increase Placeholder Width	PP 5.15	Drag sizing handle	Format | Placeholder | Size tab | Width box arrow	Format Placeholder | Size tab | Width box arrow	ALT+O | O | RIGHT ARROW | ALT+D

(continued)

MICROSOFT POWERPOINT 2000 QUICK REFERENCE SUMMARY

Microsoft PowerPoint 2000 Quick Reference Summary *(continued)*

TASK	PAGE NUMBER	MOUSE	MENU BAR	SHORTCUT MENU	KEYBOARD SHORTCUT
Increase Zoom Percentage	PP 4.13	Zoom box arrow on Standard toolbar	View | Zoom		ALT+V | Z
Insert Slide from Another Presentation	PP 5.10		Insert | Slides from Files | Find Presentation tab | Browse | Open | Insert | Close		ALT+I | F | ALT+B | ALT+O | ALT+S | I | ESC
Italicize Text	PP 1.27	Italic button on Formatting toolbar	Format | Font | Font style	Font | Font style	CTRL+I
Macro, Create by Using Macro Recorder	PP 6.16		Tools | Macro | Record New Macro		
Macro, View VBA Code	PP 6.24		Tools | Macro | Macros | Edit		ALT+T | M | V
Menu, Customize by Adding a Command	PP 6.20	More Buttons button on Standard toolbar | Add or Remove Buttons | Customize | Commands tab	View | Toolbars | Customize | Commands tab	Customize | Commands tab	
Microsoft Organization Chart, Add Co-worker Boxes	PP 4.41	Co-worker box tool on Microsoft Organization Chart icon bar			
Microsoft Organization Chart, Add Shadow Effects	PP 3.36		Boxes | Shadow	Shadow	ALT+B | W
Microsoft Organization Chart, Add Subordinate Boxes	PP 3.27	Subordinate box tool on Microsoft Organization Chart icon bar			
Microsoft Organization Chart, Change Border Style	PP 3.37		Boxes | Border Style	Border Style	ALT+B | B
Microsoft Organization Chart, Change Style	PP 3.29		Styles		ALT+S
Microsoft Organization Chart, Copy a Branch	PP 3.31		Edit | Copy	Copy	CTRL+C
Microsoft Organization Chart, Delete a Branch	PP 4.39		Edit | Select | Branch | Edit | Clear		CTRL+B | DELETE
Microsoft Organization Chart, Open	PP 3.24		Insert | Picture | Organization Chart		ALT+I | P | O
Microsoft Organization Chart, Paste a Branch	PP 3.32		Edit | Paste Boxes	Paste Boxes	CTRL+V
Microsoft Organization Chart, Quit	PP 3.38	Close button on Microsoft Organization Chart title bar	File | Close and Return to presentation		ALT+F | C